CATHOLIC SUBJECT HEADINGS

A List Designed for Use with
Library of Congress Subject Headings
or the
Sears List of Subject Headings

Edited by

Oliver L. Kapsner, O.S.B.

Under the Auspices of the

Catholic Library Association

FIFTH EDITION

With an Appendix on Names of Saints

St. John's Abbey Press

Collegeville, Minnesota

1963

Imprimi potest
✝ Baldwin Dworschak, O.S.B.
Abbot of St. John's Abbey

Imprimatur
✝ Peter W. Bartholome
Bishop of St. Cloud

September 10, 1963

First Edition 1942
Second Edition 1947
Third Edition 1953
Fourth Edition 1958
Fifth Edition 1963

Lithographed By
MAY PRINTING CO., INC.
St. Cloud, Minnesota

FOREWORD TO THE FIFTH EDITION

In 1938 when Father Kapsner was asked by the Catholic Library Association to undertake the preparation of a list of Catholic subject headings few, I am sure, had any idea that such a professional tool would become so important to the profession that a new edition would be required every five years.

This fifth edition of <u>Catholic Subject Headings</u> has been necessitated by the widespread development of Catholic libraries and ever-increasing number of Catholic publications.

The library profession, and particular Catholic librarianship, is indebted to Father Kapsner for this scholarly and authoritative publication. It is another magnificent contribution from a librarian widely renowned for his contributions to cataloging problems in general.

William A. Gillard
President
Catholic Library Association

August, 1963

Work on a list of subject headings in religion, stressing the Catholic approach but also including other important religious aspects, originated and developed, not unlike its counterparts, the Library of Congress and the Sears lists, in modest form. The first edition of the Library of Congress list of subject headings was comparatively small and issued in parts (1909-1914), printed on one side of leaf only. The second edition (1919) had a more professional and formidable appearance and can be said to have set the style and pace for subject cataloging, though it was the third edition (1928) which really took over. The first edition of the Sears list of subject headings (1923) consisted of a mere 183 pages, containing only headings and the "see" references (with their corresponding "refer froms"). The second edition of Sears, three years later, already expanded to 415 pages, largely because of the inclusion of "see also" references in addition to the "see" references, which was done at the request of users of the first edition.

The idea of preparing a list of Catholic subject headings originated in the Catholic Library Association in the early thirties. After several efforts failed to materialize, the present editor was requested in 1938 to undertake the task. His first draft must have resembled the first edition of Sears. It consisted of seventy typed pages containing 2200 headings with their "see" references (and the corresponding "refer froms"). When these first results were offered for consideration and criticism at the national convention of the Catholic Library Association they were quite enthusiastically received, so much so, in fact, that it was strongly urged to expand the list to include "see also" references, some scope notes, and classification numbers. There was special enthusiasm at the time for including classification numbers because two Catholic classification schedules had recently been published, one (the Lynn schedules) to be used with the Library of Congress tables, the other (the Walsh modification) to be used with the Dewey classification (nobody seemed to worry where the editor and publisher were to get the funds to print this additional information). When the first edition of Catholic Subject Headings was published in 1942, the first draft had expanded to 256 pages (reproduced from typed copy). The second edition five years later expanded to 426 pages and contained 3800 headings. The third edition (1953) consisted of 575 pages and included 5200 headings. Since this desk tool was beginning to get a bit bulky, the printing style for the fourth edition (1958) was changed, being set up in two columns and reduced type (achieved through photo-offset), so that, what would have been about 700 pages could be printed in 381 pages containing 6300 entries. The fifth edition is printed in the same style and includes more than 7000 entries, each with its "see" and "see also" references, with their Lynn, Walsh, and (sometimes) LC or Dewey numbers, and with scope notes whenever needed. To the third edition was added a thirty-five page appendix of names of saints, which pages are not included in the above pagination. This appendix material was considerably expanded in the fourth edition, and again, though less so, in the fifth edition.

This, then, is a brief history of the present project. Catholic interest in librarianship originated it, supported it and expanded it. It should be mentioned, however, that there has been wider general interest in the work all

along, as practically all the university libraries and not a few larger college
(non-Catholic), public and private libraries have been faithful patrons of all
editions.

PURPOSE. This list of headings aims to satisfy a longfelt need in Catholic
library circles, presenting as it does an organized arrangement of religious
subject headings from a Catholic viewpoint.

Larger Catholic libraries today follow Library of Congress practice in the
use of subject headings, smaller libraries following Sears, which is based on
Library of Congress practice. The Library of Congress list of subject headings
includes only the headings adopted for use in the dictionary catalogs of the
Library as books and library materials are cataloged there, consequently cannot
be expected to be a list of headings equally complete in all fields of knowledge.
In the preface to the third edition (1928) of the Library of Congress list of
headings it was explained that "Subjects belonging to religion and theology and
to foreign law are but sparsely and irregularly represented, owing to the fact
that the assignment of such subject headings has been discontinued until the re-
classification of these classes shall have been completed and their systematic
recataloguing is well in hand." In view of this situation it can be understood
why Catholic librarians were concerned in the early thirties about doing some-
thing for subject headings in religion and theology.   True enough, the Library
of Congress has since taken more interest in the cataloging of religious literature, but the gap is still there, owing partly to the late start and partly, it
can be safely presumed, to the limitations of its collection in that area. It
is the purpose of the present work to close that hiatus for Catholic libraries.

The organization of the list is so planned as to dovetail into Library of
Congress subject headings in non-theological fields. Accordingly, this list,
in combination with that of the Library of Congress, should satisfactorily meet
all eventualities in a Catholic library. The same applies, "mutatis mutandis",
to the Sears List of Subject Headings.

FEATURES. The features of the list are identical with those found in Subject Headings Used in the Dictionary Catalogs of the Library of Congress. Thus
they include headings, classification numbers, scope notes, cross references,
and subdivisions.

FORM OF HEADINGS. An effort was made to conform as much as possible to
Library of Congress usage. Yet this system when applied to books of a theological nature often proves very unsatisfactory for a Catholic library. Just as
Catholic students and readers when consulting a Catholic dictionary or an in-
dex to a Catholic magazine will invariably look for direct headings, so also
will they search for direct headings in a dictionary card catalog in a Catholic
library. For this reason the headings "Dogmatic theology", "Moral theology",
"Liturgy", etc., are employed directly; also the various parts of the liturgy
(Divine office, Rites and uses, etc.) and the names of liturgical books (e.g.,
Breviarium, Missale, etc.).   Catholic students should not be compelled to

examine the long files under "Catholic Church" to locate material on such important theological topics. By the same argument of convenience for consultation the forms "Asceticism", "Moral theology", "Pastoral theology", etc., have been used in preference to "Theology, Ascetical", "Theology, Moral", "Theology, Pastoral", etc., because the emphasis is plainly on asceticism, moral, pastoral, etc.

In speaking about the "aim of subject cataloging" the editor of the Sears list has this to say: "The subject catalog tries to list under one form of heading all the books on a given subject that the library possesses. In order to achieve this end efficiently, the wording of subject headings must be familiar to the users of the catalog and as specific as the material warrants." [1] In accordance with a principle of this nature the forms of entry in Catholic Subject Headings have been determined by the needs of the clientele in a Catholic library.

EXPLANATORY NOTES. Definitions or explanations have been included for those subjects which mark divisions in the field of religion or theology, and for headings which are apt to be obscure.

In most instances the meaning of terms as found in encyclopedias and as conceived in the subject content of books is identical. For that reason definitions for headings in the list are frequently chosen from authoritative Catholic reference works, where these are found well-formed, comprehensive, and intelligible.

When there was need of an explanatory note to delineate the scope of a term as comprehended in printed books, especially in relation to other terms or headings, the proper annotation has been made. Catalogers detecting specific instances where this necessary distinction was overlooked in the list will do the editor a favor by calling them to his attention.

SUBDIVISIONS. In the matter of subdivisions the list mentions all the likely subdivisions under the main subjects, including the general form divisions. Since both headings and subdivisions have been determined from an actual stock of theological books, supplemented by bibliographies on specific topics in the best theological encyclopedias and in other bibliographic guides, they should be equally applicable in the actual cataloging of theological literature.

A list of general form divisions can be found on p. xxiii after the preface. A few additions have been made to the usual list. Catholic libraries will have considerable need for using "Meditations" and "Sermons" as form divisions, also for "Prayer-books", though less frequently. The larger libraries will probably also find "Popular works" useful as a form division under headings in religion.

Under the names of countries the periodic church history subdivisions determined by Lynn have been adopted because these seem to offer a more practical

1. M.E. Sears, Sears List of Subject Headings. 8th ed. p. 11.

subdivision than do the political ones. Any other subdivisions can, of course,
be used under countries.

Headings   with which local subdivisions may be used are followed by the
phrase "Geographical subdivision" in parentheses. In the same place is indicated whether the local subdivision is direct (e.g., Church architecture - Munich,
Germany) or indirect (e.g., Abbeys - Germany - Bavaria).

Catholic libraries will hardly care to retain the mark "Catholic authors"
used as a subdivision under subject headings on Library of Congress printed
cards when this mark refers to individual authors (e.g., Spiritual life - Catholic authors).   The specification "Catholic authors" under a subject can and
should be used, however, when it implies a class of writers (e.g., Children's
literature - Catholic authors; English literature - Catholic authors).

REFERENCES. The system of references employed by both the Library of Congress and Sears in their latest editions is again carried out in this list. It
is a very complete system, consisting of See, See also, Refer from (see) and
Refer from (see also) references. As is the accepted practice by now, symbols
are used to express the last three reference terms, namely: sa for See also,
x for Refer from (see) and xx for Refer from (see also).

See references are made from forms of headings not used to those actually
used in this list.   Under the latter a corresponding x reference is made to
indicate the alternative or approximately alternative forms not used.   See
references are made from exact synonyms, from the second part of compound
headings, from the second part of inverted headings, from variant spellings,
and from opposites when these have no entry of their own.

See also references are made from a heading used to related headings in
this list.   They are usually made from general to less general and specific
headings.   They also occur between coordinate headings or subjects of approximately equal value.   Only by way of exception are they made from specific to
general subjects. For every See also reference a corresponding xx reference
is made under the heading referred to.

In Catholic Subject Headings the system of cross references was worked
out in its fulness according to steps and procedure suggested by the veteran
authority on subject headings, Charles A. Cutter.[2]

CLASSIFICATION NUMBERS. Directly following the headings two sets   of
classification numbers are included, namely, the Lynn-Library of Congress
and the Walsh-Dewey numbers.[3] It will be remembered that, for Catholic libraries, the Lynn schedules supplement the Library of Congress classification
outlines, while the Walsh schedule modifies and expands the 200 section of

2. C.A. Cutter, Rules for Dictionary Catalogue. 4th ed. p. 79-80.
3. These four classification systems are cited with their full title and latest
edition in the bibliography or "Authorities consulted".

of the Dewey decimal classification. The Lynn-LC class numbers are given first. Lynn numbers (these are taken from the second, revised edition of the Alternative Classification for Catholic Books) can be identified and distinguished from LC numbers since they invariably include the letter "Q". Four spaces following the Lynn-LC numbers the Walsh-Dewey numbers are given in parentheses. The small letter "x" is the distinguishing mark of a Walsh modification, while plain numbers are unaltered Dewey numbers. Catalogers employing the Walsh schedule understand that in actual use on cards and books the small " x" is simply omitted.

The addition of the classification numbers was incidental to the work of compiling a list of theological subject headings. In comparison to the latter task it was in a way an easy assignment. Nevertheless, the inclusion of the classification numbers easily constitutes a source of disagreement for catalogers. Several reasons may be adduced for these differences of opinion.

In the first place, even expert catalogers will persistently disagree on some choices of classification numbers because of the differences of the local character of libraries. Furthermore, the author of the Alternative Classification is very generous in offering alternatives equally acceptable. It is at times no easy task to decide on a first choice, yet in this list selective decisions had to be made.

The Walsh schedule is simpler and less comprehensive than the Lynn tables, and often provides only general places for specific headings found in this list of Catholic subject headings. It is, consequently, impossible to assign Walsh classification numbers in all cases with the same detailed accuracy as Lynn numbers. On the other hand, the cataloger's sharp eye will detect a number of bracketed Lynn numbers in the list. Bracketed numbers signify suggested additions to the Lynn tables, as for new material (e.g., Priest-worker movement) and when numbers that could have been retained were not carried over from the first to the second edition of the Alternative Classification. Bracketed numbers are also given at times for the subdivisions Bibliography, Congresses, Biblical teaching, and Papal teaching. Under the major religious orders (e.g., Dominicans, Franciscans) the subdivisions Education, Missions, and Lay Brothers have bracketed classification numbers because there is no provision for them in the Lynn subdivision table (p. 418-419 of the Alternative Classification, 2d ed.).

In assigning class numbers to books in their libraries, catalogers will, of course, always consult their respective classification schedules as well as their shelf-lists.

SCOPE. The list covers all branches of Catholic theology, as well as the Bible, Canon law, and Church history. It also includes the more important non-Catholic subject headings in religion and theology. Besides the necessary Catholic headings, any number of non-Catholic headings may be needed by the larger Catholic libraries; for example, whenever the library possesses material pertaining to non-Catholic theology and practice. In such instances

the corresponding theological heading according to creed should be used. This is
becoming more important in the era of ecumenism.

Where confusion is apt to result an explanatory note is provided in the list.
A noteworthy example is the case of "Eucharist" for the Catholic Church and
"Lord's Supper" for Protestant Churches. The Library of Congress in this in-
stance uses only the Protestant form "Lord's Supper" to cover both Protestant and
Catholic literature. Since the Protestant term is entirely foreign to the average Catholic and incorrectly applied to Catholic doctrine, Library of Congress
practice in this case is not acceptable in Catholic libraries.

A similar example, first introduced in the third edition of this list, is the
use of the term "Holy See", with subdivisions, for all diplomatic relations of
the Catholic Church. It is, for one thing, a direct entry. It also collects all
the material, both author and subject matter, proper to the heading under one
form of entry, material which is scattered under six separated entries by the
Library of Congress. As a further consequence, the vague subject heading "Papacy", which is still without a scope note in the Library of Congress list of
headings, and on LC printed cards is employed for a variety of purposes, becomes
superfluous. The entries "Catholic Church", "Holy See", and "Popes" amply cover
all exigencies.

The names of persons, places, societies, and institutions are ordinarily
omitted from the list. Only the more important names, particularly those which
are intimately related to the subject headings or under which considerable subject material is found, are included, such as Saint Augustine and Saint Thomas
Aquinas (with the determined subdivisions), the Catholic names for the books of
the Bible, the official names of liturgical books, the names of the Roman congregations, and the chief religious orders (with subdivisions), and all of these
with their classification numbers, which are sometimes complex. For the same
reason the appendix on names of saints is not out of place in connection with
this list of headings, as many of the entries for saints are used only for subject material. Augustine and Thomas Aquinas, like Lincoln and Shakespeare in
the Library of Congress list, could be considered as "key" headings of their
kind, illustrating how similar subdivisions can be used, if needed, under other
voluminous Christian writers (e.g., Ambrose, Gregory, John Chrysostom, Bonaventure, etc.). "Catholic Church - France" is another example of this type included in this list, with all subdivisions, applicable to other countries as
needed.

For the numerous religious orders of the Church, which normally occur as
subject headings, a separate guide has been made available under the title,
Catholic Religious Orders (by O.L. Kapsner. 2d ed., 1957. 594 p.).

USE WITH LIBRARY OF CONGRESS AND SEARS. Since this list purposes to supplement that of the Library of Congress on subject headings, a word on how to
use the two lists together may be instructive to catalogers in Catholic libraries. For all headings pertaining to religion this list of Catholic subject
headings should be referred to; for all other headings the Library of Congress
list should be consulted. All Library of Congress headings in theology found
acceptable have been embodied in this new list (sometimes, however, with modi-

fied meanings), so that the need for double consultation on the part of the cataloger is avoided as much as possible.[4] The same instruction obtains for users of
Sears. The deviations in Sears from Library of Congress usage in the field of
religion are very few. The necessary adaptations can readily be made by the
cataloger.

References are sometimes made to and from Library of Congress headings not
repeated in this list. Such are non-theological headings related to theological
subjects, e.g., references are made both to and from Art, Ethics, Philosophy,
etc. That is where the dovetailing has been effected between this list and the
Library of Congress and Sears lists. Catalogers must themselves check in their
LC or Sears copies respectively whatever references have been used in their own
libraries.

Borderline topics in religion (e.g., Rationalism, Skepticism, etc.) and
non-Catholic religious headings (e.g., Lord's Supper, Revivals, and names of
churches and sects) are generally settled with the note, "References as in LC"
or "Subdivisions as in LC". Such examples indicate the line of demarcation between work undertaken in Catholic Subject Headings and related work already well
done by the Library of Congress and by Sears and available to all who need it.

In time individual catalogers must make other modifications, such as, the
selection of subdivisions, cross references, and classification numbers. Small
libraries will want to use few subdivisions, carefully selected cross references, and broad classification numbers. Such problems must all be solved according to local circumstances. No guidebook of itself can solve any problems.
In these perplexities application alone will provide a solution; but no little prudence is required in making a judicious use of a guidebook. The old
adage that "practice is the best teacher" has perhaps never been more applicable than in cataloging work.

ADDENDA ET EMENDANDA. The addition of several hundred new headings (actually, nearly a thousand), occasioned either by new types of literature or as
overlooked headings, enables libraries to keep au courant in their mission to
serve the public. From these additions a selection of some of the more interesting headings can perhaps be made as follows: Almanacs, Catholic; Anniversary sermons; Archives, Monastic; Bible - Study - Papal teaching; Calendar reform; Canon law - Abbreviations; Catholic Book Week; Catholic education, Adult;
Catholic education, Preschool; Catholic social action; Chant - Discography;
Church - Biblical teaching - O.T.; Church - Indefectibility; Concursus divinus;
Eastern Churches - Ecclesiology; First Mass sermons; Good Shepherd; Gospels,
Lenten; Holy Childhood; International organizations, Catholic; Irreligion;
Jesus Christ - Iconography; Jesus Christ - Mercy; Laymen's retreat movement;
Lent - Liturgy; Liturgy and missions; Mary, Blessed Virgin - Holiness; Mis-
sions - Emigrants; Moving-pictures, Religious; Philosophy, Early Christian;
Polyphonic chant; Prayer - Confraternities; Preaching and the liturgy; Reli-

---

4. In preparing the present edition of Catholic Subject Headings the sixth
edition (1957) of the Library of Congress list and the supplements through 1961
were used for comparison. Fully one half of the total entries in Catholic Subject Headings are not in the Library of Congress list and supplements.

gion and astronautics; Sacred sciences; Servile work; State of perfection; Teachers, Catholic; Theology and history; Titular churches; Tropes (Chant); Vatican Council, 2d, 1962-   ; Virtue - Biblical teaching. A number of more specific headings were also needed in canon law, e.g., Sacred places (Canon law); Simulation (Canon law); etc.

Attention might also be called to several modifications, especially such modifications as simultaneously occasion a new heading.   The heading "Rites and ceremonies" was modified by breaking down the concept and adding the heading "Rites and ceremonies (Catholic)".   How appropriate this distinction is can readily be seen by noting the difference in subdivisions under each heading, also the entirely different classification numbers.   Now there is no longer need to file diverse material under just one heading.   Some may wonder why this important distinction was not made earlier. To which the ripe answer might be given: better late than never. The right solutions to problems rarely emerge overnight. Constant living with cataloging problems and some serious thinking about them usually generate the correct answer sooner or later.

The meaning and application of the headings "Missale" and "Missals" are explained under the headings.

The heading "Anniversary sermons" is given the same preferential treatment as "Retreats" and "Novenas" in previous editions, being divided by its subjects rather than used as a subdivision under other headings.   This procedure is based on the assumption that material on the respective topics is searched in the catalog from the approach of retreats, novenas, and anniversary sermons.

The traditional Douai forms of names for Old Testament books are retained as heretofore. During the past two decades several new English translations of the Bible have been published for Catholic readers, who for four hundred years had been accustomed to but one translation.   Some of the new translators have employed different spellings for certain Old Testament books, or even different names, while others adhere to the traditional names. Since there is no agreement as yet on new forms of name for some Biblical books, the traditional Douai forms are repeated as in the first four editions of this list.

The majority of answers to the last questionnaire, distributed to a select group of Catholic libraries, favored changing the entry "Orthodox Eastern Church" to what appears to be the more correct form, "Eastern Orthodox Church". Besides being a somewhat late idea, the change is more intricate than would appear at first sight.   It means much more than changing just one heading, since it involves all the instances where this name occurs as a subdivision under specific theological and canon law headings, also the various branches of the Orthodox Church when used as direct entries and as subdivisions, and the cross references.   It could easily become an example where inconsistencies creep in, if a thorough job is not done.   Moreover, since this is not specifically a Catholic heading, it would be desirable that the entire American library profession agrees to the change.   The idea for making the change came from a member of the Orthodox Church, who actually pleaded that we should all begin to use the correct form of name.

Somewhat parallel to the above was the request from a user of <u>Catholic Subject Headings</u> who is a member of a Catholic branch of the Eastern Churches.

He pleaded that we use the form "Divine liturgy", the only form known to them when reference is to their Mass, rather than the somewhat arbitrary western expression "Eucharistic liturgy". He won his case.

Since a new edition of the Lynn classification schedules, which are truly excellent schedules with adequate breakdown of topics throughout, will not be needed for some time yet, some larger libraries may find the following suggestions and breakdowns useful. They are indicated in their respective places in brackets in Catholic Subject Headings.
     The last number under Imitatio Christi could be broken down as follows:
     BQT 2522.1 Bibliography
          .2 Concordances
          .3 History
          .4 Authorship
Meditations on the liturgy could be subdivided to read:
     BQT 2606   Meditations on the liturgy in general
          .1   Church year
          .2   Advent
          .3   Christmas and Christmastide
          .4   Lent
          .5   Holy Week
          .6   Easter and Easter season
          .7   Pentecost and Pentecost season
Meditations on the sacraments could be subdivided thus:
     BQT 2608   Meditations on the sacraments in general
          .1   Baptism
          .2   Confirmation
          .3   Eucharist and Holy Communion
          .4   Penance
          .5   Extreme Unction
          .6   Holy Orders
          .7   Matrimony

The Library of Congress recently (1962) published greatly expanded and improved tables for the BL-BX classes, covering religion and the theological sciences. The Lynn schedules accept the Library of Congress BS tables (Bible) as is. Numbers have finally been assigned in the LC BS section for Biblical theology, though hardly adequate for an extensive and growing literature. One still looks in vain, however, for at least one classification number in those vast schedules for Biblical canticles (they are published as texts in various languages, as editions with music, and with commentaries). Even the much less pretentious Walsh classification assigns a separate number for Canticles taken from the Bible.

FILING POLICY. Some correspondents have remarked that they arrange their files somewhat differently than the order in Catholic Subject Headings. That is easily understood, since it is well known that there are three different filing systems possible, yet a published list of entries can exemplify only one system at a time. The Sears list, which is intended for small and medium-sized libraries and has but few subdivisions, employs a straight alphabetical filing system disregarding punctuation. The Library of Congress list, which is intended for large libraries and uses extensive subdivisions, employs an alphabetical arrangement and has regard for punctuation, also makes use of grouped or class arrangements under certain headings.

Catholic Subject Headings, which is planned for large theological book collections, used the Library of Congress list as a springboard from its inception, including the filing arrangement. It therefore follows an alphabetical arrangement and has regard for punctuation, with grouped arrangements of subdivisions under such headings as Asceticism, Bible, Canon law, Catholic Church, Christian literature, Christianity, Church history, Church music, Mass, Mysticism, Popes - History, Sacraments, Saints, Sermons, etc. Special grouped arrangements of subdivisions can also be seen under such major religious orders as Benedictines and Franciscans. Like the Library of Congress list of subject headings, Catholic Subject Headings is, however, not a filing manual. It is a desk tool for the cataloger. The grouped arrangements under certain headings (usually with long lists of subdivisions) are meant for the instruction and guidance of the cataloger, to enable him to determine the best form of heading and to classify correctly without loss of time (it should be noted that the classification numbers for the second and third groups of subdivisions are sometimes quite different from those under the first group).

What filing policy a local library wishes to pursue is the business and responsibility of the individual library, a matter which depends largely on the nature and size of the catalog files. In a very large catalog file it is next to inconceivable how periodic subdivisions could be interfiled with other subdivisions without creating chaos in the files. Similarly, libraries with a large catalog file are the ones more likely to prefer arranging the group of geographic subdivisions separately. A good example for study and serious reflection in the Library of Congress list would be the heading "English literature". The filing arrangement observed by the Library of Congress list and by Catholic Subject Headings is, incidentally, the same as readers meet with in Cumulative Book Index and in Readers' Guide to Periodical Literature.

ACKNOWLEDGMENTS. The form of this list of subject headings is modelled on Library of Congress practice. The Library of Congress, through the services of Mr. David J. Haykin, was very generous in granting permission to base the first edition of this list on its own both as to form and as to content, without assuming any responsibility, however, for the actual form of the list. Mr. Haykin has also enabled catalogers to benefit from his long experience as Chief of the Subject Cataloging Division in the Library of Congress through publication of his excellent manual, Subject Headings: a Practical Guide.

The theological determinations of headings in the list are based on the rules and examples of the Vatican Norme, from which the editor derived much inspiration and guidance in compiling the original edition of this work. The Vatican code was at the time the only up-to-date guide containing carefully worked out rules for subject cataloging, and still is the only guide of this kind for the cataloging of theology. Fortunately, this comprehensive manual is now available in English translation (see under "Authorities consulted").

It is again a pleasure to be able to express my gratitude to the catalogers
in many Catholic libraries, whose occasional contributions of new headings and
whose answers to questionnaires helped to make this new edition possible. As in
the previous editions, practically all their new headings will be found incorporated in this edition, while their critical suggestions helped to form important decisions.

In a special way, however, I feel indebted to the members of the library
staff at St. Vincent College, Latrobe, Pennsylvania, where this fifth edition
was for the most part prepared and brought to completion. Sincere thanks are
due, above all, to my superior, the Right Reverend Baldwin Dworschak, O.S.B.,
abbot of St. John's Abbey, Collegeville, Minnesota, for allowing me to continue
this research work for the good of the library profession in general and for
the cause of the Catholic Library profession in particular.

                                              Oliver L. Kapsner, O.S.B.

July, 1963

AUTHORITIES CONSULTED

GENERAL GUIDES

American Library Association. A.L.A. cataloging rules for author and title entries. 2d ed. Chicago, American Library Association, 1949.

Catholic Library Association. Proceedings of the ... annual conference. 1957-

Catholic Library world; official organ of the Catholic Library Association. v.1- 1929- (cf. index for articles, papers and discussions concerning cataloging problems in Catholic libraries)

Coates, E.J. Subject catalogues: headings and structure. London, Library Association, 1960.

Columbia University. School of Library Science. The subject analysis of library materials; papers presented at an institute, June 24-28, 1952, under the sponsorship of the School of Library Service, Columbia University, and the A.L.A. Division of Cataloging and Classification. Edited, with an introduction, by Maurice F. Tauber. New York, 1953.

Colvin, L.C. Cataloging sampler: a comparative and interpretative guide. Hamden, Conn., Archon Books, 1963.

Cutter, C.A. Rules for a dictionary catalogue. 4th ed., rewritten. Washington, Government Printing Office, 1904.

Haykin, D.J. Subject headings: a practical guide. Washington, Government Printing Office, 1951.

Jackson, S.L. Catalog use study; director's report. Edited by Vaclav Mostecky. Chicago, American Library Association, 1958.

Jolley, L. The principles of cataloguing. London, C. Lockwood, 1960.

Kapsner, O.L. A manual of cataloging practice for Catholic author and title entries; being supplementary aids to the A.L.A. and Vatican Library cataloging rules. Washington, Catholic University of America Press, 1953.

Metcalfe, J.W. Information indexing and subject cataloging; alphabetical, classified, coordinate, mechanical. New York, Scarecrow Press, 1957.

Pettee, Julia. Subject headings: the history and theory of the alphabetical subject approach to books. New York, H.W. Wilson, 1946.

Rovira Bertrán, Carmen. Los epígrafes en el catálogo diccionario; historia, crítica y teoría. Con un código de reglas para la asignación de epígrafes en las bibliotecas de habla española. Habana, Cultural, 1952.

Taube, Mortimer. Studies in coordinate indexing, by Mortimer Taube and associates. Washington, Documentation Incorporated, 1953-59 (v.1-5).

Vatican. Biblioteca Vaticana. Norme per il catalago degli stampati. 3. ed. Città del Vaticano, Bibllioteca Apostolica Vaticana, 1951.

Vatican. Biblioteca Vaticana. Rules for the catalog of printed books. Translated from the second Italian edition. Edited by W.E. Wright.

<u>INDEXES</u>

American Library Association. List of subject headings for use in dictionary catalogs. 3d ed. rev. and enl.   Chicago, American Library Association, 1911.

American Theological Library Association. Index to religious periodical literature; an author and subject index to periodical literature. 1949-

Biblio; catalogue des ouvrages parus en langue française dans le monde entier.   Paris, Hachette, 1934-

Bibliografia nazionale italiana; catalogo alfabetico annuale.   A cura della Biblioteca nazionale centrale di Firenze, 1958-   (Supersedes Bollettino delle pubblicazioni italiane ricevute per diritto di stampa)

Bibliothèque nationale, Paris. <u>See</u> Paris. Bibliothèque nationale.

Bollettino delle pubblicazioni italiane. <u>See</u> Florence.   Biblioteca nazionale centrale.

British Museum.   Department of Printed Books.   The British Museum Catalogue of printed books. 58 v.   London, 1881-1900 (A new edition is in progress, 1959-   )

British Museum.   Department of Printed Books.   A subject index of the modern works added to the library of the British Museum, 1881-

The British national bibliography; a subject list of the new British books. 1950-   London, Council of the British National Bibliography.

Catholic bookman; international ... survey of Catholic literature.   v.1-7, 1937-1944.   Detroit, W. Romig (Merged into Guide to Catholic literature)

The Catholic bookman's guide; a critical evaluation of Catholic literature. Edited by Sister M. Regis, I.H.M.   New York, Hawthorn, 1962.

Catholic Library Association. Catholic supplement to the standard catalog for high school libraries, selected by a committee of the Association. 1942-   New York, H.W. Wilson.

Catholic periodical index; a cumulative author and subject index to a selected list of Catholic periodicals. 1930-   Washington.

Claudia, Sister, I.H.M.   Material compiled for the purpose of formulating subject headings for church days and the liturgical year (typescript). [Detroit, Marygrove College Library]

Codex juris canonici Pii X pontificis maximi iussu digestus, Benedicti papae XV auctoritate promulgatus ... et indice analytico-alphabetico auctus.   Romae, Typis Polyglottis Vaticanis, 1918.

Cumulative book index. <u>See</u> United States catalog; books in print.   Supplement, 1928-

Deutsche Bibliographie; Verzeichnis aller in Deutschland erschienen Veröffentlichungen und der in Oesterreich und der Schweiz im Buchhandel erschienen deutschsprachigen Publikationen sowie der deutschsprachigen Veröffentlichungen anderer Länder Bücher und Karten. 1945-   Frankfurt am Main, Buchhändler-Vereinigung.

Deutsches Bücherverzeichnis; eine Zusammenstellung der im deutschen Buchhandel erschienen Bücher, Zeitschriften und Landkarten. Nebst Stich- und Schlagwortregister. 1916-   Leipzig, Börsenverein der deutschen Buchhändler.

Dewey, Melvil.   Dewey decimal classification and relative index.   16th ed. 2 v.   Lake Placid Club, N.Y., Forest Press, 1958.

Florence. Biblioteca nazionale centrale. Bollettino delle pubblicazioni ita-
    liane ricevute per diritto di stampa.   1886-1957.   Firenze (Includes
    subject index)

Florence.   Biblioteca nazionale centrale.   Soggettario per i cataloghi delle
    biblioteche italiane.   Firenze, Stamperia Il Cenacolo, 1956.

Frey, Frederic, O.S.B. Liturgical subject headings (typescript).   [College-
    ville, Minn., St. John's Abbey Library]

Guide to Catholic literature; an annotated author-title-subject bibliography
    of books and pamphlets by Catholic authors, with a selection of Catholic-
    interest books by non-Catholic authors ... v.1-   1888-   Washing-
    ton.

Kapsner, O.L., O.S.B.   Catholic religious orders; listing conventional and
    full names in English, foreign language and Latin, also abbreviations,
    date and country of origin, and founders. 2d ed., enl.   Collegeville,
    Minn., St. John's Abbey Press, 1957.

Lynn, J.M. An alternative classification for Catholic books: ecclesiastical
    Literature, theology, canon law, church history ... 2d ed., revised by
    Gilbert C. Peterson, S.J.   Washington, Catholic University of America
    Press, 1954.

The National union catalog; a cumulative author list representing Library of
    Congress printed cards and titles reported by other American libraries.
    Jan. 1956-   Washington, Library of Congress.

Paris. Bibliothèque nationale. Départment des imprimés.   Catalogue général
    des livres imprimés de la Bibliothèque nationale. Auteurs.   Paris,
    Imprimerie nationale, 1897-

Pettee, Julia.   List of theological subject headings and corporate church
    names based upon the headings in the catalogue of the Library of Union
    Theological Seminary, New York City. 2d ed.   Chicago, American Li-
    brary Association, 1947.

Primo catalogo collettivo delle biblioteche italiane. 1962-   Roma,
    Centro nazionale per il catalogo unico delle biblioteche italiane e per
    le informazioni bibliografiche.

Repertoire général de sciences religieuses; bibliographie publiee avec le
    concours de la direction générale des Affaires culturelles et techniques
    au Ministère des affaires étrangères par le service bibliographique du
    Centre d'études Saint-Louis-de-France. 1951-   Colmar-Paris, Edi-
    tions Alsatia.

Richardson, E.C.   Subject headings in theology; a synthetic index to some
    recent systems of theological library classification together with the
    A.L.A. subject headings in religion ...   Yardley, Pa., F.S. Cook,
    1928.

Sears, M.E. Sears List of subject headings. With suggestions for the be-
    ginner in subject heading work. 8th ed. by Bertha Margaret Frick.
    New York, H.W. Wilson Co., 1959.

Union Theological Seminary Library, New York City.   The shelf list of the
    Union Theological Seminary Library in New York City, in classification
    order. 10 v.   Boston, G.K. Hall, 1960.

U.S. Library of Congress. A catalog of books represented by Library of Congress printed cards issued to July 31, 1942. 167 v. Ann Arbor, Edwards Brothers, 1942-46.

------ Supplement: cards issued August 1, 1942 - December 31, 1947. 42 v. Ann Arbor, J.W. Edwards, 1948.

------ [Supplement]: Library of Congress catalog; a cumulative list of works represented by Library of Congress cards. Books: authors. 24 v. 1948-1952. Washington.

------ [Supplement] 1953- See National union catalog.

U.S. Library of Congress. Library of Congress catalog; a cumulative list of works represented by Library of Congress printed cards. Books: subjects. 1950- Washington.

U.S. Library of Congress. Classification Division. Classification: Classes A-Z. 24 v. Washington, Government Printing Office, 1910-

------ Classification: Additions and changes. List 1- March, 1928- Washington, Government Printing Office.

U.S. Library of Congress. Subject Cataloging Division. Subject headings used in the dictionary catalogs of the Library of Congress. 6th ed. Washington, 1957.

------ Supplement. Jan. 1955- Washington.

United States catalog; books in print January 1, 1912. 3d ed. New York, H.W. Wilson, 1912.

------ Supplements, 1912-1928. New York, H.W. Wilson, 1912-28.

United States catalog; books in print January 1, 1928. 4th ed. New York, H.W. Wilson, 1928.

------ Supplement: Cumulative book index, 1928- New York, H.W. Wilson, 1928-

Walsh, R.J. A modification and expansion of the Dewey decimal classification in the 200 class. Philadelphia, Peter Reilly Co., 1941 (reprint pending)

Willging, E.P. Index to Catholic pamphlets in the English language. v.1-6, 1937-52. Washington, Catholic University of America Press.

N.B.: The following printed card files, made available through either subscription or depository arrangement, were also consulted: Catholic University of American subscription series (covering current American and foreign Catholic titles); Fides Publishers (Montreal); St. Mary's College, St. Marys, Kan.; St. Mary's Seminary, Mundelein, Ill; Vatican Library.

ENCYCLOPEDIAS AND DICTIONARIES

Aigrain, René. Ecclesia; encyclopédie populaire des connaissances religieuses. Paris, Bloud & Gay, 1948.

Aigrain, René. Liturgia; encyclopédie populaire des connaissances liturgiques. Paris, Bloud & Gay, 1930.

Attwater, Donald. A Catholic dictionary. 3d ed. New York, Macmillan, 1958 (Originally published under title: The Catholic encyclopaedic dictionary)

Baudrillart, Alfred. Dictionnaire d'histoire et de géographie ecclésiastique, commencé sous la direction de Mgr. Alfred Baudrillart, continué par A. de Meyer et Et. Cauwenbergh, avec le concours d'un grand nombre de collaborateurs. v.1- Paris, Letouzey, 1912-

Bibliotheca sanctorum [dal] Istituto Giovanni XXIII nella Pontificia Università
    Lateranense. v.1-   Roma, 1961-   (Projected in 10 vols.)
Braun, Joseph, S.J. Liturgisches Handlexikon. 2. Aufl.   Regensburg, Kösel,
    1924.
Britt, Matthew, O.S.B. A dictionary of the Psalter, containing the vocabulary
    of the psalms, hymns, canticles and miscellaneous prayers of the Breviary
    Psalter. New York, Benziger, 1928.
Buchberger, Michael. Lexikon für Theologie und Kirche. 2. neubearb. Aufl.
    10 v. Freiburg i.B., Herder, 1930-38. (New edition in progress, 1957-)
Cabrol, Fernand, O.S.B. Dictionnaire d'archéologie chrétienne et de liturgie.
    15 v. in 30. Paris, Letouzey, 1907-54.
A Catholic dictionary. See Attwater, Donald.
The Catholic encyclopedia; an international work of reference on the constitu-
    tion, doctrine, discipline and history of the Catholic Church.   17 v.
    New York, Catholic Encyclopedia Press, 1907-22.
The Catholic encyclopedia dictionary ... Compiled and edited under the direc-
    tion of the editors of the Catholic encyclopedia ...   New York, The Gil-
    mary Society, 1941 (Published in 1929 under title: The New Catholic dic-
    tionary)
Catholicisme: hier, aujourd'hui, demain. Encyclopédie en sept volumes, diri-
    gée par G. Jacquemet. Paris, Letouzey, 1947-   (The original plan
    has been expanded to constitute about twice seven volumes)
Diccionario enciclopédico U. T. E. H. A. 10 v.   México, Union Tipográfica
    Editorial Hispano Americana, 1950-52.
Dictionnaire apologétique de la foi catholique, contenant les preuves de la
    verité de la religion et les réponses aux objections tirées des sciences
    humaines. 4. ed., entièrement refondue, publié sous la direction de A.
    d'Alès. 4 v. Paris, Beauchesne, 1925-28.
Dictionnaire de droit canonique, contenant tous les termes du droit cano-
    nique, avec un sommaire de l'histoire et des institutions et de l'état
    actuel de la discipline. Publié sous la direction de R. Naz ... avec le
    concours d'un grand nombre de collaborateurs. v.1-   Paris, Letouzey,
    1935-
Dictionnaire de sociologie familiale, politique, économique, spirituelle,
    générale. Publié sous la direction de G. Jacquemet ... avec le concours
    de nombreux collaborateurs. v.1-   Paris, Letouzey, 1933-
Dictionnaire de spiritualité ascétique et mystique, doctrine et histoire.
    Publié sous la direction de Marcel Viller, S.J.   Paris, G. Beauchesne,
    1937-
Dictionnaire de théologie catholique, contenant l'exposé des doctrines de la
    théologie catholique, leurs preuves et leur histoire. Commencé sous la
    direction de A. Vacant et E. Mangenot, continué sous celle de F. Amann
    ... avec le concours d'un grand nombre de collaborateurs.   Paris,
    Letouzey, 1908-
Dictionnaire du symbolisme. Par les religieuses bénédictines de la Rue mon-
    sieur, Paris. Abbaye de Saint-André [Belgique], L'Artisan liturgique,
    1934.
Dictionnaire encyclopédique de la Bible. Traduit du néerlandais [par les
    moines de l'Abbaye du Mont César à Louvain, sur la deuxième édition, re-
    vue et augmentée]. Turnout, Brepols, 1960. (Translation of Bijbels
    woordenboek)

Dictionnaire pratique des connaissances religieuses. Publié sous la direction de J. Bricout. 6 v.   Paris, Letouzey, 1925-29.

Dizionario ecclesiastico, sotto la direzione dei rev. mi mons. Angelo Mercati [e] mons. Augusto Pelzer, con la collaborazione di numerosi e noti specialisti. Redattore capo Antonio M. Bozzone.   3 v. Torino, Unione tipografico-editrice, 1953-58.

Doublas, J.D., ed. The new Bible dictionary. Consulting editors: F.F. Bruce [and others].   Grand Rapids, Eerdmans, 1962.

The Encyclopaedia of Islam. New edition, prepared by a number of leading orientalists. Edited by ... H. A. R. Gibb [and others]. Leiden , E. J. Brill, 1954-

Enciclopedia cattolica. 12 v.   Città del Vaticano, Ente per l'Enciclopedia cattolica e per il Libro cattolico, 1949-54.

Enciclopedia de la religión católica.   Barcelona, Dalmau y Jover, 1950-

Encyclopedia of religion and ethics. Edited by James Hastings, with the assistance of John A. Selbie, and other scholars. 12 v.   New York, Scribner, 1911-27.

Der Grosse Herder; Nachschlagewerk für Wissen und Leben.   5., neubearb. Aufl. von Herders Konversationslexikon. 10 v.   Freiburg i.B., Herder, 1952-56.

Hastings, James.   A dictionary of the Bible, dealing with its language, literature, and contents, including Biblical theology. 5 v.   New York, Scribner, 1898-1904.

Hastings, James.   Dictionary of the Bible. Revised edition by Frederick C. Grant and H. H. Rowley.   New York, Scribner, 1963 (in one volume).

Hoffmann, Alexius, O.S.B. A liturgical dictionary.   Collegeville, Minn., Liturgical Press, 1928.

Jewish encyclopedia; a descriptive record of the history, religion, literature, and customs of the Jewish people.   Prepared under the direction of Cyrus Adler. 12 v.   New York, Funk, 1901-06.

Julian, John. A dictionary of hymnology, setting forth the origin and history of Christian hymns of all ages and nations. 2 v.   New York, Dover Publications, 1957.

Kalt, Edmund.   Biblisches Reallexikon.   2 v.   Paderborn, F. Schöningh, 1931.

De Katholieke encyclopaedie. 2. druk. Onder redactie van P. van der Meer, O.P., F. Bauer en L. Engelbregt, O.F.M. 25 v.   Amsterdam, Uitg. Mij. Joost van den Vondel, 1949-55.

Kostler, Rudolf. Wörterbuch zum Codex iuris canonici.   München, Kösel, 1927.

Lee, F. G. A glossary of liturgical and ecclesiastical terms.   London, B. Quaritch, 1877.

Lexikon der Marienkunde. Hrsg. von Konrad Algermissen,   Ludwig Böer, Carl Feckas, Julius Tyciak.   Regensburg, F. Pustet, 1957-

The New Catholic dictionary. See The Catholic encyclopedia dictionary.

The New Jewish encyclopedia. Edited by David Bridger in association with Samuel Wolk...   New York, Behrman House, 1962 (in one volume).

Pugin, A. W.   Glossary of ecclesiastical ornament and costume ... 2d ed. London, H. G. Bohn, 1846.

Reallexikon für Antike und Christentum; Sachwörterbuch zur Auseinandersetzung des Christentums mit der antiken Welt. In Verbindung mit Franz Joseph Dölger und Hans Lietzmann ... hrsg. von Theodor Klauser. Leipzig, K. W. Hiersemann, 1950-

Die Religion in Geschichte und Gegenwart; Handwörterbuch für Theologie und Religionswissenschaft. 3., völlig neu bearb. Aufl... Hrsg. von Kurt Galling. Tübingen, Mohr, 1957-

Roberti, Francesco. Dictionary of moral theology. Compiled under the direction of Francesco Cardinal Roberti. Edited under the direction of Pietro Palazzini. Translated from the 2d Italian edition under the direction of Henry J. Yannone. Westminster, Md., Newman Press, 1962 (in one volume)

Schaff, Philip. The new Schaff-Herzog encyclopedia of religious knowledge, embracing Biblical, historical, doctrinal and practical theology and Biblical, theological and ecclesiastical biography. Based on the 3d ed. of the Real-Encyclopädie founded by J. J. Herzog and edited by Albert Hauck. S. M. Jackson, editor-in-chief. 12 v. New York, Funk, 1908-12.

Trudel, P. A dictionary of canon law. 2d ed. St. Louis, Herder, 1920.

Twentieth century encyclopedia of religious knowledge; an extension of The new Schaff-Herzog encyclopedia of religious knowledge. Editor-in-chief: Lefferts A. Loetscher. 2 v. Grand Rapids, Mich., Baker Book House, 1955.

Vigouroux, F. G. Dictionnaire de la Bible, contenant tous les noms de personnes, de lieux, de plantes, d'animaux mentionnés dans les Saintes Ecritures, les questions théologiques, archéologiques, scientifiques, critiques relatives a l'Ancien et au Nouveau Testament et des notices sur les commentateurs anciens et modernes. 5 v. Paris, Letouzey, 1907-12.

------ Supplément, publié sous la direction de Louis Pirot. v.1- Paris, Letouzey, 1926-

Wetzer, H. J. Wetzer und Welte's Kirchenlexikon; oder, Encyclopädie der katholischen Theologie und ihrer Hülfswissenschaften. 2. Aufl., in neuer Bearb. von Franz Kaulen. 12 v. and index. Freiburg i.B., Herder, 1886-1903.

FORM DIVISIONS TO BE USED UNDER SUBJECTS

Addresses, essays, lectures.
Bibliography.
Biography.
Collections.
Devotional literature.
Dictionaries.
Directories.
Drama.
Fiction.
Handbooks, manuals, etc.
History.
Meditations.
Periodicals.
Poetry.
Popular works.
Prayer-books.
Selections.
Sermons.
Statistics.
Study and teaching.
Yearbooks.

KEY TO CROSS REFERENCES

sa See also.
 x Refer from (see)
xx Refer from (see also)

KEY TO SYMBOLS AFTER EXPLANATORY NOTES

AT Attwater, Donald. A Catholic Dictionary.
LC U.S. Library of Congress. Subject Headings Used in the
      Dictionary Catalogs of the Library of Congress.
NC New Catholic Dictionary (The Catholic Encyclopedia Dic-
      tionary)

ABBESSES.   (Geog. subdiv., Indirect)
        BQX 6851; BQX 7801-8043
            (244.x9)
    xx Abbeys.
        Christian biography.
        Religious orders of women.

ABBESSES (CANON LAW)
    xx Persons (Canon law)
        Superiors, Religious (Canon law)

ABBESSES, BLESSING OF. See BLESSING
OF ABBESSES.

ABBEYS.   (Geog. subdiv., Indirect)
        BQT 5928 (Church architecture)
            (726.72)
        BQX 6801-6825 (Church history)
            (271)
    sa Abbesses.
        Abbots.
        Cathedrals.
        Convents.
        Monasteries.
        also names of individual abbeys.
    xx Architecture.
        Catholic institutions.
        Church architecture.
        Church history.
        Convents.
        Monasteries.
        Priories.

ABBEYS, BENEDICTINE, [CISTERCIAN,
ETC.]
    x Benedictine, [Cistercian, etc.]
        abbeys.

ABBOTS.   (Geog. subdiv., Indirect)
        BQX 6851; BQX 6901-7774
            (244.x9)
    sa Priors, Claustral.
    xx Abbeys.
        Christian biography.
        Monasticism.
        Prelates.
        Religious orders.
        Superiors, Religious.

ABBOTS - ELECTION.
        BQV230 506
    xx Election law (Canon law)

ABBOTS - HERALDRY.
    xx Heraldry, Sacred.

ABBOTS - INSIGNIA.

ABBOTS (CANON LAW)
        BQV230 419-517   (348.x37)
    xx Persons (Canon law)
        Superiors, Religious (Canon law)

ABBOTS, BENEDICTINE, [CISTERCIAN, ETC.]

ABBOTS, BLESSING OF. See BLESSING
OF ABBOTS.

ABBOTS, COMMENDATORY. See COMMENDA-
TORY ABBOTS.

ABBOTS NULLIUS (CANON LAW)
        BQV230 319-328   (348.x35)
    xx Bishops (Canon law)
        Persons (Canon law)

ABDIAS, BOOK OF. See BIBLE. O.T.
ABDIAS.

ABDUCTION (CANON LAW)
        BQV230 1074   (348.x427)
    xx Marriage - Impediments (Canon law)

ABORTION.   (Geog. subdiv., Indirect)
        BQT 1909 (Moral theology)
            (24x1.63)
    Other classifications and references
    as in LC.

ABORTION (CANON LAW)
        BQV230 2350   (348.x6)
    xx Crime and criminals (Canon law)

ABRAHAMITES (BOHEMIA)
    x Bohemian Deists.
        Deists, Bohemian.
        Israelites (Bohemia)

ABSENCE AND PRESUMPTION OF DEATH
(CANON LAW)
    sa Death - Proof and certification
        (Canon law)

ABSOLUTION.
     BQT 1371   (23x7.4)
sa Confession.
   Indulgences.
   Penance.
   Power of the keys.
xx Confession.
   Forgiveness of sin.
   Indulgences.
   Penance.

ABSOLUTION (CANON LAW)
     BQV230 870-892   (348.x42)
xx Censures, Ecclesiastical.
   Crime and criminals (Canon law)
   Faculties (Canon law)
   Irregularities.
   Penance (Canon law)
   Reserved cases.

ABSTINENCE.
     BQT 1989   (24x1.7)
sa Fasting.
xx Fasting.
   Temperance (Virtue)

ABYSSINIAN CHURCH. See ETHIOPIC CHURCH.

ACACIAN SCHISM. See SCHISM, ACACIAN.

ACACIANS.
     BQT 63   (273.x3)
 x Homoeans.
xx Arianism.
   Heresies and heretics - Early
     church.

ACADEMIES, EVANGELICAL. See
EVANGELICAL ACADEMIES.

ACCLAMATIONS (LITURGY)
     BQT 4319; BQT 4421
     BQT 4599; (Church music)
sa Responses (Liturgy)
 x Laudes.
   Liturgical acclamations.
xx Divine office.
   Prayers.'
   Responses (Liturgy)

ACCOMPLICES (CANON LAW)
     BQV230 884 (Confession)
     BQV230 2209 (Criminal law)
       (348.x6)
xx Criminal law (Canon law)

ACOEMETAE.
     BQX 6838
 x Akoimetae.

ACOLYTES. See ALTAR BOYS.

ACOLYTES (HOLY ORDER). See MINOR
ORDERS.

ACTA MARTYRUM.
     BQ 247; BQ 498; BQX 269
      (280.x1)
     BQ 1013 (Greek)
     BQ 5605 (Latin)
"The official records of the trials
  and execution of the martyrs." AT
xx Church history - Primitive and
    early church.
   Persecution.

ACTION, CATHOLIC. See CATHOLIC ACTION.

L'ACTION FRANCAISE.
     BQX 1795   (274.408)
xx Catholic Church - France.
   Church and state in France.

ACTIONS AND DEFENSES (CANON LAW)
     BQV230 1667-1705
sa Complaints (Canon law)
   Lis pendens (Canon law)
xx Nullity (Canon law)
   Trials, Ecclesiastical.

ACTIVE LIFE.
     BQT 2201
Here are entered works on the Christian life and the religious life
  as concerned with external activities, whether temporal (manual arts,
  education, care of the sick, etc.)
  or spiritual (cure of souls, mission
  work, preaching, etc.).
sa Mixed life.
   Perfection, Christian.

ACTS OF THE APOSTLES. See
BIBLE. N.T. ACTS.

ACTS, HUMAN. See HUMAN ACTS.

ACTUAL GRACE. See GRACE, ACTUAL.

AD DOMINUM CUM TRIBULARER CLAMAVI (MUSIC)
See PSALMS (MUSIC) - 119th PSALM.

AD LIMINA APOSTOLORUM. See VISIT AD
LIMINA.

ADAMITES.
BQT 89
xx Beghards.
Heresies and heretics - Early church.
Hussites.
Sects, Medieval.

ADELPHIANS. See MESSALIANS.

ADMINISTRATORS APOSTOLIC.
BQV230 312-318   (348.x325)
sa Vicars capitular.
x Apostolic administrators.
xx Bishops (Canon law)
Dioceses (Canon law)
Persons (Canon law)
Vicars capitular.

L ADOLESENCE x Teen age

ADONAI. See JAHVEH. x youth

ADOPTION (CANON LAW)
BQV230 1080   (348.x427)
xx Guardian and ward (Canon law)
Marriage - Impediments (Canon law)

ADOPTION (THEOLOGY)
BQT 1192   (234.x2)
Here are entered works on the spiritual
sonship which Christians receive as
an effect of sanctifying grace, whereby they become children of God and
co-heirs with Christ.
xx God - Fatherhood.
Grace (Theology)
Mystical union.

ADOPTIONISM.
BQT 49   (273.x5)
Here are entered works on the heretical
theory that Christ, as man, is the
adoptive Son of God.

ADOPTIONISM -- Continued.
sa Nestorians.
xx Heresies and heretics - Early
church.
Jesus Christ - History of doctrines.
Trinity - History of doctrines.

ADORAMUS TE (MUSIC)
M 2079

ADORATION.
BQT 1864   (24x1.61)
sa Genuflexion.
xx Religion (Virtue)
Worship.

ADORATION, PERPETUAL. See
PERPETUAL ADORATION.

ADORATION OF THE BLESSED SACRAMENT.
BQT 2589
sa Perpetual adoration.
x Blessed Sacrament, Adoration of the.
Eucharist - Adoration.
xx Eucharist - Cultus.

ADORATION OF THE BLESSED SACRAMENT -
SERMONS.
BQT 3064

ADORO TE.
BQT 2695

ADORO TE (MUSIC)
M 2079

✓ ADULT EDUCATION, CATHOLIC. See
CATHOLIC EDUCATION, ADULT.
Religious education of Adults

ADULTERY.   (Geog. subdiv., Direct)
HQ 806-808   (176.6)
BQT 1936 (Moral theology)
(24x1.64)
References as in LC.

ADULTERY (CANON LAW)
BQV230 2357 (Criminal law)
BQV230 1075; BQV230 1129 (Mar-
riage law)   (348.x427)
xx Crime and criminals (Canon law)
Marriage (Canon law)

ADULTERY (CANON LAW, ORTHODOX EASTERN)
  xx Marriage (Canon law, Orthodox
    Eastern)

✓ Adults

ADVENT.   sa Human development
      BQT 4221   (264.x5)
  sa O antiphons.
    Second advent.
  xx Church year.

ADVENT - DEVOTIONAL LITERATURE.

ADVENT - MEDITATIONS.
    [BQT 2606.2]   (24x2.1)

ADVENT - POETRY.

ADVENT - PRAYER-BOOKS.
    [BQT 2649]

ADVENT - SONGS AND MUSIC. See
  ADVENT MUSIC.

ADVENT MUSIC.
  x Advent - Songs and music.
  xx Church music.
    Sacred vocal music.

ADVENT SERMONS.
      BQT 2993   (264.x5)
  x Sermons, Advent.

ADVENTISTS.
      BX 6101-6193   (286.7)
  sa Seventh-day Adventists.
  x Second-adventists.

ADVERSE POSSESSION (CANON LAW)
  xx Possession (Canon law)

ADVERTISING - CHURCHES.
  sa Church announcements.
    Journalism, Religious.
    Public relations - Churches.

AEQUIPROBABILISM. See PROBABILISM.

AERONAUTICS IN MISSIONARY WORK.
  x Flying missionaries.

AFFINITY (CANON LAW)
      BQV230 97   (348.x3)
  xx Marriage - Impediments (Canon law)

AFFINITY (CANON LAW, ORTHODOX EASTERN)

AFFLICTION.
  sa Consolation.
  xx Consolation.
  Other references as in LC.

AFRICA - CHURCH HISTORY.
      BQX 2602-3965   (276)

AFRICA - CHURCH HISTORY - EARLY
  PERIOD.
      BQX 3621-3645

AFRICA - CHURCH HISTORY - MODERN
  PERIOD.
      BQX 3655-3659

AFRICA - RELIGION.
      BL 2400-2490

AFRICAN METHODIST EPISCOPAL CHURCH.
      BX 8440-8449

AFRICAN RITE.
      BQT 4136   (264.x82)

AGAPE.
      BQT 4073   (264.x61)
  Here are entered works dealing with
    meetings or love-feasts of the
    early Christians, which included
    a meal and sometimes were followed
    by the eucharistic celebration.
  sa Love feasts.
  xx Eucharist.
    Love feasts.
    Sacred meals.

AGE (CANON LAW)
      BQV230 88   (348.x3)
  xx Persons (Canon law)

AGE OF CONSENT (CANON LAW)
  xx Consent (Canon law)

AGED see Elderly

AGED - PRAYER-BOOKS.
      BQT 2648

AGED - RELIGIOUS LIFE.
    [BQT 2289]

AGED - SERMONS.
      BQT 3019

AGED, CHURCH WORK WITH THE. See
CHURCH WORK WITH THE AGED.

AGENCY (CANON LAW)
  sa Procurators (Canon law)

AGNOSTICISM.
      B 808 (Philosophy)   (149.7)
      BQT 123 (Theology)   (273.8)
      BD 150-232 (Theory of knowledge)
  sa Atheism.
     Belief and doubt.
     Modernism.
     Positivism.
     Rationalism.
     Skepticism.
  xx Atheism.
     Belief and doubt.
     Faith.
     Free thought.
     God.
     Irreligion.
     Modernism.
     Positivism.
     Rationalism.
     Religion.
     Secularism.
     Skepticism.
     Truth.

AGNUS DEI (SACRAMENTAL)
      BQT 4522   (23x7.8)

AGONISTS. See CIRCUMCELLIONS.

AGONY OF CHRIST. See JESUS CHRIST -
  AGONY.

AGRICULTURAL WORK OF MISSIONS. See
  MISSIONS - AGRICULTURAL WORK.

AJIVIKAS.
      BL 2020

AKOIMETAE. See ACOEMETAE.

ALASKA - CHURCH HISTORY.
      BQX 4540   (277.98)

ALBANIA - CHURCH HISTORY.
      BQX 6211-6220

ALBANIAN ORTHODOX EASTERN CHURCH. See
  ORTHODOX EASTERN CHURCH, ALBANIAN.

ALBATI. See FLAGELLANTS (SECT)

ALBIGENSES.
      BQT 91 (Theology)   (273.x61)
      DC 83.2-3 (Wars)   (944.023)
  sa Muret, Battle of, 1213.
     Waldenses.
  xx Asceticism - History - Middle Ages.
     Cathari.
     Sects, Medieval.

‾Alcoholism   (241)

ALCOHOLISM AND RELIGION.
   x Religion and alcoholism.
  xx Liquor problem.
     Temperance.

ALEXANDRIAN RITE.
      BQT 5012-5099
  "The liturgy used in the patriarchate
   of Alexandria before the Council of
   Chalcedon and the monophysite
   schism, commonly called the Liturgy
   of St. Mark." AT
  sa Liturgy of St. Mark.

ALEXANDRIAN SCHOOL.
      BJ 221-224 (Ethics)
      B 630-708 (Philosophy)
  sa Neoplatonism.
  xx Neoplatonism.

ALEXANDRIAN SCHOOL, CHRISTIAN.
      BQX 5482 (Church history)
       (273.x3)
      BQT 57 (Theology)
  sa Antiochian school.
   x Christian Alexandrian school.
     Fathers of the church, Alexandrian.
  xx Antiochian school.
     Apologetics - History - Early
        church.

ALIENATION (CANON LAW)
      BQV230 1530-1534   (348.x46)
  sa Reparation (Canon law)
  xx Church property (Canon law)
     Contracts (Canon law)

ALL SAINTS' DAY.
      BQT 4234   (264.x5)
  sa Saints.
   x Feast of All Saints.

ALL SAINTS' DAY SERMONS.

ALL SOULS' DAY.
  BQT 4234   (264.x5)
xx Purgatory.

ALL SOULS' DAY MASS. See MISSA IN COM-
MEMORATIONE OMNIUM FIDELIUM DEFUNCTORUM.

ALL SOULS' DAY NOVENA. See NOVENA -
ALL SOULS' DAY.

ALL SOULS' DAY OFFICE. See OFFICIUM IN
COMMEMORATIONE OMNIUM FIDELIUM DE-
FUNCTORUM.

ALL SOULS' DAY SERMONS.
sa Purgatory - Sermons.
xx Purgatory - Sermons.

ALLAH. See GOD (MOHAMMENDANISM)

ALLEGORIES.
  BQ 307 (Christian literature)
  BQT 2831 (Devotional literature)
References as in LC.

ALMANACS, CATHOLIC.
  AY 81.R6-7
  [BQX 36]
sa Missions - Almanacs, yearbooks, etc.
 x Catholic almanacs.
  Catholic Church - Almanacs.
xx Catholic Church - Yearbooks.
  Church calendars.

ALMS AND ALMSGIVING.
  BQT 1786   (24x1.51)
  BQT 4514
sa Charities.
  Charity.
xx Charities.
  Good works (Theology)

ALOGI.
  BQT 50   (273.x2)
xx Asceticism - History - Early
    church.
  Heresies and heretics - Early church.
  Logos.

ALOMBRADOS. See ALUMBRADOS.

ALSACE - CHURCH HISTORY.
  [BQX 1820]

ALTAR BOYS.
  [BQT 2289]   (264.x64)
sa Thurifers.
 x Acolytes.
  Servers.

ALTAR BOYS - BIOGRAPHY.

ALTAR BOYS - HANDBOOKS, MANUALS, ETC.
  BQT 4345
xx Rites and ceremonies (Catholic) -
    Handbooks, manuals, etc.

ALTAR BREADS.
  BQT 1328
sa Azyme.
  Host.
  Prosphora.
 x Breads, Altar.
  Eucharistic bread.
xx Eucharist - Elements.

ALTAR-CLOTHS.
  BQT 4361   (264.x4)
xx Church vestments.

ALTAR FURNISHINGS.
  BQT 4357

ALTAR GILDS.
  BQT 3326-3339   (256)
 x Altar societies.
  Gilds, Altar.
xx Church societies.

ALTAR GILDS - HANDBOOKS, MANUALS, ETC.

ALTAR LINENS.

ALTAR PRAYERS.
  BQT 4498   (24x3.8)
Here are entered works containing
  public prayers and devotions for
  liturgical use and for use on
  various occasions at church services.
 x Prayers, Altar.
xx Devotions, Popular.

ALTAR SCREENS. See SCREENS (CHURCH
DECORATION)

ALTAR SOCIETIES. See ALTAR GILDS.

ALTAR VESSELS. See SACRED VESSELS.

ALTAR WINE. See WINE - LITURGICAL USE.

ALTARPIECES.
      BQT 5945   (729.962)
  x Reredos.
  xx Christian art.
     Church decoration and ornament.
     Church furniture.
     Screens (Church decoration)

ALTARS.
      BQT 5943 (Church architecture)
        (729.912)
      BQT 4357 (Liturgy)   (264.x4)
  sa Baldachins.
  xx Church decoration and ornament.
     Church furniture.

ALTARS - CONSECRATION.
      BQT 4480
  x Consecration of altars.

ALTARS (CANON LAW)
      BQV230 1197-1202   (348.x413)
  xx Sacred places (Canon law)

ALTARS, PRIVILEGED.
      BQV230 916-917
  A privileged altar is "one to which
    the Apostolic See has attached a
    plenary indulgence applicable only
    to the souls in purgatory, and
    gained every time Mass is offered
    upon it." Cath. Encyc.
  x Privileged altars.
  xx Indulgences.

ALUMBRADOS.
      BQT 2461
      BQX 2945
  x Alombrados.
  xx Illuminati.
     Mysticism - History - Middle Ages.

AMALRICIANS.
      BQT 89
  x Amauriani.
  xx Pantheism.

AMAURIANI. See AMALRICIANS.

AMBASSADORS.
      JX 1621-1894
  sa Legates, Papal.
     Nuncios, Papal.
  Other references as in LC.

AMBRIES. See AUMBRIES.

AMBROSIAN CHANT.
      BQT 4918
  x Chant, Ambrosian.
  xx Chant.

AMBROSIAN RITE.
      BQT 4911-4919   (264.x82)

AMBROSIAN RITE - COLLECTIONS.

AMBROSIAN RITE - CONGRESSES.

AMBROSIAN RITE - MASS.
      BQT 4911
  sa Missale Ambrosianum.
  x Mass - Ambrosian rite.

AMBROSIAN RITE - PERIODICALS.

AMEN.
      BQT 4319

AMENS (MUSIC)
      M 2079
  xx Sacred vocal music.

AMERICANISM (CATHOLIC CONTROVERSY)
      BQX 4411   (277.38)
  By this term are understood "certain
    modifications in Christian teach-
    ing as regards both faith and con-
    duct advocated by some in order to
    increase conversions to the church
    among the people of the United
    States ... These errors were, and
    are, to be met with outside the
    United States." AT
  xx Catholic Church - France.
     Catholic Church - U.S.
     Modernism.

AMISH. See MENNONITES.

AMORAIM.
  References as in LC.

AMOS, BOOK OF. See BIBLE. O.T. AMOS.

AMUSEMENTS.
   sa Church entertainments.
   Other references as in LC.

AMUSEMENTS - MORAL AND RELIGIOUS ASPECTS.
     BQT 1935; BQT 2272

ANABAPTISTS.   (Geog. subdiv., Direct)
     BX 4930-4946   (284.3)
   References as in LC.

ANAKEPHALAIOSIS. See RECAPITULATION.

ANALOGY (RELIGION)
     BL 210   (219)
   sa Anthropomorphism.
     Correspondence, Doctrine of.

ANAPHORA.
     BQT 5115; BQT 5134; BQT 5155
      (264.x7)
   "A liturgical term for the canon of
    a eucharistic liturgy, especially
    in the Eastern rites." AT

ANATHEMA. See EXCOMMUNICATION.

ANCESTOR-WORSHIP.
     BL 467   (291.2134)
   sa Apotheosis.
    Dead (in religion, folk-lore, etc.)
    Funeral rites and ceremonies.
   x Dead, Worship of the.
   xx Funeral rites and ceremonies.
    Religion, Primitive.

ANCHORESSES.
     BQX 6842   (271.9)
   xx Christian biography.
    Hermits.
    Recluses.
    Religious orders of women.

ANCHORITES. See HERMITS.

ANECDOTES, RELIGIOUS. See RELIGION -
ANECDOTES, FACETIAE, SATIRE, ETC.

✓ ANGELS.   2 90
     BQT 649-666   (231.x6)
   sa Ark of the covenant.
    Guardian angels.

ANGELS -- Continued.
   x Cherubim.
    Seraphim.
   xx Dogmatic theology.
    Guardian angels.
    Heaven.
    Spirits.

ANGELS - ART.
     BQT 5903

ANGELS - BIBLICAL TEACHING.

ANGELS - CULTUS.

ANGELS - LEGENDS.

ANGELS - PRAYER-BOOKS.
     BQT 2683   (24x3.4)

ANGELS (JUDAISM)
     BM 645.A6)
   xx Jews - Religion.

ANGELS (MOHAMMEDANISM)
   xx Mohammedanism.

ANGELS, GUARDIAN. See GUARDIAN
ANGELS.

ANGELUS.
     BQT 2695

ANGELUS - MEDITATIONS.

ANGER.
     BJ 1535 (Ethics)   (179.8)
     BF 575 (Psychology)
     BQT 1813; BQT 1925 (Moral
      theology)   (24x1.44)
   sa Wrath.
   xx Capital sins.
    Conduct of life.

ANGER OF GOD.
     BQT 561   (231.x13)
   x God - Anger.
    God - Wrath.
    Wrath of God.
   xx Atonement.

ANGER OF GOD - SERMONS.

ANGLICAN BENEDICTINES. See
BENEDICTINES (ANGLICAN)

ANGLICAN CANON LAW. See CHURCH OF
ENGLAND - LAW.

ANGLICAN CHANT. See CHANT(ANGLICAN)

ANGLICAN CHURCH. See CHURCH OF ENGLAND.

ANGLICAN CHURCHES. See CHURCHES,
ANGLICAN.

ANGLICAN COMMUNION.
BX 5003-5009 (283)
Here are entered works dealing
with the Church of England and
related church bodies, namely,
the Episcopal churches in the
British Empire and the Protestant
Episcopal Church in the U.S.A.

ANGLICAN COMMUNION - CLERGY.

ANGLICAN COMMUNION - CONFIRMATION. See
CONFIRMATION - ANGLICAN COMMUNION.

ANGLICAN COMMUNION - LITURGICAL MOVEMENT.
See LITURGICAL MOVEMENT - ANGLICAN
CHURCH.

ANGLICAN LITURGY. See CHURCH OF
ENGLAND. LITURGY AND RITUAL.

ANGLICAN ORDERS.
BQT 350; BX 5178 (23x7.61)
"Here are entered works dealing
with the question at issue between the Anglican Communion and
the Catholic Church as to whether
the episcopate of the Anglican
Communion is in the true line of
apostolic succession." LC
x Church of England - Ordination.
Orders, Anglican.
xx Apostolic succession.
Church of England - Clergy.

ANGLICAN RELIGIOUS ORDERS. See
RELIGIOUS ORDERS, ANGLICAN.
RELIGIOUS ORDERS OF WOMEN, ANGLICAN.

ANGLO-CATHOLICISM.
BQX 5121 (283)
xx Church of England.
Oxford movement.
Protestant Episcopal Church in
the U.S.A.

ANGLO-CATHOLICISM - CONGRESSES.

ANIMA CHRISTI.
BQT 2695 (24x3.7)
x Soul of Christ (Prayer)

ANIMA CHRISTI - MEDITATIONS.
[BQT 2610.5]

ANIMA CHRISTI - SERMONS.

ANIMAL-WORSHIP.
BL 439-443 (291.2124)
References as in LC.

ANIMALS, TREATMENT OF.
sa Hunting - Moral and religious
aspects.
Other references as in LC.

ANIMISM.
GN 471 (291.211)
References as in LC.

ANNATES.
BX 1950
sa Church finance.
Tithes.
x First fruits.
xx Church finance.
Fees, Ecclesiastical.
Tithes.

ANNIHILATIONISM.
BQT 1527 (218)
"Here are entered works dealing
with the theory that at death
the body and soul of men are
annihilated." LC
sa Future punishment.
xx Nirvana.

ANNIVERSARY SERMONS.
  [BQT 3005.5]
  Here are entered sermons preached at
    silver, golden or diamond jubilees,
    centenary celebrations, etc.
  x Sermons, Anniversary.
  xx Occasional sermons.

ANNIVERSARY SERMONS - BISHOPS.
  x Bishops - Anniversary sermons.

ANNIVERSARY SERMONS - CATHEDRALS.
  x Cathedrals - Anniversary sermons.

ANNIVERSARY SERMONS - CONVENTS.
  x Convents - Anniversary sermons.

ANNIVERSARY SERMONS - DIOCESES.
  x Dioceses - Anniversary sermons.

ANNIVERSARY SERMONS - MONASTERIES.
  x Monasteries - Anniversary sermons.

ANNIVERSARY SERMONS - PARISHES.
  x Parishes - Anniversary sermons.

ANNIVERSARY SERMONS - PRIESTS.
  x Priests - Anniversary sermons.

ANNIVERSARY SERMONS - RELIGIOUS
  PROFESSION.
  x Profession, Religious - Anniversary
    sermons.

ANNO SANTO. See HOLY YEAR.

✓ ANNULMENT ~~OF MARRIAGE~~. ~~See~~
  ~~MARRIAGE - ANNULMENT.~~ 265.5

ANNUNCIATION.
  BQT 1054
  sa Incarnation.
  x Mary, Blessed Virgin - Annun-
    ciation.

ANNUNCIATION - ART.
  BQT 5882
  xx Mary, Blessed Virgin - Art.

ANNUNCIATION, FEAST OF THE.
  BQT 4230   (23x3.72)
  x Feast of the Annunciation.

ANNUNCIATION, MASS OF THE. See
MISSA IN ANNUNTIATIONE BEATAE
MARIAE VIRGINIS.
✓ Anointing of the Sick
  ANOINTINGS.   x Extreme Unction
  BQT 4509
  sa Extreme Unction.
    Holy oils.
  x Unction.
  xx Holy oils.

ANTE-NICENE FATHERS. See FATHERS
OF THE CHURCH, ANTE-NICENE.

ANTHEM.
  BQT 4596   (245.x2; 783.4)
  xx Church music.

ANTHROPOLOGY, BIBLICAL. See
MAN (THEOLOGY) - BIBLICAL TEACHING.

ANTHROPOLOGY, THEOLOGICAL. See
MAN (THEOLOGY)

ANTHROPOMORPHISM.
  BQT 529   (215)
  BL 215
  xx Analogy (Religion)
    Ejection (Psychology)
    God.
    Nature-worship.
    Symbolism.

ANTHROPOSOPHY.
  BP 595
  References and subdivisions as
    in LC.

ANTI-CATHOLIC POLEMIC.   (Geog.
  subdiv.)
    BQT 425-445
  Here are entered works which attack
    the Catholic Church.
  sa Anti-clericalism.
    Church history - Errors, in-
      ventions, etc.
    Ultramontanism.
    also subdivision "Controversial
      literature" under such head-
      ings as Indulgences, Jesuits,
      Mass, Popes - Infallibility,
      Religious orders.

ANTI-CATHOLIC POLEMIC -- Continued.
   x Catholic Church - Anti-Catholic
      polemic.
     Polemic, Anti-Catholic.
   xx Apologetics.
     Persecution.

ANTI-CATHOLIC POLEMIC - BIBLIOGRAPHY.

ANTI-CATHOLIC POLEMIC - FICTION.

ANTI-CATHOLIC POLEMIC - HISTORY.

ANTI-CATHOLIC POLEMIC - PERIODICALS.

ANTI-CATHOLIC POLEMIC - PERSONAL
  NARRATIVES.

ANTICHRIST.
     BQT 1462   (236.x92)
  sa End of the world.
  xx End of the world.
    Eschatology.
    Jesus Christ.

ANTI-CLERICALISM.   (Geog. subdiv.,
  Direct)
     BQX 1079
  xx Anti-Catholic polemic.
    Clergy.
    Freemasons and Catholic Church.
    Secularism.

ANTI-CLERICALISM - FICTION.

ANTINOMIANISM.
     BT 1330; BQT 48 (273.x11)
  sa Neonomianism.
    Ranters.
  xx Calvinism.
    Congregationalism.
    Good works (Theology)

ANTIOCH, SCHOOL OF. See ANTIOCHIAN
  SCHOOL.

ANTIOCHENE RITE.
  "The original liturgy of Antioch,
  called 'of the Apostolic constitutions,' said to be the
  oldest and most apostolic of
  all known liturgies. Super-
  seded by the 'Liturgy of St.
  James'." AT

ANTIOCHENE RITE - CANON LAW.
    BQV 1171-1187

ANTIOCHENE RITE - HISTORY.
    BQX 5551-5659

ANTIOCHENE RITE. LITURGY AND RITUAL.
    BQT 5101-5170 (264.x7)

ANTIOCHENE SCHOOL. See ANTIOCHIAN
  SCHOOL.

ANTIOCHIAN SCHOOL.
    BQT 57 (273.x3)
  "Here are entered works dealing
  with the theories of a group of
  early Christian theologians at
  Antioch. Common to all of them
  was a grammatico-historical
  method of the Alexandrian school
  and a dogmatic theory which tended
  to separate the divine and human
  in the person of Christ." LC
  sa Alexandrian school, Christian.
  x Antioch, School of.
    Antiochene school.
  xx Alexandrian school, Christian.
    Bible - Criticism, interpreta-
     tion, etc. - History.
    Dogmatic theology - History -
     Early church.
    Jesus Christ - History of doc-
     trines.

ANTIPATHIES AND PREJUDICES (RELIGION).
  See PREJUDICES AND ANTIPATHIES
  (RELIGION)

ANTIPHONAL CHANT.
    BQT 4626
  sa Communion verse (Music)
    Introits (Music)
    Offertories (Chant)
  x Chant, Antiphonal.

ANTIPHONARIUM.
    BQT 4262; BQT 4385 (783.24)
  "A liturgical book containing the
  chant not only of the antiphons
  but of all sung parts of the
  Divine Office." AT
  x Antiphonary.
  xx Divine Office.

ANTIPHONARIUM - ART.
    ND 3380

ANTIPHONARIUM MISSAE.
    BQT 4252
  A liturgical book containing the
    antiphonal and responsorial chants
    of the Mass.
  sa Graduale.

ANTIPHONARY. See ANTIPHONARIUM.

ANTIPHONS.
    BQT 4393

ANTIPHONS (MUSIC)
  xx Sacred vocal music.

ANTIPOPES.
    BQX   101-104
  xx Popes.

ANTI-PROTESTANT POLEMIC.
   x Polemic, Anti-Protestant.
  xx Protestantism - Controversial
    literature.

ANTIQUITIES, BIBLICAL. See
  BIBLE - ANTIQUITIES.

ANTIQUITIES, CHRISTIAN. See
  CHRISTIAN ANTIQUITIES.

ANTIQUITIES, ECCLESIASTICAL. See
  CHRISTIAN ANTIQUITIES.

ANTISEMITISM.
  References and subdivisions as in LC.

ANTITRINITARIANS.
    BQT 85   (273.x7)
  xx Trinity - History of doctrines.

APHORISMS AND APOTHEGMS (RELIGION)
    BQT 2512   (244.x8)
  sa Ejaculations.

APOCALYPSE OF ST. JOHN. See
  BIBLE. N.T. APOCALYPSE.

APOCALYPTIC LITERATURE.
   x Literature, Apocalyptic.
  xx Bible - Prophecies.
    Prophecies.

APOCRYPHA.
  According to Catholic usage the
    term "Apocrypha" refers to
    spurious writings which once
    claimed rank with the canonical
    or inspired books of the Bible.
    Catholics and non-Catholics dif-
    fer in the use of the term; the
    books which Catholics call apo-
    crypha non-Catholics call pseud-
    epigrapha and apply the term
    "Apocrypha" to the deutero-
    canonical books, which latter the
    Catholic Church recognizes to be
    canonical.
  In this list the non-Catholic apo-
    crypha are entered under "Bible.
    O.T. Deutero-canonical Books"
    for collective works, while
    single apocrypha are entered the
    same way as other Biblical books,
    e.g., Bible. O.T. Baruch.
  Catholic apocrypha (the non-Catholic
    pseudepigrapha) are entered under
    "Apocryphal Books (O.T.)" and
    "Apocryphal Books (N.T.)" for
    collective works, while single
    books are entered directly under
    their name, e.g., Apocalypse of
    Abraham; Gospel of Barnabas; etc.
  Cf. note under Apocryphal Books.

√APOCRYPHAL BOOKS.
  As used by the Library of Congress,
    the entries "Bible. O.T. Apo-
    cryphal Books" and "Bible. N.T.
    Apocryphal Books" include the
    Catholic apocrypha and the non-
    Catholic pseudepigrapha.
  Since these books are more correctly
    considered anonymous classics
    rather than Biblical literature
    (they have never been included in
    any Bible, Jewish, Catholic or
    Protestant) the individual books
    are preferably entered directly
    under their accepted names.
  For lists of these apocryphal books
    see the Vatican Norme or the
    Walsh classification schedule or
    the New Catholic Dictionary or
    Kapsner's Manual of Cataloging
    Practice for Catholic Author and
    Title Entries.

APOCRYPHAL BOOKS. COPTIC, [ENGLISH,
FRENCH, HEBREW, ETC.]

APOCRYPHAL BOOKS - BIBLIOGRAPHY.

APOCRYPHAL BOOKS - COMMENTARIES.

APOCRYPHAL BOOKS - CRITICISM,
INTERPRETATION, ETC.

APOCRYPHAL BOOKS - HISTORY AND
CRITICISM.

APOCRYPHAL BOOKS - INTRODUCTIONS.

APOCRYPHAL BOOKS - THEOLOGY.

APOCRYPHAL BOOKS (O.T.)
BS 1691-1830   (22x8)
x Bible. O.T. Apocryphal Books.
Pseudepigrapha (O.T.)
With subdivisions as under Apocryphal
Books.

APOCRYPHAL BOOKS (N.T.)
BS 2820-2825   (22x8.4-22x8.8)
x Bible. N.T. Apocryphal Books.
Jesus Christ - Apocryphal life.
Pseudepigrapha (N.T.)
With subdivisions as under Apocryphal
Books.

APOLLINARIANISM.
BQT 64

APOLOGETICAL SERMONS. See
APOLOGETICS - SERMONS.

APOLOGETICS.   238
BQT 202-396   (239.x7)
Here used to signify the theological science which explains and
defends the Catholic Church as
the true church of Christ. For
works explaining and justifying
the Christian religion, as by
non-Catholic authors, see
Christianity - Evidences.
sa Anti-Catholic polemic.
Belief and doubt.
Bible - Evidences, authority, etc.
Christianity - Evidences.

APOLOGETICS -- Continued.
sa Church.
Irenics.
Natural theology.
Religion and science.
x Catholic Church - Apologetics.
Catholic evidences.
Christian evidences.
Evidences of Christianity.
Evidences of the Catholic Church.
Fundamental theology.
Polemics (Theology)
Theology, Fundamental.
xx Christianity - Evidences.
Dogmatic theology.
Free thought.
Religion.
Religion and science.

APOLOGETICS - BIBLIOGRAPHY.
[BQT 200]
Z 7863   (016.239)

APOLOGETICS - CATECHISMS, QUESTION-
BOOKS.
BQT 221   (239.x721)

APOLOGETICS - COLLECTIONS.

APOLOGETICS - DEBATES.
BQT 230
x Debates with non-Catholics.
xx Catholic Church - Controversial
literature.
Theology, Comparative.

APOLOGETICS - DICTIONARIES.
[BQT 204]

APOLOGETICS - FICTION.

APOLOGETICS - HISTORY.
BQT 211
Here are entered works on the history of apologetic theology and
apologetic literature, subdivided by period, e.g., Giordani,
Igino. La prima polemica cris-
tiana: gli apologeti greci del
secondo secolo (APOLOGETICS -
HISTORY - EARLY CHURCH).

14

APOLOGETICS - HISTORY -- Continued.
   Individual apologetical treatises
      are entered under Apologetics
      with direct period subdivision,
      e.g., Arnobius Afer, 4th cent.
      Adversus gentes (APOLOGETICS -
      EARLY CHURCH)

APOLOGETICS - HISTORY - EARLY CHURCH.
   sa Alexandrian school, Christian.
   xx Church history - Primitive and
      early church.

APOLOGETICS - HISTORY - MIDDLE AGES.
   xx Church history - Middle Ages.

APOLOGETICS - HISTORY - MODERN
   PERIOD.
      xx Catholic Church - History -
         Modern period.

APOLOGETICS - HISTORY - 16th CENTURY.

APOLOGETICS - HISTORY - 17th CENTURY.

APOLOGETICS - HISTORY - 18th CENTURY.

APOLOGETICS - HISTORY - 19th CENTURY.

APOLOGETICS - HISTORY - 20th CENTURY.

APOLOGETICS - METHODOLOGY.
      BQT 205
   xx Theology - Methodology.

APOLOGETICS - PERSONAL NARRATIVES. See
   CONVERSION - PERSONAL NARRATIVES.

APOLOGETICS - POPULAR WORKS.
      BQT 216-217

APOLOGETICS - SERMONS.
   x Apologetical sermons.
      Sermons, Apologetical.

APOLOGETICS - TEXTBOOKS.
      BQT 213

################

APOLOGETICS - EARLY CHURCH.
   See note under Apologetics - History.

APOLOGETICS - MIDDLE AGES.

APOLOGETICS - MODERN PERIOD.

APOLOGETICS - 16th CENTURY.

APOLOGETICS - 17th CENTURY.

APOLOGETICS - 18th CENTURY.

APOLOGETICS - 19th CENTURY.

APOLOGETICS - 20th CENTURY.

################

APOLOGETICS - EASTERN CHURCHES. See
   EASTERN CHURCHES - APOLOGETICS.

APOLOGETICS, MISSIONARY.
      BQT 3299   (266.x02)
   "Here are entered works on methods
      of presenting Christianity in
      the foreign mission fields, as
      well as works on Christianity
      which are prepared for the
      foreign mission fields." LC
   x Mission methods.
      Missionary apologetics.

APOSTASY.
      BQV230 1325   (348.x44)
   sa Heresy.
      Schism.
      Sects.
   xx Catholics, Lapsed.
      Faith.
      Non-Catholics.
      Offenses against religion.

APOSTASY (JUDAISM)
      BM 720.H5

APOSTLES.
      BS 2440 (Biography)
         (225.x931)
      BS 2618-19 (Teaching)
      BQT 867 (Calling of)
   sa Evangelists (Bible)
      Jesus Christ - Brethren.
   x Disciples, Twelve.
   xx Bible - Biography.
      Christian biography.
      Christianity.
      Church history - Primitive and
         early church.
      Disciples.
      Evangelists (Bible)
      Saints.

APOSTLES - ART.
      BQT 5891
  xx Saints - Art.

APOSTLES - DRAMA.

APOSTLES - LEGENDS.

APOSTLES - SERMONS.
      [BQT 3090]

APOSTLES' CREED.
      BQT 146   (238.1)
  xx Creeds.

APOSTLES' CREED - CATHECHISMS,
  QUESTION-BOOKS.
      BQT 3197

APOSTLES' CREED - EARLY WORKS TO
1800.

APOSTLES' CREED - JUVENILE
LITERATURE.

APOSTLES' CREED - MEDITATIONS.

APOSTLES' CREED - PICTURES,
ILLUSTRATIONS, ETC.

APOSTLES' CREED - SERMONS.
      BQT 3089

APOSTOLATE.
      BQT 3518-3527
  Here are entered general works on
    the Christian apostolate or ef-
    forts to make the name and work
    of Christ known to others, which
    mission can be carried out in any
    walk of life and has been exer-
    cised since the beginning of
    Christianity.
  Works on the more recent organized
    cooperation of the laity with the
    apostolic hierarchy are entered
    under Catholic action.
  sa Catholic action.
    Episcopacy.
    Laity.

APOSTOLATE -- Continued.
  sa Missions.
    Priesthood.
    also names of movements promoting
      the apostolate, e.g., Christo-
      pher movement, Grail movement,
      etc.
  x Christian apostolate.

APOSTOLATE - BIBLIOGRAPHY.
      [BQT 3518.2]; [Z 7763]

APOSTOLATE - CONGRESSES.

APOSTOLATE - EARLY CHURCH.
      [BQT 3520]

APOSTOLATE - PAPAL TEACHING.

APOSTOLATE, LAY. See CATHOLIC
ACTION; LAITY.

APOSTOLATE, LITURGICAL. See
LITURGICAL MOVEMENT.

APOSTOLIC ADMINISTRATORS. See
ADMINISTRATORS, APOSTOLIC.

APOSTOLIC CHANCERY. See
CANCELLARIA APOSTOLICA.

APOSTOLIC CHURCH. See
CHURCH HISTORY - PRIMITIVE AND
EARLY CHURCH.

APOSTOLIC CONSTITUTIONS.
  x Constitutiones apostolorum.

APOSTOLIC DATARY. See
DATARIA APOSTOLICA.

APOSTOLIC DELEGATES. See
DELEGATES, APOSTOLIC.

APOSTOLIC FATHERS.
      BQ 172·(History and criticism)
      (280.x1)
      BQ 1080 (Texts)
  "Those Christian writers who lived
    near enough to apostolic times to
    have had personal intercourse
    with the Apostles, or at any rate

APOSTOLIC FATHERS -- Continued.
    to have come within their near
    and unmodified influence." AT
    x Fathers, Apostolic.
      Fathers of the church, Apostolic.
    xx Christian biography.
      Church history - Primitive and
        early church.
      Fathers of the church.

APOSTOLIC PREFECTS. See
  VICARS APOSTOLIC.

APOSTOLIC PROTONOTARIES. See
  PROTONOTARIES APOSTOLIC.

APOSTOLIC SIGNATURA. See
  SIGNATURA APOSTOLICA.

APOSTOLIC SUCCESSION.
    BQT 352   (2x39.31)
  "The authoritative and unbroken
  transmission of the mission and
  powers conferred by Jesus Christ
  on St. Peter and the apostles
  [and] from them to the present
  pope and hierarchy." AT
  sa Anglican orders.
    Bishops.
    Clergy.
    Episcopacy.
    Popes.
    Priesthood.
  xx Bishops.
    Church - Apostolicity.
    Episcopacy.

APOSTOLIC VICARS. See
  VICARS APOSTOLIC.

APOSTOLIC VISITORS. See
  VISITORS APOSTOLIC.

APOSTOLICITY OF THE CHURCH. See
  CHURCH - APOSTOLICITY.

APOSTOLOS.
    BQT 5245
  A liturgical book of the Byzantine
  rite containing selections from
  the Epistles and from the Acts
  of the Apostles.

APOTHEOSIS.
    BL 465   (291.213)
  x Deification.
  Other references as in LC.

APPARITIONS.
    BQT 556; BQT 971-973
      (23x9.12)
  sa Demonology.
    Ghosts.
    Hallucinations and illusions.
    Jesus Christ - Apparitions and
      miracles (Modern)
    Mary, Blessed Virgin - Appari-
      tions and miracles.
    Miracles.
    Spiritualism.
    Visions.
  xx Demonology.
    Ghosts.
    Hallucinations and illusions.
    Psychical research.
    Spiritualism.
    Superstition.
    Theophanies.
    Visions.

APPEAL AS FROM AN ABUSE.
  xx Appellate procedure (Canon law)
    Church and state.
    Jurisdiction (Canon law)

APPELLATE PROCEDURE (CANON LAW)
    BQV230 1879-1891   (348.x5)
  sa Appeal as from abuse.
  xx Procedure (Canon law)
    Trials, Ecclesiastical.

APPROPRIATION (THEOLOGY)

ARABIA - CHURCH HISTORY.
    BQX 3121

ARAMAIC LANGUAGE.
    PJ 5201-5530   (482.1)
  Explanation as in LC.
  x Biblical Aramaic language.

ARCANA DISCIPLINA. See
  DISCIPLINE OF THE SECRET.

ARCHAEOLOGY, BIBLICAL. See
  BIBLE - ANTIQUITIES.

ARCHAEOLOGY, CHRISTIAN. See
  CHRISTIAN ANTIQUITIES.

ARCHAEOLOGY, MEDIEVAL.
  sa Art, Medieval.

ARCHBISHOPRICS. See DIOCESES.

ARCHBISHOPS.   (Geog. subdiv.,
  Indirect)
      BQX 181   (922.2)
  xx Bishops.
     Prelates.

ARCHBISHOPS (CANON LAW)
      BQV230 270-280   (348.x324)
  sa Pallium.
  xx Bishops (Canon law)
     Persons (Canon law)

ARCHCONFRATERNITIES. See
  CONFRATERNITIES.

ARCHDEACONS.
  sa Chorepiscopi.
     Rural chapters.
  xx Deans.

ARCHITECTURE, CHURCH. See
  CHURCH ARCHITECTURE.

ARCHITECTURE, CISTERCIAN.
      BQT 5989
   x Cistercian architecture.
  xx Church architecture, Gothic.
     Cistercians and art.

ARCHITECTURE, CLUNIAC.
   x Cluniac architecture.

ARCHITECTURE, ECCLESIASTICAL. See
  CHURCH ARCHITECTURE.

ARCHITECTURE AND RELIGION.
  sa Church architecture.
   x Religion and architecture.
  xx Church architecture.

ARCHIVES (CANON LAW)

ARCHIVES, CHURCH.
      CD 1218
   x Church archives.
     Ecclesiastical archives.

ARCHIVES, DIOCESAN.
   x Diocesan archives.

ARCHIVES, MONASTIC.
      CD 1218
   x Monastic archives.
     Religious orders - Archives.

ARCHIVES, PARISH.
      BQT 3323
   x Parish archives.

ARCHPRIESTS.
  xx Bishops.
     Clergy.
     Deans.

ARGENTINE REPUBLIC - CHURCH HISTORY.
      BQX 4751-4759

ARIANISM.
      BQT 63; BQT 583   (273.x31)
  "The heresy propagated by Arius
   denying the divinity of Jesus
   Christ." New Cath. Dict.
  sa Acacians.
     Eunomianism.
     Socinianism.
   x Eusebians.
     Semi-Arianism.
  xx Heresies and heretics - Early
       church.
     Jesus Christ - Divinity.
     Jesus Christ - History of doc-
       trines.
     Socinianism.
     Trinity - History of doctrines.
     Unitarianism.

ARK OF THE COVENANT.
  References as in LC.

ARK OF THE LAW.
      BM 657.A85
  References as in LC.

ARMED FORCES - PRAYER-BOOKS.
      BQT 2648
  sa Soldiers - Prayer-books.

ARMED FORCES - PRAYER-BOOKS, ENGLISH,
  [FRENCH, GERMAN, ETC.]

18

ARMED FORCES - RELIGIOUS LIFE.
   [BQT 2289]
   sa Seamen - Religious life.
      Soldiers - Religious life.

ARMENIAN CHURCH.

ARMENIAN CHURCH - HISTORY.
      BQX 5662-5699   (28x1.9)

ARMENIAN CHURCH - LAW.
      BQV 1321-1339   (348.x7)

ARMENIAN CHURCH. LITURGY AND RITUAL.
      BQT 5171-519°   (264.x9)

ARMENIAN FATHERS OF THE CHURCH. See
   FATHERS OF THE CHURCH, ARMENIAN.

ARMENIAN RITE.

ARMENIAN RITE - CANON LAW.
      BQV 1251-1257   (348.x7)

ARMENIAN RITE - HISTORY.
      BQX 5701-5713   (28x2.7)

ARMENIAN RITE. LITURGY AND RITUAL.
      BQT 5201-5229   (264.x77)

ARMINIANISM.
      BQT 1145   (273.x7)
   "The doctrines and following of
   Jacobus Arminius who revolted
   from Calvinism, denying its
   formulated doctrines of predestination, election and grace." AT
   sa Calvinism.
      Neonomianism.
      Remonstrants.
   xx Calvinism.

ARMINIANS.
      BX 6195-6197   (284.9x1)
   References as in LC.

ARNOLDISTS.
      BQT 89
   xx Asceticism - History - Middle
         Ages.
      Cathari.

ART, BEURONESE.
      BQT 5672
   x Beuronese art.

ART, CATHOLIC. See CHRISTIAN ART.

ART, CHRISTIAN. See CHRISTIAN ART. for x refs
   sa Church art + environment

ART, CLUNIAC.
      BQT 5664
   x Cluniac art.

ART, ECCLESIASTICAL. See
   CHRISTIAN ART.

ART, MEDIEVAL.
      N 5940-6311   (709.02)
   References as in LC.

ART, MISSION. See MISSIONS AND ART.

ART, RELIGIOUS. See CHRISTIAN ART.

ART AND LITURGY. See
   LITURGY AND ART.

ART AND MORALS.
      N 70-72.
   sa Art, Immoral.
      Music and morals.
      Nude in art.
      Theater - Moral and religious
         aspects.
   x Morals and art.
   xx Aesthetics.
      Art, Immoral.
      Nude in art.

ART AND RELIGION.
   sa Christian art.
      Gods in art.
   x Religion and art.
   xx Christian art.

ASCENSION DAY.
      BQT 4225
   x Feast of the Ascension.
   xx Jesus Christ - Ascension.

ASCENSION DAY - SERMONS.
      BQT 2999

ASCENSION OF CHRIST. See
  JESUS CHRIST - ASCENSION.

ASCETICAL THEOLOGY.
  Some Catholic libraries may prefer
    to use the heading "Ascetical
    theology" for Catholic asceticism,
    and the heading "Asceticism" for
    works on asceticism in general.

ASCETICISM.
    BQT 2102-2396   (24x7)
  "Self-discipline in all its forms,
    particularly those voluntarily
    undertaken out of love of God and
    desire for spiritual improve-
    ment." AT
  sa Christian life.
    Contemplative life.
    Devotional literature.
    Good works (Theology)
    Hedonism.
    Martyrdom.
    Mysticism.
    Pastoral theology.
    Penance (Virtue)
    Perfection, Christian.
    Prayer.
    Psychology, Religious.
    Religious life.
    Spiritual life.
  x Catholic Church - Discipline.
    Theology, Ascetical.
  xx Church discipline.
    Ethics.
    Fanaticism.
    Fasting.
    Mysticism.
    Perfection, Christian.
    Religion.
    Religious life.
    Spiritual life.
    Theology.

ASCETICISM - BIBLICAL TEACHING.

ASCETICISM - BIBLIOGRAPHY.
  [BQT 2130.5]; Z 7819
    (016.24x7)

ASCETICISM - BIOGRAPHY.
    BQT 2169
  Ascetics.

ASCETICISM - CATECHISM, QUESTION-BOOKS.
  xx Spiritual life - Catechisms,
    question-books.

ASCETICISM - COLLECTED WORKS.
    BQT 2134

ASCETICISM - COLLECTIONS.
    BQT 2132-2133   (24x7.08)

ASCETICISM - CONGRESSES.
    BQT 2132

ASCETICISM - DICTIONARIES.
    BQT 2131   (24x7.03)

ASCETICISM - HISTORY.
    BQT 2164-2169   (24x7.09)
  Here are entered works on the his-
    tory of asceticism and of ascet-
    ical doctrine, subdivided by
    period, e.g., Keusch, Karl. Die
    Aszetik des hl. Alfons Maria von
    Liguori im Lichte der Lehre vom
    geistlichen Leben in alter und
    neuer Zeit (ASCETICISM - HISTORY -
    18th CENTURY).
  Individual ascetical treatises are
    entered under Asceticism with
    direct period subdivision, e.g.,
    Maria Antonia de Jesus, O.C.D.,
    1700-1760. Edificio espiritual
    (ASCETICISM - 18th CENTURY).

ASCETICISM - HISTORY - EARLY CHURCH.
    BQT 2165
  sa Alogi.
    Messalians.
    Montanism.
    Novatianists.
  x Fathers of the desert.
  xx Church history - Primitive and
    early church.

ASCETICISM - HISTORY - MIDDLE AGES.
    BQT 2166
  sa Albigenses.
    Arnoldists.
    Brothers of the Common Life.
    Cathari.
  xx Church history - Middle Ages.

ASCETICISM - HISTORY - MODERN PERIOD.
    BQT 2167

ASCETICISM - HISTORY - 16th CENTURY.

ASCETICISM - HISTORY - 17th CENTURY.

ASCETICISM - HISTORY - 18th CENTURY.

ASCETICISM - HISTORY - 19th CENTURY.

ASCETICISM - HISTORY - 20th CENTURY.

ASCETICISM - METHODOLOGY.
    [BQT 2171]

ASCETICISM - PERIODICALS.
    BQT 2130

#################

ASCETICISM - EARLY CHURCH.

ASCETICISM - MIDDLE AGES.

ASCETICISM - MODERN PERIOD.

ASCETICISM - 16th CENTURY.

ASCETICISM - 17th CENTURY.

ASCETICISM - 18th CENTURY.

ASCETICISM - 19th CENTURY.

ASCETICISM - 20th CENTURY.

#################

ASCETICISM - EASTERN CHURCHES.
    BQX 5444
    x Eastern Churches - Asceticism.

ASCETICISM - JUDAISM.
    x Jewish asceticism.
      Judaism - Asceticism.

ASCETICISM - ORTHODOX EASTERN CHURCH.
    BQX 5881
    x Orthodox Eastern Church -
      Asceticism.

#################

ASCETICISM AND DOGMATIC THEOLOGY.
    BQT 2173
    x Dogmatic theology and asceticism.

ASCETICISM AND MORAL THEOLOGY.
    BQT 2174
    x Moral theology and asceticism.

ASCETICISM AND PSYCHOLOGY.
    BQT 2176
    x Psychology and asceticism.
    xx Psychology, Religious.

ASCETICS. See
ASCETICISM - BIOGRAPHY.

ASH WEDNESDAY.
    BQT 4222
    sa Lent.
    xx Lent.

ASIA - RELIGION.
    BL 1000-2370
    BQX 3072-3567; BQX 5401-6539

ASIA MINOR - CHURCH HISTORY.
    BQX 3125

ASMONEANS. See MACCABEES.

ASSASSINS (ISMAILITES)
    BP 185
    References as in LC.

ASSISTANT PASTORS.
    BQV230 476   (348.x36)
    x Curates.
      Pastors, Assistant.
    xx Clergy.
      Vicars, Parochial.

ASSOCIATE PRESBYTERIAN CHURCH.
    Scope note and references as in
    LC supplement 1959-60.

ASSOCIATE REFORMED PRESBYTERIAN CHURCH.
    Scope note and references as in
    LC supplement 1959-60.

ASSOCIATIONS, BAPTIST. See
BAPTIST ASSOCIATIONS.

ASSOCIATIONS, PIOUS. See
CONFRATERNITIES.

ASSUMPTION.
    BQT 1058   (23x3.2)
  sa Mary, Blessed Virgin - Death.
   x Mary, Blessed Virgin - Assumption.

ASSUMPTION - ART.
    BQT 5885

ASSUMPTION - BIBLIOGRAPHY.

ASSUMPTION - CONGRESSES.

ASSUMPTION - CONTROVERSIAL LITERATURE.

ASSUMPTION - HISTORY OF DOCTRINES -
  EARLY CHURCH.

ASSUMPTION - HISTORY OF DOCTRINES -
  MIDDLE AGES.

ASSUMPTION - HISTORY OF DOCTRINES -
  MODERN PERIOD.

ASSUMPTION - LITURGY.
  xx Mary, Blessed Virgin, in liturgy.

ASSUMPTION - MEDITATIONS.

ASSUMPTION - PAPAL TEACHING.

ASSUMPTION - POETRY.

ASSUMPTION - SERMONS.

ASSUMPTION, FEAST OF THE.
    BQT 4230   (23x3.72)
   x Feast of the Assumption.

ASSUMPTION, MASS OF THE. See
  MISSA IN ASSUMPTIONE BEATAE
  MARIAE VIRGINIS.

ASSURANCE (THEOLOGY)
    BQT 239; BQT 1135
  sa Faith.

ASSURANCE (THEOLOGY) - HISTORY OF
  DOCTRINES.

ASSYRIANS, MODERN.
  "Here are entered works dealing
    with the modern adherents of the
    Nestorian Church as an element
    in the population of both Asiatic
    Turkey and Iraq. The name "As-
    syrian" is based on an alleged
    racial affinity for the ancient
    Assyrians. The term "Assyrian"
    was used in the 18th century by
    Assemani." LC
  sa Nestorians.
   x Modern Assyrians.
  xx Nestorians.

ASSYRO-BABYLONIAN PRAYERS.
    PJ 3785
   x Prayers, Assyro-Babylonian.
  xx Assyro-Babylonian religion.

ASSYRO-BABYLONIAN RELIGION.
    BL 1620-1625   (299.219)
  sa Assyro-Babylonian prayers.
   x Religion, Assyro-Babylonian.

ASTRONAUTICS AND RELIGION. See
  RELIGION AND ASTRONAUTICS.

ASYLUM, RIGHT OF.
  Classification and references as
    in LC.

ASYLUMS - RELIGIOUS LIFE.

ATHANASIAN CREED.
    BQT 148   (238.1)
  xx Creeds.

ATHANASIANISM.
  xx Trinity - History of doctrines.

ATHEISM.
    BL 2700-2790; BQT 529
     (211; 23x9)
  sa Agnosticism.
    Deism.
    Lokayata.
    Rationalism.
    Skepticism.
    Theism.

ATHEISM -- Continued.
  xx Agnosticism.
     Deism.
     Faith.
     God.
     Irreligion.
     Rationalism.
     Religion.
     Theism.
     Theology.

ATHEISM - CONTROVERSIAL LITERATURE.

ATHEISM - SERMONS.

  Other subdivisions under Atheism
  as in LC.

ATOMIC WARFARE - ~~MORAL ASPECTS.~~
     see NUCLEAR WARFARE

ATONEMENT.
     BQT 766 (Christology)
     BQT 1117 (Soteriology)
        (232.x8)
  Here are entered works on the reconciliation of man to God through
  Christ.
  sa Anger of God.
     Satisfaction.
   x Jesus Christ - Atonement.
  xx Dogmatic theology.
     Guilt.
     Jesus Christ.
     Redemption.
     Sacrifice.
     Salvation.
     Satisfaction.
     Sin.

ATONEMENT - BIBLICAL TEACHING.

ATONEMENT - HISTORY OF DOCTRINES.

ATONEMENT - HISTORY OF DOCTRINES -
  EARLY CHURCH.

ATONEMENT - HISTORY OF DOCTRINES -
  MIDDLE AGES.

ATONEMENT - HISTORY OF DOCTRINES -
  MODERN PERIOD.

ATONEMENT - HISTORY OF DOCTRINES -
  16th, [17th, etc.] CENTURY.

ATONEMENT - SERMONS.

ATONEMENT (BRAHMANISM)
  xx Brahmanism.

ATONEMENT (JUDAISM)

ATONEMENT, DAY OF. See YOM KIPPUR.

ATTENDANCE, CHURCH. See
  CHURCH ATTENDANCE.

ATTENTATS (CANON LAW)
     BQV230 1854-1857
  xx Trials, Ecclesiastical.
✓ ATTITUDE
ATTRIBUTES OF GOD. See
  GOD - ATTRIBUTES.

ATTRITION.
     BQT 1375   (23x7.4)
  xx Contrition.
     Repentance.

AUDITORS (CANON LAW)
     BQV230 1580-1584
  xx Trials, Ecclesiastical.

AUGSBURG, DIET OF, 1518.
     BQX 853   (270.6)
  x Diet of Augsburg, 1518.

AUGSBURG, DIET OF, 1530.
     BQX 853   (270.6)
  x Diet of Augsburg, 1530.

AUGSBURG, DIET OF, 1548.
     BQX 853   (270.6)
  x Diet of Augsburg, 1548.

AUGSBURG, RELIGIOUS PEACE OF.
     BQX 858   (270.6)

AUGSBURG CONFESSION.
     BX 8069   (284.1)
  x Confession of Augsburg.
  xx Lutheran Church.
     Reformation - Germany.

AUGUSTANA EVANGELICAL LUTHERAN
  CHURCH.

AUGUSTINE, SAINT, BP. OF HIPPO,
354-430.
Omit dates when used with subheading.

AUGUSTINE, SAINT - ADDRESSES, ESSAYS,
LECTURES.
BQ 5737; BQ 5740

AUGUSTINE, SAINT - AESTHETICS.
BQ 5816
x subdivision Art.

AUGUSTINE, SAINT - ANGELS (THEOLOGY)
BQ 5795

AUGUSTINE, SAINT - ANNIVERSARIES.
[with date]
BQ 5737

AUGUSTINE, SAINT - ANTAGONISTS.
BQ 5790

AUGUSTINE, SAINT - APOLOGETICS.
BQ 5824

AUGUSTINE, SAINT - AS APOLOGIST.
BQ 5783
x subdivision As Polemicist.

AUGUSTINE, SAINT - ART. See
subdivision Aesthetics.

AUGUSTINE, SAINT - ASCETICISM.
BQ 5807

AUGUSTINE, SAINT - AUTHORSHIP.
BQ 5778

AUGUSTINE, SAINT - AUTOBIOGRAPHY. See
Augustine, Saint. Confessions.
AUGUSTINE, SAINT - BIOGRAPHY.

AUGUSTINE, SAINT - BIBLICAL SCHOLAR-
SHIP.
BQ 5782

AUGUSTINE, SAINT - BIBLIOGRAPHY.
BQ 5732
x subdivision Editions.

AUGUSTINE, SAINT - BIOGRAPHY.
BQ 5739' BQ 5750-5776
x subdivision Autobiography.

AUGUSTINE, SAINT - BIOGRAPHY -
CONVERSION.
BQ 5772
x subdivision Conversion.

AUGUSTINE, SAINT - BIOGRAPHY -
EDUCATION. See subdivision
Education.

AUGUSTINE, SAINT - BIOGRAPHY -
EPISCOPATE. See subdivision
Episcopate.

AUGUSTINE, SAINT - BIOGRAPHY -
SOURCES.
BQ 5771

AUGUSTINE, SAINT - BIOGRAPHY -
YOUTH.
BQ 5772

AUGUSTINE, SAINT - CATECHETICS.
[BQ 5809.1]

AUGUSTINE, SAINT - CAUSATION (META-
PHYSICS)
BQ 5811

AUGUSTINE, SAINT - CHRISTOLOGY.
BQ 5796

AUGUSTINE, SAINT - CHRONOLOGY OF
WORKS.
BQ 5779

AUGUSTINE, SAINT - CHURCH (THEORY)
See subdivision Ecclesiology.

AUGUSTINE, SAINT - CONTEMPORARIES.
BQ 5788

AUGUSTINE, SAINT - CONVERSION.
See subdivision Biography - Conversion.

AUGUSTINE, SAINT - COSMOLOGY.
BQ 5824

AUGUSTINE, SAINT - CREATION.
BQ 5795

AUGUSTINE, SAINT - CRITICISM,
TEXTUAL.
BQ 5747

AUGUSTINE, SAINT - CRITICISM AND
    INTERPRETATION.
        BQ 5732-5748

AUGUSTINE, SAINT - DEVOTIONAL
    LITERATURE.
        BQ 5740

AUGUSTINE, SAINT - DICTIONARIES,
    INDEXES, ETC.
        BQ 5829

AUGUSTINE, SAINT - ECCLESIOLOGY.
        BQ 5803
    x subdivision Church (theory)

AUGUSTINE, SAINT - EDITIONS. See
    subdivision Bibliography.

AUGUSTINE, SAINT - EDUCATION.
        BQ 5772
    x subdivision Biography - Education.

AUGUSTINE, SAINT - EDUCATION (THEORY)
        BQ 5824
    x subdivision Pedagogy.

AUGUSTINE, SAINT - AS EDUCATOR.
        BQ 5780
    x subdivision As Teacher.

AUGUSTINE, SAINT - EPISCOPATE.
        BQ 5774
    x subdivision Biography - Episco-
        pate.

AUGUSTINE, SAINT - EPISTEMOLOGY.
        BQ 5815

AUGUSTINE, SAINT - ESCHATOLOGY.
        BQ 5804

AUGUSTINE, SAINT - ETHICS.
        BQ 5807
    xx subdivision Moral theology.

AUGUSTINE, SAINT - EVOLUTION THEORY.
        BQ 5822

AUGUSTINE, SAINT - FICTION.
        [BQ 5741]

AUGUSTINE, SAINT - FREE WILL.
        BQ 5800

AUGUSTINE, SAINT - GOD (THEOLOGY)
        BQ 5792
    sa subdivision Natural theology.

AUGUSTINE, SAINT - GRACE.
        BQ 5799

AUGUSTINE, SAINT - HISTORY, PHILO-
    SOPHY OF. See subdivision
    Philosophy of history.

AUGUSTINE, SAINT - ICONOGRAPHY.
        BQ 5776

AUGUSTINE, SAINT - INFLUENCE.
        BQ 5785

AUGUSTINE, SAINT - INFLUENCE -
    CALVIN, [DANTE, ROSMINI, ETC.]

AUGUSTINE, SAINT - INFLUENCE -
    ST. THOMAS AQUINAS.
        BQ 6886

AUGUSTINE, SAINT - LANGUAGE,
    STYLE, ETC.
        BQ 5828
    x subdivision Style.

AUGUSTINE, SAINT - LITURGY.
        [BQ 5810]

AUGUSTINE, SAINT - MAN (THEOLOGY)
        BQ 5798

AUGUSTINE, SAINT - MARIOLOGY.
        BQ 5797

AUGUSTINE, SAINT - METAPHYSICS.
        BQ 5814

AUGUSTINE, SAINT - MONASTICISM.
        BQ 5824

AUGUSTINE, SAINT - MORAL THEOLOGY.
        BQ 5807
    sa subdivision Ethics.

AUGUSTINE, SAINT - MUSIC (THEORY)

AUGUSTINE, SAINT - MYSTICISM.
        [BQ 5808.5]

AUGUSTINE, SAINT - NATURAL SCIENCES.
     BQ 5821
     x subdivision Science.

AUGUSTINE, SAINT - NATURAL THEOLOGY.
     BQ 5813
     x subdivision Theodicy.
     xx subdivision God (theology)

AUGUSTINE, SAINT - NEO-PLATONISM.
     BQ 5812

AUGUSTINE, SAINT - AS ORATOR.
     BQ 5781
     xx subdivision Rhetoric.

AUGUSTINE, SAINT - PASTORAL THEOLOGY.
     BQ 5809

AUGUSTINE, SAINT - PEDAGOGY. See
     subdivision Education (theory)

AUGUSTINE, SAINT - PERIODICALS. See
     subdivision Societies, periodicals,
     etc.

AUGUSTINE, SAINT - PHILOSOPHY.
     BQ 5811

AUGUSTINE, SAINT - PHILOSOPHY OF
     HISTORY.
     BQ 5818
     x subdivision History, Philosophy
       of.

AUGUSTINE, SAINT - AS POLEMICIST.
     See subdivision As Apologist.

AUGUSTINE, SAINT - POLITICAL SCIENCE.
     BQ 5819

AUGUSTINE, SAINT - PRAYER-BOOKS.
     BQ 5740

AUGUSTINE, SAINT - PREDESTINATION.
     BQ 5800

AUGUSTINE, SAINT - PROVIDENCE.
     BQ 5800
     x subdivision Theodicy.

AUGUSTINE, SAINT - PSYCHOLOGY.
     BQ 5798

AUGUSTINE, SAINT - REDEMPTION. See
     subdivision Soteriology.

AUGUSTINE, SAINT - RELICS.
     [BQ 5777]
     x subdivision Tomb.

AUGUSTINE, SAINT - RELIGIOUS PSY-
     CHOLOGY.
     BQ 5824

AUGUSTINE, SAINT - RHETORIC.
     BQ 5778
     sa subdivision As Orator.

AUGUSTINE, SAINT - SACRAMENTS.
     BQ 5806

AUGUSTINE, SAINT - SACRAMENTS -
     BAPTISM.
     [BQ 5806.1]

AUGUSTINE, SAINT - SACRAMENTS.
     EUCHARIST.
     BQ 5805

AUGUSTINE, SAINT - SACRAMENTS.
     MARRIAGE.
     [BQ 5806.5]

AUGUSTINE, SAINT - SACRAMENTS -
     PENANCE.
     [BQ 5806.3]

AUGUSTINE, SAINT - SALVATION. See
     subdivision Soteriology.

AUGUSTINE, SAINT - SCIENCE. See
     subdivision Natural sciences.

AUGUSTINE, SAINT - SERMONS.
     BQ 5824

AUGUSTINE, SAINT - SIN (THEOLOGY)
     BQ 5802

AUGUSTINE, SAINT - SOCIETIES,
     PERIODICALS, ETC.
     BQ 5733
     x subdivision Periodicals.

AUGUSTINE, SAINT - SOCIOLOGY.
     BQ 5820

AUGUSTINE, SAINT - SOTERIOLOGY.
BQ 5796
x subdivisions Redemption and
Salvation.

AUGUSTINE, SAINT - SOUL (THEORY)
BQ 5798

AUGUSTINE, SAINT - SOURCES.
BQ 5787

AUGUSTINE, SAINT - SOURCES - CICERO,
[PLATO, PLOTINUS, ST. AMBROSE, ETC.]
BQ 5789

AUGUSTINE, SAINT - SPIRITUAL LIFE.
BQ 5772

AUGUSTINE, SAINT - STUDY.
BQ 5826

AUGUSTINE, SAINT - STYLE. See
subdivision Language, style, etc.

AUGUSTINE, SAINT - AS TEACHER. See
subdivision As Educator.

AUGUSTINE, SAINT - THEODICY. See
subdivisions Natural theology and
Providence.

AUGUSTINE, SAINT - THEOLOGY.
BQ 5792

AUGUSTINE, SAINT - TOMB. See
subdivision Relics.

AUGUSTINE, SAINT - TRANSLATIONS.
BQ 5825

AUGUSTINE, SAINT - TRINITY.
BQ 5792

AUGUSTINE, SAINT - VIRTUE.
BQ 5824

AUGUSTINIAN CANONESSES.
BQX 7833
x Canonesses Regular of St.
Augustine.
St. Augustine, Canonesses
Regular of.

AUGUSTINIAN CANONS.
BQX 7151-7200
x Austin Canons.
Black Canons.
Canons Regular of St. Augustine.
Ordo Canonicorum Regularium
Sancti Augustini.
St. Augustine, Canons Regular of.

AUGUSTINIAN FRIARS. See
AUGUSTINIANS.

AUGUSTINIAN HERMITS. See
AUGUSTINIANS.

AUGUSTINIAN SAINTS. See
SAINTS, AUGUSTINIAN.

AUGUSTINIANS. (Geog. subdiv., Direct)
BQX 6971-7020 (271.x1)
x Augustinian Friars.
Augustinian Hermits.
Austin Friars.
Hermits of St. Augustine.
Ordo Fratrum Eremitarum Sancti
Augustini.
St. Augustine, Order of.
xx Friars.

AUGUSTINIANS - BIBLIOGRAPHY.
BQX 6971

AUGUSTINIANS - BIOGRAPHY.
BQX 7019-7020
sa Saints, Augustinian.

AUGUSTINIANS - CANON LAW.
[BQX 6984.7]

AUGUSTINIANS - COLLECTIONS.
BQX 6973

AUGUSTINIANS - EDUCATION.
[BQX 6984.5]

AUGUSTINIANS - HISTORY.
BQX 6981-7014

AUGUSTINIANS - MISSIONS.
[BQX 6984.6]
x Missions, Augustinian.

AUGUSTINIANS - PERIODICALS.
    BQX 6972

AUGUSTINIANS - RULES.
    BQX 6975-6978

AUGUSTINIANS - SPIRITUAL LIFE.
    BQX 6984

        ################

AUGUSTINIANS - AUSTRIA, [FRANCE,
    GERMANY, ETC.]
    BQX 6981-7005

        ################

AUGUSTINIANS. LAY BROTHERS.
    [BQX 7015]

AUGUSTINIANS. LITURGY AND RITUAL.
    BQT 4721-4729

AUGUSTINIANS. PROVINCES.
    BQX 7006-7014

        ################

AUMBRIES.
    BQT 5929   (729.912)
  sa Sacrament houses.
   x Ambries.
  xx Church decoration and ornament.
     Church furniture.
     Eucharist - Reservation.

AURICULAR CONFESSION.
    BQT 1377
  sa Penance - History.
  xx Confession.

AUSTIN CANONS. See
    AUGUSTINIAN CANONS.

AUSTIN FRIARS. See AUGUSTINIANS.

AUSTRALIA - CHURCH HISTORY.
    BQX 4961-4993

AUTHORITY (RELIGION)
    BQT 238
  sa Bible - Evidences, authority, etc.
     Church - Authority.
     Church - Infallibility.

AUTHORITY (RELIGION) -- Continued.
  sa Church - Teaching office.
     Conciliar theory.
     Liberty of speech in the church.
     Popes - Infallibility.
     Tradition (Theology)

AUTHORS, CATHOLIC. See
CATHOLIC AUTHORS.

AUTHORSHIP, CATHOLIC.
  sa Catholic authors.
   x Catholic authorship.

AUTO-DA-FE SERMONS.
  xx Inquisition.

AVARICE.
    BQT 1813   (24x1.44)
   x Covetousness.
  xx Capital sins.
     Conduct of life.

AVE MARIA.
    BQT 2695   (24x3.7)
   x Hail Mary.
  xx Mary, Blessed Virgin.
     Prayers.

AVE MARIA - MEDITATIONS.

AVE MARIA - SERMONS.

AVE MARIA (MUSIC)
    BQT 4682; M 2079

AVE MARIA STELLA.
    BQT 2695   (24x3.7)

AVE MARIA STELLA (MUSIC)
    BQT 4682; M 2079

AVIGNON, POPES AT. See
    POPES - HISTORY - 1309-1378.

AZARIAS, PRAYER OF. See BIBLE. O.T.
DANIEL. chap. III, 24-25.

AZYME.
    BQV230 816   (348.x42)
  "A name given to the unleavened
   bread used in the Mass of the
   Western Church." AT
  xx Altar breads.
     Eucharist - Elements.

28

BAAL (DEITY)
BL 1671

BABEL, TOWER OF. See TOWER OF BABEL.

BABISM.
BP 340   (297)
References as in LC.

BABYLONIAN CAPTIVITY, PAPAL. See
POPES - HISTORY - 1309-1378.

BACCALAUREATE ADDRESSES.
BQT 3006   (252.x5)
x Graduation sermons.
Sermons, Baccalaureate.
Sermons, Graduation.
xx Occasional sermons.

BAHAISM.   (Geog. subdiv.)
BP 300-395
References as in LC.

BALANISM.
BQT 115; BQT 1129

BALDACHINS.
BQT 4361; BQT 5946
xx Altars.
Church furniture.

BALTIMORE CATECHISM.
BQT 3161   (25x3.1)
x Catechism, Baltimore.

BANKRUPTCY (CANON LAW)

BANNERS, CHURCH. See
CHURCH PENNANTS.

BANNS OF MARRIAGE.
BQV230 1019-1034   (348.x427)
xx Marriage (Canon law)

BANTUS - RELIGION.
xx Prayer (Bantu religion)

BAPTISM.
BQT 1253-1280 (Dogmatic
theology)   (23x7.1)
BQT 2043 (Moral theology)
sa Fonts
Infant baptism.

BAPTISM -- Continued.
sa Innocence (Theology)
Regeneration (Theology)
Sponsors.
x Christening.
Immersion, Baptismal.
xx Initiations (in religion,
folk-lore, etc.)
Sacraments.

BAPTISM - BIBLICAL TEACHING.
BQT 1255

BAPTISM - DEVOTIONAL LITERATURE.
[BQT 2608.1]

BAPTISM - DOUBTFUL CASES.
BQT 1269

BAPTISM - EARLY WORKS TO 1800.

BAPTISM - HISTORY.
BQT 1253-1258

BAPTISM - HISTORY - EARLY CHURCH.
BQT 1256

BAPTISM - HISTORY - MIDDLE AGES.
BQT 1257

BAPTISM - HISTORY - MODERN PERIOD.
BQT 1258

BAPTISM - HISTORY - 16th, [17th, etc.]
CENTURY.

BAPTISM - JUVENILE LITERATURE.

BAPTISM - MINISTER.

#################

BAPTISM - ANGLICAN COMMUNION,
[BAPTISTS, ORTHODOX EASTERN
CHURCH, ETC.]

#################

BAPTISM (CANON LAW)
BQV230 737-799   (348.x42)
xx Sacraments (Canon law)

BAPTISM (HINDUISM)

BAPTISM (LITURGY)
     BQT 4444   (264.x63)
  xx Sacraments (Liturgy)

BAPTISM, SECOND. See MARTYRDOM.

BAPTISM OF BLOOD.
     BQT 1279
  "Consists in suffering martyrdom for
     the Faith or for some Christian
     virtue, which infuses sanctifying
     grace into the soul and forgives
     sin." AT
  xx Martyrdom.

BAPTISM OF CHRIST. See
  JESUS CHRIST - BAPTISM.

BAPTISM OF DESIRE.
     BQT 1280
  "When it is not possible to be
     baptized, an act of perfect con-
     trition or pure love of God will
     supply the omission." AT
  x Desire, Baptism of.

BAPTISM OF HERETICS.
     BQT 50
  x Heretics, Baptism of.

BAPTISMAL FONTS. See FONTS.

BAPTISMAL NAMES. See
  NAMES, PERSONAL.

BAPTISMAL WATER.
     BQT 4482; BQT 4522
  x Water, Baptismal.
  xx Water (in religion, folklore,
     etc.)

BAPTIST ASSOCIATIONS.
  x Associations, Baptist.
  Explanatory note and other
     references as in LC.

BAPTIST CHURCHES. See
  CHURCHES, BAPTIST.

BAPTISTERIES.
     BQT 5931 (Church architecture)
        (726.43)
     BQX 70 (Christian archaeology)
  x Fonts.
  xx Churches.

BAPTISTS.   (Geog. subdiv.)
     BX 6201-6495   (286)
  sa Separate Baptists.
     Other references and subdivisions
     as in LC.

BAPTISTS, NEGRO.
     BX 6440-6460   (286)
  References as in LC.

BARETTINI. See HUMILIATI.

BAROQUE CHURCH ARCHITECTURE. See
  CHURCH ARCHITECTURE, BAROQUE.

BARREN FIG-TREE (PARABLE)
     BQT 888   (226.x6)

BARTHIANISM. See DIALECTICAL
  THEOLOGY.

BARTHOLOMEW, SAINT, MASSACRE OF. See
  ST. BARTHOLOMEW'S DAY, MASSACRE OF.
  1572.

BARUCH, BOOK OF. See BIBLE. O.T.
  BARUCH.

BASEL, COUNCIL OF, 1431-1449.
     BQX 823   (26x2.39)

BASILIANS.
     BQX 7031-7038   (271.x1)
     BQX 5458
  x Order of St. Basil the Great.
     Ordo Sancti Basilii Magni.
     St. Basil the Great, Order of.

BASILIANS - ALBANIA, [ASIA MINOR,
  U.S., ETC.]

BASILICAS.
     BQT 5963-5964
  sa Minor basilicas.
  xx Architecture, Ancient.
     Church architecture.
     Churches.

BATINITES.
  References as in LC.

BAVARIA - CHURCH HISTORY.
    [BQX 1870]

BAZAARS, CHARITABLE.
  References as in LC.

BEADS.
     NK 3650 (Art industries)
     TT 860 (Technology)
  sa Rosary.

BEATI IMMACULATI IN VIA (MUSIC). See
PSALMS (MUSIC) - 118th PSALM.

BEATIFIC VISION.
     BQT 1549   (236.x61)
  x Vision, Beatific.
  xx Desire for God.
    Future life.
    Glory (Theology)
    Heaven.

BEATIFICATION.
     BQV230 1999-2135 (Canon law)
     BQT 4437.6 (Liturgy)
  sa Canonization.
  xx Canonization.

BEATITUDES.
     BQT 893; BQT 1220   (226.x23)
  x Jesus Christ - Beatitudes.
  xx Sermon on the Mount.

BEATITUDES - ILLUSTRATIONS.

BEATITUDES - MEDITATIONS.

BEATITUDES - POETRY.

BEATITUDES - SERMONS.

BEATITUDES - STORIES.

BEATUS VIR, QUI NON ABIIT IN CONSILIO
IMPIORUM (MUSIC). See PSALMS (MUSIC) -
1st PSALM.

BEATUS VIR, QUI TIMET DOMINUM (MUSIC).
  See PSALMS (MUSIC) - 111th PSALM.

BEGHARDS.
     BQT 89 (History of theology)
     BQX 7039 (Religious orders)
      (271.x1)
  sa Adamites.
    Beguines.
    Bohemian Brethren.
  xx Beguines.
    Mysticism - Middle Ages.

BEGUINAGES.   (Geog. subdiv., Indirect)
  xx Beguines.
    Convents.
    Religious orders of women.

BEGUINES. (Geog. subdiv., Indirect)
     BQT 89 (History of theology)
     BQX 7805 (Religious orders)
      (271.9)
  sa Beghards.
    Beguinages.
  xx Beghards.
    Mysticism - Middle Ages.

BEKTASHI.
     BP 175.D4
  xx Mohammedan sects.

BEL AND THE DRAGON. See
    BIBLE. O.T. DANIEL. chap. XIV.

BELGIAN MISSIONS. See
  MISSIONS, BELGIAN.

BELGIUM - CHURCH HISTORY.
     BQX 1562-1598   (274.93)

BELGIUM - CHURCH HISTORY - EARLY PERIOD.

BELGIUM - CHURCH HISTORY - 1501-

BELGIUM - CHURCH HISTORY - 19th CENTURY.

BELGIUM - CHURCH HISTORY - 20th CENTURY.

BELIEF AND DOUBT.
      BQT 239 (Apologetics)
        (23x9.52)
      BD 215 (Philosophy)   (121)
      BF 773 (Psychology)
  sa Agnosticism.
     Error.
     Evidence.
     Faith.
     Rationalism.
     Skepticism.
     Truth.
   x Certainty.
     Conviction.
     Doubt.
     Religious belief.
  xx Agnosticism.
     Knowledge, Theory of (Religion)
     Rationalism.
     Religion.

BELLS.
      BQT 4522 (Sacramentals)
      BQT 5959 (Church architecture)
        (246.x9)
  Other classifications and references
    as in LC.

BELLS - DEDICATION.
      BQT 4484

BENEDIC, ANIMA MEA DOMINO, DOMINE
  DEUS MEUS (MUSIC). See
  PSALMS (MUSIC) - 103d PSALM.

BENEDIC, ANIMA MEA DOMINO ET OMNIA QUAE
  INTRA ME SUNT (MUSIC). See
  PSALMS (MUSIC) - 102d PSALM.

BENEDICT, SAINT, MEDAL OF. See
  MEDAL OF ST. BENEDICT.

BENEDICTINE BROTHERS. See
  BENEDICTINES. LAY BROTHERS.

BENEDICTINE MISSIONS. See
  BENEDICTINES - MISSIONS.

BENEDICTINE NUNS.   (Geog. subdiv., Direct)
  x Benedictines. Second Order.
    Moniales Ordinis Sancti Benedicti.
  xx Benedictine Sisters.

BENEDICTINE OBLATES. See
  BENEDICTINES. OBLATES.

BENEDICTINE SAINTS. See
  SAINTS, BENEDICTINE.

BENEDICTINE SISTERS.   (Geog. subdiv.,
  Direct)
      BQX 7806-7829   (271.9)
  sa Benedictine Nuns.
   x Benedictines. Third Order.
    St. Benedict, Sisters of the
      Order of.
    Sisters of the Order of St.
      Benedict.
    Sorores Ordinis Sancti Benedicti.

BENEDICTINES.   (Geog. subdiv., Direct)
      BQX 7041-7111   (271.x1)
  sa Camaldolese.
     Celestines (Benedictine)
     Cistercians.
     Cluniacs.
     Mechitarists.
     Olivetans.
     Sylvestrines.
     Trappists.
     Vallumbrosians.
   x Black Monks.
    Order of St. Benedict.
    Ordo Sancti Benedicti.
    St. Benedict, Order of.
  xx Cistercians.
    Cluniacs.

BENEDICTINES - BIBLIOGRAPHY.
      BQX 7041; Z 7840

BENEDICTINES - BIO-BIBLIOGRAPHY.

BENEDICTINES - BIOGRAPHY.
      BQX 7110-7111
  sa Martyrologium. Benedictine.
    Saints, Benedictine.

BENEDICTINES - CANON LAW.
  [BQX 7054.7]

BENEDICTINES - COLLECTIONS.
      BQX 7043

BENEDICTINES - DIRECTORIES.
      BQX 7044

32

BENEDICTINES - DRAMA.

BENEDICTINES - EDUCATION.
    [BQX 7054.5]
 sa Benedictines and education.

BENEDICTINES - FICTION.

BENEDICTINES - GOVERNMENT.

BENEDICTINES - HISTORY.
    BQX 7051-7075

BENEDICTINES - HISTORY - EARLY PERIOD.

BENEDICTINES - HISTORY - MIDDLE AGES.

BENEDICTINES - HISTORY - MODERN PERIOD.

BENEDICTINES - HISTORY - 16th, [17th,
 ETC.] CENTURY.

BENEDICTINES - MEDITATIONS.

BENEDICTINES - MISSIONS.
    [BQX 7054.6]
  x Benedictine missions.
   Missions, Benedictine.

BENEDICTINES - MISSIONS - PERIODICALS.

BENEDICTINES - NOVITIATE. See
 NOVITIATE - BENEDICTINES.

BENEDICTINES - OBITUARIES.

BENEDICTINES - ORGANIZATION.

BENEDICTINES - PERIODICALS.
    BQX 7042

BENEDICTINES - PRAYER-BOOKS.
    BQX 7049

BENEDICTINES - PROFESSION. See
 PROFESSION, RELIGIOUS - BENEDICTINES.

BENEDICTINES - RECRUITING.

BENEDICTINES - RETREATS. See
 RETREATS FOR BENEDICTINES.

BENEDICTINES - RULES.
    BQX 7045-7048

BENEDICTINES - SPIRITUAL LIFE.
    BQX 7054

BENEDICTINES - YEARBOOKS.
    BQX 7050

################

BENEDICTINES - AUSTRIA, [ENGLAND,
 FRANCE, ETC.]
    BQX 7060-7075

################

BENEDICTINES. CONGREGATIONS.
    BQX 7076-7096

BENEDICTINES. CONGREGATIONS. AMER-
 ICAN-CASSINESE, [BEURONESE,
 BURSFELD, ETC.]

BENEDICTINES. CONGREGATIONS. CLUNY.
 See CLUNIACS.

BENEDICTINES. CONGREGATIONS. ST. MAUR.
    BQX 7093; BQX 41
  x Maurists.

BENEDICTINES. LAY BROTHERS.
    [BQX 7108]
  x Benedictine Brothers.

BENEDICTINES. LITURGY AND RITUAL.
    BQT 4731-4739

BENEDICTINES. LITURGY AND RITUAL. ANTI-
 PHONARIUM, [BREVIARIUM, ETC.] See
 ANTIPHONARIUM. BENEDICTINE; BREVIARIUM.
 BENEDICTINE; ETC.

BENEDICTINES. OBLATES.
    BQX 7109
  x Benedictine Oblates.
   Benedictines. Third Order.
   Oblates of St. Benedict.

BENEDICTINES. SECOND ORDER. See
 BENEDICTINE NUNS.

BENEDICTINES. THIRD ORDER. See
 BENEDICTINE SISTERS; BENEDICTINES.
 OBLATES.

################

BENEDICTINES (ANGLICAN)
    BX 5184-85
    x Anglican Benedictines.

BENEDICTINES (EPISCOPALIAN)
    BX 5971

BENEDICTINES (EVANGELICAL)
    x Evangelical Benedictines.

BENEDICTINES, CAMALDOLESE. See
    CAMALDOLESE.

BENEDICTINES, CELESTINE. See
    CELESTINES (BENEDICTINE)

BENEDICTINES, CLUNIAC. See
    CLUNIACS.

BENEDICTINES, MECHITARIST. See
    MECHITARISTS.

BENEDICTINES, OLIVETAN. See
    OLIVETANS.

BENEDICTINES, SYLVESTRINE. See
    SYLVESTRINES.

BENEDICTINES, VALLUMBROSIAN. See
    VALLUMBROSIANS.

BENEDICTINES AND AGRICULTURE.
    BQX 7057

BENEDICTINES AND ART.

BENEDICTINES AND CHURCH MUSIC.

BENEDICTINES AND CULTURE.

BENEDICTINES AND EDUCATION.
    xx Benedictines - Education.

BENEDICTINES AND HUMILITY.

BENEDICTINES AND LITURGY.

BENEDICTINES AND MYSTICISM.

BENEDICTINES AND PHILOSOPHY.

BENEDICTINES AND POPULAR DEVOTIONS.

BENEDICTINES AND PRINTING.

BENEDICTINES AND SCIENCE.

BENEDICTINES AND THEOLOGY.

BENEDICTINES AND WORK.
    xx Work.

BENEDICTION OF THE BLESSED SACRAMENT.
    BQT 4349   (264.x64)
    sa Divine praises.
    x Blessed Sacrament, Benediction
      of the.
    xx Devotions, Popular.
    Eucharist - Cultus.

BENEDICTION OF THE BLESSED SACRAMENT -
HYMNS.
    BQT 4681

BENEDICTIONALE.
    BQT 4273   (26x5.9)
    "A book containing various forms
    of blessing extracted from the
    Missal, the Pontificale, the
    Rituale, etc." AT
    sa Blessings.
    Pontificale romanum.
    Rituale.
    xx Blessings.

BENEDICTIONS. See BLESSINGS.

BENEDICTUS DOMINUS, DEUS MEUS (MUSIC).
  See PSALMS (MUSIC) - 143d PSALM.

BENEFICES, ECCLESIASTICAL.   (Geog.
subdiv.)
    A benefice is "an ecclesiastical
    foundation permanently constituted,
    consisting of a sacred office and
    the right of the holder to the
    annual revenue from the endowment."
    AT
    sa Clergy - Salaries, pensions, etc.
    Commendatory abbots.
    also subdivision "Benefices" under
      the names of churches other than
      the Catholic Church (e.g., Church
      of England - Benefices)
    x Ecclesiastical benefices.
    xx Church property.

BENEFICES, ECCLESIASTICAL (CANON LAW)
     BQV230 1409-1488   (348.x45)
  sa Devolution (Canon law)
     Distributions (Canon law)
     Excardination (Canon law)
     Incardination (Canon law)
     Parishes (Canon law)
     Pensions (Canon law)
     Prebends.
     Renunciation (Canon law)
  xx Things (Canon law)

BENEFIT OF CLERGY. See
  PRIVILEGIUM FORI.

BENIGNITY (THEOLOGY) See
  KINDNESS (THEOLOGY)

BETROTHAL.
   x Engagement.
    Marriage, Promise of.
   Other references as in LC.

BETROTHAL (CANON LAW)
     BQV230 1017   (348.x427)
  xx Marriage (Canon law)

BEURONESE ART. See ART, BEURONESE.

BIANCHI. See FLAGELLANTS (SECT).

BIBLE.
     BS   (220)
   x Holy Scriptures.
    Sacred Scriptures.
    Scriptures, Holy.
  xx Hebrew literature.
    History, Ancient.
    Jewish literature.
    Sacred sciences.
    Theology.

BIBLE - ADDRESSES, ESSAYS, LECTURES.
     BS 540

BIBLE - ANIMALS. See
  BIBLE - NATURAL HISTORY.

BIBLE - ANTHROPOLOGY. See
  MAN (THEOLOGY) - BIBLICAL TEACHING.

BIBLE - ANTIQUITIES.
     BS 620-625   (220.93)
  sa Christian antiquities.
    Dancing (Religious ceremony)
    Ephod.
    Jews - Antiquities.
    Musical instruments, Jewish.
    Phylacteries.
    also subdivision "Antiquities"
    under names of Biblical countries
    and cities.
   x Antiquities, Biblical.
    Archaeology, Biblical.
    Bible - Archaeology.
    Biblical archaeology.

BIBLE - APPRECIATION.
     BS 538.5

BIBLE - ARCHAEOLOGY. See
  BIBLE - ANTIQUITIES.

BIBLE - ASTRONOMY.
     BS 655   (220.852)
  xx Astronomy.

BIBLE - ATLASES. See
  BIBLE - GEOGRAPHY - MAPS.

BIBLE - AUTHORITY. See BIBLE -
  EVIDENCES, AUTHORITY, ETC.

BIBLE - BIBLIOGRAPHY.
    [BS 444]; Z 7770-7772   (016.22)
  "Here are entered works containing
    bibliographies of texts of the
    Bible in two or more languages." LC
  sa Bible - Study - Bibliography.

BIBLE - BIBLIOGRAPHY - CATALOGS.

BIBLE - BIOGRAPHY.
     BS 570-580   (220.92)
  sa Apostles.
    Children in the Bible.
    Disciples.
    Patriarchs (Bible)
    Prophets.
    Saints, Biblical.
    Women in the Bible.
   x Bible - Characters.
    Biography, Biblical.

BIBLE - BIOGRAPHY - SERMONS.
BS 571.5

BIBLE - BIRDS. See
BIBLE - NATURAL HISTORY.

BIBLE - BOTANY. See
BIBLE - NATURAL HISTORY.

BIBLE - CANON.
BS 465   (220.x61)
x Canon of the Holy Scriptures.

BIBLE - CARTOONS, SATIRE, ETC.

BIBLE - CATALOGING. See
CATALOGING OF THE BIBLE.

BIBLE - CATALOGS. See
BIBLE - PICTURES, ILLUSTRATIONS,
ETC. - CATALOGS; BIBLE. MANUS-
CRIPTS - CATALOGS.

BIBLE - CATECHISMS, QUESTION-BOOKS.
BS 612
"Here are entered catechisms and
books with questions intended
for juvenile use." LC
sa Sunday-schools - Question-books.
xx Bible - Study.
Catechisms.
Sunday-schools - Question-books.

BIBLE - CATENAE. See CATENAE.

BIBLE - CHAPTERS AND VERSES. See
BIBLE - NUMERICAL DIVISION.

BIBLE - CHARACTERS. See
BIBLE - BIOGRAPHY.

BIBLE - CHILDREN. See
CHILDREN IN THE BIBLE.

BIBLE - CHRONOLOGY.
BS 637   (220.94)
x Chronology, Biblical.
xx Chronology, Hebrew.

BIBLE - CODICES. See
BIBLE. MANUSCRIPTS.

BIBLE - COINS. See
BIBLE - NUMISMATICS.

BIBLE - COLLECTED WORKS.
BS 413-415   (220.08)
"Here are entered collections of
works on Biblical subjects (by
one or more authors) too varied
in character to admit of a
specific subdivision. For collections of texts of the Bible
see Bible - Bibliography." LC

BIBLE - COLPORTAGE. See BIBLE -
PUBLICATION AND DISTRIBUTION.

BIBLE - COMMENTARIES.
BS 485-498   (220.7)
sa Catenae.
Scholia.
x Bible - Exegesis.
Bible - Interpretations.
Commentaries, Biblical.

BIBLE - CONCORDANCES. 220.A17
BS 420-429
xx Concordances.

BIBLE - CONCORDANCES, ENGLISH,
[FRENCH, GERMAN, ETC.]

BIBLE - CONGRESSES.
BS 411

BIBLE - COPIES, CURIOUS.
x Bible - Curiosa.

BIBLE - COSTUME. See
BIBLICAL COSTUME.

BIBLE - COVENANTS. See
COVENANTS (THEOLOGY)

BIBLE - CRITICISM, HIGHER.
BS 503-518
x Bible - Higher criticism.
Criticism, Higher.
Higher criticism.
xx Bible - Criticism, interpretation,
etc.
Bible - Hermeneutics.

BIBLE - CRITICISM, TEXTUAL.
　　　BS 471; BS 525　　(220.x65)
　x Bible - Textual criticism.
　xx Bible - Criticism, interpretation,
　　　etc.
　　　Bible - Hermeneutics.

BIBLE - CRITICISM, INTERPRETATION, ETC.
　　　BS 500-534　　(220.x66)
　sa Bible - Criticism, Higher.
　　　Bible - Criticism, Textual.
　　　Bible as literature.
　　　Modernist-fundamentalist con-
　　　　troversy.
　x Bible - Interpretation.
　　　Bible - Literary criticism.
　　　Interpretation, Biblical.
　xx Bible as literature.
　　　Criticism.

BIBLE - CRITICISM, INTERPRETATION, ETC. -
HISTORY.
　　　BS 500
　sa Antiochian school.
　x Bible - Hermeneutics - History.

BIBLE - CRITICISM, INTERPRETATION, ETC. -
THEORY, METHODS, ETC.　See
BIBLE - HERMENEUTICS.

BIBLE - CURIOSA.　See
　BIBLE - COPIES, CURIOUS.
　BIBLE - EDITIONS, CURIOUS.
　BIBLE - MISCELLANEA.

BIBLE - DICTIONARIES.
　　　BS 440-443　　(220.x5)
　x Bible - Glossaries, vocabularies,
　　　etc.

BIBLE - DICTIONARIES, ENGLISH,
[FRENCH, GERMAN, ETC.]

BIBLE - DRAMA.　See
　BIBLE AS LITERATURE.
　BIBLE PLAYS.
　MYSTERIES AND MIRACLE-PLAYS.

BIBLE - ECONOMICS.
　　　BS 670　　(220.733)
　x Christianity and economics -
　　　Biblical teaching.
　xx Sociology, Biblical.

BIBLE - EDITIONS, CURIOUS.
　x Bible - Curiosa.

BIBLE - ETHICS.
　　　BS 680　　(220.717)
　sa Sociology, Biblical.
　x Biblical ethics.
　　　Ethics, Biblical.
　　　Moral theology - Biblical
　　　　teaching.
　xx Sociology, Biblical.

BIBLE - ETHNOLOGY.
　　　BS 661　　(220.8572)
　sa Lost Tribes of Israel.
　xx Ethnology.
　　　Man (Theology)

BIBLE - EVIDENCES, AUTHORITY, ETC.
　　　BS 480　　(220.x63)
　sa Bible - Quotations, Early.
　　　Miracles.
　x Bible - Authority.
　　　Bible - Sources.
　　　Evidences of the Bible.
　xx Apologetics.
　　　Authority (Religion)
　　　Bible - Inspiration.
　　　Christianity.
　　　Free thought.

BIBLE - EXAMINATIONS, QUESTIONS, ETC.
　　　BS 612
　"Here are entered works containing
　　examinations and questions on the
　　Bible intended for advanced and
　　adult use."　LC
　x Questions and answers - Bible.

BIBLE - EXEGESIS.　See
　BIBLE - COMMENTARIES.
　BIBLE - HEREMENEUTICS

BIBLE - FESTIVALS.　See
　FEASTS, ECCLESIASTICAL.
　FESTIVALS - JEWS.
　also names of special festivals,
　e.g., Passover.

BIBLE - FICTION.　See　BIBLE - HISTORY
OF BIBLICAL EVENTS - FICTION.

BIBLE - FOLK-LORE.　See
　FOLKLORE - JEWS.

BIBLE - GARDENS. See
BIBLE - NATURAL HISTORY.

BIBLE - GENEALOGY.
        BS 569
    sa Jesus Christ - Genealogy.

BIBLE - GEOGRAPHY.
        BS 630-633; DS 44-108
            (220.9)
    sa Ecclesiastical geography.
    x Geography, Biblical.
    xx Ecclesiastical geography.

BIBLE - GEOGRAPHY - MAPS.
        BS 631; G 2230-2239
    x Bible - Atlases.
        Bible - Maps.

BIBLE - GEOGRAPHY - MAPS - To 1800.

BIBLE - GEOGRAPHY - MOVING-PICTURES.

BIBLE - GEOLOGY. See
BIBLE AND GEOLOGY.

BIBLE - GLOSSARIES, VOCABULARIES, ETC.
    See BIBLE - DICTIONARIES.

BIBLE - HANDBOOKS, MANUALS, ETC.
        BS 417   (220.02)

BIBLE - HARMONIES.
        BS 481

BIBLE - HERMENEUTICS.
        BS 476   (220.x67)
    "Here are entered works on the
        principles of Biblical criticism.
        For critical works on the Bible
        see Bible - Criticism, interpre-
        tation, etc." LC
    sa Bible - Criticism, Higher.
        Bible - Criticism, Textual.
    x Bible - Criticism, interpretation,
        etc. - Theory, methods, etc.
        Bible - Exegesis.
        Bible - Interpretation.
        Hermeneutics, Biblical.

BIBLE - HERMENEUTICS - HISTORY. See
    BIBLE - CRITICISM, INTERPRETATION,
    ETC. - HISTORY.

BIBLE - HIEROGLYPHIC BIBLES. See
    HIEROGLYPHIC BIBLES.

BIBLE - HIGHER CRITICISM. See
    BIBLE - CRITICISM, HIGHER.

BIBLE - HISTORIOGRAPHY.
    "Here are entered works on the
        representation of historical
        events in the Bible." LC
    x Bible - History of Biblical
        events - Historiography.
    xx Jews - History - Historiography.

BIBLE - HISTORY.
        BS 445-460   (220.09)
    Here are entered works dealing with
        the history of the Bible as a
        book. For the history of the
        events contained in the Bible
        see Bible - History of Biblical
        events.

BIBLE - HISTORY BIBLES.

BIBLE - HISTORY OF BIBLICAL EVENTS.
        BS 550-558; BS 635   (220.95)
    sa Bible stories.
    x Bible history.
        History, Biblical.
    xx Palestine - History - To 70 A.D.

BIBLE - HISTORY OF BIBLICAL EVENTS -
    FICTION.
    x Bible - Fiction.

BIBLE - HISTORY OF BIBLICAL EVENTS -
    HISTORIOGRAPHY. See
    BIBLE - HISTORIOGRAPHY.

BIBLE - HISTORY OF BIBLICAL EVENTS -
    JUVENILE LITERATURE. See
    BIBLE STORIES.

BIBLE - HISTORY OF BIBLICAL EVENTS -
    POETRY.

BIBLE - HISTORY OF CONTEMPORARY
    EVENTS, ETC.
        BS 635   (220.95)
        BS 1197 (Old Testament)
            (221.95)
        BS 2410 (New Testament)
            (225.95)
    xx Palestine - History - To 70 A.D.

BIBLE - HOMILETICAL USE.
    BQT 2965
  xx Bible - Use.

BIBLE - ILLUSTRATIONS. See
  BIBLE - PICTURES, ILLUSTRATIONS, ETC.

BIBLE - INDEXES, TOPICAL.
    BS 432

BIBLE - INFLUENCE.
    BS 538.7

BIBLE - INSPIRATION.
    BS 480   (220.x62)
  sa Bible - Evidences, authority, etc.
    Inspiration.
    Revelation.
   x Bible - Revelation.
  xx Inspiration.

BIBLE - INTERLINEAR TRANSLATIONS.

BIBLE - INTERPRETATION. See
  BIBLE - COMMENTARIES.
  BIBLE - CRITICISM, INTERPRETATION, ETC.
  BIBLE - HERMENEUTICS.

BIBLE - INTRODUCTIONS.
    BS 474-475   (220.x6)
  "Here are entered works dealing
    with the origin, authorship,
    authenticity, general character-
    istics, contents, and aim of the
    different books of the Bible." LC
   x Bible - Literary criticism.
    Bible - Propaedeutics.

BIBLE - JUVENILE LITERATURE.

BIBLE - LANGUAGE, STYLE.
    BS 537   (220.84)
  sa Aramaic language.
    Bible - Parables.
    Bible as literature.
    Greek language, Biblical.
    Hebrew language.
  xx Languages - Religious aspects.

BIBLE - LAW. See
  JEWISH LAW.
  LAW (THEOLOGY)

BIBLE - LEGENDS.
  "Here are entered works on legends
    in the whole Bible. Works on
    legends in the Old Testament are
    entered under the heading Legends,
    Jewish. Works on legends in the
    New Testament are entered under
    the heading Bible. N.T. -
    Legends." LC
  sa Bible stories.
  xx Bible stories.

BIBLE - LITERARY CRITICISM. See
  BIBLE - CRITICISM, INTERPRETATION, ETC.
  BIBLE - INTRODUCTIONS.
  BIBLE AS LITERATURE.

BIBLE - LITURGICAL USE.
    BQT 4064
  xx Bible - Use.

BIBLE - LOVE AND MARRIAGE.
   x Bible - Marriage.

BIBLE - MANUSCRIPTS. See
  BIBLE. MANUSCRIPTS.

BIBLE - MAPS. See
  BIBLE - GEOGRAPHY - MAPS.

BIBLE - MARGINAL READINGS.

BIBLE - MARRIAGE. See
  BIBLE - LOVE AND MARRIAGE.

BIBLE - MEDICINE, HYGIENE, ETC.
    BS 640   (220.8614
  xx Christian science.

BIBLE - MEDITATIONS.
    [BQT 2607]

BIBLE - MENSURATION. See
  MENSURATION IN THE BIBLE.

BIBLE - METALLURGY.

BIBLE - METICAL VERSIONS.

BIBLE - MILITARY HISTORY.
  xx Military history, Ancient.

BIBLE - MINEROLOGY.
    BS 667

BIBLE - MIRACLES. See
  JESUS CHRIST - MIRACLES.
  MIRACLES.

BIBLE - MISCELLANEA.
    BS 534   (220.08)
  x Bible - Curiosa.

BIBLE - MUSIC.
    ML 166   (220.878)
  sa Music - Jews.
    Musical instruments, Jewish.
  x Bible. O.T. Psalms - Music.
    Bible and music.
  xx Synagogue music - History and
      criticism.

BIBLE - NAMES.
    BS 435
  sa God - Name.
    Israel - Name.
    Jesus Christ - Name.
    Jews - Name.
  x Biblical names.
    Names, Biblical.

BIBLE - NATURAL HISTORY.
    BS 660-667   (220.857)
  sa Nature in the Bible.
    Nature - Religious interpretations.
  x Bible - Animals.
    Bible - Birds.
    Bible - Botany.
    Bible - Gardens.
    Bible - Zoology.
    Botany of the Bible.
    Natural history, Biblical.
    Zoology of the Bible.

BIBLE - NUMERICAL DIVISION.
  x Bible - Chapters and verses.

BIBLE - NUMISMATICS.
    CJ 255
  x Bible - Coins.
    Coins of the Bible.
  xx Numismatics, Ancient.

BIBLE - OUTLINES, SYLLABI, ETC. See
  BIBLE - STUDY - OUTLINES, SYLLABI, ETC.

BIBLE - PARABLES.
    BS 680
  sa Jesus Christ - Parables.
  x Parables, Biblical.
    Parables, Christian.
  xx Bible - Language, style.
    Bible as literature.
    Parables.

BIBLE - PARAPHRASES.
    BS 550-558

BIBLE - PATRISTIC QUOTATIONS. See
  BIBLE - QUOTATIONS, EARLY.

BIBLE - PERIODICALS.
    BS 410   (220.05)

BIBLE - PHILOLOGY. See
  GREEK LANGUAGE, BIBLICAL.

BIBLE - PHILOSOPHY.
    BS 645   (220.01)

BIBLE - PICTURE BIBLES.
    N 8020-8037; BS 560
    (704.9484)
    ND 3355 (Illuminated manuscripts)
  "Here are entered works, especially
  medieval works, containing pictorial
  illustrations exclusively, or with
  only short passages of text accom-
  panying the pictures. If pictures
  accompany the complete text, the
  subdivision 'Pictures, illustrations, etc.' is used." LC
  sa Hieroglyphic Bibles.
  x Picture Bibles.
  xx Christian art.
    Jesus Christ - Art.

BIBLE - PICTURE·BIBLES - BIBLIOGRAPHY.
  Z 7771.13

BIBLE - PICTURES, ILLUSTRATIONS, ETC.
    BQT 5888-5893   (246.x64-65)
    N 8020-8185   (704.9484)
    BS 560 (Juvenile)

BIBLE - PICTURES, ILLUSTRATIONS, ETC. --
Continued.
　sa Bible and art.
　　also subdivision Art under names
　　　of Bible characters and under
　　　Biblical subjects, e.g., Jesus
　　　Christ - Art; Judgment Day - Art.
　　also subdivision Pictures, illus-
　　　trations, etc. under parts of
　　　the Bible, e.g., Bible. O.T. -
　　　Pictures, illustrations, etc.
　x Bible - Illustrations.
　xx Bible and art.
　　Christian art.
　　Jesus Christ - Art.

BIBLE - PICTURES, ILLUSTRATIONS, ETC. -
CATALOGS.
　x Bible - Catalogs.

BIBLE - POETRY.　See　HEBREW POETRY.

BIBLE - POPULAR WORKS.
　　BS 538

BIBLE - PRAYERS.
　　BV 228-235
　sa Jesus Christ - Prayers.
　　Lord's prayer.
　　Prayer - Biblical teaching.
　x Bible and prayer.

BIBLE - PROPAEDEUTICS.　See
　BIBLE - INTRODUCTIONS.

BIBLE - PROPHECIES.
　　BS 647-649
　　BS 1198 (Old Testament)
　　　(220.x64)
　　BS 2827 (New Testament)
　　D 524 (European War)
　sa Apocalyptic literature.
　　Jesus Christ - Prophecies.
　x Prophecies, Biblical.
　xx Prophecies.

BIBLE - PROPHECIES - CHRONOLOGY.

BIBLE - PROPHECIES - JEWS.

BIBLE - PROPHECIES - MESSIAH.　See
　MESSIAH - PROPHECIES.

BIBLE - PROPHECIES - NEGROES.

BIBLE - PROPHECIES - RUSSIA.

BIBLE - PROPHECIES - U.S.

BIBLE - PSYCHOLOGY.
　　BS 645　　(220.815)
　x Biblical psychology.
　　Psychology, Biblical.
　　Bible and Psychology

BIBLE - PUBLICATION AND DISTRIBUTOR.
　　BV 2369
　sa Language question in the church.
　x Bible - Colportage.
　xx Language question in the church.
　　Religious literature - Publication
　　and distribution.

BIBLE - PUBLICATION AND DISTRIBUTION -
PERIODICALS.

BIBLE - PUBLICATION AND DISTRIBUTION -
SOCIETIES.
　　BV 2369-2372
　x Bible societies.

BIBLE - QUESTION-BOOKS.　See
　BIBLE - CATECHISMS, QUESTION-BOOKS.

BIBLE - QUOTATIONS.
　　BS 390-399

BIBLE - QUOTATIONS, EARLY.
　　BS 391.A2
　"Here are entered works on quota-
　tions from the Bible found in the
　early Christian literature and
　allusions and references thereto."
　LC
　x Bible - Patristic quotations.
　　Fathers of the church - Biblical
　　quotations.
　xx Bible - Evidences, authority, etc.

BIBLE - READING.
　　bs 617

BIBLE - REFERENCE EDITIONS.

BIBLE - REVELATION.　See
　BIBLE - INSPIRATION.

BIBLE - RITES AND CEREMONIES.

BIBLE - SCIENCE. See
    BIBLE AND SCIENCE.

BIBLE - SERMONS.
    [BQT 3090]

BIBLE - SOCIETIES.
        BS 411
    "This heading is used for societies
    organized for professional and
    scholarly study of the Bible. For
    societies concerned with the pub-
    lication and distribution of the
    Bible see Bible - Publication and
    distribution - Societies." LC

BIBLE - SOCIOLOGY. See
    SOCIOLOGY, BIBLICAL.

BIBLE - SOURCES. See
    BIBLE - EVIDENCES, AUTHORITY, ETC.

BIBLE - STORIES. See BIBLE STORIES.

BIBLE - STUDY.
        BS 585-613   (220.07)
    sa Bible - Catechisms, question-books.
    x Bible study.
    xx Religious education.
        Sunday-schools.

BIBLE - STUDY - AIDS AND DEVICES.

BIBLE - STUDY - BIBLIOGRAPHY.
    [BS 444]
    xx Bible - Bibliography.

BIBLE - STUDY - BIOGRAPHY.
        BS 501
    sa Theologians.

BIBLE - STUDY - OUTLINES, SYLLABI, ETC.
        BS 590-5.2
    x Bible - Outlines, syllabi, etc.

BIBLE - STUDY - PAPAL TEACHING.

BIBLE - STUDY - TEXTBOOKS.
        BS 604-613
        BQT 3191
    "Here are entered textbooks of
    elementary and high-school
    grade." LC
    sa Bible stories.
        Sunday-schools - Question-books.
    xx Religious education - Textbooks.

BIBLE - SYMBOLISM.
        BS 477

BIBLE - TEXTUAL CRITICISM. See
    BIBLE - CRITICISM, TEXTUAL.

BIBLE - THEOLOGY.
        BS 543   (220.x96)
    Here are entered works which present
    a systematic exposition of Christian
    belief as contained in the Bible.
    sa subdivision "Theology" under
        parts and books of the Bible,
        and subdivision "Biblical
        teaching" under specific topics,
        e.g., Peace - Biblical teaching.
    x Biblical theology.
        Theology, Biblical.

BIBLE - TRANSLATIONS. See
    BIBLE - VERSIONS.

BIBLE - TYPOLOGY. See
    TYPOLOGY (THEOLOGY)

BIBLE - USE.
        BS 538.3
    "Here are entered works that show
    how the Bible is applied to
    problems of doctrine and life,
    as well as works that indicate
    its purpose and function." LC
    sa Bible - Homiletical use.
        Bible - Liturgical use.

BIBLE - VERSIONS.
        BS 450-460
    sa Language question in the church.
    x Bible - Translations.
    xx Language question in the church.
        Languages - Religious aspects.

42

BIBLE - VERSIONS - FILMSTRIPS.

BIBLE - VERSIONS - PERIODICALS.

BIBLE - VERSIONS, CATHOLIC.
        BS 453
  Here are entered works about the
  Catholic versions of the Bible.
  For texts of the Vulgate version
    see Bible.   Latin. [date]. Vul-
    gate. For works about the Vul-
    gate see Bible. Latin - Versions -
    Vulgate.
  For texts of the English Catholic
    versions see Bible. English. Cath-
    olic Biblical Association, [Douai,
    Westminster, etc.]; and Bible. N.T.
    English. Knox, [Rheims, etc.]
    x Catholic Bibles.

BIBLE - VERSIONS - CATHOLIC VS.
  PROTESTANT.
        BS 470

BIBLE - VERSIONS, LATIN. See
  BIBLE. LATIN - VERSIONS.

BIBLE - VERSIONS, POLYGOT, [ANGLO-
  SAXON, DANISH, FRENCH, ETC.]
        BS 1-355   (220.x3)
    x Polygot Bibles.

BIBLE - WEIGHTS AND MEASURES. See
  WEIGHTS AND MEASURES, JEWISH.

BIBLE - WOMEN. See
  WOMEN IN THE BIBLE.

BIBLE - ZOOLOGY. See
  BIBLE - NATURAL HISTORY.

        ################

BIBLE. MANUSCRIPTS.
    x Bible - Codices.
      Bible - Manuscripts.

BIBLE. MANUSCRIPTS - CATALOGS.
    x Bible - Catalogs.

BIBLE. MANUSCRIPTS - FACSIMILES.

BIBLE. MANUSCRIPTS, COPTIC, [GREEK,
  LATIN, ETC.]

        ################

BIBLE. O.T.
        BS 701-1830   (221-224)
    x Old Testament.
      Testament, Old.

With subdivisions as under Bible.
The Catholic names for the books of
  the Bible are listed below, together with references from all
  forms in use, Catholic as well as
  non-Catholic. The references
  from non-Catholic forms are necessary in order to interpret
  Library of Congress printed cards
  correctly, which follow Protestant
  usage, specifically the English
  Authorized version.

Modified classification outlines
  for the books of the Bible for
  use in Catholic libraries to fit
  both the Library of Congress classification and the Dewey Decimal
  classification can be found in the
  Catholic Library World, vol. 10,
  p.63-64. Libraries using the Walsh
  schedule can also follow the Bible
  classification outlined therein.
  The LC classification numbers in
  brackets under the individual books
  listed below indicate suggested
  modifications.

BIBLE. O.T. - BIOGRAPHY.
    x Biography, Biblical.

BIBLE. O.T. - PARABLES.
   xx Parables, Jewish.

BIBLE. O.T. - PICTORIAL ILLUSTRATIONS.
   sa Commandments, Ten - Art.

BIBLE. O.T. - PROPHECIES.
    x Prophecies, Biblical.

BIBLE. O.T. - THEOLOGY.
        BM 605; BS 1192.5
    x Biblical theology (O.T.)
      Theology, Biblical (O.T.)

        ################

BIBLE. O.T. ABDIAS.
    BS 1591-1595   (224.91)
  x Abdias, Book of.
    Bible. O.T. Obadiah.
    Obadiah, Book of.

BIBLE. O.T. AGGEUS.
    BS 1651-1655
  x Aggeus, Book of.
    Bible. O.T. Haggai.
    Haggai, Book of.

BIBLE. O.T. AMOS.
    BS 1581-1585   (224.8)
  x Amos, Book of.

BIBLE. O.T. APOCRYPHA. See
  BIBLE. O.T. DEUTERO-CANONICAL
  BOOKS.
  The Library of Congress uses the
    term "Apocrypha" in the Protes-
    tant sense to denote the deutero-
    canonical books of the Old Testa-
    ment. On LC printed cards the
    entry should be corrected as in-
    dicated above.
  Individual books so represented
    on LC printed cards should be
    amended to conform to Catholic
    usage, as follows.

BIBLE. O.T. APOCRYPHA. BARUCH.
  See BIBLE. O.T. BARUCH.

BIBLE. O.T. APOCRYPHA. BEL AND
  THE DRAGON. BIBLE. O.T. DANIEL.
  chap. XIV.

BIBLE. O.T. APOCRYPHA. ECCLESIAS-
  TICUS. See BIBLE. O.T. ECCLESI-
  ASTICUS.

BIBLE. O.T. APOCRYPHA. 1 ESDRAS.
  See ESDRAS, THIRD BOOK OF (APO-
  CRYPHAL)

BIBLE. O.T. APOCRYPHA. 2 ESDRAS.
  See ESDRAS, FOURTH BOOK OF (APO-
  CRYPHAL)

BIBLE. O.T. APOCRYPHA. HISTORY OF
  SUSANNA. See BIBLE. O.T. DANIEL.
  chap. XIII.

BIBLE. O.T. APOCRYPHA. JUDITH.
  See BIBLE. O.T. JUDITH.

BIBLE. O.T. APOCRYPHA. 1-2 MACCABEES.
  See BIBLE. O.T. 1-2 MACCABEES.

BIBLE. O.T. APOCRYPHA. PRAYER OF
  AZARIAH. See BIBLE. O.T. DANIEL.
  chap. III, 24-25.

BIBLE. O.T. APOCRYPHA. PRAYER OF
  MANASSES. See PRAYER OF MANASSES.

BIBLE. O.T. APOCRYPHA. REST OF ESTHER.
  See BIBLE. O.T. ESTHER.

BIBLE. O.T. APOCRYPHA. SONG OF THE
  THREE HOLY CHILDREN. See BIBLE. O.T.
  DANIEL. chap. III,57-90.

BIBLE. O.T. APOCRYPHA. TOBIT. See
  BIBLE. O.T. TOBIAS.

BIBLE. O.T. APOCRYPHA. WISDOM OF
  SOLOMON. See BIBLE. O.T. WISDOM.

BIBLE. O.T. APOCRYPHAL BOOKS. See
  APOCRYPHAL BOOKS (O.T.)

BIBLE. O.T. BARUCH.
    [BS 1536-1537]; BS 1771-1775
  x Baruch, Book of.
    Bible. O.T. Apocrypha. Baruch.
    Jeremias, Epistle of.

BIBLE. O.T. CANTICLE OF CANTICLES.
    BS 1481-1490   (223.x6)
  x Bible. O.T. Song of Solomon.
    Canticle of Canticles.
    Solomon, Song of.
    Song of Solomon.

BIBLE. O.T. CHRONICLES. See
  BIBLE. O.T. PARALIPOMENON.

BIBLE. O.T. DANIEL.
    BS 1551-1556   (224.x5)
  x Daniel, Book of.

44

BIBLE. O.T. DANIEL. chap. III, 24-25.
  x Azarias, Prayer of.
    Bible. O.T. Apocrypha. Prayer of
      Azariah.
    Prayer of Azarias.

BIBLE. O.T. DANIEL. chap. III, 57-90.
  x Bible. O.T. Apocrypha. Song of
    the Three Holy Children.

BIBLE. O.T. DANIEL. chap. XIII.
  x Bible. O.T. Apocrypha. History
    of Susanna.
    History of Susanna.
    Susanna, History of.

BIBLE. O.T. DANIEL. chap. XIV.
  x Bel and the Dragon.
    Bible. O.T. Apocrypha. Bel and
      the Dragon.

BIBLE. O.T. DEUTERO-CANONICAL BOOKS.
    [BS 1681-1690]
  x Apocrypha.
    Bible. O.T. Apocrypha.
    Deutero-canonical Books (Bible)

BIBLE. O.T. DEUTERONOMY.
    BS 1271-1275   (222.x17)
  x Deuteronomy, Book of.

BIBLE. O.T. ECCLESIASTES.
    BS 1471-1476   (223.x5)
  x Ecclesiastes, Book of.
    Kohelet, Book of.

BIBLE. O.T. ECCLESIASTICUS.
    [BS 1493-1494]; BS 1761-1765
      (223.x7)
  x Bible. O.T. Apocrypha. Ecclesi-
    asticus.
    Bible. O.T. Sirach.
    Ecclesiasticus, Book of.
    Sirach, Book of.

BIBLE. O.T. 1-2 ESDRAS.
    BS 1351-1365   (222.x6)
  x Esdras and Nehemias, Book of.

BIBLE. O.T. 1 ESDRAS.
    BS 1351-1355
  x Bible. O.T. Ezra.
    Esdras, First Book of.
    Ezra, Book of.

BIBLE. O.T. 2 ESDRAS.
    BS 1261-1265
  x Bible. O.T. Nehemiah.
    Esdras, Second Book of.
    Nehemias, Book of.

BIBLE. O.T. ESTHER.
    BS 1371-1375   (222.x7)
  x Bible. O.T. Apocrypha. Rest of
    Esther.
    Esther, Book of.
    Rest of Esther.

BIBLE. O.T. EXODUS.
    BS 1241-1245   (222.x14)
  x Exodus, Book of.

BIBLE. O.T. EZECHIEL.
    BS 1541-1545   (224.x4)
  x Bible. O.T. Ezekiel.
    Ezechiel, Book of.
    Ezekiel, Book of.

BIBLE. O.T. EZEKIEL. See
  BIBLE. O.T. EZECHIEL.

BIBLE. O.T. EZRA. See
  BIBLE. O.T. 1 ESDRAS.

BIBLE. O.T. FIVE SCROLLS.
  x Five Scrolls.

BIBLE. O.T. GENESIS.
    BS 1231-1235   (222.x13)
  x Genesis, Book of.

BIBLE. O.T. HABACUC.
    BS 1631-1635
  x Bible. O.T. Habakkuk.
    Habacuc, Book of.
    Habakkuk, Book of.

BIBLE. O.T. HABAKKUK. See
  BIBLE. O.T. HABACUC.

BIBLE. O.T. HAGGAI. See
    BIBLE. O.T. AGGEUS.

BIBLE. O.T. HAGIOGRAPHA.
    x Hagiographa (Bible)

BIBLE. O.T. HEPTATEUCH.
    x Heptateuch (Bible)

BIBLE. O.T. HEXATEUCH.
        BS 1211-1215   (222.x1)
    x Hexateuch (Bible)

BIBLE. O.T. HISTORICAL BOOKS.
        BS 1201-1375   (222)

BIBLE. O.T. HOSEA. See
    BIBLE. O.T. OSEE.

BIBLE. O.T. ISAIAH. See
    BIBLE. O.T. ISAIAS.

BIBLE. O.T. ISAIAS.
        BS 1511-1515   (224.x2)
    x Bible. O.T. Isaiah.
    Isaiah, Book of.
    Isaias, Book of.

BIBLE. O.T. JEREMIAH. See
    BIBLE. O.T. JEREMIAS.

BIBLE. O.T. JEREMIAS.
        BS 1521-1525   (224.x3)
    x Bible. O.T. Jeremiah.
    Jeremiah, Book of.
    Jeremias, Book of.

BIBLE. O.T. JOB.
        BS 1411-1417   (223.x2)
        BS 1411-1417
    x Job, Book of.

BIBLE. O.T. JOEL.
        BS 1571-1575   (224.7)
    x Joel, Book of.

BIBLE. O.T. JONAH. See
    BIBLE. O.T. JONAS.

BIBLE. O.T. JONAS.
        BS 1601-1605   (224.92)
    x Bible. O.T. Jonah.
    Jonah, Book of.
    Jonas, Book of.

BIBLE. O.T. JOSHUA. See
    BIBLE. O.T. JOSUE.

BIBLE. O.T. JOSUE.
        BS 1291-1295   (222.x18)
    x Bible. O.T. Joshua.
    Joshua, Book of.
    Josue, Book of.

BIBLE. O.T. JUDGES.
        BS 1301-1305   (222.x2)
    x Judges, Book of.

BIBLE. O.T. JUDITH.
        [BS 1368-1369]; BS 1731-1735
        (222.x7)
    x Bible. O.T. Apocrypha. Judith.
    Judith, Book of.

BIBLE. O.T. KINGS.
        BS 1321-1335
    x Kings, Books of.

BIBLE. O.T. 1-2 KINGS.
        BS 1321-1325   (222.x3)
    x Bible. O.T. Samuel.
    Samuel, Books of.

BIBLE. O.T. 1 KINGS.

BIBLE. O.T. 2 KINGS.

BIBLE. O.T. 3-4 KINGS.
        BS 1331-1335   (222.x4)
    These are called 1-2 Kings in
    Protestant Bibles.

BIBLE. O.T. 3 KINGS.

BIBLE. O.T. 4 KINGS.

BIBLE. O.T. LAMENTATIONS.
        BS 1531-1535   (224.x3)
    x Jeremiah, Lamentations of.
    Jeremias, Lamentations of.
    Lamentations of Jeremias.

BIBLE. O.T. LESSONS, LITURGICAL.

BIBLE. O.T. LEVITICUS.
        BS 1251-1255   (222.x15)
    x Leviticus, Book of.

BIBLE. O.T. 1-2 MACHABEES.
        [BS 1676-1677]; BS 1821-1825
        (222.x9)
    x Bible. O.T. Apocrypha. 1-2 Mac-
        cabees.
      Maccabees, 1-2 Books of.
      Machabees, 1-2 Books of.

BIBLE. O.T. 1 MACHABEES.

BIBLE. O.T. 2 MACHABEES.

BIBLE. O.T. MAJOR PROPHETS.
        BS 1501-1556   (224)
    x Major Prophets.
      Prophets, Major.
    xx Bible. O.T. Prophets.

BIBLE. O.T. MALACHI. See
    BIBLE. O.T. MALACHIAS.

BIBLE. O.T. MALACHIAS.
        BS 1671-1675   (224.x99)
    x Bible. O.T. Malachi.
      Malachi, Book of.
      Malachias, Book of.

BIBLE. O.T. MICAH. See
    BIBLE. O.T. MICHEAS.

BIBLE. O.T. MICHEAS.
        BS 1611-1615   (224.93)
    x Bible. O.T. Micah.
      Micah, Book of.
      Micheas, Book of.

BIBLE. O.T. MINOR PROPHETS.
        BS 1560-1675   (224.9)
    x Minor Prophets.
      Prophets, Minor.
    xx Bible. O.T. Prophets.

BIBLE. O.T. NAHUM.
        BS 1621-1625   (224.94)
    x Nahum, Book of.

BIBLE. O.T. NEHEMIAH. See
    BIBLE. O.T. 2 ESDRAS.

BIBLE. O.T. NUMBERS.
        BS 1261-1265   (222.x16)
    x Numbers, Book of.

BIBLE. O.T. OBADIAH. See
    BIBLE. O.T. ABDIAS.

BIBLE. O.T. OCTATEUCH.
    x Octateuch (Bible)

BIBLE. O.T. OSEE.
        BS 1561-1565   (224.6)
    x Bible. O.T. Hosea.
      Hosea Book of.
      Osee, Book of.

BIBLE. O.T. PARALIPOMENON.
        BS 1341-1345   (222.x5)
    x Bible. O.T. Chronicles.
      Chronicles, Books of.
      Paralipomenon, Books of.

BIBLE. O.T. 1 PARALIPOMENON.

BIBLE. O.T. 2 PARALIPOMENON.

BIBLE. O.T. PENTATEUCH.
        BS 1221-1225   (222.x12)
    x Pentateuch (Bible)

BIBLE. O.T. POETICAL BOOKS.
        BS 1401-1490   (223)

BIBLE. O.T. PROPHETS.
        BS 1501-1675   (224)
    sa Bible. O.T. Major Prophets.
       Bible. O.T. Minor Prophets.
    x Prophets, Books of the.

BIBLE. O.T. PROVERBS.
        BS 1461-1465   (223.x4)
    x Proverbs, Book of.

BIBLE. O.T. PSALMS.
        BS 1419-1451   (223.x3)
    sa Psalterium.
    x Psalms.
    xx Psalmody.

BIBLE. O.T. PSALMS - COMMENTARIES.
  x Psalterium - Commentaries.

BIBLE. O.T. PSALMS - LITURGICAL USE.
  BS 1435

BIBLE. O.T. PSALMS - MUSIC See
  BIBLE - MUSIC; PSALMS (MUSIC)

BIBLE. O.T. PSALMS - TITLES.

BIBLE. O.T. PSALMS I, [II, III, etc.]
  BS 1450
  The corresponding numbering of the
  150 psalms according to Catholic
  and Protestant practice is listed
  below.

Catholic	Protestant
1-8	1-8
9	9-10
10-112	11-113
113	114-115
114-115	116
116-145	117-146
146-147	147
148-150	148-150

BIBLE. O.T. PSALMS. L.
  x Miserere mei, Deus.

BIBLE. O.T. PSALMS. CXXIX.
  x De profundis.

BIBLE. O.T. PSALMS, GRADUAL.
  BS 1445
  These comprise "fifteen psalms,
  namely, nos. 119-133, which in
  Hebrew bear a superscription which
  is variously rendered as "gradual
  canticle," "song of degrees,"
  "song of ascents." AT
  x Gradual Psalms.
  Psalms, Gradual.
  Songs of degrees.

BIBLE. O.T. PSALMS, MESSIANIC.
  BS 1445
  x Messianic Psalms.
  Psalms, Messianic.

BIBLE. O.T. PSALMS, PENITENTIAL.
  BS 1445   (223.32)
  BQT 4421 (Liturgy)
  "The seven Penitential Psalms are
  nos. 6, 31, 37, 50, 101, 129 and
  142, wherein penitence for sin
  and desire for pardon are expressed." AT
  x Penitential Psalms.
  Psalms, Penitential.

BIBLE. O.T. RUTH.
  BS 1311-1315   (222.x2)
  x Ruth, Book of.

BIBLE. O.T. SAMUEL. See
  BIBLE. O.T. 1-2 KINGS.

BIBLE. O.T. SIRACH. See
  BIBLE. O.T. ECCLESIASTICUS.

BIBLE. O.T. SONG OF SOLOMON. See
  BIBLE. O.T. CANTICLE OF CANTICLES.

BIBLE. O.T. SOPHONIAS.
  BS 1641-1645   (224.96)
  x Bible. O.T. Zephoniah.
  Sophonias, Book of.
  Zephaniah, Book of.

BIBLE. O.T. TOBIAS.
  [BS 1366-1367]; BS 1721-1725
  (222.x8)
  x Bible. O.T. Apocrypha. Tobit.
  Tobias, Book of.
  Tobit, Book of.

BIBLE. O.T. WISDOM.
  [BS 1491-1492]; BS 1751-1755
  (223.x8)
  x Bible. O.T. Apocrypha. Wisdom
  of Solomon.
  Solomon, Wisdom of.
  Wisdom, Book of.
  Wisdom of Solomon.

BIBLE. O.T. WISDOM LITERATURE.
  BS 1455-1456   (223.x9)
  x Wisdom Literature (Bible)

48

BIBLE. O.T. ZACHARIAS.
       BS 1661-1665   (224.98)
    x Bible. O.T. Zechariah.
    Zacharias, Book of.
    Zechariah Book of.

BIBLE. O.T. ZECHARIAH. See
    BIBLE. O.T. ZACHARIAS.

BIBLE. O.T. ZEPHANIAH. See
    BIBLE. O.T. SOPHONIAS.

          #################

BIBLE. N.T.
       BS 1901-2970   (225-227)
    x New Testament.
    Testament, New.

    With subdivisions as under Bible.

BIBLE. N.T. - BIOGRAPHY.
       BS 2430-2520
    x Biography, Biblical.

BIBLE. N.T. - CRITICISM, INTERPRETATION,
    ETC.
    sa Demythologization.
    Bible. N.T. — History of biblical events
BIBLE. N.T. - LEGENDS.
    See note under Bible - Legends.

BIBLE. N.T. - PROPHECIES.
       BS 2545
    x Prophecies, Biblical.

BIBLE. N.T. - RELATION TO O.T.
       BS 2387

BIBLE. N.T. - THEOLOGY.
       BS 2397
    x Biblical theology (N.T.)
    Theology, Biblical (N.T.)

          ################

BIBLE. N.T. ACTS.
       BS 2620-2628   (226.x4)
    x Acts of the Apostles.

BIBLE. N.T. APOCALYPSE.
       BS 2820-2825   (227.x98)
    x Apocalypse of St. John.
    Bible. N.T. Revelation.
    Revelation, Book of.

BIBLE. N.T. APOCRYPHAL BOOKS. See
    APOCRYPHAL BOOKS (N.T.)

BIBLE. N.T. CAPTIVITY EPISTLES.
    x Captivity, Epistles of the.
    Epistles of the Captivity.
    xx Bible. N.T. Epistles of Paul.

BIBLE. N.T. CATHOLIC EPISTLES.
       BS 2777   (227.9)
    x Catholic Epistles.
    Epistles, Catholic.

BIBLE. N.T. COLOSSIANS.
       BS 2710-2715   (227.7)
    x Colossians, Epistle to the.

BIBLE. N.T. CORINTHIANS.
       BS 2670-2675   (227.x3)
    x Corinthians, Epistles to the

BIBLE. N.T. 1 CORINTHIANS.

BIBLE. N.T. 2 CORINTHIANS.

BIBLE. N.T. EPHESIANS.
       BS 2690-2695   (227.5)
    x Ephesians, Epistles to the.

BIBLE. N.T. EPISTLES. use Letters
       BS 2630-2635   (227)
    x Epistles (Bible)

BIBLE. N.T. EPISTLES, LITURGICAL.
    sa Epistolarium.
    x Epistles, Liturgical.

BIBLE. N.T. EPISTLES AND GOSPELS,
    LITURGICAL.
       BQT 4297-4298
    sa Lectionarium.
    x Epistles and Gospels, Liturgical.

BIBLE. N.T. - EPISTLES AND GOSPELS,
    LITURGICAL - COMMENTARIES.
       BQT 2992

BIBLE. N.T. EPISTLES AND GOSPELS,
   LITURGICAL - MEDITATIONS.
      BQT 2606

BIBLE. N.T. EPISTLES AND GOSPELS,
   LITURGICAL - SERMONS.
      BQT 2992
   xx Church year - Sermons.

BIBLE. N.T. EPISTLES OF JOHN.
      BS 2800-2805   (227.94-227.96)
   x Bible. N.T. John, Epistles of.
   John, Saint, Epistles of.

BIBLE. N.T. 1 EPISTLE OF JOHN.

BIBLE. N.T. 2 EPISTLE OF JOHN.

BIBLE. N.T. 3 EPISTLE OF JOHN.

BIBLE. N.T. EPISTLES OF PAUL.
      BS 2640-2657   (227.x1)
   sa Bible. N.T. Captivity Epistles.
   Bible. N.T. Pastoral Epistles.
   x Epistles, Pauline.
   Paul, Saint, Epistles of.

BIBLE. N.T. GALATIANS.
      BS 2680-2685   (227.4)
   x Galatians, Epistles to the.

BIBLE. N.T. GOSPELS.
      BS 2549-2961   (226)
   sa name of individual Gospel, e.g.,
      Bible. N.T. Matthew.
   x Gospels.

BIBLE. N.T. GOSPELS - RELATION
   TO O.T.

BIBLE. N.T. GOSPELS, LITURGICAL.
      BQT 4297-4298
   sa Evangeliarium.
   Gospels, Lenten.
   x Gospels, Liturgical.

BIBLE. N.T. HEBREWS.
      BS 2770-2775   (227.87)
   x Hebrews, Epistle to the.

BIBLE. N.T. JAMES.
      BS 2780-2785   (227.91)
   x James, Saint, Catholic Epistle of.

BIBLE. N.T. JOHANNINE LITERATURE.
   x Johannine Literature (Bible)

BIBLE. N.T. JOHN.
      BS 2610-2617   (226.x26)
   x John, Saint, Gospel of.

BIBLE. N.T. JOHN, EPISTLES OF. See
   BIBLE. N.T. EPISTLES OF JOHN.

BIBLE. N.T. JUDE.
      BS 2810-2815   (227.97)
   x Jude, Saint, Catholic Epistle of.

BIBLE. N.T. LUKE.
      BS 2590-2597   (226.x25)
   x Luke, Saint, Gospel of.

BIBLE. N.T. MARK.
      BS 2580-2587   (226.x24)
   x Mark, Saint, Gospel of.

BIBLE. N.T. MATTHEW.
      BS 2570-2577   (226.x23)
   x Matthew, Saint, Gospel of.

BIBLE. N.T. PASTORAL EPISTLES.
      BS 2730-2735
   x Epistles, Pastoral.
   Pastoral Epistles.
   xx Bible. N.T. Epistles of Paul.

BIBLE. N.T. PETER.
      BS 2790-2795   (227.92-227.93)
   x Peter, Saint, Epistles of.

BIBLE. N.T. 1 PETER.

BIBLE. N.T. 2 PETER.

BIBLE. N.T. PHILEMON.
      BS 2760-2765   (227.86)
   x Philemon, Epistle to.

BIBLE. N.T. PHILIPPIANS.
      BS 2700-2705   (227.6)
   x Philippians, Epistle to the.

BIBLE. N.T. REVELATION. See
   BIBLE. N.T. APOCALYPSE.

BIBLE. N.T. ROMANS.
      BS 2660-2665   (227.x2)
   x Romans, Epistle to the.

BIBLE. N.T. THESSALONIANS.
    BS 2720-2725   (227.81-227.82)
  x Thessalonians, Epistles to the.

BIBLE. N.T. 1 THESSALONIANS.

BIBLE. N.T. 2 THESSALONIANS.

BIBLE. N.T. TIMOTHY.
    BS 2740-2745   (227.83-227.84)
  x Timothy, Saint, Epistles to.

BIBLE. N.T. 1 TIMOTHY.

BIBLE. N.T. 2 TIMOTHY.

BIBLE. N.T. TITUS.
    BS 2750-2755   (227.85)
  x Titus, Epistle to.

################

BIBLE AND ART.
    BS 680
    BQT 5888-5889
  sa Bible - Pictures, illustrations,
    etc.
  xx Bible - Pictures, illustrations,
    etc.

BIBLE AND GEOLOGY.
    BS 657   (220.855)
  x Bible - Geology.
    Biblical geology.
    Geology and Bible.
    Geology and religion.
    Religion and geology.

BIBLE AND LAW.
    BS 639   (220.834)
  "Here are entered works on the in-
    fluence of the Bible upon secular
    law. Works on Biblical law are
    entered under the heading Jewish
    law." LC
  x Law and the Bible.

BIBLE AND LITURGY. See
  LITURGY AND BIBLE.

BIBLE AND MUSIC. See BIBLE - MUSIC.

BIBLE AND MYTHOLOGY.
    BS 680
  x Mythology and Bible.

BIBLE AND PEACE. See
  PEACE - BIBLICAL TEACHING.

BIBLE AND PRAYER. See
  BIBLE - PRAYERS.
  PRAYER - BIBLICAL TEACHING.
  √Bible + Psychology see Bible - Psycho
BIBLE AND SCIENCE.
    BS 650-667   (220.85)
    BQT 237 (Apologetics)
  sa Creation.
    Modernist-fundamentalist con-
      troversy.
    Nature - Religious interpretations.
  x Bible - Science.
  xx Religion and science.

BIBLE AND SPIRITUALISM.
    BF 1275   (220.82899)

BIBLE AND TEMPERANCE. See
  TEMPERANCE - BIBLICAL TEACHING.

BIBLE AS LITERATURE.
    BS 535   (220.88)
  sa Bible - Criticism, interpreta-
      tion, etc.
    Bible - Parables.
  x Bible - Drama.
    Bible - Literary criticism.
  xx Bible - Criticism, interpreta-
      tion, etc.
    Bible - Language, style.
    Religious literature.

BIBLE-CHRISTIAN CHURCH.
    BX 6510.B48

BIBLE CHRISTIANS.
    BX 6510.B5   220.C45
  BIBLE for Children x Children - Bible
BIBLE GAMES AND PUZZLES.
    GV 1507
  x Bible puzzles.
  xx Crossword puzzles.
    Games.
    Literary recreations.
    Puzzles.

BIBLE HISTORY. See BIBLE -
  HISTORY OF BIBLICAL EVENTS.

BIBLE IN LITERATURE.
        PN 49 (General)
        PN 1077 (Poetry; general)
        BQ 66 (Christian literature)
  xx Religion in literature.

BIBLE IN THE SCHOOLS.
        BS 601-603
  xx Church and education.
     Religious education.

✓ BIBLE PLAYS.
        PN 6120.R4
  "Here are entered works on the
    dramatization of Biblical
    events, collections of such
    dramatizations, and such indi-
    vidual plays as are not entered
    under the name of a principal
    character or other specific
    heading." LC
  sa Biblical costume.
     Hebrew drama.
     Liturgical drama.
     also subdivision "Drama" under
       names of Biblical characters
       (e.g., Joseph, the Patriarch -
       Drama)
  ✓ x Bible ⊣ Drama.
  ✓   Plays, Bible.
  xx Mysteries and miracle-plays.

BIBLE PROTESTANT CHURCH.

BIBLE PUZZLES. See
  BIBLE GAMES AND PUZZLES.

BIBLE SOCIETIES. See BIBLE - PUBLI-
  CATION AND DISTRIBUTION - SOCIETIES.

✓ BIBLE STORIES.
        BS 546-559   (220.95)
        BQT 3191-3195 (Catechetics)
          (25x3.4)
  sa Bible - Legends.
   x Bible - History of Biblical
       events - Juvenile literature.
     Bible - Stories.
     Religious education - Stories.
     Stories, Bible.

BIBLE STORIES -- Continued.
  xx Bible - History of Biblical
       events.
     Bible - Legends.
     Bible - Study - Textbooks.
     Catechism stories.
     Story-telling - Religion.

BIBLE STORIES, ENGLISH, [FRENCH,
  GERMAN, ETC.]

BIBLE STORIES - O.T.

BIBLE STORIES - N.T.

BIBLE STUDY. See BIBLE - STUDY.

BIBLES FOR THE BLIND. See
  BLIND, BIBLES FOR THE.

BIBLICAL ANTHROPOLOGY. See
  MAN (THEOLOGY) - BIBLICAL TEACHING.

BIBLICAL ARAMAIC LANGUAGE. See
  ARAMAIC LANGUAGE.

BIBLICAL ARCHAEOLOGY. See
  BIBLE - ANTIQUITIES.

BIBLICAL COMMISSION. See
  COMMISSIO DE RE BIBLICA.

BIBLICAL COSTUME.
  sa Costume, Jewish.
   x Bible - Costume.
     Costume, Biblical.
  xx Bible plays.
     Costume, Jewish.

BIBLICAL ETHICS. See BIBLE - ETHICS.

BIBLICAL GEOLOGY. See
  BIBLE AND GEOLOGY.

BIBLICAL GREEK. See
  GREEK LANGUAGE, BIBLICAL.

BIBLICAL LAW. See JEWISH LAW.

BIBLICAL LANGUAGES. See
  LANGUAGES - RELIGIOUS ASPECTS.

BIBLICAL NAMES. See BIBLE - NAMES.

52

BIBLICAL SAINTS. See
SAINTS, BIBLICAL.

✓ BIBLICAL PSYCHOLOGY. See
BIBLE - PSYCHOLOGY.

BIBLICAL THEOLOGY. See
BIBLE - THEOLOGY.

BIBLICAL THEOLOGY (O.T.). See
BIBLE. O.T. - THEOLOGY.

BIBLICAL THEOLOGY (N.T.). See
BIBLE. N.T. - THEOLOGY.

BIBLIOGRAPHY - BEST BOOKS - CATHOLIC
LITERATURE.
x Catholic literature - Bibliography -
Best books.

BIBLIOGRAPHY - BEST BOOKS - THEOLOGY.
x Theology - Bibliography - Best
books.

BIBLIOGRAPHY - BIBLIOGRAPHY -
CATHOLIC LITERATURE.

BIGAMY (CANON LAW)
BQV230 2356 (Criminal law)
(348.x6)
BQV230 884 (Marriage law)
(348.x427)
xx Crime and criminals (Canon law)
Marriage (Canon law)

BILLS OF COMPLAINT (CANON LAW). See
COMPLAINTS (CANON LAW)

BINATION.
BQV230 806
"The offering of Mass twice in the
same day by the same priest." AT
xx Mass - Celebration.

BINDING AND LOOSING. See
POWER OF THE KEYS.

BIOGRAPHY, BIBLICAL. See
BIBLE - BIOGRAPHY.
BIBLE. O.T. - BIOGRAPHY.
BIBLE. N.T. - BIOGRAPHY.

BIOGRAPHY, CATHOLIC. See
CATHOLIC CHURCH - BIOGRAPHY.

BIOGRAPHY, CHRISTIAN. See
CHRISTIAN BIOGRAPHY.

BIRTH CONTROL - MORAL AND RELIGIOUS
ASPECTS.
BQT 1937   (24x1.64)
sa Family Planning   610

BIRTHS, REGISTERS OF. See
REGISTERS OF BIRTHS, ETC.

BISHOPRICS. See DIOCESES.

✓ BISHOPS.   (Geog. subdiv., Indirect)
BQT 348 (Hierarchy)
BQX 181 (Biography)   (922.2)
sa Apostolic succession.
Archbishops.
Archpriests.
Cathedraticum.
Chanceries, Diocesan.
Chapters, Cathedral, collegiate,
etc.
Chorepiscopi.
Dioceses.
Episcopacy.
Exarchs.
Investiture.
Ordination.
Patriarchs and patriarchate.
Popes - Primacy.
Primates (Ecclesiastical)
Rural deans.
Staff, Pastoral.
Vicars apostolic.
Vicars-general.
xx Apostolic succession.
Catholic Church - Government.
Christian biography.
Church history.
Clergy.
Curia, Diocesan.
Episcopacy.
Ordination.
Popes - Primacy.
Prelates.
Vicars apostolic.

BISHOPS - ANNIVERSARY SERMONS. See
ANNIVERSARY SERMONS - BISHOPS.

BISHOPS - BIOGRAPHY.
BQX 181; BQX 8258
xx Catholic Church - Biography.

BISHOPS - CONSECRATION. See
CONSECRATION OF BISHOPS.

BISHOPS - CORRESPONDENCE, REMINIS-
CENCES, ETC.

BISHOPS - ELECTION.
BQV230 329 332   (348.x35)
xx Election law (Canon law)

BISHOPS - HERALDRY.
xx Heraldry, Sacred.

BISHOPS - INSIGNIA.
xx Insignia, Pontifical.

BISHOPS - QUINQUENNIAL REPORT.
BQV230 340-342
x Quinquennial report of bishops.

BISHOPS - RESIDENCE.
"Here are entered works dealing
with the requirement that bishops
reside in their diocese." LC

BISHOPS - TEMPORAL POWER.
BQX 184
x Temporal power of bishops.
xx Church and state.

BISHOPS (CANON LAW)
BQV230 329-349   (348.x35)
sa Abbots nullius (Canon law)
Adminstrators apostolic.
Archbishops (Canon law)
Coadjutor bishops.
Consultors, Diocesan.
Jurisdiction (Canon law)
Trials, Ecclesiastical (Bishops)
Vicars capitular.
Visit ad limina.
xx Dioceses (Canon law)
Jurisdiction (Canon law)
Persons (Canon law)

BISHOPS (CANON LAW) - HISTORY.

BISHOPS, CEREMONIAL OF. See
CAEREMONIALE EPISCOPORUM.

BLACK CANONS. See AUGUSTINIAN CANONS.

BLACK CARDINALS.
"The cardinals who, because they
refused to be amenable to the
wishes of Napoleon I, were forbidden to wear red robes." LC
x Cardinals, Black.

BLACK FRIARS. See DOMINICANS.

BLACK MASS. See MASS, REQUIEM.

BLACK MASS (SATANISM). See SATANISM.

BLACK MONKS. See BENEDICTINES.

BLACK SCAPULAR OF THE PASSION. See
SCAPULAR OF THE PASSION (BLACK)

BLASPHEMY.   (Geog. subdiv.
BQT 1874   (24x1.61)
"Here are entered works on blasphemy
in the legal and theological sense
'maliciously reviling God or reli-
gion'. Works on profane language
are entered under 'Swearing'.
Works on judicial or official oaths
are entered under 'Oaths'." LC
sa Liberty of the press.
Prohibited books.
Sacrilege.
xx Libel and slander.
Liberty of speech.
Liberty of the press.
Offenses against religion.
Prohibited books.
Religion (Virtue)
Religious liberty.

BLESSED.
BQX 8203-8279
By this term such venerated persons
are referred to as, e.g., Blessed
Oliver Plunkett, and must be distinguished from fully canonized
saints.

BLESSED -- Continued.
  sa Saints.
  xx Christian biography.

BLESSED SACRAMENT. See EUCHARIST.

BLESSED SACRAMENT, ADORATION OF THE. See
  ADORATION OF THE BLESSED SACRAMENT.

BLESSED SACRAMENT, BENEDICTION OF THE.
  See BENEDICTION OF THE BLESSED
  SACRAMENT.

BLESSED SACRAMENT, FEAST OF THE. See
  CORPUS CHRISTI.

BLESSED SACRAMENT, MASS OF THE. See
  MISSA DE SANCTISSIMO EUCHARISTIAE
  SACRAMENTO.

BLESSED SACRAMENT, OFFICE OF THE. See
  OFFICIUM DE SANCTISSIMO SACRAMENTO.

BLESSED SACRAMENT, OUR LADY OF THE. See
  OUR LADY OF THE BLESSED SACRAMENT.

BLESSED SACRAMENT, PROCESSION OF THE. See
  PROCESSION OF THE BLESSED SACRAMENT.

BLESSED TRINITY. See TRINITY.

BLESSED VIRGIN MARY. See
  MARY, BLESSED VIRGIN.

BLESSED WATER. See HOLY WATER.

BLESSING, PAPAL. See PAPAL BLESSING.

BLESSING AND CURSING.
  Here are entered works dealing with
    blessing and cursing in the ab-
    stract. For works dealing with
    the liturgical function for blessing
    persons and objects see Blessings.
  x Cursing and blessing.
    Execration.
    Imprecation.
    Malediction.
  xx Blessings.

BLESSING OF ABBESSES.
  [BQT 4464.6]
  x Abbesses, Blessing of.

BLESSING OF ABBOTS.
  BQT 4464.5; BQT 4679
  x Abbots, Blessing of.

BLESSING OF HOUSES. See
  HOUSES, BLESSING OF.

BLESSING OF ORGAN. See
  ORGAN, BLESSING OF.

BLESSING OF VIRGINS. See
  CONSECRATION OF VIRGINS.

✓ BLESSINGS.
  BQT 4461-4484; BQT 4516-4518
  (23x7.8)
  Here are entered works dealing with
    the liturgical rites by which per-
    sons, places or things are dedi-
    cated to a sacred purpose.
  sa Benedictionale.
    Blessing and cursing.
  x Benedictions.
  xx Benedictionale.
    Sacramentals.

BLESSINGS - SERMONS.
  BQT 3089

BLESSINGS, TABLE. See
  GRACE AT MEALS.

BLIND, BIBLES FOR THE.
  x Bibles for the blind.
  xx Missions - Blind.

BLOOD (IN RELIGION, FOLKLORE, ETC.)
  References as in LC.

BLOOD COVENANT.
  References as in LC.

BLOOD OF JESUS. See PRECIOUS BLOOD.

BLUE SCAPULAR OF THE IMMACULATE
  CONCEPTION.
  BQT 4522
  x Immaculate Conception, Blue
    scapular of the.

BOA-HO. See BON (TIBETAN RELIGION)
BODY, HUMAN   610
BODY, HUMAN - PAPAL TEACHING.

BODY, RESURRECTION OF. See
  RESURRECTION.

BOGOMILES.
      BQT 89
      BQX 1612; BQX 5446; BQX 5933
  xx Cathari.
     Sects, Medieval.

BOHEMIAN BRETHREN.
      BX 4 20-4921   (284.3)
  xx Beghards.
     Moravians.

BOHEMIAN DEISTS. See
  ABRAHAMITES (BOHEMIA)

BOLIVIA - CHURCH HISTORY.
      BQX 4761-5769

BOLLANDISTS.
      BQT 1576; BQX 41
  sa Hagiography.
  xx Jesuits.

BON (TIBETAN RELIGION)
  References as in LC.

BONA FIDES (CANON LAW)
      BQV230 1512   (348.x46)
  xx Prescription (Canon law)

BONJOURS, LES FRERES. See
  FAREINISTES.

BOOK OF COMMON PRAYER. See
  CHURCH OF ENGLAND. BOOK OF COMMON
    PRAYER.
  PROTESTANT EPISCOPAL CHURCH IN THE
    U.S.A. BOOK OF COMMON PRAYER.

BOOK OF LIFE.
  x Life, Book of.
  xx Heaven.
     Predestination.

BOOK OF MORMON.
  References and subdivisions as
    in LC.

BOOKS, CONDEMNED. See
  CONDEMNED BOOKS.

BOOKS, EXPURGATED. See
  EXPURGATED BOOKS.

BOOKS, FORBIDDEN. See
  PROHIBITED BOOKS.

BOOKS, LITURGICAL. See
  LITURGICAL BOOKS.

BOOKS, PROHIBITED. See
  PROHIBITED BOOKS.

BOOKS, SACRED. See SACRED BOOKS.

BOOKS AND READING - MORAL ASPECTS.
      BQT 1866   (24x1.61)
  sa Prohibited books.
  xx Literature and morals.

BOOKS OF HOURS. See DIURNALE.

BOOKS OF PRAYER. See PRAYER-BOOKS.

BOTANY OF THE BIBLE. See
  BIBLE - NATURAL HISTORY.

BOWING OF THE HEAD (POSTURE IN
  WORSHIP). See POSTURE IN WORSHIP.

BOXING - MORAL ASPECTS.
      BQT 1907   (175.6)

BOY SCOUTS - PRAYER-BOOKS.
      BQT 2648

BOY SCOUTS - RELIGIOUS LIFE.

BOY SCOUTS, CATHOLIC.
      BQT 3590
  x Catholic Boy Scouts.

BOYS - MEDITATIONS.
      BQT 2566

BOYS - PRAYER-BOOKS.
      BQT 2648

BOYS - RELIGIOUS LIFE.
      BQT 2283   (24x1.8)
  sa Retreats for young men.
  xx Youth - Religious life.

BOYS - RETREATS. See
  RETREATS FOR CHILDREN.
  RETREATS FOR YOUNG MEN.

BOYS - SERMONS.
    BQT 3015
  xx Children's sermons.

BOYS IN THE BIBLE. See
  CHILDREN IN THE BIBLE.

BRAHMANISM.
    BL 1100-1245   (294)
  References as in LC.

BRAZEN SERPENT.
  x Serpent, Brazen.
  xx Jews - Antiquities.
    Serpent-worship.

BRAZIL - CHURCH HISTORY.
    BQX 4771-4818

BREADS, ALTAR. See ALTAR BREADS.

BRETHREN AND SISTERS OF THE FREE SPIRIT.
    BQT 89
  xx Mysticism - History - Middle Ages.

BRETHREN OF JESUS. See
  JESUS CHRIST - BRETHREN.

BREVES, PAPAL. See BRIEFS, PAPAL.

BREVIARIUM.
    BQT 4259; BQT 4371-4427
      (26x5.3)
  A liturgical book which contains all
    the prayers and readings to be re-
    cited daily by clerics in major
    orders and by certain religious,
    who thereby fulfill their obliga-
    tion of saying the Divine Office.
  sa Commune sanctorum.
    Completorium.
    Diurnale.
    Divine Office.
    Matutinale.
    Octavarium romanum.
    Officia propria.
    Officium pro defunctis.
    Psalterium.
    Vesperale.

BREVIARIUM -- Continued.
  x Breviary.
  xx Divine Office.
    Prayer-books.

BREVIARIUM - ART.
    ND 3365

BREVIARIUM - COMMENTARIES.

BREVIARIUM - HISTORY.
    BQT 4171-4172

BREVIARIUM - INSTRUCTION AND STUDY.
    BQT 4174

BREVIARIUM - MANUSCRIPTS.
    Z 113Z

BREVIARIUM - MANUSCRIPTS - FACSIMILES.

BREVIARIUM - MEDITATIONS.

BREVIARIUM - RUBRICS. See
  DIVINE OFFICE - RITES AND CEREMONIES.

BREVIARIUM. BENEDICTINE, [CARMELITE,
  CISTERCIAN, ETC.]

BREVIARIUM ROMANUM.
  x Roman Breviary.

BREVIARIUM ROMANUM. ENGLISH, [FRENCH,
  GERMNA, ETC.]

BREVIARIUM ROMANUM - BIBLIOGRAPHY.

BREVIARIUM ROMANUM - COMMENTARIES.
  [BQT 4377.5]

BREVIARIUM ROMANUM - HISTORY.
    BQT 4172-4174

BREVIARY. See BREVIARIUM.

BRIEFS, PAPAL.
    BQV 2-8   (26x3)
  "A compendious papal letter lacking
    some of the solemnity and formal-
    ity of a papal bull." NC
  x Breves, Papal.
    Papal briefs.
    Popes - Briefs.

BRIEFS, PAPAL -- Continued.
  xx Canons, decretals, etc. (Eccles-
      iastical)
    Documents, Papal.
    Letters, Papal.
    Rescripts, Papal.

BRITISH MISSIONS. See
  MISSIONS, BRITISH.

BROTHERHOODS, RELIGIOUS. See
  BROTHERS.
  LAY BROTHERS.

BROTHERS.   (geog. subdiv.)
      BQX 6838; BQX 6901-7774
      (271.x1)
  Here are entered works on members
    of religious communities who are
    engaged in teaching or in hospital
    or some other charitable work but
    do not receive holy orders, e.g.,
    Brothers of the Christian Schools,
    Alexian Brothers, Brothers of
    Charity. They constitute a com-
    plete community by themselves,
    differing thereby from Lay Brothers
    who are a part of a community.
    See note under Lay Brothers.
  sa Lay Brothers.
  x Brotherhoods, Religious.
  xx Lay Brothers.
    Religious orders.

BROTHERS - BIOGRAPHY.

BROTHERS - MEDITATIONS.

BROTHERS - PRAYER-BOOKS.

BROTHERS - SPIRITUAL LIFE.

BROTHERS - VOCATION.
      BQT 2309; [BQT 2346]
  xx Vocation, Ecclesiastical.

BROTHERS (CANON LAW)

BROTHERS, CONVERSE. See
  LAY BROTHERS.

BROTHERS, LAY. See LAY BROTHERS.

BROTHERS OF JESUS. See
  JESUS CHRIST - BRETHREN.

BROTHERS OF THE CHRISTIAN SCHOOLS.
      BQX 7123-7130
  x Christian Brothers.
    De La Salle Brothers.
    Freres des Ecoles Chretiennes.
    Institutum Fratrum Scholarum
      Christianarum.

BROWN SCAPULAR. See
  SCAPULAR OF MOUNT CARMEL.

BROWNISTS.
  sa Pilgrim Fathers.
  xx Congregationalism.

BUDDHA AND BUDDHISM.
      BL 1400-1480   (294.3)
  References and subdivisions as
  in LC.

BUDDHISM AND SCIENCE.
      BL 1435.S35
  x Science and Buddhism.
  xx Religion and science.

BUDDHISM AND SOCIAL PROBLEMS.
  x Religion and social problems.
    Social problems and Buddhism.
  xx Religion and sociology.

BUDDHIST COUNCILS AND SYNODS.
      BL 1422.A1
  x Councils and synods, Buddhist.
    Synods, Buddhist.

BUDDHIST MISSIONS. See
  MISSIONS - BUDDHISTS.

BUDDHIST MONASTERIES. See
  MONASTERIES, BUDDHIST.

BUDDHIST MONASTICISM. See
  MONASTICISM,.BUDDHIST.

BUDDHIST PARABLES. See
  PARABLES, BUDDHIST.

BUDDHIST PRIESTS. See
  PRIESTS, BUDDHIST.

BUDDHIST SECTS.
 BL 1480   (294.3)
 References as in LC.

BUDDHIST SERMONS.
 x Sermons, Buddhist.

BUDDHIST SHRINES.   (Geog. subdiv., Direct)
 x Shrines, Buddhist.

BUILDINGS - REPAIR AND RECONSTRUCTION.
 xx Church maintenance and repair.

BULGARIA - CHURCH HISTORY.
 BQX 1602-1619; BQX 6225-6238
  (274.97)

BULGARIA - CHURCH HISTORY - EARLY
 PERIOD TO 1453.

BULGARIA - CHURCH HISTORY - 1453-

BULGARIAN CATHOLIC RITE. See
 BYZANTINE RITE, BULGARIAN.

BULGARIAN CHURCH SLAVIC LANGUAGE. See
 CHURCH SLAVIC LANGUAGE.

BULGARIAN ORTHODOX CHURCH. See
 ORTHODOX EASTERN CHURCH, BULGARIAN.

BULLA CRUCIATA. See CRUSADE BULLS.

BULLS, BYZANTINE.
 x Byzantine Bulls.

BULLS, CRUSADE. See CRUSADE BULLS.

BULLS, IN COENA DOMINI. See
 IN COENA DOMINI BULLS.

BULLS, PAPAL.
 BQV 2-8   (26x3)
 "The most solemn and weighty form
  of papal letter." AT
 sa Crusade bulls.
  In coena Domini bulls.
 x Papal bulls.
  Popes - Bulls.
 xx Canons, decretals, etc. (Ecclesi-
  astical)
  Documents, Papal.
  Letters, Papal.
  Rescripts, Papal.

BURIAL.
 BQT 1998 (Moral theology)
 Other classifications and references
  as in LC.

BURIAL CUSTOMS. See
 FUNERAL RITES AND CEREMONIES.

BURIAL LAWS (CANON LAW)
 BQV230 1203-1242   (348.x414)
 sa Cemeteries (Canon law)

BURIAL SERVICE. See
 FUNERAL SERVICE.

BUSINESS ETHICS.
 BQT 1947 (Moral theology)
 sa Clergy and business.
 Other classifications and references
  as in LC.

BYZANTINE BULLS. See
 BULLS, BYZANTINE.

BYZANTINE CHANT. See
 CHURCH MUSIC - BYZANTINE RITE.

BYZANTINE CHURCH ARCHITECTURE. See
 CHURCH ARCHITECTURE, BYZANTINE.

BYZANTINE RITE.
 "The system and forms of worship
  and administration of the sacraments proper at first to the
  church of Constantinople, but
  now used by the whole of what is
  now the Orthodox Eastern Church
  and also by some Catholics. It
  includes the three eucharistic
  liturgies, that of St. John
  Chrysostom, of St. Basil and of
  the Presanctified." AT
 The term is here used to refer
  mainly to the Catholic part.
  For works dealing with the non-
  Catholics using the Byzantine
  ritual see Orthodox Eastern
  Church.
 sa Orthodox Eastern Church.
 x Greek Rite.
 xx Orthodox Eastern Church.

BYZANTINE RITE - BIBLIOGRAPHY.

BYZANTINE RITE - CANON LAW.
    BQV 1188-1240   (348.x7)

BYZANTINE RITE - CHURCH MUSIC. See
  CHURCH MUSIC - BYZANTINE RITE.

BYZANTINE RITE - HISTORY.
    BQX 5721-6405   (28x2.1)

BYZANTINE RITE - HYMNS.
    BQT 5258
  sa Kanones (Liturgy)
     Troparion.

BYZANTINE RITE. LITURGY AND RITUAL.
    BQT 5232-5397   (264.x76)
  sa Liturgy of St. Basil.
     Liturgy of St. James.
     Liturgy of St. John Chrysostom.
     Liturgy of the Presanctified.

BYZANTINE RITE. LITURGY AND RITUAL -
  DIVINE LITURGY.
    BQT 5243-5245
  x Divine liturgy.
    Eucharistic liturgy (Byzantine rite)

BYZANTINE RITE. LITURGY AND RITUAL -
  DIVINE OFFICE.
    BQT 5251-5255

BYZANTINE RITE, BULGARIAN.
  x Bulgarian Catholic Rite.

BYZANTINE RITE, BULGARIAN - CANON LAW.
    BQV 1201-1204   (348.x7)

BYZANTINE RITE, BULGARIAN - HISTORY.
    BQX 6225-6238   (28x2.1)

BYZANTINE RITE, BULGARIAN. LITURGY
  AND RITUAL.
    BQT 6365-6366   (264.x76)

BYZANTINE RITE, GEORGIAN.
  x Georgian Rite.

BYZANTINE RITE, GEORGIAN - HISTORY.
    BQX 6241-6248

BYZANTINE RITE, GEORGIAN. LITURGY
  AND RITUAL.

BYZANTINE RITE, GREEK.
  x Greek Catholic Rite.

BYZANTINE RITE, GREEK - CANON LAW.
    BQV 1206-1209   (348.x7)

BYZANTINE RITE, GREEK - HISTORY.
    BQX 6251-6258   (28x2.1)

BYZANTINE RITE, GREEK. LITURGY AND
  RITUAL.
    BQT 5369-5370   (264.x76)

BYZANTINE RITE, ITALO-ALBANIAN.
  x Byzantine Rite, Italo-Greek.
    Italo-Albanian Rite.
    Italo-Greek Rite.

BYZANTINE RITE, ITALO-ALBANIAN -
  CANON LAW.
    BQV 1217-1219   (348.x7)

BYZANTINE RITE, ITALO-ALBANIAN -
  HISTORY.
    BQX 6271-6298   (28x2.14)

BYZANTINE RITE, ITALO-ALBANIAN.
  LITURGY AND RITUAL.
    BQT 5377-5378   (264.x76)

BYZANTINE RITE, ITALO-GREEK. See
  BYZANTINE RITE, ITALO-ALBANIAN.

BYZANTINE RITE, MELKITE.
  x Melkite Rite.

BYZANTINE RITE, MELKITE - CANON LAW.
    BQV 1226-1230   (348.7)

BYZANTINE RITE, MELKITE - HISTORY.
    BQX 6311-6344   (28x4.11)

BYZANTINE RITE, MELKITE. LITURGY
  AND RITUAL.
    BQT 5385-5386   (264.x76)

BYZANTINE RITE, RUMANIAN.
  x Rumanian Catholic Rite.

BYZANTINE RITE, RUMANIAN - CANON LAW.
    BQV 1233-1235   (348.x7)

BYZANTINE RITE, RUMANIAN - HISTORY.
    BQX 6351-6475   (28x2.13)

BYZANTINE RITE, RUMANIAN - PRAYER-BOOKS.

BYZANTINE RITE, RUMANIAN. LITURGY
  AND RITUAL.
      BQT 5389-5390   (264.x76)

BYZANTINE RITE, RUSSIAN.
  x Russian Catholic Rite.

BYZANTINE RITE, RUSSIAN. LITURGY
  AND RITUAL.
      BQT 5395

BYZANTINE RITE, RUTHENIAN.
  x Ruthenian Catholic Rite.
    Ukrainian Catholic Rite.

BYZANTINE RITE, RUTHENIAN - CANON LAW.
      BQV 1237-1240   (348.x7)

BYZANTINE RITE, RUTHENIAN - HISTORY.
      BQX 6381-6405   (28x2.12)

BYZANTINE RITE, RUTHENIAN. LITURGY
  AND RITUAL.
      BQT 5393-5394   (264.x76)

CABALA.
      BM 525 (Jewish religion)
      BF 1585-1623 (Occult sciences)
    References as in LC.

CABIRI.
      BL 313

CAEREMONIALE.
  x Ceremonial (Book)
  xx Rites and ceremonies (Catholic)

CAEREMONIALE. BENEDICTINE, [FRAN-
CISCAN, ETC.]

CAEREMONIALE EPISCOPORUM.
      BQT 4433   (26x5.8)
  A liturgical book containing: 1.
  General detailed directions for
  pontifical functions and for
  everything connected with the
  Mass; 2. Ritual directions for
  the singing of the Mass and Divine
  Office in cathedral and collegiate
  churches; 3. Directions for various
  extra-liturgical functions.

CAEREMONIALE EPISCOPORUM -- Continued.
  x Bishops, Ceremonial of.
    Ceremonial of Bishops.
  xx Pontifical service.

CAEREMONIALE EPISCOPORUM. ENGLISH,
  [FRENCH, GERMAN, ETC.]

CAEREMONIALE ROMANUM.
      BQT 4437   (26x5.9)
  A book containing directions for
  the ceremonies of the election
  and coronation of the pope, the
  canonization of saints, the
  creation of cardinals, and other
  papal functions and services.
  Also called Caeremoniale papale.
  x Papal Ceremonial.
    Roman Ceremonial.
  xx Popes - Rites and ceremonies.

CAESAROPAPISM.
      BQX 5419
  Here are entered works on the
  relationship between Church and
  state, wherein the Church is
  dominated by the state. The
  situation obtained originally
  and primarily in the Byzantine
  Empire.
  xx Church and state.

CALENDAR, ECCLESIASTICAL. See
CHURCH CALENDAR.

CALENDAR REFORM.
      CE 73
      [BQT 4194.5]

CALENDARS, DEVOTIONAL. See
DEVOTIONAL LITERATURE (DAILY
READINGS)

CALIFORNIA - CHURCH HISTORY.
      BQX 4423

CALLING. See VOCATION.

CALVINISM.   (Geog. subdiv.)
      BX 9401-9595   (284.2)
    sa Antionomianism.
      Arminianism.
      Congregationalism.

CALVINISM -- Continued.
  sa Neonominism.
    New England theology.
    Predestination.
    Presbyterianism.
    Puritans.
    Zwinglianism.
  xx Arminianism.
    Congregationalism.
    Puritans.
    Reformation.
    Reformed Church.

CALVINISTS.

CAMALDOLESE.
    BQX 7098-7100   (271.x1)
  x Benedictines, Camaldolese.
  xx Benedictines.

CAMERA APOSTOLICA.
    BQV230 262   (348.x34)
    BQV 89-90 (Documents)
      (348.x16)
  The office which is entrusted with
    the administration of the temporal
    goods of the Catholic Church.

CAMPBELLITES. See
  DISCIPLES OF CHRIST.

CAMPS (CHURCH). See CHURCH CAMPS.

CANA, MARRIAGE IN. See
  MARRIAGE IN CANA (MIRACLE)

CANA CONFERENCE MOVEMENT.
    BQT 3536
  xx Family, Christian.

CANADA - CHURCH HISTORY.
    BQX 4061-4165   (277.1)

CANADA - CHURCH HISTORY - EARLY
  PERIOD TO 1763.

CANADA - CHURCH HISTORY - 1763-1867.

CANADA - CHURCH HISTORY - 1867-

CANADA - CHURCH HISTORY - 20th CENTURY.

CANCELLARIA APOSTOLICA.
    BQV230 260   (348.x34)
    BQV 85-86 (Documents)
      (348.x16)
  x Apostolic Chancery.
    Chancery, Apostolic.

CANDLEHOLDERS. See CANDLESTICKS.

CANDLEMAS.
    BQT 4230   (264.x5)
  sa Candles and lights.
    Missa in Purificatione Beatae
      Mariae Virginis.
  x Feast of the Presentation of
    Jesus Christ.
    Presentation of Jesus Christ,
    Feast of the.
  xx Jesus Christ - Presentation.

CANDLES, LITURGICAL. See
CANDLES AND LIGHTS.

CANDLES AND LIGHTS.
    BQT 4362; BQT 4522   (264.x4)
  "Here are entered works on the use
    of candles and lights in religious
    worship." LC
  sa Hanukkah lamp.
    Paschal candle.
  x Candles, Liturgical.
    Lights, Litrugical.
    Lights and candles.
    Liturgical cnadles.
    Liturgical lights.
  xx Church furniture.
    Fire (in religion, folklore, etc.)

CANDLESTICKS.
  x Candleholders.

CANON LAW.   (Geog. subdiv)
    BQV   (348)
  Here are entered works dealing with
    the statutes and regulations of
    the highest authorities in the
    Catholic Church for the govern-
    ment of ecclesiastical affairs.
  Works dealing with church laws in
    general are entered under Ecclesi-
    astical law.

CANON LAW -- Continued.
  sa Canons, decretals, etc. (Ecclesias-
      tical)
    Censures, Ecclesiastical.
    Codex juris canonici.
    Councils and synods.
    Ecclesiastical law.
    Letters, Papal.
    Moral theology.
    Pastoral theology.
    Penalties, Ecclesiastical.
    Persons (Canon law)
    Religious orders (Canon law)
    Sacraments (Canon law)
    Sacred places (Canon law)
    Things (Canon law)
    Trials. Ecclesiastical.

    x Catholic Church - Discipline.
      Catholic Church - Law.
      Church law.
      Law, Church.
      Public law (Canon law)

    xx Catholic Church - Government.
      Church discipline.
      Church orders, Ancient.
      Ecclesiastical law.
      Moral theology.
      Sacred sciences.
      Theology.

CANON LAW - ABBREVIATIONS.

CANON LAW - ADDRESSES, ESSAYS,
  LECTURES.
      BQV 219

CANON LAW - BIBLIOGRAPHY.
      BQV 1o1; Z 7776   (o16.348)

CANON LAW - BIOGRAPHY.
      BQV 130-132

CANON LAW - CASES.
      BQV 194; BQV 221
   x Canon law - Decisions.

CANON LAW - CATECHISMS, QUESTION-BOOKS.

CANON LAW - CODIFICATION.
      BQV 127

CANON LAW - COLLECTED WORKS.
      BQV 192-193   (348.x08)

CANON LAW - COLLECTED WORKS - MIDDLE
  AGES.

CANON LAW - COLLECTED WORKS - 16th
  CENTURY.

CANON LAW - COLLECTED WORKS - 17th
  CENTURY.

CANON LAW - COLLECTED WORKS - 18th
  CENTURY.

CANON LAW - COLLECTED WORKS - 19th
  CENTURY.

CANON LAW - COLLECTED WORKS - 20th
  CENTURY.

CANON LAW - COLLECTIONS.
      BQV 2-99; BQV 104; BQV 191
        (348.x14)

CANON LAW - COMPENDS.

CANON LAW - CONCORDANCES.

CANON LAW - CONFLICT OF LAWS. See
  CONFLICT OF LAWS (CANON LAW)

CANON LAW - CONGRESSES.
    [BQV 103]

CANON LAW - DECISIONS. See
  CANON LAW - CASES.

CANON LAW - DICTIONARIES.
      BQV 105   (348.x03)

CANON LAW - DIGESTS.
      BQV 218   (348.x02)

CANON LAW - EARLY CHURCH.
  xx Church history - Primitive and
    early church.

CANON LAW - HANDBOOKS, MANUALS, ETC.
      BQV 218

CANON LAW - HISTORY.
      BQV 116-132   (348.x09)
   sa Glossators.

CANON LAW - HISTORY - EARLY CHURCH.

CANON LAW - HISTORY - MIDDLE AGES.

CANON LAW - HISTORY - 1140-1234.

CANON LAW - HISTORY - 1234-1582.

CANON LAW - HISTORY - 1582-1917.

CANON LAW - HISTORY - 1917-

CANON LAW - INTERPRETATION AND
   CONSTRUCTION.
      BQV230 8-24
   sa Epikaia.
      Legislation (Canon law)

CANON LAW - INTRODUCTIONS.
   x Canon law - Propaedeutics.

CANON LAW - MANUSCRIPTS.

CANON LAW - METHODOLOGY.
      BQV 107

CANON LAW - PERIODICALS.
      BQV 102   (348.x05)

CANON LAW - PHILOSOPHY.
      BQV 107

CANON LAW - PROPAEDEUTICS. See
   CANON LAW - INTRODUCTIONS.

CANON LAW - SOCIETIES.
      [BQV 102.5]

CANON LAW - SOURCES.
      BQV 135-136   (348.x1)

CANON LAW - STUDY AND TEACHING.
      BQV 138-139

CANON LAW - TEXTBOOKS.
      BQV 198   (348.x02)
      BQV 214 (New Code)

CANON LAW - TEXTBOOKS - 16th CENTURY.

CANON LAW - TEXTBOOKS - 17th CENTURY.

CANON LAW - TEXTBOOKS - 18th CENTURY.

CANON LAW - TEXTBOOKS - 1800-1870.

CANON LAW - TEXTBOOKS - 1871-1917.

CANON LAW - TEXTBOOKS - 1918-

################

CANON LAW - AUGUSTINIANS, [BENEDIC-
   TINES, FRANCISCANS, ETC.]. See
   AUGUSTINIANS, [BENEDICTINES, FRAN-
   CISCANS, ETC.]. - CANON LAW.

CANON LAW - EASTERN CHURCHES. See
   EASTERN CHURCHES - CANON LAW.

################

CANON LAW, ANGLICAN. See
   CHURCH OF ENGLAND - LAW.

CANON LAW, CODE OF. See
   CODEX JURIS CANONICI.

CANON LAW, ORIENTAL. See
   CODEX JURIS CANONICI ORIENTALIS.
   EASTERN CHURCHES - CANON LAW.

CANON LAW AND CIVIL LAW.
      BQV 110
   x Civil law and canon law.

CANON LAW AND MEDICINE.
      BQV 115
   x Medicine and canon law.

CANON LAW AND MORAL THEOLOGY.
      BQV 113
   x Moral theology and canon law.

CANON LAW AND NATURAL LAW.
      BQV 109
   x Natural law and canon law.

CANON LAW AND ROMAN LAW.
   x Roman law and canon law.

CANON LAW AND THEOLOGY.
    BQT 25
    x Theology and canon law.

CANON MISSAE.
    BQT 4296
    Here are entered texts for the
      Canon of the Mass, as used by
      bishops during pontifical mass.
    For works on the function of this
      part of the Mass see Canon of
      the Mass.
    xx Canon of the Mass.
      Orinarium Missae.

CANON OF THE HOLY SCRIPTURES. See
    BIBLE - CANON.

CANON OF THE MASS.
    BQT 4166.5; BQT 4296
        (264.x61; 23x7.31)
    See note under Canon Missae.
    sa Canon Missae.
      Consecration at mass.
    x Mass - Canon.
    xx Mass of the faithful.

CANONESSES.
    BQX 6842   (271.2)
    xx Religious orders of women.

CANONESSES REGULAR OF ST. AUGUSTINE.
    See AUGUSTINIAN CANONESSES.

CANONICAL FACULTIES. See
    FACULTIES (CANON LAW)

CANONICAL HOURS. See DIVINE OFFICE.

CANONICAL PRECEPT. See
    PRECEPTS (CANON LAW)

CANONICAL TRIALS. See
    TRIALS, ECCLESIASTICAL.

CANONIZATION.
    BQT 1579; BQT 4437   (23x5.3)
    BQV230 1999-2141   (348.x57)
    "A public and official declaration
      of the heroic virtue of a person
      and the inclusion of his or her
      name in the canon (roll or regis-
      ter) of the saints." AT

CANONIZATION -- Continued.
    sa Beatification.
    x Saints - Canonization.
    xx Beatification.
      Rites and ceremonies (Catholic)

CANONIZATION SERMONS.
    x Sermons, Canonization.

CANONS, MINOR. See
    MINOR CANONS, CATHEDRAL, COLLEGIATE,
    ETC.

CANONS, DECRETALS, ETC. (ECCLESIASTICAL)
    BQV 2-99; BQV 142-189
        (348.x14)
    Here are entered general collections
      of legislative enactments of the
      Church, as by popes, congregations,
      councils, etc. They are found in
      papal constitutions, apostolic
      letters, decrees, etc. The name
      "decrees" is often applied to any
      or all of them.
    sa Briefs, Papal.
      Bulls, Papal.
    x Catholic Church - Canons, de-
      cretals, etc.
      Decrees, Ecclesiastical.
      Decretals, Ecclesiastical.
    xx Canon law.

CANONS, DECRETALS, ETC. (ECCLESIASTICAL) -
    BIBLIOGRAPHY.

CANONS, DECRETALS, ETC. (ECCLESIASTICAL) -
    DICTIONARIES.
    BQV 13

CANONS, DECRETALS, ETC. (ECCLESIASTICAL) -
    HISTORY.

CANONS, DECRETALS, ETC. (ECCLESIASTICAL) -
    INDEXES.

CANONS, DECRETALS, ETC. (ECCLESIASTICAL) -
    1918-
    BQV 212

CANONS REGULAR.   (Geog. subdiv.,
    Indirect)
    BQX 6838   (271.x1)
    By this term are understood priests
      bound by the vows of religion and

CANONS REGULAR -- Continued.
    living in community under a rule.
    They differ from monks in that
    they are at all times prepared to
    undertake the works of the active
    apostolate.
  sa names of Canons regular, e.g.,
    Augustinian Canons, Premon-
    stratensians, etc.
  xx Religious orders.

CANONS REGULAR - HISTORY.

CANONS REGULAR OF ST. AUGUSTINE. See
  AUGUSTINIAN CANONS.

CANONS SECULAR.
  By this term are understood the
    members of cathedral and collegiate
    chapters.
  x Secular canons.
  xx Chapters, Cathedral, collegiate,
    etc.

CANOPIES.
    BQT 4361; BQT 5946
  xx Church furniture.

CANTATAS, SACRED.
    M 2020-2030
  sa Christmas cantatas.
    Easter cantatas.
  x Sacred cantatas.
  Other references and subdivisions
    as in LC.

CANTATE DOMINO CANTICUM NOVUM, CANTATE
  DOMINO (MUSIC). See
  PSALMS (MUSIC) - 95th PSALM.

CANTICLE OF CANTICLES. See
  BIBLE. O.T. CANTICLE OF CANTICLES.

CANTICLE OF OUR LADY. See MAGNIFICAT.

CANTICLE OF SIMEON. See NUNC DIMITTIS.

CANTICLES.
    (223.x6)
  "Sacred songs whose words are taken
   from the Bible." AT
  sa Hymns.
  xx Hymns.

CANTORS, JEWISH.
    BM 652
  References as in LC.

CANTUS PASSIONIS DOMINI NOSTRI JESU
  CHRISTI.
    BQT 4326
  xx Jesus Christ - Passion.

CANVASSING (CHURCH WORK)
  sa Visitations (Church work)
    Visitations (Religious education)
  xx Social surveys.
    Visitations (Church work)

CAODISM.
  References as in LC.

CAPITAL SINS.
    BQT 1813   (24x1.44)
  sa Anger.
    Avarice.
    Envy.
    Gluttony.
    Lust.
    Pride and vanity.
    Sloth.
  x Deadly sins.
    Sins, Capital.
    Sins, Deadly.

CAPITAL SINS - SERMONS.

CAPITULAR VICARS. See
  VICARS, CAPITULAR.

CAPITULARE EVANGELIORUM. See COMES.

CAPITULARIES.
    BQV 151
  xx Ecclesiastical law.

CAPTIVES, RANSOM OF. See
  RANSOM OF CAPTIVES.

CAPTIVITY, EPISTLES OF THE. See
  BIBLE. N.T. CAPTIVITY EPISTLES.

CAPUCHINS.   (Geog. subdiv., Direct)
    BQX 7406   (271.x1)
  x Friars Minor Capuchin.
    Order of Friars Minor Capuchin.
    Ordo Fratrum Minorum Capuccinorum.

CAPUCHINS - BIBLIOGRAPHY.
    BQX 7406

CAPUCHINS - BIOGRAPHY.
    BQX 7406.8

CAPUCHINS - CANON LAW.
    [BQX 7406.57]

CAPUCHINS - DICTIONARIES.
    BQX 7406

CAPUCHINS - EDUCATION.
    [BQX 7406.55]

CAPUCHINS - HISTORY.
    BQX 7406.3

CAPUCHINS - MISSIONS.
    [BQX 7406.56]

CAPUCHINS - PERIODICALS.
    BQX 7406.1

CAPUCHINS - POPULAR DEVOTIONS.

CAPUCHINS - POPULAR DEVOTIONS -
    BLESSED VIRGIN MARY.

CAPUCHINS - POPULAR DEVOTIONS -
    THREE "HAIL MARYS". See
    THREE HAIL MARYS".

CAPUCHINS - RULES.
    BQX 7406.2

CAPUCHINS - SPIRITUAL LIFE.
    BQX 7406.4

################

CAPUCHINS - ENGLAND, [GERMANY,
    ITALY, ETC.]
    BQX 7406.5

################

CAPUCHINS. LAY BROTHERS.
    [BQX 7406.9]

CAPUCHINS. LITURGY AND RITUAL.
    BQT 4801-4809

CAPUCHINS. PROVINCES. BOLOGNA,
    [LYON, PARMA, ETC.]
    BQX 7406.6

################

CAPUCHINS AND PARISH MISSIONS.

CAPUCHINS AND PREACHING.

CARDINAL PROTECTORS.
    "A cardinal protector is a cardinal
    appointed to keep an eye on the
    interests of a particular religious
    order, congregation, church, nation,
    etc., but without any jurisdiction
    over them." AT
  xx Religious orders.

CARDINAL VIRTUES. See
    VIRTUES, MORAL.

CARDINALS.   (Geog. subdiv., Direct)
    BQX 157-159   (922.2)
  xx Catholic Church - Government.
    Christian biography.
    Prelates.

CARDINALS - BIO-BIBLIOGRAPHY.
    Z 7838

CARDINALS - BIOGRAPHY.
    BQT 159; BQX 8254
  xx Catholic Church - Biography.

CARDINALS - CORRESPONDENCE, REMINIS-
    CENCES, ETC.

CARDINALS - PORTRAITS.

CARDINALS (CANON LAW)
    BQV230 230-241   (348.x322)
  xx Persons (Canon law)

CARDINALS, BLACK. See
    BLACK CARDINALS.

CARDS - MORAL AND RELIGIOUS ASPECTS.

CARE OF SOULS. See
    PASTORAL COUNSELLING.
    PASTORAL THEOLOGY.

CARILLONS.   (Geog. subdiv., Direct)
  References as in LC.

CARMATHIANS. See KARMATHIANS.

CARMELITE SAINTS. See
  SAINTS, CARMELITE.

CARMELITES.   (Geog. subdiv., Direct)
      BQX 7211-7260   (271.x1)
    x Friars, White.
      Order of Our Lady of Mount Carmel.
      Ordo Fratrum Beatissimae Virginis
        Mariae de Monte Carmelo.
      Ordo Fratrum Carmelitarum.
      Our Lady of Mount Carmel, Order of.
      White Friars.
    xx Friars.

CARMELITES - BIBLIOGRAPHY.
      BQX 7211; Z 7840

CARMELITES - BIO-BIBLIOGRAPHY.

CARMELITES - BIOGRAPHY.
      BQX 7259-7260
    sa Saints, Carmelite.

CARMELITES - CANON LAW.
      [BQX 7224.7]

CARMELITES - COLLECTIONS.
      BQX 7213

CARMELITES - DRAMA.

CARMELITES - EDUCATION.
      [BQX 7224.5]

CARMELITES - FICTION.

CARMELITES - HISTORY.
      BQX 7221-7245

CARMELITES - MEDITATIONS.

CARMELITES - MISSIONS.   (Geog.
    subdiv.)
      [BQX 7224.6]

CARMELITES - PERIODICALS.
      BQX 7212

CARMELITES - PRAYER-BOOKS.

CARMELITES - RULES.
      BQX 7215-7218

CARMELITES - SPIRITUAL LIFE.
      BQX 7224

          ################

CARMELITES - ENGLAND, [FRANCE,
  GERMANY, ETC.]
      BQX 7228-7245

          ################

CARMELITES. LAY BROTHERS.

CARMELITES. LITURGY AND RITUAL.
      BQT 4751-4759

CARMELITES. PROVINCES.
      BQX 7246-7254

CARMELITES. THIRD ORDER.
      BQX 7256-7258

CARMELITES. THIRD ORDER - HANDBOOKS,
  MANUALS, ETC.

CARMELITES. THIRD ORDER - PRAYER-
  BOOKS.

CARMELITES, DISCALCED.
      BQX 7247
    x Discalced Carmelites.
      Ordo Fratrum Carmelitarum Dis-
        calceatorum.

CARMELITES AND MYSTICISM.

CARNIVAL.
    sa Shrovetide.
    Other references as in LC.

CAROLS.
      ML 2880; PR 1195

CARTHAGE, COUNCIL OF, 256.
      BQX 306   (270.1)

CARTHUSIANS.   (geog. subdiv., Direct)
    BQX 7262   (271.x1)
  x Chartreux.
    Ordo Cartusianorum.
    Ordre de Chartreux.

CARTHUSIANS.   LITURGY AND RITUAL.
    BQX 4701-4709

CASES, RESERVED. See RESERVED CASES.

CASES OF CONSCIENCE. See CASUISTRY.

CASUISTRY.
    BQT 1735-1736 (Moral theology)
      (24x1.x07)
    BJ 1440-1448 (Ethics)
  "The method followed by moral
   theologians of explaining moral
   principles through the presentation and solution of concrete
   cases." NC
  sa Conscience.
    Pastoral psychology.
    Probabilism.
  x Cases of conscience.
  xx Conscience.
    Moral theology.

CATACOMBS.
    BQX (General)
    BQ 631 (Inscriptions) (246.5)
    BQT 5682 (Art)
    BQT 5930 (Architecture)
  sa Christian art.
    Church history - Primitive and
     early church.
  xx Cemeteries.
    Christian antiquities.
    Christian art.
    Church history - Primitive and
     early church.
    Tombs.

CATACOMBS - DRAMA.

CATACOMBS - FICTION.

CATALOGING OF CATHOLIC LITERATURE.
    Z 695.1
  x Catholic literature - Cataloging.

CATALOGING OF SACRED BOOKS.
  sa Cataloging of the Bible.
  x Sacred books - Cataloging.

CATALOGING OF THE BIBLE.
    Z 695.1. T3
  x Bible - Cataloging.
  xx Cataloging of sacred books.

CATALOGING OF THEOLOGY.
  x Theology - Cataloging.

CATECHETICAL ILLUSTRATIONS.
    BQT 3193   (25x3)
  sa Catechism stories.
    Homiletical illustrations.
  x Catechisms - illustrations.
  xx Homiletical illustrations.

CATECHETICAL SERMONS.
    [BQT 3021]   (252.x6)
  x Catechisms - Sermons.
    Sermons, Catechetical.
  xx Dogmatic theology - Sermons.
    Religious education.

✔ CATECHETICS.
    BQT 3103-3197   (25x3)   268
  "Here are entered works dealing
   with the theory and method of
   catechising: a means of imparting
   knowledge of the fundamental
   teachings of Christianity in the
   form of question and answers." LC
  sa Catechisms.
    Questioning.
  x Christian doctrine.
    Instruction, Religious.
    Religious instruction.
  xx Church - Teaching office.
    Pastoral theology.
    Religion.
    Religious education - Teaching
     methods.
    Theology - Study and teaching.

CATECHETICS - BIBLIOGRAPHY.
    [BQT 3101]

CATECHETICS - EARLY CHURCH.

CATECHETICS - HISTORY.   (Geog. subdiv.)
    BQT 3106-3107   (25x3.09)

################

CATECHETICS - LUTHERAN CHURCH, [ETC.]

################

CATECHETICS (CANON LAW)
    BQV230 1328-1336   (348.x44)

CATECHETICS AND LITURGY. See
    LITURGY AND CATECHETICS.

CATECHISM, BALTIMORE. See
    BALTIMORE CATECHISM.

CATECHISM OF THE COUNCIL OF TRENT. See
    CATECHISMUS ROMANUS.

CATECHISM STORIES.
    BQT 3195
    sa Bible stories.
    x Religious education - Stories.
      Stories, Catechism.
    xx Catechetical illustrations.
      Story-telling - Religion.

CATECHISMS.
    BQT 3161-3197   (25x3.1)
    "A series of questions and answers
      summarizing Christian doctrine,
      formulated and published by
      authority." AT
    sa Bible - Catechisms, question-
        books.
      Creeds.
      Religious education - Textbooks.
      Also subdivision "Catechisms and
        creeds" under names of churches,
        e.g., Church of England - Cate-
        chisms and creeds; and subdivi-
        sion "Catechisms, question-books"
        under such headings as Canon
        law, Dogmatic theology, Liturgy,
        Moral theology, Religious orders.
    x Catholic Church - Catechisms and
        creeds.

CATECHISMS - HISTORY AND CRITICISM.

CATECHISMS - ILLUSTRATIONS. See
    CATECHETICAL ILLUSTRATIONS.
    CATECHISMS - PICTORIAL ILLUSTRATIONS.

CATECHISMS - MEDITATIONS.
    BQT 2579
    xx Dogmatic theology - Meditations.

CATECHISMS - PICTORIAL ILLUSTRATIONS.
    x Catechisms - Illustrations.

CATECHISMS - SERMONS. See
    CATECHETICAL SERMONS.

CATECHISMS, ENGLISH, [FRENCH,
    GERMAN, ETC.]

CATECHISMUS ROMANUS.
    BQT 154   (25x3.11)
    x Catechism of the Council of Trent.
      Roman Catechism.
      Trent, Council of. Catechism.

CATECHUMENS.

CATECHUMENS - EARLY CHURCH.

CATECHUMENS - MIDDLE AGES.

CATECHUMENS, MASS OF THE. See
    MASS OF THE CATECHUMENS.

CATENAE.
    BS 483-498 (Bible commentaries)
    BQT 304 (Patristics)
    Here are entered commentaries con-
      sisting of extracts from various
      authors. Biblical "Catenae" were
      especially popular among the Greeks.
    x Bible - Catenae.
    xx Bible - Commentaries.
      Fathers of the church.

CATHARI.
    BQT 89
    sa Albigenses.
      Arnoldists.
      Bogomiles.
    xx Asceticism - History - Middle
        Ages.
      Dualism (Theology)
      Sects, Medieval.

CATHEDRA. See CHAIRS (CATHEDRA)

CATHEDRA PETRI. See
ST. PETER'S CHAIR.

CATHEDRAL CHAPTERS. See
CHAPTERS, CATHEDRAL, COLLEGIATE,
ETC.

CATHEDRALS.   (Geog. subdiv.,
    Indirect)
        BQT 5923   (264.x3)
    sa Architecture, Gothic.
        Chairs (Cathedral)
        Chapters, Cathedral, collegiate,
          etc.
        Minor canons, Cathedral,
          collegiate, etc.
        also names of cathedrals, e.g.,
          New York (City). St. Patrick's
          Cathedral; Paris. Notre-Dame
          (Cathedral)
    x Religious art.
    xx Abbeys.
        Architecture.
        Architecture, Gothic.
        Architecture, Medieval.
        Christian art.
        Church architecture.
        Churches.

CATHEDRALS - ANNIVERSARY SERMONS. See
ANNIVERSARY SERMONS - CATHEDRALS.

CATHEDRALS (CANON LAW)
    xx Church architecture (Canon law)
        Churches (Canon law)
        Sacred places (Canon law)

CATHEDRATICUM.
        BQV230 1504   (348.x46)
    "An annual contribution to the sup-
    port of a diocesan bishop payable
    from all churches or benefices
    under his jurisdiction." AT
    xx Bishops.
        Catholic Church - Finance.
        Councils and synods, Diocesan.

CATHOLIC ACTION.   (Geog. subdiv.,
    Direct)
        BQT 3503-3653   (24x8.5)
    Here are entered works on the par-
    ticipation of the Catholic layman

CATHOLIC ACTION -- Continued.
    in the hierarchical apostolate of
    the Church.
    sa Catholic youth movement.
        Christian democracy.
        Christopher movement.
        Missionaries, Lay.
    x Action, Catholic.
        Apostolate, Lay.
        Lay apostolate.
    xx Apostolate.
        Catholic Church and social
          problems.
        Christian democracy.
        Laity.
        Pastoral theology.
        Sociology, Christian.

CATHOLIC ACTION - BIBLIOGRAPHY.

CATHOLIC ACTION - CONGRESSES.

CATHOLIC ACTION - PAPAL TEACHING.

CATHOLIC ACTION - PERIODICALS.

CATHOLIC ALMANACS. See
    ALMANACS, CATHOLIC.

CATHOLIC AUTHORS.
        BQ
        [PN 485]
        Z 7837
    sa Catholic poets.
        also subdivision "Catholic
          authors" under names of
          literature, e.g., American
          literature - Catholic authors.
    x Authors, Catholic.
    xx Authorship, Catholic.
        Catholic Church - Biography.
        Catholic literature.

CATHOLIC AUTHORS - PORTRAITS.

CATHOLIC AUTHORS - QUOTATIONS.

CATHOLIC AUTHORS, AMERICAN.
    [PS 152]

CATHOLIC AUTHORS, ENGLISH
    PR 120

CATHOLIC AUTHORS, FRENCH.
PQ 150

CATHOLIC AUTHORS, GERMAN.
PT 170

CATHOLIC AUTHORSHIP. See
AUTHORSHIP, CATHOLIC.

CATHOLIC BIBLES. See
BIBLE - VERSIONS, CATHOLIC.
See also note under that heading.

CATHOLIC BIOGRAPHY. See
CATHOLIC CHURCH - BIOGRAPHY.

CATHOLIC BOOK WEEK.
xx Catholic literature.

CATHOLIC BOY SCOUTS. See
BOY SCOUTS, CATHOLIC.

CATHOLIC CAMPAIGNERS FOR CHRIST.

CATHOLIC CHARITIES. See
CATHOLIC CHURCH - CHARITIES.

CATHOLIC CHURCH.   (Geog. subdiv.,
Direct)
sa Christianity.
   Church.
   Holy See.
   Non-Catholics.
 x Catholicism.   x Ecclesiology
   Roman Catholic Church.
xx Christianity.
   Church.

CATHOLIC CHURCH - ADDRESSES, ESSAYS,
LECTURES.
BQ 5271-5283

CATHOLIC CHURCH - ALMANACS. See
ALMANACS, CATHOLIC.

CATHOLIC CHURCH - ANTI-CATHOLIC
POLEMIC. See ANTI-CATHOLIC
POLEMIC.

CATHOLIC CHURCH - APOLOGETICS. See
APOLOGETICS.

CATHOLIC CHURCH - ART. See
CHRISTIAN ART.

CATHOLIC CHURCH - BIBLIOGRAPHY.
Z 7837-7840
sa Catholic literature.

CATHOLIC CHURCH - BIBLIOGRAPHY -
CATALOGS.

CATHOLIC CHURCH - BIO-BIBLIOGRAPHY.

CATHOLIC CHURCH - BIOGRAPHY.
BQX 8203-8279
sa Bishops - Biography.
   Cardinals - Biography.
   Catholic authors.
   Catholic historians.
   Christian biography.
   Converts.
   Priests - Biography.
   Religious orders - Biography.
 x Biography, Catholic.
   Catholic biography.
xx Christian biography.

CATHOLIC CHURCH - BIOGRAPHY -
BIBLIOGRAPHY.
Z 7837

CATHOLIC CHURCH - BIOGRAPHY -
DICTIONARIES.
BQX 8203

CATHOLIC CHURCH - CANONS, DECRETALS,
ETC. See CANONS, DECRETALS, ETC.
(ECCLESIASTICAL)

CATHOLIC CHURCH - CARTOONS, SATIRE, ETC.

CATHOLIC CHURCH - CATECHISMS AND CREEDS.
See CATECHISMS; CREEDS.

CATHOLIC CHURCH - CEREMONIES AND
PRACTICES. See
CHURCH ETIQUETTE.
RITES AND CEREMONIES (CATHOLIC)

CATHOLIC CHURCH - CHARITIES.
BQT 3658-3699
sa Social service, Catholic.
 x Catholic charities.
   Charities, Catholic.

CATHOLIC CHURCH - CHARITIES - Continued.
  xx Catholic Church - Government.
    Charities.
    Church charities.
    Social service, Catholic.

CATHOLIC CHURCH - CHARITIES -
  CONGRESSES.
    [BQT 3404]

CATHOLIC CHURCH - CHARITIES -
  SOCIETIES.
    BQT 3663; [BQT 3404]

CATHOLIC CHURCH - CLERGY. See
  CLERGY.

CATHOLIC CHURCH - COLLECTED WORKS.
  Here are entered the collected
    works of individual Catholic
    authors writing on various sub-
    jects, e.g., the collected works
    of Cardinal Newman.
  The collected works of individual
    theological writers are entered
    under Theology - Collected works,
    and of writers in a more specific
    branch of theology under the name
    of the subject, e.g., Asceticism -
    Collected works.

CATHOLIC CHURCH - COLLECTIONS.
  Here are entered general collections
    from various Catholic authors.

CATHOLIC CHURCH - CONCORDATS. See
  CONCORDATS.

CATHOLIC CHURCH - CONGREGATIONS, ROMAN.
  See CONGREGATIONS, ROMAN.

CATHOLIC CHURCH - CONGRESSES.
    BQT 2824

CATHOLIC CHURCH - CONTROVERSIAL
  LITERATURE.
    BQT 219; BQT 230; BQT 425-445
    BX 1760-1780
  sa Apologetics - Debates.
    also the subdivision "Controver-
     sial literature" under specific
    topics, e.g., Mary, Blessed
    Virgin - Controversial litera-
    ture; Popes - Infallibility -
    Controversial literature.

CATHOLIC CHURCH - CONVERTS. See
  CONVERTS.

CATHOLIC CHURCH - COUNCILS. See
  COUNCILS AND SYNODS.

CATHOLIC CHURCH - DICTIONARIES.
    BQT 6-7
  x Catholic Church - Encyclopedias.
    Catholic dictionaries.
    Dictionaries, Catholic.

CATHOLIC CHURCH - DICTIONARIES -
  DUTCH, [FRENCH, ITALIAN, ETC.]

CATHOLIC CHURCH - DICTIONARIES,
  JUVENILE.

CATHOLIC CHURCH - DIPLOMATIC SERVICE.
  See HOLY SEE - DIPLOMATIC SERVICE.

CATHOLIC CHURCH - DIRECTORIES.
    BQX 21   (209)
  x Catholic directories.
    Directories, Catholic.

CATHOLIC CHURCH - DISCIPLINE. See
  ASCETICISM.
  CANON LAW.
  MORAL THEOLOGY.

[CATHOLIC CHURCH - DOCTRINAL AND
  CONTROVERSIAL WORKS]
  This heading is used as a catchall
    by the Library of Congress. The
    subdivision "Doctrinal and con-
    troversial works" is in itself
    already an unfortunate combina-
    tion of ideas, as if all doctrinal
    works in theology were controver-
    sial. Nor does the cumbersome
    subheading lend itself to proper
    subdividing in a field where the
    literature is extensive.
  In this list the subdivision "Doc-
    trinal and controversial works" is
    never used, but is broken down in-
    to two subheadings, namely, "Doc-
    trine" and "Controversial litera-
    ture," e.g., Lutheran Church -
    Doctrine; Lutheran Church - Con-
    troversial literature, not, however,
    for the same book.
  When the heading "Catholic Church -
    Doctrinal and controversial works"

CATHOLIC CHURCH - DOCTRINAL AND
CONTROVERSIAL WORKS -- Continued.
appears in the tracing on LC
printed cards, it will be necessary for the cataloger to examine
the book in order to determine the
correct heading for the subject
matter of the book. In some instances the headings "Dogmatic
theology" or "Apologetics" can be
substituted, with or without a
more detailed subdivision, but a
dozen and more other specific
headings are also applicable,
since the Library of Congress gives
this subheading a wide range of
meaning.

CATHOLIC CHURCH - DOCTRINE. See
DOGMATIC THEOLOGY.

CATHOLIC CHURCH - EASTERN RITES. See
EASTERN CHURCHES.

CATHOLIC CHURCH - EDUCATION. See
CATHOLIC EDUCATION.

CATHOLIC CHURCH - ENCYCLOPEDIAS. See
CATHOLIC CHURCH - DICTIONARIES.

CATHOLIC CHURCH - EXHIBITIONS AND
MUSEUMS.
BQX 61   (270.x074)
x Catholic Church - Museums.

CATHOLIC CHURCH - FINANCE.
sa Cathedraticum.
Investments (Canon law)
Peter's pence.
Taxation, Papal.
xx Church finance.

CATHOLIC CHURCH - FOREIGN RELATIONS.
See HOLY SEE - RELATIONS (DIPLOMATIC)
Cf. note under Holy See.

CATHOLIC CHURCH - GOVERNMENT.
BQX 153-191   (23x9.4)
sa Bishops.
Canon law.
Cardinals.
Catholic Church - Charities.

CATHOLIC CHURCH - FINANCE -- Continued.
sa Church and state.
Church finance.
Church property.
Clergy.
Curia Romana.
Legislative bodies (Canon law)
Popes.
Religious orders.
xx Church polity.
Public law (Canon law)

CATHOLIC CHURCH - HANDBOOKS,
MANUALS, ETC.
BQT 186

CATHOLIC CHURCH - HISTORY.
BQX   (270-279)
Individual libraries must determine according to the size
and nature of their book collection whether the entry "Church
history" suffices for their
needs or whether in addition the
entry "Catholic Church - History"
is also required. Libraries with
large collections will need both
entries, since the two terms are
not synonymous for the period
after the Protestant Reformation.
sa Church history.
Councils and synods.
Counter-Reformation.
Heresies and heretics.
Missions.
Popes.
Reformation.
Religious orders.
Schism, Eastern and Western
Church.
Schism, The great western, 1378-
1417.
Most of the see also references
under Church History also
apply here.
x Christianity - History.
xx Church history.

CATHOLIC CHURCH - HISTORY - ADDRESSES,
ESSAYS, LECTURES.

CATHOLIC CHURCH - HISTORY - BIBLIO-
GRAPHY.
BQX 1; Z 7777-7779   (016.27)

CATHOLIC CHURCH - HISTORY - ERRORS,
INVENTIONS, ETC.

CATHOLIC CHURCH - HISTORY - HISTORIO-
GRAPHY.

CATHOLIC CHURCH - HISTORY - JUVENILE
LITERATURE.
BQX 83

CATHOLIC CHURCH - HISTORY - MAPS.
BQX 34
sa Ecclesiastical geography - Maps.

CATHOLIC CHURCH - HISTORY - POPULAR
WORKS.
BQX 83

CATHOLIC CHURCH - HISTORY - SOCIETIES.

CATHOLIC CHURCH - HISTORY - SOURCES.

CATHOLIC CHURCH - HISTORY - TEXTBOOKS.
BQX 81-82   (270.x02)

CATHOLIC CHURCH - HISTORY - EARLY
PERIOD. See CHURCH HISTORY -
PRIMITIVE AND EARLY CHURCH.

CATHOLIC CHURCH - HISTORY - MIDDLE
AGES. See CHURCH HISTORY -
MIDDLE AGES.

CATHOLIC CHURCH - HISTORY - MODERN
PERIOD.
BQX 931-1131   (270.6)
sa Apologetics - History - Modern
period.
Church history - Modern period.
xx Church history - Modern period.

CATHOLIC CHURCH - HISTORY - MODERN
PERIOD - SOURCES.
BQX 931

CATHOLIC CHURCH - HISTORY - 16th
CENTURY.

CATHOLIC CHURCH - HISTORY - 17th
CENTURY.

CATHOLIC CHURCH - HISTORY - 18th
CENTURY.

CATHOLIC CHURCH - HISTORY - 19th
CENTURY.

CATHOLIC CHURCH - HISTORY - 20th
CENTURY.

Further subdivisions under "Catholic
Church - History" can be made by
reign of individual popes.

CATHOLIC CHURCH - HYMNS. See HYMNS.

CATHOLIC CHURCH - INFALLIBILITY. See
CHURCH - INFALLIBILITY.

CATHOLIC CHURCH - INFLUENCE.

CATHOLIC CHURCH - LAW. See
CANON LAW.

CATHOLIC CHURCH - LITERATURE. See
CATHOLIC LITERATURE.

CATHOLIC CHURCH - LITURGY. See
LITURGY.
RITES AND CEREMONIES (CATHOLIC)

CATHOLIC CHURCH - MEMBERSHIP.

CATHOLIC CHURCH - MISSIONS. See
MISSIONS.

CATHOLIC CHURCH - MUSEUMS. See
CATHOLIC CHURCH - EXHIBITIONS AND
MUSEUMS.

CATHOLIC CHURCH - MUSIC. See
CHURCH MUSIC.

CATHOLIC CHURCH - NAME.
sa Church - Catholicity.

CATHOLIC CHURCH - ORIENTAL RITES. See
EASTERN CHURCHES.

CATHOLIC CHURCH - PASTORAL LETTERS.
See PASTORAL LETTERS.

CATHOLIC CHURCH - PERIODICALS. See
CATHOLIC PERIODICALS.

CATHOLIC CHURCH - PICTURES, ILLUSTRA-
TIONS, ETC.
[BQX 35]
"Here are entered pictorial works
descriptive of the activities of
the Catholic Church." LC
sa Missions - Pictures, illustrations, etc.

CATHOLIC CHURCH - POPULAR WORKS.

CATHOLIC CHURCH - PRAYER-BOOKS. See
PRAYER-BOOKS.

CATHOLIC CHURCH - RELATION TO THE
STATE. See CHURCH AND STATE -
CATHOLIC CHURCH.

CATHOLIC CHURCH - RELATIONS.
BQT 413-418
Subdivided by churches with whom
relations are conducted, e.g.,
Catholic Church - Relations -
Orthodox Eastern Church, Russian
(With duplicate entry under Ortho-
dox Eastern Church, Russian -
Relations - Catholic Church.

CATHOLIC CHURCH - RELATIONS - ORTHO-
DOX EASTERN CHURCH.
BQX 5428
sa Schism - Eastern and Western
Church.
Schism, Acacian, 484-519.

CATHOLIC CHURCH - RELATIONS (CANON
LAW)

CATHOLIC CHURCH - RELATIONS (DIPLO-
MATIC). See HOLY SEE - RELATIONS
(DIPLOMATIC)
Cf. note under Holy See.

CATHOLIC CHURCH - SCHOOLS, PAROCHIAL.
See CHURCH SCHOOLS.

CATHOLIC CHURCH - SERMONS.
Here are entered sermon works
dealing specifically with the
Catholic Church.

CATHOLIC CHURCH - SOCIETIES. See
CATHOLIC SOCIETIES.

CATHOLIC CHURCH - STATISTICS.

CATHOLIC CHURCH - TERMINOLOGY.

CATHOLIC CHURCH - YEARBOOKS.
BQX 21
sa Almanacs, Catholic.
x Catholic yearbooks.
Yearbooks, Catholic.

################

CATHOLIC CHURCH - AUSTRIA, [BELGIUM,
FRANCE, ETC.]

It is recommended that instead of
the form "Catholic Church in ..."
the usual method of geographic
subdivision by use of the dash be
applied. Below, under the entry
"Catholic Church - France" as an
example, are given the further
subdivisions ordinarily needed
under subdivision of Catholic
Church by country.
sa Catholics in Austria, [Belgium,
France, etc.]

CATHOLIC CHURCH - FRANCE.
BQX 1701-1878
sa L'Action francaise.
Americanism (Catholic contro-
versy)
Fareinistes.
Gallicanism.
Louisets.
Nonjurors, French Catholic.
Priest-worker movement.
x Gallican Church.

CATHOLIC CHURCH - FRANCE - BIBLIOGRAPHY.

CATHOLIC CHURCH - FRANCE - BIOGRAPHY.
BQX 1715

CATHOLIC CHURCH - FRANCE - CHARITIES.

CATHOLIC CHURCH - FRANCE - CLERGY.

CATHOLIC CHURCH - FRANCE - CONGRESSES.
[BQX 1705]

76

CATHOLIC CHURCH - FRANCE - DIOCESES.
    BQX 1830-1878

CATHOLIC CHURCH - FRANCE - EDUCATION.
    See CATHOLIC EDUCATION - FRANCE.

CATHOLIC CHURCH - FRANCE - HISTORY.
    BQX 1713-1817
    Smaller libraries may prefer to use
    only the entry "France - Church
    history," with period subdivisions
    as indicated under that heading.
    xx France - Church history.

CATHOLIC CHURCH - FRANCE - HISTORY -
    BIBLIOGRAPHY.

CATHOLIC CHURCH - FRANCE - HISTORY -
    HISTORIOGRAPHY.

CATHOLIC CHURCH - FRANCE - HISTORY -
    PERIODICALS.
    BQX 1701

CATHOLIC CHURCH - FRANCE - HISTORY -
    SOURCES.
    BQX 1706

CATHOLIC CHURCH - FRANCE - MISSIONS.

CATHOLIC CHURCH - FRANCE - MISSIONS -
    SOCIETIES.

CATHOLIC CHURCH - FRANCE - SOCIETIES.

CATHOLIC CHURCH - FRANCE - YEARBOOKS.
    BQX 1703

CATHOLIC CHURCH - GERMANY.
    sa German Catholicism.
    Kulturkampf.

CATHOLIC CHURCH - U.S.
    sa Americanism (Catholic contro-
    versy)

CATHOLIC CHURCH - U.S. - HISTORY -
    1785-1865.
    sa Trusteeism.

################

CATHOLIC CHURCH. CODEX JURIS CANONICI.
    See CODEX JURIS CANONICE.

CATHOLIC CHURCH. COLLEGIUM CARDINA-
    LIUM. See COLLEGIUM CARDINALIUM.

CATHOLIC CHURCH. CORPUS JURIS CANONICI.
    See CORPUS JURIS CANONICI.

CATHOLIC CHURCH. CURIA ROMANA. See
    CURIA ROMANA.

CATHOLIC CHURCH. LEGATES, NUNCIOS,
    ETC. See HOLY SEE. LEGATES,
    NUNCIOS, ETC.

CATHOLIC CHURCH. LITURGY AND RITUAL.
    See LITURGY.
        RITES AND CEREMONIES (CATHOLIC)

CATHOLIC CHURCH. LITURGY AND RITUAL.
    ANTIPHONARIUM, [BREVIARIUM, MISSALE,
    ETC.]. See ANTIPHONARIUM.
        BREVIARIUM.
        MISSALE.
        etc.

The individual Catholic liturgical
    books are listed directly under
    their names, as exemplified above.

CATHOLIC CHURCH. POPE. See POPES.

CATHOLIC CHURCH. TREATIES, ETC. See
    HOLY SEE. TREATIES, ETC.
    Cf. note under Holy See.

################

CATHOLIC CHURCH AND ART.
    BQT 3498; BQT 5615
    xx Christian art.

CATHOLIC CHURCH AND COMMUNISM. See
    COMMUNISM AND CATHOLIC CHURCH.

CATHOLIC CHURCH AND CULTURE.
    BQT 3483-3498

CATHOLIC CHURCH AND FREEMASONRY. See
    FREEMASONS AND CATHOLIC CHURCH.

CATHOLIC CHURCH AND JEWS.
    BQT 413; BQT 3423
    x Jews and Catholic Church.

CATHOLIC CHURCH AND LABOR. See
    CHURCH AND LABOR.

CATHOLIC CHURCH AND MOVING-PICTURES. See
    MOVING-PICTURES AND CATHOLIC CHURCH.

CATHOLIC CHURCH AND OTHER RELIGIONS.
    BQT 159; BQT 403-418
    Here are entered works consisting of
      comparative studies in doctrinal
      and practical theology between
      the Catholic religion and other
      religions.

CATHOLIC CHURCH AND OTHER RELIGIONS -
    CHURCH OF ENGLAND, [LUTHERAN CHURCH,
    NEEDERLANDSCHE HERFORMDE KERK, ETC.]

CATHOLIC CHURCH AND PEACE.
    BQT 3473
    xx Catholic Church and war.
       Peace.

CATHOLIC CHURCH AND POLITICS.
    BQT 3451-3469
    xx Christianity and politics.

CATHOLIC CHURCH AND REUNION.
    BQT 403-418
    Here is entered Catholic literature
      dealing with the reunion of Chris-
      tendom.
    For works on Protestant ideas and
      efforts to achieve a unity of
      Christendom see Christian union.
    sa Christian union.
       Church - Unity.
       Church unity octave.
       Communicatio in sacris.
     x Church unity.
       Reunion of Christendom.
    xx Christian union.
       Church.
       Irenics.

CATHOLIC CHURCH AND REUNION - CON-
    GRESSES.

CATHOLIC CHURCH AND REUNION - HISTORY.
    BQX 869; BQX 5829

CATHOLIC CHURCH AND REUNION - PAPAL
    TEACHING.

CATHOLIC CHURCH AND REUNION - PERI-
    ODICALS.
    BQT 405

        #################

CATHOLIC CHURCH AND REUNION - CHURCH OF
    ENGLAND.
    BQT 414

CATHOLIC CHURCH AND REUNION - EASTERN
    CHURCHES.
    BQX 5428; BQX 5829
    sa Ferrara-Florence, Council of,
       1438-1439.

CATHOLIC CHURCH AND REUNION - ETHIOPIC
    CHURCH.
    BQX 5527

CATHOLIC CHURCH AND REUNION - ORTHODOX
    EASTERN CHURCH.
    BQX 6043

        #################

CATHOLIC CHURCH AND RURAL SOCIOLOGY. See
    SOCIOLOGY, RURAL (CATHOLIC)

CATHOLIC CHURCH AND SALVATION. See
    SALVATION OUTSIDE THE CHURCH.

CATHOLIC CHURCH AND SCIENCE.
    BQT 3491   (215)
    x Christianity and science.
      Church and science.
      Science and the Catholic Church.
    xx Religion and science.

CATHOLIC CHURCH AND SCIENCE - CONGRESSES.

CATHOLIC CHURCH AND SECRET SOCIETIES.
    See SECRET SOCIETIES AND CATHOLIC
    CHURCH.

CATHOLIC CHURCH AND SOCIAL PROBLEMS.
      BQT 3413-3429
  sa Catholic action.
     Christian democracy.
     Clergy and social problems.
     Priest-worker movement.
     Sociology, Rural (Catholic)
     Syndicalism, Catholic.
     Trade-unions, Catholic.
   x Church and social problems -
     Catholic Church.
     Social justice.
  xx Social service, Catholic.
     Sociology, Christian.

CATHOLIC CHURCH AND SOCIAL PROBLEMS -
PAPAL TEACHING.
   x Social encyclicals.

CATHOLIC CHURCH AND SOCIALISM. See
SOCIALISM AND CATHOLIC CHURCH.

CATHOLIC CHURCH AND STATE. See
CHURCH AND STATE - CATHOLIC CHURCH.

CATHOLIC CHURCH AND THEATER. See
THEATER AND CATHOLIC CHURCH.

CATHOLIC CHURCH AND WAR.
      BQT 1913
  sa Catholic Church and peace.
  xx War and religion.

CATHOLIC CHURCH IN ...
  See entry above "Catholic Church -
    Austria, [Belgium, France, etc.]"

CATHOLIC CHURCHES. See
CHURCHES, CATHOLIC.

CATHOLIC DICTIONARIES. See
CATHOLIC CHURCH - DICTIONARIES.

CATHOLIC DIRECTORIES. See
CATHOLIC CHURCH - DIRECTORIES.

CATHOLIC DRAMA.
   x Drama, Catholic.
  xx Catholic literature.
     Church and theater.

CATHOLIC EASTERN CHURCHES. See
EASTERN CHURCHES, CATHOLIC.

CATHOLIC EDUCATION. (Geog. subdiv.,
  Indirect)
     LC 461-510 (377.82; 261.5)
  sa Catholics in education.
     Church schools.
     Educators, Catholic.
     Moral education.
     Newman Club.
     Religious education.
     Rural schools, Catholic.
     Students, Catholic.
     Teachers, Catholic.
     Vacation schools, Catholic.
   x Catholic Church - Education.
     Education, Catholic.
     Religion and education.
  xx Church and education.

CATHOLIC EDUCATION - ADDRESSES,
ESSAYS, LECTURES.

CATHOLIC EDUCATION - AIMS AND
OBJECTIVES.

CATHOLIC EDUCATION - BIBLIOGRAPHY.

CATHOLIC EDUCATION - CONGRESSES.

CATHOLIC EDUCATION - CURRICULA.

CATHOLIC EDUCATION - DIRECTORIES.

CATHOLIC EDUCATION - FINANCE.

CATHOLIC EDUCATION - HISTORY.

CATHOLIC EDUCATION - LAY TEACHERS.
    [LC 480]
   x Lay teachers, Catholic.
  xx Teachers, Catholic.

CATHOLIC EDUCATION - PAPAL TEACHING.

CATHOLIC EDUCATION - PERIODICALS.

CATHOLIC EDUCATION - PHILOSOPHY.

CATHOLIC EDUCATION - SERMONS.

CATHOLIC EDUCATION - SOCIETIES.

CATHOLIC EDUCATION - STANDARDS.

CATHOLIC EDUCATION - STUDY AND
 TEACHING.

CATHOLIC EDUCATION - U.S.
     BQX 4351-4360

CATHOLIC EDUCATION (CANON LAW)
     BQV230 1372-1383
 sa Universities and colleges,
     Catholic (Canon law)

CATHOLIC EDUCATION, ADULT.
 x Adult education, Catholic.
 see Religious education of Adults

CATHOLIC EDUCATION, ELEMENTARY.
 x Elementary education, Catholic.

CATHOLIC EDUCATION, HIGHER.
 sa Universities and colleges,
     Catholic.
 x Higher education, Catholic.

CATHOLIC EDUCATION, PRESCHOOL.
 x Preschool education, Catholic.

CATHOLIC EDUCATION, SECONDARY.
 x Secondary education, Catholic.

CATHOLIC EDUCATORS. See
 EDUCATORS, CATHOLIC.

CATHOLIC EMANCIPATION.
     BQX 2085-2089   (274.207)
 sa Gordon riots, 1780.
 x Emancipation, Catholic.

CATHOLIC EPISTLES. See
 BIBLE. N.T. CATHOLIC EPISTLES.

CATHOLIC ESSAYS.
 x Essays, Catholic.
 xx Catholic literature.

CATHOLIC ETHICS. See
 MORAL THEOLOGY.

CATHOLIC EVIDENCES. See APOLOGETICS.

CATHOLIC FICTION.
 sa Short stories, Catholic.
 x Fiction, Catholic.
   Stories, Catholic.
 xx Catholic literature.

CATHOLIC HISTORIANS.
     BQX 47
 sa Church historians.
 x Historians, Catholic.
 xx Catholic Church - Biography.
   Church historians.

CATHOLIC HOME. See FAMILY, CHRISTIAN.

CATHOLIC HOSPITALS. See
 HOSPITALS, CATHOLIC.

CATHOLIC INSTITUTIONS.   (Geog.
 subdiv.)
 sa Abbeys.
   Church schools.
   Convents.
   Hospitals, Catholic.
   Monasteries.
   Priories.
   Theological seminaries.
   Universities and colleges,
     Catholic.
 x Institutions, Catholic.
 xx Corporations, Ecclesiastical.

CATHOLIC INTERNATIONAL ORGANIZATIONS.
 See INTERNATIONAL ORGANIZATIONS,
 CATHOLIC.

CATHOLIC JUVENILE LITERATURE. See
 CHILDREN'S LITERATURE - CATHOLIC
 AUTHORS.

CATHOLIC LABOR UNIONS. See
 TRADE-UNIONS, CATHOLIC.

CATHOLIC LEAGUE, 1609-1648.
 xx Thirty Years' War, 1618-1648.

CATHOLIC LEARNING AND SCHOLARSHIP.
     BQT 3489
 sa Catholics as scientists.
 x Learning and scholarship -
     Catholic Church.

CATHOLIC LIBRARIES. See
LIBRARIES, CATHOLIC.

CATHOLIC LITERATURE.
        BQ   (280)
        BQT 3495
        PN 485
sa Catholic authors.
   Catholic Book Week.
   Catholic drama.
   Catholic essays.
   Catholic fiction.
   Catholic pamphlets.
   Catholic poetry.
   Catholic readers and speakers.
   Catholic speeches, addresses,
      etc.
   Catholic wit and humor.
   Index librorum prohibitorum.
   Short stories, Catholic.
   also subdivision "Catholic
      authors" under names of
      special literatures, e.g.,
      German literature - Catholic
      authors.
 x Catholic Church - Literature.
xx Catholic Church - Bibliography.
   Christian literature.
   Religious literature.

CATHOLIC LITERATURE - ADDRESSES,
ESSAYS, LECTURES.

CATHOLIC LITERATURE - BIBLIOGRAPHY.
   Z 7837-7840

CATHOLIC LITERATURE - BIBLIOGRAPHY -
BEST BOOKS. See BIBLIOGRAPHY -
BEST BOOKS - CATHOLIC LITERATURE.

CATHOLIC LITERATURE - BIBLIOGRAPHY -
CATALOGS.

CATHOLIC LITERATURE - BIBLIOGRAPHY -
PERIODICALS.

CATHOLIC LITERATURE - BIO-BIBLIOGRAPHY.

CATHOLIC LITERATURE - CATALOGING. See
CATALOGING OF CATHOLIC LITERATURE.

CATHOLIC LITERATURE - COLLECTIONS.

CATHOLIC LITERATURE - HISTORY AND
CRITICISM.

CATHOLIC LITERATURE - SELECTIONS.

CATHOLIC LITERATURE - SUBJECT HEADINGS.
See SUBJECT HEADINGS - CATHOLIC
LITERATURE.

CATHOLIC LITERATURE - YEARBOOKS -
ENGLISH, [FRENCH, GERMAN, ETC.]

CATHOLIC NEWSPAPERS.
   x Newspapers, Catholic.
   xx Catholic press.
      Religious newspapers and
      periodicals.

CATHOLIC NONJURORS, ENGLISH. See
NONJURORS, ENGLISH CATHOLIC.

CATHOLIC NONJURORS, FRENCH. See
NONJURORS, FRENCH CATHOLIC.

CATHOLIC PAMPHLETS.
     BQ 5322-5390
   x Pamphlets, Catholic.
   xx Catholic literature.

CATHOLIC PERIODICALS.   (Geog. subdiv.,
   Direct)
   x Catholic Church - Periodicals.
     Periodicals, Catholic.
   xx Catholic press.
      Religious newspapers and
      periodicals.

CATHOLIC PERIODICALS - BIBLIOGRAPHY.

CATHOLIC PERIODICALS - DIRECTORIES.

CATHOLIC PERIODICALS - HISTORY.

CATHOLIC PERIODICALS - INDEXES.

CATHOLIC POETRY.
     BQ 265-268; BQ 5081-5103
   x Poetry, Catholic.
   xx Catholic literature.
      Christian poetry.

CATHOLIC POETS.
   x Poets, Catholic.
  xx Catholic authors.

CATHOLIC PRESS.   (Geog. subdiv.,
  Direct)
      BQT 3604-3616   (070.1)
  sa Catholic newspapers.
     Catholic periodicals.
     Catholic propaganda.
   x Press, Catholic.
  xx Communication - Religious
     aspects.

CATHOLIC PRESS - ENGLAND,
[GERMANY, U.S., ETC.]

CATHOLIC PROPAGANDA.
      BQT 3617
   x Propaganda, Catholic.
  xx Catholic press.
     Communication - Religious
     aspects.

CATHOLIC READERS AND SPEAKERS.
      BQ 288; BQ 5183
   x Readers and speakers, Catholic.
  xx Catholic literature.

CATHOLIC RURAL LIFE. See
  SOCIOLOGY, RURAL (CATHOLIC)

CATHOLIC RURAL SCHOOLS. See
  RURAL SCHOOLS, CATHOLIC.

CATHOLIC SCHOOL SONG-BOOKS. See
  SCHOOL SONG-BOOKS, CATHOLIC.

CATHOLIC SCIENTISTS. See
  SCIENTISTS, CATHOLIC.

CATHOLIC SHORT STORIES. See
  SHORT STORIES, CATHOLIC.

CATHOLIC SOCIAL ACTION.
      BQT 3525
   x Social action, Catholic.
  xx Laity.
     Sociology, Christian.

CATHOLIC SOCIAL SERVICE. See
  SOCIAL SERVICE, CATHOLIC.

CATHOLIC SOCIETIES.
  sa Confraternities.
     International organizations,
     Catholic.
    also subdivision "Societies"
     under Catholic Church divided
     by country, e.g., Catholic
     Church - France - Societies.
   x Catholic Church - Societies.
     Societies.
  xx Church societies.

CATHOLIC SOCIETIES - HISTORY,
ORGANIZATION, ETC.

CATHOLIC SONG-BOOKS. See
  SONG-BOOKS, CATHOLIC.

CATHOLIC SPEECHES, ADDRESSES, ETC.
   x Speeches, addresses, etc.,
     Catholic.
  xx Catholic literature.

CATHOLIC STUDENTS. See
  STUDENTS, CATHOLIC.

CATHOLIC SYNDICALISM. See
  SYNDICALISM, CATHOLIC.

CATHOLIC TEACHERS. See
  TEACHERS, CATHOLIC.

CATHOLIC TRADE-UNIONS. See
  TRADE-UNIONS, CATHOLIC.

CATHOLIC UNIVERSITIES AND COLLEGES. See
  UNIVERSITIES AND COLLEGES, CATHOLIC.

CATHOLIC VACATION SCHOOLS. See
  VACATION SCHOOLS, CATHOLIC.

CATHOLIC WIT AND HUMOR. See
  * Wit and humor, Catholic.
  xx Catholic literature.

CATHOLIC WIT AND HUMOR, PICTORIAL.

CATHOLIC YEARBOOKS. See
  CATHOLIC CHURCH - YEARBOOKS.

CATHOLIC YOUTH MOVEMENT. (Geog.
  subdiv.)
   x Youth movement, Catholic.
  xx Catholic action.

✓ CATHOLICISM. See
✓ CATHOLIC CHURCH.
  CATHOLICITY.

CATHOLICISM, OLD. See
  OLD CATHOLICISM.

CATHOLICS.

CATHOLICS, COLORED. See
  CATHOLICS, NEGRO.

CATHOLICS, LAPSED.
  sa Apostasy.
    Heresies and heretics.
    Non-Catholics.
    Schism.
  x Lapsed Catholics.

CATHOLICS, NEGRO.
    BQX 4337
  sa Priests, Negro.
  x Catholics, Colored.
    Colored Catholics.
    Negro Catholics.
  xx Negroes - Religion.

CATHOLICS, CROATION, [LETTISH, ETC.]
  "Here are entered works on Catholics
    living outside their native country
    but using their native language." LC
  x Croation, [Lettish, etc.] Catholics.

CATHOLICS AS SCIENTISTS.
  "Here are entered works on the
    attainments of Catholics as
    scientists. Works mainly bio-
    graphical are entered under the
    heading Scientists, Catholic." LC
  xx Catholic learning and scholarship.
    Scientists, Catholic.

CATHOLICS IN EDUCATION.
  xx Catholic education.

CATHOLICS IN LITERATURE.

CATHOLICS IN NON-CATHOLIC COUNTRIES.
  xx Man - Migrations.
    Minorities.

CATHOLICS IN BOSTON, [CANADA,
  ENGLAND, ETC.]
  "Used for works treating Catholics,
    not as an ecclesiastical body,
    but as a distinct element or group
    in the population (cf. Germans in
    the U.S.). Reference is made from
    Catholic Church (e.g. Catholic
    Church - Minnesota. See also
    Catholics in Minnesota)" LC
  xx Catholic Church - Austria,
    [Belgium, France, etc.]

CATHOLICS IN ENGLAND.
  x Recusants.

CAVE CHURCHES.
    NA 4910; NA 5201-6113
  x Monolithic churches.
    Rock churches.

✓ CELEBRANTS. —
    BQT 4331
  xx Priests.
    x - Presiders

CELEBRET.
    BQV230 804
  "A letter which a bishop gives to
    a priest, that he may obtain per-
    mission in another diocese to say
    Mass ..." CE
  xx Mass (Canon law)

CELESTINES (BENEDICTINE)
    BQX 7101
  x Benedictines, Celestine.
    Hermits of Murrone.
    Murrone, Hermits of.
  xx Benedictines.

CELESTINES (FRANCISCAN)
    BQX 7408
  x Franciscans, Celestine.

✓ CELIBACY.
    BQT 2299   (24x1.82)
  sa Chastity (Vow)
    Marriage of clergy.
    Patarines.
  x Clergy - Celibacy.
  xx Chastity.
    Marriage.
    Religious life.
    Virginity.

CELIBACY - HISTORY.

CELIBACY (CANON LAW)
      BQV230 132   (348.x31)
  xx Clergy (Canon law)

CELTIC MONASTICISM. See
  MONASTICISM, IRISH.

CELTIC RITE.
      BQT 4138   (264.x82)

CEMETERIES. (Geog. subdiv.,
  Indirect)
      RA 626-630
        BQX 68 (Christian archaeology)
  References as in LC.

CEMETERIES - CONSECRATION.
  x Consecration of cemeteries.
  xx Dedication services.

CEMETERIES - VIOLATION.
      BQV230 1207

CEMETERIES (CANON LAW)
      BQV230 1205   (348.x414)
  xx Burial law (Canon law)
    Sacred places (Canon law)

CENSORSHIP (CANON LAW)
      BQV230 1384-1405   (348.x443)
  sa Index librorum prohibitorum.
    Prohibited books (Canon law)
  x Ecclesiastical censorship.
  xx Church - Teaching office.

CENSURES, ECCLESIASTICAL.
      BQV230 2241-2285   (348.x6)
  "Penalties by which a baptized
  person, guilty of a crime and
  contumacious, is deprived of
  certain spiritual benefits." AT
  sa Absolution (Canon law)
    Excommunication.
    Interdict (Canon law)
    Reserved cases.
    Suspension (Canon law)
  xx Canon law.
    Penalties, Ecclesiastical.

CENSUS (CANON LAW)

CENSUS, CHURCH. See CHURCH CENSUS.

CENTRAL AMERICA - CHURCH HISTORY.
      BQX 4602-4682

CEREMONIAL (BOOK). See CAEREMONIALE.

CEREMONIAL OF BISHOPS. See
  CAEREMONIALE EPISCOPORUM.

CEREMONIES. See RITES AND CEREMONIES.

CERTAINTY. See
  BELIEF AND DOUBT.
  FAITH.
  PROBABILITIES.
  TRUTH.

CERTAINTY, JUDICIAL. See
  JUDICIAL CERTAINTY.

CHAINS OF ST. PETER. See
  ST. PETER'S CHAINS.

CHAIR OF PETER. See
  ST. PETER'S CHAIR.

CHAIR OF UNITY OCTAVE. See
  CHURCH UNITY OCTAVE.

CHAIRS (CATHEDRA)
      BQT 5948
  x Cathedra.
  xx Cathedrals.
    Church furniture.

CHALCEDON, COUNCIL OF, 451.
      BQX 426

CHALDEAN CHURCH. See
  NESTORIAN CHURCH.

CHALDEAN RITE.
  x Syrian Rite, East.
    Syro-Chaldean Rite.

CHALDEAN RITE - CANON LAW.
      BQV 1261-1270   (348.x7)

CHALDEAN RITE - HISTORY.
      BQX 6461-6479   (28x1)

CHALDEAN RITE. LITURGY AND RITUAL.
BQT 5431-5439   (264.x74)

CHALICES.
BQT 4358; BQT 6026   (264.x4)
xx Sacred vessels.

CHAMBERLAINS, PAPAL. See
PAPAL CHAMBERLAINS.

CHANCELLORS, DIOCESAN.
BQV230 372-373   (348.x35)
sa Notaries (Canon law)
x Diocesan chancellors.
xx Curia, Diocesan.
Dioceses.
Persons (Canon law)

CHANCERIES, DIOCESAN.   (Geog.
subdiv., Direct)
x Diocesan chanceries.
Episcopal chanceries.
xx Bishops.
Dioceses.

CHANCERY, APOSTOLIC. See
CANCELLARIA APOSTOLICA.

CHANT.   (Geog. subdiv.)
BQT 4611-4630   (783,5)
sa Ambrosian chant.
Choral.
Mozarabic chant.
Neumes.
x Gregorian chant.
Plain chant.
Plainsong.
xx Choral music.
Church music.
Liturgy.

CHANT - ACCOMPANIMENT.
BQT 4630
sa Hymns - Accompaniment.
xx Hymns - Accompaniment.

CHANT - ADDRESSES, ESSAYS, LECTURES.

CHANT - BIBLIOGRAPHY.
[BQT 4610]

CHANT - COLLECTIONS.
BQT 4651-4654
xx Choir books.

CHANT - DISCOGRAPHY.
[BQT 4610.5]
[ML 156.5]
x Phonorecords - Catalogs.
xx Music - Discography.

CHANT - HISTORY AND CRITICISM.
BQT 4614-4618

CHANT - HISTORY AND CRITICISM -
EARLY PERIOD TO 604.

CHANT - HISTORY AND CRITICISM -
605-1246.

CHANT - HISTORY AND CRITICISM -
1247-1599.

CHANT - HISTORY AND CRITICISM -
1600-1857.

CHANT - HISTORY AND CRITICISM -
1858-

CHANT - INSTRUCTION AND STUDY.
BQT 4621
x Chant - Study and teaching.

CHANT - INSTRUCTION AND STUDY - To 1800.
xx Music - Theory - Medieval.

CHANT - MANUALS, TEXTBOOKS, ETC.
BQT 4620

CHANT - MANUSCRIPTS.
M 2147
xx Church music - Manuscripts.
Music - Manuscripts.
Paleography, Musical.

CHANT - MANUSCRIPTS - FACSIMILES.

CHANT - MODES AND TONES.
BQT 4624
x Gregorian modes.
Modes, Musical (Chant)

CHANT - PERIODICALS.
BQT 4532

CHANT - RHYTHM.
BQT 4628
x Rhythm (Church music)
xx Musical meter and rhythm
(Church music)

CHANT - STUDY AND TEACHING. See
CHANT - INSTRUCTION AND STUDY.

CHANT (ANGLICAN)
M 2168.6-.7
x Anglican chant.

CHANT (JEWISH)
x Jewish chant.

CHANT, AMBROSIAN. See
AMBROSIAN CHANT.

CHANT, ANTIPHONAL. See
ANTIPHONAL CHANT.

CHANT, BYZANTINE. See
CHURCH MUSIC - BYZANTINE RITE.

CHANT, MOZARABIC. See
MOZARABIC CHANT.

CHANT, POLYPHONOC. See
POLYPHONIC CHANT.

CHANTRIES.
xx Monasteries.

CHAPELS. (Geog. subdiv., Indirect)
BQT 5926 (726.41)
sa Oratories.
also names of individual chapels,
and subdivision "Chapels" under
names of cities.
xx Church architecture.
Churches.

CHAPELS (CANON LAW)
BQV230 1188 (348.x413)
xx Sacred places (Canon law)

CHAPELS, COURT.
x Chapels royal.
Court chapels.

CHAPELS ROYAL. See CHAPELS, COURT.

CHAPLAINS.
BQX 8261
Here are entered works on clergymen
appointed to exercise the sacred
ministry in the armed forces, in
institutions (convents, hospitals,
schools, orphanages, prisons), for
sodalities, for courts and families.
sa Legislative bodies - Chaplains'
prayers.
also specific types of chaplains
listed below, and subdivision
"Chaplains" under names of
particular bodies, e.g.,
U.S. Congress - Chaplains.
xx Clergy.

CHAPLAINS (CANON LAW)
BQV230 698 (348.x36)
xx Clergy (Canon law)
Persons (Canon law)

CHAPLAINS, COURT.
x Court chaplains.

CHAPLAINS, HOSPITAL.
x Hospital chaplains.
Hospitals - Chaplains.

CHAPLAINS, HOSPITAL - LUTHERAN
CHURCH, [METHODIST CHURCH, ETC.]

CHAPLAINS, INDUSTRIAL.
x Industrial chaplains.
xx Church work.
Welfare work in industry.

CHAPLAINS, MILITARY. (Geog. subdiv.,
Direct)
x Chaplains, Naval.
Military chaplains.
Naval chaplains.
xx Clergy and military service.

CHAPLAINS, MILITARY - CORRESPONDENCE,
REMINISCENCES, ETC.

CHAPLAINS, MILITARY - PERIODICALS.

CHAPLAINS, MILITARY - LUTHERAN CHURCH,
[METHODIST CHURCH, ETC.]

86

CHAPLAINS, MILITARY (CANON LAW)
        BQV230 451,3   (348.x36)

CHAPLAINS, NAVAL. See
    CHAPLAINS, MILITARY.

CHAPLAINS, PRISON.
    sa Prisons - Religious life.
    x Prison chaplains.

CHAPLAINS, PRISON - CORRESPONDENCE,
    REMINISCENCES, ETC.

CHAPLAINS, SCHOOL.
    x School chaplains.
    xx Chaplains, University and college.
    Church work with students.

CHAPLAINS, UNIVERSITY AND COLLEGE.
    sa Chaplains, School.
    x College chaplains.
    Universities and colleges -
        Chaplains.
    University chaplains.
    xx Church work with students.

CHAPLAINS FOR SISTERS.
    x Religious orders of women -
        Chaplains.

CHAPLAINS FOR SISTERS (CANON LAW)
        BQV230 479,2   (348.x37)
    xx Religious orders of women (Canon
       law)

CHAPLAINS' PRAYERS. See LEGISLATIVE
    BODIES - CHAPLAINS' PRAYERS.

CHAPTERS, CATHEDRAL, COLLEGIATE, ETC.
    (Geog. subdiv., Indirect)
    sa Canons secular.
    Deans.
    Minor canons, Cathedral, col-
        legiate, etc.
    Rural chapters.
    Vicars capitular.
    x Cathedral chapters.
    Collegiate chapters.
    xx Bishops.
    Cathedrals.
    Dioceses.
    Vicars capitular.

CHAPTERS, CATHEDRAL, COLLEGIATE, ETC.
    (CANON LAW)
        BQV230 394-422   (348.x35)
    sa Deans (Canon law)
    xx Dioceses (Canon law)
    Persons (Canon law)

CHAPTERS, CONVENTUAL. See
    CHAPTERS OF FAULTS.

CHAPTERS, RURAL. See
    RURAL CHAPTERS.

CHAPTERS OF FAULTS.
        BQT 2323   (24x1.83)
    Here are entered works on the daily
        or periodical meeting held in
        monasteries, usually after prime,
        for the reading of the martyrology,
        the self-accusation and correction
        of faults, and the assignment of
        the daily tasks.
    x Chapters, Conventual.
    Conventual chapters.
    Culpa.
    Faults, Chapters.
    xx Religious life.

CHARACTER.
    Classifications and references as
    in LC.

CHARACTER (SACRAMENTS)
        BQT 1243
    Here are entered works on the in-
        delible mark produced on the soul
        by certain sacraments, namely,
        Baptism, Confirmation, and Holy
        Orders.
    x Sacramental character.
    Sacraments - Character.

CHARACTER EDUCATION. See
    MORAL EDUCATION.

CHARISMATA.
        BQT 1217   (234.15)
    x Gifts, Spiritual.
    xx Discernment of spirits.
    Gifts of the Holy Spirit.

✓Charismatic Renewal

CHARITABLE BEQUESTS.   (Geog. subdiv.,
  Direct)
    x Religious bequests.
      Religious legacies.
    Other references as in LC supple-
      ment 1956-58.

CHARITABLE BEQUESTS (CANON LAW)

CHARITIES.   (Geog. subdiv., Indirect)
        HV 1-4959   (360)
        BQT 3658-3699 (Catholic)
    References as in LC, with the follow-
      ing additional references.
    sa Alms and almsgiving.
       Catholic Church - Charities.
    xx Alms and almsgiving.

CHARITIES - TAXATION.   See
    CHURCH PROPERTY - TAXATION.

CHARITIES, CATHOLIC.   See
    CATHOLIC CHURCH - CHARITIES.

CHARITY.
        BQT 1203 (Dogmatic theology)
        BQT 1786 (Moral theology)
          (24x1.51)
        BQT 2395 (Asceticism) (24x7.12)
    Here are entered works on the love
      which man manifests towards his
      neighbor. For works on the love
      which man accords God see Love
      (Theology).
    sa Altruism.
       Correction, Fraternal.
       Humanity.
       Kindness.
       Love.
       Social service, Catholic.
       Women in charitable work.
     x Love of neighbor.
    xx Alms and almsgiving.
       Begging.
       Benevolence.
       Church work.
       Conduct of life.
       Ethics.
       Humanity.
       Perfection, Christian.

CHARITY - SERMONS.
        [BQT 3073.5]

CHARITY, SISTERS OF.   See
    SISTERS OF CHARITY.

CHARTREUX.   See CARTHUSIANS.

CHASIDISM.   See HASIDISM.

CHASTITY.
        BQT 1933 (Commandments)
          (24x1.64)
        BQT 1793 (Virtue)   (24x1.52)
    sa Celibacy.
       Continence.
       Lust.
       Modesty.
    xx Evangelical counsels.
       Purity.
       Temperance (Virtue)
       Virginity.

CHASTITY - SERMONS.

CHASTITY (VOW)
        BQT 2313   (24x1.83)
    xx Celibacy.
       Vows.

CHERUBIM. See ANGELS.
✓ Child study x Child psychology development
CHICAGO-LAMBETH QUADRILATERAL. See ✗Child development
    LAMBETH QUADRILATERAL.
✓ Child + Parent see Parenting
✓ Child welfare
CHILDERMAS. See
    HOLY INNOCENTS, FEAST OF THE.

CHILDHOOD, HOLY. See
    HOLY CHILDHOOD.
CHILDREN - BIBLE see Bible for children
CHILDREN - BIBLICAL TEACHING. See
    CHILDREN IN THE BIBLE.

CHILDREN - BIOGRAPHY.
        BQT 2706 (Pius biography)
    References as in LC.

CHILDREN - CONVERSION TO CHRISTIANITY.

CHILDREN - DEATH AND FUTURE STATE.

CHILDREN - MEDITATIONS.

CHILDREN - MISSIONS. See
    MISSIONS - CHILDREN.

88

CHILDREN - PRAYER-BOOKS.
BQT 2645
x Prayer-books for children.

CHILDREN - PRAYER-BOOKS - ENGLISH,
[FRENCH, GERMAN, ETC.]

CHILDREN - RELIGIOUS EDUCATION. See
RELIGIOUS EDUCATION OF CHILDREN.

CHILDREN - RELIGIOUS LIFE.
BQT 2287
sa Retreats for children.

CHILDREN - RETREATS. See
RETREATS FOR CHILDREN.
√ Children as artists

CHILDREN (CANON LAW). See
MINORS (CANON LAW)

CHILDREN, CHURCH WORK WITH. See
CHURCH WORK WITH CHILDREN.

CHILDREN IN THE BIBLE.
BS 576-578
BS 2446 (New Testament)
x Bible - Children.
Boys in the Bible.
Children - Biblical teaching.
Girls in the Bible.
xx Bible - Biography.

CHILDREN OF GOD.
BS 2545
sa God - Fatherhood.
Kingdom of God.
xx God - Fatherhood.
Mystical union.
CHILDREN'S BIBLE See Bible for children

CHILDREN'S CRUSADE, 1212.
BQX 662 (270.5)
xx Crusades.

CHILDREN'S LITERATURE - CATHOLIC
AUTHORS.
x Catholic juvenile literature.
Juvenile literature, Catholic.

CHILDREN'S LITERATURE - MORAL AND
RELIGIOUS ASPECTS.
xx Literature and morals.

CHILDREN'S SERMONS.
,BQT 3017 (252.x6)
sa Boys - Sermons.
x Sermons for children.

CHILDREN'S STORIES.
sa Missionary stories.
Other references as in LC.

CHILE - CHURCH HISTORY.
BQX 4821-4829

CHILIASM. See MILLENNIUM.

CHINA - CHURCH HISTORY.
BQX 3141-3216 (275.1)

CHINA - CHURCH HISTORY - EARLY
PERIOD TO 1552.

CHINA - CHURCH HISTORY - 1552-1900.

CHINA - CHURCH HISTORY - 19th CENTURY.

CHINA - CHURCH HISTORY - 20th CENTURY.

CHINA - RELIGION.
BL 1801-1940

CHINESE RITES.
BQX 3164
"Here are entered works dealing with
the controversy concerning the
participation of Christian converts in Chinese rites and ceremonies." LC
sa Malabar rites.
x Rites, Chinese.
xx Malabar rites.

CHIVALRY.
sa Crusades.
xx Crusades.
Other references as in LC.

CHOIR BOOKS.
BQT 4651-4654
Here are entered collections of
church songs, polyphonic and/or
chant, for use by choirs, or by
choirs and congregations.

CHOIR BOOKS -- Continued.
  sa Chants - Collections.
    Hymnals.
    also names of official chant
      books, e.g., Antiphonarium,
      Graduale, Kyriale, Liber
      usualis, Vesperale.
  x Church music - Choruses and
    choir books.
  xx Hymnals.

CHOIR BOOKS - CHURCH OF ENGLAND,
  [LUTHERAN CHURCH, ETC.]

CHOIR-STALLS.
      BQT 5932
  x Stalls, Choir.
  xx Church decoration and ornament.
    Church furniture.

CHOIRBOY TRAINING.

CHOIRS (CHURCH MUSIC)
      BQT 4581-4586   (783.8)
  xx Church music.

CHORAL MUSIC.   (Geog. subdiv.)
  "Here are entered works on choral
    music. Church compositions are
    entered under the heading
    'Choruses'." LC
  Classifications and references as
    in LC.

CHORAL VICARS. See
  MINOR CANONS, CATHEDRAL, COLLEGIATE,
  ETC.

CHORALE.
  Classifications and references as
    in LC.

CHOREPISCOPI.
  x Rural bishops.
  xx Archdeacons.
    Bishops.

CHORUSES, SACRED.
      M 1999-2101
  References and subdivisions as
    in LC.

CHRISM.
      BQT 4483
  xx Holy oils.

CHRIST. See JESUS CHRIST.

CHRIST THE KING, FEAST OF. See
  JESUS CHRIST THE KING, FEAST OF.

CHRISTENING. See BAPTISM.

CHRISTIAN ALEXANDRIAN SCHOOL. See
  ALEXANDRIAN SCHOOL, CHRISTIAN.

CHRISTIAN ANTIQUITIES.   (Geog.
  subdiv., Direct)
  sa Architecture, Gothic.
    Catacombs.
    Christian art.
    Church architecture.
    Church furniture.
    Church vestments.
    Crosses.
    Feasts, Ecclesiastical.
    Fonts.
    Heraldry, Sacred.
    Inscriptions, Christian.
    Relics and reliquaries.
    Sarcophagi.
    Sepulchral monuments.
    Staff, Pastoral.

  x Antiquities, Christian.
    Antiquities, Ecclesiastical.
    Archaeology, Christian.
    Christian archaeology.
    Church antiquities.
    Ecclesiastical antiquities.
    Ecclesiology (Archaeology)

  xx Archaeology.
    Bible - Antiquities.
    Christian art.
    Church history.

CHRISTIAN ANTIQUITIES - BIBLIOGRAPHY.
  [BQT 54]; Z 7779

CHRISTIAN ANTIQUITIES - COLLECTED
  WORKS.

CHRISTIAN ANTIQUITIES - COLLECTIONS.
  BQX 55

90

CHRISTIAN ANTIQUITIES - CONGRESSES.

CHRISTIAN ANTIQUITIES - DICTIONARIES.
BQX 57

CHRISTIAN ANTIQUITIES - PICTURES,
ILLUSTRATIONS, ETC.

CHRISTIAN APOSTOLATE. See
APOSTOLATE.

CHRISTIAN ARCHAEOLOGY. See
CHRISTIAN ANTIQUITIES.

CHRISTIAN ART. *see Art, Christian* (Geog. subdiv.,
Direct)
BQT 5601-6278   (246.x6)
sa Altarpieces.
Art and religion.
Bible - Picture Bibles.
Bible - Pictures, illustrations,
etc.
Catacombs.
Cathedrals.
Catholic Church and art.
Christian antiquities.
Church architecture.
Church decoration and ornament.
Church furniture.
Church vestments.
Commandments, Ten - Art.
Custodials.
Devil - Art.
Emblems.
Eucharist - Art.
Fish (in religion, etc.)
Flabella.
Fonts.
God - Art.
Heaven - Art.
Hell - Art.
Heraldry, Sacred.
Holy Spirit - Art.
Illumination of books and
manuscripts.
Jesus Christ - Art.
Judgment-day - Art.
Magi - Art.
Mary, Blessed Virgin - Art.
Mosaics.
Nimbus - Art.
Painting, Religious.

CHRISTIAN ART -- Continued.
sa Paradise in art.
Pieta.
Relics and reliquaries.
Saints - Art.
Sarcophagi.
Screens (Church decoration)
Sculpture, Religious.
Ship models (Church decoration)
Soul in art.
Staff, Pastoral.
Symbolism, Christian.
Symbolism of numbers.

x Art, Catholic.
Art, Christian.
Art, Ecclesiastical.
Art, Religious.
Catholic art.
Catholic Church - Art.
Ecclesiastical art.
Ecclesiology (Church decoration
and ornament)
Iconography.
Liturgical art.
Religious art.
Sacred art.

xx Archaeology.
Art and religion.
Catacombs.
Christian antiquities.
Church decoration and ornament.
Jesus Christ - Art.
Liturgy.
Saints - Art.
Symbolism, Christian.
Symbolism in art.

CHRISTIAN ART - ADDRESSES, ESSAYS,
LECTURES.

CHRISTIAN ART - BIBLIOGRAPHY.
BQT 5601; Z 5963

CHRISTIAN ART - COLLECTED WORKS.
BQT 5607-5608

CHRISTIAN ART - CONGRESSES.
BQT 5603

CHRISTIAN ART - DICTIONARIES.
BQT 5609

CHRISTIAN ART - EXHIBITIONS.

CHRISTIAN ART - GALLERIES AND
    MUSEUMS.
        BQT 5803-6808

CHRISTIAN ART - HISTORY.
        BQT 5616-5798

CHRISTIAN ART - HISTORY - EARLY
    PERIOD.
        BQT 5663

CHRISTIAN ART - HISTORY - MIDDLE
    AGES.
        BQT 5664-5667

CHRISTIAN ART - HISTORY - MODERN
    PERIOD.
        BQT 5668

CHRISTIAN ART - HISTORY - 19th
    CENTURY.

CHRISTIAN ART - HISTORY - 20th
    CENTURY.

CHRISTIAN ART - JUVENILE LITERATURE.

CHRISTIAN ART - MUSEUMS. See
    CHRISTIAN ART - GALLERIES AND
    MUSEUMS.

CHRISTIAN ART - PERIODICALS.
        BQT 5602

CHRISTIAN ART - PHILOSOPHY.
        BQT 5611-5615

CHRISTIAN ART - STUDY AND TEACHING.
        BQT 5801

            ################

CHRISTIAN ART - EASTERN CHURCHES.
    See EASTERN CHURCHES - ART.

            ################

CHRISTIAN ART (CANON LAW)
    xx Liturgical law.

CHRISTIAN BIOGRAPHY.
        BQT 2703-2771   (244.x9)
        BQX 8203-8399   (922)
    sa Abbesses
       Abbots.
       Anchoresses.
       Apostles.
       Apostolic fathers.
       Bishops.
       Blessed.
       Cardinals.
       Catholic Church - Biography.
       Clergy.
       Fathers of the church.
       Hermits.
       Martyrs.
       Missionaries.
       Pilgrim fathers.
       Popes - Biography.
       Priests - Biography.
       Puritans.
       Reformers.
       Religious biography.
       Religious orders - Biography.
       Saints.
       Theologians.

     x Biography, Christian.
       Church biography.
       Ecclesiastical biography.

    xx Biography.
       Catholic Church - Biography.
       Religious biography.

CHRISTIAN BIOGRAPHY - JUVENILE
    LITERATURE.

CHRISTIAN BIOGRAPHY - SERMONS.
        BQT 3089

CHRISTIAN BROTHERS. See
    BROTHERS OF THE CHRISTIAN SCHOOLS.

CHRISTIAN CATHOLICISM. See
    OLD CATHOLICISM.

CHRISTIAN CIVILIZATION. See
    CIVILIZATION, CHRISTIAN.

92

CHRISTIAN DEMOCRACY.
sa Catholic action.
Church and labor.
Socialism, Christian.
Trade-unions, Catholic.
xx Catholic action.
Catholic Church and social
problems.

CHRISTIAN DOCTRINE. See
CATECHETICS.
DOGMATIC THEOLOGY.
RELIGIOUS EDUCATION.

CHRISTIAN EDUCATION. See
RELIGIOUS EDUCATION.

CHRISTIAN EPIGRAPHY. See
INSCRIPTIONS, CHRISTIAN.

CHRISTIAN ETHICS.
BJ 1201-1278 (Ethics)
(170-179)
BQT 1703-2073 (Moral theology)
(24x1)
Catholic libraries will hardly have
any need for this heading. The
headings "Ethics" and "Moral
theology" should cover all situa-
tions.

CHRISTIAN EVIDENCES. See
APOLOGETICS.
CHRISTIANITY - EVIDENCES.

CHRISTIAN FAMILY. See
FAMILY, CHRISTIAN.

CHRISTIAN FLAGS. See
CHURCH PENNANTS.

CHRISTIAN GIVING.
References as in LC.

CHRISTIAN HEALING. See FAITH CURE.

CHRISTIAN HUMANISM. See
HUMANISM, CHRISTIAN.

CHRISTIAN INSCRIPTIONS. See
INSCRIPTIONS, CHRISTIAN.

CHRISTIAN LABOR UNIONS. See
TRADE-UNIONS, CATHOLIC.

CHRISTIAN LEGENDS. See
LEGENDS, CHRISTIAN.

√ CHRISTIAN LIFE.
BQT 2187-2188   (24x7)
BQT 2003-2021; BQT 2271-2287
Here are entered works dealing with
the principles of Christianity as
put into practice. The Christian
life is a conduct of life fashioned
along the teachings and ideals of
Christ and the New Testament.
sa Character.
Conduct of life.
Conversion.
Faith.
Family, Christian.
Liturgical life.
Mixed life.
Prayer.
Religious education.
Sanctification.
Spiritual life.
Third orders.
also subdivision "Religious
life" under names of classes
of persons and of institutions,
e.g., Children - Religious life;
Prisons - Religious life.
xx Asceticism.
Conduct of life.
Moral theology.
Spiritual life.

CHRISTIAN LIFE - ADDRESSES, ESSAYS,
LECTURES.

CHRISTIAN LIFE - BIBLICAL TEACHING.
xx Life - Biblical teaching.

CHRISTIAN LIFE - BIBLIOGRAPHY.

CHRISTIAN LIFE - MEDITATIONS.

CHRISTIAN LIFE - PERIODICALS.

CHRISTIAN LIFE - PICTURES, ILLUSTRA-
TIONS, ETC.
xx Homilectical illustrations.

CHRISTIAN LIFE - POETRY.

CHRISTIAN LIFE - POPULAR WORKS.
    BQT 2188

CHRISTIAN LIFE - SERMONS.

CHRISTIAN LIFE - STORIES.

CHRISTIAN LIFE - STUDY AND TEACHING.

        #################

CHRISTIAN LIFE - EARLY CHURCH.

CHRISTIAN LIFE - MIDDLE AGES.

CHRISTIAN LIFE - MODERN TIMES.

CHRISTIAN LIFE - 16th CENTURY.

CHRISTIAN LIFE - 17th CENTURY.

CHRISTIAN LIFE - 18th CENTURY.

CHRISTIAN LIFE - 19th CENTURY.

CHRISTIAN LIFE - 20th CENTURY.

        #################

CHRISTIAN LITERATURE.
        BQ   (280)
    sa Catholic literature.
       Christian poetry.
    x Literature, Christian.

CHRISTIAN LITERATURE - ADDRESSES,
    ESSAYS, LECTURES.

CHRISTIAN LITERATURE - BIBLIOGRAPHY.
        BQ 1; Z 7751   (016.28)

CHRISTIAN LITERATURE - BIO-BIBLIO-
    GRAPHY.
        BQ 95-99   (280.x091)

CHRISTIAN LITERATURE - CHARTS,
    TABLES, ETC.

CHRISTIAN LITERATURE - COLLECTIONS.
        BQ 25; BQ 302-379   (280.x08)

CHRISTIAN LITERATURE - DICTIONARIES,
    INDEXES, ETC.
        BQ 31

CHRISTIAN LITERATURE - HISTORY AND
    CRITICISM.
        BQ 87-288

CHRISTIAN LITERATURE - MANUSCRIPTS.

CHRISTIAN LITERATURE - PERIODICALS.
        BQ 2

CHRISTIAN LITERATURE - SELECTIONS.
        BQ 304-307   (280.x08)

CHRISTIAN LITERATURE - STUDY AND
    TEACHING.
        BQ 83

CHRISTIAN LITERATURE - TERMS AND
    PHRASES.

        #################

CHRISTIAN LITERATURE - GEORGIAN
    AUTHORS.
        BQ 499
    x Georgian Christian literature.

CHRISTIAN LITERATURE - GREEK AUTHORS.
        BQ 403-498
    sa Fathers of the Church, Greek.
    x Greek Christian literature.

CHRISTIAN LITERATURE - HUNGARIAN
    AUTHORS.
        BQ 499
    x Hungarian Christian literature.

CHRISTIAN LITERATURE - LATIN AUTHORS.
        BQ 5003-5318
    sa Fathers of the Church, Latin.
    x Latin Christian literature.

CHRISTIAN LITERATURE - RUSSIAN AUTHORS.
        BQ 499
    x Russian Christian literature.

        #################

CHRISTIAN LITERATURE, EARLY.
BQ 142-180   (280.x1)
sa Fathers of the church.
Literature, Medieval.
x Early Christian literature.
xx Church orders, Ancient.
Fathers of the church.
Religious literature.

CHRISTIAN LITERATURE, EARLY -
ADDRESSES, ESSAYS, LECTURES.

CHRISTIAN LITERATURE, EARLY -
BIBLIOGRAPHY.

CHRISTIAN LITERATURE, EARLY -
BIO-BIBLIOGRAPHY.
BQ 142-147

CHRISTIAN LITERATURE, EARLY -
COLLECTIONS.

CHRISTIAN LITERATURE, EARLY -
HISTORY AND CRITICISM.

CHRISTIAN LITERATURE, EARLY -
PERIODICALS.

CHRISTIAN LITERATURE, EARLY -
SELECTIONS.

################

CHRISTIAN LITERATURE, EARLY -
ARABIC AUTHORS.
BQ 3101-3198   (280.x39)

CHRISTIAN LITERATURE, EARLY -
ARMENIAN AUTHORS.
BQ 3301-3398   (280.x31)

CHRISTIAN LITERATURE, EARLY -
COPTIC AUTHORS.
BQ 3501-3598   (280.x32)

CHRISTIAN LITERATURE, EARLY -
ETHIOPIAN AUTHORS.
BQ 3701-3798   (280.x39)

CHRISTIAN LITERATURE, EARLY -
GREEK AUTHORS.
BQ 434-439   (280.x41)

CHRISTIAN LITERATURE, EARLY -
LATIN AUTHORS.
BQ 5034-5038   (280.x51)

CHRISTIAN LITERATURE, EARLY -
SYRIAC AUTHORS.
BQ 3901-3998   (280.x33)

################

CHRISTIAN LITERATURE, MEDIEVAL.
BQ 184-189   (280.x61)

CHRISTIAN LITERATURE, MODERN.
BQ 192-195   (280.x71)

CHRISTIAN NAMES. See
NAMES, PERSONAL.

CHRISTIAN PERFECTION. See
PERFECTION, CHRISTIAN.

CHRISTIAN PHILOSOPHY, EARLY. See
PHILOSOPHY, EARLY CHRISTIAN.

CHRISTIAN POETRY.
BQ 265-268
sa Catholic poetry.
x Poetry, Christian.
xx Christian literature.
Religious poetry.

CHRISTIAN POETRY, EARLY.
x Early Christian poetry.

CHRISTIAN REFORMED CHURCH.
Subdivisions and references as
in LC.

CHRISTIAN SCIENCE.   (Geog. subdiv.)
BX 6901-6997   (289.5)
References as in LC.

CHRISTIAN SCIENCE, JEWISH. See
JEWISH SCIENCE.

CHRISTIAN SCIENCE CHURCHES. See
CHURCHES, CHRISTIAN SCIENCE.

CHRISTIAN SECTS. See SECTS.

CHRISTIAN SOCIALISM. See
SOCIALISM, CHRISTIAN.

CHRISTIAN SOCIOLOGY. See
SOCIOLOGY, CHRISTIAN.

CHRISTIAN SYMBOLISM. See
SYMBOLISM, CHRISTIAN.

CHRISTIAN UNION.
        BX 1-9   (261.x8)
    Here are entered works dealing
      with Protestant views and
      efforts to unite the Christian
      denominations.
    For works on the Catholic theory
      for establishing a reunion of
      Christendom see Catholic Church
      and reunion.
    sa Catholic Church and reunion.
        Church - Unity.
        Ecumenical movement.
        Irenics.
        Lambeth Quadrilateral.
        Local church councils.
        Simultaneum.
        Unionism (Religion)
     x Church unity.
        Reunion of Christendom.
        Union, Christian.
    xx Catholic Church and reunion.
        Church.
        Ecumenical movement.
        Irenics.

CHRISTIAN YEAR. See CHURCH YEAR.

CHRISTIANITY.   (Geog. subdiv., Direct)
        BR   (200-219)
    sa Apostles.
        Catholic Church.
        Civilization, Christian.
        Councils and synods.
        Deism.
        Ecumenical movement.
        God.
        Jesus Christ.
        Miracles.
        Missions.
        Protestantism.
        Reformation.

CHRISTIANITY -- Continued.
    sa Socialism, Christian.
        Theism.
        Theology.
        also headings beginning "Christian"
          and "Church", and names of
          Christian churches and sects
          (e.g., Lutheran Church; Huguenots)
    xx Catholic Church.
        Church.
        Deism.
        God.
        Jesus Christ.
        Religions.
        Theism.
        Theology.

CHRISTIANITY - ADDRESSES, ESSAYS,
LECTURES.

CHRISTIANITY - CONGRESSES.

CHRISTIANITY - CONTROVERSIAL LITERATURE.
    sa Rationalism.

CHRISTIANITY - ESSENCE, GENIUS, NATURE.
        BR 120-121
    sa Demythologization.

CHRISTIANITY - EVIDENCES.
        BQ 1095-1255   (239.x78)
    Here are entered works in defense
      of Christianity in general. Such
      works are mostly by non-Catholic
      writers. Treatises on the evi-
      dences of Christianity from the
      Catholic viewpoint are entered
      under Apologetics.
    sa Apologetics.
        Bible - Evidences, authority, etc.
     x Christian evidences.
        Evidences of Christianity.
    xx Apologetics.
        Free thought.
        Religion and science.

CHRISTIANITY - HISTORY. See
    CATHOLIC CHURCH - HISTORY.
    CHURCH HISTORY.

CHRISTIANITY - INFLUENCE.

96

CHRISTIANITY - JUVENILE LITERATURE.
    BR 125.5

CHRISTIANITY - MISCELLANEA.

CHRISTIANITY - ORIGIN. See
    CHURCH HISTORY - PRIMITIVE AND
    EARLY CHURCH.

CHRISTIANITY - PERIODICALS.

CHRISTIANITY - PHILOSOPHY.
    BQT 234-235
  sa Transcendence of God.

CHRISTIANITY - PSYCHOLOGY.
    BR 100; BQT 245

CHRISTIANITY - QUESTIONS AND ANSWERS.
  See QUESTIONS AND ANSWERS - THEOLOGY.

CHRISTIANITY - SOURCES.
    BR 129

################

CHRISTIANITY - EARLY CHURCH.
    BR 165

CHRISTIANITY - MIDDLE AGES.
    BR 250-270

CHRISTIANITY - MODERN PERIOD.

CHRISTIANITY - 16th CENTURY.
    BR 280

CHRISTIANITY - 17th CENTURY.
    BR 120; BR 440

CHRISTIANITY - 18th CENTURY.
    BR 120; BR 470

CHRISTIANITY - 19th CENTURY.
    BR 121-125; BR 477

CHRISTIANITY - 20th CENTURY.
    BR 121-125; BR 479

################

CHRISTIANITY AND ECONOMICS.
    BR 115; BQT 3432
  sa Capitalism.
    Church and labor.
    Communism and religion.
    Economics.
    Religion and labor.
    Socialism, Christian.
    Socialism and religion.
    Sociology, Christian.
    Wealth, Ethics of.

CHRISTIANITY AND ECONOMICS - BIBLICAL
  TEACHING. See BIBLE - ECONOMICS.

CHRISTIANITY AND INTERNATIONAL AFFAIRS.
    BR 115; BQT 3469
  x Church and international affairs.
    International affairs and Chris-
    tianity.
  xx Church and social problems.

CHRISTIANITY AND LAW. See
  RELIGION AND LAW.

CHRISTIANITY AND OTHER RELIGIONS.
    BR 127-128   (290)
  sa Paganism.

CHRISTIANITY AND OTHER RELIGIONS -
  BUDDHISM, [CHINESE, GREEK, ETC.]

√ CHRISTIANITY AND OTHER RELIGIONS -
  JUDAISM.
    BM 535
  x Jews and Christianity.
  xx Judaism.

CHRISTIANITY AND OTHER RELIGIONS -
  JUDAISM - EARLY CHURCH.

CHRISTIANITY AND OTHER RELIGIONS -
  JUDAISM - MIDDLE AGES.

CHRISTIANITY AND OTHER RELIGIONS -
  JUDAISM - MODERN PERIOD.

CHRISTIANITY AND PAGANISM.
    BQX 291-299
  Here are entered works on the
    struggle of the early church
    with paganism.

CRISTIANITY AND PAGANISM -- Continued.
    x Paganism and Christianity.
    xx Church history - Primitive and
        early church.

CHRISTIANITY AND POLITICS.
      BQT 3451-3473   (261)
    sa Church and international
        organization.
       Church and state.
       Political science - Papal teaching.
     x Politics and Christianity.
       Religion and politics.
    xx Church and state.

CHRISTIANITY AND SCIENCE. See
    CATHOLIC CHURCH AND SCIENCE.
    RELIGION AND SCIENCE.

CHRISTIANITY AND WAR. See
    WAR AND RELIGION.

CHRISTIANITY IN LITERATURE.
      PN 49

CHRISTIANITY IN THE MIDRASH.
    sa Christianity in the Talmud.
    xx Christianity in the Talmud.
       Midrash.

CHRISTIANITY IN THE TALMUD.
    sa Christianity in the Midrash.
    xx Christianity in the Midrash.
       Talmud.

CHRISTIANS.

CHRISTIANS - NAME.

CHRISTIANS, JEWISH. See
    JEWISH CHRISTIANS.

CHRISTIANS IN AFRICA, [CHINA,
    INDIA, ETC.]

CHRISTIANS OF ST. JOHN. See
    MANDAEANS.

CHRISTIANS OF ST. THOMAS. See
    ST. THOMAS CHRISTIANS.

CHRISTMAS.   (Geog. subdiv., Indirect)
      GT 4985; BQT 4221
    sa Circumcision, Feast of the.
       Epiphany.
       Jesus Christ - Nativity.
     x Christmas books.
       Feast of Christmas.
    xx Jesus Christ - Nativity.

CHRISTMAS - ART.
      BQT 5858

CHRISTMAS - BIBLIOGRAPHY.
      Z 5711

CHRISTMAS - CONTROVERSIAL LITERATURE.

CHRISTMAS - DRAMA. See
    CHRISTMAS PLAYS.

CHRISTMAS - HISTORY.

CHRISTMAS - JUVENILE FILMS.

CHRISTMAS - MEDITATIONS.
      [BQT 2606.3]

CHRISTMAS - MOVING-PICTURES.

CHRISTMAS - POETRY.
      PN 6110
    sa Carols.
    xx Carols.
       Hymns.

CHRISTMAS - PRAYER-BOOKS.
      [BQT 2649]

CHRISTMAS - YEARBOOKS.

CHRISTMAS BOOKS. See
    CHRISTMAS.
    CHRISTMAS PLAYS.
    CHRISTMAS STORIES.
    GIFT-BOOKS (ANNUALS, ETC.)

CHRISTMAS CANTATAS.
    xx Cantatas, Sacred.

CHRISTMAS CARDS.
    sa Greeting cards.

98

CHRISTMAS CAROLS. See CAROLS.

CHRISTMAS DECORATIONS.
TT 157

CHRISTMAS MASS. See MISSA IN NATIVI-
TATE DOMINI NOSTRI JESU CHRISTI.

CHRISTMAS MUSIC.
M 2018-2037; M 2045; M 2065;
M 2075; M 2095   (783.28)
sa Carols.
xx Carols.
Holidays - Songs and music.
Music.

CHRISTMAS PLAYS.
PN 6120
BQ 5157
sa Crib in Christian art and
tradition.
x Christmas - Drama.
Christmas books.
Plays, Christmas.
xx Drama.
Religious drama.

CHRISTMAS PLAYS, MEDIEVAL.
x Plays, Medieval.
xx Drama, Medieval.
Religious drama.

CHRISTMAS SEALS. See
SEALS (CHRISTMAS, ETC.)

CHRISTMAS SEASON.
BQT 4221
xx Church year.

CHRISTMAS SEASON - MEDITATIONS.
[BQT 2606.3]

CHRISTMAS SERMONS.
BQT 2994   (252.x21)
x Sermons, Christmas.

CHRISTMAS SERVICE.
BQT 4221
sa Officium in Nativitate Domini
Nostri Jesu Christi.

CHRISTMAS STORIES.
PN 6071
x Christmas books.

CHRISTMAS TREES.

CHRISTMAS TREES - JUVENILE LITERATURE.

CHRISTOLOGY. See JESUS CHRIST.

CHRISTOPHER MOVEMENT.
BQT 3531
xx Catholic action.

CHRONICLES, BOOKS OF. See
BIBLE. O.T. PARALIPOMENON.

CHRONOLOGY, BIBLICAL. See
BIBLE - CHRONOLOGY.

CHRONOLOGY, ECCLESIASTICAL.
BQX 43
sa Church calendar.
Feasts, Ecclesiastical.
x Church chronology.
Church history - Chronology.
Ecclesiastical chronology.
xx Church calendar.
Feasts, Ecclesiastical.

CHRONOLOGY, ECCLESIASTICAL - CHARTS.

CHRONOLOGY, HEBREW.
CE 35
sa Bible - Chronology.
Other references as in LC.

CHURCH.
BQT 302-396   (23x9.3)
sa Catholic Church.
Catholic Church and reunion.
Christian union.
Christianity.
Communion of saints.
Ecumenical movement.
Kingdom of God.
Mystical Body of Christ.
Salvation outside the church.
x Ecclesiology.

CHURCH -- Continued.
  xx Apologetics.
     Catholic Church.
     Dogmatic theology.
     Mystical Body of Christ.

CHURCH - ADDRESSES, ESSAYS, LECTURES.

CHURCH - APOSTOLICITY.
     BQT 393   (23x9.36)
  sa Apostolic succession.
     Popes - Primacy.
   x Apostolicity of the Church.
  xx Church - Marks.

CHURCH - AUTHORITY.
     BQT 324-361
  sa Liberty of speech in the church.
  xx Authority (Religion)

CHURCH - BIBLICAL TEACHING.

CHURCH - BIBLICAL TEACHING - O.T.

CHURCH - BIBLICAL TEACHING - N.T.

CHURCH - CATHOLICITY.
     BQT 394   (23x9.36)
  xx Catholic Church - Name.
     Catholicity.
     Church - Marks.

CHURCH - FOUNDATION.
     BQT 305
  sa Popes - Primacy.
   x Church - Historicity.
     Jesus Christ - Foundation of
      the church.

CHURCH - HISTORICITY. See
  CHURCH - FOUNDATION.

CHURCH - HISTORY OF DOCTRINES.
  sa Church - Biblical teaching.

CHURCH - HISTORY OF DOCTRINES -
  EARLY CHURCH.

CHURCH - HISTORY OF DOCTRINES -
  MIDDLE AGES.

CHURCH - HISTORY OF DOCTRINES -
  MODERN PERIOD.

CHURCH - HISTORY OF DOCTRINES -
  16th, [17th, etc.] CENTURY.

CHURCH - HOLINESS.
     BQT 395   (23x9.36)
  xx Church - Marks.

CHURCH - INDEFECTIBILITY.
     BQT 381
  Here are entered works on the
     quality of unfailingness in the
     Church, externally and internally.

CHURCH - INFALLIBILITY. *See Infallibility*
     BQT 381   (23x9.32)
  sa Popes - Infallibility.
   x Catholic Church - Infallibility.
  xx Authority (Religion)
     Church - Teaching office.

CHURCH - JUVENILE LITERATURE.

CHURCH - MARKS.
     BQT 391-396   (23x9.36)
  sa Church - Apostolicity.
     Church - Catholicity.
     Church - Holiness.
     Church - Unity.
   x Marks of the church.

CHURCH - MISSION.
     BQT 344
   x Mission of the Church
CHURCH - MOTHERHOOD.
     BQT 381
   x Mater ecclesia.

CHURCH - NECESSITY.
     BQT 381

CHURCH - PICTORIAL WORKS.

CHURCH - SERMONS.
     BQT 303; BQT 3062

CHURCH - STUDY AND TEACHING.

✓ CHURCH - TEACHING ~~OFFICE~~ *authority*
    BQT 249; BQT 327
    BQV230 1322-1408 (Canon law)
      (348.x44)
  Here are entered works dealing with
    the Church's divinely appointed
    authority to teach the truths of
    religion.
  sa Catechetics.
    Censorship (Canon law)
    Church - Infallibility.
    Church and education.
    Index librorum prohibitorum.
    Missions.
    Preaching.
    Profession of faith.
    Religious education.
    Rule of faith.
    Theological seminaries.
 ✓ x Magisterium ~~ecclesiae~~. *authority*
  ✓ Teaching ~~office~~ of the church.
  xx Authority (Religion)

CHURCH - TYPOLOGY.
  xx Typology (Theology)

CHURCH - UNITY.
    BQT 396   (23x9.36)
  Here are entered theological
    treatises proving that unity is a
    mark of the true Church of Christ.
  xx Catholic Church and reunion.
    Christian union.
    Church - Marks.

CHURCH - UNITY - HISTORY OF DOCTRINES.

CHURCH - VISIBILITY.
    BQT 381

CHURCH (CANON LAW)

CHURCH (THE WORD)

CHURCH, APOSTOLIC. See CHURCH
  HISTORY - PRIMITIVE AND EARLY
  CHURCH.

CHURCH ACCOUNTING. See
  CHURCH FINANCE - ACCOUNTING.

CHURCH AND COLLEGE.   (Geog. subdiv.)
    LC 383   (377.8; 261.5)
  sa Church and education.
    Education and state.
    Universities and colleges -
     Religion.
  x College and church.
    Education and church.
  xx Church and education.
    Religious education.

CHURCH AND COLLEGE - GREAT BRITAIN,
[INDIA, U.S., ETC.]
    LA (History of education)
    LC 321-629 (Religion and
     education)

CHURCH AND ECONOMICS.
  sa Church and industry.

CHURCH AND EDUCATION.
    BQV 313-315   (261.5)
    LC 351-629   (377.1)
    LA 91-131 (History of
     education)
  "Here are entered treatises on the
    relation of the church to educa-
    tion in general, and works on the
    history of the part that the
    church has taken in secular edu-
    cation. Works limited to any
    special denomination are entered
    under that denomination with
    subdivision "Education" (e.g.,
    Presbyterian Church in the
    U.S.A. - Education)
  "Works on the history and theory of
    religious education are entered
    under Religious education." LC

  sa Bible in the schools.
    Catholic education.
    Church and college.
    Church schools.
    Missions - Educational work.
    Teaching, Freedom of.
    Theology - Study and teaching.

  x Education and church.
    Education and religion.
    Religion and education.

CHURCH AND EDUCATION -- Continued.
  xx Church - Teaching office.
    Church and college.
    Church and state.
    Religious education.
    Theology - Study and teaching.

CHURCH AND EDUCATION IN CONNECTICUT,
  [ITALY, U.S., ETC.]

CHURCH AND INDUSTRY.
    BV 628
  x Industry and the church.
  xx Church and economics.
    Church and labor.
    Church and social problems.
    Sociology, Christian.

CHURCH AND INTERNATIONAL AFFAIRS. See
  CHRISTIANITY AND INTERNATIONAL
  AFFAIRS.

CHURCH AND INTERNATIONAL ORGANIZATION.
  x International organization and
    the church.
  xx Christianity and politics.
    Church and social problems.
    Church and state.

CHURCH AND INTERNATIONAL ORGANIZATION -
  CATHOLIC CHURCH.

CHURCH AND LABOR.
    BQT 3440   (261)
  sa Christianity and economics.
    Church and industry.
    Judaism and labor.
    Labor Day Mass.
    Priest-worker movement.
    Trade-unions, Catholic.
  x Catholic Church and labor.
    Labor and the church.
  xx Christian democracy.
    Christianity and economics.
    Church and social problems.
    Religion and labor.

CHURCH AND MOVING-PICTURES, CATHOLIC.
  See MOVING-PICTURES AND CATHOLIC
  CHURCH.

CHURCH AND SCIENCE. See
  CATHOLIC CHURCH AND SCIENCE.
  RELIGION AND SCIENCE.

CHURCH AND SLAVERY. See
  SLAVERY AND THE CHURCH.

CHURCH AND SOCIAL PROBLEMS.   (Geog.
  subdiv.)
  "Here are entered works dealing
    with the origin and treatment of
    social problems from the point of
    view of the church. The rela-
    tionship of this heading to So-
    ciology, Christian, is that of
    the concrete to abstract, prac-
    tice to theory, and works to
    which these headings are appro-
    priate are classified respec-
    tively in social reform or the-
    ology. Works covering both as-
    pects are entered under the one
    heading which more nearly ex-
    presses the primary interest of
    the work." LC
  sa Christianity and international
    affairs.
    Church and industry.
    Church and international organi-
      zation.
    Church and labor.
    Church charities.
    Civilization, Christian.
    Integrated churches.
    Judaism and social problems.
    Non church-allliated people.
    Slavery and the church.
    Socialism, Christian.
    Sociology, Christian.
  x Religion and social problems.
    Social problems and the church.
  xx Church and labor.
    Church work.
    Civilization, Christian.
    Religion and sociology.
    Social service.
    Socialism, Christian.
    Sociology, Christian.
  Cf. note under Sociology, Christian.

CHURCH AND SOCIAL PROBLEMS - ADDRESSES,
  ESSAYS, LECTURES.

CHURCH AND SOCIAL PROBLEMS - CATHOLIC
  CHURCH. See CATHOLIC CHURCH AND
  SOCIAL PROBLEMS.

CHURCH AND SOCIAL PROBLEMS - CONGRESSES.

✓ CHURCH + POLITICS x Church and
world politics
Politics and
the church

102

CHURCH AND SOCIAL PROBLEMS - HISTORY.

CHURCH AND SOCIAL PROBLEMS - STUDY
AND TEACHING.

CHURCH AND SOCIAL PROBLEMS - ANGLICAN
COMMUNION, [LUTHERAN CHURCH, ETC.]

CHURCH AND STATE.
      BQT 3464-3466   (23x9.43)
      BQV 267-296
   sa Appeal as from abuse.
      Asylum, Right of.
      Bishops - Temporal power.
      Caesaropapism.
      Christianity and politics.
      Church and education.
      Church and international organi-
        zation.
      Church lands.
      Church polity.
      Church property.
      Church representation.
      Concordats.
      Ecclesiastical law.
      Government, Resistance to.
      Investiture.
      Jus primarium precum.
      Jus reformandi.
      Liberty of conscience.
      Nationalism and religion.
      Patronage, Ecclesiastical.
      Placitum regium.
      Popes - Temporal power.
      Pragmatic sanctions.
      Religion and state.
      Religious education - Law and
        legislation.
      Religious liberty.
      Secularization.
      Taxation, Exemption from.
      Theocracy.
    x Catholic Church - Relation to
        the state.
      State and Church.
   xx Catholic Church - Government.
      Christianity and politics.
      Church history.
      Nationalism and religion.
      Political science.
      Popes - Temporal power.
      Religion and state.
      Religious liberty.

CHURCH AND STATE - ADDRESSES,
   ESSAYS, LECTURES.

CHURCH AND STATE - BIBLICAL TEACHING.

CHURCH AND STATE - HISTORY.

CHURCH AND STATE - HISTORY - SOURCES.

CHURCH AND STATE - PAPAL TEACHING.

CHURCH AND STATE - SERMONS.

CHURCH AND STATE - STUDY AND TEACHING.

################

CHURCH AND STATE - CATHOLIC CHURCH.
   x Catholic Church and state.

CHURCH AND STATE - JUDAISM. See
   SOCIOLOGY, JEWISH.

CHURCH AND STATE - MOHAMMEDANISM. See
   SOCIOLOGY, MOHAMMEDAN.

CHURCH AND STATE - PRESBYTERIAN
   CHURCH, [ETC.]

################

CHURCH AND STATE IN CANADA, [FRANCE,
   ITALY, ETC.]
      BQV 272

CHURCH AND STATE IN AUSTRIA.
   sa Josephinism.

CHURCH AND STATE IN BAVARIA.
   sa Concordat of 1924 (Bavaria)

CHURCH AND STATE IN FRANCE.
   sa L'Action francaise.
      Gallicanism.

CHURCH AND STATE IN GERMANY.
   sa Kulturkampf.

CHURCH AND STATE IN GERMANY - 1933-1945.
   sa Concordat of 1933 (Germany)

CHURCH AND STATE IN GERMANY - 1945-
      BQX 1957.5

CHURCH AND STATE IN GREAT BRITAIN.
  Explanatory note, classifications and
    references as in LC.

CHURCH AND STATE IN RUSSIA.
    BQX 6046

CHURCH AND STATE IN RUSSIA - 1917-
    BQX 6066

CHURCH AND STATE IN SWEDEN.
  sa Konventikelplakatet, 1726.

CHURCH AND STATE IN THE U.S.
    BQX 4325

CHURCH AND THEATER.
    BQT 3498
  sa Catholic drama.
   x Theater and church.
  xx Religious drama.

CHURCH AND WAR. See
  WAR AND RELIGION.
CHURCH and WORLD POLITICS see
church + politics
CHURCH ANNOUNCEMENTS. (Geog. subdiv.,
  Direct)
  xx Advertising - Churches.
    Church work.

CHURCH ANTIQUITIES. See
  CHRISTIAN ANTIQUITIES.

CHURCH ARCHITECTURE.   (Geog. subdiv.,
  Direct)
    BQT 5912-5989   (726)
  sa Abbeys.
    Architecture and religion.
    Basilicas.
    Cathedrals.
    Chapels.
    Church decoration and
      ornament.
    Crypts.
    Jaquemarts.
    Lichgates.
    Martyria.
    Mosques.
    Orientation (Architecture)
    Orientation (Religion)
    Orientation of churches.
    Spires.

CHURCH ARCHITECTURE -- Continued.
  sa Sunday-school buildings.
    Temples.
    Towers.
    Vaults.
   x Architecture, Church.
    Architecture, Ecclesiastical.
    Church building.
    Ecclesiastical architecture.
    Religious art.
  xx Architecture.
    Architecture and religion.
    Christian antiquities.
    Christian art.
    Churches.

CHURCH ARCHITECTURE - DECORATION AND
  ORNAMENT. See CHURCH DECORATION
  AND ORNAMENT.

CHURCH ARCHITECTURE - DESIGNS AND
  PLANS.
    BQT 5918   (726.5)

CHURCH ARCHITECTURE - DETAILS.
    BQT 5932-5934   (726.59)

CHURCH ARCHITECTURE - HANDBOOKS,
  MANUALS, ETC.
    BQT 5914

CHURCH ARCHITECTURE - HISTORY.
    BQT 5962-6989

CHURCH ARCHITECTURE - HISTORY -
  EARLY PERIOD.

CHURCH ARCHITECTURE - HISTORY -
  MIDDLE AGES.

CHURCH ARCHITECTURE - HISTORY -
  MODERN PERIOD.

CHURCH ARCHITECTURE - HISTORY -
  20th CENTURY.

CHURCH ARCHITECTURE - PERIODICALS.
    BQT 5912

CHURCH ARCHITECTURE - VIEWS.
    BQT 5917

104

CHURCH ARCHITECTURE (CANON LAW)
  sa Cathedrals (Canon law)

CHURCH ARCHITECTURE, BAROQUE.
      BQT 5983-5984
  x Baroque church architecture.

CHURCH ARCHITECTURE, BYZANTINE.
      BQT 5965-5966
  x Byzantine church architecture.

CHURCH ARCHITECTURE, GOTHIC.
      BQT 5971-5980
  sa Architecture, Cistercian.
  x Gothic church architecture.

CHURCH ARCHITECTURE, RENAISSANCE.
      BQT 5981-5982
  x Renaissance church architecture.

CHURCH ARCHITECTURE, ROCOCO.
      BQT 5983-5984
  x Rococo church architecture.

CHURCH ARCHITECTURE, ROMAN.
      BQT 5963-5964
  x Roman church architecture.

CHURCH ARCHITECTURE, ROMANESQUE.
      BQT 5967-5968
  x Romanesque church architecture.

CHURCH ARCHITECTURE, RURAL.
  x Rural church architecture.

CHURCH ARCHIVES. See
  ARCHIVES, CHURCH.

Church art + environment
  x Church decoration + ornament
CHURCH ATTENDANCE.
  sa Public worship.
  x Attendance, Church.
    Church going.
  xx Worship.

CHURCH ATTENDANCE - LAW AND
  LEGISLATION.

CHURCH ATTENDANCE (CANON LAW)
  xx Mass (Canon law)

CHURCH BANNERS. See
  CHURCH PENNANTS.

CHURCH BELLS. See BELLS.

CHURCH BENEFICES. See
  BENEFICES, ECCLESIASTICAL.

CHURCH BIOGRAPHY. See
  CHRISTIAN BIOGRAPHY.

CHURCH BUILDINGS. See
  CHURCH ARCHITECTURE.
  CHURCHES.

CHURCH CALENDAR. prefer Church year
      BQT 4192-4214   (529.44)
      [BQX 36]
  sa Almanacs, Catholic.
    Chronology, Ecclesiastical.
    Easter controversy.
    Fast days.
    Feasts, Ecclesiastical.
  x Calendar, Ecclesiastical.
    Computus ecclesiastical.
    Ecclesiastical calendar.
    Heortology.
    Liturgy - Calendar.
  xx Chronology, Ecclesiastical.
    Church year.
    Feasts, Ecclesiastical.

CHURCH CALENDAR - EASTERN CHURCHES. See
  EASTERN CHURCHES - CHURCH CALENDAR.

CHURCH CAMPS.
      BV 1650
      BX 7830 (Church of Brethren)
  x Camps (Church)
  xx Church work with children.
    Church work with youth.
    Vacation schools, Religious.

CHURCH CENSUS.
      BQT 3309
  sa Registers of births, etc. (Canon
      law)
  x Census, Church.
  xx Church statistics.

CHURCH CHARITIES.
      BQT 3658-3699
      HV 530
  sa Catholic Church - Charities.
    also subdivision "Charities"
      under names of churches and

CHURCH CHARITIES -- Continued.
     denominations, e.g., Methodist
     Episcopal Church - Charities.
  x Religious social work.
 xx Church and social problems.
   Church finance.

CHURCH CHRONOLOGY. See
  CHRONOLOGY, ECCLESIASTICAL.

CHURCH COMMANDMENTS. See
  COMMANDMENTS OF THE CHURCH.

CHURCH CONSECRATION. See
  CHURCH DEDICATION.

CHURCH CORRESPONDENCE.
    BV 652
  x Correspondence, Church.
 xx Church work.

CHURCH COSTUME. See
  CHURCH VESTMENTS.

CHURCH COUNCILS. See
  COUNCILS AND SYNODS.

CHURCH COUNCILS, LOCAL. See
  LOCAL CHURCH COUNCILS.

CHURCH COURTS. See
  ECCLESIASTICAL COURTS.

CHURCH DECORATION AND ORNAMENT. *see*
  (Geog. subdiv., Indirect) *Church art*
    BQT 5936-5939 (246) *+ environment*
 sa Altarpieces.
   Altars.
   Aumbries.
   Choir-stalls.
   Christian art.
   Church furniture.
   Flower arrangement in churches.
   Fonts.
   Glass painting and decoration.
   Mosaics.
   Mural painting and decoration.
   Sacrament houses.
   Screens (Church decoration)
   Ship models (Church decoration)

CHURCH DECORATION AND ORNAMENT -- Con-
  tinued.
  x Church architecture - Decoration
    and ornament.
   Church ornament.
   Decoration, Church.
   Ecclesiastical decoration and
    ornament.
 xx Christian art.
   Church architecture.
   Churches.
   Decoration and ornament.
   Interior decoration.

CHURCH DEDICATION.
    BQT 4479
 sa Corner stones, Laying of.
  x Church consecration.
   Churches - Dedication and con-
    secration.
   Consecration of churches.
   Dedication of churches.
 xx Dedication services.

CHURCH DEDICATION - SERMONS.
    BQT 3005   (252.x5)
 xx Occasional sermons.
   Sermons, Church dedication.

CHURCH DEDICATION (CANON LAW)
    BQV230 1165-1167   (348.x413)
 xx Churches (Canon law)

CHURCH DESECRATION. See SACRILEGE.

CHURCH DISCIPLINE.
 sa Asceticism.
   Canon law.
   Moral theology.
  x Discipline, Ecclesiastical.
   Ecclesiastical discipline.

CHURCH DISCIPLINE - EARLY CHURCH.
 xx Church history - Primitive and
    early church.
   Church orders, Ancient.

CHURCH DISCIPLINE (CANON LAW)
 sa Precepts (Canon law)

CHURCH ENTERTAINMENTS.
    x Church sociables.
    xx Amusements.

CHURCH ETIQUETTE.
        BQT 223
        BJ 2018
    sa Clergy - Etiquette.
    x Catholic Church - Ceremonies
        and practices.
        Etiquette, Church.
    xx Conduct of life.
        Rites and ceremonies (Catholic)

CHURCH EXTENSION. See
    MISSIONS, HOME.

CHURCH FABRIC. See
    CHURCH MAINTENANCE AND REPAIR.

CHURCH FAIRS. See
    BAZAARS, CHARITABLE.

CHURCH FATHERS. See
    FATHERS OF THE CHURCH.

CHURCH FESTIVALS. See
    FEASTS, ECCLESIASTICAL.

CHURCH FINANCE.   (Geog. subdiv.,
    Direct)
        BQT 3311-3321   (259)
        BV 770-777
    sa Annates.
        Catholic Church - Finance.
        Church charities.
        Church lands.
        Church property.
        Church support.
        Church tax.
        Church work - Forms, blanks,
            etc.
        Easter dues.
        Parishes - Finance.
        Pews and pew rights.
        Taxation, Exemption from.
        Tithes.
        also subdivision "Finance" under
            names of churches (e.g., Church
            of England - Finance) and under
            special topics (e.g., Missions -
            Finance)

CHURCH FINANCE -- Continued.
    x Finance, Church.
    xx Annates.
        Catholic Church - Government.

CHURCH FINANCE - ACCOUNTING.
    x Church accounting.

CHURCH FLAGS. See
    CHURCH PENNANTS.

CHURCH FLOWER ARRANGEMENT. See
    FLOWER ARRANGEMENT IN CHURCHES.

CHURCH FURNITURE.
        BQT 5941-5959   (254.x4)
    sa Altarpieces.
        Altars.
        Aumbries.
        Baldachins.
        Candles and lights.
        Canopies.
        Chairs (Cathedra)
        Choir-stalls.
        Confessionals (Architecture)
        Crucifixes.
        Easter sepulcher.
        Fonts.
        Pulpits.
        Sacrament houses.
        Sacred vessels.
        Screens (Church decoration)
        Tabernacles.
     x Ecclesiastical furniture.
    xx Christian antiquities.
        Christian art.
        Church decoration and ornament.
        Furniture.

CHURCH-GOING. See CHURCH ATTENDANCE.

CHURCH GOODS. See CHURCH SUPPLIES.

CHURCH GOVERNMENT. See
    CHURCH POLITY.

CHURCH GROUP WORK.
    x Group work, Church.
    xx Church societies.
        Church work.

CHURCH HISTORIANS.
     BQ 239; BQX 46-47
  sa Catholic historians.
   x Historians, Church.
  xx Catholic historians.

CHURCH HISTORY.
     BQX   (270)
  sa Abbeys.
    Bishops.
    Catholic Church - History.
    Christian antiquities.
    Church and state.
    Convents.
    Councils and synods.
    Creeds.
    Dioceses.
    Ecclesiastical geography.
    Episcopacy.
    Fathers of the church.
    Hagiography.
    Inquisition.
    Martyrs.
    Miracles.
    Missions.
    Persecution.
    Popes.
    Protestant churches.
    Protestantism.
    Reformation.
    Religious orders.
    Sects.
    also headings beginning with
      the word "Christian"; the
      subdivision "Church history"
      under names of countries,
      cities, etc.; and names of
      denominations, sects,
      churches, councils, etc.
   x Christianity - History.
    Ecclesiastical history.
    History, Church.
    Religious history.
  xx Catholic Church - History.
    History.
    Sacred sciences.

CHURCH HISTORY - ADDRESSES, ESSAYS,
  LECTURES.
     BQX 85   (270.x04)

CHURCH HISTORY - ATLASES. See
  ECCLESIASTICAL GEOGRAPHY - MAPS.

CHURCH HISTORY - BIBLIOGRAPHY.
     BQX 1
     Z 7777-7779   (016.27)

CHURCH HISTORY - BIOGRAPHY.

CHURCH HISTORY - CATECHISMS,
  QUESTION-BOOKS.

CHURCH HISTORY - CHRONOLOGY. See
  CHRONOLOGY, ECCLESIASTICAL.

CHURCH HISTORY - COLLECTED WORKS.

CHURCH HISTORY - CRUSADES. See
  CRUSADES.

CHURCH HISTORY - DICTIONARIES.
     BQX 31   (270.x03)

CHURCH HISTORY - ERRORS, INVENTIONS,
  ETC.
     BQX 87
  xx Anti-Catholic polemic.

CHURCH HISTORY - HISTORIOGRAPHY.

CHURCH HISTORY - INQUISITION. See
  INQUISITION.

CHURCH HISTORY - JUVENILE LITERATURE.
     BQX 83

CHURCH HISTORY - MAPS. See
  ECCLESIASTICAL GEOGRAPHY - MAPS.

CHURCH HISTORY - OUTLINES, SYLLABI,
  ETC.
     BQX 73   (270.x02)

CHURCH HISTORY - PERIODICALS.
     BQX 3   (270.x05)

CHURCH HISTORY - PERSECUTIONS. See
  PERSECUTIONS.

CHURCH HISTORY - PHILOSOPHY.
     BQX 38   (270.x01)

108

CHURCH HISTORY - PHILOSOPHY - SOURCES.

CHURCH HISTORY - PICTURES, ILLUSTRA-
TIONS, ETC.
[BQX 35]

CHURCH HISTORY - POPULAR WORKS.
BQX 83

CHURCH HISTORY - SERMONS.
BQX 85; BQT 3089

CHURCH HISTORY - SOCIETIES.
BQX 11

CHURCH HISTORY - SOURCES.
BQX 24

CHURCH HISTORY - STUDY AND TEACHING.
BQX 71

CHURCH HISTORY - TEXTBOOKS.
BQX 81-82   (270.x02)

CHURCH HISTORY - TEXTBOOKS - 19th
CENTURY.

CHURCH HISTORY - TEXTBOOKS - 20th
CENTURY.

################

CHURCH HISTORY - PRIMITIVE AND
EARLY CHURCH.
BQX 232-449   (270.1)
sa Acta martyrum.
Apologetics - History - Early
church.
Apostles.
Apostolic Fathers.
Asceticism - History - Early
church.
Canon law - Early church.
Catacombs.
Church discipline - Early church.
Church orders, Ancient.
Church polity - Early church.
Dogmatic theology - History -
Early church.
Fathers of the church.
Funeral rites and ceremonies -
Early church.

CHURCH HISTORY - PRIMITIVE AND
EARLY CHURCH -- Continued.
sa Heresies and heretics - Early
church.
Italy - Church history - Early
period to 570.
Jewish Christians - Early church.
Liturgy - History - Early church.
Missions - History - Early period.
Moral theology - History - Early
church.
Mysticism - History - Early church.
Neoplatonism.
Persecutions - Early church.
Religious life - Early church.
Religious orders - History -
Early church.
Religious thought - Ancient
period.
Schism, Acacian, 484-519.
x Apostolic church.
Catholic Church - History -
Early period.
Christianity - Origin.
Church, Apostolic.
Primitive Christianity.
xx Catacombs.
Church orders, Ancient.
Fathers of the church.

CHURCH HISTORY - PRIMITIVE AND
EARLY CHURCH - BIBLIOGRAPHY.

CHURCH HISTORY - PRIMITIVE AND
EARLY CHURCH - BIOGRAPHY.

CHURCH HISTORY - PRIMITIVE AND
EARLY CHURCH - FICTION.

CHURCH HISTORY - PRIMITIVE AND
EARLY CHURCH - SOURCES.

CHURCH HISTORY - APOSTOLIC AGE TO 313.
BQX 241-355   (270.1)

CHURCH HISTORY - 313-590.
BQX 371-449   (270.21-270.25)

CHURCH HISTORY - 4th CENTURY.

CHURCH HISTORY - MIDDLE AGES.
  BQX 451-920 (270.3-270.5)
 sa Apologetics - History - Middle
   Ages.
  Asceticism - History - Middle
   Ages.
  Crusades.
  Inquisition.
  Missions - History - Middle Ages.
  Mysticism - History - Middle
   Ages.
  Popes - Temporal power.
  Reformation - Early movements.
  Religious life - Middle Ages.
  Religious orders - History -
   Middle Ages.
  Religious thought - Middle Ages.
  Schism, The Great Western,
   1378-1417.
  Sects, Medieval.
 x Catholic Church - History -
  Middle Ages.
 xx Middle Ages.

CHURCH HISTORY - 590-1049.
  BQX 463-622 (270.3)

CHURCH HISTORY - 1049-1305.
  BQX 631-750 (270.4)

CHURCH HISTORY - 11th CENTURY.

CHURCH HISTORY - 1305-1447.
  BQX 752-828 (270.5)

CHURCH HISTORY - 1447-1564.
  BQX 831-920

CHURCH HISTORY - REFORMATION. See
 REFORMATION.

CHURCH HISTORY - MODERN PERIOD.
  BQX 931-1131 (270.6-270.8)
 sa Catholic Church - History -
  Modern period.
  Counter-Reformation.
  Missions - History - Modern period.
  Protestantism - History.
  Reformation.
  Religious life - Modern period.

CHURCH HISTORY - MODERN PERIOD --
 Continued.
 sa Religious orders - History -
  Modern period.
  Religious thought - Modern
   period.
  Sects.
 xx Catholic Church - History -
  Modern period.

CHURCH HISTORY - 1564-1648.
  BQX 931-975

CHURCH HISTORY - 1648-1789.
  BQX 983-1014 (270.7)

CHURCH HISTORY - 17th CENTURY.

CHURCH HISTORY - 18th CENTURY.

CHURCH HISTORY - 1789-1869.
  BQX 1021-1057 (270.8)

CHURCH HISTORY - 19th CENTURY.

CHURCH HISTORY - 1870-
  BQX 1063-

CHURCH HISTORY - 20th CENTURY.

CHURCH HISTORY - 1945-
  BQX 1103

   #################

CHURCH IN LITERATURE.
 PN 56

CHURCH IN WALES.
 sa Church of England in Wales.

CHURCH LANDS. (Geog. subdiv.,
 Indirect)
 sa Parsonages.
 x Glebes.
 xx Church and state.
  Church finance.
  Church property.

CHURCH LATIN. See
 LATIN LANGUAGE - CHURCH LATIN.

CHURCH LAW. See
  CANON LAW.
  ECCLESIASTICAL LAW.

CHURCH LIBRARIES. See
  LIBRARIES, CHURCH.

CHURCH MAINTENANCE AND REPAIR.
  x Church fabric.
    Churches - Maintenance and
      repair.
  xx Buildings - Repair and recon-
      struction.

CHURCH MAINTENANCE AND REPAIR (CANON
  LAW) See CHURCH MAINTENANCE AND
  REPAIR (ECCLESIASTICAL LAW)

CHURCH MAINTENANCE AND REPAIR (EC-
  CLESIASTICAL LAW).   (Geog. subdiv., Direct)
  x Church maintenance and repair
      (Canon law)

CHURCH MEMBERSHIP.
  sa Integrated churches.
    See also subdivision "Member-
      ship" under names of churches,
      e.g., Catholic Church - Mem-
      bership.

CHURCH MUSIC.   (Geog. subdiv.,
  Indirect)
      BQT 4531-4689   (246.x8)
  Subdivided, when desirable, by
    denomination and rite as well as
    by locality (e.g., 1. Church
    music - Church of England;
    2. Church music - Byzantine rite;
    3. Church music - England)
  sa Advent music.
    Anthem.
    Carillons.
    Carols.
    Chant.
    Chapels (Music)
    Chimes and chiming.
    Choirs (Church music)
    Choral.
    Chorale.
    Conducting.
    Epiphany music.

CHURCH MUSIC -- Continued.
  sa Hymns.
    Liturgy.
    Motet.
    Music in churches.
    Oratorio.
    Organ music.
    Passion music - History and
      criticism.
    Psalmody.
    Religion and music.
    Religious drama.
    Sequences (Liturgy)
  x Catholic Church - Music.
    Ecclesiastical music.
    Liturgical music.
    Music, Church.
    Music, Sacred.
    Religious music.
    Sacred music.
  xx Liturgy.
    Music.
    Psalmody.
    Religion and music.

CHURCH MUSIC - ADDRESSES, ESSAYS,
  LECTURES.

CHURCH MUSIC - ALMANACS, YEARBOOKS,
  ETC.
  x Church music - Yearbooks.

CHURCH MUSIC - BIBLIOGRAPHY.
      BQT 4531; ML 128

CHURCH MUSIC - BIBLIOGRAPHY - CATALOGS.

CHURCH MUSIC - BIOGRAPHY. See
  MUSICIANS (CHURCH MUSIC)

CHURCH MUSIC - CHORUSES AND CHOIR
  BOOKS. See CHOIR BOOKS.

CHURCH MUSIC - COLLECTED WORKS.
      BQT 4536

CHURCH MUSIC - COLLECTIONS.
      BQT 4651-4659

CHURCH MUSIC - CONGRESSES.
      BQT 4534

CHURCH MUSIC - DICTIONARIES.
    BQT 4538

CHURCH MUSIC - HISTORY AND CRITICISM.
    BQT 4541-4575

CHURCH MUSIC - HISTORY AND CRITICISM -
    EARLY PERIOD TO 604.
    BQT 4543-4544

CHURCH MUSIC - HISTORY AND CRITICISM -
    605-1570.
    BQT 4545-4551

CHURCH MUSIC - HISTORY AND CRITICISM -
    1571-1857.
    BQT 4553-4555

CHURCH MUSIC - HISTORY AND CRITICISM -
    1858-
    BQT 4557-4559

CHURCH MUSIC - INSTRUCTION AND STUDY.
    BQT 4575

CHURCH MUSIC - LISTS OF MUSIC.
    BQT 4649

CHURCH MUSIC - MANUALS, TEXTBOOKS, ETC.
    BQT 4578

CHURCH MUSIC - MANUSCRIPTS.
    sa Chant - Manuscripts.

CHURCH MUSIC - PAPAL TEACHING.
    BQT 4539

CHURCH MUSIC - PERIODICALS.
    BQT 4532

CHURCH MUSIC - SOCIETIES.
    BQT 4534
    "Here are entered both works about
    societies for the cultivation of
    church music and publications of
    such societies." LC

CHURCH MUSIC - TERMINOLOGY.

CHURCH MUSIC - THEMATIC CATALOGS.

CHURCH MUSIC - THEORY.
    BQT 4577

CHURCH MUSIC - YEARBOOKS. See
    CHURCH MUSIC - ALMANACS, YEARBOOKS,
    ETC.

################

CHURCH MUSIC - ANGLICAN COMMUNION.

CHURCH MUSIC - BYZANTINE RITE.
    BQT 5258
    x Byzantine chant.
      Byzantine rite - Church music.
      Chant, Byzantine.

CHURCH MUSIC - CHURCH SLAVIC.
    x Church Slavic music.

CHURCH MUSIC - CHURCH OF ENGLAND.
    ML 3166
    x Church of England - Church music.

CHURCH MUSIC - CONGREGATIONAL CHURCHES.

CHURCH MUSIC - EASTERN CHURCHES.
    x Eastern Churches - Church music.

CHURCH MUSIC - LUTHERAN CHURCH.
    ML 3168

CHURCH MUSIC - MARONITE RITE.
    BQT 5164
    x Maronite Rite - Church music.

CHURCH MUSIC - ORTHODOX EASTERN
    CHURCH.
    BQT 5258; ML 3060
    x Orthodox Eastern Church - Church
      music.

CHURCH MUSIC - PROTESTANT CHURCHES.
    ML 3100-3188

CHURCH MUSIC - PROTESTANT EPISCOPAL
    CHURCH IN THE U.S.A.
    ML 3166

################

CHURCH MUSIC (CANON LAW)
    BQT 4578-4579
    BQC230 1264   (348.x415)
xx Liturgical law.

CHURCH MUSIC, POLYPHONIC. See
POLYPHONIC CHURCH MUSIC.

CHURCH-NIGHT SERVICES.
  sa Vespers.
   x Mid-week services.
     Week-night services.
  xx Church work.
     Prayer-meetings.
     Public worship.
     Vespers.

CHURCH OF ABYSSINIA. See
ETHIOPIC CHURCH.

CHURCH OF CHRIST, SCIENTIST.
     BX 6901-6997   (289.5)
  "Here are entered official pub-
     lications of the church, in-
     cluding hymn-books, etc. For
     other works about the church
     see Christian science." LC

CHURCH OF CHRIST OF LATTER-DAY SAINTS.
  See CHURCH OF JESUS CHRIST OF
  LATTER-DAY SAINTS.
  also MORMONS AND MORMONISM.

CHURCH OF ENGLAND.
     BX 5011-5207   (283)
  References as in LC.

CHURCH OF ENGLAND - BIOGRAPHY.

CHURCH OF ENGLAND - CLERGY.
   x Clergy - Church of England.

CHURCH OF ENGLAND - LAW.
     BX 5150-5173
   x Anglican canon law.
     Canon law, Anglican.

Other subdivisions under Church
  of England as in LC.

################

CHURCH OF ENGLAND. ARTICLES OF
  RELIGION.
   x Thirty-nine articles.

CHURCH OF ENGLAND. BOOK OF COMMON
  PRAYER.
   x Book of Common Prayer.
     Prayer Book - Church of England.

CHURCH OF ENGLAND. LITURGY AND RITUAL.
   x Anglican Liturgy.
     Subdivisions as in LC.

################

CHURCH OF ENGLAND IN AMERICA.
     BX 5881   (283.073)
  Explanatory note and references as
  in LC.

CHURCH OF ENGLAND IN CONNECTICUT,
  [MARYLAND, ETC.]

CHURCH OF ENGLAND IN IRELAND. See
  CHURCH OF IRELAND.

CHURCH OF ENGLAND IN SCOTLAND. See
  EPISCOPAL CHURCH IN SCOTLAND.

CHURCH OF ENGLAND IN WALES.
  xx Church in Wales.

CHURCH OF ETHIOPIA. See
  ETHIOPIC CHURCH.

CHURCH OF GOD.
     BX 7020
  "Here are entered works on the
     various religious bodies using
     the words "Church of God" in
     their name." LC
  sa Holiness churches.
  xx Holiness churches.
     Pentecostal churches.

CHURCH OF IRELAND.
     BX 5410-5595
   x Church of England in Ireland.
     Episcopal Church.
     Established Church of Ireland.
     Irish Church.
  Subdivisions as in LC.

CHURCH OF JESUS CHRIST OF LATTER-DAY
SAINTS.
BX 8601-8695
"Here are entered the official publications of the church, including
also its liturgy and ritual,
hymn-books, etc. For other works
about the church see Mormons and
Mormonism." LC
x Church of Christ of Latter-day
Saints.
xx Mormons and Mormonism.

CHURCH OF SCOTLAND.
BX 9075-9079   (285.2)
sa Covenanters.
Presbyterian Church.
Presbyterianism.
Subdivisions as in LC.

CHURCH OF THE BRETHREN.
BX 7801-7843
x Dunkards.
German Baptist Brethren.
xx Anabaptists.

CHURCH OF THE NAZARENE.

CHURCH OF THE NEW JERUSALEM. See
NEW JERUSALEM CHURCH.

CHURCH OFFICERS.
sa Church secretaries.
Church ushers.
Installation service (Church
officers)

CHURCH ORDERS, ANCIENT.
BQ 1250-1261
"Here are entered works dealing with
one or more of a group of closely
related early compositions containing rules and regulations,
usages and practices governing the
discipline, cult and management
of church affairs in general,
which were believed to have been
formulated by the apostles. They
are prominent among the sources
of liturgy and of later compila-
tions of canon law, with which
they are not to be confused." LC

CHURCH ORDERS, ANCIENT -- Continued.
sa Canon law.
Christian literature, Early.
Church discipline - Early church.
Church history - Primitive and
early church.
Dogmatic theology - History -
Early church.
Fathers of the church.
Liturgy - History - Early church.
xx Church history - Primitive and
early church.

CHURCH ORDERS, LUTHERAN, [PROTESTANT,
REFORMED, ETC.]

CHURCH ORNAMENT. See
CHURCH DECORATION AND ORNAMENT.

CHURCH PENNANTS. see BANNERS, CHURCH/
BQT 5846
x Banners, Church.
Christian flags.
Church banners.
Church flags.
Pennants, Church.

CHURCH PLATE.   (Geog. subdiv., Direct)
NK 7100-7215
sa Sacred vessels.

CHURCH POLITY.
BQX 101-230
BV 646-651
sa Catholic Church - Government.
Integrated churches.
Local church councils.
x Church government.
Ecclesiastical polity.
Polity, Ecclesiastical.
xx Church and state.

CHURCH POLITY - EARLY CHURCH.
xx Church history - Primitive and
early church.

CHURCH POLITY - MIDDLE AGES.

CHURCH PRECEPTS. See
COMMANDMENTS OF THE CHURCH.

CHURCH PROPERTY.   (Geog. subdiv.,
  Indirect)
       BQT 3319-3321   (259)
  sa Benefices, Ecclesiastical.
     Church lands.
     Convents.
     Corporations, Ecclesiastical.
     Monasteries.
     Parsonages.
     Patronage, Ecclesiastical.
     Pews and pew rights.
     Religious orders.
     Secularization.
   x Ecclesiastical property.
     Property, Church.
  xx Catholic Church - Government.
     Church and state.
     Church finance.

CHURCH PROPERTY - MAINTENANCE AND
  REPAIR.

CHURCH PROPERTY - TAXATION.
   x Charities - Taxation.
  xx Corporations, Nonprofit - Taxa-
       tion.
     Land - Taxation.
     Property tax.

CHURCH PROPERTY (CANON LAW)
       BQV230 1495-1551   (348.x46)
  sa Alienation (Canon law)
     Incorporation (Canon law)
     Mortgages (Canon law)
     Prescription (Canon law)
     Spoliation (Canon law)
     Wills (Canon law)

CHURCH PROPERTY (CANON LAW, EASTERN)

CHURCH PROPERTY (CANON LAW, ORTHODOX
  EASTERN)

CHURCH RATES.
  sa Church tax.
  xx Church tax.
     Churchwardens' accounts.

CHURCH REFORM.
     [BQT 329]
  Here are entered works dealing
    with the principles which under-
    lie any reform in the Church.

CHURCH REFORM -- Continued.
  sa Counter-Reformation.
     Reformation.
   x Reform, Church.
   x Church Renewal
CHURCH REGISTERS. See
  REGISTERS OF BIRTHS, ETC.

CHURCH REPRESENTATION.   (Geog. subdiv., Direct)
  xx Church and state.

CHURCH SCHOOLS.   (Geog. subdiv.,
  Indirect)
       BQT 3373   (257)
       LC 427-629   (377.5)
  "Here are entered works dealing
    with church schools in general,
    including buildings (site,
    equipment, sanitary provisions),
    finances, statistics, etc. Works
    treating of the educational func-
    tion of the church are entered
    under Church and education (cf.
    note under this heading.)
  "Works dealing with the schools of
    any special denomination are
    entered under that denomination,
    e.g., Presbyterian Church in the
    U.S.A. - Education." LC
  sa Rural schools, Catholic.
     Universities and colleges,
       Catholic.
     Vacation schools, Religious.
   x Catholic Church - Schools,
       Parochial.
     Denominational schools.
     Diocesan schools.
     Parish schools.
     Parochial schools.
     Schools, Denominational.
     Schools, Parochial.
  xx Catholic education.
     Catholic institutions.
     Church and education.
     Private schools.
     Religious education.

CHURCH SCHOOLS - CURRICULA.

CHURCH SCHOOLS - MANAGEMENT AND
  ORGANIZATION.

CHURCH SCHOOLS (CANON LAW)
    BQV230 1372-1383   (348.x442)

CHURCH SLAVIC LANGUAGE.
    PG 601-699   (491.81701)
 sa Liturgical language - Slavic.
  x Bulgarian Church Slavic language.
    Old Bulgarian language.
    Old Church Slavic language.
    Old Slovenian language.
    Serbian Church Slavic language.
    Slovenian language (Old)
 xx Liturgical language - Slavic.
    Subdivisions as in LC.

CHURCH SLAVIC LITERATURE.
    Subdivisions as in LC.

CHURCH SLAVIC MUSIC. See
    CHURCH MUSIC - CHURCH SLAVIC.

CHURCH SOCIABLES. See
    CHURCH ENTERTAINMENTS.

CHURCH SOCIETIES.
    BQT 3326-3339   (256)
 sa Altar gilds.
    Catholic societies.
    Church group work.
    Confraternities.
  x Societies, Church.

CHURCH SOCIETIES (CANON LAW)

CHURCH STATISTICS.   (Geog. subdiv.,
  Indirect)
 sa Church census.
    Church work - Forms, blanks, etc.
  x Ecclesiastical statistics.
    Statistics, Church.
 xx Ecclesiastical geography.
    Religious surveys.

CHURCH SUFFERING. See
    PURGATORY.

CHURCH SUPPLIES.
  x Church goods.
    Ecclesiastical supplies.
    Goods, Ecclesiastical.

CHURCH SUPPLIES (CANON LAW)
    BQV230 1296-1306   (348.x415)

CHURCH SUPPORT.
    BQT 3313-3317
 sa Pews and pew rights.
 xx Church finance.

CHURCH SUPPORT (CANON LAW)

CHURCH SYNODS. See
    COUNCILS AND SYNODS.

CHURCH TAX.   (Geog. subdiv.)
  "Here are entered works on taxes
    levied by the state for the
    support of the established church
    or of recognized religious
    bodies." LC
 sa Church rates.
    Tithes.
 xx Church finance.
    Church rates.
    Taxation.
    Tithes.

CHURCH TOWERS. See TOWERS.

CHURCH TRIUMPHANT. See
    COMMUNION OF SAINTS.
    HEAVEN.

CHURCH UNITY. See
    CATHOLIC CHURCH AND REUNION.
    CHRISTIAN UNION.

CHURCH UNITY OCTAVE.
    BQT 407
  x Chair of unity octave.
 xx Catholic Church and reunion.

CHURCH USHERS.
 xx Church officers.
    Church work.
    Ushers.

CHURCH VACATION SCHOOLS. See
    VACATION SCHOOLS, RELIGIOUS.

CHURCH VESTMENTS. *See VESTMENTS*
    BQT 4365   ~~(264.x41)~~
  sa Altar-cloths.
    Clergy - Costume.
    Colors, Liturgical.
    Costume.
    Pallium.
    Religious orders - Habit.
    Sacristans.
    Scapulars.
    Staff, Pastoral.
  x Church costume.
    Ecclesiastical costume.
    Ecclesiastical vestments.
    Liturgical vestments.
    Vestments.
  xx Christian antiquities.
    Christian art.
    Clergy - Costume.

CHURCH WORK.
    BQT 3403-3699 (Catholic)
    BV 4400-4470 (Protestant)
  Some Catholic libraries may prefer
    to enter works dealing with
    Catholic social work under Social
    service, Catholic.
  sa Chaplains, Industrial.
    Charity.
    Church and social problems.
    Church announcements.
    Church correspondence.
    Church-night services.
    Church secretaries.
    City clergy.
    Local church councils.
    Missions.
    Moving-pictures in church work.
    Pastoral counseling.
    Pastoral psychology.
    Public relations - Churches.
    Radio in religion.
    Rural clergy.
    Suburban churches.
    Television in religion.
    Visitations (Church work)

CHURCH WORK - AUDIO-VISUAL AIDS.
  xx Religious education - Audio-
    visual aids.

CHURCH WORK - CONGRESSES.

CHURCH WORK - DIRECTORIES.

CHURCH WORK - FORMS, BLANKS, ETC.
    BQT 3316
  xx Church finance.
    Church statistics.
    Registers of births, etc.

CHURCH WORK, RURAL. See
  RURAL CHURCHES.

CHURCH WORK WITH ADULTS. ~~See~~
× CHURCH WORK WITH MEN.

CHURCH WORK WITH BOYS. See
  CHURCH WORK WITH CHILDREN.

CHURCH WORK WITH CHILDREN. *See Children - Church work in*
    BQT 3541-3583
  sa Church camps.
  x Children, Church work with.
    Church work with boys.
    Church work with girls. *Church work with problem children*

CHURCH WORK WITH CRIMINALS.
    BQT 3699
  x Criminals, Church work with.

CHURCH WORK WITH EXCEPTIONAL CHILDREN.
  x Exceptional children, Church work
    with.

CHURCH WORK WITH FOREIGNERS.
    BQT 3638
  x Foreigners, Church work with.

CHURCH WORK WITH GIRLS. See
  CHURCH WORK WITH CHILDREN.

CHURCH WORK WITH JUVENILE DELINQUENTS.
  See CHURCH WORK WITH PROBLEM
  CHILDREN.

CHURCH WORK WITH MEN. *See Church Work with adults*
  ~~sa Men in church work.~~
  ~~x Church work with adults.~~
  ~~xx Men in church work.~~

CHURCH WORK WITH MENTALLY HANDICAPPED
  CHILDREN.
  x Mentally handicapped children,
    Church work with.

CHURCH WORK WITH MIGRANTS.
[3685]
sa Missions - Emigrants.
x Migrants, Church work with.

CHURCH WORK WITH PRISONERS.
BQT 3698
x Prisoners, Church work with.

CHURCH WORK WITH PROBLEM CHILDREN.
x Church work with juvenile
delinquents.
Problem children, Church work
with. *See Church work with children*

CHURCH WORK WITH SINGLE PEOPLE.
x Single people, Church work with.

CHURCH WORK WITH STUDENTS.
BQT 3652-3653
sa Chaplains, School.
Chaplains, University and
college.
Newman Club.
x Students, Church work with.

CHURCH WORK WITH THE AGED.
BQT 3669
x Aged, Church work with the.

CHURCH WORK WITH THE DEAF.
x Deaf, Church work with the.

CHURCH WORK WITH THE HANDICAPPED.
x Handicapped, Church work with the.

CHURCH WORK WITH THE INSANE. See
CHURCH WORK WITH THE MENTALLY ILL.

CHURCH WORK WITH THE MENTALLY ILL.
BQT 3694
x Church work with the insane.
xx Mentally ill - Care and treatment.

CHURCH WORK WITH THE POOR.
BQT 3668
x Poor, Church work with the.

CHURCH WORK WITH THE SICK. *See Ministry to the Sick*
BQT 3685-3694
sa Sick-calls.
x Sick, Church work with the.

CHURCH WORK WITH VETERANS.
BQT 3639-3640
x Veterans, Church work with.
xx Soldiers - Religious life.

CHURCH WORK WITH YOUTH.
BQT 3541-3590
sa Church camps.
x Youth, Church work with.

CHURCH YEAR.
BQT 4192-4236   (264.x5)
"Here are entered works on the
Christian festivals with their
cycles, as making up the Christian
or church year." LC
sa Advent.
Christmas season.
Church calendar.
Easter season.
Fast days.
Feasts, Ecclesiastical.
Lent.
Liturgy.
Pentecost season.
Septuagesima.
x Christian year.
Ecclesiastical year.
Heortology.
Liturgical year.
Year, Christian.
Year, Church.
Year, Ecclesiastical.
Year, Liturgical.
xx Feasts, Ecclesiastical.
Liturgy.

CHURCH YEAR - BIBLIOGRAPHY.

CHURCH YEAR - CATECHISMS, QUESTION-
BOOKS.

CHURCH YEAR - MEDITATIONS.
[BQT 2606.1]   (24x2.1)
xx Liturgy - Meditations.

CHURCH YEAR - POETRY.

CHURCH YEAR - POPULAR WORKS.

CHURCH YEAR - SERMONS.
　　[BQT 4208]　　(252.x1)
　　Here are entered sermons explaining
　　　the meaning of the church year.
　　For series of sermons designed to
　　　be given during the complete
　　　course of the church year see
　　　Sermons, Church year.
　　sa Bible. N.T. Epistles and gospels,
　　　Liturgical - Sermons.
　　x Church year sermons.
　　xx Sermons, Church year.

CHURCH YEAR SERMONS.　See
　　CHURCH YEAR - SERMONS.
　　SERMONS, CHURCH YEAR.

CHURCHES.　　(Geog. subdiv., Indirect)
　　　BQT 5924　　(726.5)
　　sa Baptisteries.
　　　Basilicas.
　　　Cathedrals.
　　　Chapels.
　　　Church architecture.
　　　Church decoration and ornament.
　　　Oratories.
　　　Parish houses.
　　　Parsonages.
　　　also names of individual churches,
　　　　and subdivision "Churches" under
　　　　names of cities.
　　x Church buildings.

CHURCHES - DEDICATION AND CONSECRATION.
　　See　CHURCH DEDICATION.

CHURCHES - LIBRARIES.　See
　　LIBRARIES, CHURCH.

CHURCHES - LOCATION.
　　xx Cities and towns - Planning.

CHURCHES - MAINTENANCE AND REPAIR.
　　See　CHURCH MAINTENANCE AND REPAIR.

CHURCHES - ORIENTATION.　See
　　ORIENTATION OF CHURCHES.

CHURCHES - PUBLIC RELATIONS.　See
　　PUBLIC RELATIONS - CHURCHES.

CHURCHES (CANON LAW)
　　　BQV230 1161-1187　　(348.x4)
　　sa Cathedrals (Canon law)
　　　Church dedication (Canon law)
　　　Oratories (Canon law)
　　xx Sacred places (Canon law)

CHURCHES, ANGLICAN.
　　　NA 4821
　　"Here are entered works dealing
　　　with Anglican church buildings."
　　　LC
　　x Anglican churches.
　　　Churches, Episcopal.
　　　Churches, Protestant Episcopal.
　　　Episcopal churches.
　　　Protestant Episcopal churches.

CHURCHES, BAPTIST.
　　　NA 4821
　　"Here are entered works dealing
　　　with Baptist church buildings."
　　　LC
　　x Baptist churches.

CHURCHES, CATHOLIC.
　　　NA 4820; NA 5200-6113
　　"Here are entered works dealing
　　　with Catholic church buildings."
　　　LC
　　x Catholic churches.

CHURCHES, CHRISTIAN SCIENCE.
　　"Here are entered works dealing
　　　with Christian Science church
　　　buildings."　LC
　　x Christian Science churches.

CHURCHES, CITY.　See　CITY CHURCHES.

CHURCHES, COMMUNITY.　See
　　COMMUNITY CHURCHES.

CHURCHES, COUNTRY.　See
　　RURAL CHURCHES.

CHURCHES, EASTERN.　See
　　EASTERN CHURCHES.

CHURCHES, EPISCOPAL.　See
　　CHURCHES, ANGLICAN.

CHURCHES, FEDERATED. See
    FEDERATED CHURCHES.

CHURCHES, FRIEND.
    "Here are entered works dealing
        with the meeting-houses or
        churches of the Society of
        Friends." LC
    x Friend churches.
      Friend meeting-houses.
      Meeting-houses, Friend.
    xx Friends, Society of.

CHURCHES, INTEGRATED. See
    INTEGRATED CHURCHES.

CHURCHES, METHODIST.
    "Here are entered works dealing
        with Methodist church buildings."
        LC
    x Methodist churches.

CHURCHES, MORMON.
    "Here are entered works dealing
        with Mormon church buildings."
        LC
    x Mormon churches.

CHURCHES, PROTESTANT.
        NA 5200-6113
    "Here are entered works dealing
        with Protestant church buildings.
        For the organizations worshipping
        in such buildings see Protestant
        Churches." LC

CHURCHES, PROTESTANT EPISCOPAL. See
    CHURCHES, ANGLICAN.

CHURCHES, RURAL. See
    RURAL CHURCHES.

CHURCHES, SIMULTANEOUS. See
    SIMULTANEUM.

CHURCHES, SUBURBAN. See
    SUBURBAN CHURCHES.

CHURCHES, TITULAR. See
    TITULAR CHURCHES.

CHURCHES, TOWN. See CITY CHURCHES.

CHURCHES, UNDENOMINATIONAL. See
    COMMUNITY CHURCHES.

CHURCHES, URBAN. See CITY CHURCHES.

CHURCHES IN ART.
        BQT 5896
    xx Art.

CHURCHES OF CHRIST. (Geog. subdiv.)
    Subdivisions as in LC.

CHURCHING OF WOMEN.
        BQT 4472

CHURCHWARDENS' ACCOUNTS.
    sa Church rates.

CHURCHYARDS. See CEMETERIES.

CIRCUMCELLIONS.
        BQT 75   (273.x41)
    x Agonists.
    xx Donatists.
       Heresies and heretics - Early
           church.
       Sects, Medieval.

CIRCUMCISION.
        BQT 846 (Jesus Christ)
        (225.x91)
    Other classifications and refer-
    ences as in LC.

CIRCUMCISION, FEAST OF THE.
        BQT 4225
    x Feast of the Circumcision.
    xx Christmas.

CIRCUMCISION, FEAST OF THE - SERMONS.

CISTERCIAN ARCHITECTURE. See
    ARCHITECTURE, CISTERCIAN.

CISTERCIAN BROTHERS. See
    CISTERCIANS. LAY BROTHERS.

CISTERCIAN NUNS.
        BQX 7880   (271.9)
    x Cistercians. Second Order.

CISTERCIAN NUNS, REFORMED. See
    TRAPPISTINES.

120

CISTERCIAN RITE. See
    CISTERCIANS. LITURGY AND RITUAL.

CISTERCIANS.
        BQX 7271-7278   (271.x1)
    sa Benedictines.
       Trappists.
       also individual Cistercian abbeys.
     x Citeaux, Order of.
       Order of Citeaux.
       Sacer Ordo Cisterciensis.
       White Monks.
    xx Benedictines.
       Trappists.

CISTERCIANS - BIBLIOGRAPHY.
    BQX 7273

CISTERCIANS - BIOGRAPHY.
    BQX 7273

CISTERCIANS - CANON LAW.

CISTERCIANS - DIRECTORIES.
    BQX 7272

CISTERCIANS - HISTORY.
    BQX 7272; BQX 7275

CISTERCIANS - MEDITATIONS.
    BQX 7274

CISTERCIANS - PERIODICALS.
    BQX 7271

CISTERCIANS - PRAYER-BOOKS.
    BQX 7274

CISTERCIANS - RETREATS. See
    RETREATS FOR CISTERCIANS.

CISTERCIANS - RULES.
    BQX 7272

CISTERCIANS - SPIRITUAL LIFE.
    BQX 7274

################

CISTERCIANS. CONGREGATIONS.
    BQX 7276

CISTERCIANS. LAY BROTHERS.
    [BQX 7277.8]
    x Cistercian Brothers.

CISTERCIANS. LITURGY AND RITUAL.
    BQT 4761-4769

CISTERCIANS. OBLATES.
    [BQX 7277.9]

CISTERCIANS. SECOND ORDER. See
    CISTERCIAN NUNS.

################

CISTERCIANS AND ART.
    sa Architecture, Cistercian.

CISTERCIANS AND THEOLOGY.

CITEAUX, ORDER OF. See CISTERCIANS.

CITIES AND TOWNS - RELIGIOUS LIFE.
    xx City churches.

CITY CHURCHES.   (Geog. subdiv.,
    Indirect)
        BQT 3352
        BV 637
    sa Cities and towns - Religious
        life.
       City clergy.
       Suburban churches.
     x Churches, City.
       Churches, Town.
       Churches, Urban.
       Town churches.
       Urban churches.
    xx City clergy.
       Suburban churches.

CITY CLERGY.
        BV 637.5
    sa City churches.
     x Clergy, City.
       Clergy, Urban.
       Ministry, Urban.
       Urban clergy.
       Urban ministry.
    xx Church work.
       City churches.

CIVIL ECCELSIASTICAL LAW. See
  ECCLESIASTICAL LAW.

CIVIL LAW AND CANON LAW. See
  CANON LAW AND CIVIL LAW.

CIVIL PROCEDURE (CANON LAW)
  sa Complaints (Canon law)
     Judicial sentence (Canon law)
     Lis pendens (Canon law)
     Matrimonial actions (Canon law)
     Prorogation (Canon law)
     Summons (Canon law)
  xx Procedure (Canon law)
     Trials, Ecclesiastical.

CIVIL RIGHTS.   (Geog. subdiv.,
  Direct)
  sa Religious liberty.
  Other references as in LC.

CIVILIZATION, CHRISTIAN.
  sa Church and social problems.
   x Christian civilization.
  xx Christianity.
     Church and social problems.

CIVILIZATION, CHRISTIAN - SERMONS.

CIVILIZATION, SECULAR.
  xx Secularism.
  Other references as in LC supple-
     ment 1959-60.

CLAIMS AGAINST DECEDENTS' ESTATES.
  (CANON LAW)

CLANDESTINITY (CANON LAW)
       BQV230 1094-1103   (348.x427)
  xx Marriage (Canon law)

CLAPHAM SECT.
  References as in LC.

CLARES, POOR. See POOR CLARES.

CLARISSES. See POOR CLARES.

CLASSIFICATION - BOOKS - RELIGION.

CLAUSURA. See ENCLOSURE (MONASTICISM)

CLAUSTRAL PRIORS. See
  PRIORS, CLAUSTRAL.

CLEANSING OF THE LEPER (MIRACLE)

CLEMENTINE LITURGY.
       BQ 1256
  "An early form of liturgy found in
     the eighth book of the Apostolic
     Constitutions." AT

CLERGY.   (Geog. subdiv., Direct)
       BQT 2293-2299   (24x8.3)
  Here are entered works dealing with
     persons in the Church legitimately
     deputed to exercise the power of
     holy orders and jurisdiction. In
     the Catholic Church a person be-
     comes a cleric by receiving the
     tonsure.
  sa Anti-clericalism.
     Archpriests.
     Assistant pastors.
     Bishops.
     Chaplains.
     Directors of religious education.
     Major orders.
     Minor canons, Cathedral,
        collegiate, etc.
     Minor orders. *Ministry*
     Ordination.
     Parishes.
     Parsonages.
     Pastoral theology.
     Pastors.
     Priests.
     Religious orders.
     Spiritual directors.
     Theologians.
     Tonsure.
     Vicars, Parochial.
     also subdivision "Clergy" under
        names of churches (e.g., Church
        of England - Clergy)
   x Catholic Church - Clergy.
     Clerics.
     Hierarchy.
     Ministers of the gospel.
     ~~Ministry.~~
  xx Apostolic succession.
     Catholic Church - Government.
     Christian biography.
     Pastoral theology.

122

CLERGY - ANECDOTES, FACETIAE,
SATIRE, ETC. See
PASTORAL THEOLOGY - ANECDOTES,
FACETIAE, SATIRE, ETC.

CLERGY - APPOINTMENT, CALL, AND
ELECTION. See
CLERGY - VOCATION.

CLERGY - BIBLICAL TEACHING.

CLERGY - BOOKS AND READING.
   x Priests - Books and reading.

CLERGY - CELIBACY. See CELIBACY.

CLERGY - COMMON LIFE.

CLERGY - CONFERENCES. See
CLERGY CONFERENCES.

CLERGY - CONFIDENTIAL COMMUNICATIONS.
See CONFIDENTIAL COMMUNICATIONS -
CLERGY.

CLERGY - CORRESPONDENCE, REMIN-
ISCENCES, ETC.

CLERGY - COSTUME.
      BQT 2299
   "Here are entered works on the
   costume worn by the clergy in
   daily life and on the street.
   Works on the costume worn at
   liturgical functions are entered under the heading Church
   vestments." LC
   sa Church vestments.
      Religious orders - Habit.
    x Clerical costume.
      Clerical dress.
      Clerical habit.
      Costume, Clerical.
      Costume, Ecclesiastical.
      Dress, Clerical.
      Dress, Ecclesiastical.
      Ecclesiastical costume.
      Ecclesiastical dress.
      Ecclesiastical habit.
      Habit, Clerical.
      Habit, Ecclesiastical.
   xx Church vestments.
      Religious orders - Habit.

CLERGY - DEPOSITION.
      BQV230 2303-05
   sa Pastors - Removal.
      Renunciation (Canon law)
   xx Renunciation (Canon law)

CLERGY - EDUCATION.
      BQX 194-199
   sa Theological seminaries.
    x Priests - Education.

CLERGY - ETIQUETTE.
      BQT 2299; BQT 2926
      BV 4012
    x Clerical etiquette.
      Etiquette, Clerical.
   xx Church etiquette.

CLERGY - HANDBOOKS, MANUALS, ETC.

CLERGY - HISTORY.
      BQX 181-199

CLERGY - INSTALLATION. See
   INSTALLATION (CLERGY)

CLERGY - MARRIAGE. See
   MARRIAGE OF CLERGY.

CLERGY - OFFICE.

CLERGY - PERIODICALS.
    x Priests - Periodicals.

CLERGY - POPULAR WORKS.

CLERGY - PRAYER-BOOKS.
   sa Itinerarium.

CLERGY - PRAYER-BOOKS - ENGLISH,
   [FRENCH, GERMAN, ETC.]

CLERGY - RESIDENCE.
   sa subdivision "Residence" under
      special types of clergymen,
      e.g., Bishops - Residence.
    x Pastors - Residence.
      Residence, Clerical.

CLERGY - RETIREMENT.
   xx Clergy - Salaries, pensions, etc.

CLERGY - RETREATS. See
RETREATS FOR CLERGY.

CLERGY - SALARIES, PENSIONS, ETC.
BQT 3317
sa Clergy - Retirement.
x Ecclesiastical pensions.
Pensions, Ecclesiastical.
xx Benefices, Ecclesiastical.

CLERGY - SERMONS.

CLERGY - SPIRITUAL LIFE.

CLERGY - VOCATION.
BQT 2294   (24x8.3)
sa Priests - Vocation.
x Clergy - Appointment, call,
and election.
xx Vocation, Ecclesiastical.

################

CLERGY - CHURCH OF ENGLAND, LUTHERAN
CHURCH, ETC. See
CHURCH OF ENGLAND, [LUTHERAN CHURCH,
ETC.] - CLERGY.

CLERGY - EASTERN CHURCHES. See
EASTERN CHURCHES - CLERGY.

################

CLERGY (CANON LAW)
BQV230 108-486; BQV230 2142-94
(348.x31-348.x36)
sa Celibacy (Canon law)
Chaplains (Canon law)
Deposition (Canon law)
Excardination (Canon law)
Incardination (Canon law)
Irregularities.
Native clergy (Canon law)
Offices, Ecclesiastical.
Ordination (Canon law)
Parishes (Canon law)
Pastors.
Profession of faith (Canon law)
Suspension (Canon law)
Trials, Ecclesiastical (Clergy)
xx Persons (Canon law)

CLERGY (CANON LAW, ORTHODOX EASTERN)

CLERGY, CITY. See CITY CLERGY.

CLERGY, COUNTRY. See RURAL CLERGY.

CLERGY, INDIGENOUS. See
NATIVE CLERGY.

CLERGY, ITINERANT. See
ITINERANCY (CHURCH POLITY)

CLERGY, NATIVE. See NATIVE CLERGY.

CLERGY, PRIVILEGE OF. See
PRIVILEGIUM FORI.

CLERGY, RATING OF.
sa subdivision Clergy, Rating of,
under church denominations,
e.g., Methodist Church -
Clergy, Rating of.
x Rating of clergymen.

CLERGY, RURAL. See RURAL CLERGY.

CLERGY, URBAN. See CITY CLERGY.

CLERGY AND BUSINESS.
BQV230 142
xx Business ethics.

CLERGY AND LAITY.
x Laity and clergy.

CLERGY AND MEDICINE.
xx Pastoral medicine.

CLERGY AND MILITARY SERVICE.
sa Chaplains, Military.
xx Military service, Compulsory.

CLERGY AND POLITICS.

CLERGY AND SOCIAL PROBLEMS.   (Geog.
subdiv.)
[BQT 2939]
x Priests and social problems.
xx Catholic Church and social
problems.
Pastoral theology.

CLERGY CONFERENCES.
  x Clergy - Conferences.
    Clerical conferences.
    Conferences, Clergy.
    Pastoral conferences.
  xx Councils and synods.

CLERGY CONFERENCES (CANON LAW)
    BQV230 131   (348.x31)

CLERGY IN LITERATURE.
    PR 151
    x Priests in literature.

CLERGYMEN AS AUTHORS.
  x Ministers as authors.
    Priests as authors.

CLERGYMEN'S FAMILIES.
    BV 4396
    References as in LC supple-
    ment 1959-60.

CLERGYMEN'S WIVES.
    References as in LC.

CLERGYMEN'S WIVES - RELIGIOUS LIFE.

CLERICAL CONFERENCES. See
    CLERGY CONFERENCES.

CLERICAL COSTUME. See
    CLERGY - COSTUME.

CLERICAL DRESS. See
    CLERGY - COSTUME.

CLERICAL ETIQUETTE. See
    CLERGY - ETIQUETTE.

CLERICAL HABIT. See
    CLERGY - COSTUME.

CLERICAL MEDICINE. See
    PASTORAL MEDICINE.

CLERICAL PSYCHOLOGY. See
    PASTORAL PSYCHOLOGY.

CLERICAL RETREATS. See
    RETREATS FOR CLERGY.

CLERICS. See CLERGY.

CLERMONT, COUNCIL OF, 1095.
    BQX 656   (270.4)

CLOAK OF ST. MARTIN. See
    ST. MARTIN'S CLOAK.

CLOISTERS. See
    CONVENTS.
    ENCLOSURE (MONASTICISM)

CLOTHING AND DRESS - MORAL ASPECTS.

CLUNIAC ARCHITECTURE. See
    ARCHITECTURE, CLUNIAC.

CLUNIAC ART. See ART, CLUNIAC.

CLUNIACS.
    BQX 7102   (271.x1)
  sa Benedictines.
  x Benedictines.   Congregations.
    Cluny.
    Benedictines, Cluniac.
    Cluny, Congregation of.
  xx Benedictines.

CLUNIACS - ENGLAND, [FRANCE,
    ITALY, ETC.]

CLUNY, CONGREGATION OF. See
    CLUNIACS.

COADJUTOR BISHOPS.
    BQV230 350-355   (348.x35)
  xx Bishops (Canon law)
    Persons (Canon law)

COADJUTOR VICARS. See
    VICARS, COADJUTOR.

CODEX JURIS CANONICI.
    BQV 126-127 (History)
    (348.x148)
    BQV 207-231 (Text and com-
    mentary   (348.x149)
  Here are entered texts of and works
    dealing with the collection of the
    laws of the Catholic Church of the
    Latin rite which came into force
    in 1918.

CODEX JURIS CANONICI -- Continued.
   sa Corpus juris canonici.
    x Canon law, Code of.
      Catholic Church. Codex juris
        canonici.
    xx Canon law.
      Corpus juris canonici.

CODEX JURIS CANONICI - COMMENTARIES.
     BQV 214

CODEX JURIS CANONICI - COPYRIGHT. See
  COPYRIGHT - CODEX JURIS CANONICI.

CODEX JURIS CANONICI - CRITICISM,
  INTERPRETATION, ETC.

CODEX JURIS CANONICI - DICTIONARIES.

CODEX JURIS CANONICI - INDEXES.

CODEX JURIS CANONICI - OUTLINES,
  SYLLABI, ETC.

CODEX JURIS CANONICI ORIENTALIS.
    [BQV 1119]
    x Canon law, Oriental.
      Oriental canon law.
    xx Eastern Churches - Canon law.

COENA DOMINI BULLS. See
  IN COENA DOMINI BULLS.

COERCION (CANON LAW). See
  DURESS (CANON LAW)

COINS, PAPAL.
    CJ 2928
    x Papal coins.

COINS IN THE BIBLE. See
  BIBLE - NUMISMATICS.

COLLABORATION   x Team. work
COLLECTARIUM.
    BQT 4264.5   (26x5.9)
    "A liturgical book of the Middle
      Ages containing the collects of
      the divine office." Braun
    xx Collects.

COLLECTIO RITUUM.
    BQT 4434.6
  A selection from the Rituale romanum,
    containing a vernacular along with
    the Latin text.
  Can be subdivided by diocese or by
    country.
  xx Rituale romanum.

COLLECTS.
    BQT 4166.5
    sa Collectarium.
    x Orations (Liturgy)
    xx Prayers.

COLLECTS - MEDITATIONS.

COLLEGE AND CHURCH. See
  CHURCH AND COLLEGE.

COLLEGE CHAPLAINS. See
  CHAPLAINS, UNIVERSITY AND COLLEGE.

COLLEGE OF CARDINALS. See
  COLLEGIUM CARDINALIUM.

COLLEGE SERMONS. See UNIVERSITIES
  AND COLLEGES - SERMONS.

COLLEGES, CATHOLIC. See
  UNIVERSITIES AND COLLEGES, CATHOLIC.

COLLEGIATE CHAPTERS. See CHAPTERS,
  CATHEDRAL, COLLEGIATE, ETC.

COLLEGIUM CARDINALIUM.
    x Catholic Church. Collegium
      cardinalium.
      College of cardinals.

COLOMBIA - CHURCH HISTORY.
    BQX 4831-4854

COLORED BAPTISTS. See
  BAPTISTS, NEGRO.

COLORED CATHOLICS. See
  CATHOLICS, NEGRO.

COLORED LUTHERANS. See
  LUTHERANS, NEGRO.

COLORED METHODIST EPISCOPAL CHURCH.
    BX 8460-8469

COLORED METHODISTS. See
  METHODISTS, COLORED.

COLORED PRIESTS. See
  PRIESTS, NEGRO.

COLORS, LITURGICAL.
    BQT 4367
  x Liturgical colors.
  xx Church vestments.

COLOSSIANS, EPISTLE TO THE. See
  BIBLE. N.T. COLOSSIANS.

COMES.
    BQT 4246
  An ancient liturgical book con-
    taining readings from the
    Epistles or Gospels or from
    both.
  sa Plenarium.
  x Capitulare evangeliorum.
    Liber comitis.
  xx Evangeliarium.
    Lectionarium.

COMMANDMENTS (JUDAISM)
  References as in LC.

COMMANDMENTS, SIX HUNDRED AND
  THIRTEEN.
    BM 646
  References as in LC.

COMMANDMENTS, TEN.
    BQT 1856-1959   (24x1.6)
  sa Evangelical counsels.
    Revelation on Sinai.
  x Commandments of God.
    Decalogue.
    Ten Commandments.
  xx Commandments (Judaism)
    Moral theology.

COMMANDMENTS, TEN - ART.
    BQT 5909   (246.x66)
  xx Bible. O.T. - Pictorial
    illustrations.
    Christian art.

COMMANDMENTS, TEN - CATECHISMS,
  QUESTION-BOOKS.
    BQT 3197

COMMANDMENTS, TEN - JUVENILE
  LITERATURE.

COMMANDMENTS, TEN - MEDITATIONS.
    BQT 2593

COMMANDMENTS, TEN - NUMERICAL
  DIVISION.

COMMANDMENTS, TEN - SERMONS.
    BQT 1859; BQT 3071

COMMANDMENTS OF GOD. See
  COMMANDMENTS, TEN.

COMMANDMENTS OF THE CHURCH.
    BQT 1982-1998   (24x1.7)
  "Here are entered works dealing
    with certain precepts of the
    church, disciplinary rather than
    doctrinal in character (e.g. to
    observe Sundays and fast days,
    to pay tithes, to go to confes-
    sion, etc.). If used for any
    church other than the Catholic,
    the name of the denomination is
    added as a subdivision." LC
  x Church commandments.
    Church precepts.
    Precepts of the church.
  xx Moral theology.

COMMANDMENTS OF THE CHURCH -
  CATECHISMS, QUESTION-BOOKS.

COMMANDMENTS OF THE CHURCH -
  MEDITATIONS.
    BQT 2593

COMMANDMENTS OF THE CHURCH -
  SERMONS.

COMMEMORATION OF SAINTS. See
  SAINTS - COMMEMORATION.

COMMENDATORY ABBOTS.
  Here are entered works on prel-
    ates or laymen who held abbeys
    "in commendam," that is, who

COMMENDATORY ABBOTS -- Continued.
   had charge of religious houses
   and drew their revenues without
   being members of the community.
   x Abbots, Commendatory.
    In commendam.
   xx Benefices, Ecclesiastical.

COMMENTARIES, BIBLICAL. See
  BIBLE - COMMENTARIES.

COMMISSIO AD CODICIS CANONES
  AUTHENTICE INTERPRETANDOS.
    BQV 98   (348.x33)

COMMISSIO DE RE BIBLICA.
    BQV 98   (348.x33)
   x Biblical Commission.

COMMISSIO PRO RUSSIA.
    BQV 98   (348.x33)
   x Russia, Commissio pro.

COMMISSIO SACRAE ARCHAEOLOGIAE.
    BQV 98   (348.x33)

COMMISSIO VULGATAE EMENDANDAE.
    BQV 98   (348.x33)
   x Vulgate Commission.

COMMON LIFE (RELIGIOUS ORDERS) See
  RELIGIOUS ORDERS - COMMON LIFE.

COMMON OF THE SAINTS. See
  COMMUNE SANCTORUM.

COMMON PRIESTHOOD. See
  PRIESTHOOD, UNIVERSAL.

COMMUNE SANCTORUM.
    BQT 4319 (Missal)
    BQT 4393 (Breviary)
  "A division of the Missal and
   Breviary in which are found
   Masses and Offices for all those
   saints who have not special ones
   assigned to them, or who have
   only certain parts proper." AT
   x Common of the Saints.
   xx Breviarium.
    Missale.

COMMUNICATIO IN SACRIS.
    BQT 1866   (24x1.61)
  "Here are entered works dealing
   with the participation of
   Catholics with non-Catholics
   in prayer and other forms of
   worship.
  "For the corresponding term used
   among Lutherans see Unionism
   (Religion)". LC
  sa Intercommunion.
    Unionism (Religion)
   x Communication in worship.
    Participation in non-Catholic
     worship.
    Worship, Communication in.
   xx Catholic Church and reunion.
    Intercommunion.
    Non-Catholics.
    Unionism (Religion)

COMMUNICATIO IN SACRIS (CANON LAW)
    BQV 230 1258
Communication, human see Human Relations

COMMUNICATION - RELIGIOUS ASPECTS.
   [BQT 3603]
  sa Catholic press.
    Catholic propaganda.

COMMUNICATION IN WORSHIP. See
  COMMUNICATIO IN SACRIS.

COMMUNION, FIRST. See
  FIRST COMMUNION.

COMMUNION, FREQUENT.
    BQT 1347   (24x8.6)
   x Daily communion.
    Frequent communion.
   xx Communion, Holy.
    Eucharist.

COMMUNION, FREQUENT - SERMONS.
   [BQT 3064.5]
   x Communion sermons.
    Sermons, Communion.

COMMUNION, HOLY.
    BQT 1339-1359   (23x7.3)
  Here are entered works on the
   reception of the Eucharist.

COMMUNION, HOLY -- Continued.
    sa Communion, Frequent.
       Communion, Spiritual.
       Easter duty.
       Eucharist.
       First communion.
       Mass.
       Viaticum.
     x Holy communion.
    xx Eucharist.
       Mass.

COMMUNION, HOLY - DEVOTIONAL
    LITERATURE.
       [BQT 2608.3]

COMMUNION, HOLY - EFFICACY. See
    EUCHARIST - EFFICACY.

COMMUNION, HOLY - MEDITATIONS.
       [BQT 2608.3]
    xx Eucharist - Meditations.

COMMUNION, HOLY - MINISTER.
       BQV230 845

COMMUNION, HOLY - PRAYER-BOOKS.
       BQT 2665-2669   (24x3.1)

COMMUNION, HOLY - PRAYER-BOOKS -
    ENGLISH, [FRENCH, GERMAN, ETC.]

COMMUNION, HOLY - RITES AND CEREMONIES.
       BQT 4347

COMMUNION, HOLY - SERMONS.
       [BQT 3064.5]
     x Communion sermons.
       Sermons, Communion.

COMMUNION, HOLY - EASTERN CHURCHES.

COMMUNION, HOLY (CANON LAW)
       BQV230 845-869

COMMUNION, INFANT. ·See
    INFANT COMMUNION.

COMMUNION, SPIRITUAL.
       BQT 1354   (24x8.71)
    By this term is meant "An earnest
       desire, especially during Mass,

COMMUNION, SPIRITUAL -- Continued.
       to receive the blessed sacrament,
       when one is not able actually to
       do so." AT
     x Spiritual communion.
    xx Communion, Holy.

COMMUNION IN BOTH ELEMENTS.
       BQT 1341

COMMUNION OF SAINTS.
       BQT 313   (23x5.1)
     x Church triumphant.
       Saints, Communion of.
    xx Church.

COMMUNION SERMONS. See
    COMMUNION, FREQUENT - SERMONS.
    COMMUNION, HOLY - SERMONS.
    EUCHARIST - SERMONS.

COMMUNION VERSE (MUSIC)
    xx Antiphonal chant.

COMMUNISM AND CATHOLIC CHURCH.
       BQT 3463
       BQX 1073; BQX 1116
    sa Communists (Canon law)
     x Catholic Church and communism.
    xx Communism and religion.
       Socialism and Catholic Church.

COMMUNISM AND JUDAISM.
     x Judaism and communism.
    xx Communism and religion.

COMMUNISM AND RELIGION.
       BQT 3463
    sa Christianity and economics.
       Communism and Catholic Church.
       Communism and Judaism.
       Socialism and Catholic Church.
     x Religion and communism.
    xx Socialism and Catholic Church.

COMMUNISM AND ZIONISM.
    References as in LC.

COMMUNISTS (CANON LAW)
    xx Communism and Catholic Church.

COMMUNITY CHURCHES.
BV 636
Explanatory note and references
as in LC.

COMPANIONATE MARRIAGE. See
MARRIAGE, COMPANIONATE.

COMPANY OF JESUS. See JESUITS.

COMPARATIVE RELIGION. See
RELIGIONS.

COMPARATIVE SYMBOLICS. See
CREEDS - COMPARATIVE STUDIES.

COMPARATIVE THEOLOGY. See
THEOLOGY, COMPARATIVE.

COMPLAINTS (CANON LAW)
BQV230 1706-1710
x Bills of complaint (Canon law)
xx Actions and defenses (Canon law)
Civil procedure (Canon law)
Ecclesiastical courts.

COMPLETORIUM.
BQT 4383
A liturgical book containing the
prayers for the last hour (Compline) of the Divine Office.
xx Breviarium.
Compline.

COMPLINE.
BQT 4175
sa Completorium.
xx Divine Office.

COMPROMISE (CANON LAW)

COMPUTUS ECCLESIASTICAL. See
CHURCH CALENDAR.

CONCELEBRATION.
"The saying of Mass by several
priests together, all conse-
crating the same bread and
wine ... This usage is very
common among all users of the
Byzantine rite, Catholic or
dissident." AT
xx Mass - Celebration.

CONCILIAR THEORY.
BQT 369
Here are entered works dealing
with the theory that an ecumen-
ical council is essentially
superior to the Pope.
xx Authority (Religion)
Councils and synods, Ecumenical.
Gallicanism.
Popes - Primacy.

CONCLAVES, PAPAL. See
POPES - ELECTION.

CONCORDAT OF 1122 (HOLY ROMAN EMPIRE)
See CONCORDAT OF WORMS, 1122.

CONCORDAT OF 1448 (HOLY ROMAN EMPIRE)
See CONCORDAT OF VIENNA, 1448.

CONCORDAT OF 1516 (FRANCE)
BQX 1778

CONCORDAT OF 1753 (SPAIN)
BQX 2958

CONCORDAT OF 1784 (VENICE)

CONCORDAT OF 1801 (FRANCE)
BQX 1787   (274.404)
sa Louisets.

CONCORDAT OF 1817 (BAVARIA)
BQX 1941   (274.33)

CONCORDAT OF 1818 (NAPLES)

CONCORDAT OF 1826 (BELGIUM)
BQX 1576

CONCORDAT OF 1841 (SARDINIA)
BQX 2637   (274.59)

CONCORDAT OF 1851 (SPAIN)
BQX 2966   (274.607)

CONCORDAT OF 1851 (TUSCANY)
BQX 2576   (274.55)

CONCORDAT OF 1855 (AUSTRIA)
BQX 1545   (274.36)

CONCORDAT OF 1857 (PORTUGAL)
BQX 2811   (274.69)

CONCORDAT OF 1860 (HAITI)
BQX 4631   (277.294)

CONCORDAT OF 1862 (ECUADOR)
BQX 4866   (278.6)

CONCORDAT OF 1862 (VENEZUELA)
BQX 4926   (278.7)

CONCORDAT OF 1881 (ECUADOR)
BQX 4866   (278.6)

CONCORDAT OF 1886 (PORTUGAL)
BQX 2811   (274.69)

CONCORDAT OF 1887 (COLOMBIA)
BQX 4836   (274.6)

CONCORDAT OF 1914 (SERBIA)
BQX 2684   (274.97)

CONCORDAT OF 1922 (LATVIA)

CONCORDAT OF 1924 (BAVARIA)
BQX 1953   (274.33)
xx Church and state in Bavaria.

CONCORDAT OF 1925 (POLAND)
BQX 2769   (274.38)

CONCORDAT OF 1927 (LITHUANIA)
BQX 2694   (274.75)

CONCORDAT OF 1927 (RUMANIA)
BQX 2840   (274.96)

CONCORDAT OF 1929 (ITALY)
BQX 137   (27x2.62)

CONCORDAT OF 1929 (PRUSSIA)
BQX 1953   (274.31)

CONCORDAT OF 1932 (BADEN)
BQX 1979   (274.34)

CONCORDAT OF 1933 (AUSTRIA)
BQX 1545   (274.36)

CONCORDAT OF 1933 (GERMANY)
BQX 1957   (274.308x5)
xx Church and state in Germany -
1933-1945.

CONCORDAT OF 1940 (PORTUGAL)
BQX 2811   (274.69)

CONCORDAT OF 1953 (SPAIN)
BQX 2967

CONCORDAT OF VIENNA, 1448.
BQX 1541   (274.302)
x Concordat of 1448 (Holy Roman
Empire)
Vienna, Concordat of, 1448.

CONCORDAT OF WORMS, 1122.
BQX 644   (27x2.3)
x Concordat of 1122 (Holy Roman
Empire)
Worms, Concordat of, 1122.
xx Investiture.

CONCORDATS.   (Geog. subdiv.)
BQV 93-94 (Texts)   (348.x81)
BQV 257 (Treatises)
x Catholic Church - Concordats.
xx Church and state.
International law.
International relations.

CONCUPISCENCE.
BQT 643; BQT 1755   (231.x73)
xx Free will and determinism.
Sin, Original.

CONCURSUS DIVINUS.
BQT 609
"That act by which God's energy
flows into all operations of
creatures." AT
x Divine concursus.
xx Creation.

CONDEMNED BOOKS.
BQT 1992-1994   (24x1.7)
sa Censorship.
Expurgated books.
Index librorum prohibitorum.
Liberty of the press.
Prohibited books.
x Books, Condemned.
xx Expurgated books.
Prohibited books.

131

CONDEMNED BOOKS - BIBLIOGRAPHY.
  Z 1919-1920

CONDEMNED SOCIETIES.
  x Forbidden societies.
    Prohibited societies.
    Societies, Condemned.
    Societies, Forbidden.

CONDEMNED SOCIETIES (CANON LAW)
  BQV230 2335   (348.x6)

CONDUCT OF LIFE.
  BJ 1545-1695 (Ethics) (170)
  BQT 2364-2396 (Christian
    perfection) (24x7)
  References as in LC, with the
    following additional references.
  sa Moral theology.
  xx Moral theology.

CONFERENCES, CLERGY. See
  CLERGY CONFERENCES.

CONFESSION. See Penance
  BQT 1364-1391 (Dogmatic
    theology) (23x7.4)
  BQT 2058 (Moral theology)
    (24x1.94)
  BQV230 870-936 (Canon law)
    (348.x42)
  sa Absolution.
    Auricular confession.
    Confessors.
    Conscience, Examination of.
    Easter duty.
    General confession.
    Lay confession.
    Penance.
    Sin.
  xx Absolution.
    Forgiveness of sin.
    Moral theology.
    Penance.

CONFESSION - EFFICACY. See
  PENANCE - EFFICACY.

CONFESSION - FREQUENCY.
  x Frequency of confession.

CONFESSION - HANDBOOKS, MANUALS, ETC.
  BQT 1724
  sa Confessors - Handbooks, manuals,
    etc.

CONFESSION - HANDBOOKS, MANUALS, ETC. -
  POLYGLOT.
  BQT 1731

CONFESSION - HISTORY.

CONFESSION - HISTORY - EARLY PERIOD.

CONFESSION - HISTORY - MIDDLE AGES.

CONFESSION - HISTORY - MODERN PERIOD.

CONFESSION - HISTORY - 16th, [17th,
  etc.] CENTURY.

CONFESSION - INSTRUCTION AND STUDY.
  [BQT 3153]

CONFESSION - JUVENILE LITERATURE.

CONFESSION - PRAYER-BOOKS - ENGLISH,
  [FRENCH, GERMAN, ETC.]
  BQT 2670

CONFESSION - PSYCHOLOGY.
  xx Psychology, Religious.

CONFESSION - ORTHODOX EASTERN CHURCH.
  x Orthodox Eastern Church - Con-
    fession.

CONFESSION (CANON LAW)
  sa Conscience, Manifestation of
    (Canon law)

CONFESSION, JUDICIAL (CANON LAW)
  BQV230 1750-1753
  xx Trials, Ecclesiastical.

CONFESSION, SEAL OF. See
  SEAL OF CONFESSION.

CONFESSION OF AUGSBURG. See
  AUGSBURG CONFESSION.

CONFESSIONALS (ARCHITECTURE)
  BQT 5953
  xx Church furniture.

CONFESSIONS OF FAITH. See CREEDS.

CONFESSORS.
BQT 1388 (24x1.94)
sa Spiritual directors.
xx Confession.

CONFESSORS - HANDBOOKS, MANUALS, ETC.
BQT 1725-1734 (24x1.941)
xx Confession - Handbooks, manuals,
etc.

CONFESSORS - HANDBOOKS, MANUALS, ETC. -
POLYGLOT

CONFESSORS (CANON LAW)
BQV230 518-530
BQV230 871-892 (348.x42)
sa Faculties (Canon law)
Solicitation (Canon law)
xx Penance (Canon law)
Persons (Canon law)

CONFESSORS (SAINTS)
BQX 8227

CONFESSORS FOR RELIGIOUS.
BQV230 518-530 (348.x37)
sa Confessors for sisters.
x Religious confessors.
Religious orders - Confessors.

CONFESSORS FOR SISTERS.
BQV230 520-527 (348.x37)
x Religious confessors.
Religious orders of women -
Confessors.
xx Confessors for religious.

CONFIDENCE IN GOD. See
TRUST IN GOD.

CONFIDENTIAL COMMUNICATIONS - CLERGY.
x Clergy - Confidential communications.

CONFIRMATION.
BQT 1283 (Dogma) (23x7.2)
BQT 2048 (Moral) (24x1.92)

CONFIRMATION - CATECHISMS, QUESTION-
BOOKS.

CONFIRMATION - DEVOTIONAL LITERATURE.
[BQT 2608.2]

CONFIRMATION - HISTORY.

CONFIRMATION - HISTORY - EARLY CHURCH.

CONFIRMATION - HISTORY - MIDDLE AGES.

CONFIRMATION - INSTRUCTION AND STUDY.
BQT 3154
x Confirmation - Manuals of instruction.

CONFIRMATION - MANUALS OF INSTRUCTION.
See CONFIRMATION - INSTRUCTION AND
STUDY.

CONFIRMATION - MINISTER.
BQV230 782-785

CONFIRMATION - SERMONS.
BQT 3003
x Sermons, Confirmation.
xx Occasional sermons.

################

CONFIRMATION - ANGLICAN COMMUNION,
[LUTHERAN CHURCH, ETC.]
x Anglican Communion, [Lutheran
Church, etc.] - Confirmation.

################

CONFIRMATION (CANON LAW)
BQV230 780-800 (348.x42)
xx Sacraments (Canon law)

CONFIRMATION (JEWISH RITE)
BM 675.06; BM 707

CONFIRMATION (LITURGY)
BQT 4445
xx Sacraments (Liturgy)

CONFITEBOR TIBI DOMINE IN TOTO CORDE
MEO, NARRABO (MUSIC). See
PSALMS (MUSIC) - 9th PSALM.

CONFITEBOR TIBI DOMINE IN TOTO CORDE
MEO, QUONIAM AUDISTI VERBA ORIS
MEI (MUSIC). See
PSALMS (MUSIC) - 137th PSALM.

CONFITEMINI DOMINO QUONIAM BONUS, QUONIAM
IN AETRNUM MISERICORDIA EJUS (MUSIC).
See PSALMS (MUSIC) - 135th PSALM.

CONFLICT OF LAWS (CANON LAW)
   x Canon law - Conflict of laws.

CONFORMITY (RELIGION). See DISSENTERS.

CONFRATERNITIES.
      BQT 2810-2817   (24x8.8)
      BQT 3326-3339   (256)
  sa Eucharist - Confraternities.
     Holy Childhood - Confraternities.
     Mary, Blessed Virgin - Confra-
       ternities.
     Prayer - Confraternities.
     Precious Blood - Confraternities.
     Priests - Confraternities.
     Religious orders - Confraternities.
   x Archconfraternities.
     Associations, Pious.
     Parish societies.
     Pious associations.
     Religious societies.
     Societies, Religious.
     Sodalities.
  xx Catholic societies.
     Church societies.
     Corporations, Ecclesiastical.
     Laity.
     Pastoral theology.

CONFRATERNITIES - ADDRESSES, SERMONS,
ETC.
      BQT 3319

CONFRATERNITIES - HISTORY.

CONFRATERNITIES (CANON LAW)
      BQV230 684-725   (348.x391)

CONFRATERNITIES, MONASTIC. See
  RELIGIOUS ORDERS - CONFRATERNITIES.

CONFUCIAN PARABLES. See
  PARABLES, CONFUCIAN.

CONFUCIUS AND CONFUCIANISM.
      BL 1830-1870   (299.51)
      B 128.C6-8 (Philosophy) (181.1)
  References as in LC.

CONGREGATIO CAEREMONIALIS.
      BQV230 254   (348.x34)
      BQV 43-46 (Documents) (348.x16)

CONGREGATIO CONCILII.
      BQV230 250   (348.x34)
      BQV 27-30 (Documents) (348.x16)
   x Council, Congregation of the.

CONGREGATIO CONSISTORIALIS.
      BQV230 248   (348.x34)
      BQV 19-22 (Documents) (348.x16)
   x Consistory, Congregation of the.

CONGREGATIO DE DISCIPLINA SACRAMEN-
TORUM.
      BQV230 249   (348.x34)
      BQV 23-26 (Documents) (348.x16)
   x Sacraments, Congregation of the.

CONGREGATIO DE PROPAGANDA FIDE.
      BQV230 252   (348.x34)
      BQV 35-38 (Documents) (348.x161)
   x Propagation of the Faith, Congre-
     gation of the.

CONGREGATIO DE RELIGIOSIS.
      BQV230 251   (348.x34)
      BQV 31-34 (Documents) (348.x16)

CONGREGATIO DE SEMINARIIS ET STUDIORUM
UNIVERSITATIBUS.
      BQV230 256   (348.x16)
      BQV 51-54 (Documents) (348.x16)
   x Seminary and University Studies,
     Congregation of.

CONGREGATIO EPISCOPORUM ET REGULARIUM.
      BQV 69   (348.x16)

CONGREGATIO INDICIS.
      BQV 69.K6   (348.x16)
   x Index, Congregation of the.

CONGREGATIO INDULGENTIARUM ET
SACRARUM RELIQUIARUM.
      BQV 69.17   (348.x16)
   x Indulgences and Sacred Relics,
     Congregation of.

CONGREGATIO PRO ECCLESIA ORIENTALI.
      BQV230 257   (348.x34)
      BQV 55-58 (Documents) (348.x16)
   x Oriental Church, Congregation of
     the.

CONGREGATIO PRO NEGOTIIS ECCLESIASTICIS
  EXTRAORDINARIIS.
      BQV230 255   (348.x34)
      BQV 47-50 (Documents) (348.x16)
  x Ecclesiastical Affairs, Congre-
    gation for Extraordinary.

CONGREGATIO REVERENDAE FABRICAE
  SANCTI PETRI.
      BQV 69   (348.x16)

CONGREGATIO SACRORUM RITUUM.
      BQV230 253   (348.x34)
      BQV 39-42 (Documents) (264.x68)
  x Rites, Congregation of Sacred.

CONGREGATIO SANCTI OFFICII.
      BQV230 246-247   (348.x34)
      BQV 15-18 (Documents) (348.x16)
  x Holy Office, Congregation of the.
    Inquisition, Holy Roman and
    Universal.

CONGREGATIO SUPER CORRECTIONE LIBRORUM
ECCLESIASTICORUM ECCLESIAE ORIENTALIS.

CONGREGATIONAL CHURCHES.
  Subdivisions as in LC.

CONGREGATIONAL SINGING.
      BQT 4598

CONGREGATIONALISM.
      BX 7101-7620   (285.8)
  sa Antinomianism.
    Brownists.
    Calvinism.
    Dissenters.
    Friends, Society of.
    New England theology.
    Presbyterianism.
    Puritans.
    Unitarianism.
  xx Calvinism.
    Dissenters.
    Puritans.

CONGREGATIONALISTS, FINNISH,
  [GERMAN, ETC.]
  "Here are entered works on Congre-
    gationalists living outside of
    their native country whose church
    services are conducted in their
    native tongue." LC

CONGREGATIONS, RELIGIOUS. See
  RELIGIOUS ORDERS.

CONGREGATIONS, ROMAN.
      BQV230 246-257   (348.x34)
      BQV 13-69 (Documents) (348.x16)
      BQX 161 (History)
  sa Curia Romana.
    also names of individual congre-
      gations, e.g., Congregatio
      Sacrorum Rituum.
  x Catholic Church - Congregations,
    Roman.
    Roman congregations.
  xx Curia Romana.
    Holy See.

CONJUGAL STATE.
      BQT 1938   (24x1.97)
  Here are entered works on the
    rights and duties husband and
    wife are obliged to exercise
    mutually.
  xx Husband and wife.
    Marriage.

CONSANQUINITY (CANON LAW)
      BQV230 96   (348.x3)
  xx Marriage - Impediments (Canon
    law)

CONSCIENCE.
      BQT 1759   (24x1.2)
      BJ 1471 (Philosophy)
  sa Casuistry.
    Doubt (Canon law)
    Free will and determinism.
    Guilt.
    Liberty of conscience.
    Super-ego.
  x Freedom of conscience.
  xx Casuistry.
    Duty.

CONSCIENCE, EXAMINATION OF.
      BQT 1724 (general) (24x1.94)
      BQT 2215 (Means of perfection)
        (24x7.51)
  sa Particular examen.
    Scruples.
  x Examination of conscience.
    Self-examination.
  xx Confession.
    Penance.

CONSCIENCE, MANIFESTATION OF.
    [BQT 2236]
  "Laying open the whole state of
   one's spiritual life to another
   for guidance." AT
  x Manifestation of conscience.
  xx Spiritual direction.

CONSCIENCE, MANIFESTATION OF (CANON
  LAW)
     BQV230 530
  xx Confession (Canon law)
    Superiors, Religious (Canon law)

CONSCIENCE, MARRIAGE OF. See
  MARRIAGE OF CONSCIENCE.

CONSECRATION.
  xx Holiness.

CONSECRATION AT MASS.
    BQT 1330; BQT 4077   (23x7.31)
  sa Epiklesis.
  x Mass, Consecration at.
  xx Canon of the Mass.
    Epiklesis.
    Mass.

CONSECRATION OF ALTARS. See
  ALTARS - CONSECRATION.

CONSECRATION OF BISHOPS.
    BQT 4464   (26x5.9)
  x Bishops - Consecration.

CONSECRATION OF CEMETERIES. See
  CEMETERIES - CONSECRATION.

CONSECRATION OF CHURCHES. See
  CHURCH DEDICATION.

CONSECRATION OF VIRGINS.
    BQT 4468
    BQX 307
  x Blessing of virgins.
    Virgins, Consecration of.
  xx Deaconesses.

CONSECRATION SERVICES. See
  DEDICATION SERVICES.

CONSENT (CANON LAW)
    BQV230 1081
  sa Age of consent (Canon law)
    Declaration of intention (Canon
     law)
    Silence (Canon law)
  xx Declaration of intention (Canon
     law)
    Marriage (Canon law)

CONSERVATIVE JUDAISM.
    BM 197.5
  x Judaism, Conservative.
  xx Jewish sects.

CONSISTORY, CONGREGATION OF THE. See
  CONGREGATIO CONSISTORIALIS.

CONSOLATION.
  sa Affliction.
    Sorrow.
  xx Affliction.

CONSTANCE, COUNCIL OF, 1414-1418.
    BQV 12 (Documents)
    BQX 820 (Church history)

CONSTANTINE, DONATION OF. See
  DONATION OF CONSTANTINE.

CONSTANTINOPLE, COUNCIL OF, 1st, 381.
    BQX 409   (26x2.22)
    BQV 12 (Documents)

CONSTANTINOPLE, COUNCIL OF, 2d, 553.
    BQX 444   (26x2.25)
    BQV 12 (Documents)

CONSTANTINOPLE, COUNCIL OF, 3d, 680-681.
    BQX 534   (26x2.26)
    BQV 12 (Documents)

CONSTANTINOPLE, COUNCIL OF, 4th, 869-870.
    BQX 571   (26x2.28)
    BQV 12 (Documents)

CONSTANTINOPOLITAN CREED.
    BQT 149   (238)
  xx Creeds.

CONSTITUTIONES APOSTOLORUM. See
  APOSTOLIC CONSTITUTIONS.

136

CONSULTORS, DIOCESAN.
     BQV230 423-428   (348.x35)
  x Diocesan consultors.
  xx Dioceses.
     Persons (Canon law)

CONTEMPLATION.
     BQT 2468   (24x9.1)
  "A prayer which dispenses with
    reasoning or discourse and with
    distinct perceptions of God,
    and concentrates on Him in
    simple gaze and a wordless act
    of love." AT
  sa Contemplative life.
     Mystical union.
     Mysticism.
     Prayer, Mental.

   x Mystic prayer.
     Prayer, Mystic.
  xx Meditation.
     Mysticism.
     Prayer, Mental.

CONTEMPLATIVE LIFE.
     BQT 2202
  Here are entered works on that form
    of the religious life in which
    external activities are excluded,
    allowing the individuals to de-
    vote much time to prayer and to
    aim at attaining the prayer of
    contemplation.
  sa Mixed life.
     also names of contemplative or-
       ders, e.g., Camaldolese, Poor
       Clares, Trappists, etc.
  xx Asceticism.
     Contemplation.
     Monasticism.
     Nuns.
     Perfection, Christian.
     Religious life.

CONTENTMENT.
     BJ 1533
  sa Happiness.
  xx Happiness.
  Other references as in LC

CONTINENCE.
     BQT 1933
  xx Chastity.

CONTRACTS (CANON LAW)
     BQV230 1529-1543   (348.x46)
  sa Alienation (Canon law)
     Restitutio in integrum (Canon
      law)
     Simulation (Canon law)

CONTRITION.
     BQT 1375 (Confession)
      (23x7.4)
     BQT 1170 (Grace)   (234.5)
  sa Attrition.
     Repentance.
   x Sorrow for sin.
  xx Penance.
     Repentance.

CONTRITION - HISTORY OF DOCTRINES.

CONTUMACY (CANON LAW)
     BQV230 1842-1851   (348.x5)
  xx Trials, Ecclesiastical.

CONVENTICLE ACT, 1870.
  xx Assembly, Right of.
     Church and state in Great
      Britain.

CONVENTS.   (Geog. subdiv., In-
    direct)
     BQX 6801-8043   (271.9)
     BQT 5928 (Architecture)
  sa Abbeys.
     Beguinages.
     Enclosure (Monasticism)
     Monasteries.
     Priories.
     Secularization.
     also names of individual
      convents.
   x Cloisters.
     Nunneries.
     Religious houses.
     Women in religion.
  xx Abbeys.
     Catholic institutions.
     Church history.
     Church property.

CONVENTS -- Continued.
  sa Monasteries.
     Nuns.
       Religious orders of women.

CONVENTS - ANNIVERSARY SERMONS. See
  ANNIVERSARY SERMONS - CONVENTS.

CONVENTUAL CHAPTERS. See
  CHAPTERS OF FAULTS.

CONVENTUAL MASS. See
  MASS, CONVENTUAL.

CONVERSE BROTHERS. See
  LAY BROTHERS.

CONVERSION.
     BQT 245
  Here are entered works dealing
     with the turning towards God
     either from a lax or sinful life,
     or from heresy and unbelief.
  sa Converts.
     Grace (Theology)
     Regeneration (Theology)
     Repentance.
     Salvation.
   x Religious conversion.
  xx Christian life.

CONVERSION - BIBLICAL TEACHING.

CONVERSION - BIOGRAPHY.
     BQT 227
  Here are entered individual bio-
     graphies of converts in which
     conversion is the principal
     point of interest. For auto-
     biographies of converts see
     Conversion - Personal narratives.

CONVERSION - CATECHISMS, QUESTION-
  BOOKS.

CONVERSION - METHODS AND MANUALS. See
  CONVERT MAKING.

CONVERSION - PERSONAL NARRATIVES.
     BQT 227   (239.x9)
  Here are entered apologies by con-
     verts, mainly autobiographies,
     especially such as stress the
     process of conversion.
   x Apologetics - Personal narratives.

CONVERSION - POPULAR WORKS.

CONVERSION - PSYCHOLOGY.
     BQT 245
  xx Psychology, Religious.

CONVERSION - SERMONS.

CONVERT MAKING. use CONVERSION or EVANGELIZATION
     BQT 3145
  Here are entered works on ways
     and means of winning converts
     and instructing them.
  For the corresponding term used
     by Protestants see Evangelistic
     work.
   x Conversion - Methods and manuals.
  xx Parish missions.
     Pastoral theology.

CONVERTS.
     BQT 228
  Here are entered collective trea-
     tises on converts, mainly collec-
     tive biographies. Individual
     autobiographies by converts are
     entered under Conversion - Per-
     sonal narratives.
   x Catholic Church - Converts.
     Neophytes.
  xx Catholic Church - Biography.
     Conversion.

CONVERTS (CANON LAW)
     BQV230 1350-1351   (348.x44)
  Here are entered works on the
     regulations of canon law regard-
     ing the reception of converts
     into the Church.

CONVERTS, ANGLICAN, [MOHAMMEDAN,
  MORMON, ETC.]
  Here are entered works dealing
     with persons who have become
     affiliated with these respective
     faiths.

CONVICTION. See
  BELIEF AND DOUBT.
  TRUTH.

CONVULSIONARIES.
   x Convulsionists.
  xx Jansenists.

CONVULSIONISTS. See
CONVULSIONARIES.

COOPERATION (CANON LAW)

COPTIC CHURCH.

COPTIC CHURCH - HISTORY.
 BQX 5504-5510 (28x2.4)

COPTIC CHURCH - LAW.
 BQV 1311-1316 (348.x7)

COPTIC CHURCH - RELATIONS -
CATHOLIC CHURCH.

COPTIC CHURCH. LITURGY AND RITUAL.
 BQT 5022-5039 (264.x78)

COPTIC FATHERS OF THE CHURCH. See
FATHERS OF THE CHURCH, COPTIC.

COPTIC MONASTICISM. See
MONASTICISM, COPTIC.

COPTIC RITE.

COPTIC RITE - CANON LAW.
 BQV 1131-1147

COPTIC RITE - HISTORY.
 BQX 5511-5519

COPTIC RITE. LITURGY AND RITUAL.
 BQT 5040-5059

COPYRIGHT - CODEX JURIS CANONICI.
 x Codex juris canonici - Copyright.

COPYRIGHT - LECTURES, SERMONS, ETC.
(Geog. subdiv., Direct)
 x Sermons - Copyright.

CO-REDEMPTION.
 BQT 1033
sa Mary, Blessed Virgin - Mediation.
 Mary, Blessed Virgin - Motherhood (spiritual)
 x Mary, Blessed Virgin - Co-redemption.
xx Mary, Blessed Virgin - Mediation.
 Redemption.

CORINTHIANS, EPISTLES TO THE. See
BIBLE. N.T. CORINTHIANS.

CORNER STONES, LAYING OF.
xx Church dedication.
Other references as in LC supplement 1956-58.

CORONATIONS. (Geog. subdiv., Indirect)
 BQT 4471 (Church rite)
xx Rites and ceremonies.
Other classifications and references as in LC.

CORPORAL WORKS OF MERCY.
 BQT 2393-2396
 x Works of mercy, Corporal.
xx Good works (Theology)

CORPORATIONS, ECCLESIASTICAL.
(Geog. subdiv., Indirect)
sa Catholic institutions.
 Confraternities.
 Dioceses.
 Parishes.
 Pious foundations.
 Religious orders.
 Theological seminaries.
 x Ecclesiastical corporations.
 Moral persons.
 Religious corporations.
xx Church property.
 Religious orders.

CORPORATIONS, ECCLESIASTICAL (CANON
LAW)
 BQV230 99-106

CORPORATIONS, NONPROFIT - TAXATION.
sa Church property - Taxation.
Other references as in LC.

CORPUS CHRISTI FESTIVAL.
 BQT 4225
sa Officium Corporis Christi.
 x Blessed Sacrament, Feast of the.
xx Eucharist.

CORPUS CHRISTI FESTIVAL - MEDITATIONS.

CORPUS CHRISTI FESTIVAL - SERMONS.

CORPUS CHRISTI MYSTICUM. See
MYSTICAL BODY OF CHRIST.

CORPUS JURIS CANONICI.
        BQV 119-123 (History) (348.x141)
        BQV 154-177 (Texts)   (348.x142)
Here are entered collections of
  ecclesiastical laws of several
  early collectors, as, Gratian,
  Pope Gregory IX, Pope Boniface VIII,
  etc. The collective name was of-
  ficially established in 1560.
sa Codex juris canonici.
 x Catholic Church. Corpus juris
      canonici.
xx Canon law.
      Codex juris canonici.

CORPUS JURIS CANONICI - COMMENTARIES.
        BQV 191-192

CORRECTION, FRATERNAL.
        BQT 1786
   x Fraternal correction.
  xx Charity.

CORRESPONDENCE, CHURCH. See
CHURCH CORRESPONDENCE.

CORRESPONDENCE, DOCTRINE OF.
        BX 8727
  xx Analogy (Religion)

CORYBANTES.
  xx Cultus, Greek.
      Mythology, Greek.
      Priests, Greek.

COSMOGONY.
  sa Universe, Destruction of.
  Other references as in LC.

COSMOGONY, BIBLICAL. See CREATION.

COSMOLOGY, BIBLICAL. See CREATION.

COSTS (CANON LAW)
        BQV230 1908-1916

COSTUME, BIBLICAL. See
BIBLICAL COSTUME.

COSTUME, CLERICAL. See
CLERGY - COSTUME.

COSTUME, ECCLESIASTICAL. See
CLERGY - COSTUME.

COSTUME, JEWISH.
        GT 540
  sa Biblical costume.
   x Jewish costume.
  xx Biblical costume.

COUNCIL, CONGREGATION OF THE. See
CONGREGATIO CONCILII.

COUNCIL OF CHALCEDON, [CONSTANCE,
  NICAEA, ETC.]. See CHALCEDON,
  [CONSTANCE, NICAEA, ETC.], COUNCIL
  OF.

COUNCILS AND SYNODS.   (Geog. subdiv.,
  Direct)
        BQX 175   (26x2)
  sa Clergy conferences.
      Local church councils.
      Popes - Primacy.
   x Catholic Church - Councils and
      synods.
      Church synods.
      Synods.
  xx Canon law.
      Catholic Church - History.
      Christianity.
      Church history.
      Popes - Primacy.

COUNCILS AND SYNODS - COLLECTIONS.
        BQV 11   (26x2.08)

COUNCILS AND SYNODS - COLLECTIONS -
  HISTORY.

COUNCILS AND SYNODS - DICTIONARIES.

COUNCILS AND SYNODS - HISTORY.
        BQX 175   (26x2.09)

COUNCILS AND SYNODS - EASTERN CHURCHES.
   x Eastern Churches - Councils and
      synods.

COUNCILS AND SYNODS (CANON LAW)
BQV230 222-229
BQV230 281-292

COUNCILS AND SYNODS, BUDDHIST. See
BUDDHIST COUNCILS AND SYNODS.

COUNCILS AND SYNODS, DIOCESAN.
(Geog. subdiv.)
BQV230 356-362 (General)
(26x2.8)
BQV 341-1020 (Local) (26x2.81)
"A meeting of the chief clergy of
his diocese summoned by a bishop
at least every ten years to dis-
cuss the maintenance of the faith
and good order in the diocese."
AT
sa Cathedraticum.
also names of individual diocesan
synods, e.g., La Crosse, Wis.
(Diocese), Synod, 1887; Malines,
Belgium (Archdiocese), Synod,
1924.
x Diocesan synods.
xx Dioceses.

COUNCILS AND SYNODS, DIOCESAN (CANON
LAW)

COUNCILS AND SYNODS, ECUMENICAL.
BQV230 222-229 (General)
(348.x13)
BQV 12 (Individual councils)
(26x2.2-.3)
sa Conciliar theory.
also names of individual ecumenical councils, e.g., Nicaea,
Council of, 325; Vatican Council, 1st, 1869-1870.
x Councils and synods, General.
Ecumenical councils.
General councils.
Oecumenical councils.

COUNCILS AND SYNODS, ECUMENICAL -
HISTORY.
BQX 175   (26x2.2-.5; 270.2)

COUNCILS AND SYNODS, GENERAL. See
COUNCILS AND SYNODS, ECUMENICAL.

COUNCILS AND SYNODS, NATIONAL. See
PLENARY COUNCILS.

COUNCILS AND SYNODS, PLENARY. See
PLENARY COUNCILS.

COUNCILS AND SYNODS, PROVINCIAL.
(Geog. subdiv.)
BQV230 283-292 (General)
(26x2.7)
BQV 341-1020 (Local) (26x2.71)
"A meeting of the bishops of a
province, convened by the metro-
politan at least once in every
twenty years, chiefly for the
purposes of any necessary dis-
ciplinary legislation." AT
sa names of individual provincial
councils, e.g., Baltimore (Ecclesiastical province), Council,
1829; Milwaukee (Ecclesiastical
province), Council, 1886.
x Provincial councils.

COUNCILS AND SYNODS, PROVINCIAL
(CANON LAW)

COUNSELLING, PASTORAL. See
X PASTORAL COUNSELLING.

COUNSELS, EVANGELICAL. See
EVANGELICAL COUNSELS.

COUNTER-REFORMATION.   (Geog. subdiv.)
BQX 863-866   (270.6)
sa Franciscans and the Counter-
Reformation.
Jesuits and the Counter-
Reformation.
Reformation.
Thirty Years' War, 1618-1648.
Trent, Council of, 1545-1563.
xx Catholic Church - History.
Church history - Modern period.
Church reform.
Reformation.
Trent, Council of, 1545-1563.

COUNTER-REFORMATION - GERMANY.
BQX 1931

COUNTRY CHURCHES. See
RURAL CHURCHES.

COUNTRY CLERGY. See
RURAL CLERGY.

COUNTRY MINISTRY. See
RURAL CLERGY.

COURT, PAPAL. See PAPAL COURT.

COURT CHAPELS (BUILDING). See
CHAPELS, COURT.

COURT CHAPLAINS. See
CHAPLAINS, COURT.

COURT SERMONS.
BQT 3009
x Sermons, Court.

COURTS, CHURCH. See
ECCLESIASTICAL COURTS.

COURTS, ECCLESIASTICAL. See
ECCLESIASTICAL COURTS.

COURTS, JEWISH.
sa Rabbinical courts.
Other references as in LC.

COURTS, RABBINICAL. See
RABBINICAL COURTS.

COVENANTERS.
BX 9081-9082 (274.1)
References as in LC.

COVENANTS (CHURCH HISTORY). See
COVENANTERS.
SOLEMN LEAGUE AND COVENANT.

COVENANTS (CHURCH POLITY)
BT 1010 (General)
BX 7234 (Congregational)
BX 9183 (Presbyterian)
"Here are entered works dealing
with covenants as expressions of
church polity, creeds, member-
ships, etc." LC
References as in LC.

COVENANTS (RELIGION)
BL 617
"Here are entered works dealing
with covenants in various religions, especially primitive. For

COVENANTS (RELIGION) -- Continued.
that use of the covenant idea
which makes it the organizing
principle of a theological system, see Covenants (Theology)."
LC
References as in LC.

COVENANTS (THEOLOGY)
BT 155 (238)
"Here are entered works which give
the covenant idea a central impor-
tance not elsewhere assigned to
it, and use it as the organizing
principle of an entire theological system describing the relations of God and man under the
form of a covenant of works and
a covenant of grace." LC
sa Dispensationalism.
Other references as in LC.

COVETOUSNESS. See AVARICE.

CREATION.
BQT 603-666 (231.x5)
sa Bible and science.
Concursus divinus.
Cosmology.
Deluge.
Dualism (Theology)
Earth.
Evolution.
Geology.
God.
Hexaemeron.
Man.
Mythology.
Nebular hypothesis.
Teleology.
Universe.
x Cosmogony, Biblical.
Cosmology.
God - Creator.
xx Cosmogony.
Cosmology.
Dogmatic theology.
God.
Nebular hypothesis.
Philosophy.
Religion and science.
Teleology.
Universe.

CREATION - ART.

CREATION - EARLY WORKS TO 1800.

CREATION - JUVENILE LITERATURE.

CREATION - MEDITATIONS.

CREATION - MISCELLANEA.

CREATION - POPULAR WORKS.

CREATION - POETRY.

CREATIVITY

CREDO (MUSIC) Creation (Literary, artistic, etc.)
   M 2079.L3; M 2099.L3

CREEDS.
      BQT 141-159   (238)
  sa Apostles' Creed.
    Athanasian Creed.
    Catechisms.
    Constantinopolitan Creed.
    Covenants (Church polity)
    Nicene Creed.
    Rule of faith.
    also subdivision "Catechisms and
      creeds" under names of Chris-
      tian denominations, sects, etc.
      (e.g., Baptists - Catechisms
      and creeds)
  x Catholic Church - Catechisms and
     creeds.
    Confessions of faith.
    Faith, Confessions of.
    Symbolics.
    Symbols (Religion)
  xx Catechisms.
    Church history.
    Dogmatic theology.

CREEDS - COMPARATIVE STUDIES.
      BQT 159
  sa Theology, Comparative.
  x Comparative symbolics.
    Symbolics, Comparative.
  xx Theology, Comparative.

CREEDS - HISTORY AND CRITICISM.
      BQT 143

CREEDS - SUBSCRIPTION.
  sa Profession of faith.

CREEDS, ECUMENICAL.
  "Here are entered works that com-
  bine in one study the Apostles'
  Nicene, and Athanasian creeds."
  LC

CREMATION.
      BQT 1998 (Moral theology)
  Other classifications and references as in LC.

CRIB IN CHRISTIAN ART AND TRADITION.
      BQT 5846
  x Manger in Christian art and
    tradition.
  xx Christmas plays.

CRIME AND CRIMINALS (CANON LAW)
      BQV230 2195-2213 (General)
        (348.x6)
      BQV230 1075 (Marriage impedi-
        ment)   (348.x427)
  sa Abortion (Canon law)
    Absolution (Canon law)
    Adultery (Canon law)
    Bigamy (Canon law)
    Dueling (Canon law)
    Rape (Canon law)
    Trials, Ecclesiastical.
  xx Irregularities.
    Marriage - Impediments (Canon
    law)

CRIMES, RELIGIOUS. See
OFFENSES AGAINST RELIGION.

CRIMINAL LAW (CANON LAW)
      BQV230 1933-1953
  sa Accomplices (Canon law)
    Denunciation (Canon law)

CRIMINAL LAW (CANON LAW, ORTHODOX
EASTERN)

CRIMINAL LIABILITY (CANON LAW)

CRIMINAL PROCEDURE (CANON LAW)
      BQV230 1933-1959   (348.x56)
  xx Procedure (Canon law)
    Trials, Ecclesiastical.

CRIMINALS, CHURCH WORK WITH. See
CHURCH WORK WITH CRIMINALS.

CRISIS THEOLOGY. See
DIALECTICAL THEOLOGY.

CRITICISM, HIGHER. See
BIBLE - CRITICISM, HIGHER.

CROATIAN CATHOLICS. See
CATHOLICS, CROATIAN.

CROSIER. See STAFF, PASTORAL.

CROSIER INDULGENCE.
        BQT 1397
    xx Indulgences.
       Rosary.

CROSS.
        BQT 4522
    Here are entered works on the
       cross as a symbol of the
       Christian religion.

CROSS - APPARITIONS AND MIRACLES.

CROSS - ART.

CROSS - DEVOTIONAL LITERATURE.

CROSS - LEGENDS.

CROSS - MEDITATIONS.

CROSS - POETRY.

CROSS - PRAYER-BOOKS.
    sa Missa de Sancta Cruce.

CROSS - SERMONS.

CROSS, ADORATION OF THE.
        BQT 4462
    x Adoration of the cross.

CROSS, FINDING OF THE.
        BQT 942
    sa Missa in Inventione Sanctae
       Crucis.
    x Finding of the cross.

CROSS, FINDING OF THE - DRAMA.

CROSS, FINDING OF THE - SERMONS.

CROSS, RELICS OF THE.
        BQT 942; BQT 4522
    x Relics of the cross.
    xx Jesus Christ - Passion -
       Instruments.

CROSS, SIGN OF THE.
        BQT 4517   (23x7.8)
    x Sign of the cross.

CROSS, STATIONS OF THE. See
STATIONS OF THE CROSS.

CROSS OF LORRAINE.
    x Lorraine, Cross of.
    xx Crosses.

CROSSES.   (Geog. subdiv., Indirect)
        BQT 5872
    Here are entered works on figures
       or structures in the form of a
       cross.
    sa Christian art.
       Cross of Lorraine.
       Crucifixes.
       Crucifixion.
       Red Cross (Symbol)
       Swastika.
       Symbolism.
    xx Christian antiquities.
       Christian art.
       Signs and symbols.

CROSSES (IN HERALDRY)
        CR 41

CROWN, FRANCISCAN. See
FRANCISCAN CROWN.

CROWN OF THORNS.
        BQT 942
    x Thorns, Crown of.
    xx Jesus Christ - Passion -
       Instruments.

CROWN OF THORNS - SERMONS.
        BQT 3055

CROZIER. See STAFF, PASTORAL.

CRUCIFIXES.
        BQT 4522   (24x8.6)
    xx Church furniture.
       Crosses.

CRUCIFIXES - ART.
     BQT 5872   (246.x66)

CRUCIFIXION OF CHRIST. See
  JESUS CHRIST - CRUCIFIXION.

CRUSADE BULLS.
  "Here are assembled texts of and
  critical works on the many bulls
  issued by the popes granting
  indulgences and other benefits
  to participants in the crusades
  and by extension down to the
  present times to others, especially in the Hipanic world."
  LC
  x Bulla cruciata.
    Bulls, Crusade.
    Cruzada, Bula de.
  xx Bulls, Papal.
    Crusades - Finance.
    Indulgences.

CRUSADES.
     BQX 654-663   (270.4)
     BQX 5831-5839 (Eastern Church)
  sa Children's Crusade, 1212.
    Chivalry.
    Jerusalem - History - Latin
      Kingdom, 1099-1244.
    Latin Orient.
    Military religious orders.
    Templars.
  x Church history - Crusades.
  xx Chivalry.
    Church history - Middle Ages.
    Latin Orient.
    Middle Ages - History.
    Saracens.

CRUSADES - BIBLIOGRAPHY.
   [BQX 654]
     Z 6207   (016.94018)

CRUSADES - FICTION.

CRUSADES - FINANCE.
  sa Crusade bulls.

CRUSADES - INFLUENCE.
    D 157-160

CRUSADES - POETRY.

CRUSADES - FIRST, 1096-1099.
    BQX 656   (270.4)

CRUSADES - SECOND, 1147-1149.
    BQX 657   (270.4)

CRUSADES - THIRD, 1189-1192.
    BQX 658   (270.4)

CRUSADES - FOURTH, 1202-1204.
    BQX 659   (270.5)
  sa Istanbul - Siege, 1203-1204.
    Latin Orient.
  xx Istanbul - Siege, 1203-1204.

CRUSADES - FIFTH, 1218-1221.
    BQX 660   (270.5)

CRUSADES - SIXTH, 1228-1229.
    BQX 660   (270.5)

CRUSADES - SEVENTH, 1248-1250.
    BQX 660   (270.5)

CRUSADES - EIGHTH, 1270.
    BQX 660   (270.5)

CRUSADES - LATER, 13th, 14th, and
  15th CENTURIES.

CRUZADA, BULA DE. See
  CRUSADE BULLS.

CRYPTS.
    BQT 5929; NA 2880
  xx Church architecture.

CUBA - CHURCH HISTORY.
    BQX 4623-4624

CULDEES.
    BQX 2210   (274.1)
  xx Monasticism, Irish.

CULPA. See CHAPTERS OF FAULTS.

CULT, DISPARITY OF. See
  DISPARITY OF CULT.

CULTURAL ADAPTATION IN LITURGY
    See
  LITURGY & CULTURE ADAPTATION

CULTUS.   (Geog. subdiv., Direct)
        BL 550-620   (217)
    sa Postures in worship.
        Shrines.
        also subdivision "Cultus" under
            specific headings, e.g., Mary,
            Blessed Virgin - Cultus.
    xx Mysteries, Religious.
        Religion.
        Rites and ceremonies.
        Sacrifice.
        Worship.

CULTUS (CANON LAW)
        BQV230 1255-1321

CULTUS, ALEXANDRIAN, [EGYPTIAN,
    GREEK, ETC.]
    References as in LC.

CUM INVOCAREM, EXAUDIVIT ME DEUS (MUSIC).
    See PSALMS (MUSIC) - 4th PSALM.

CURATES. See
    ASSISTANT PASTORS.
    PASTORS.
    VICARS, PAROCHIAL.

CURE OF SOULS. See
    PASTORAL COUNSELLING.
    PASTORAL THEOLOGY.

CURETES.
        BL 820
    xx Demonology.
        Mythology.

CURIA, DIOCESAN.
        BQV230 363-390
    sa Bishops.
        Vicars-general.
        Chancellors, Diocesan.
    x Diocesan Curia.

CURIA ROMANA.
        BQV230 242-264   (348.x32)
        BQV 13-99 (Documents)
            (348.x16)
        BQX 163-167 (Church history)
    "The totality of organized bodies
    which assist the pope in the
    government and administration of
    the church, namely, the congre-
    gations, the tribunals, and the
    curial offices." AT

CURIA ROMANA -- Continued.
    sa Congregations, Roman.
        Papal Court.
        Prelates.
        also names of individual
            congregations, tribunals,
            and offices (e.g., Congre-
            gatio de Propaganda Fide,
            Romana Rota, Cancelleria
            Apostolica, etc.)
    x Catholic Church. Curia
        Romana.
        Roman Curia.
        Roman tribunals.
        Tribunals, Roman.
    xx Catholic Church - Government.
        Congregations, Roman.
        Holy See.
        Papal Court.

CURSING. See SWEARING.

CURSING AND BLESSING. See
    BLESSING AND CURSING.

CUSTODIALS.
        BQT 4358; BQT 6026
    xx Christian art.
        Relics and reliquaries.
        Sacred vessels.

CUSTOMARY LAW (CANON LAW)
        BQV230 25-30   (348.x22)

CZECHOSLOVAK REPUBLIC - CHURCH
    HISTORY.
        BQX 1621-1649   (274.37)

CZECHOSLOVAK REPUBLIC - CHURCH
    HISTORY - EARLY PERIOD.

CZECHOSLOVAK REPUBLIC - CHURCH
    HISTORY - 1454-

CZECHOSLOVAK REPUBLIC - RELIGION.
        BR 1050

DAILY COMMUNION. See
    COMMUNION, FREQUENT.

DAILY DEVOTIONAL READINGS. See
    DEVOTIONAL LITERATURE (DAILY
    READINGS)

146

DAMAGES (CANON LAW)
   sa Reparation (Canon law)
      Restitution (Canon law)

DAMNED.
      BQT 1521-1528   (236.x4)
   sa Reprobation.
   xx Hell.

DANCING - MORAL ASPECTS.
      GV 1740-1741

DANCING (IN RELIGION, FOLK-LORE, ETC.)
      BL 605
   sa Indians of North America -
      Dances.

DANIEL, BOOK OF. See
   BIBLE. O.T. DANIEL.

DANITES.
      BX 8601-8695
   xx Mormons and Mormonism.

DATARIA APOSTOLICA.
      BQV230 261   (348.x32)
      BQV 87-88 (Documents)
         (348.x15)
   x Apostolic Datary.

DAY HOURS. See DIURNALE.

DAY OF ATONEMENT (JEWISH HOLIDAY)
   See YOM KIPPUR.

DAY OF JEHOVAH.
      BS 1199
   References as in LC.

DAY OF JUDGMENT. See JUDGMENT-DAY.

DE PROFUNDIS. See
   BIBLE. O.T. PSALMS CXXIX.

DE PROFUNDIS (MUSIC). See
   PSALMS (MUSIC) - 129th PSALM.

DEACONESSES.
      BQX 307
   sa Consecration of virgins.

DEACONESSES (PROTESTANT)
      BV 4423-4425
   References as in LC under
   Deaconesses.

DEACONS.
      BQT 356   (23x7.6)
   sa Major orders.
   x Diaconate.
   xx Deans.
      Major orders.
      Ordination.

DEACONS (PROTESTANT)
      BV 680

DEAD.
   Classifications and references as
   in LC.

DEAD (IN RELIGION, FOLKLORE, ETC.)
   References as in LC.

DEAD, MASS FOR THE. See
   MASS, REQUIEM.

DEAD, OFFICE FOR THE. See
   OFFICIUM PRO DEFUNCTIS.

DEAD, PRAYERS FOR THE. See
   PRAYERS FOR THE DEAD.

DEAD, WORSHIP OF THE. See
   ANCESTOR-WORSHIP.

DEAD SEA SCROLLS.
      BM 487-488
   x Quamran scrolls.

DEADLY SINS. See CAPITAL SINS.

DEAF, CHURCH WORK WITH THE. See
   CHURCH WORK WITH THE DEAF.

DEANERIES (BUILDINGS). See
   PARSONAGES.

DEANS.
   "The usual name for the chief
   dignitary of a diocesan or
   collegiate chapter ..." AT

DEANS -- Continued.
  sa Archdeacons.
    Archpriests.
    Deacons.
    Vicars-general.
  xx Chapters, Cathedral,
    collegiate, etc.

DEANS (CANON LAW)
  xx Chapters, Cathedral, collegi-
    ate, etc. (Canon law)

DEANS, RURAL. See RURAL DEANS.

DEATH.
      BQT 1459 (Theology)   (236.x2)
  Other classifications and sub-
    divisions as in LC.
  sa Dead.
    Future life.
    Future punishment.
    Heaven.
    Hell.
    Martyrdom.
    Mortality.
    Rigor mortis.
    Translation into heaven.
    Violent deaths.
  xx Biology.
    Eschatology.
    Future life.
    Life.

DEATH - ART.
      BQT 5902
      N 8217

DEATH - BIBLICAL TEACHING.

DEATH - MEDITATIONS.
      BQT 2609   (24x2.5)

DEATH - PRAYER-BOOKS.
      [BQT 2690]

DEATH - PROOF AND CERTIFICATION
  (CANON LAW)
  xx Absence and presumption of
    death (Canon law)

DEATH - SERMONS.

DEATHS, REGISTERS OF. See
REGISTERS OF BIRTHS, ETC.

DEBATES WITH NON-CATHOLICS. See
APOLOGETICS - DEBATES.

DECALOGUE. See
COMMANDMENTS, TEN.
Decision making
DECLARATION OF INTENTION (CANON LAW)
  sa Consent (Canon law)
    Silence (Canon law)
    Simulation (Canon law)
  xx Consent (Canon law)

DECORATION, CHURCH. See
CHURCH DECORATION AND ORNAMENT.

DECORATIONS OF HONOR, PAPAL.
      CR 4701; CR 5577
  x Papal decorations of honor.

DECREES, ECCLESIASTICAL. See
CANONS, DECRETALS, ETC. (ECCLESI-
ASTICAL)

DECRETALS, ECCLESIASTICAL. See
CANONS, DECRETALS, ETC. (ECCLESI-
ASTICAL)

DEDICATION, FEAST OF. See
HANUKKAH (FEAST OF LIGHTS)

DEDICATION OF CHURCHES. See
CHURCH DEDICATION.

DEDICATION SERVICES.
  sa Cemeteries - Consecration.
    Church dedication.
  x Consecration services.
    Services, Dedication.

DEFAMATION. See LIBEL AND SLANDER.

DEFECTIVE AND DELINQUENT CLASSES.
  sa Vice.
  Other references as in LC.

DEFENDER OF THE MARRIAGE BOND.
      BQV230 1586   (348.x5)
  sa Promotors of justice (Canon
     law)
   x Defensor vinculi.
    Marriage bond, Defender of the.
  xx Divorce (Canon law)
    Marriage - Annulment (Canon law)
    Matrimonial actions (Canon law)
    Promotors of justice (Canon law)

DEFENSOR VINCULI. See
  DEFENDER OF THE MARRIAGE BOND.

DEGRADATION (CANON LAW). See
  DEPOSITION (CANON LAW)

DEGREES, DOCTRINE OF.
  References as in LC.

DEIFICATION. See APOTHEOSIS.

DEISM.
      BQT 123
      BL 2700-2790   (211)
  sa Atheism.
    Christianity.
    Cosmology.
    Free thought.
    God.
    Positivism.
    Rationalism.
    Theism.
  xx Atheism.
    Christianity.
    God.
    Pantheism.
    Rationalism.
    Religion.
    Theism.
    Theology.

DEISTS, BOHEMIAN. See
  ABRAHAMITES (BOHEMIA)

DEITIES. See GODS.

DE LA SALLE BROTHERS. See
  BROTHERS OF THE CHRISTIAN
  SCHOOLS.

DELEGATES, APOSTOLIC.   (Geog.
  subdiv.)
      BQV230 265-270   (348.x324)
  sa Legates, Papal.
   x Apostolic delegates.
  xx Legates, Papal.

DELEGATION OF POWERS (CANON LAW)
      BQV230 197-210   (348.x31)
  sa Vicars delegate.
  xx Jurisdiction (Canon law)

DELUGE.
      BS 658 (Bible)   (222.x13)
      QE 507 (Biology)   (551.92)
  sa Noah's Ark.
   x Flood, Biblical.
  xx Creation.
    Earth.
    Geology.

DEMONIAC POSSESSION.
      BF 1555 (Occult sciences)
      (133.4)
      BQT 666; BQT 2491
      BS 2545 (New Testament)
  sa Demonomania.
    Exorcism.
    Satanism.
   x Possession, Demoniac.
  xx Demonomania.

DEMONOLOGY.
      BL 480 (Comparative religion)
      GR 525-540 (Folklore)
      BF 1501-1561 (Occult sciences)
      (133.4)
      BQT 661 (Theology)   (231.x61)
      BQT 5906 (Art)
  sa Amulets.
    Apparitions.
    Charms.
    Curetes.
    Demonomania.
    Devil.
    Devil-worship.
    Discernment of spirits.
    Evil eye.
    Exorcism.
    Magic.
    Occult sciences.
    Satanism.

DEMONOLOGY -- Continued.
  sa Superman.
     Superstition.
     Witchcraft.
   x Evil spirits.
  xx Apparitions.
     Devil.
     Devil-worship.
     Exorcism.
     Ghosts.
     Occult sciences.
     Spirits.
     Superstition.
     Witchcraft.

DEMONOMANIA.
     RC 616
  sa Obsession.
  xx Obsession.
  Other references as in LC.

DEMYTHOLOGIZATION.
     BS 2378
  "Divesting (a writing) of mytholo-
     gical forms in order to uncover
     the meaning underlying such
     forms." Webster's unabridged
     dict., 1961.
  xx Bible. N.T. - Criticism, inter-
     pretation, etc.
     Christianity - Essence, genius,
        nature.
     History - Philosophy.
     Mythology.

DENMARK - CHURCH HISTORY.
     BQX 1651-1669   (274.89)

DENMARK - CHURCH HISTORY - EARLY
  PERIOD TO 1524.

DENMARK - CHURCH HISTORY - 20th
  CENTURY.

DENOMINATIONAL SCHOOLS. See
  CHURCH SCHOOLS.

DENOMINATIONS, RELIGIOUS. See
  RELIGIONS.
  SECTS.
  also names of churches and sects.

DENUNCIATION (CANON LAW)
     BQV230 1934-1938   (348.x56)
  xx Criminal law (Canon law)
     Trials, Ecclesiastical.

DEPOSITION (CANON LAW)
     BQV230 2303   (348.x6)
   x Degradation (Canon law)
  xx Clergy (Canon law)

DERVISHES.
     BP 175   (297)
  References as in LC.

DESCENT INTO HELL. See
  JESUS CHRIST - DESCENT INTO HELL.

DESECRATION. See SACRILEGE.

DESIRE FOR GOD.
     BQT 620
  sa Beatific vision.
   x God, Desire for.
  xx God - Knowableness.
     Happiness.
     Love (Theology)
     Man (Theology)

DESIRE OF BAPTISM. See
  BAPTISM OF DESIRE.

DESPAIR.
     BQT 1816
  sa Hope.
  xx Hope.

DESTRUCTION OF THE UNIVERSE. See
  UNIVERSE, DESTRUCTION OF THE.

DETACHMENT.
  xx Recollection (Spiritual)

DETERMINISM AND INDETERMINISM. See
  FREE WILL AND DETERMINISM.

DETRACTION. See SLANDER.

DEUS, IN ADJUTORIUM MEUM INTENDE (MUSIC)
  See PSALMS (MUSIC) - 69th PSALM.

DEUS, IN NOMINE TUO SALVUM ME FAC (MUSIC)
  See PSALMS (MUSIC) - 53d PSALM.

150

DEUS MISEREATUR NOSTRI (MUSIC). See
    PSALMS (MUSIC) - 66th PSALM.

DEUS NOSTER REFUGIUM ET VIRTUS (MUSIC).
    See PSALMS (MUSIC) - 45th PSALM.

DEUTERO-CANONICAL BOOKS (BIBLE). See
    BIBLE. O.T. DEUTERO-CANONICAL
    BOOKS.

DEUTERONOMY, BOOK OF. See
    BIBLE. O.T. DEUTERONOMY.

DEUTSCHER RITTER-ORDEN. See
    TEUTONIC KNIGHTS.

DEUTSCHKATHOLIZISMUS. See
    GERMAN CATHOLICISM.

DEVELOPMENT, Human
    see HUMAN DEVELOPMENT

DEVELOPMENT OF DOGMA. See
    DOGMA, DEVELOPMENT OF.

DEVIL.
        BL 480 (Comparative religion)
        BF 1546-1561 (Demonology)
          (291.216)
        BQT 659-666 (Theology)
          (231.x61)
    sa Demonology.
       Hell.
       Satanism.
       Serpent (in Paradise)
     x Satan.
    xx Demonology.
       Dogmatic theology.

DEVIL - ART.
        BQT 5906
        N 8140   (704.9487)
    xx Christian art.

DEVIL - BIBLICAL TEACHING.
        BS 680; BS 2545

DEVIL - BIBLIOGRAPHY.

DEVIL - DRAMA.
        BQ 5157

DEVIL - POETRY.

DEVIL IN LITERATURE.

DEVIL-WORSHIP.
        BL 480 (Comparative religion)
        BF 1546-1550 (Demonology)
          (291.216)
    sa Demonology.
       Occult sciences.
       Satanism.
       Yezidis.
    xx Demonology.

DEVOLUTION (CANON LAW)
    xx Benefices, Ecclesiastical
          (Canon law)
       Election law (Canon law)

DEVOTIO MODERNA.
        BQT 2166; BQX 797.5
    "Here are entered works on the
       medieval movement initiated by
       Gerard Groote, which resulted
       in the founding of the Brothers
       of the Common Life and the
       Windesheim congregation of
       Augustinian Canons." LC
     x New Devotion.

DEVOTION.
        [BQT 2238.5]
    xx Prayer.
       Religion (Virtue)

DEVOTIONAL CALENDARS. See
    DEVOTIONAL LITERATURE (DAILY
    READINGS)

DEVOTIONAL LITERATURE.
        BQT 2233
    Here are entered works which treat
       about devotional literature or
       spiritual reading. Devotional
       books as such, unless they treat
       of a specific topic (e.g.,
       Jesus Christ - Devotional liter-
       ature) are best classified under
       BQ or 280 (Christian authors)
       and entered in the catalog only
       by author and title.
    Devotional books in the form of
       meditations or prayer-books are
       classified under BQT 2503-2771
       or 242-243 (Meditations and
       Prayer-books). They are entered

DEVOTIONAL LITERATURE -- Continued.
   in the catalog under the form-
   headings "Meditations" or "Prayer-
   books" and generally also under
   a specific heading with the corresponding subdivision "Meditations" or "Prayer-books" (e.g.,
   Eucharist - Meditations; Eucharist - Prayer-books)
   sa Meditations.
      Prayer-books.
      Saints.
    x Literature, Devotional.
      Spiritual reading.
   xx Asceticism.
      Religious literature.
      Spiritual life.

DEVOTIONAL LITERATURE - BIBLIOGRAPHY.

DEVOTIONAL LITERATURE - COLLECTIONS.

DEVOTIONAL LITERATURE - HISTORY AND
   CRITICISM.

DEVOTIONAL LITERATURE - SELECTIONS.

DEVOTIONAL LITERATURE (DAILY
   READINGS)
      BQT 2512
    x Calendars, Devotional.
      Daily devotional readings.
      Devotional calendars.
   xx Meditations.

DEVOTIONAL MEDALS. See
   MEDALS, DEVOTIONAL.

DEVOTIONS, MONTHLY.
      BQT 4495   (24x8.7)
   sa individual monthly devotions,
      e.g., May devotions; June
      devotions; etc.
    x Monthly devotions.
   xx Devotions, Popular.

DEVOTIONS, POPULAR.
      BQT 4089; BQT 4487-4498
      (24x8.7)
   "Spontaneous pious movements of
      the Christian body towards this
      or that feature of the faith,

DEVOTIONS, POPULAR -- Continued.
   sanctified individual, or historical event, approved by
   authority and usually expressed
   in authorized vernacular formu-
   las and observances." AT
   sa Altar prayers.
      Benediction of the Blessed
         Sacrament.
      Devotions, Monthly.
      First Friday devotions.
      Five wounds, Devotion to the.
      Forty hours' devotion.
      Fourteen holy helpers.
      Holy hour.
      Holy Name, Devotion to.
      July devotions.
      June devotions.
      Litanies.
      March devotions.
      May devotions.
      November devotions.
      October devotions.
      Perpetual adoration.
      Prayer-books.
      Prayers.
      Prayers for the dead.
      Rosary.
      Stations of the cross.
      Three hours.
      also subdivision "Prayer-books"
         under names of mysteries
         (e.g., Eucharist - Prayer-
         books) and saints (e.g.,
         Joseph, Saint - Prayer-books)
    x Popular devotions.
   xx Liturgy.

DEVOTIONS, POPULAR - HISTORY.

DIABOLISM. See SATANISM.

DIACONATE. See DEACONS.

DIALECTICAL THEOLOGY.
      BT 78
   sa Neo-orthodoxy.
    x Barthianism.
      Crisis theology.
      Theology, Crisis.
      Theology, Dialectical.
   xx Theology - Methodology.

152

DIALOGUE MASS. See
MASS, DIALOGUE.

DICTIONARIES, CATHOLIC. See
CATHOLIC CHURCH - DICTIONARIES.

DIDACHE. See
TEACHING OF THE TWELVE APOSTLES.

DIES IRAE.
BQT 4312

DIET OF AUGSBURG, 1518. See
AUGSBURG, DIET OF, 1518.

DIET OF AUGSBURG, 1530. See
AUGSBURG, DIET OF, 1530.

DIET OF AUGSBURG, 1548. See
AUGSBURG, DIET OF, 1548.

DIET OF RATISBON, 1532. See
RATISBON, DIET OF, 1532.

DIET OF RATISBON, 1653-1654. See
RATISBON, DIET OF, 1653-1654.

DIET OF SPIRES, 1526. See
SPIRES, DIET OF, 1526.

DIET OF WORMS, 1521. See
WORMS, DIET OF, 1521.

DIOCESAN ARCHIVES. See
ARCHIVES, DIOCESAN.

DIOCESAN CHANCELLORS. See
CHANCELLORS, DIOCESAN.

DIOCESAN CHANCERIES. See
CHANCERIES, DIOCESAN.

DIOCESAN CONSULTORS. See
CONSULTORS, DIOCESAN.

DIOCESAN CURIA. See
CURIA, DIOCESAN.

DIOCESAN RELIGIOUS ORDERS. See
RELIGIOUS ORDERS, DIOCESAN.

DIOCESAN SCHOOLS. See
CHURCH SCHOOLS.

DIOCESAN SYNODS. See
COUNCILS AND SYNODS, DIOCESAN.

DIOCESES.   (Geog. subdiv.)
sa Chancellors, Diocesan.
   Chanceries, Diocesan.
   Chapters, Cathedral, collegiate,
      etc.
   Consultors, Diocesan.
   Councils and synods, Diocesan.
   Eparchies.
   Rural chapters.
   Rural deans.
   Vicars general.
 x Archbishoprics.
   Bishoprics.
xx Bishops.
   Church history.
   Corporations, Ecclesiastical.

DIOCESES - ANNIVERSARY SERMONS. See
ANNIVERSARY SERMONS - DIOCESES.

DIOCESES, TITULAR. See
TITULAR DIOCESES.

DIOCESES (CANON LAW)
     BQV230 215-217   (348.x35)
sa Administrators apostolic.
   Bishops (Canon law)
   Chapters, Cathedral, collegiate,
      etc. (Canon law)
   Parishes (Canon law)
   Vicars capitular.
   Visitations, Ecclesiastical
      (Canon law)

DIPTYCHS.
     BQT 4156

DIRECTION, SPIRITUAL. See
SPIRITUAL DIRECTION.

DIRECTORIES, CATHOLIC. See
CATHOLIC CHURCH - DIRECTORIES.

DIRECTORIUM. See
ORDO DIVINI OFFICII.

DIRECTORS, SPIRITUAL. See
SPIRITUAL DIRECTORS.

DIRECTORS OF RELIGIOUS EDUCATION.
    BV 1531
  xx Clergy.
    Religious education.

DISABLED - RELIGIOUS LIFE.

DISCALCED CARMELITES. See
  CARMELITES, DISCALCED.

DISCERNMENT OF SPIRITS.
    BQT 2445   (24x7.02)
  sa Charismata.
   x Spirits, Discernment of.
  xx Demonology.
    Experience (Religion)
    Psychology, Religious.

DISCIPLES.
  Here are entered works on the
    early followers of Our Lord,
    particularly the seventy-two
    referred to in the Gospels.
  sa Apostles.
    Jesus Christ - Brethren.
  xx Bible - Biography.

DISCIPLES, TWELVE. See APOSTLES.

DISCIPLES OF CHRIST.
    BX 7301-7343   (266.6)
   x Campellites.
    Subdivisions as in LC.

DISCIPLES OF CHRIST, NEGRO.
  References as in LC.

DISCIPLES OF ST. JOHN. See
  MANDAEANS.

DISCIPLINA ARCANI. See
  DISCIPLINE OF THE SECRET.

DISCIPLINE, ECCLESIASTICAL. See
  CHURCH DISCIPLINE.

DISCIPLINE, PENITENTIAL. See
  PENITENTIAL DISCIPLINE.

DISCIPLINE OF THE SECRET.
   x Arcani disciplina.
    Disciplina arcani.
    Secret discipline.

DISMISSAL OF RELIGIOUS.
    BQV230 646-672   (348.x37)
  xx Religious orders (Canon law)

DISPARITY OF CULT.
    BQV230 1070-1071
  "A diriment impediment to marriage
    arising when one of the parties
    has been baptized in the Catholic
    Church or converted thereto and
    the other is an unbaptized per-
    son." AT
   x Cult, Disparity of.
  xx Marriage - Impediments (Canon law)
    Marriage, Mixed.

DISPENSATIONALISM.
    BT 157
   x Theology, Dispensational.
  xx Covenants (Theology)

DISPENSATIONS.
  sa Epikeia.
    Indults.
  xx Irregularities.
    Marriage - Impediments.

DISPENSATIONS (CANON LAW)
    BQV230 80-86   (348.x24)
  xx Irregularities (Canon law)
    Marriage - Impediments (Canon
    law)

DISPENSATIONS FOR MARRIAGE. See
  MARRIAGE - DISPENSATIONS.

DISPUTATIONS, THEOLOGICAL. See
  THEOLOGY - DISPUTATIONS.

DISSENTERS.   (Geog. subdiv.)
    BX 5202-5207 (Church of
      England)   (274.2)
  sa Congregationalism.
    Methodism.
    Presbyterianism.
   x Conformity (Religion)
  xx Church of England.
    Congregationalism.
    Liberty of conscience.

DISSIDENT EASTERN CHURCHES. See
  EASTERN CHURCHES, ORTHODOX.

DISSOLUTION OF MARRIAGE. See
   MARRIAGE - DISSOLUTION.

DISTRIBUTIONS (CANON LAW)
   "Distributions, canonically
      termed 'distributiones quoti-
      dianae", are certain portions
      of the revenue of a church."
      Cath. Encyc.
   xx Benefices, Ecclesiastical
         (Canon law)

DIURNALE.
         BQT 4381   (26x5.3)
   A liturgical book containing the
      divine office from lauds to com-
      pline inclusively, or, all the
      "hours" except matins.
    x Books of hours.
      Day hours.
      Horae diurnae.
      Hours, Books of.
   xx Breviarium.
      Divine office.
      Prayer-books.

DIVES AND LAZARUS (PARABLE)
         BQT 888
    x Lazarus and Dives.

DIVINATION.
         BL 613 (Comparative religion)
         BQT 1866 (Moral theology)
            (24x1.61)
         BF 1745-1779 (Occult sciences)
            (133.3)
   References as in LC.

DIVINE CONCURSUS. See
   CONCURSUS DIVINUS.

DIVINE HEALING. See
   CHRISTIAN SCIENCE.
   FAITH-CURE.
   MIRACLES.

DIVINE IMMANENCE. See
   IMMANENCE OF GOD.

DIVINE LAW.
         BQT 1831-1959   (24x1.x3-x7)
   sa God - Sovereignty.
    x Law, Divine.
   xx Justice.
      Natural law.

DIVINE LITURGY. See
   BYZANTINE RITE. LITURGY AND
   RITUAL - DIVINE LITURGY.
   EASTERN CHURCHES. LITURGY AND
   RITUAL - DIVINE LITURGY.

DIVINE OFFICE.
         BQT 4171-4175   (26x5.3)
   "The service of prayer and praise,
      psalms, lessons, hymns, etc.,
      ancillary to and distinct from
      the sacrifice of the mass,
      which all priests and certain
      other clerics are obliged to
      recite daily, which is said or
      sung in choir by monks, friars,
      many nuns and some others, and
      in which the laity are exhorted
      to take part according to their
      ability and opportunity. It is
      also recited or sung daily in
      the choirs of cathedrals by the
      canons." AT
   sa Acclamations (Liturgy)
      Antiphonarium.
      Breviarium.
      Compline.
      Diurnale.
      Mass. Conventual.
      Matins.
      Prime.
      Responses (Liturgy)
      Rites and ceremonies.
      Vespers.
    x Canonical hours.
      Office, Divine.
   xx Breviarium.
      Liturgy.
      Prayer.
      Rites and ceremonies.

DIVINE OFFICE - HISTORY.

DIVINE OFFICE - INSTRUCTION AND
   STUDY.

DIVINE OFFICE - RITES AND CEREMONIES.
    x Breviarium - Rubrics.

              ################

DIVINE OFFICE - EASTERN CHURCHES. See
   EASTERN CHURCHES. LITURGY AND
   RITUAL - DIVINE OFFICE.

DIVINE OFFICE - MOZARABIC RITE. See
MOZARABIC RITE - DIVINE OFFICE.

################

DIVINE OFFICE (CANON LAW)
BQV230 135   (348.x31)

DIVINE PRAISES.
BQT 2695
xx Benediction of the Blessed
Sacrament.

DIVINE PROVIDENCE. See
PROVIDENCE, DIVINE.

DIVINE TRANSCENDENCE. See
TRANSCENDENCE OF GOD.

DIVINITY OF CHRIST. See
JESUS CHRIST - DIVINITY.

DIVORCE.   (Geog. subdiv., Direct)
HQ 811-960   (173.1)
References as in LC, with the
following additional references.
sa Marriage - Dissolution.
xx Marriage - Dissolution.

DIVORCE - BIBLICAL TEACHING.
BS 2417

DIVORCE (CANON LAW)
BQV230 1118-1132   (24x1.97)
sa Defender of the marriage bond.
Marriage - Annulment (Canon law)
Marriage - Dissolution (Canon
law)
Pauline privilege.
Separation (Canon law)
xx Marriage (Canon law)
Separation (Canon law)

DIVORCE (CANON LAW, ORTHODOX
EASTERN)

DIVORCE SUITS (CANON LAW)
xx Matrimonial actions (Canon law)

DIXI, CUSTODIAM VIAS MEAS (MUSIC). See
PSALMS (MUSIC) - 38th PSALM.

DIXIT DOMINUS DOMINO MEO (MUSIC). See
PSALMS (MUSIC) - 109th PSALM.

DIXIT INJUSTUS UT DELINQUAT IN
SEMETIPSO (MUSIC). See
PSALMS (MUSIC) - 35th PSALM.

DOCETISM.
BQT 48
Here are entered works on the
heretical theory that Christ was
not man, but only seemed to have
a human body and to lead a human
life.
xx Gnosticism.
Heresies and heretics - Early
church.
Jesus Christ - History of doctrines.

DOCTORS OF THE CHURCH.
[BQX 8227
xx Fathers of the church.
Saints.
Theologians.

DOCTRINA APOSTOLORUM. See
TEACHING OF THE TWELVE APOSTLES.

DOCTRINAL SERMONS. See
DOGMATIC THEOLOGY - SERMONS.

DOCUMENTS, PAPAL.
BQV 4-5
sa Briefs, Papal.
Bulls, Papal.
Encyclicals, Papal.
Letters, Papal.
Rescripts, Papal.
xx Popes.
x Papal documents
DOCUMENTS, PAPAL - BIBLIOGRAPHY.

DOCUMENTS, PAPAL - DICTIONARIES.

DOCUMENTS, PAPAL - INDEXES.

DOCUMENTS, PAPAL - PERIODICALS.

DOGMA.
BQT 277-289
"A truth directly proposed by the
church for our belief as an article
of divine revelation." AT

156

DOGMA -- Continued.
  sa Rule of faith.
  xx Dogmatic theology.
    Faith.
    Revelation.'

DOGMA, DEVELOPMENT OF.
      BQT 29
  "The process, under the infallible
    guidance of the Holy Spirit, by
    which the contents of the Deposit
    of Faith are explicitly drawn
    out." AT
  x Development of dogma.

DOGMATIC THEOLOGY.
      BQT 506-1589   (230-238)
  "The science of Christian doc-
    trine; the systematic presen-
    tation of the faith, establish-
    ing the church as the depository
    of revealed truth, setting out
    the relations between faith and
    reason and between religion and
    philosophy. The subject matter
    of dogmatic theology may be
    found reduced to its bare bones
    in 'The Penny Catechism'." AT
  sa Angels.
    Apologetics.
    Atonement.
    Catechisms.
    Church.
    Creation.
    Creeds.
    Devil.
    Dogma.
    Eschatology.
    Faith.
    Fall of man.
    God.
    Good and evil.
    Grace (Theology)
    Holy Spirit.
    Immortality.
    Incarnation.
    Jesus Christ.
    Man (Theology)
    Mary, Blessed Virgin.
    Mass.
    Natural theology.
    Predestination.
    Providence, Divine.

DOGMATIC THEOLOGY -- Continued.
  sa Redemption.
    Repentance.
    Resurrection.
    Revelation.
    Sacraments.
    Sacrifice.
    Salvation.
    Sanctification.
    Sin.
    Transubstantiation.
    Trinity.
  x Catholic Church - Doctrine.
    Christian doctrine.
    Doctrinal theology.
    Theology, Doctrinal.
    Theology, Dogmatic.
  xx Religion.
    Theology.

DOGMATIC THEOLOGY - ADDRESSES,
  ESSAYS, LECTURES.
      BQT 511

DOGMATIC THEOLOGY - BIBLIOGRAPHY.
  See THEOLOGY - BIBLIOGRAPHY.

DOGMATIC THEOLOGY - CATECHISMS,
  QUESTION-BOOKS.

DOGMATIC THEOLOGY - COLLECTED WORKS.

DOGMATIC THEOLOGY - COLLECTED WORKS -
  EARLY CHURCH.

DOGMATIC THEOLOGY - COLLECTED WORKS -
  MIDDLE AGES.

DOGMATIC THEOLOGY - COLLECTED WORKS -
  MODERN PERIOD.

DOGMATIC THEOLOGY - COLLECTIONS.
      BQT 4

DOGMATIC THEOLOGY - CONTROVERSIAL
  LITERATURE.

DOGMATIC THEOLOGY - DICTIONARIES.
  See THEOLOGY - DICTIONARIES.

DOGMATIC THEOLOGY - HANDBOOKS,
  MANUALS, ETC.
      BQT 509

DOGMATIC THEOLOGY - HISTORY.
BQT 31-137   (230.x9)

DOGMATIC THEOLOGY - HISTORY - EARLY
CHURCH.
sa Antiochian school.
Heresies and heretics - Early church.
Messalians.
xx Church history - Primitive and
early church.
Church orders, Ancient.

DOGMATIC THEOLOGY - HISTORY - MIDDLE
AGES.
sa Sects, Medieval.

DOGMATIC THEOLOGY - HISTORY - MODERN
PERIOD.
sa Sects.

DOGMATIC THEOLOGY - HISTORY - 19th
CENTURY.

DOGMATIC THEOLOGY - HISTORY - 20th
CENTURY.

DOGMATIC THEOLOGY - INTRODUCTIONS.
See   THEOLOGY - INTRODUCTIONS.

DOGMATIC THEOLOGY - MEDITATIONS.
sa Catechisms - Meditations.

DOGMATIC THEOLOGY - METHODOLOGY.
See   THEOLOGY - METHODOLOGY.

DOGMATIC THEOLOGY - PERIODICALS.
See   THEOLOGY - PERIODICALS.

DOGMATIC THEOLOGY - POPULAR WORKS.

DOGMATIC THEOLOGY - SELECTIONS.

DOGMATIC THEOLOGY - SERMONS.
BQT 511   (252.3)
sa Catechetical sermons.
x Doctrinal sermons.
Sermons, Doctrinal.

DOGMATIC THEOLOGY - SOURCES. See
THEOLOGY - SOURCES.

DOGMATIC THEOLOGY - TEXTBOOKS.
BQT 509   (230.x2)

DOGMATIC THEOLOGY - TEXTBOOKS -
MIDDLE AGES.

DOGMATIC THEOLOGY - TEXTBOOKS -
16th CENTURY.

DOGMATIC THEOLOGY - TEXTBOOKS -
17th CENTURY.

DOGMATIC THEOLOGY - TEXTBOOKS -
18th CENTURY.

DOGMATIC THEOLOGY - TEXTBOOKS -
19th CENTURY.

DOGMATIC THEOLOGY - TEXTBOOKS -
20th CENTURY.

#################

DOGMATIC THEOLOGY - EASTERN CHURCHES.
See   EASTERN CHURCHES - DOCTRINE.

#################

DOGMATIC THEOLOGY AND ASCETICISM. See
ASCETICISM AND DOGMATIC THEOLOGY.

DOLORS OF OUR LADY. See
SORROWS OF THE BLESSED VIRGIN MARY.

DOLUS (CANON LAW)
xx Guilt (Canon law)
Simulation (Canon law)

DOMESTIC RELATIONS (CANON LAW)

DOMICILE (CANON LAW)
BQV230 90-95   (348.x3)
sa Quasi-domicile (Canon law)
xx Marriage (Canon law)
Persons (Canon law)

DOMINE, DOMINUS NOSTER (MUSIC). See
PSALMS (MUSIC) - 8th PSALM.

DOMINE, EXAUDI ORATIONEM MEAM, AURIBUS
PERCIPE OBSECRATIONEM MEAM (MUSIC).
See PSALMS (MUSIC) - 142d PSALM.

DOMINE, EXAUDI ORATIONEM MEAM, ET CLAMOR
MEUS AD TE VENIAT (MUSIC). See
PSALMS (MUSIC) - 101st PSALM.

158

DOMINE, NE IN FURORE TUO ARGUAS ME
    (MUSIC). See
PSALMS (MUSIC) - 6th PSALM.

DOMINICAN NUNS.
        BQX 7883-7886   (271.9)
    x Dominicans. Second Order.
    xx Dominican Sisters.

DOMINICAN RITE.
        BQT 4781-4789   (264.x81)
    x Dominicans. Liturgy and ritual.

DOMINICAN SAINTS. See
SAINTS, DOMINICAN.

DOMINICAN SISTERS.   (Geog. subdiv.,
    Direct)
        BQX 7888-7891
    sa Dominican Nuns.
    xx Dominicans. Third Order.
        Sisters of the Third Order of
        St. Dominic.

DOMINICANS.   (Geog. subdiv., Direct)
        BQX 7301-7350   (271.x1)
    x Black Friars.
        Friars, Black.
        Friars Preachers.
        Order of Friars Preachers.
        Ordo Fratrum Praedicatorum.
        Preachers, Order of.
        Preaching Friars.
        Predicadores.
        St. Dominic, Order of.
    xx Friars.

DOMINICANS - BIBLIOGRAPHY.
        BQX 7301; Z 7840

DOMINICANS - BIO-BIBLIOGRAPHY.

DOMINICANS - BIOGRAPHY.
        BQX 7349-7350
    sa Saints, Dominican.

DOMINICANS - CANON LAW.
        [BQX 7314.7]

DOMINICANS - COLLECTED WORKS.
        BQX 7303

DOMINICANS - DIRECTORIES.
        BQX 7304

DOMINICANS - EDUCATION.
        [BQX 7314.5]

DOMINICANS - HISTORY.
        BQX 7311-7335

DOMINICANS - MEDITATIONS.

DOMINICANS - MISSIONS.
        [BQX 7314.6]

DOMINICANS - PERIODICALS.
        BQX 7302

DOMINICANS - RULES.
        BQX 7305-7308

DOMINICANS - SPIRITUAL LIFE.
        BQX 7314

        ################

DOMINICANS - FRANCE, [GERMANY,
    ITALY, ETC.]
        BQX 7319-7335

DOMINICANS - FRANCE.
    sa Jacobins (Dominicans)

        ################

DOMINICANS. LAY BROTHERS.
        [BQX 7345]

DOMINICANS. LITURGY AND RITUAL.
    See DOMINICAN RITE.

DOMINICANS. PROVINCES.
        BQX 7336-7344

DOMINICANS. SECOND ORDER. See
DOMINICAN NUNS.

DOMINICANS. THIRD ORDER.
        BQX 7346-7348
    sa Dominican Sisters.

DOMINICANS. THIRD ORDER - CONGRESSES.

        ################

DOMINICANS AND ART.

DOMINICANS AND MYSTICISM.

DOMINICANS AND PREACHING.

DOMINUS ILLUMINATIO MEA, ET SALUS
  MEA (MUSIC). <u>See</u>
  PSALMS (MUSIC) - 26th PSALM.

DONATION OF CONSTANTINE.
     BQX 380
  x Constantine, Donation of.

DONATION OF PEPIN.
  x Pepin, Donation of.
  xx Popes - Temporal power.

DONATISTS.
     BQT 76; BQX 391   (273.x3)
  sa Circumcellions.
  xx Heresies and heretics - Early
    church.
    Sacraments - Efficacy.

DOOR-KEEPERS (HOLY ORDER). <u>See</u>
  MINOR ORDERS.

DOUBLE MONASTERIES.
  Here are entered works on those
    religious institutions which
    sheltered both monks and nuns,
    usually under the supreme com-
    mand of the abbess; they met
    only in church for the litur-
    gical offices.
  x Monasteries, Double.
  xx Religious orders.

DOUBT. <u>See</u> BELIEF AND DOUBT.

DOUBT (CANON LAW)
  x Moral doubt.
  xx Conscience.
    Probabilism.

DOVE (IN RELIGION, FOLKLORE, ETC.)
     BQT 5840
  x Doves.
    Folklore of doves.
  xx Holy Spirit - Art.

DOWRY (CANON LAW)
     BQV230 547-551   (348.x37)
  xx Religious orders of women
    (Canon law)

DOXOLOGY.

DRAGONNADES.
     DC 127
  xx Persecution.

DRAMA.
  sa Religion in drama.
  Other references as in LC.

DRAMA, CATHOLIC. <u>See</u>
  CATHOLIC DRAMA.

DRAMA, LITURGICAL. <u>See</u>
  LITURGICAL DRAMA.

DRAMA, MEDIEVAL.
     PN 1751
  sa Christmas plays, Medieval.
    Liturgical drama.
    Moralities.
    Mysteries and miracle-plays.
    Passion-plays.
  x Plays, Medieval.
  xx Easter - Drama.
    Moralities.
    Mysteries and miracle-plays.

DRAMA, RELIGIOUS. <u>See</u>
  RELIGIOUS DRAMA.

DRAMA AND LITURGY. <u>See</u>
  LITURGY AND DRAMA.
  ✓ DREAMS
DRESS, CLERICAL. <u>See</u>
  CLERGY - COSTUME.

DRESS, ECCLESIASTICAL. <u>See</u>
  CLERGY - COSTUME.
  ✓ Drug abuse
DRUIDS AND DRUIDISM.
     BL 910   (299.16)
  References as in LC.

DRUSES.
     BL 1695; BP 195   (297)
  xx Mohammedan sects.
    Mohammedanism.
    Religions.

DUALISM (THEOLOGY)
"A philosophic and religious system according to which the universe is the work of two co-
eternal and opposed principles,
the one good, the other bad." AT
sa Cathari.
Manichaeism.
xx Creation.

DUELING (CANON LAW)
BQT 1907
BQV230 2351   (348.x6)
xx Crime and criminals (Canon law)

DUKHOBORS.
[BQX 6157]; BX 7433
xx Sects, Russian.

DULIA. See SAINTS - CULTUS.

DUNKARDS. See
CHURCH OF THE BRETHREN.

DURESS (CANON LAW)
x Coercion (Canon law)
Force (Canon law)
Violence (Canon law)
xx Fear (Canon law)
Legal responsibility (Canon law)

DUTCH REFORMED CHURCH. See
NEDERLANDSE HERVORMDE KERK.

EARLY CHRISTIAN LITERATURE. See
CHRISTIAN LITERATURE, EARLY.

EARLY CHRISTIAN PHILOSOPHY. See
PHILOSOPHY, EARLY CHRISTIAN.

EARLY CHRISTIAN POETRY. See
CHRISTIAN POETRY, EARLY.

EARTHQUAKES - RELIGIOUS INTER-
PRETATIONS.

EAST (FAR EAST) - RELIGION.
BL 1055
BQX 3072-3113

EAST SYRIAN CHURCH. See
NESTORIAN CHURCH.

EASTER.
BQT 4224
GT 4935 (Manners and customs)
sa Easter controversy.
Jesus Christ - Resurrection.
x Feast of Easter.
xx Holy Week.
Jesus Christ - Resurrection.
Lent.

EASTER - BIBLIOGRAPHY.
Z 5711

EASTER - DRAMA.
BQ 5157
sa Drama, Medieval.
Mysteries and miracle-plays.
xx Jesus Christ - Drama.
Religious drama.

EASTER - MEDITATIONS.
[BQT 2606.6]

EASTER - POETRY.
PN 6110
sa Carols.
xx Carols.
Hymns.

EASTER - SERMONS.
BQT 2996
sa Easter season - Sermons.
Jesus Christ - Resurrection -
Sermons.
x Sermons, Easter.

EASTER CANTATAS.
xx Cantatas, Sacred.

EASTER CONTROVERSY.
BQT 4202
Here are entered works about the
dispute over the exact date for
the celebration of Easter.
xx Church calendar.
Easter.

EASTER DUES.
x Easter offerings.
xx Church finance.
Tithes.

EASTER DUTY.
> BQT 1987   (24x1.93)
x Paschal precept.
xx Communion, Holy.
> Confession.

EASTER MUSIC.
References as in LC.

EASTER OFFERINGS. See EASTER DUES.

EASTER OFFICE. See
OFFICIUM PASCHATIS.

EASTER SEALS. See
SEALS (CHRISTMAS, ETC.)

EASTER SEASON.
> BQT 4224
sa Lent.
> Pentecost season.
xx Church year.

EASTER SEASON - SERMONS.
> BQT 2966
xx Easter - Sermons.

EASTER SEPULCHER.
> BQT 5959
x Sepulcher, Easter.
xx Church furniture.

EASTER VIGIL.
> [BQT 4224.2]
> BQT 4391 (Text)
sa Ordo Sabbati Sancti.
> Paschal candle.
x Paschal Vigil.
> Vigil of Easter.
xx Holy Saturday.

EASTERN CHURCHES.   (Geog. subdiv.)
> BQX 5401-5409 (General)
> BQV 1102-1481) (Canon law)
> (348.x7)
> BQX 5410-6539 (History)
> (28x1-28x2)
> BQT 5003-5449 (Liturgy)
> (264.x7)
This term is here used to include
all the Eastern churches and rites.
The Orthodox or separated churches

EASTERN CHURCHES -- Continued.
and the Catholic or uniate churches (rites) differ very little from
each other in doctrine, practice, and liturgy. Catholic
libraries will find it conven-
ient to keep almost all material
on the Eastern churches under the
heading "Eastern churches", with
the subdivisions as listed below,
rather than distribute it under
"Eastern churches, Catholic", and
"Eastern churches, Orthodox".
The latter two headings should be
used only when a book treats
specifically about either of
those topics.
Throughout the list the individual
Eastern bodies are called "church"
if Orthodox (e.g., Armenian
Church) and "rite" if Catholic
(e.g., Armenian Rite).
The subdivisions listed below can
in general also be used under
any particular Eastern rite or
church, e.g., under Byzantine
Rite, Coptic Church, etc.
> x Catholic Church - Eastern
> rites.
> Catholic Church - Oriental
> rites.
> Churches, Eastern.
> Eastern rites.
> Oriental churches.

EASTERN CHURCHES - ADDRESSES,
ESSAYS, LECTURES.
> BQX 5404-5405

EASTERN CHURCHES - ANTIQUITIES.
> BQX 5414

EASTERN CHURCHES - APOLOGETICS.
> BQX 6555
x Apologetics - Eastern churches.

EASTERN CHURCHES - ART.
> BQT 5631-5654
x Christian art - Eastern churches.

EASTERN CHURCHES - ASCETICISM. See
ASCETICISM - EASTERN CHURCHES.

EASTERN CHURCHES - BIBLIOGRAPHY.
        BQX 5401
        Z 7842

EASTERN CHURCHES - BIOGRAPHY.

EASTERN CHURCHES - CANON LAW.
        BQV 1102-1481   (348.x7)
    Individual topics in canon law of
        the Eastern churches should be
        treated as seen in the following
        example: Church property (Canon
        law, Eastern)
    sa Codex juris canonici Orientalis.
        Persons (Canon law, Eastern)
        Religious orders (Canon law,
        Eastern)
    x Canon law - Eastern Churches.
        Canon law, Oriental.
        Oriental canon law.

EASTERN CHURCHES - CANON LAW -
    PERIODICALS.
        BQV 1111

EASTERN CHURCHES - CHURCH CALENDAR.
    x Church calendar - Eastern churches.

EASTERN CHURCHES - CHURCH MUSIC. See
    CHURCH MUSIC - EASTERN CHURCHES.

EASTERN CHURCHES - CLERGY.
        BQV 1120
    x Clergy - Eastern churches.

EASTERN CHURCHES - COLLECTED WORKS.
        BQ 3001-3041
        BQX 5405

EASTERN CHURCHES - COLLECTIONS.
        BQ 3003; BQX 5404

EASTERN CHURCHES - COUNCILS AND
    SYNODS. See COUNCILS AND SYNODS -
    EASTERN CHURCHES.

EASTERN CHURCHES - DICTIONARIES.
        BQX 5406

EASTERN CHURCHES - DISCIPLINE.

EASTERN CHURCHES - DOCTRINE.
        BQX 5444
    x Dogmatic theology - Eastern
        churches.

EASTERN CHURCHES - ECCLESIOLOGY.
        BQX 5443
    x Ecclesiology (Eastern churches)

EASTERN CHURCHES - HISTORY.
        BQX 5410-5436   (28x1)

EASTERN CHURCHES - HOMILETICS. See
    HOMILETICS - EASTERN CHURCHES.

EASTERN CHURCHES - LITERATURE.
        BQ 3001-3998

EASTERN CHURCHES - MARIOLOGY.
        BQX 5443
    x Mary, Blessed Virgin - Eastern
        churches.

EASTERN CHURCHES - MISSIONS.
        BQX 5415
    Here is entered literature dealing
        with missionary work carried on
        by the Eastern churches.
    For material about missionary work
        of the Western or Latin church
        among the Orthodox Eastern
        churches see Missions - Eastern
        churches.

EASTERN CHURCHES - MONASTICISM. See
    MONASTICISM, EASTERN.

EASTERN CHURCHES - MORAL THEOLOGY.

EASTERN CHURCHES - MYSTICISM. See
    MYSTICISM - EASTERN CHURCHES.

EASTERN CHURCHES - PERIODICALS.
        BQX 5402

EASTERN CHURCHES - POPULAR DEVOTIONS.

EASTERN CHURCHES - RELATIONS.

EASTERN CHURCHES - RELATIONS -
    CATHOLIC CHURCH.

EASTERN CHURCHES - SACRAMENTS.
BQX 5443
x Sacraments - Eastern churches.

EASTERN CHURCHES - SAINTS.
BQX 5415; BQX 5436

EASTERN CHURCHES - SAINTS - CALENDAR.
BQT 5242

EASTERN CHURCHES - THEOLOGY.
BQX 5442-5446
x Theology - Eastern churches.

EASTERN CHURCHES - THEOLOGY -
BIBLIOGRAPHY.

EASTERN CHURCHES - THEOLOGY -
COLLECTED WORKS.

EASTERN CHURCHES - THEOLOGY -
HANDBOOKS, MANUALS, ETC.

EASTERN CHURCHES - THEOLOGY -
HISTORY.

EASTERN CHURCHES - YEARBOOKS.

##################

EASTERN CHURCHES. LITURGY AND RITUAL.
BQT 5002-5007   (264.x7)
Works on specific topics of the
Eastern liturgy generally treat
of the liturgy of a particular
church or rite, and will come
under such headings as, Byzantine Rite. Liturgy and ritual -
Divine liturgy.
x Liturgy - Eastern churches.

EASTERN CHURCHES. LITURGY AND RITUAL -
COLLECTED WORKS.

EASTERN CHURCHES. LITURGY AND RITUAL -
COLLECTIONS.
BQT 5003-5004

EASTERN CHURCHES. LITURGY AND RITUAL -
DIVINE OFFICE.
x Divine office - Eastern churches.

EASTERN CHURCHES. LITURGY AND RITUAL -
DIVINE LITURGY.
x Eucharistic liturgy (Eastern
churches)
Divine liturgy.

EASTERN CHURCHES. LITURGY AND RITUAL -
HISTORY.

EASTERN CHURCHES. LITURGY AND RITUAL -
LANGUAGE.

##################

EASTERN CHURCHES, CATHOLIC.
This term is here used to signify
all Eastern churches (rites or
uses) of the Byzantine and other
rites which are united to Rome,
located in Europe and elsewhere.
sa names of Eastern Catholic rites,
e.g., Byzantine Rite, Bulgarian;
Maronite Rite; etc.
x Catholic Eastern churches.
Eastern churches, Uniate.
Uniate Eastern churches.

EASTERN CHURCHES, CATHOLIC - CANON
LAW.
BQV 1102-1270   (348.x7)

EASTERN CHURCHES, CATHOLIC - HISTORY.
BQX 5451-6539   (28x2)

EASTERN CHURCHES, CATHOLIC. LITURGY
AND RITUAL.
BQT 5007   (264.x7)

EASTERN CHURCHES, DISSIDENT. See
EASTERN CHURCHES, ORTHODOX.

EASTERN CHURCHES, ORTHODOX.
This term is here used to signify
all non-Catholic Eastern churches,
of the Byzantine and other groups,
located in Europe and in other
parts of the world.
sa names of Eastern non-Catholic
churches, e.g., Jacobite Church;
Orthodox Eastern Church, Bulgarian; etc.

EASTERN CHURCHES, ORTHODOX -- Continued.
   x Dissident Eastern churches.
     Eastern churches, Dissident.
     Eastern churches, Schismatic.
     Eastern churches, Separated.
     Schismatic Eastern churches.
     Separated Eastern churches.

EASTERN CHURCHES, ORTHODOX - HISTORY.
     BQX 5401-6539   (28x1)

EASTERN CHURCHES, ORTHODOX - LAW.
     BQV 1301-1484

EASTERN CHURCHES, ORTHODOX - THEOLOGY.
     BQX 5442-5446

EASTERN CHURCHES, ORTHODOX. LITURGY
  AND RITUAL.
     BQT 5002-5443   (264.x7)

EASTERN CHURCHES, SCHISMATIC. See
  EASTERN CHURCHES, ORTHODOX.

EASTERN CHURCHES, SEPARATED. See
  EASTERN CHURCHES, ORTHODOX.

EASTERN CHURCHES, UNIATE. See
  EASTERN CHURCHES, CATHOLIC.

EASTERN ORTHODOX CHURCH. See
  ORTHODOX EASTERN CHURCH.

EASTERN RITES. See
  EASTERN CHURCHES.

EASTERN SCHISM. See
  SCHISM - EASTERN AND WESTERN CHURCH.

EBIONISM.
     BQT 47   (273.x1)
  xx Gnosticism.
     Heresies and heretics - Early
      church.

ECCLESIASTES, BOOK OF. See
  BIBLE. O.T. ECCLESIASTES.

ECCLESIASTICAL AFFAIRS, CONGREGATION
  FOR EXTRAORDINARY. See
  CONGREGATIO PRO NEGOTIIS ECCLESI-
  ASTICIS EXTRA-ORDINARIIS.

ECCLESIASTICAL ANTIQUITIES. See
  CHRISTIAN ANTIQUITIES.

ECCLESIASTICAL ARCHITECTURE. See
  CHURCH ARCHITECTURE.

ECCLESIASTICAL ARCHIVES. See
  ARCHIVES, CHURCH.

ECCLESIASTICAL ART. See
  CHRISTIAN ART.

ECCLESIASTICAL BENEFICES. See
  BENEFICES, ECCLESIASTICAL.

ECCLESIASTICAL BIOGRAPHY. See
  CHRISTIAN BIOGRAPHY.

ECCLESIASTICAL CALENDAR. See
  CHURCH CALENDAR.

ECCLESIASTICAL CENSORSHIP. See
  CENSORSHIP (CANON LAW)

ECCLESIASTICAL CHRONOLOGY. See
  CHRONOLOGY, ECCLESIASTICAL.

ECCLESIASTICAL CORPORATIONS. See
  CORPORATIONS, ECCLESIASTICAL.

ECCLESIASTICAL COSTUME. See
  CLERGY - COSTUME.
  CHURCH VESTMENTS.
  RELIGIOUS ORDERS - HABIT.

ECCLESIASTICAL COURTS.   (Geog.
  subdiv., Direct)
  sa Complaints (Canon law)
    Judges (Canon law)
    Jurisdiction (Canon law)
    Privilegium fori.
  x Church courts.
    Courts, Church.
    Courts, Ecclesiastical.
    Ecclesiastical tribunals.
    Forum ecclesiasticum.
    Tribunals, Ecclesiastical.

ECCLESIASTICAL DECORATION AND
  ORNAMENT. See CHURCH DECORATION
  AND ORNAMENT.

ECCLESIASTICAL DISCIPLINE. See
CHURCH DISCIPLINE.

ECCLESIASTICAL DIVISIONS. See
ECCLESIASTICAL GEOGRAPHY.

ECCLESIASTICAL DRESS. See
CLERGY - DRESS.

ECCLESIASTICAL FEASTS. See
FEASTS, ECCLESIASTICAL.

ECCLESIASTICAL FEES. See
FEES, ECCLESIASTICAL.

ECCLESIASTICAL FURNITURE. See
CHURCH FURNITURE.

ECCLESIASTICAL GEOGRAPHY. (Geog.
subdiv., Indirect)
        BQX 34
    "Here are entered works dealing
    with the geographical expansion
    of the Christian religion and
    its creeds, sects, orders, mon-
    asteries, shrines, etc., and
    also with its territorial or-
    ganization into patriarchates,
    dioceses, provinces, national
    churches, etc." LC
sa Bible - Geography.
    Church statistics.
    Geography, Historical.
    Missions - Geography.
 x Ecclesiastical divisions.
    Geography, Ecclesiastical.
xx Bible - Geography.
    Church history.
    Religion and geography.

ECCLESIASTICAL GEOGRAPHY -
DICTIONARIES.
        BQX 31

ECCLESIASTICAL GEOGRAPHY -
MAPS.
        BQX 34.
 x Church history - Maps.
xx Catholic Church - History -
    Maps.

ECCLESIASTICAL HABIT. See
CLERGY - COSTUME.

ECCLESIASTICAL HISTORY. See
CHURCH HISTORY.

ECCLESIASTICAL IMMUNITY. See
IMMUNITY, ECCLESIASTICAL.

ECCLESIASTICAL LANGUAGES. See
LANGUAGES - RELIGIOUS ASPECTS.

ECCLESIASTICAL LATIN. See
LATIN LANGUAGE - CHURCH LATIN.

ECCLESIASTICAL LAW. (Geog. subdiv.,
Direct)
        BQV 301-325   (348.x8)
sa Canon law.
    Capitularies.
    also subdivision "Government"
    under names of churches, e.g.,
    Presbyterian Church - Govern-
    ment.
 x Church law.
    Civil ecclesiastical law.
    Law, Church.
    Law, Ecclesiastical.
xx Canon law.

ECCLESIASTICAL MUSIC. See
CHURCH MUSIC.

ECCLESIASTICAL OFFICES. See
OFFICES, ECCLESIASTICAL.

ECCLESIASTICAL PATRONAGE. See
PATRONAGE, ECCLESIASTICAL.

ECCLESIASTICAL PENALTIES. See
PENALTIES, ECCLESIASTICAL.

ECCLESIASTICAL PENSIONS. See
CLERGY - SALARIES, PENSIONS, ETC.

ECCLESIASTICAL PERSONS. See
PERSONS (CANON LAW)

ECCLESIASTICAL POLITY. See
CHURCH POLITY.

ECCLESIASTICAL PROCESSIONS. See
PROCESSIONS, ECCLESIASTICAL.

ECCLESIASTICAL RITES AND CEREMONIES.
See RITES AND CEREMONIES (CATHOLIC)

ECCLESIASTICAL STATISTICS. See
CHURCH STATISTICS.

ECCLESIASTICAL SUPPLIES. See
CHURCH SUPPLIES.

ECCLESIASTICAL TRIALS. See
TRIALS, ECCLESIASTICAL.

ECCLESIASTICAL TRIBUNALS. See
ECCLESIASTICAL COURTS.

ECCLESIASTICAL VESTMENTS. See
CHURCH VESTMENTS.

ECCLESIASTICAL VISITATIONS. See
VISITATIONS, ECCLESIASTICAL.

ECCLESIASTICAL VOCATION. See
VOCATION, ECCLESIASTICAL.

ECCLESIASTICAL YEAR. See
CHURCH YEAR.

ECCLESIASTICUS, BOOK OF. See
BIBLE. O.T. ECCLESIASTICUS.

ECCLESIOLOGY. See CHURCH.

ECCLESIOLOGY (ARCHAEOLOGY). See
CHRISTIAN ANTIQUITIES.

ECCLESIOLOGY (CHURCH DECORATION AND
ORNAMENT). See CHRISTIAN ART.

ECCLESIOLOGY (EASTERN CHURCHES). See
EASTERN CHURCHES - ECCLESIOLOGY.

ECONOMICS

ECONOMICS - PAPAL TEACHING.

ECONOMICS AND CHRISTIANITY. See
CHRISTIANITY AND ECONOMICS.

ECSTASY.
BQT (Mysticism) (24x9.2)
BF 1321 (Spiritualism) (132.5)

ECSTASY -- Continued.
sa Enthusiasm.
Hysteria.
Trance.
xx Mysticism.

ECUMENICAL COUNCILS. See
COUNCILS AND SYNODS, ECUMENICAL.

ECUMENICAL MOVEMENT.
BQT 403-418 (Catholic)
BX 1-9 (Protestant)
Here are entered works dealing
with the movement begun in the
20th century, toward worldwide
interconfessional Christian
unity.
sa Christian union.
Local church councils.
Missions - Cooperative movement.
x Catholicity.
Christian union.
Christianity.
Church.

ECUMENICAL MOVEMENT - HISTORY.

ECUMENICAL MOVEMENT - PERIODICALS.

EDEN.
BS 1237
BQT 634   (231.x71)
sa Fall of man.
Tree of life.
x Garden of Eden.
xx Paradise.

EDICT OF NANTES.
BQX 1774   (274.4)
sa France - History - Wars of the
Huguenots, 1562-1598.
x Nantes, Edict of.
xx Huguenots in France.

EDUCATION, CATHOLIC. See
CATHOLIC EDUCATION.

EDUCATION, CHRISTIAN. See
RELIGIOUS EDUCATION.

EDUCATION, ETHICAL. See
  MORAL EDUCATION.
  RELIGIOUS EDUCATION.

EDUCATION, MORAL. See
  MORAL EDUCATION.

EDUCATION, RELIGIOUS. See
  RELIGIOUS EDUCATION.

EDUCATION AND CHURCH. See
  CHURCH AND COLLEGE.
  CHURCH AND EDUCATION.

EDUCATION AND LITURGY. See
  LITURGY AND EDUCATION.

EDUCATION AND RELIGION. See
  CHURCH AND EDUCATION.

EDUCATION OF CHILDREN - SERMONS.
      BQT 3089

EDUCATION OF CHILDREN, RELIGIOUS. See
  RELIGIOUS EDUCATION OF CHILDREN.

EDUCATIONAL LAW AND LEGISLATION (CANON
  LAW)
    sa Universities and colleges (Canon
        law)

EDUCATIONAL MISSIONS. See
  MISSIONS - EDUCATIONAL WORK.

EDUCATORS, CATHOLIC.
    sa Teachers, Catholic.
     x Catholic educators.
    xx Catholic education.
       Teachers, Catholic.

EGYPT - CHURCH HISTORY.
      BQX 5471-5519 (General)
        (276.2)
      BQX 3695-3699 (Latin Church)

EGYPTIAN PRIESTS. See
  PRIESTS, EGYPTIAN.

EJACULATIONS.
      BQT 4504
     x Prayers, Ejaculatory.
    xx Aphorisms and apothegms
        (Religion)
       Indulgences.

ELECTION (THEOLOGY)
      BQT 1135
    sa Predestination.
       Semi-Pelagianism.
    xx Predestination.

ELECTION (THEOLOGY) - BIBLICAL
  TEACHING.

ELECTION (THEOLOGY) - SERMONS.

ELECTION LAW (CANON LAW)
      BQV230 160-178   (348.x31)
    sa Abbots - Election.
       Bishops - Election.
       Devolution (Canon law)
       Majorities (Canon law)
       Popes - Election.
    xx Offices, Ecclesiastical.

ELECTION SERMONS.
      BQT 3009
     x Sermons, Election.
    xx Occasional sermons.

ELECTIONS, PAPAL. See
  POPES - ELECTION.

ELEMENTARY EDUCATION, CATHOLIC. See
  CATHOLIC EDUCATION, ELEMENTARY.

ELVIRA, SYNOD OF, ca. 300.
      BQX 352

EMANCIPATION, CATHOLIC. See
  CATHOLIC EMANCIPATION.

EMBER DAYS.
      BQT 4236
    xx Fast days.

EMBLEMS.
    Classification and references as
      in LC.

EMIGRATION AND IMMIGRATION - MISSIONS.
  See MISSIONS - EMIGRANTS.

EMIGRATION AND IMMIGRATION (CANON LAW)

EMMANUEL.
    xx God - Name.
       Jesus Christ - Name.

✓ELDERLY
    x Aged
      Senior Citizens
      Gerentology

EMOTIONS.
    BQT 1773
sa Joy.
xx Human acts.
Other classifications and
    references as in LC.

ENCLOSURE (MONASTICISM)
    BQT 2325; BQV230 597
x Clausura.
    Cloisters.
xx Convents.
    Monasteries.

ENCYCLICALS, PAPAL.
    BQV 2-8   (25x3)
x Papal encyclicals.
    Popes - Encyclicals.
xx Documents, Papal.
    Letters, Papal.

ENCYCLICALS, PAPAL - BIBLIOGRAPHY.

END OF THE WORLD.
    BQT 1461-1473   (236.x9)
"Here are entered works dealing
    not only with judgment-day,
    but also with all preceding
    events, signs, fulfilments of
    prophecies, etc." LC
sa Antichrist.
    Judgment-day.
    One thousand, A.D.
    Universe, Destruction of.
xx Antichrist.

ENGAGEMENT. See BETHROTHAL.

ENGLAND - CHURCH HISTORY. See
    GREAT BRITAIN - CHURCH HISTORY.

ENGLISH CATHOLIC NONJURORS. See
    NONJURORS, ENGLISH CATHOLIC.

ENGLISH LANGUAGE - LITURGICAL USE.
    See LITURGICAL LANGUAGE - ENGLISH.

ENGLISH LITERATURE - CATHOLIC AUTHORS.
    PR 1110 (Collections)
    PR 1195 (Collections of
        poetry)
x English poetry - Catholic
    authors.

ENGLISH LITERATURE - CATHOLIC AUTHORS -
    BIBLIOGRAPHY.

ENGLISH LITERATURE - CATHOLIC AUTHORS -
    HISTORY AND CRITICISM.

ENGLISH MARTYRS. See
    MARTYRS - ENGLAND.

ENGLISH ORDER OF ST. JOHN OF JERUSALEM.
    See ORDER OF ST. JOHN OF JERUSALEM
    (ANGLICAN)

ENGLISH POETRY - CATHOLIC AUTHORS. See
    ENGLISH LITERATURE - CATHOLIC AUTHORS.

ENTHRONEMENT OF THE SACRED HEART. See
    SACRED HEART - ENTHRONEMENT.

ENTHUSIASM.
    BF 575 (Psychology)
    BQT 125; BQT 2178
sa Sacramentarians.
xx Ecstasy.
    Fanaticism.
    Inspiration.
    Mysticism.
    Psychology, Religious.
    Revivals.

ENTHUSIASTS (MESSALIANS). See
    MESSALIANS.

ENVY.
    BQT 1813
xx Capital sins.

EPARCHIES.
    Here are entered works on ecclesi-
    astical divisions in the Eastern
    churches, similar to dioceses in
    the Western Church, especially
    in the Russian Orthodox Church.
xx Dioceses.

EPHESIANS, EPISTLE TO THE. See
    BIBLE. N.T. EPHESIANS.

EPHESUS, COUNCIL OF, 431.
    BQX 422   (26x2.23)

EPHESUS, SEVEN SLEEPERS OF. See
    SEVEN SLEEPERS OF EPHESUS.

EPHOD.
     BM 657
  xx Bible - Antiquities.
     Christian antiquities.
     Cultus, Jewish.
     Jews - Antiquities.

EPIGRAPHY, CHRISTIAN. See
  INSCRIPTIONS, CHRISTIAN.

EPIKEIA.
  By this term is understood "the
     interpretation of a law whereby
     it is held not to bind in a
     particular case because some
     special hardship would result."
     AT
  xx Canon law - Interpretation and
        construction.
     Dispensations.

EPIKLESIS.
     BQT 4077
  sa Consecration at mass.
  xx Consecration at mass.

EPIPHANY.
     BQT 845 (Christology)
     [BQT 4221.3] (Liturgy)
  sa Magi.
     Officium in Epiphania Domini
        Nostri Jesu Christi.
   x Feast of the Epiphany.
     Twelfth Day.
     Twelfth Night.
  xx Christmas.

EPIPHANY - ART.
     BQT 5858
  xx Jesus Christ - Art.

EPIPHANY - DRAMA.

EPIPHANY - POETRY.

EPIPHANY - SERMONS.

EPIPHANY MUSIC.
  xx Church music.
     Sacred vocal music.

EPISCOPACY.
     BQT 348   (23x9.31)
     BQX 184
  sa Apostolic succession.
     Bishops.
  xx Apostolate.
     Apostolic succession.
     Bishops.
     Church history.
     State of perfection.

EPISCOPACY - HISTORY.

EPISCOPAL CHANCERIES. See
  CHANCERIES, DIOCESAN.

EPISCOPAL CHURCH. See
  CHURCH OF ENGLAND.
  CHURCH OF IRELAND.
  EPISCOPAL CHURCH IN SCOTLAND.
  PROTESTANT EPISCOPAL CHURCH IN
     THE U.S.A.

EPISCOPAL CHURCHES. See
  CHURCHES, ANGLICAN.

EPISCOPALIAN RELIGIOUS ORDERS. See
  RELIGIOUS ORDERS, EPISCOPALIAN.

EPISCOPALIANS.

EPISCOPALIANS, NEGRO.
     BX 5979-5980

EPISTLES (BIBLE). See
  BIBLE. N.T. EPISTLES.

EPISTLES, CATHOLIC. See
  BIBLE. N.T. CATHOLIC EPISTLES.

EPISTLES, LITURGICAL. See
  BIBLE. N.T. EPISTLES, LITURGICAL.
  EPISTOLARIUM.
  LECTIONARIUM.
  For commentaries, meditations, and
     sermons on the liturgical epis-
     tles, see Bible. N.T. Epistles,
     Liturgical - Commentaries,
     [Meditations, Sermons, etc.]

EPISTLES, PASTORAL. See
  BIBLE. N.T. EPISTLES OF PAUL.

170

EPISTLES, PAULINE. See
  BIBLE. N.T. EPISTLES OF PAUL.

EPISTLES AND GOSPELS, LITURGICAL. See
  BIBLE. N.T. EPISTLES AND GOSPELS,
  LITURGICAL.

EPISTLES OF THE CAPTIVITY. See
  BIBLE. N.T. CAPTIVITY EPISTLES.

EPISTOLARIUM.
      BQT 4247; BQT 4299
  "A book containing the liturgical
    epistles for the use of the
    subdeacon at high mass." AT
  x Epistles, Liturgical.
    Lessons (Mass)
  xx Bible. N.T. Epistles,
      Liturgical.
    Lectionarium.

EQUIPROBABILISM. See PROBABILISM.

ERROR.
      BD 171
  xx Belief and doubt.
  Other references as in LC supple-
    ment 1961.

ERROR (CANON LAW). See
  MISTAKE (CANON LAW)

ESCHATOLOGY.
      BQT 1453-1563   (236)
  "That branch of theology which is
    concerned with death and the
    last things, the destruction and
    renewal of the world, the eternal
    reign of Christ when all men are
    judged and all things fulfilled,
    etc." AT
  sa Antichrist.
    Death.
    Future life.
    Future punishment.
    Heaven.
    Hell.
    Immortality.
    Judgment-day.
    Millenium.
    Purgatory.
    Recapitulation.

ESCHATOLOGY -- Continued.
  sa Resurrection.
    Second advent.
    Universe, Destruction of.
  x Last things.
  xx Dogmatic theology.
    Future life.
    Immortality.

ESCHATOLOGY - BIBLICAL TEACHING.

ESCHATOLOGY - HISTORY OF DOCTRINES.

ESCHATOLOGY - HISTORY OF DOCTRINES -
  EARLY CHURCH.

ESCHATOLOGY - HISTORY OF DOCTRINES -
  MIDDLE AGES.

ESCHATOLOGY - MEDITATIONS.

ESCHATOLOGY - MISCELLANEA.

ESCHATOLOGY - SERMONS.
      BQT 1456

ESCHATOLOGY, ANCIENT.

ESCHATOLOGY, ASSYRO-BABYLONIAN,
  [EGYPTIAN, ETC.]

ESCHATOLOGY, JEWISH.
  sa Messianic era (Judaism)

ESCHATOLOGY, MOHAMMEDAN.
  sa Intercession (Mohammedanism)
    Mahdism.
  x Mohammedan eschatology.

ESCHATOLOGY IN LITERATURE.

ESDRAS, FIRST BOOK OF. See
  BIBLE. O.T. 1 ESDRAS.

ESDRAS, SECOND BOOK OF. See
  BIBLE. O.T. 2 ESDRAS.

ESDRAS, THIRD BOOK OF (APOCRYPHAL)
      BS 1711-1715
  x Bible. O.T. Apocrypha.
    1 Esdras.

ESDRAS, FOURTH BOOK OF (APOCRYPHAL)
     BS 1711-1715
  x Bible. O.T. Apocrypha.
    2 Esdras.

ESDRAS AND NEHEMIAS, BOOK OF. <u>See</u>
  BIBLE. O.T. 1-2 ESDRAS.

ESKIMOS - MISSIONS.

ESKIMOS - RELIGION AND MYTHOLOGY.

ESSAYS, CATHOLIC. <u>See</u>
  CATHOLIC ESSAYS.

ESSENES.
     BQT 47 (Heresy)
     BM 175 (Judaism)   (22x9.79)
  sa Qumran community.
    Zealots (Jewish party)
  xx Jewish sects.
    Monasticism, Jewish.

ESTABLISHED CHURCH OF IRELAND. <u>See</u>
  CHURCH OF IRELAND.

ESTHER, BOOK OF. <u>See</u>
  BIBLE. O.T. ESTHER.

ESTHER, FEAST OF. <u>See</u>
  PURIM (FEAST OF ESTHER)

ESTHONIA - CHURCH HISTORY.
     BQX 1682-1687 (Latin Church)
     BQX 5961-5967 (Orthodox Church)

ETERNAL LIFE. <u>See</u>
  FUTURE LIFE.
  IMMORTALITY.

ETERNAL PUNISHMENT. <u>See</u>
  FUTURE PUNISHMENT.

ETERNITY.
     BQT 1512   (236.x11)
  sa Future life.
  xx Future life.

ETERNITY - MEDITATIONS.
     BQT 2610

ETERNITY - SERMONS.
     BQT 3089

ETHICAL EDUCATION. <u>See</u>
  MORAL EDUCATION.
  RELIGIOUS EDUCATION.

ETHICAL MOVEMENT (DUTCH REFORMED
  CHURCH)
  "Here are entered works dealing
    with a theological -- not moral --
    movement which originated about
    1853 with Daniel Chantepie de la
    Saussaye. It emphasized the per-
    sonal nature of religion as
    against contemporary rational
    and humanistic theories." LC
  x Dutch Ethical Movement.
    Ethische Richting.
  xx Nederlands Hervormde Kerk -
     Parties and movements.

ETHICS.
     BJ   (170)
  References as in LC, with the
    following additional references.
  sa Moral theology.
  xx Moral theology.

ETHICS, BIBLICAL. <u>See</u>
  BIBLE - ETHICS.

ETHICS, CATHOLIC. <u>See</u>
  MORAL THEOLOGY.

ETHICS AND RELIGION. <u>See</u>
  RELIGION AND ETHICS.

ETHICS OF WEALTH. <u>See</u>
  WEALTH, ETHICS OF.

ETHIOPIA - CHURCH HISTORY.
     BQX 5522-5529

ETHIOPIA - CHURCH HISTORY - EARLY
  PERIOD.
     BQX 5526

ETHIOPIA - CHURCH HISTORY - MODERN
  PERIOD.
     BQX 5527-5529

ETHIOPIA - CHURCH HISTORY - 19th
  CENTURY.

ETHIOPIA - CHURCH HISTORY - 20th
  CENTURY.

172

ETHIOPIC CHURCH.
  x Abyssinian Church.
    Church of Abyssinia.
    Church of Ethiopia.

ETHIOPIC CHURCH - HISTORY.
    BQX 5532-5538   (28x1.4)

ETHIOPIC CHURCH - LAW.
    BQV 1317-1320   (348.x7)

ETHIOPIC CHURCH. LITURGY AND RITUAL.
    BQT 5061-5079   (264.x79)

ETHIOPIC MONASTICISM. See
  MONASTICISM, ETHIOPIC.

ETHIOPIC RITE.

ETHIOPIC RITE - CANON LAW.
    BQV 1154-1157

ETHIOPIC RITE - HISTORY.
    BQX 5542-5545

ETHIOPIC RITE. LITURGY AND RITUAL.
    BQT 5080-5099

ETHISCHE RICHTING. See
  ETHICAL MOVEMENT (DUTCH REFORMED
  CHURCH)

ETIQUETTE, CHURCH. See
  CHURCH ETIQUETTE.

ETIQUETTE, CLERICAL. See
  CLERGY - ETIQUETTE.

EUCHARIST.
    BQT 1303-1359 (Doctrine)
      (23x7.3)
    BQT 4071-4079 (Liturgy)
      (264.x63)
  Here are entered general works on
    the Blessed Sacrament or the Holy
    Eucharist.
  Works treating of the sacrificial
    aspect of the Holy Eucharist are
    entered under Mass.
  Works dealing with the reception of
    the Holy Eucharist are entered
    under Communion, Holy.

EUCHARIST -- Continued.
  Similar Protestant literature is
    entered under Lord's Supper
    (cf. note under that heading)
  sa Agape.
    Communion, Frequent.
    Communion, Holy.
    Corpus Christi Festival.
    First communion.
    Last Supper.
    Mass.
    Procession of the Blessed
      Sacrament.
  x Blessed Sacrament.
    Holy Eucharist.
    Sacrament, Blessed. x Mass
  xx Communion, Holy.
    Jesus Christ.
    Mass.
    Sacraments.
    Sacraments (Liturgy)
    Transubstantiation.

EUCHARIST - ADDRESSES, ESSAYS,
  LECTURES.

EUCHARIST - ADORATION. See
  ADORATION OF THE BLESSED SACRAMENT.

EUCHARIST - ART.
    BQT 5898   (246.x66)
  xx Christian art.
    Jesus Christ - Art.

EUCHARIST - BIBLICAL TEACHING.
    [BQT 1305.2]

EUCHARIST - BIBLIOGRAPHY.

EUCHARIST - BIOGRAPHY.

EUCHARIST - CATECHISMS, QUESTION-BOOKS.
    BQT 3197

EUCHARIST - COLLECTIONS.
    BQT 1303

EUCHARIST - CONFRATERNITIES.
    BQT 2814
  xx Confraternities.

EUCHARIST - CONGRESSES. See
  EUCHARISTIC CONGRESSES.

EUCHARIST - CULTUS.
    sa Adoration of the Blessed
        Sacrament.
        Benediction of the Blessed
        Sacrament.
        Eucharist - Miracles.
        Forty Hours' Devotion.
        Perpetual Adoration.

EUCHARIST - DEVOTIONAL LITERATURE.
    [BQT 2608.3]

EUCHARIST - DRAMA.
    [BQT 1313]

EUCHARIST - EARLY WORKS.

EUCHARIST - EFFICACY.
    BQT 1343
    x Communion, Holy - Efficacy.

EUCHARIST - ELEMENTS.
    BQT 1328
    BQV230 814-817 (Canon law)
      (348.x42)
  sa Altar breads.
    Azyme.
    Host.
    Wine - Liturgical use.

EUCHARIST - FICTION.

EUCHARIST - HISTORY.
    BQT 1305   (23x7.3)

EUCHARIST - HISTORY - SOURCES.

EUCHARIST - HISTORY - EARLY CHURCH.

EUCHARIST - HISTORY - MIDDLE AGES.

EUCHARIST - HISTORY - MODERN PERIOD.

EUCHARIST - HISTORY - 16th CENTURY.

EUCHARIST - HISTORY - 17th CENTURY.

EUCHARIST - HISTORY - 18th CENTURY.

EUCHARIST - HISTORY - 19th CENTURY.

EUCHARIST - HISTORY - 20th CENTURY.

EUCHARIST - INSTITUTION.
    x Institution of the Eucharist.

EUCHARIST - MEDIEVAL WORKS.

EUCHARIST - MEDITATIONS.
    BQT 2589; [BQT 2608.3]
      (24x2.3)
    x Communion, Holy - Meditations.

EUCHARIST - MIRACLES.
    BQT 1359
  xx Eucharist - Cultus.
    Miracles.

EUCHARIST - PAPAL TEACHING.
    [BQT 1305.7]

EUCHARIST - PRAYER-BOOKS.
    BQT 2665-2669
  sa Missa de Sanctissimo
    Eucharistico Sacramento.

EUCHARIST - PRAYER-BOOKS - ENGLISH,
[FRENCH, GERMAN, ETC.]

EUCHARIST - PROPHECIES.

EUCHARIST - REAL PRESENCE. See
TRANSUBSTANTIATION.

EUCHARIST - RESERVATION.
    BQT 4348
  sa Aumbries.
    x Reservation of the Eucharist.

EUCHARIST - RESERVATION (CANON LAW)
    BQV230 1265-1275
  xx Eucharist (Canon law)

EUCHARIST - SERMONS.
    BQT 1313; BQT 3064
      (252.x54)
    x Communion sermons.
    Sermons, Communion.
  xx Mass - Sermons.

EUCHARIST - TYPOLOGY.
  xx Typology (Theology)

174

EUCHARIST (CANON LAW)
    BQV230 801-869   (343.x42)
  sa Eucharist - Reservation (Canon
      law)
    First Communion (Canon law)
    Mass (Canon law)
  xx Mass (Canon law)
    Sacraments (Canon law)

EUCHARIST IN LITERATURE.

EUCHARISTIC BREAD. See
  ALTAR BREADS.

EUCHARISTIC CONGRESSES.
    BQT 1307-1308   (24x8.712)
  x Eucharist - Congresses.

EUCHARISTIC FAST.
    BQT 1345
  xx Fasting.

EUCHARISTIC FAST (CANON LAW)
    BQV230 858

EUCHARISTIC LITURGY. See MASS.

EUCHARISTIC LITURGY (BYZANTINE
  RITE). See BYZANTINE RITE.
  LITURGY AND RITUAL - DIVINE LITURGY.

EUCHARISTIC LITURGY (EASTERN
  CHURCHES). See EASTERN CHURCHES.
  LITURGY AND RITUAL - DIVINE LITURGY.

EUCHITES. See MESSALIANS.

EUCHOLOGION.
    BQT 5243
  "A liturgical book of the Byzan-
    tine rite containing the text
    of the three eucharistic litur-
    gies, the ceremonies and prayers
    of the priest and deacon at the
    divine office and for the adminis-
    tration of the sacraments, sacra-
    mentals, blessings, etc." AT
  xx Byzantine Rite. Liturgy and
      ritual - Divine Liturgy.

EUNOMIANISM.
    BQT 63   (273.x3)
  x Anomeans.
  xx Arianism.
    Heresies and heretics - Early
      church.
    Jesus Christ - History of
      doctrines.

EUROPEAN WAR, 1914-1918 - CATHOLIC
  CHURCH.
    BQX 1076
  xx War and religion.

EUROPEAN WAR, 1914-1918 - RELIGIOUS
  ASPECTS.
    D 524; D 639   (940.478)
  xx War and religion.

EUSEBIANS. See ARIANISM.

EUTHANASIA.
    R 725 (Ethics)   (179.7)
    BQT 1908 (Moral theology)
      (24x1.63)
  sa Aged, Killing of the.

EUTYCHIANS.
    BQT 66
  xx Monophysites.

EVANGELIARIUM.
    BQT 4246; BQT 4300
      (26x5.9)
  "A book containing the liturgical
    gospels for the use of the
    deacon at high mass." AT
  sa Comes.
    Plenarium.
  x Gospels, Liturgical.
  xx Bible. N.T. Gospels,
    Liturgical.

EVANGELIARIUM - ART.

EVANGELIARIUM - MANUSCRIPTS.

EVANGELIARIUM - MANUSCRIPTS -
  FACSIMILES.

EVANGELICAL ACADEMIES.
  x Academies, Evangelical.

EVANGELICAL AND REFORMED CHURCH.

EVANGELICAL BENEDICTINES. See
  BENEDICTINES (EVANGELICAL)

EVANGELICAL CHURCH.

EVANGELICAL COUNSELS.
        BQT 2208   (24x7.14)
  Here are entered works dealing
    with the evangelical counsels
    of voluntary poverty, per-
    petual chastity and entire
    obedience, the observance of
    which is recommended for those
    striving after a higher per-
    fection than that contained in
    the Ten Commandments.
  For works dealing with the solemn
    and permanent promise to ob-
    serve the evangelical counsels
    see Vows.
  sa Chastity.
     Obedience.
     Poverty.
     Vows.
   x Counsels, Evangelical.
  xx Commandments, Ten.
     Perfection, Christian.
     Religious life.

EVANGELICAL FREE CHURCH OF AMERICA.

EVANGELICAL LUTHERAN CHURCH.

EVANGELICAL ORDER OF ST. JOHN OF
  JERUSALEM. See ORDER OF ST. JOHN
  OF JERUSALEM (EVANGELICAL)

EVANGELICAL REVIVAL.
  References as in LC.

EVANGELICALISM.
        BX 5125
   x Protestantism, Evangelical.
  Other references and subdivisions
    as in LC.

EVANGELISTARION.
        BQT 5245
  A liturgical book of the Byzantine
    rite containing selections from
    the gospels.

EVANGELISTIC SERMONS.
        BV 3797
   x Revival sermons.
     Sermons, Revival.

EVANGELISTIC WORK.
  Here are entered works on methods
    employed by various Protestant
    churches to win converts.
  For literature dealing with
    similar work done by Catholics
    see Convert making.
  Classification and references as
    in LC.

EVANGELISTS.
        BV 3780-3785
   x Revivalists.

EVANGELISTS (BIBLE)
  sa Apostles.
  xx Apostles.

EVANGELISTS (BIBLE) - ART.
        BQT 5892-5893
  xx Saints - Art.

EVANGELISTS (BIBLE) - SERMONS. *EVANGELIZATION x Convent Making*
EVENING MASS. See MASS, EVENING.

EVIDENCE (CANON LAW)
        BQV230 1747-1836   (348.x5)
  sa Presumptions (Canon law)
   x Proof (Canon law)
  xx Witnesses (Canon law)

EVIDENCE (CANON LAW, ORTHODOX EASTERN)

EVIDENCE, EXPERT (CANON LAW)
  xx Witnesses (Canon law)

EVIDENCES OF CHRISTIANITY. See
  APOLOGETICS.
  CHRISTIANITY - EVIDENCES.

EVIDENCES OF THE BIBLE. See
  BIBLE - EVIDENCES, AUTHORITY, ETC.

EVIDENCES OF THE CATHOLIC CHURCH.
  See APOLOGETICS.

EVIL. See GOOD AND EVIL.

EVIL SPIRITS. See DEMONOLOGY.

EVOLUTION.
      BQT 237 (Theology)
      [BS 651] (Bible)
   Other classifications and
    references as in LC.

EX POST FACTO LAWS (CANON LAW)

EXALTABO TE, DEUS MEUS, REX (MUSIC).
  See PSALMS (MUSIC) - 144th PSALM.

EXAMINATION OF CONSCIENCE. See
  CONSCIENCE, EXAMINATION OF.

EXARCHS.
  sa Primates (Ecclesiastic)
  xx Bishops.
     Primates (Ecclesiastic)

EXCARDINATION (CANON LAW)
      BQV230 111-117 (348.x31)
  sa Incardination (Canon law)
  xx Benefices, Ecclesiastical
     (Canon law)
     Clergy (Canon law)
     Incardination (Canon law)

EXCEPTIONAL CHILDREN, CHURCH
  WORK WITH. See CHURCH WORK
  WITH EXCEPTIONAL CHILDREN.

EXCEPTIONS (CANON LAW)

EXCLAUSTRATION.
      BQV230 638-639 (348.x37)
  "A religious who received a temporary permission to remain
   outside the community, e.g.,
   because of financial difficul-
   ties of his or her parents,
   etc., is said to be exclaus-
   trated." Lyon
  xx Indults.
     Religious orders (Canon law)

EXCOMMUNICATION.
      BQV230 2257-2267 (348.x6)
  sa Interdict (Canon law)
  x Anathema.
  xx Censures, Ecclesiastical.
     Interdict (Canon law)

EXECRATION. See
  BLESSING AND CURSING.

EXECUTION SERMONS.
      BQT 3009 (252.x5)
  "Here are entered sermons preached
   at the execution of criminals."
   LC
  x Sermons, Execution.

EXECUTIONS (CANON LAW)

EXECUTIVE POWER (CANON LAW)

EXEMPTION (CANON LAW)
      BQV230 615-618 (348.x37)
  xx Privilege (Canon law)
     Religious orders (Canon law)

EXEQUATUR. See PLACITUM REGIUM.

EXERCISES, SPIRITUAL. See
  RETREATS.

EXISTENCE OF GOD. See
  GOD - EXISTENCE.

EXODUS, BOOK OF. See
  BIBLE. O.T. EXODUS.

EXORCISM.
      BQT 666
      BQT 1874 (Moral theology)
       (24x1.61)
      BQT 4516 (Sacramentals)
      BQT 4473 (Text) (264.x64)
  sa Demonology.
     Witchcraft.
  xx Demoniac possession.
     Demonology.
     Demonomania.
     Sacramentals.

EXORCISM IN ART.

EXORCISTS (HOLY ORDER). See
  MINOR ORDERS.

EXPERIENCE (RELIGION)
      BQT 245
  sa Discernment of spirits.

EXPURGATED BOOKS.
  sa Condemned books.
    Index librorum prohibitorum.
    Liberty of the press.
    Printing - Cancels.
    Prohibited books.
   x Books, Expurgated.
  xx Condemned books.
    Prohibited books.

EXTEMPORANEOUS PREACHING. See
  PREACHING, EXTEMPORANEOUS.

EXTRA ECCLESIAM NULLA SALUS. See
  SALVATION OUTSIDE THE CHURCH.

EXTREME UNCTION. *see Anointing of the sick*
    BQT 1407   (23x7.5)
    BQT 2063 (Moral theology)
    BQT 4455 (Ritual)
   x Last sacraments.
    Unction, Extreme.
  xx Anointings.
    Sacraments.

EXTREME UNCTION - DEVOTIONAL
  LITERATURE.
    [BQT 2608.2]

EXTREME UNCTION (CANON LAW)
    BQV230 937-947   (348.x42)
  xx Sacraments (Canon law)

EXTREME UNCTION (LITURGY)
    BQT 4455
  xx Sacraments (Liturgy)

EXULTATE, JUSTI, IN DOMINO (MUSIC).
  See PSALMS (MUSIC) - 33d PSALM.

EXULTET (PREFACE)
    BQT 4391
  xx Holy Saturday.
    Prefaces (Liturgy)

EZECHIEL, BOOK OF. See
  BIBLE. O.T. EZECHIEL.

EZEKIEL, BOOK OF. See
  BIBLE. O.T. EZECHIEL.

EZRA, BOOK OF. See
  BIBLE. O.T. 1 ESDRAS.

FABRICA ECCLESIAE. See
  CHURCH MAINTENANCE AND REPAIR.

FACULTIES (CANON LAW)
    BQV230 66 (General) (348.x25)
    BQV230 872-884 (Confessors)
    BQT 1388
  sa Absolution (Canon law)
   x Canonical faculties.
    Faculties, Canonical.
  xx Confessors (Canon law)

FACULTIES (CHURCH OF ENGLAND)

FACULTIES, CANONICAL. See
  FACULTIES (CANON LAW)

FAITH.
    BQT 236-289 (Apologetics)
      (23x9.5)
    BQT 1197; BQT 1781 (Virtue)
      (24x9.3)
  "Here are entered works on religious faith and doubt. For works
  on belief and doubt from the
  philosophical standpoint see
  Belief and doubt." LC
  sa Agnosticism.
    Apostasy.
    Atheism.
    Dogma.
    Evidence.
    Fideism.
    Hope.
    Revelation.
    Revelations, Private.
    Rule of faith.
    Salvation.
    Sanctification.
    Skepticism.
    Truth.
   x Certainty.
    Religious belief.
  xx Assurance (Theology)
    Belief and doubt.
    Christian life.
    Dogmatic theology.
    Justification.
    Knowledge, Theory of (Religion)
    Religion.
    Spiritual life.
    Trust in God.
    Virtues, Theological.

FAITH - HISTORY OF DOCTRINES.

FAITH - HISTORY OF DOCTRINES -
EARLY CHURCH.

FAITH - HISTORY OF DOCTRINES -
MIDDLE AGES.

FAITH - HISTORY OF DOCTRINES -
MODERN PERIOD.

FAITH - HISTORY OF DOCTRINES -
16th, [17th, etc.] CENTURY.

FAITH - JUVENILE LITERATURE.

FAITH - MEDITATIONS.

FAITH - SERMONS.

FAITH, CONFESSIONS OF. See
CREEDS.

FAITH, PROFESSION OF. See
PROFESSION OF FAITH.

FAITH, RULE OF. See
RULE OF FAITH.

FAITH AND REASON.
BQT 236
x Reason and faith.
xx Religion and science.

FAITH-CURE. See Healing
RZ 400-401   (615.852)
References as in LC.

FAKIRS.
BL 2015   (297)
References as in LC.

FALL OF MAN.
BQT 641-643   (231.x72)
sa Good and evil.
Paradise.
Serpent (in Paradise)
Sin, Original.
x Man, Fall of.
xx Dogmatic theology.
Eden.
Justice, Original.

FALL OF MAN -- Continued.
xx Man (Theology)
Sin.
Sin, Original.

FALL OF MAN - HISTORY OF DOCTRINES.

FALSE MESSIAHS. See
PSEUDO-MESSIAHS.

FALSEHOOD. See
TRUTHFULNESS AND FALSEHOOD.

FAMILISTS.
BX 7575
x Family of Love (Religious sect)

FAMILY.
Classifications and references
as in LC.

FAMILY - PRAYER-BOOKS.
BQT 2641
x Family devotions.
Family prayers.
Prayers, Family.

FAMILY - RELIGIOUS LIFE.
BQT 2277

FAMILY, CHRISTIAN.
BQT 2277-2281
BQT 3535-3537
sa Cana Conference Movement.
Children.
Fathers.
Mothers.
Parents.
x Catholic home.
Christian family.
Home, Catholic.
xx Christian life.
Religious education - Home
training.
Vocation.

FAMILY, CHRISTIAN - BIBLIOGRAPHY.

FAMILY, CHRISTIAN - PERIODICALS.

FAMILY, CHRISTIAN - SERMONS.

FAMILY, HOLY. See
   HOLY FAMILY.

✓ Family Celebrations 249

FAMILY DEVOTIONS. See
   FAMILY - PRAYER-BOOKS.

FAMILY OF LOVE (RELIGIOUS SECT).
   See FAMILISTS.

✓ FAMILY PLANNING

FAMILY PRAYERS. See
   FAMILY - PRAYER-BOOKS.

✓ Family relationships (649)

FANATICISM.
   BF 575 (Psychology)   *sa human*
   BR 114   *relations*
   sa Asceticism.
      Enthusiasm.
   x Intolerance.

FAQUIRS. See FAKIRS.

FAREINISTES.
   BX 7577
   Here are entered works dealing
      with a Jansenist sect founded
      at the end of the 17th century
      in the village of Farein by
      Claude and Francois Bonjours.
   x Bonjours, Les frères.
   xx Catholic Church - France.
      Flagellants and flagellation.
      Jansenists.

FAREWELL SERMONS.
   BQT 3009   (252.x5)
   x Sermons, Farewell.
   xx Occasional sermons.

FAST-DAY MENUS. See LENTEN MENUS.

FAST-DAY SERMONS.
   BQT 2997
   x Sermons, Fast-day.

FAST DAYS.
   sa Ember days.
      Lent.
      Stations, Roman.
   xx Church calendar.
      Church year.
      Fasting.
      Penance (Virtue)

FASTING.
   BQT 1989   (24x1.7)
   sa Abstinence.
      Asceticism.
      Eucharistic fast.
      Fast days.
   xx Abstinence.
      Good works (Theology)
      Penance (Virtue)

FASTING - DISPENSATION.

FASTING - HISTORY.

FASTING (CANON LAW)
   BQV230 1250-1254   (348.x412)

FASTNACHT. See SHROVETIDE.

FATE AND FATALISM.
   BJ 1460-1466 (Ethics)
   BD 411 (Philosophy)   (149.8)
   BL 235 (Religion)   (214)
   References as in LC.

FATE AND FATALISM (MOHAMMEDANISM)
   BP 166.3
   xx God (Mohammedanism)
      Mohammedan theology.

FATHERS.
   BQT 2279 (Christian family)
   HQ 756 (Sociology)   (173.5)
   sa Parents.
   xx Family.
      Family, Christian.
      Parents.

FATHERS - RELIGIOUS LIFE.

FATHERS - SERMONS.
   BQT 3001

FATHERS, APOSTOLIC. See
   APOSTOLIC FATHERS.

FATHERS OF THE CHURCH.
   BQ 142-180   (280.x1)
   "All those writers of the first
      twelve centuries whose works on
      Christian doctrine are considered
      of weight and worthy of respect.

FATHERS OF THE CHURCH -- Continued.
  "More strictly, those teachers of
    the first twelve, and especially
    the first six, centuries, who
    added notable holiness and
    complete orthodoxy to their
    learning." AT
  Here are entered works on the study
    of the writings of the Fathers of
    the church and the science of
    their contents.
  sa Apostolic Fathers.
    Catenae.
    Christian literature, Early.
    Church history - Primitive and
      early church.
    Doctors of the church.
    Saints.
    Scholia.
   x Church Fathers.
    Patristics.
    Patrology.
  xx Christian biography.
    Christian literature, Early.
    Church history.
    Church history - Primitive and
      early church.
    Church orders, Ancient.
    Saints.

FATHERS OF THE CHURCH - ADDRESSES,
  ESSAYS, LECTURES.

FATHERS OF THE CHURCH - BIBLICAL
  QUOTATIONS. See
  BIBLE - QUOTATIONS, EARLY.

FATHERS OF THE CHURCH - BIBLIOGRAPHY.
    BQ 1
    Z 7791   (016.x28)

FATHERS OF THE CHURCH - BIO-BIBLIOGRAPHY.

FATHERS OF THE CHURCH - BIOGRAPHY.
    BQ 142-147   (280.x091)

FATHERS OF THE CHURCH - COLLECTIONS.
    BQ 302-369   (280.x08)

FATHERS OF THE CHURCH - CONGRESSES.
    BQ 11

FATHERS OF THE CHURCH - DICTIONARIES.
    BQ 31

FATHERS OF THE CHURCH - HISTORY AND
  CRITICISM.
    BQ 142-147

FATHERS OF THE CHURCH - HOMILETICAL
  USE.

FATHERS OF THE CHURCH - INDEXES.

FATHERS OF THE CHURCH - INFLUENCE.

FATHERS OF THE CHURCH - INFLUENCE -
  EDUCATION.

FATHERS OF THE CHURCH - INFLUENCE -
  LITERATURE.

FATHERS OF THE CHURCH - LITURGICAL
  USE.

FATHERS OF THE CHURCH - QUOTATIONS.

FATHERS OF THE CHURCH - SELECTIONS.

FATHERS OF THE CHURCH - SERMONS.
  Here are entered sermons about
    the Church Fathers.

FATHERS OF THE CHURCH - STUDY AND
  TEACHING.
    BQ 83

FATHERS OF THE CHURCH, ALEXANDRIAN.
  See ALEXANDRIAN SCHOOL, CHRISTIAN.

FATHERS OF THE CHURCH, ANTE-NICENE.
    BQ 151-172   (280.x21)
  x Ante-Nicene Fathers.

FATHERS OF THE CHURCH, APOSTOLIC.
  See APOSTOLIC FATHERS.

FATHERS OF THE CHURCH, ARMENIAN.
    BQ 3501-3398   (280.x31)
  x Armenian Fathers of the church.

FATHERS OF THE CHURCH, COPTIC.
    BQ 3501-3598   (280.x32)
  x Coptic Fathers of the church.

FATHERS OF THE CHURCH, GREEK.
    BQ 403-443 (History and
        criticism)
    BQ 500-699 (Collections)
        (280.x41)
    BQ 1006-1949 (Individual
        authors)   (280.x4)
    x Greek Fathers of the church.
    xx Christian literature - Greek
        authors.

FATHERS OF THE CHURCH, LATIN.
    BQ 5034-5044 (History and
        criticism)
    BQ 5200-5225 (Collections)
        (280.x51)
    BQ 5601-6285 (Individual
        authors)   (280.x5)
    x Latin Fathers of the church.
    xx Christian literature - Latin
        authors.

FATHERS OF THE CHURCH, SYRIAC.
    BQ 3901-3998   (280.x33)
    x Syriac Fathers of the church.

FATHERS OF THE CHURCH AS CHURCH
    HISTORIANS.

FATHERS OF THE CHURCH AS HAGIOLO-
    GISTS.

FATHERS OF THE CHURCH AS MORALISTS.

FATHERS OF THE CHURCH AS MYSTICISTS.

FATHERS OF THE CHURCH AS PHILOSOPHERS.

FATHERS OF THE CHURCH AS SOCIOLOGISTS.

FATHERS OF THE DESERT. See
    ASCETICISM - HISTORY - EARLY CHURCH.
    HERMITS.

FATIMA, PORTUGAL (SHRINE)
    BQT 1073   (23x2.61)
    [BQX 2802.4]   (274.69)
    x Nossa Senhora da Fatima (Shrine)
    Our Lady of Fatima (Shrine)

FAULTS, CHAPTERS OF. See
    CHAPTERS OF FAULTS.

FAULTS (THEOLOGY). See
    IMPERFECTIONS (THEOLOGY)

FEAR (CANON LAW)
    sa Duress (Canon law)
    xx Guilt (Canon law)

FEAR OF GOD.
    BQT 1793
    Here are entered works on the fear
    man has of punishment inflicted
    by God for sin, which fear may
    be salutary in preventing man
    from turning away from God.
    x God, Fear of.
    xx Gifts of the Holy Spirit.
    Hell.

FEAR OF GOD - SERMONS.

Feast days x Feasts, ecclesiastical

FEAST OF ALL SAINTS. See
    ALL SAINTS' DAY.

FEAST OF CHRISTMAS. See
    CHRISTMAS.

FEAST OF DEDICATION. See
    HANUKKAH (FEAST OF LIGHTS)

FEAST OF EASTER. See
    EASTER.

FEAST OF ESTHER. See
    PURIM (FEAST OF ESTHER)

FEAST OF JESUS CHRIST THE KING. See
    JESUS CHRIST THE KING, FEAST OF.

FEAST OF LIGHTS. See
    HANUKKAH (FEAST OF LIGHTS)

FEAST OF OUR LADY OF GUADALUPE. See
    OUR LADY OF GUADALUPE, FEAST OF.

FEAST OF OUR LADY OF LOURDES. See
    OUR LADY OF LOURDES, FEAST OF.

FEAST OF OUR LADY OF MOUNT CARMEL. See
    OUR LADY OF MOUNT CARMEL, FEAST OF.

FEAST OF PENTECOST. See
    PENTECOST FESTIVAL.

182

FEAST OF ST. JOSEPH. See
JOSEPH, SAINT, FEAST OF.

FEAST OF TABERNACLES. See
SUKKOTH.

FEAST OF THE ANNUNCIATION. See
ANNUNCIATION, FEAST OF THE.

FEAST OF THE ASCENSION. See
ASCENSION DAY.

FEAST OF THE ASSUMPTION. See
ASSUMPTION, FEAST OF THE.

FEAST OF THE CIRCUMSION. See
CIRCUMCISION, FEAST OF THE.

FEAST OF THE EPIPHANY. See
EPIPHANY.

FEAST OF THE HOLY INNOCENTS. See
HOLY INNOCENTS, FEAST OF THE.

FEAST OF THE HOLY LANCE AND NAILS.
See HOLY LANCE AND NAILS, FEAST
OF THE.

FEAST OF THE IMMACULATE CONCEPTION.
See IMMACULATE CONCEPTION, FEAST
OF THE.

FEAST OF THE IMMACULATE HEART OF
MARY. See IMMACULATE HEART OF
MARY, FEAST OF THE.

FEAST OF THE MACCABEES. See
HANUKKAH (FEAST OF THE)

FEAST OF THE PRECIOUS BLOOD. See
PRECIOUS BLOOD, FEAST OF THE.

FEAST OF THE PRESENTATION OF JESUS
CHRIST. See CANDLEMAS.

FEAST OF THE PRESENTATION OF THE
BLESSED VIRGIN MARY. See
PRESENTATION OF THE BLESSED VIRGIN
MARY, FEAST OF THE.

FEAST OF THE SACRED HEART. See
SACRED HEART, FEAST OF THE.

FEAST OF THE SEVEN DOLORS OF MARY.
See SORROWS OF OUR LADY, FEAST
OF THE.

FEAST OF WEEKS. See
SHAVU'OTH (FEAST OF WEEKS)

FEASTS, ECCLESIASTICAL. (Geog. use Feast days
subdiv.)
    BQT 4219-4236   (264.x5)
sa Chronology, Ecclesiastical.
   Church calendar.
   Church year.
   Festivals.
   Holidays.
   Jesus Christ - Feasts.
   Mary, Blessed Virgin - Feasts.
   Namedays.
   Patron saints.
   Rogation days.
   Saints.
   Vigils (Liturgy)
   also names of individual ecclesi-
     astical feasts, e.g., All Saints'
     Day; Christmas; Sacred Heart,
     Feast of the; etc.
 x Bible - Festivals.
   Church festivals.
   Ecclesiastical feasts.
   Festivals, Church.
   Heortology.
   Holy days.
   Religious festivals.
   Saints - Feasts.
xx Christian antiquities.
   Chronology, Ecclesiastical.
   Church calendar.
   Festivals.
   Holidays.
   Liturgy.

FEASTS, ECCLESIASTICAL - MEDITATIONS.
    BQT 2602-2603   (24x2.1)

FEASTS, ECCLESIASTICAL - POETRY.

FEASTS, ECCLESIASTICAL - SERMONS.
    [BQT 2992.5]   (252.x2)
 sa Saints - Sermons.
  x Festival-day sermons.
    Sermons, Festival.
 xx Saints - Sermons.

FEASTS, ECCLESIASTICAL - CHURCH OF
ENGLAND, [JUDAISM, LUTHERAN
CHURCH, ETC.]

FEBRONIANISM.
        BQT 120; BQT 369 (Theology)
        BQX 987; BQX 1946 (Church
            history)
    xx Popes - Primacy.

FEDERAL THEOLOGY. See
    COVENANTS (THEOLOGY)

FEDERATED CHURCHES.
        BV 636
    "Here are entered works dealing
        with such local churches as are
        themselves a federation of two
        or more denominational churches
        united for local worship, but
        with each unit retaining its
        denominational affiliation. For
        that type of local church which
        seeks to serve all in a communi-
        ty but without any denomination-
        al affiliation see Community
        churches." LC
    x Churches, Federated.
    xx Christian union.
        Rural churches.

FEDERATIONS, LOCAL CHURCH. See
    LOCAL CHURCH COUNCILS.

FEEDING OF THE FIVE THOUSAND (MIRACLE).
    See FIVE THOUSAND, FEEDING OF THE
    (MIRACLE)

FEES, ECCLESIASTICAL.
    sa Annates.
        Mass stipends.
        Tithes.
    x Ecclesiastical fees.
        Stole fees.

FEET, WASHING OF. See
    WASHING OF FEET.

FERRARA-FLORENCE, COUNCIL OF, 1438-
    1439.
        BQX 827
    x Florence, Council of, 1438-1439.
    xx Catholic Church and reunion -
        Eastern Churches.

FESTIVAL-DAY SERMONS. See
    FEASTS, ECCLESIASTICAL - SERMONS.

FESTIVAL OF HANUKKAH. See
    HANUKKAH (FEAST OF LIGHTS)

FESTIVALS, CHURCH. See
    FEASTS, ECCLESIASTICAL.

FETISHISM.
        GN 472 (Ethnology) (291.211)
    References as in LC.

FICTION, CATHOLIC. See
    CATHOLIC FICTION.

FICTIONS (CANON LAW)
    xx Presumptions (Canon law)

FIDEISM.
        BQT 123
    "The doctrine that faith is the
        foundation of philosophy." AT
    sa Traditionalism (Theology)
    xx Faith.
        Revelation.
        Traditionalism (Theology)

FILIOQUE CONTROVERSY.
        BQT 70
    sa Nicene creed.
    xx Holy Spirit - Procession.

FINANCE, CHURCH. See
    CHURCH FINANCE.

FINDING OF THE CROSS. See
    CROSS, FINDING OF THE.

FINLAND - CHURCH HISTORY.
        BQX 1692-1697 (Latin Church)
        BQX 5971-5977 (Orthodox
            Church)

FIRE (IN RELIGION, FOLKLORE, ETC.)
    sa Candles and lights.

FIRE-WORSHIPPERS.
        BL 453
    References as in LC.

184

FIRST COMMUNION.
        BQT 1352   (23x7.3)
    x Communion, First.
    xx Communion, Holy.
        Eucharist.

FIRST COMMUNION - BIOGRAPHY.

FIRST COMMUNION - CATECHISMS,
    QUESTION-BOOKS.
        BQT 3197

FIRST COMMUNION - DEVOTIONAL
    LITERATURE.
        BQT 2646

FIRST COMMUNION - INSTRUCTION
    AND STUDY.
        BQT 3154

FIRST COMMUNION - PRAYER-BOOKS.
        BQT 2646   (252.x54)

FIRST COMMUNION - SERMONS.   See
    FIRST COMMUNION SERMONS.

FIRST COMMUNION - STORIES.   See
    FIRST COMMUNION STORIES.

FIRST COMMUNION (CANON LAW)
        BQV230 854
    xx Eucharist (Canon law)

FIRST COMMUNION SERMONS.
        BQT 3009   (252.x54)
    x First Communion - Sermons.
      Sermons, Communion.
      Sermons, First communion.
    xx Occasional sermons.

FIRST COMMUNION STORIES.
    x First communion - Stories.
      Stories, First communion.

FIRST FRIDAY DEVOTIONS.
        BQT 2670   (24x8.71)
    x Nine First Fridays.
    xx Devotions, Popular.

FIRST FRIDAY DEVOTIONS - SERMONS.

FIRST FRUITS.   See
    ANNATES.
    TITHES.

FIRST MASS SERMONS.
        BQT 3004
    xx Ordination sermons.

FIRST SATURDAY DEVOTIONS.
        BQT 2679
    x Five First Saturdays.

FISH (IN RELIGION, FOLKLORE, ETC.)
        BQT 5840
    x Folklore of fishes.
      Ichthys.
    xx Christian art.
       Jesus Christ - Art.

FISHING IN THE BIBLE.
    xx Sea in the Bible.

FIVE FIRST SATURDAYS.   See
    FIRST SATURDAY DEVOTIONS.

FIVE SCROLLS.   See
    BIBLE. O.T. FIVE SCROLLS.

FIVE THOUSAND, FEEDING OF THE (MIRACLE)
    See FEEDING OF THE FIVE THOUSAND
    (MIRACLE)

FIVE WOUNDS, DEVOTION TO.
        BQT 2593; BQT 2670   (24x8.71)
    sa Missa Sacrorum Quinque Vulnerum.
    x Jesus Christ - Five wounds,
        Devotion to.
      Wounds of Christ, Devotion to.
    xx Devotions, Popular.
       Jesus Christ - Passion.

FLABELLA.
        BQT 5959
    xx Fans.

FLAGELLANTS (SECT)
        BQX 668 (Church history)
        BQX 89 (Heresies)
    x Albati.
      Bianchi.
    xx Sects, Medieval.

FLAGELLANTS AND FLAGELLATION.
    BQT 2221 (Asceticism)
      (24x1.4)
    HV 8613-8621 (Punishment)
      (343.2)
  References as in LC, with the
    following additional references.
  sa Fareinistes.
  xx Penance (Virtue)

FLIGHT INTO EGYPT. See
  JESUS CHRIST - FLIGHT INTO EGYPT.

FLOOD, BIBLICAL. See DELUGE.

FLORENCE, COUNCIL OF, 1438-1439. See
  FERRARA-FLORENCE, COUNCIL OF, 1438-
  1439.

FLOWER ARRANGEMENT IN CHURCHES.
    SB 449.5.C4
  x Church flower arrangement.
  xx Church decoration and ornament.

FLOWERS (IN RELIGION, FOLKLORE, ETC.)
    BQT 4522

FLYING MISSIONARIES. See
  AERONAUTICS IN MISSIONARY WORK.

FOLKLORE OF DOVE, [FIRE, FISHES, ETC.]
  See DOVE, [FIRE, FISH, ETC.] (IN
  RELIGION, FOLKLORE, ETC.)

FOLLOWING OF CHRIST. See
  IMITATIO CHRISTI.

FONTS.
    BQT 5952 (246)
  sa Holy water fonts.
  x Baptismal fonts.
  xx Baptism.
    Baptisteries.
    Christian antiquities.
    Christian art.
    Church decoration and ornament.
    Church furniture.

FOOT, WASHING OF. See
  WASHING OF FEET.

FORBIDDEN BOOKS. See
  PROHIBITED BOOKS.

FORBIDDEN SOCIETIES. See
  CONDEMNED SOCIETIES.

FORCE (CANON LAW). See
  DURESS (CANON LAW)

FOREIGN MISSIONS. See
  MISSIONS, FOREIGN.

FOREIGNERS, CHURCH WORK WITH. See
  CHURCH WORK WITH FOREIGNERS.

FOREKNOWLEDGE OF GOD. See
  GOD - FOREKNOWLEDGE.

FORENAMES. See NAMES, PERSONAL.

FORGERY (CANON LAW)

FORGIVENESS OF SIN.
    BQT 1190 (234.4)
  sa Absolution.
    Confession.
    Penance.
    Repentance.
  x Sin, Forgiveness of.

FORMS (CANON LAW)
    BQV 196

FORTITUDE.
    BQT 1209; BQT 1789 (24x1.52)
  "A cardinal virtue and one of the
  gifts of the Holy Ghost, whereby
  man is inclined to face those
  evils which he most dreads and to
  resist the motions of mere reck-
  lessness; it involves the control,
  not the absence, of fear." AT
  sa Patience.
    Perseverance.
  xx Virtues, Moral.

FORTY HOURS' DEVOTION.
    BQT 2668; BQT 4351 (24x8.71)
  xx Devotions, Popular.
    Eucharist - Cultus.

FORTY HOURS' DEVOTION - HANDBOOKS,
  MANUALS, ETC.
    BQT 4351

FORTY HOURS' DEVOTION - SERMONS.
    BQT 3009 (252.x54)

FORUM ECCLESIASTICUM. See
ECCLESIASTICAL COURTS.

FOUNDATION MASS.
BQV230 826
Here are entered works on Masses
for which stipends are received
from endowments canonically
established for this purpose.
x Mass, Foundation.
xx Pious foundations.

FOUNDATIONS, PIOUS. See
PIOUS FOUNDATIONS.

FOURTEEN HOLY HELPERS.
x Devotions, Popular.
Helpers, Fourteen holy.
Holy helpers, Fourteen.

FOURTEEN HOLY HELPERS - PRAYER-BOOKS.
BQT 2689

FRANCE - CHURCH HISTORY.
BQX 1701-1878   (274.4)
x Gallican Church.

FRANCE - CHURCH HISTORY - SOURCES.

FRANCE - CHURCH HISTORY - EARLY
PERIOD TO 741.
BQX 1717-1739

FRANCE - CHURCH HISTORY - 742-1285.
BQX 1731-1744

FRANCE - CHURCH HISTORY - 1285-1483.
BQX 1748-1759

FRANCE - CHURCH HISTORY - 1483-1789.
BQX 1762-1779

FRANCE - CHURCH HISTORY - 1789-
BQX 1781-1798

FRANCE - CHURCH HISTORY - 20th
CENTURY.
BQX 1794

FRANCE - HISTORY - REVOLUTION -
RELIGIOUS HISTORY.
BQX 1783-1785   (274.404)
sa Nonjurors, French Catholic.

FRANCE - RELIGION.

FRANCISCAN BROTHERS. See
FRANCISCANS. LAY BROTHERS.

FRANCISCAN CROWN.
x Crown, Franciscan.
Rosary, Seraphic.
Seraphic rosary.
xx Mary, Blessed Virgin -
Prayer-books.

FRANCISCAN RECOLLETS. See
RECOLLETS (FRANCISCAN)

FRANCISCAN SAINTS. See
SAINTS, FRANCISCAN.

FRANCISCAN SISTERS.   (Geog.
subdiv., Direct)
BQX 7901-7914   (271.9)
Here are entered works on the
Franciscan Sisters in general.
Works dealing with any of the
numerous individual Franciscan
Sisterhoods are entered under
the specific name of the order,
e.g., Franciscan Missionary
Sisters of the Sacred Heart.
sa Poor Clares.

FRANCISCAN THEOLOGIANS. See
THEOLOGIANS, FRANCISCAN.

FRANCISCANS.   (Geog. subdiv.,
Direct)
BQX 7371-7420   (271.x1)
sa Capuchins.
Fraticelli.
Recollets (Franciscan)

x Friars, Grey.
Friars Minor.
Gray Friars.
Grey Friars.
Minorites.
Order of Friars Minor.
Ordo Fratrum Minorum.
St. Francis, Order of.
xx Friars.

FRANCISCANS - BIBLIOGRAPHY.
BQX 7371
Z 7840

FRANCISCANS - BIO-BIBLIOGRAPHY.

FRANCISCANS - BIOGRAPHY.
BQX 7419-7420
sa Saints, Franciscan.

FRANCISCANS - CANON LAW.
[BQX 7384.7]

FRANCISCANS - CHARITIES.

FRANCISCANS - COLLECTED WORKS.
BQX 7373

FRANCISCANS - COLLECTIONS.
BQX 7373

FRANCISCANS - DIRECTORIES.
BQX 7374

FRANCISCANS - EDUCATION.
[BQX 7384.5]
sa Franciscans and education.

FRANCISCANS - FICTION.

FRANCISCANS - HABIT.

FRANCISCANS - HISTORY.
BQX 7381-7405

FRANCISCANS - MEDITATIONS.

FRANCISCANS - MISSIONS.   (Geog.
subdiv.)
[BQX 7384.6]
x Missions, Franciscans.

FRANCISCANS - NOVITIATE. See
NOVITIATE - FRANCISCANS.

FRANCISCANS - PERIODICALS.
BQX 7372

FRANCISCANS - POPULAR DEVOTIONS.

FRANCISCANS - POPULAR DEVOTIONS -
PASSION OF CHRIST.

FRANCISCANS - POPULAR DEVOTIONS -
SACRED HEART OF JESUS.

FRANCISCANS - PRAYER-BOOKS.

FRANCISCANS - PROFESSION. See
PROFESSION, RELIGIOUS - FRANCISCAN.

FRANCISCANS - RECRUITING.

FRANCISCANS - RETREATS. See
RETREATS FOR FRANCISCANS.

FRANCISCANS - RULES.
BQX 7375-7378

FRANCISCANS - SPIRITUAL LIFE.
BQX 7384

################

FRANCISCANS - ARIZONA, [CALIFORNIA,
ENGLAND, ETC.]
BQX 7389-7405

################

FRANCISCANS. LAY BROTHERS.
[BQX 7415]
x Franciscan Brothers.

FRANCISCANS. LITURGY AND RITUAL.
BQT 4791-4799

FRANCISCANS. PROVINCES. ASSUMPTION,
[IMMACULATE CONCEPTION, ETC.]
BQX 7414

FRANCISCANS. SECOND ORDER. See
POOR CLARES.

FRANCISCANS. THIRD ORDER.   (Geog.
subdiv.)
BQX 7416
x Third Order Secular of St.
Francis.

FRANCISCANS. THIRD ORDER -
BIOGRAPHY.
BQX 7416.8

FRANCISCANS. THIRD ORDER -
CANON LAW.

FRANCISCANS. THIRD ORDER -
CONGRESSES.

188

FRANCISCANS. THIRD ORDER -
DEVOTIONAL LITERATURE.

FRANCISCANS. THIRD ORDER -
DIRECTORIES.

FRANCISCANS. THIRD ORDER -
HANDBOOKS, MANUALS, ETC.
[BQX 7416.25]

FRANCISCANS. THIRD ORDER -
HISTORY.
BQX 7416.3

FRANCISCANS. THIRD ORDER -
MEDITATIONS.

FRANCISCANS. THIRD ORDER -
PRAYER-BOOKS.

FRANCISCANS. THIRD ORDER -
PRAYER-BOOKS - ENGLISH, [FRENCH,
ETC.]

FRANCISCANS. THIRD ORDER -
PROFESSION. See
PROFESSION, RELIGIOUS - FRANCISCANS.
THIRD ORDER.

FRANCISCANS. THIRD ORDER -
RULES.
BQX 7416.2

FRANCISCANS. THIRD ORDER -
SERMONS.
BQX 7416.4

################

FRANCISCANS. THIRD ORDER - ENGLAND,
GERMANY, U.S., ETC.]
BQX 7416.5

################

FRANCISCANS. THIRD ORDER (PRO-
TESTANT)
x Franciscans, Protestant.
Protestant Franciscans.

FRANCISCANS. THIRD ORDER REGULAR.
BQX 7408   (271.9)

FRANCISCANS, CELESTINE. See
CELESTINES (FRANCISCANS)

FRANCISCANS, PROTESTANT. See
FRANCISCANS. THIRD ORDER (PRO-
TESTANT)

FRANCISCANS AND EDUCATION.
xx Franciscans - Education.

FRANCISCANS AND MARIOLOGY.

FRANCISCANS AND MYSTICISM.

FRANCISCANS AND PHILOSOPHY.

FRANCISCANS AND POVERTY.

FRANCISCANS AND PREACHING.

FRANCISCANS AND SCIENCE.

FRANCISCANS AND THE COUNTER-
REFORMATION.
xx Counter-reformation.

FRANCISCANS AND THEOLOGY.
sa Theologians, Franciscan.

FRANCISCANS IN ART.

FRANCISCANS IN LITERATURE.

FRATERNAL CORRECTION. See
CORRECTION, FRATERNAL.

FRATICELLI.
BQT 89
BQX 7408
xx Franciscans.
Mysticism - History - Middle
Ages.

FREE AGENCY. See
FREE WILL AND DETERMINISM.

FREE CHURCH OF SCOTLAND.
BX 9084   (285.6)

FREE METHODIST CHURCH.

FREE THOUGHT.
    BQT 123   (211)
sa Agnosticism.
  Apologetics.
  Bible - Evidences, authority,
    etc.
  Christianity - Evidences.
  Rationalism.
  Religious liberty.
  Skepticism.
 x Freethinkers.
xx Deism.
  God.
  Irreligion.
  Liberty of conscience.
  Rationalism.

FREE WILL AND DETERMINISM.
    BJ 1460-1468 (Ethics) (171)
    BF 620-628 (Psychology)
     (159.1)
    BQT 1132 (Free will and grace)
     (234.x2)
    BQT 1753-1755 (Moral theology)
sa Concupiscence.
  Freedom (Theology)
  Inhibition.
  Necessity (Philosophy)
  Responsibility.
  Use of reason.
 x Determinism and indeterminism.
  Free agency.
  Freedom of the will.
  Indeterminism.
  Liberty of the will.
xx Conscience.
  Fate and fatalism.
  Human acts.
  Necessity (Philosophy)
  Philosophy.
  Predestination.
  Responsibility.
  Will.

FREEDOM (THEOLOGY)
 x Liberty (Theology)
 xx Free will and determinism.
  Law and gospel.

FREEDOM OF CONSCIENCE. See
 CONSCIENCE.

FREEDOM OF RELIGION. See
 RELIGIOUS LIBERTY.

FREEDOM OF SPEECH IN THE CHURCH. See
 LIBERTY OF SPEECH IN THE CHURCH.

FREEDOM OF THE WILL. See
 FREE WILL AND DETERMINISM.

FREEDOM OF WORSHIP. See
 RELIGIOUS LIBERTY.

FREEMASONS.
    HS 351-929   (366.1)
  References and subdivisions as
  in LC.

FREEMASONS AND CATHOLIC CHURCH.
    HS 495
  sa Anti-clericalism.
   x Catholic Church and Free-
    masonry.
  xx Secret societies and Catholic
    Church.

FREETHINKERS. See FREE THOUGHT.

FRENCH CATHOLIC NONJURORS. See
 NONJURORS, FRENCH CATHOLIC.

FRENCH LITERATURE - CATHOLIC AUTHORS.
  BQ 150

FRENCH PROTESTANTS. See
 HUGUENOTS.
 PROTESTANTS IN FRANCE.

FRENCH SAINTS. See
 SAINTS, FRENCH.

FREQUENCY OF CONFESSION. See
 CONFESSION - FREQUENCY.

FREQUENT COMMUNION. See
 CONFESSION - FREQUENT.

FRERES DES ECOLES CHRETIENNES. See
 BROTHERS OF THE CHRISTIAN SCHOOLS.

190

FRIARS.
      BQX 6838
  sa Augustinians.
     Carmelites.
     Dominicans.
     Franciscans.
     Religious orders.
  xx Mendicant orders.
     Religious orders.

FRIARS, BLACK. See DOMINICANS.

FRIARS, GRAY. See FRANCISCANS.

FRIARS, WHITE. See CARMELITES.

FRIARS MINOR. See FRANCISCANS.

FRIARS MINOR CAPUCHIN. See
  CAPUCHINS.

FRIARS PREACHERS. See DOMINICANS.

FRIEND CHURCHES. See
  CHURCHES, FRIEND.

FRIEND MEETING-HOUSES. See
  CHURCHES, FRIEND.

FRIENDS, SOCIETY OF.
      BX 7601-7797   (289.6)
  sa Churches, Friend.
   x Quakers.
  xx Congregationalism.
  Subdivisions as in LC.

Friendship see Human Relations

FRUITS OF THE HOLY SPIRIT.
      BQT 1220
  sa Kindness (Theology)
   x Holy Spirit, Fruits of the.
  xx Grace, Habitual.

FUNDAMENTAL THEOLOGY. See
  APOLOGETICS.

✓ FUNDAMENTALISM.
      BT 78
  Scope note and references
    as in LC.

FUNERAL RITES AND CEREMONIES.
  (Geog. subdiv., Indirect)
     GN 486 (Ethnology)
     BT 3150-3390 (Manners and
       customs)   (393)
     BQT 1998 (Moral theology)
  sa Ancestor-worship.
     Cremation.
     Dead.
     Funeral service.
     Indians of North America -
      Mortuary customs.
     Indians of South America -
      Mortuary customs.
     Lanterns of the dead.
     Lecythi.
     Memorial service.
     Mourning customs.
     Scaffold burial.
     Urns.
   x Burial customs.
     Obsequies.
     Rites and ceremonies, Funeral.
  xx Ancestor-worship.
     Cremation.
     Dead.
     Funeral service.
     Rites and ceremonies.

FUNERAL RITES AND CEREMONIES - EARLY
  CHURCH.
  xx Church history - Primitive and
    early church.
  Other subdivisions as in LC.

FUNERAL RITES AND CEREMONIES (CANON
  LAW)
      BQV230 1203-1242   (348.x414)

FUNERAL SERMONS.
      BQT 3002   (252.x7)
  sa Obituaries.
   x Sermons, Funeral.
  xx Funeral orations.
     Occasional sermons.

FUNERAL SERMONS - OUTLINES.

FUNERAL SERMONS, ENGLISH, [FRENCH,
  GERMAN, ETC.]

FUNERAL SERVICE.
>BQT 4456
sa Funeral rites and ceremonies.
 x Burial service.
xx Funeral rites and ceremonies.

FUNERAL SERVICE - ORTHODOX EASTERN
CHURCH.

FUTURE LIFE.
>BL 535-547 (Comparative
>religion)   (291.x23)
>BQT 1503-1563 (Theology)
>(236.x1)
sa Beatific vision.
Death.
Elysium.
Eschatology.
Eternity.
Future punishment.
Heaven.
Hell.
Immortality.
Judgment-day.
Millenium.
Purgatory.
Resurrection.
Reward (Theology)
Salvation.
Soul.
Spiritualism.
Transmigration.
Translation into heaven.
Universe, Destruction of.
 x Eternal life.
Hades.
Life, Future.
Life after death.
xx Death.
Eschatology.
Eternity.
Future punishment.
Heaven.
Immortality.
Purgatory.
Resurrection.
Soul.

FUTURE LIFE - BIBLICAL TEACHING.
>BQT 1510

FUTURE LIFE - BIBLIOGRAPHY.

FUTURE LIFE - MEDITATIONS.

FUTURE LIFE - SERMONS.

FUTURE PUNISHMENT.
>BQT 1514-1528   (236.x51)
sa Future life.
Hell.
Purgatory.
Universalism.
 x Eternal punishment.
xx Annihilationism.
Death.
Eschatology.
Future life.
Hell.
Punishment.
Purgatory.
Universalism.

FUTURE PUNISHMENT - HISTORY OF
DOCTRINES.

GALATIANS, EPISTLE TO THE. See
BIBLE. N.T. GALATIANS.

GALLICAN CHURCH. See
CATHOLIC CHURCH - FRANCE.
FRANCE - CHURCH HISTORY.

GALLICAN RITE.
>BQT 4137   (264.x82)

GALLICAN SACRAMENTARY. See
SACRAMENTARIUM GALLICANUM.

GALLICANISM.
>BQX 987; BQX 1750; BQX 1774;
>BQX 1793 (Church history)
>(274.404-274.408)
>BQT 119; BQT 369 (Theology)
"Here are entered works dealing
with the theories advocated by
[some] French Catholics, assert-
ing the supremacy of the French
state and clergy as opposed to
the asserted supremacy of the
pope." LC
sa Conciliar theory.
Josephinism.
Pragmatic Sanction of
Charles VII, 1438.
xx Catholic Church - France.
Church and state in France.

GARDEN OF EDEN. See EDEN.

GAUL - CHURCH HISTORY.
      BQX 1717-1729   (274.401)

GAULS - RELIGION.

GELASIAN SACRAMENTARY. See
  SACRAMENTARIUM GELASIANUM.

GENERAL CHURCH OF THE NEW JERUSALEM.

GENERAL CONFESSION.
     [BQT 1724.5]
  xx Confession.

GENERAL COUNCILS. See
  COUNCILS AND SYNODS, ECUMENICAL.

GENERAL ZIONISM.
  References as in LC.

GENESIS, BOOK OF. See
  BIBLE. O.T. GENESIS.

GENUFLEXION.
     BQT 4518
  xx Adoration.
    Posture in worship.

GEOGRAPHY, BIBLICAL. See
  ECCLESIASTICAL GEOGRAPHY.

GEOGRAPHY AND RELIGION. See
  RELIGION AND GEOGRAPHY.

GEOLOGY AND BIBLE. See
  BIBLE AND GEOLOGY.

GEOLOGY AND RELIGION. See
  BIBLE AND GEOLOGY.
  RELIGION AND SCIENCE.

GEORGIA (TRANSCAUCASIA) - CHURCH
  HISTORY.
     BQX 5981-5990

GEORGIAN CHRISTIAN LITERATURE. See
  CHRISTIAN LITERATURE - GEORGIAN
  AUTHORS.

GEORGIAN RITE. See
  BYZANTINE RITE, GEORGIAN.

GERMAN CATHOLICISM.
     BX 4740
  "Here are entered works on an
    antipapal, nationalistic move-
    ment among Catholics in Germany
    started by J. Ronge and J.
    Czerski in 1844. The movement
    was subsequently merged into the
    "free religious" movement." LC
  x Deutschkatholizismus.
  xx Catholic Church - Germany.

GERMAN PRESBYTERIANS. See
  PRESBYTERIANS, GERMAN.

GERMANIC TRIBES - RELIGION.
  sa Salvation (Germanic religion)

GERMANY - CHURCH HISTORY.
     BQX 1881-1986   (274.3)

GERMANY - CHURCH HISTORY - 843-1517.
     BQX 1904-1919

GERMANY - CHURCH HISTORY - 1517-1648.
     BQX 1921-1939

GERMANY - CHURCH HISTORY - REFORMATION.
  See REFORMATION - GERMANY.

GERMANY - CHURCH HISTORY - 1648-
     BQX 1941-1959

GERMANY - CHURCH HISTORY - 19th
  CENTURY.

GERMANY - CHURCH HISTORY - 20th
  CENTURY.

GERMANY - CHURCH HISTORY - 1933-1945.
     BQX 1957

GERMANY - CHURCH HISTORY - 1945-
     BQX 1957.5

GERMANY - RELIGION.

GERMANY - RELIGION - MIDDLE AGES.

GERMANY - RELIGION - 18th CENTURY.

GERMANY - RELIGION - 19th CENTURY.

GERMANY - RELIGION - 20th CENTURY.

GERMANY - RELIGION - 1933-1945.
  BR 856

GERMANY - RELIGION - 1945-
  BR 856.3

GHIBELLINES. See
 GUELFS AND GHIBELLINES.

GHOSTS.
  BF 1445-1543 (133.1)
  GR 580 (Folklore) (398.4)
 sa Apparitions.
  Demonology.
  Hallucinations and illusions.
  Psychical research.
  Spiritualism.
  Superstition.
 xx Apparitions.
  Spirits.

GIFT OF TONGUES. See
 GLOSSOLALIA.

GIFTS (CANON LAW)

GIFTS, SPIRITUAL. See
 CHARISMATA.

GIFTS OF THE HOLY SPIRIT.
  BQT 1217-1218 (234.15)
 sa Charismata.
  Fear of God.
 x Holy Spirit, Gifts of the.
  Seven gifts of the Holy Spirit.
 xx Grace, Habitual.

GIFTS OF THE HOLY SPIRIT - SERMONS.
 xx Holy Spirit - Sermons.

GILBERTINE RITE.
  BQT 4811-4819

GILDS, ALTAR. See ALTAR GILDS.

GIRLS - PRAYER-BOOKS.
  BQT 2645

GIRLS - RELIGIOUS LIFE.
  BQT 2284 (24x8.3)
 sa Retreats for young women.
 xx Youth - Religious life.

GIRLS - RETREATS. See
 RETREATS FOR CHILDREN.
 RETREATS FOR YOUNG WOMEN.

GIRLS IN THE BIBLE. See
 CHILDREN IN THE BIBLE.

GIROVAGUES.
  BQX 6838
 x Gyrovagi.
 xx Religious orders - History -
  Early period.

GIVING, CHRISTIAN. See
 CHRISTIAN GIVING.

GLAGOLITIC LITURGY. See
 SLAVONIC USE.

GLEBES. See CHURCH LANDS.

GLORIA IN EXCELSIS DEO.

GLORY (THEOLOGY)
  [BQT 1550]
  [BQT 1192.5]
 sa Beatific vision.
 xx Saints.

GLOSSATORS.
 xx Canon law - History.
  Roman law - History.

GLOSSOLALIA.
  BL 54
 sa Pentecostal churches.
 x Gift of tongues.
  Speaking with tongues.
  Tongues, Gift of.

GLUTTONY.
  BQT 1813 (24x1.44)
 xx Capital sins.
  Temperance (Virtue)

GNOSTICISM.
  BQ 686 (Christian literature)
  BQT 48; BQT 72; BQT 1114
   (Theology)
  BQX 3625 (Church history)
   (273.x11)
 sa Docetism.
  Ebionism.

GNOSTICISM -- Continued.
   sa Mandaeans.
      Priscillianists.
   xx Religions.
      Theosophy.

GOD.
      BQT 514-568   (231)
   sa Agnosticism.
      Anthropomorphism.
      Atheism.
      Christianity.
      Creation.
      Deism.
      Free thought.
      Holy, The.
      Holy Spirit.
      Jesus Christ.
      Metaphysics.
      Mythology.
      Natural theology.
      Nihilianism.
      Occasionalism.
      Ontologism.
      Pantheism.
      Polytheism.
      Providence, Divine.
      Rationalism.
      Religion.
      Teleology.
      Trinity.
   xx Christianity.
      Creation.
      Deism.
      Dogmatic theology.
      Natural theology.
      Philosophy.
      Religion.
      Theism.
      Theology.
      Trinity.

GOD - ADDRESSES, ESSAYS, LECTURES.
      BQT 515

GOD - ANGER. See ANGER OF GOD.

GOD - ART.
      BQT 5851-5854   (246.x64)
   sa Gods in art.
      Holy Spirit - Art.
      Jesus Christ - Art.
      Trinity - Art.
   xx Christian art.

GOD - ATTRIBUTES.
      BQT 531-568   (231.x12)
   x Attributes of God.

GOD - ATTRIBUTES - SERMONS.

GOD - BEAUTY.
      BQT 561   (231.x16)

√ GOD - BIBLICAL TEACHING.
      [BQT 512]
      BM 610
      BT 99

GOD - CREATOR. See CREATION.

GOD - EXEMPLARY CAUSE.
      BQT 605
   sa Image of God.

GOD - EXISTENCE.
      BQT 516   (231.x11)
   sa Causation.
      Natural theology.
   x Existence of God.
      God - Proof.

GOD - EXISTENCE - EMPIRICAL ARGUMENT.

GOD - EXISTENCE - MORAL ARGUMENT.

GOD - EXISTENCE - ONTOLOGICAL ARGUMENT.

GOD - EXISTENCE - SERMONS.
      BQT 3052

GOD - EXISTENCE - TELEOLOGICAL ARGUMENT.

GOD - FATHERHOOD.
      BQT 585
   sa Adoption (Theology)
      Children of God.
   xx Children of God.
      Kingdom of God.

GOD - FATHERHOOD - PRAYER-BOOKS.
      BQT 2652

GOD - FOREKNOWLEDGE.
      BQT 547   (231.x18)
   x Foreknowledge of God.
      Knowledge of God.
   xx Predestination.

GOD - GOODNESS.
     BQT 561

GOD - HISTORY OF DOCTRINES.
     BQT 528-529
  x God (Theory of knowledge)

GOD - HISTORY OF DOCTRINES - ANCIENT
  PERIOD.
   sa God (Assyro-Babylonian religion)
     God (Brahmanism)
     God (Chinese religion)
     God (Egyptian religion)
     God (Greek religion)

GOD - HISTORY OF DOCTRINES - EARLY
  CHRISTIAN PERIOD.

GOD - HISTORY OF DOCTRINES - MIDDLE
  AGES.

GOD - HISTORY OF DOCTRINES - MODERN
  PERIOD.

GOD - HISTORY OF DOCTRINES - 16th,
  [17th, etc.] CENTURY.

GOD - IMMANENCE. See
  IMMANENCE OF GOD.

GOD - IMMUTABILITY..
     BQT 540   (231.x12)

GOD - IMPASSIBILITY.
     BQT 540   (231.x12)

GOD - INDWELLING. See
  IMMANENCE OF GOD.

GOD - JUSTICE.
     BQT 563   (231.x16)
  x God - Righteousness.

GOD - JUVENILE LITERATURE.
     BQT 515

GOD - KINGSHIP.

GOD - KNOWABLENESS.
     BQT 517   (231.x11)
  sa Desire for God.
  x God (Theory of knowledge)
    Knowledge of God.
  xx Knowledge, Theory of (Religion)

GOD - LOVABLENESS. See
  LOVE (THEOLOGY)

GOD - LOVE.
     BQT 567   (231.x16)
  Here are entered works on God's
   love toward man. For works on
   the love which man accords God
   see Love (Theology).
  Cf. note under Love (Theology).
  xx Love (Theology)

GOD - MEDITATIONS.
     BQT 2580   (24x2.9)

GOD - MERCY.
     BQT 567   (231.x16)
  sa Jesus Christ - Mercy.
  x Mercy of God.

GOD - MOTHERHOOD.

GOD - NAME.
     BQT 520   (231)
  sa Emmanuel.
    Jahve.
    Holy Name, Devotion to.
    Memra (The word)
  xx Bible - Names.

GOD - OMNIPOTENCE.
     BQT 540   (231.x12)

GOD - OMNIPRESENCE.
     BQT 540   (231.x12)
  sa Immanence of God.
    Presence of God, Practice of.

GOD - OMNISCIENCE.
     BQT 547   (231.x12)
  x Knowledge of God.

GOD - PERSONALITY.
     BQT 526; BQT 575   (231.x12)

GOD - POETRY.

GOD - PROMISES.

GOD - PROOF. See
  GOD - EXISTENCE.

GOD - PROVIDENCE. See
  PROVIDENCE, DIVINE.

GOD - RIGHTEOUSNESS.   See
GOD - JUSTICE.

GOD - SERMONS.
     BQT 3052

GOD - SOVEREIGNTY.
     BQT 552-556   (231.x13)
xx Divine law.

GOD - TRANSCENDENCE. See
TRANSCENDENCE OF GOD.

GOD - WILL.
     BQT 551   (231.x16)

GOD - WISDOM.
     BQT 561   (231.x14)

GOD - WORSHIP AND LOVE.   See
LOVE (THEOLOGY).
WORSHIP.

GOD - WRATH.   See   ANGER OF GOD.

GOD (ASSYRO-BABYLONIAN RELIGION)
xx God - History of doctrines -
     Ancient period.

GOD (BRAHMANISM)
xx God - History of doctrines -
     Ancient period.

GOD (CHINESE RELIGION)
xx God - History of doctrines -
     Ancient period.

GOD (EGYPTIAN RELIGION)
xx God - History of doctrines -
     Ancient period.

GOD (GREEK RELIGION)
xx God - History of doctrines -
     Ancient period.

GOD (HINDUISM)

GOD (JUDAISM)
     BM 610

GOD (MOHAMMEDANISM)
sa Fate and fatalism (Mohammedanism)
   Trust in God (Mohammedanism)

GOD (THEORY OF KNOWLEDGE).   See
GOD - HISTORY OF DOCTRINES.
GOD - KNOWABLENESS.

GOD, DESIRE FOR.   See
DESIRE FOR GOD.

GOD, FEAR OF. See FEAR OF GOD.

GOD, IMAGE OF. See IMAGE OF GOD.

GOD AND MAN, MYSTICAL UNION OF.   See
MYSTICAL UNION.

GOD IN LITERATURE.
sa Gods in literature.
   Jesus Christ in literature.
xx Gods in literature.
   Religion in literature.

GODDESSES, MOTHER.   See
MOTHER-GODDESSES.

GODDESSES IN LITERATURE.   See
GODS IN LITERATURE.

GODFATHERS.   See   SPONSORS.

GODMOTHERS.   See   SPONSORS.

GODS.
     BL 473   (290; 291.21)
sa Healing gods.
   Mother-goddesses.
   Mythology.
   Religions.
   Titans (Mythology)
   also names of deities, e.g.,
     Athena; Baal (Deity); etc.
 x Deities.
xx Religions.

GODS - COSTUME. See IDOLS AND
IMAGES - COSTUME AND ADORNMENT.

GODS - LANGUAGE.
     P 141

GODS, HEALING. See
HEALING GODS.

GODS, HINDU.
 x Hindu gods.
 xx Hinduism.

GODS IN ART.
 sa Idols and images.
 x Goddesses in art.
 xx Art and religion.
 God - Art.
 Idols and images.

GODS IN LITERATURE.
 sa God in literature.
 x Goddesses in literature.
 xx Art and religion.
 God - Art.
 God in literature.
 Religion in literature.

GOD'S TRUCE. See
 TRUCE OF GOD.

GOLDEN RULE.
 Classifications and references
 as in LC.

GOOD AND EVIL.
 BJ 1400-1408 (Philosophy)
 (111.84; 170)
 BQT 565 (Theology) (231.x61)
 sa Evil in literature.
 Providence, Divine.
 Sin.
 Suffering.
 x Evil.
 Theodicy.
 xx Dogmatic theology.
 Fall of man.
 Suffering.

GOOD FAITH (CANON LAW)

GOOD FRIDAY.
 BQT 4223 (264.x52)
 sa Holy Week.
 Three Hours.
 x Mass of the Presanctified.
 Presanctified, Mass of the.
 xx Holy Week.

GOOD FRIDAY - LITURGY.
 BQT 4223

GOOD FRIDAY - MEDITATIONS.

GOOD FRIDAY SERMONS.
 BQT 2999
 x Sermons, Good Friday.
 xx Jesus Christ - Passion -
 Sermons.

GOOD INTENTION. See INTENTION.

GOOD SAMARITAN (PARABLE)
 BQT 888 (226.x6)

GOOD SHEPHERD.
 BQT 888

GOOD SHEPHERD - ART.
 BQT 5876

GOOD SHEPHERD - SERMONS.
 BQT 3057

GOOD WORKS (THEOLOGY)
 sa Alms and almsgiving.
 Antinomianism.
 Corporal works of mercy.
 Fasting.
 Indulgences.
 Justification.
 Prayer.
 Reward (Theology)
 Spiritual works of mercy.
 xx Asceticism.
 Justification.
 Sanctification.

GOOD WORKS (THEOLOGY) - EARLY WORKS
 TO 1800.

GOODS, ECCLESIASTICAL. See
 CHURCH SUPPLIES.

GORDON RIOTS, 1780.
 DA 510 (975.836)
 x No-popery riots, 1780.
 xx Catholic emancipation.

GOSPEL AND LAW. See
 LAW AND GOSPEL.

GOSPELS. See
 BIBLE. N.T. GOSPELS.

GOSPELS (APOCRYPHAL)
      BS 2850-2851

GOSPELS (APOCRYPHAL). ENGLISH,
   [FRENCH, LATIN, ETC.]
      BS 2850

GOSPELS (APOCRYPHAL) - CRITICISM,
   INTERPRETATION, ETC.
      BS 2851

GOSPELS, LENTEN.
   x Lenten gospels.
   xx Bible. N.T. Gospels, Liturgical.
      Lent - Liturgy.

GOSPELS, LITURGICAL. See
   BIBLE. N.T. GOSPELS, LITURGICAL.
   EVANGELIARIUM.
   LECTIONARIUM.
   For commentaries, meditations, and
      sermons on the liturgical gospels,
      see Bible. N.T. Gospels, Litur-
      gical - Commentaries, [Meditations,
      Sermons].

GOTHIC CHURCH ARCHITECTURE. See
   CHURCH ARCHITECTURE, GOTHIC.

GOTHIC RITE. See MOZARABIC RITE.

GRACE (THEOLOGY)
      BQT 1126-1220   (234.x1)
   "A supernatural gift of God to an
      intellectual creature, bestowed
      with a view to eternal life." AT
   sa Adoption (Theology)
      Illumination of intellect.
      Merit.
      Molinism.
      Pelagianism.
      Predestination.
      Sacramentals.
      Semi-Pelagianism.
      Spiritual life.
      Virtues, Infused.
   xx Conversion.
      Covenants (Theology)
      Dogmatic theology.
      Salvation.

GRACE (THEOLOGY) - BIBLICAL TEACHING.

GRACE (THEOLOGY) - CATECHISMS,
   QUESTION-BOOKS.

GRACE (THEOLOGY) - EARLY WORKS.

GRACE (THEOLOGY) - HISTORY OF
   DOCTRINES.
      BQT 1129-1148

GRACE (THEOLOGY) - HISTORY OF
   DOCTRINES - EARLY CHURCH.

GRACE (THEOLOGY) - HISTORY OF
   DOCTRINES - MIDDLE AGES.

GRACE (THEOLOGY) - HISTORY OF
   DOCTRINES - MODERN PERIOD.

GRACE (THEOLOGY) - HISTORY OF
   DOCTRINES - 16th, [17th, etc.]
   CENTURY.

GRACE (THEOLOGY) - MEDIEVAL WORKS.

GRACE (THEOLOGY) - MEDITATIONS.

GRACE (THEOLOGY) - POPULAR WORKS.

GRACE (THEOLOGY) - SERMONS.

GRACE, ACTUAL.
      BQT 1151   (234.x11)
   "Any supernatural and transient
      aid by which God enlightens the
      mind or assists the will to
      produce supernatural acts." AT
   x Actual grace.

GRACE, HABITUAL.
      BQT 1161-1220   (234.x12)
   "An absolutely supernatural quality,
      intrinsically and permanently in-
      hering in the soul, by which we
      are made friends of God, adopted
      sons, coheirs with Christ, par-
      takers of the divine nature." AT
   sa Fruits of the Holy Spirit.
      Gifts of the Holy Spirit.
      Perfection, Christian.
      Perseverance (Theology)
      Regeneration (Theology)
      Repentance.

GRACE, HABITUAL -- Continued.
   sa Sanctification.
      Virtues, Moral.
      Virtues, Theological.
   x Grace, Sanctifying.
      Habitual grace.
      Sanctifying grace.

GRACE, SANCTIFYING. See
   GRACE, HABITUAL.

GRACE AT MEALS.
      BQT 4421
   x Blesssings, Table.
      Prayers, Table.
      Table blessings.
      Table prayers.
   xx Prayers.

GRADUAL (LITURGICAL BOOK). See
   GRADUALE.

GRADUAL PSALMS. See
   BIBLE. O.T. PSALMS, GRADUAL.

GRADUALE.
      BQT 4305-4307   (783.23)
   "A liturgical book containing all
   the chants required for the
   Mass, both ordinary and proper,
   throughout the year." AT
   sa Antiphonarium Missae.
      Kyriale.
      Liber usualis.
   x Gradual (Liturgical book)
   xx Mass - Music.

GRADUALE ROMANUM.
   x Roman Gradual.

GRADUALS.
      BQT 4319
   By this term are understood the
   psalm verses and the alleluja
   verse occurring immediately
   after the epistle at Mass.

GRADUALS (MUSIC)
      M 2079.L416
      M 2099.L416
      M 2149
   xx Propers (Music)

GRADUATION SERMONS. See
   BACCALAUREATE ADDRESSES.

GRAIL MOVEMENT.   (Geog. subdiv.)
      BQT 3586

GRAPES (IN RELIGION, FOLKLORE, ETC.)
      BQT 5858

GRATEFULNESS. See GRATITUDE.

GRATITUDE.
      BQT 1793; BQT 2396   (24x1.52)
   x Gratefulness.
      Thankfulness.
   xx Justice.

GRATITUDE - SERMONS.
      BQT 3089

GRAVEYARDS. See CEMETERIES.

GRAY FRIARS. See FRANCISCANS.

GREAT AWAKENING.
      BR 520
   "Here are entered works dealing
   with the revival of religion that
   occurred in the American colonies
   in the 18th century." LC
   References as in LC.

GREAT BRITAIN - CHURCH HISTORY.
      BQX 2001-2187   (274.2)
   x England - Church history.

GREAT BRITAIN - CHURCH HISTORY -
   EARLY PERIOD TO 1066.
      BQX 2031-2039

GREAT BRITAIN - CHURCH HISTORY -
   1066-1485.
      BQX 2041-2051

GREAT BRITAIN - CHURCH HISTORY -
   REFORMATION. See
   REFORMATION - ENGLAND.

GREAT BRITAIN - CHURCH HISTORY -
   1485-1603.
      BQX 2055-2079

GREAT BRITAIN - CHURCH HISTORY -
1603-1829
        BQX 2081-2089

GREAT BRITAIN - CHURCH HISTORY -
1829-
        BQX 2091-2099

GREAT BRITAIN - CHURCH HISTORY -
20th CENTURY.

GREAT BRITAIN - RELIGION.
        BR 759

GREAT SCHISM. See
    SCHISM - EASTERN AND WESTERN CHURCH.
    SCHISM, THE GREAT WESTERN, 1378-1417.

GREAT SUPPER (PARABLE)
    x Supper, Parable of.

GREAT WESTERN SCHISM. See
    SCHISM, THE GREAT WESTERN, 1378-1417.

GREATER ANTIPHONS. See
    O ANTIPHONS.

GRECO-ROMAN SCHISM. See
    SCHISM - EASTERN AND WESTERN CHURCH.
    SCHISM, ACACIAN, 484-519.

GREECE - CHURCH HISTORY.
        BQX 2301-2320   (274.95)

GREECE - CHURCH HISTORY - EARLY
    PERIOD TO 1200.

GREECE - CHURCH HISTORY - 1200-1669.

GREECE - CHURCH HISTORY - 1669-

GREECE - CHURCH HISTORY - 20th CENTURY.

GREECE - RELIGION.

GREEK CATHOLIC RITE. See
    BYZANTINE RITE, GREEK.

GREEK CHRISTIAN LITERATURE. See
    CHRISTIAN LITERATURE - GREEK
    AUTHORS.

GREEK CHURCH. See
    ORTHODOX EASTERN CHURCH.

GREEK FATHERS OF THE CHURCH. See
    FATHERS OF THE CHURCH, GREEK.

GREEK LANGUAGE, BIBLICAL.
        PA 700-791; PA 800-891
        (487.3)
    x Bible - Philology.
      Biblical Greek.
      New Testament Greek.
    xx Bible - Language, style.
      Languages - Religious aspects.

GREEK ORTHODOX EASTERN CHURCH. See
    ORTHODOX EASTERN CHURCH, GREEK.

GREEK PRIESTS. See
    PRIESTS, GREEK.

GREEK RITE. See BYZANTINE RITE.

GREGORIAN CHANT. See CHANT.

GREGORIAN MASS.
    A Gregorian Mass consists of thirty
    masses offered for a departed
    soul on thirty consecutive days.
    x Mass, Gregorian.
    xx Mass intentions.

GREGORIAN MODES. See
    CHANT - MODES AND TONES.

GREGORIAN SACRAMENTARY. See
    SACRAMENTARIUM GREGORIANUM.

GREY FRIARS. See FRANCISCANS.

GRIEF. See SORROW.

GROUP WORK, CHURCH. See
    CHURCH GROUP WORK.

GROVES, SACRED. See
    SACRED GROVES.

GUADALUPE, MEXICO (SHRINE)
        BQT 1075   (23x3.61)
        BQX 4196   (277.2)
    x Our Lady of Guadalupe (Shrine),
      Mexico.
      Nuestra Señora de Guadalupe
      (Shrine), Mexico.

GUADALUPE, SPAIN (SHRINE)
    BQT 1075   (23x3.61)
    BQX 2897   (274.6)
    x Our Lady of Guadalupe (Shrine),
      Spain.
      Nuestra Señora de Guadalupe
        (Shrine), Spain.

GUARDIAN AND WARD (CANON LAW)
  sa Adoption (Canon law)
     Parent and child (Canon law)

GUARDIAN ANGELS.
    BQT 651   (231.x6)
  sa Angels.
  x Angels, Guardian.
  xx Angels.

GUARDIAN ANGELS - DEVOTIONAL
  LITERATURE.

GUARDIAN ANGELS - PRAYER-BOOKS.
    BQT 2683

GUARDIAN ANGELS - SERMONS.
    BQT 3089

GUARDS, PAPAL. See PAPAL GUARDS.

GUELFS AND GHIBELLINES.
    BQX 758   (274.504)
    x Ghibellines and Guelfs.

GUILT.
    [BQT 1759.5] (Moral theology)
  sa Atonement.
     Responsibility.
     Sin.
  xx Conscience.
     Free will and determinism.
     Sin.
     Subconsciousness.

GUILT (CANON LAW)
  sa Dolus (Canon law)
     Fear (Canon law)
  xx Legal responsibility (Canon
     law)

GYROVAGI. See GIROVAGUES.

HABACUC, BOOK OF. See
  BIBLE. O.T. HABACUC.

HABAKKUK, BOOK OF. See
  BIBLE. O.T. HABACUC.

HABIT.
    BF 335-337
    BQT 1775
  References as in LC, with the
    following additional references.
  xx Human acts.
     Virtues, Infused.

HABIT, CLERICAL. See
  CLERGY - COSTUME.

HABIT, MONASTIC. See
  RELIGIOUS ORDERS - HABIT.

HABITUAL GRACE. See
  GRACE, HABITUAL.

HADES. See
  FUTURE LIFE.
  HELL.

HADITH.
    BP 135
  References as in LC.

HADRAN.
  xx Sermons, Jewish.

HAGGAI, BOOK OF. See
  BIBLE. O.T. AGGEUS.

HAGIOGRAPHA (BIBLE). See
  BIBLE. O.T. HAGIOGRAPHA.

HAGIOGRAPHY.
    BQT 1576   (23x5)
  "Here are entered works on lives
    of the saints, and how to write
    them. For the lives themselves
    see Saints." LC
  x Hagiology.
  xx Bollandists.
     Church history.
     Saints.

HAGIOLOGY. See HAGIOGRAPHY.

HAIL MARY. See AVE MARIA.

HAIL MARYS, THREE. See
  THREE "HAIL MARYS".

HALAYA.
    BM 515
  References as in LC.

HALLAH.
  xx Priests, Jewish.

HANDICAPPED, CHURCH WORK WITH THE. See
CHURCH WORK WITH THE HANDICAPPED.

HANDS, IMPOSITION OF. See
  IMPOSITION OF HANDS.

HANUKKAH (FEAST OF LIGHTS)
  sa Hanukkah lamp.
   x Dedication, Feast of.
    Feast of dedication.
    Feast of lights.
    Feast of the Maccabees.
    Maccabees, Feast of the.
    Festival of Hanukkah.
    Lights, Feast of.

HANUKKAH LAMP.
    BM 657
  References as in LC.

HAPPINESS.
    BQT 1541-1551 (Theology)
      (236.6)
    BJ 1480-1486   (171.4)
  sa Cheerfulness.
    Contentment.
    Desire for God.
    Joy.
    Pleasure.
  xx Contentment.
    Ethics.
    Heaven.
    Joy.
    Pleasure.

HASIDIC PARABLES. See
  PARABLES, HASIDIC.

HASIDISM.
    BM 198
  sa Parables, Hasidic.
   x Chasidism.
  xx Jewish sects.
  Subdivisions as in LC.

HASKALAH.
  References as in LC.

HASMONAENS. See MACCABEES.
✓ HEALING x Faith-cure
HEALING GODS. Divine Healing
    BL 325   (290) Spiritual Healing

HEALING OF THE MAN BORN BLIND (MIRACLE)
  x Man born blind (Miracle)

HEALING OF THE NOBLEMAN'S SON (MIRACLE)
  x Nobleman's son (Miracle)

HEALING OF THE SICK. See
  FAITH-CURE.
  MENTAL HEALING.

HEART (IN RELIGION, FOLKLORE, ETC.)
  References as in LC.

HEART OF JESUS. See SACRED HEART.

HEART OF MARY, IMMACULATE. See
  IMMACULATE HEART OF MARY.

HEATHENISM. See PAGANISM.

✓ HEAVEN.
    BQT 1541-1551   (236.6)
  sa Angels.
    Beatific vision.
    Book of life.
    Future life.
    Happiness.
    Paradise.
   x Church triumphant.
  xx Death.
    Eschatology.
    Future life.
    Happiness.
    Immortality.
    Paradise.

HEAVEN - ART.
  xx Christian art.

HEAVEN - MEDITATIONS.
    BQT 2610

HEAVEN - SERMONS.
    BQT 1545; BQT 3067

HEAVENLY RECOGNITION.
   BQT 1551 (236.x63)
  x Recognition, Heavenly.

HEBDOMADA MAJOR. See HOLY WEEK.

HEBREW POETRY.
   PJ 4775 (892.41)
   BS 1405 (Bible) (223)
  sa Psalmody.
  x Bible - Poetry.

HEBREW. See JEWS.

HEBREWS, EPISTLE TO THE. See
  BIBLE. N.T. HEBREWS.

HELL.
   BL 735 (Classical mythology)
   BL 545 (Comparative religion)
   BQT 1521-1528 (Theology)
    (236.x4)
  sa Damned.
   Fear of God.
   Future punishment.
  x Eternal punishment.
   Hades.
   Punishment, Eternal.
  xx Death.
   Devil.
   Eschatology.
   Future life.
   Future punishment.

HELL - ART.
   BQT 5906
  xx Christian art.

HELP OF CHRISTIANS.
   BQT 2598
  sa Missa Beatae Mariae Virginis
    Auxilium Christianorum.
  x Our Lady Help of Christians.
  xx Mary, Blessed Virgin - Titles.

HELPERS, FOURTEEN HOLY. See
  FOURTEEN HOLY HELPERS.

HEORTOLOGY. See
  CHURCH CALENDAR.
  CHURCH YEAR.
  FEASTS, ECCLESIASTICAL.
  SAINTS - CALENDAR.

HEPTATEUCH (BIBLE). See
  BIBLE. O.T. HEPTATEUCH.

HERALDRY, SACRED.
   BQX 67
   CR 1101-1131
  sa Abbots - Heraldry.
   Bishops - Heraldry.
   Popes - Heraldry.
   Religious orders - Heraldry.
  xx Christian antiquities.
   Christian art.

HERESIES AND HERETICS.
   BQ 215-218 (Collected writings)
   BQT 35-135 (History of heresy)
    (273-273.8x1)
  Here are entered works dealing
   with baptized persons, and their
   theories, who profess Christianity but reject or doubt any article of faith as determined by
   the authority of the Catholic
   Church. For works about the
   various bodies or denominations
   which have broken away from the
   established Protestant churches
   of the 16th century, see Sects.
  For works about heresy in the ab-
   stract see Heresy.
  sa In coena Domini bulls.
   also names of individual here-
    sies, e.g., Adoptionism;
    Arianism; etc.
  xx Catholic Church - History.
   Catholics, Lapsed.
   Non-Catholics.
   Theology - History.

HERESIES AND HERETICS - DICTIONARIES.

HERESIES AND HERETICS - EARLY CHURCH.
   BQ 5286 (Collections)
   BQT 41-67 (History) (273.x1)
  sa Acacians.
   Adamites.
   Alogi.
   Arianism.
   Circumcellions.
   Docetism.
   Donatists.
   Ebionism.
   Eumonianism.

HERESIES AND HERETICS - EARLY
CHURCH -- Continued.
sa Melchisedechians.
Messalians.
Monarchianism.
Monophysites.
Monothelism.
Montanism.
Nestorians.
Novatianists.
Paulicians.
Pelagianism.
Prescilianists.
Quartodecimans.
Sabellianism.
Semi-Pelagianism.
xx Church history - Primitive
and early church.

HERESIES AND HERETICS - MIDDLE
AGES.
BQT 81-103
sa Sects, Medieval.

HERESIES AND HERETICS - MODERN
PERIOD.
BQT 112-139
sa Sects.

HERESIES AND HERETICS - 16th
CENTURY.

HERESIES AND HERETICS - 17th
CENTURY.

HERESIES AND HERETICS - 18th
CENTURY.

HERESIES AND HERETICS - 19th
CENTURY.

HERESIES AND HERETICS - 20th
CENTURY.

################

HERESIES AND HERETICS - EASTERN
CHURCHES.
BQX 5421
BQX 5445-5446

HERESIES AND HERETICS - ORTHODOX
EASTERN CHURCH.
BQX 5883
sa Hesychasm.
x Orthodox Eastern Church -
Heresies and heretics.

################

HERESIES AND HERETICS (CANON LAW)

HERESIES AND HERETICS, MOHAMMEDAN.
BP 167.5
x Mohammedan heresies and heretics.
xx Mohammedan sects.

HERESY.
BQT 330   (23x9.4)
Cf. note under Heresies and
heretics.
sa Liberty of speech in the
church.
xx Apostasy.
Offenses against religion.
Schism.

HERESY (CANON LAW)
BQV230 2314-2316   (348.x6)
xx Irregularities.

HERETICS, BAPTISM OF. See
BAPTISM OF HERETICS.

HERMENEUTICS, BIBLICAL. See
BIBLE - HERMENEUTICS.

HERMITAGES. See HERMITS.

HERMITS.   (Geog. subdiv., Indirect)
BQX 6814; BQX 6838   (271)
BQT 2708; BQX 5495; BQX 8261
sa Anchoresses.
Inclusi.
Recluses.
x Anchorites.
Fathers of the desert.
Hermitages.
xx Christian biography.
Religious orders.
Saints.

HERMITS OF MURRONE. See
CELESTINES (BENEDICTINE)

HERMITS OF ST. AUGUSTINE. See
AUGUSTINIANS.

HEROIC ACT OF CHARITY.
BQT 1537
xx Purgatory.

HEROIC VIRTUE.
BQT 1579
"The virtue of Christian heroes,
of those who lived as saints or
who achieved heroism in the
moment of martyrdom." AT
x Virtue, Heroic.
xx Martyrdom.
Saints.

HERRNHUTER. See MORAVIANS.

HESYCHASM.
BQX 5883
"A theory of mysticism upheld by
the Orthodox Eastern Church in
defense of a system of contemplation practiced by the Antonine
monks in the 14th century." AT
xx Heresies and heretics - Orthodox
Eastern Church.
Mysticism - Orthodox Eastern
Church.

HEXAEMERON.
BS 651   (222.x13)
Here are entered works on the six
days of creation as described in
chapter one of Genesis.
xx Creation.

HEXATEUCH (BIBLE). See
BIBLE. O.T. HEXATEUCH.

HIERARCHY. See CLERGY.

HIEROGLYPHIC BIBLES.
BS 560
x Bible - Hieroglyphic Bibles.
xx Bible - Picture Bibles.
Children's literature.
Picture-books for children.

HIGH HOLY DAY SERMONS.
xx Sermons, Jewish.

HIGH HOLY DAYS.
BM 693
References as in LC.

HIGH MASS.
x Mass, High.

HIGH MASS - RITES AND CEREMONIES.
BQT 4333
xx Mass - Rites and ceremonies.

HIGHER CRITICISM. See
BIBLE - CRITICISM, HIGHER.

HIGHER EDUCATION, CATHOLIC. See
CATHOLIC EDUCATION, HIGHER.

HINDU GODS. See GODS, HINDU.

HINDU SAINTS. See SAINTS, HINDU.

HINDU SECTS.
BL 1245.A1
References as in LC supplement
1959-60.

HINDUISM.
Classifications and references as
in LC.

HIRE (CANON LAW)

HISTORIANS, CATHOLIC. See
CATHOLIC HISTORIANS.

HISTORIANS, CHURCH. See
CHURCH HISTORIANS.

HISTORY.
sa Church history.
Other references as in LC.

HISTORY - PHILOSOPHY.
D 16.7-9
sa Theology and history.
Other references as in LC.

HISTORY, BIBLICAL. See
BIBLE - HISTORY OF BIBLICAL
LITERATURE.

HISTORY, CHURCH. See
   CHURCH HISTORY.

HISTORY AND THEOLOGY. See
   THEOLOGY AND HISTORY.

HISTORY OF SUSANNA. See
   BIBLE. O.T. DANIEL. chap. XIII.

HITTITE CULTUS. See
   CULTUS, HITTITE.

HITTITE PRIESTS. See
   PRIESTS, HITTITE.

HITTITES - RELIGION.
   BL 2370

HOLIDAYS.   (Geog. subdiv., Indirect)
   Classifications and references
     as in LC.

HOLINESS.
   BQT 1192
  sa Consecration.
     Sanctification.
   x Sanctity.

HOLINESS CHURCHES.
   "Here are entered works dealing
    with the various modern church
    bodies stressing the doctrine of
    holiness." LC
  sa Church of God.
  xx Church of God.
     Pentecostal churches.

HOLY, THE.
   x Numinous, The.
  xx God.
     Holiness.
     Mysticism.
     Religion.
     Theism.

HOLY ARK. See ARK OF THE LAW.

HOLY CHILDHOOD.
  sa Infant Jesus of Prague (Statue)
     Litany of the Holy Infancy.
   x Childhood, Holy.
  xx Jesus Christ - Childhood.

HOLY CHILDHOOD - CONFRATERNITIES.
   BQT 2814
  xx Confraternities.

HOLY CHILDHOOD - CULTUS.
   BQT 2659

HOLY CHILDHOOD - DEVOTIONAL
   LITERATURE.

HOLY CHILDHOOD - MEDITATIONS.
   BQT 2586

HOLY CHILDHOOD - POETRY.

HOLY CHILDHOOD - PRAYER-BOOKS.
   BQT 2659

HOLY CHILDHOOD - SERMONS.
   BQT 3057

HOLY COAT.
   BQT 942
   x Jesus Christ - Holy coat.
  xx Jesus Christ - Relics of the
     Passion.

HOLY COMMUNION. See
   COMMUNION, HOLY.

HOLY CROSS, MASS OF THE. See
   MISSA DE SANCTA CRUCE.

HOLY DAYS. See
   FEASTS, ECCLESIASTICAL.

HOLY EUCHARIST. See EUCHARIST.

HOLY FACE.
   BQT 942
  sa Veil of Veronica.
   x Jesus Christ - Holy face.
  xx Jesus Christ - Passion.

HOLY FACE - MEDITATIONS.
   BQT 2593   (24x8.71)

HOLY FACE - PRAYER-BOOKS.
   BQT 2670

HOLY FACE, LITANY OF THE. See
   LITANY OF THE HOLY FACE.

HOLY FAMILY.
        BQT 833
    sa Jesus Christ - Family.
    x Family, Holy.
    xx Jesus Christ - Family.

HOLY FAMILY - DEVOTIONAL LITERATURE.

HOLY FAMILY - MEDITATIONS.

HOLY FAMILY - PRAYER-BOOKS.
    [BQT 2672]

HOLY FAMILY - SERMONS.
        BQT 3057

HOLY GHOST. See HOLY SPIRIT.

HOLY HELPERS, FOURTEEN. See
    FOURTEEN HOLY HELPERS.

HOLY HOUR.
        BQT 2668; BQT 4492.5
        (24x8.7)
    xx Devotions, Popular.

HOLY HOUR - HYMNS.

HOLY HOUR - MEDITATIONS.
        BQT 2589

HOLY INFANCY, LITANY OF THE. See
    LITANY OF THE HOLY INFANCY.

HOLY INNOCENTS, FEAST OF THE.
        BQT 4234   (23x5.31)
    x Childermas.
      Feast of the Holy Innocents.
      Innocents, Feast of the Holy.

HOLY INNOCENTS, MASSACRE OF THE.
        BQT 848
    x Innocents, Massacre of the.
      Massacre of the Innocents.

HOLY LANCE.
    x Lance, Holy.

HOLY LANCE AND NAILS, FEAST OF THE.
    x Feast of the Holy Lance and
      Nails.

HOLY LAND. See X PALESTINE.

HOLY NAILS.
        BQT 942
    x Nails, Holy.

HOLY NAME, DEVOTION TO.
        BQT 2593   (24x8.71)
    xx Devotions, Popular.
       God - Name.
       Jesus Christ - Name.

HOLY NAME, DEVOTION TO - HYMNS.

HOLY NAME, DEVOTION TO - POETRY.

HOLY NAME, DEVOTION TO - SERMONS.
        BQT 3057

HOLY NAME, LITANY OF THE. See
    LITANY OF THE HOLY NAME.

HOLY OFFICE, CONGREGATION OF THE.
    See CONGREGATIO SANCTI OFFICII.

HOLY OILS.
        BQT 4483   (23x7.8)
    sa Anointings.
       Chrism.
    x Oil, Holy.
    xx Anointings.
       Sacramentals.

HOLY ORDERS. See ORDINATION.

HOLY ORTHODOX EASTERN CATHOLIC AND
    APOSTOLIC CHURCH. See
    ORTHODOX EASTERN CHURCH.

HOLY PLACES. See SACRED PLACES.

HOLY SATURDAY.
        BQT 4223; BQT 4326; BQT 4391
        (264.x52)
    sa Easter vigil.
       Exultet (Preface)
       Ordo Sabbati Sancti.
    xx Holy Week.

HOLY SATURDAY MASS. See
    MISSA IN SABBATO SANCTO.

HOLY SCRIPTURES. See
    BIBLE.

HOLY SEE.
      BQV 244-256 (Canon law)
        (348.x8)
      BQX 101-173 (Church history)
        (27x2)
  "In diplomatic and international
    relations the Catholic Church is
    always spoken of as the Holy See."
    Vatican Code, n. 118.
  sa Congregations, Roman.
    Curia Romana.
    Popes.
  x Papacy.
    See, Holy.
  xx Catholic Church.
    Popes.

HOLY SEE - DIPLOMATIC SERVICE.
      JC 1801-1802 (International
        law)
      BQX 107 (Church history)
  sa Nuncios, Papal.
  x Catholic Church - Diplomatic
    service.

HOLY SEE - DIPLOMATIC SERVICE -
  HISTORY.

HOLY SEE - RELATIONS (DIPLOMATIC)
      BQV 241-295 (Canon law)
        (348.x81)
      BQX 105-108; BQX 941-947
        (Church history)   (23x9.43)
  Subdivided by country, e.g., Holy
    See - Relations (diplomatic) with
    France (with duplicate entry under
    France - Foreign relations - Holy
    See.
  x Catholic Church - Foreign rela-
    tions.
    Catholic Church - Relations (Dip-
    lomatic)

HOLY SEE - RELATIONS (DIPLOMATIC) WITH
  ITALY.
  sa Roman Question.

HOLY SEE - RELATIONS (GENERAL) WITH
  FRANCE, [GERMANY, ITALY, ETC.]
  Duplicate entry is made under
    France, [Germany, Italy, etc.] -
    Relations (general) with the
    Holy See.

#################

HOLY SEE. LEGATES, NUNCIOS, ETC.
  x Catholic Church. Legates,
    nuncios, etc.

HOLY SEE. TREATIES, ETC.
      BQV 93-94   (348.x81)
  x Catholic Church. Treaties, etc.

#################

HOLY SEE (INTERNATIONAL LAW)
      BQV 246-251
  xx International law.
    Persons (International law)

HOLY SEE, VACANCY OF THE. See
  VACANCY OF THE HOLY SEE.

HOLY SEPULCHER.
      BQT 942
      BQT 5929
  x Jesus Christ - Tomb.
    Sepulcher, Holy.

HOLY SHROUD.
      BQT 942
  x Jesus Christ - Holy shroud.
    Shroud, Holy.
  xx Jesus Christ - Passion.
    Jesus Christ - Relics of the
    Passion.

HOLY SPIRIT.
      BQT 587-599   (231.3)
  sa Pentecost.
    Pneumatology (Theology)
    Trinity.
  x Holy Ghost.
    Paraclete.
    Spirit, Holy.
  xx Dogmatic theology.
    God.
    Trinity.

HOLY SPIRIT - ART.
      BQT 5853   (246.x64)
  sa Dove (in religion, folklore,
    etc.)
  xx Christian art.
    God - Art.

HOLY SPIRIT - BIBLICAL TEACHING.
      BQT 589

HOLY SPIRIT - DEVOTIONAL LITERATURE.
BQT 2582

HOLY SPIRIT - HISTORY OF DOCTRINES.

HOLY SPIRIT - HISTORY OF DOCTRINES -
EARLY CHURCH.

HOLY SPIRIT - HISTORY OF DOCTRINES -
MIDDLE AGES.

HOLY SPIRIT - HISTORY OF DOCTRINES -
MODERN PERIOD.

HOLY SPIRIT - INDWELLING.
BQT 593; BQT 1215
 x Indwelling of the Holy Spirit.
 xx Immanence of God.

HOLY SPIRIT - MEDITATIONS.
BQT 2582   (24x2.9)

HOLY SPIRIT - NAME.

HOLY SPIRIT - POPULAR WORKS.

HOLY SPIRIT - PRAYER-BOOKS.
BQT 2655
 sa Missa de Spiritu Sancto.
    Veni Creator Spiritus.
    Veni Sancte Spiritus.

HOLY SPIRIT - PROCESSION.
BQT 579
 sa Filioque controversy.
 x Procession of the Holy Spirit.
 xx Trinity - Procession.

HOLY SPIRIT - SERMONS.
BQT 3053
 sa Gifts of the Holy Spirit - Sermons.

HOLY SPIRIT, FRUITS OF THE. See
  FRUITS OF THE HOLY SPIRIT.

HOLY SPIRIT, GIFTS OF THE. See
  GIFTS OF THE HOLY SPIRIT.

HOLY THURSDAY. See
  MAUNDY THURSDAY.

HOLY TRINITY. See TRINITY.

HOLY WAR, JEWISH. See
  JEWISH HOLY WAR.

HOLY WAR, MOSLEM. See JIHAD.

HOLY WATER.
BQT 4510; BQT 4482   (23x7.8)
 x Blessed water.
   Water, Blessed.
   Water, Holy.
 xx Water (in religion, folklore,
    etc.)

HOLY WATER FONTS.
BQT 5955
 xx Fonts.

HOLY WEEK.
BQT 4223   (264.x52)
 sa Easter.
    Good Friday.
    Holy Saturday.
    Maundy Thursday.
    Officium Hebdomadae Sanctae.
    Ordo Hebdomadae Sanctae.
    Palm Sunday.
    Tenebrae.
 x Hebdomada Major.
 xx Good Friday.
    Jesus Christ - Passion.
    Lent.
    Passiontide.

HOLY WEEK - HANDBOOKS, MANUALS, ETC.
  [BQT 4391.3]
  Here are collected the various
  guides or unofficial service-
  books, which usually include
  text material, for use during
  Holy Week. The guidebooks
  themselves are entered under
  editor or title (main entry).

HOLY WEEK - MEDITATIONS.
  [BQT 2606.5]

HOLY WEEK - RITES AND CEREMONIES.
BQT 4337-4339

HOLY WEEK - SERMONS.
  [BQT 2995.5]   (252.x53)
 x Sermons, Holy-week.
 xx Jesus Christ - Passion - Sermons.

210

HOLY-WEEK MUSIC.
xx Sacred vocal music.

HOLY-WEEK OFFICE. See
OFFICIUM HEBDOMADAE SANCTAE.

HOLY WELLS.
GR 690
BQT 4525-4526
References as in LC.

HOLY YEAR.
BQT 1399-1401
x Anno santo.
Jubilee Year.
Year, Holy.
Year, Jubilee.
xx Jubilee indulgences.

HOLY YEAR, 1300, [1475, etc.]
BQT 1401

HOME, CATHOLIC. See
FAMILY, CHRISTIAN.

HOME MISSIONS. See
MISSIONS, HOME.

HOMILETICAL ILLUSTRATIONS.
BQT 2967   (252.x02)
sa Allegories.
Catechetical illustrations.
Christian life - Pictures,
illustrations, etc.
Parables.
x Sermons - Illustrations.
xx Catechetical illustrations.
Homiletics.
Preaching.

HOMILETICS.
BQT 2952-3089   (251)
sa Homiletical illustrations.
Preaching.
Sermons.
xx Preaching.
Sermons.

HOMILETICS - EASTERN CHURCHES.
BQX 5444
x Eastern Churches - Homiletics.

HOMILIES. See SERMONS.

HOMOEANS. See ACACIANS.
Homosexuality - 261
HOPE.
BQT 1201; BQT 1782   (24x7.12)
sa Despair.
xx Despair.
Faith.
Virtues, Theological.

HORAE BEATAE MARIAE VIRGINIS.
BQT 4397   (24x8.72)
x Hours of the Blessed Virgin Mary.
Mary, Blessed Virgin, Hours of the.
xx Mary, Blessed Virgin - Prayer-books.

HORAE DIURNAE. See DIURNALE.

HORAE MATUTINALES. See MATUTINALE.

HORAE SANCTI SPIRITUS.
BQT 4396   (24x8.7)

HOSEA, BOOK OF. See
BIBLE. O.T. OSEE.

HOSPITAL CHAPLAINS. See
CHAPLAINS, HOSPITAL.

HOSPITALLERS.
BQX 6838
sa names of individual hospitaller
orders, e.g., Brothers Hospitallers of St. John of God;
Knights of Malta; etc.
x Religious orders, Hospital.
xx Medicine, Medieval.
Military religious orders.
Religious orders.
Social service, Catholic.

HOSPITALLERS - RELIGIOUS LIFE.

HOSPITALLERS OF ST. JOHN OF
JERUSALEM, ORDER OF. See
KNIGHTS OF MALTA.

HOSPITALS - CHAPLAINS. See
CHAPLAINS, HOSPITAL.

HOSPITALS (CANON LAW)

HOSPITALS, CATHOLIC.
  x Catholic hospitals.
  xx Catholic institutions.

HOST.
    BQT 1328
  "The consecrated eucharistic
    Elements, particularly the
    species of bread." AT
  xx Altar breads.
    Eucharist - Elements.

HOURS, BOOKS OF. See DIURNALE.

HOURS OF THE BLESSED VIRGIN MARY.
  See HORAE BEATAE MARIAE VIRGINIS.

HOUSES, BLESSING OF.
  x Blessing of houses.

HUGUENOTS.
    BQX 1766-1773
  Other classifications and
    references as in LC.

HUMAN ACTS.
    BQT 1767-1816.   (24x1.x1)
  sa Emotions.
    Free will and determinism.
    Habit.
    Intention.
    Sin.
    Virtue.
  x Acts, Human.
  xx Moral theology.

HUMAN SCIENCE. See
  ANTHROPOSOPHY.

HUMANISM, CHRISTIAN.
  x Christian humanism.

HUMANISM, RELIGIOUS.
  "Here are entered works dealing
    with a movement, originating in
    American Unitarianism, which
    stressed the idea that man can
    satisfy all his religious needs
    from within himself and discarded
    in its advanced thought all
    theistic concepts." LC

HUMANISM, RELIGIOUS -- Continued.
  x Religious humanism.
  xx Man (Theology)
    Philosophy, Modern.
    Religions.
    Unitarianism.

HUMILIATI.
    BQT 89; BQT 4851-4859
  x Barettini.
  xx Mysticism - History - Middle
    Ages.

HUMILITY.
    BQT 1793   (24x1.52)
  xx Pride and vanity.

Humor see wit + humor

HUNGARIAN CHRISTIAN LITERATURE. See
  CHRISTIAN LITERATURE - HUNGARIAN
  AUTHORS.

HUNGARIAN PRESBYTERIANS. See
  PRESBYTERIANS, HUNGARIAN.

HUNGARY - CHURCH HISTORY.
    BQX 2338-2349   (274.39)

HUNGARY - CHURCH HISTORY - EARLY
  PERIOD TO 1222.

HUNGARY - CHURCH HISTORY - 1222-1526.

HUNGARY - CHURCH HISTORY - 1526-1711.

HUNGARY - CHURCH HISTORY - 1711-

HUNGARY - CHURCH HISTORY - 20th CENTURY.

HUNGARY - RELIGION.

HUNTERS' MASS.

HUNTING - MORAL AND RELIGIOUS ASPECTS.
  xx Animals, Treatment of.

HUSBAND AND WIFE.
  sa Conjugal state.
  x Spouses.
  Other references as in LC

Human Relations, sa Family Relations
x Interpersonal Relations, Communications, human

Human development
x Adult development
Child development
Personal growth
Development, Human

HUSBAND AND WIFE (CANON LAW)
      BQV230 1128-1132

HUSSITES.
      BX 4913-4918
  sa Adamites.
  Other references as in LC.

HYMN PLAYING. See
  HYMNS - ACCOMPANIMENT.

HYMN WRITERS.
      BV 325
  x Hymnists.
  xx Hymns - History and criticism.
    Poets.

HYMNALS.
      BQT 4681-4689 (Catholic); M 2119
      BV 360-465 (non-Catholic);
      M 2115-2146
  Here are entered collections of
    hymns with music, particularly
    for use by congregations. See
    also note under Choir books.
  sa Choir books.
  xx Choir books.

HYMNARIUM.
      BQT 4253; BQT 4268; [BQT 4384]
  A liturgical book containing the
    hymns from the Breviary and
    Missal.
  sa Hymns, Liturgical.
  x Hymnary.
  xx Hymns.

HYMNARIUM. ENGLISH, [FRENCH,
GERMAN, ETC.]

HYMNARY. See HYMNARIUM.

HYMNISTS. See HYMN WRITERS.

HYMNOLOGY. See HYMNS.

HYMNS.   (Geog. subdiv.)
      BQT 4598-4603; BQT 4681-4689
      (Church music)
      M 2115-2145 (Hymns with music)
      BQ 5253 (Latin hymns; Collections)
      BQ 5081-5103 (Latin hymns:
      Literary history)
      BQ 268 (Literary history)
      (245.x09)

HYMNS -- Continued.
  sa Canticles.
    Christmas - Poetry.
    Easter - Poetry.
    Funeral hymns.
    Hymnarium.
    Psalmody.
    Sequences (Music)
    Sunday-schools - Hymns.
    also subdivision "Hymns" under
      names of churches and denom-
      inations, e.g., Church of Eng-
      land - Hymns, Presbyterian
      Church - Hymns; and under such
      headings as Mary, Blessed Vir-
      gin - Hymns, Missions - Hymns,
      Sacred Heart - Hymns; Sol-
      diers - Hymns, etc,; also
      names of hymns, e.g., Gloria
      in excelsis Deo.
  x Catholic Church - Hymns.
    Hymnology.
    Song-books, Sunday-school.
  xx Canticles.
    Church music.
    Music.
    Poetry.
    Psalmody.
    Religious poetry.
    Songs.
    Vocal music.

HYMNS - ACCOMPANIMENT.
  sa Chant - Accompaniment.
  x Hymn playing.
  xx Chant - Accompaniment.

HYMNS - BIBLIOGRAPHY.
      BQ 5081
      Z 7813

HYMNS - COLLECTIONS.

HYMNS - DEVOTIONAL USE.

HYMNS - DICTIONARIES.

HYMNS - HISTORY AND CRITICISM.
      BQ 268   (245.x09)
  sa Hymn writers.

HYMNS - INDEXES.

           ################

HYMNS - AUSTRIA, [BOHEMIA,
FRANCE, ETC.]

################

HYMNS - BYZANTINE RITE. See
BYZANTINE RITE - HYMNS.

HYMNS - CHURCH OF ENGLAND,
[LUTHERAN CHURCH, ETC.]. See
CHURCH OF ENGLAND, [LUTHERAN
CHURCH, ETC. - HYMNS.

################

HYMNS, ENGLISH, [FRENCH,
GERMAN, ETC.]

HYMNS, ENGLISH, [ETC] - TRANSLATIONS
FROM LATIN, [ETC.]

HYMNS, ENGLISH, [ETC.] - TRANSLATIONS
INTO GERMAN, [ETC.]

HYMNS, JEWISH. See
JEWS - HYMNS.

HYMNS, LITURGICAL.
BQ 5085
"Liturgical humns are those appointed for use in the liturgy
and consist principally of some
175 hymns with their tunes which
form part of the Divine Office."
AT
sa Sequences (Liturgy)
x Liturgical hymns.
xx Hymnarium.

HYMNS, LITURGICAL - BIBLIOGRAPHY.

HYMNS, LITURGICAL - SERMONS.

HYMNS, MISSION. See
MISSIONS - HYMNS.

HYMNS, MOHAMMEDAN.
x Mohammedan hymns.

HYPERDULIA. See
MARY, BLESSED VIRGIN - CULTUS.

HYPNOTISM - MORAL AND RELIGIOUS ASPECTS.

HYPOSTASIS.
BD 331 (Philosophy)   (111.32)
BQT 575-583 (Theology)
(231.x2)
x Subsistence (Philosophy)
xx Substance (Philosophy)

HYPOSTATIC UNION.
BQT 704   (232.x41)
"The union of the two distinct
natures of God and man in the
one person of Jesus Christ." AT
sa Jesus Christ - Divinity.
x Jesus Christ - Hypostatic union.
Union, Hypostatic.
xx Jesus Christ - Person.

HYSTERECTOMY - MORAL ASPECTS.
BX 1759

ICHTHYS. See
FISH (IN RELIGION, FOLKLORE, ETC.)

ICONOCLASM.
BQX 485; BQX 5742 (Church
history)
BQT 77 (Heresy)   (273.x51)
xx Images, Veneration of.

ICONOGRAPHY. See
ART.
CHRISTIAN ART.
IDOLS AND IMAGES.
PORTRAITS.
also special subjects (e.g.,
Saints - Art; Musicians - Por-
traits) and subdivisions "Icono-
graphy", "Portraits", and
"Portraits, caricatures, etc."
under names of persons.

ICONS.
N 7956 (Russian art)
BQX 6134 (Church history)
x Ikons.

Identity, Personal see Personal Development

IDOLATRY. See
IDOLS AND IMAGES - WORSHIP.

IDOLS AND IMAGES.
sa Gods in art.
x Iconography.
Images and idols.
Religious art.
xx Gods in art.

IDOLS AND IMAGES - COSTUME AND
  ADORNMENT.
    x Gods - Costume.

IDOLS AND IMAGES - WORSHIP.
     BL 485   (291.218)
     BQT 1866   (24x1.61)
    x Idolatry.
    xx Religion (Virtue)
      Worship.

IGNORANCE (CANON LAW)
     BQV230 16   (348.x2)
     BQV230 2229   (348.x6)
    xx Legal responsibility (Canon
      law)
      Nullity (Canon law)
      Penalties, Ecclesiastical.

IGNORANCE, INVINCIBLE.
     BQT 1755
    x Invincible ignorance.
    xx Responsibility.

IKONS. See ICONS.

ILLEGITIMACY (CANON LAW)
     BQV230 1114-1117   (348.x427)
    x Legitimacy (Canon law)
    xx Irregularities.

ILLUMINATI.
     BQT 2461
     HS 142
    sa Alumbrados.
      Enlightenment.
    xx Mysticism - History - Middle
      Ages.

ILLUMINATION OF INTELLECT.
  Here are entered works on the
    theory, particularly propounded
    by St. Augustine, that a divine
    light is communicated to the
    soul, by which the intellect be-
    comes capable of thinking and
    judging according to norms tran-
    scending space and time.
  For works on the Protestant theory
    concerning a somewhat similar
    interior religious experience,
    especially as taught by the
    Society of Friends, see Inner
    light.

ILLUMINATION OF INTELLECT -- Continued.
    xx Grace (Theology)
      Knowledge, Theory of (Religion)

ILLUMINATIVE WAY TO PERFECTION.
     BQT 2207
    xx Perfection, Christian.

IMAGE OF GOD.
     BQT 625
    x God, Image of.
    xx God - Exemplary cause.
      Man (Theology)

IMAGE OF GOD - EARLY WORKS TO 1900.

IMAGE OF GOD - HISTORY OF DOCTRINES.

IMAGES, VENERATION OF.
     BQT 1589
    sa Iconoclasm.
      Relics and reliquaries.
      Saints - Cultus.
    x Veneration of images.
    xx Relics and reliquaries.
      Saints - Cultus.

IMAGES AND IDOLS. See
  IDOLS AND IMAGES.

IMITATIO CHRISTI.
     BQT 2514-2522   (24x8.71)
    x Following of Christ.
      Imitation of Christ (Book)

IMITATIO CHRISTI - ADAPTATIONS.

IMITATIO CHRISTI - AUTHORSHIP.
    [BQT 2522.4]

IMITATIO CHRISTI - BIBLIOGRAPHY.
    [BQT 2522.1]

IMITATIO CHRISTI - COMMENTARIES.
    BQT 2522

IMITATIO CHRISTI - CRITICISM, TEXTUAL.
    BQT 2522

IMITATIO CHRISTI - CONCORDANCES.
    [BQT 2522.2]

IMITATIO CHRISTI - HISTORY.
    [BQT 2522.3]

IMITATIO CHRISTI - PARAPHRASES.

IMITATIO CHRISTI - ENGLISH, [FRENCH, GERMAN, ETC.]

IMITATION OF CHRIST. See
JESUS CHRIST - EXAMPLE.

IMITATION OF CHRIST (BOOK). See
IMITATIO CHRISTI.

IMITATION OF THE SAINTS.
     BQT 2196   (24x7.5)
 x Saints, Imitation of the.
xx Perfection, Christian.
  Sanctification.

IMMACULATE CONCEPTION.
     BQT 1022   (23x3.2)
sa Mary, Blessed Virgin - Sinlessness.
 x Mary, Blessed Virgin - Immaculate Conception.
xx Mary, Blessed Virgin - Prerogatives.

IMMACULATE CONCEPTION - ART.
     BQT 5887
xx Mary, Blessed Virgin - Art.

IMMACULATE CONCEPTION - BIBLICAL
  TEACHING.

IMMACULATE CONCEPTION - BIBLIO-
  GRAPHY.

IMMACULATE CONCEPTION - CONGRESSES.

IMMACULATE CONCEPTION - CULTUS.

IMMACULATE CONCEPTION - HISTORY OF
  DOCTRINES.

IMMACULATE CONCEPTION - HISTORY OF
  DOCTRINES - EARLY CHURCH.

IMMACULATE CONCEPTION - HISTORY OF
  DOCTRINES - MIDDLE AGES.

IMMACULATE CONCEPTION - HISTORY OF
  DOCTRINES - 16th, [17th, etc.]
  CENTURY.

IMMACULATE CONCEPTION - MEDITATIONS.
     BQT 2598

IMMACULATE CONCEPTION - PAPAL
  TEACHING.

IMMACULATE CONCEPTION - POETRY.

IMMACULATE CONCEPTION - SERMONS.
     BQT 3060

IMMACULATE CONCEPTION, BLUE SCAPULAR
  OF THE. See BLUE SCAPULAR OF THE
  IMMACULATE CONCEPTION.

IMMACULATE CONCEPTION, FEAST OF THE.
     BQT 4230   (23x3.72)
 x Feast of the Immaculate Conception.

IMMACULATE CONCEPTION, MASS OF THE.
  See MISSA IN CONCEPTIONE IMMACU-
LATA BEATAE MARIAE VIRGINIS.

IMMACULATE CONCEPTION, OFFICE OF THE.
  See OFFICIUM IN CONCEPTIONE IMMA-
CULATA BEATAE MARIAE VIRGINIS.

IMMACULATE HEART OF MARY.
  x Heart of Mary, Immaculate.
    Mary, Blessed Virgin - Immacu-
     late Heart.
    Mary, Blessed Virgin - Sacred
     Heart.
    Sacred Heart of Mary.
 xx Sacred Hearts.

IMMACULATE HEART OF MARY - DEVOTIONAL
  LITERATURE.

IMMACULATE HEART OF MARY - MEDITA-
  TIONS.
     BQT 2598

IMMACULATE HEART OF MARY - NOVENAS.
  See NOVENAS - IMMACULATE HEART OF
MARY.

IMMACULATE HEART OF MARY - PRAYER-
  BOOKS.
     BQT 2679

IMMACULATE HEART OF MARY, FEAST OF THE.
    BQT 4230
    x Feast of the Immaculate Heart of
       Mary.

IMMACULATE HEART OF MARY, MASS OF THE.
    See MISSA IMMACULATI CORDIS MARIAE
    VIRGINIS.

IMMANENCE (PHILOSOPHY)
    References as in LC.

IMMANENCE OF GOD.
        BQT 1215   (231.x13)
    The meaning of this term is that
       "in God we live and move and have
       our being; God made us with all
       our faculties, and we have the
       constant aid of His concursus."
       AT
    For works in the Modernistic sense
       of this term, that we are emana-
       tions of the divine substance,
       see Modernism.
    sa Holy Spirit - Indwelling.
       Mystical union.
       Presence of God, Practice of the.
       Transcendence of God.
     x Divine immanence.
       God - Immanence.
       God - Indwelling.
       Indwelling of God.
    xx God - Omnipresence.

IMMERSION, BAPTISMAL. See
    BAPTISM.

IMMORAL LITERATURE. See
    LITERATURE, IMMORAL.

IMMORTALITY.
        BL 530 (Comparative religion)
        BD 420-422 (Philosophy)
           (129.6)
        BQT 629 (Theology)   (218;
           236.x12)
    sa Eschatology.
       Future life.
       Heaven.
       Materialism.
       Soul.
     x Eternal life.
       Life after death.

IMMORTALITY -- Continued.
    xx Dogmatic theology.
       Eschatology.
       Future life.
       Soul.

IMMORTALITY - POETRY.

IMMORTALITY - SERMONS.

IMMUNITY, ECCLESIASTICAL.
    "Exemption granted by law in favor
       of ecclesiastical persons,
       places or property." AT
    sa Privilegium fori.
     x Ecclesiastical immunity.
    xx Asylum, Right of.
       Privileges (Canon law)

IMPEDIMENTS (CANON LAW)
    sa Irregularities.
       Marriage - Impediments (Canon
          law)
       Ordination - Impediments.
       Religious orders - Impediments.

IMPEDIMENTS TO MARRIAGE. See
    MARRIAGE - IMPEDIMENTS.

IMPEDIMENTS TO ORDINATION. See
    IRREGULARITIES.
    ORDINATION - IMPEDIMENTS.

IMPEDIMENTS TO RELIGIOUS LIFE. See
    RELIGIOUS ORDERS - IMPEDIMENTS.

IMPENITENCE.
        BQT 1811
    xx Penance (Virtue)

IMPENITENCE - SERMONS.

IMPERFECTIONS (THEOLOGY)
        BQT 1810; BQT 2240
     x Faults (Theology)
    xx Perfection, Christian.
       Vice.
       Virtue.

IMPERFECTIONS (THEOLOGY) - SERMONS.

IMPORTUNATE WIDOW (PARABLE). See
    UNJUST JUDGE (PARABLE)

IMPOSITION OF HANDS.
      BQT 4474
      BM 715 (Jewish rite)
   x Hands, Imposition of.
    Laying-on of hands.

IMPOTENCE (CANON LAW)
  xx Marriage - Impediments (Canon law)

IMPRECATION. See
  BLESSING AND CURSING.

IMPROPRIATION. See
  SECULARIZATION.

IN COENA DOMINI BULLS.
   x Bulls, In coena Domini.
    Coena Domini bulls.
  xx Bulls, Papal.
    Heresies and heretics.

IN COMMENDAM. See
  COMMENDATORY ABBOTS.

IN EXITU ISRAEL DE EGYPTO (MUSIC). See
  PSALMS (MUSIC) - 113th PSALM.

IN TE, DOMINE, SPERAVI (MUSIC). See
  PSALMS (MUSIC) - 30th PSALM.

INCARDINATION (CANON LAW)
      BQV230 111-118 (348.x31)
  sa Excardination (Canon law)
  xx Benefices, Ecclesiastical (Canon
    law)
    Clergy (Canon law)
    Excardination (Canon law)
    Ordination (Canon law)

INCARNATION.
      BQT 731 (232.x2)
  sa Jesus Christ.
    Kenosis.
   x Jesus Christ - Incarnation.
  xx Annunciation.
    Dogmatic theology.
    Jesus Christ.
    Theophanies.

INCARNATION - HISTORY OF DOCTRINES.

INCARNATION - HISTORY OF DOCTRINES -
  EARLY CHURCH.

INCARNATION - HISTORY OF DOCTRINES -
  MIDDLE AGES.

INCARNATION - HISTORY OF DOCTRINES -
  MODERN PERIOD.

INCENSE.
      BQT 4369; BQT 4522 (23x7.8)

INCLINA, DOMINE, AUREM TUAM (MUSIC).
  See PSALMS (MUSIC) - 85th PSALM.

INCLUSI.
      BQX 6838
  Here are entered works about religious persons who, with permission
  of ecclesiastical authority, were
  voluntarily walled-up in a cell.
  xx Hermits.
    Religious orders.

INCOMMUNICANTS. See LOUISETS.

INCOMPATIBILITY OF OFFICES (CANON
  LAW)

INCORPORATION (CANON LAW)
  xx Church property (Canon law)

INDETERMINISM. See
  FREE WILL AND DETERMINISM.

INDEX, CONGREGATION OF THE. See
  CONGREGATIO INDICIS.

INDEX LIBRORUM PROHIBITORUM.
      BQT 1993-1994
      BQV230 1384-1405 (348.x444)
      Z 1020 (098.x11)
  xx Catholic literature.
    Censorship (Canon law)
    Church - Teaching office.
    Condemned books.
    Expurgated books.
    Prohibited books.

INDEX LIBRORUM PROHIBITORUM - BIBLIO-
  GRAPHY.

INDIA - CHURCH HISTORY.
      BQX 3221-3297 (275.4)
  sa Missions - India.

INDIA - CHURCH HISTORY - EARLY
  PERIOD TO 1498.

INDIA - CHURCH HISTORY - 1498-1774.

INDIA - CHURCH HISTORY - 1774-

INDIA - CHURCH HISTORY - 20th CENTURY.

INDIA - RELIGION.
    BL 2000-2030

INDIANS - MISSIONS.
    x Missions - Indians.
    Missions, Indian.

INDIANS - MYTHOLOGY. See
  INDIANS - RELIGION AND MYTHOLOGY.

INDIANS - RELIGION AND MYTHOLOGY.
    E 59.R
    x Indians - Mythology.

INDIANS OF CENTRAL AMERICA - MISSIONS.
    x Missions - Indians.
    Missions, Indian.

INDIANS OF CENTRAL AMERICA - RELIGION
  AND MYTHOLOGY.
    F 1434.2.R
    References as in LC.

INDIANS OF MEXICO - MISSIONS.
    BQX 4202
    x Missions - Indians.
    Missions, Indian.

INDIANS OF MEXICO - RELIGION AND
  MYTHOLOGY.
    References as in LC.

INDIANS OF MEXICO - RITES AND
  CEREMONIES.

INDIANS OF NORTH AMERICA - MISSIONS.
    BQX 4041-4049
    sa Jesuits - Missions.
       also subdivision "Missions" under
       names of Indian tribes, e.g.,
       Illinois Indians - Missions.
    x Missions - Indians.
    Missions, Indian.
    xx Missions.

INDIANS OF NORTH AMERICA - RELIGION
  AND MYTHOLOGY.
    E 98.R
    References as in LC.

INDIANS OF NORTH AMERICA - RITES AND
  CEREMONIES.
    References as in LC.

INDIANS OF SOUTH AMERICA - MISSIONS.
    BQX 4724-4734
    x Missions - Indians.
    Missions, Indian.

INDIANS OF SOUTH AMERICA - RELIGION
  AND MYTHOLOGY.
    F 2230.1.R
    References as in LC.

INDIANS OF THE WEST INDIES - RELIGION
  AND MYTHOLOGY.
    F 1619

INDIFFERENCE, RELIGIOUS. See
  INDIFFERENTISM (RELIGION)

INDIFFERENTISM (RELIGION)
    BQT 242   (23x9.44)
    sa Toleration.
       Unionism (Religion)
    x Indifference, Religious.
    Religious indifference.
    xx Irreligion.
    Rationalism.

INDIGENOUS CLERGY. See
  NATIVE CLERGY.

INDISSOLUBILITY OF MARRIAGE. See
  MARRIAGE - INDISSOLUBILITY.

INDULGENCES.
    BQT 1394-1397   (23x7.41)
    sa Absolution.
       Altars, Privileged.
       Crosier indulgence.
       Crusade bulls.
       Ejaculations.
       Marian Year.
       Portiuncula indulgence.
       Purgatory.
       Scapulars.

INDULGENCES -- Continued.
  xx Absolution.
    Good works (Theology)
    Penance.
    Prayers.
    Purgatory.

INDULGENCES - COLLECTIONS.
    BQT 4506

INDULGENCES - CONTROVERSIAL
  LITERATURE.
    [BQT 1398]

INDULGENCES - HISTORY.
    BQT 1394

INDULGENCES - SERMONS.

INDULGENCES (CANON LAW)
    BQV230 911-936   (348.x42)

INDULGENCES AND SACRED RELICS,
  CONGREGATION OF. See
  CONGREGATIO INDULGENTIARUM ET
  SACRARUM RELIQUIAUM.

INDULTS.
  An indult is "a faculty granted by
    the Holy See to bishops and others
    to do something not permitted by
    the common law of the Church,
    e.g., to a priest in charge of a
    foreign mission to administer the
    sacrament of confirmation." AT
  sa Exclaustration.
    Secularization (Canon law)
  xx Dispensation.
    Privileges (Canon law)

INDUSTRIAL CHAPLAINS. See
  CHAPLAINS, INDUSTRIAL.

INDUSTRIAL MISSIONS. See
  MISSIONS - INDUSTRIAL WORK.

INDUSTRY AND THE CHURCH. See
  CHURCH AND INDUSTRY.

INDWELLING OF GOD. See
  IMMANENCE OF GOD.

INDWELLING OF THE HOLY SPIRIT. See
  HOLY SPIRIT - INDWELLING.
INFALLIBILITY
INFALLIBILITY OF THE CHURCH. See
  CHURCH - INFALLIBILITY.

INFALLIBILITY OF THE POPE. See
  POPES - INFALLIBILITY.

INFAMY (CANON LAW)
    BQV230 2293 (348.x6)
  xx Penalties, Ecclesiastical.

INFANT BAPTISM.
    BQT 1266 (23x7.1)
  sa Predestination.
  xx Baptism.

INFANT COMMUNION.
  x Communion, Infant.

INFANT JESUS OF PRAGUE (STATUE)
    [BQT 2659.1]
  x Prague, Infant Jesus of (Statue)
    Pražské Jezulátko.
  xx Holy Childhood.

INFANT SALVATION.
    BQT 1563 (236.7)
  Here are entered works on the
    state of infants who die without
    baptism.
  sa Limbo.
  xx Salvation.

INFIDELS.
  sa Paganism.
  xx Non-Catholics.

INFUSED VIRTUES. See
  VIRTUES, INFUSED.

INHERITANCE AND SUCCESSION (CANON
  LAW)
  sa Legitime (Canon law)
    Wills (Canon law)
  xx Wills (Canon law)

INITIATIONS (IN RELIGION, FOLKLORE,
  ETC.)
    BL 615
  sa Baptism.
    Circumcision.
    Profession, Religious.

INNER LIGHT.
    BX 7748.I
  For works on the Catholic theory
    of divine or interior illumina-
    tion see Illumination of in-
    tellect.
  References as in LC.

INNER MISSIONS.
    BV 2950
  Here are entered works dealing
    with the free-will activities of
    Protestants to improve the reli-
    gious, moral, and social status
    of their fellow-citizens, which
    work is carried on over and above
    the official church and parish
    activities.
  x Missions, Inner.
  xx Charities - Germany.
    Protestant Churches - Germany -
    Charities.

INNOCENCE (THEOLOGY).
  xx Baptism.

INNOCENTS, FEAST OF THE HOLY. See
HOLY INNOCENTS, FEAST OF THE.

INNOCENTS, MASSACRE OF THE HOLY. See
HOLY INNOCENTS, MASSACRE OF THE.

INQUISITION. (Geog. subdiv., Direct)
    BQX 781-7.6 (270.6)
  sa Auto-da-fe sermons.
    Persecution.
  x Church history - Inquisition.
  xx Church history.
    Church history - Middle Ages.
    Persecution.

INQUISITION - BOHEMIA.
    BQX 791

INQUISITION - FRANCE.
    BQX 792

INQUISITION - GERMANY.
    BQX 794

INQUISITION - ITALY.
    BQX 795

INQUISITION - MEXICO.
    BQX 2930

INQUISITION - NETHERLANDS.
    BQX 2330

INQUISITION - PORTUGAL.
    BQX 796

INQUISITION - SPAIN.
    BQX 2923-2935 (274.604)
  x Spanish Inquisition.

INQUISITION, HOLY ROMAN AND
UNIVERSAL. See
CONGREGATIO SANCTI OFFICII.

INSANITY.
  sa Use of reason.
  Other references as in LC.

INSANITY (CANON LAW)
  sa Use of reason (Canon law)
  xx Irregularities.
    Mental illness (Canon law)

INSCRIPTIONS, CHRISTIAN.
    BQ 631 (Latin)
    BQ 5237 (Greek)
    BQX 65   (264.x13)
  x Christian epigraphy.
    Christian inscriptions.
    Epigraphy, Christian.
  xx Christian antiquities.

INSIGNIA, PONTIFICAL.
    BQT 5959
  Here are entered works on cere-
    monial ornaments proper to
    popes, cardinals, bishops,
    abbots, canons and princes.
  sa Bishops - Insignia.
  x Pontifical insignia.

INSPIRATION.
    BS 480 (Bible)
    BQT 268 (Theology)
  sa Bible - Inspiration.
    Enthusiasm.
    Revelation.
  xx Bible - Inspiration.
    Supernatural.

INSTALLATION (CLERGY)
  sa Installation sermons.
  x Clergy - Installation.

INSTALLATION (RABBIS)
  x Rabbis - Installation.

INSTALLATION SERMONS.
  x Sermons, Installation.
  xx Installation (Clergy)

INSTALLATION SERVICE (CHURCH
  OFFICERS)
  References as in LC.

INSTITUTE OF THE BROTHERS OF THE
  CHRISTIAN SCHOOLS. See
  BROTHERS OF THE CHRISTIAN SCHOOLS.

INSTITUTES, RELIGIOUS. See
  RELIGIOUS ORDERS.

INSTITUTES, SECULAR. See
  SECULAR INSTITUTES.

INSTITUTION OF THE EUCHARIST. See
  EUCHARIST - INSTITUTION.

INSTITUTIONAL MISSIONS. (Geog.
  subdiv.)
        BV 2000-3705
  x Missions, Institutional.

INSTITUTIONS, CATHOLIC. See
  CATHOLIC INSTITUTIONS.

INSTITUTUM FRATRUM SCHOLARUM
  CHRISTIANARUM. See
  BROTHERS OF THE CHRISTIAN SCHOOLS.

INSTRUCTION, RELIGIOUS. See
  CATECHETICS.
  RELIGIOUS EDUCATION.

INSTRUMENTAL MASSES. See
  ORGAN MASSES.

INSTRUMENTS, MUSICAL (CHURCH MUSIC).
  See MUSICAL INSTRUMENTS (CHURCH
  MUSIC)

INSTRUMENTS OF THE PASSION. See
  JESUS CHRIST - PASSION - INSTRU-
  MENTS.

INSUBORDINATION (CANON LAW)
  xx Offenses against religion.

INTEGRATED CHURCHES.
  x Churches, Integrated.
  xx Church and social problems.
  Church membership.
  Church polity.
  Race problems.

INTEMPERANCE. See
  ALCOHOLISM.
  INEBRIATES - HOSPITALS AND ASYLUMS.
  LIQUOR PROBLEM.
  TEMPERANCE.

INTENTION.
        BQT 1769 (Moral theology)
        BQT 2227 (Means of perfection)
  x Good intention.
  xx Human acts.
  Perfection, Christian.

INTENTION - SERMONS.

INTENTION, DECLARATION OF. See
  DECLARATION OF INTENTION.

INTENTIONS, MASS.
  x Mass Intentions.

INTERCESSION (MOHAMMEDANISM)
  xx Eschatology, Mohammedan.

INTERCOMMUNION.
        BQT 1866
        BX 9.5.I
  sa Communicatio in sacris.
  xx Communicatio in sacris.
  Other references as in LC.

INTERDENOMINATIONAL COOPERATION.
        BV 625
  References as in LC.

INTERDICT (CANON LAW)
        BQV230 2268-2277   (348.x6)
  sa Excommunication.
  xx Censures, Ecclesiastical.
  Excommunication.

INTEREST AND USURY.
        BQT 1947 (Moral theology)
  Other classifications and
  references as in LC.

INTEREST AND USURY (CANON LAW)
    BQV230 1543   (348.x46)
    x Usury (Canon law)

INTERMARRIAGE. See
    MARRIAGE, MIXED.
    MISCEGENATION.

INTERNATIONAL AFFAIRS AND CHRISTIANITY.
    See CHRISTIANITY AND INTERNATIONAL
    AFFAIRS.

INTERNATIONAL ORGANIZATION AND THE
    CHURCH. See CHURCH AND INTER-
    NATIONAL ORGANIZATION.

INTERNATIONAL ORGANIZATIONS, CATHOLIC.
    BQT 3512
    x Catholic international organi-
        zations.
    xx Catholic societies.

INTERPELLATION (CANON LAW)
    BQV230 1121-1123

Interpersonal Relations see

INTERPRETATION, BIBLICAL. See   *Human relations*
    BIBLE - CRITICISM, INTERPRETATION,
    ETC.

INTERRACIAL MARRIAGE. See
    MISCEGENATION.

INTOLERANCE. See
    FANATICISM.
    LIBERTY OF CONSCIENCE.
    RELIGIOUS LIBERTY.
    TOLERATION.

INTROITS.
    BQT 4319
    The introit is "the first variable
        portion of the Mass, consisting
        of an antiphon (usually from the
        Psalms), a psalm-verse, Gloria
        Patri, and the antiphon re-
        peated. It is really the be-
        ginning of the Mass." AT
    xx Mass.

INTROITS (MUSIC)
    BQT 4626
    xx Antiphonal chant.
        Propers (Music)
        Psalms (Music)

INTUITION (THEOLOGY)
    BQT 19
    xx Theology - Methodology.

INVESTITURE.
    BQX 643-644; BQX 1908
    sa Concordat of Worms, 1122.
    xx Bishops.
        Church and state.

INVESTMENTS (CANON LAW)
    xx Catholic Church - Finance.

INVINCIBLE IGNORANCE. See
    IGNORANCE, INVINCIBLE.

INVITATORIUM.
    BQT 4393
    x Venite exultemus Domino (In-
        vitatory)
    xx Matins.
        Psalms (Music) - 94th Psalm.

IRELAND - CHURCH HISTORY.
    BQX 2201-2269   (274.15)
    sa Monasticism, Irish.

IRELAND - CHURCH HISTORY - EARLY
    PERIOD TO 1169.

IRELAND - CHURCH HISTORY - 1169-1603.

IRELAND - CHURCH HISTORY - 16th
    CENTURY.

IRELAND - CHURCH HISTORY - 1603-1829.

IRELAND - CHURCH HISTORY - 1829-

IRELAND - CHURCH HISTORY - 20th
    CENTURY.

IRENICS.
    BQT 403-418
    Here are entered works on the
        attitude that peace is to be
        sought in religious matters.
    sa Catholic Church and reunion.
        Christian union.
        Schism.
    xx Apologetics.
        Christian union.

IRISH CHURCH. See
    CHURCH OF IRELAND.

IRISH MISSIONS. See
    MISSIONS, IRISH.

IRISH MONASTICISM. See
    MONASTICISM, IRISH.

IRISH SAINTS. See SAINTS, IRISH.

IRREGULARITIES.
    BQV230 983-991   (348.x426)
    "A canonical impediment, of its
    nature permanent, rendering
    unlawful, though not invalid,
    the reception or/and the exer-
    cise of the sacrament of
    orders." AT
    sa Absolution (Canon law)
       Crime and criminals (Canon
       law)
       Dispensations (Canon law)
       Heresy (Canon law)
       Illegitimacy (Canon law)
       Insanity (Canon law)
       Marriage (Canon law)
    xx Clergy (Canon law)
       Impediments (Canon law)
       Ordination - Impediments.
       Ordination (Canon law)

IRRELIGION.
    "Here are entered works dealing
    with a condition of complete
    absence of religion." LC sup-
    plement 1961.
    sa Agnosticism.
       Atheism.
       Free thought.
       Indifferentism (Religion)
       Non church-affiliated people.
       Rationalism.
       Secularism.
    xx Religion.

ISAIAH, BOOK OF. See
    BIBLE. O.T. ISAIAS.

ISAIAS, BOOK OF. See
    BIBLE. O.T. ISAIAS.

ISHMAELITES.
    "Not to be confused with the
    Mohammedan sect 'Ismailites'."
    LC

ISLAM. See MOHAMMEDANISM.

ISMAILITES.
    BP 195.I   (297)
    References as in LC.

ISRAEL - NAME.
    xx Bible - Names.
       Jews - Name.

ISRAEL, TEN LOST TRIBES OF. See
    LOST TRIBES OF ISRAEL.

ISRAEL, TWELVE TRIBES OF. See
    TWELVE TRIBES OF ISRAEL.

ISRAELITES (BOHEMIA). See
    ABRAHAMITES (BOHEMIA)

ITALIAN PRESBYTERIANS. See
    PRESBYTERIANS, ITALIAN.

ITALO-ALBANIAN RITE. See
    BYZANTINE RITE, ITALO-ALBANIAN.

ITALO-GREEK RITE. See
    BYZANTINE RITE, ITALO-ALBANIAN.

ITALY - CHURCH HISTORY.
    BQX 2361-2660   (274.5)

ITALY - CHURCH HISTORY - SOURCES.

ITALY - CHURCH HISTORY - EARLY
    PERIOD TO 590.
    xx Church history - Primitive and
       early church.

ITALY - CHURCH HISTORY - 590-1250.

ITALY - CHURCH HISTORY - 1250-1517.

ITALY - CHURCH HISTORY - 1517-1870.

ITALY - CHURCH HISTORY - 19th CENTURY.

ITALY - CHURCH HISTORY - 20th CENTURY.

ITALY - RELIGION.

ITALY - RELIGIOUS AND ECCLESIASTICAL
   INSTITUTIONS.

ITINERANCY (CHURCH POLITY)
        BV 664
      x Clergy, Itinerant.

ITINERANCY (CHURCH POLITY) - METHODIST
   CHURCH, [ETC.]
        BX 8345 (Methodist Church)

ITINERARIUM.
        BQT 4421
      "A form of blessing for a cleric
        about to undertake a journey."
        AT
      xx Clergy - Prayer-books.

IUS. See
   JUS.

JACOBINS (DOMINICANS)
      xx Dominicans - France.

JACOBITE CHURCH.

JACOBITE CHURCH - HISTORY.
        BQX 5581-5594   (28x1.5)

JACOBITE CHURCH - LAW.
        BQV 1341-1346   (348.x7)

JACOBITE CHURCH - THEOLOGY.

JACOBITE CHURCH. LITURGY AND
   RITUAL.
        BQT 5111-5129   (264.x72)

JACOBITE CHURCH, MALABAR. See
   MALABAR JACOBITE CHURCH.

JAHAD. See JIHAD.

JAHVE.
      x Adonai.
        Jehovah.
        Yahweh.

JAINA SECTS.
      References as in LC.

JAINA SHRINES.
      x Shrines, Jaina.

JAINISM.
        BL 1305-1365   (294.4)
      References as in LC.

JAINS.
        BL 1305-1365   (294.4)
      References as in LC.

JAMES, SAINT, CATHOLIC EPISTLE OF.
   See BIBLE. N.T. JAMES.

JANITORS.   (Geog. subdiv., Direct)
        TX 339
      sa Sacristans.
      Other references as in LC.

JANSENISTS.
        BQX 988; BQX 1776 (Church
           history)
        BQT 116; BQT 1142 (Theology)
           (284.84)
      sa Convulsionaries.
         Fareinistes.
         Old Catholic Church.

JAPAN - CHURCH HISTORY.
        BQX 3341-3388   (275.2)
      sa Missions - Japan.

JAPAN - CHURCH HISTORY - EARLY
   PERIOD TO 1640.

JAPAN - CHURCH HISTORY - 1640-

JAPAN - CHURCH HISTORY - 16th
   CENTURY.

JAPAN - CHURCH HISTORY - 17th
   CENTURY.

JAPAN - CHURCH HISTORY - 20th
   CENTURY.

JAPAN - RELIGION.
        BL 2200-2220

JEHOVAH. See JAHVE.

JEHOVAH, DAY OF. See
   DAY OF JEHOVAH.

JEHOVAH, SERVANT OF. See
    SERVANT OF JEHOVAH.

JEHOVAH'S WITNESSES.
        BX 8525.7
    x Witnesses of Jehovah.

JEREMIAH, BOOK OF. See
    BIBLE. O.T. JEREMIAS.

JEREMIAH, LAMENTATIONS OF. See
    BIBLE. O.T. LAMENTATIONS.

JEREMIAS, BOOK OF. See
    BIBLE. O.T. JEREMIAS.

JEREMIAS, EPISTLE OF. See
    BIBLE. O.T. BARUCH.

JEREMIAS, LAMENTATIONS OF. See
    BIBLE. O.T. LAMENTATIONS.

JERUSALEM - HISTORY - LATIN
    KINGDOM, 1099-1244.
        BQX 5574
        D 175-195
    x Latin Kingdom of Jerusalem.
    xx Crusades.
        Latin Orient.

JERUSALEM. TEMPLE.
        BM 655
    sa Tabernacle.
    x Temple of Jerusalem.

JERUSALEM, COUNCIL OF, 50 or 51.
        BQX 322

JERUSALEM, ORDER OF THE KNIGHTS OF
    ST. JOHN. See
    KNIGHTS OF MALTA.

JERUSALEM IN THE BIBLE.

JESU DULCIS MEMORIA.
        BQT 2695   (24x3.7)

JESU DULCIS MEMORIA (MUSIC)
        BQT 4682

JESUIT BROTHERS. See
    JESUITS. LAY BROTHERS.

JESUIT DRAMA. See
    JESUITS AND DRAMA.

JESUIT MISSIONS. See
    JESUITS - MISSIONS.

JESUIT SAINTS. See
    SAINTS, JESUIT.

JESUIT THEOLOGIANS. See
    THEOLOGIANS, JESUIT.

JESUIT WAR, 1754-1756 (SOUTH AMERICA)
    See SEVEN REDUCTIONS, WAR OF THE,
    1754-1756.

JESUITS.   (Geog. subdiv., Direct)
        BQX 7451-7500   (271.x1)
    sa Bollandists.
    x Company of Jesus.
        Jesus, Society of.
        Societas Jesu.
        Society of Jesus.

JESUITS - BIBLIOGRAPHY.
        BQX 7451
        Z 7840

JESUITS - BIOGRAPHY.
        BQX 7499-7500
    sa Saints, Jesuit.

JESUITS - CANON LAW.
        [BQX 7464.7]

JESUITS - CONTROVERSIAL LITERATURE.

JESUITS - DICTIONARIES.

JESUITS - DIRECTORIES.
        BQX 7454

JESUITS - EDUCATION.
        [BQX 7464.5]
    sa Jesuits and education.

JESUITS - EDUCATION - DIRECTORIES.

JESUITS - HISTORY.
        BQX 7461-7485

226

JESUITS - MEDITATIONS.

JESUITS - MISSIONS.   (Geog. subdiv.)
     [BQX 7464.6]
      BQX 4043 (Indian missions)
   x Jesuit missions.
     Missions, Jesuit.
   xx Indians of North America -
      Missions.

JESUITS - NOVITIATE. See
  NOVITIATE - JESUITS.

JESUITS - PERIODICALS.
      BQX 7452

JESUITS - PORTRAITS.

JESUITS - PRAYER-BOOKS.

JESUITS - PROPERTY.

JESUITS - RETREATS. See
  RETREATS FOR JESUITS.

JESUITS - RULES.
      BQX 7455-7458

JESUITS - SPIRITUAL LIFE.
      BQX 7464

JESUITS - SUPPRESSION.
      BQX 995; BQX 7467
   x Suppression of the Jesuits.

      ################

JESUITS - AUSTRIA, [BAVARIA,
  JAPAN, ETC.]
      BQX 7469-7485

      ################

JESUITS. LAY BROTHERS.
      BQX 7495-7498   (271.x1)
   x Jesuit Brothers.

JESUITS. LETTERS FROM MISSIONS.

JESUITS. PROVINCES. CHICAGO,
  [MEXICO, PARAGUAY, ETC.]
      BQX 7486-7494

      ################

JESUITS AND AGRICULTURE.

JESUITS AND ARCHITECTURE.

JESUITS AND ASTRONOMY.

JESUITS AND DRAMA.
   x Jesuit drama.

JESUITS AND EDUCATION.
   xx Jesuits - Education.

JESUITS AND MORAL THEOLOGY.

JESUITS AND OBEDIENCE.

JESUITS AND PHILOSOPHY.

JESUITS AND PREACHING.

JESUITS AND THE COUNTER-REFORMATION.
      BQX 866
   xx Counter-reformation.

JESUITS AND THEOLOGY.

JESUS, SOCIETY OF. See JESUITS.

JESUS AND MARY, SACRED HEARTS OF.
  See SACRED HEARTS.

√ JESUS CHRIST.
      BQT 682-981   (232)
   sa Antichrist.
      Atonement.
      Christianity.
      Eucharist.
      Incarnation.
      Logos.
      Mary, Blessed Virgin.
      Mass.
      Messiah.
      Millennium.
      Recapitulation.
      Redemption.
      Salvation.
      Second advent.
      Trinity.
    x Christ.
      Christology.
   xx Christianity.
      Dogmatic theology.
      God.

JESUS CHRIST -- Continued.
  sa Incarnation.
     Messiah.
     Trinity.

JESUS CHRIST - ADDRESSES, ESSAYS,
  LECTURES.
       BQT 685

JESUS CHRIST - AGONY.
       BQT 921
   x Agony of Christ.
  xx Jesus Christ - Passion.

JESUS CHRIST - APOCRYPHAL AND LEGENDARY
  LITERATURE. See
  JESUS CHRIST - BIOGRAPHY - APOCRYPHAL
  AND LEGENDARY LITERATURE.

JESUS CHRIST - APOCRYPHAL LIFE. See
  APOCRYPHAL BOOKS (N.T.)

JESUS CHRIST - APPARITIONS AND
  MIRACLES (MODERN)
       BQT 971-973
  xx Apparitions.
     Jesus Christ - Miracles.

JESUS CHRIST - APPEARANCES.
       BQT 951
  "Here are entered works dealing
   with the appearances of Jesus
   Christ after His resurrection."
   LC
  xx Jesus Christ - Forty days.
     Theophanies.

JESUS CHRIST - APPRECIATION.

JESUS CHRIST - ART.
       BQT 5854-5876   (246.x64)
  sa Bible - Pictures, illustrations,
       etc.
     Bible - Picture Bibles.
     Christian art.
     Epiphany - Art.
     Eucharist - Art.
     Fish (in religion, folklore,
       etc.)
     Jesus Christ - Iconography.
     Magi - Art.
     Mary, Blessed Virgin - Art.
     Pieta.

JESUS CHRIST - ART -- Continued.
   x Jesus Christ - Nativity - Art.
     Jesus Christ - Passion - Art.
     Jesus Christ - Pictures, illus-
       trations, etc.
     Jesus Christ in art.
  xx Christian art.
     God - Art.

JESUS CHRIST - ASCENSION.
       BQT 957
  sa Ascension Day.
   x Ascension of Christ.

JESUS CHRIST - ATONEMENT. See
  ATONEMENT.

JESUS CHRIST - ATTITUDE TOWARDS
  WOMEN.
       BQT 981

JESUS CHRIST - BAPTISM.
       BQT 863
   x Baptism of Christ.

JESUS CHRIST - BEATITUDES. See
  BEATITUDES.

JESUS CHRIST - BIBLIOGRAPHY.
  [BQT 680]
   Z 8455

JESUS CHRIST - BIOGRAPHY. *Use: Jesus Christ*
       BQT 803-961   (225.x91)
   x Jesus Christ - Ministry.
     Life of Christ.

JESUS CHRIST - BIOGRAPHY - APOCRYPHAL
  AND LEGENDARY LITERATURE.
       BQT 961
   x Jesus Christ - Apocryphal and
     legendary literature.
     Jesus Christ - Legends.

JESUS CHRIST - BIOGRAPHY - CATECHISMS,
  QUESTION-BOOKS.

JESUS CHRIST - BIOGRAPHY - CONTRO-
  VERSIAL LITERATURE.

JESUS CHRIST - BIOGRAPHY - DEVOTIONAL
  LITERATURE.

JESUS CHRIST - BIOGRAPHY - EARLY LIFE.
sa Jesus Christ - Childhood.

JESUS CHRIST - BIOGRAPHY - EARLY
WORKS TO 1800.

JESUS CHRIST - BIOGRAPHY - FICTION.

JESUS CHRIST - BIOGRAPHY - HISTORY
AND CRITICISM.

JESUS CHRIST - BIOGRAPHY - JUVENILE
LITERATURE.
BQT 810

JESUS CHRIST - BIOGRAPHY - MEDITA-
TIONS.
BQT 2585-2587

JESUS CHRIST - BIOGRAPHY - PASSION
WEEK.
BQT 911-942
sa Jesus Christ - Passion.

JESUS CHRIST - BIOGRAPHY - PRAYER-
BOOKS.
BQT 2657
xx Jesus Christ - Prayer-books.

JESUS CHRIST - BIOGRAPHY - PUBLIC
LIFE.
BQT 861-957

JESUS CHRIST - BIOGRAPHY - SERMONS.
xx Jesus Christ - Sermons.

JESUS CHRIST - BIOGRAPHY - SOURCES.
BQT 823
xx Jesus Christ - Historicity.

JESUS CHRIST - BIOGRAPHY - SOURCES,
BIBLICAL.
BQT 803

JESUS CHRIST - BIOGRAPHY - SOURCES,
JEWISH.

JESUS CHRIST - BIOGRAPHY - STUDY.
BQT 827

JESUS CHRIST - BIRTH. See
JESUS CHRIST - NATIVITY.

JESUS CHRIST - BLESSING OF CHILDREN.

JESUS CHRIST - BRETHREN.
x Brethren of Jesus.
Brothers of Jesus.
xx Apostles.
Disciples.
Mary, Blessed Virgin - Virginity.

JESUS CHRIST - BURIAL.
BQT 937
x Jesus Christ - Descent from
the cross.

JESUS CHRIST - CHARACTER.
[BQT 818]

JESUS CHRIST - CHARACTER - JUVENILE
LITERATURE.

JESUS CHRIST - CHARITY.
BQT 981

JESUS CHRIST - CHILDHOOD.
BQT 831-850
sa Holy Childhood.
xx Jesus Christ - Biography - .
Early life.

JESUS CHRIST - CHRONOLOGY.
BQT 825

JESUS CHRIST - CONFLICTS.
"Here are entered works dealing
with the controversies which
Jesus Christ had with His
opponents." LC

JESUS CHRIST - CRUCIFIXION.
BQT 931
sa Jesus Christ - Transfixion.
x Crucifixion of Christ.
Jesus Christ - Death.

JESUS CHRIST - CULTUS.
BQT 2657-2670

JESUS CHRIST - DEATH. See
JESUS CHRIST - CRUCIFIXION.
JESUS CHRIST - PASSION.

JESUS CHRIST - DESCENT FROM THE CROSS.
See JESUS CHRIST - BURIAL.

JESUS CHRIST - DESCENT INTO HELL.
    BQT 945
  x Descent into hell.

JESUS CHRIST - DEVOTIONAL LITERATURE.
    BQT 2585-2593

JESUS CHRIST - DIVINITY.
    BQT 708   (232.32; 23x9.2)
  sa Arianism.
     Socinianism.
     Trinity.
     Unitarianism.
   x Divinity of Christ.
  xx Hypostatic union.
     Socinianism.
     Unitarianism.

JESUS CHRIST - DRAMA.
    BQT 967
  sa Easter - Drama.
     Passion-plays.
   x Jesus Christ - Passion - Drama.

JESUS CHRIST - EDUCATION.

JESUS CHRIST - ENTRY INTO JERUSALEM.
    BQT 913

JESUS CHRIST - ETHICS.

JESUS CHRIST - EXALTATION.

JESUS CHRIST - EXAMPLE.
    BQT 2195
  "Here are entered works dealing
    with Jesus Christ as an example
    or pattern to be followed." LC
   x Imitation of Christ.
  xx Perfection, Christian.

JESUS CHRIST - EXAMPLE - SERMONS.

JESUS CHRIST - FAMILY.
  sa Holy Family.
  xx Holy Family.

JESUS CHRIST - FEASTS.
    BQT 4219-4225
  sa individual feasts in honor
     of Christ, e.g., Ascension
     Day, Christmas, etc.
  xx Feasts, Ecclesiastical.

JESUS CHRIST - FEASTS - SERMONS.
  xx Jesus Christ - Sermons.

JESUS CHRIST - FICTION.
    BQT 969
  xx Jesus Christ in literature.
     Religion in literature.

JESUS CHRIST - FIVE WOUNDS, DEVOTION
  TO. See FIVE WOUNDS, DEVOTION TO.

JESUS CHRIST - FLIGHT INTO EGYPT.
    BQT 850
   x Flight into Egypt.

JESUS CHRIST - FORTY DAYS.
    BQT 949
  "Here are entered works descrip-
    tive of the forty days between
    the resurrection and ascension."
    LC
  sa Jesus Christ - Appearances.

JESUS CHRIST - FORTY DAYS IN THE
  WILDERNESS. See
  JESUS CHRIST - TEMPTATION.

JESUS CHRIST - FOUNDATION OF THE
  CHURCH. See
  CHURCH - FOUNDATION.

JESUS CHRIST - FRIENDS AND
  ASSOCIATES.
    BQT 981

JESUS CHRIST - GENEALOGY.
    BQT 837
  xx Bible - Genealogy.

JESUS CHRIST - HISTORICITY.
    BQT 816
  xx Jesus Christ - Biography -
     Sources.

JESUS CHRIST - HISTORY OF DOCTRINES.
    BQT 688-773
  sa Adoptionism.
     Antiochian school.
     Arianism.
     Docetism.
     Eunomianism.
     Monophysites.
     Monothelism.

230

JESUS CHRIST - HISTORY OF DOCTRINES --
Continued.
sa Nestorians.
Nihilianism.
Valentinians.

JESUS CHRIST - HISTORY OF DOCTRINES -
EARLY CHURCH.
BQT 691

JESUS CHRIST - HISTORY OF DOCTRINES -
MIDDLE AGES.
BQT 693

JESUS CHRIST - HISTORY OF DOCTRINES -
MODERN PERIOD.
BQT 694

JESUS CHRIST - HISTORY OF DOCTRINES -
16th, [17th, etc.] CENTURY.

JESUS CHRIST - HOLY COAT. See
HOLY COAT.

JESUS CHRIST - HOLY FACE. See
HOLY FACE.

JESUS CHRIST - HOLY SHROUD. See
HOLY SHROUD.

JESUS CHRIST - HUMANITY.
BQT 712-718 (232.x4)
sa Precious Blood.
Sacred Heart.

JESUS CHRIST - HUMILIATION.
BQT 981

JESUS CHRIST - HYPOSTATIC UNION.
See HYPOSTATIC UNION.

JESUS CHRIST - ICONOGRAPHY.
BQT 981
xx Jesus Christ - Art.

JESUS CHRIST - INCARNATION. See
INCARNATION.

JESUS CHRIST - INFLUENCE.

JESUS CHRIST - INTELLECTUAL LIFE.
BQT 981

JESUS CHRIST - INTERCESSION.

JESUS CHRIST - JEWISH INTERPRETATIONS.
BQT 697
xx Judaism.

JESUS CHRIST - JOURNEYS.
BQT 981

JESUS CHRIST - KENOSIS. See
KENOSIS.

JESUS CHRIST - KINGDOM. See
KINGDOM OF GOD.

JESUS CHRIST - KINGSHIP.
BQT 1123 (232.x7)
sa Jesus Christ the King,
Feast of.
x Jesus Christ - Royal office.
Kingship of Christ.

JESUS CHRIST - LAMB OF GOD. See
LAMB OF GOD.

JESUS CHRIST - LANGUAGE.
"Here are entered works dealing
with the problem of the language
used by Jesus Christ, specifically whether he spoke Hebrew,
Aramaic, or Greek." LC

JESUS CHRIST - LAST SUPPER. See
LAST SUPPER.

JESUS CHRIST - LAST WORDS. See
JESUS CHRIST - SEVEN LAST WORDS.

JESUS CHRIST - LEGENDS. See
JESUS CHRIST - BIOGRAPHY - APO-
CRYPHAL AND LEGENDARY LITERATURE.

JESUS CHRIST - LOGOS DOCTRINE. See
LOGOS.

JESUS CHRIST - MEDITATIONS.
BQT 2585-2593 (24x2.2)

JESUS CHRIST - MERCY.
BQT 981
xx God - Mercy.

JESUS CHRIST - MESSIAHSHIP.
    BQT 744-746 (232.x1)
sa Messiah.

JESUS CHRIST - MINISTRY. See
  JESUS CHRIST - BIOGRAPHY.

JESUS CHRIST - MIRACLES.
    BQT 871-874; BQT 971-973
    (23x9.2)
sa Jesus Christ - Apparitions
    and miracles (Modern)
    also names of miracles, e.g.,
    Healing of the man born blind
    (Miracle); Healing of the
    nobleman's son (Miracle).
 x Bible - Miracles.
  Miracles of Christ.
xx Miracles.

JESUS CHRIST - MISCELLANEA.

JESUS CHRIST - MOHAMMEDAN
  INTERPRETATIONS.
    BQT 697
xx Mohammedanism.

JESUS CHRIST - MONOGRAMS.
    BQT 5872 (246.x64)
sa Labarum.
xx Monograms.

JESUS CHRIST - MORMON
  INTERPRETATIONS.
    BQT 697
xx Mormons and Mormonism.

JESUS CHRIST - MUSIC. See
  JESUS CHRIST IN MUSIC.

JESUS CHRIST - MYSTICAL BODY. See
  MYSTICAL BODY OF CHRIST.

JESUS CHRIST - NAME.
sa Emmanuel.
  Holy Name, Devotion to.
  Lamb of God.
  Servant of Jehovah.
  Son of Man.
 x Jesus Christ - Titles.
xx Bible - Names.

JESUS CHRIST - NAME - SERMONS.

JESUS CHRIST - NATIVITY.
    BQT 843 (225.x91)
sa Christmas.
 x Jesus Christ - Birth.
  Nativity of Christ.
xx Christmas.

JESUS CHRIST - NATIVITY - ART.
  See JESUS CHRIST - ART.

JESUS CHRIST - NEW THOUGHT INTER-
  PRETATIONS.
    BQT 697

JESUS CHRIST - ORIENTAL INTER-
  PRETATIONS.
    BQT 813

JESUS CHRIST - PARABLES.
    BQT 881-888 (226.x6)
sa names of special parables, e.g.,
  Good Samaritan (Parable)
 x Parables, Biblical.
  Parables, Christian.
xx Bible - Parables.

JESUS CHRIST - PARABLES - FILMSTRIPS.

JESUS CHRIST - PARABLES - JUVENILE
  LITERATURE.

JESUS CHRIST - PARABLES - MEDITATIONS.
    BQT 885

JESUS CHRIST - PARABLES - PICTURES,
  ILLUSTRATIONS, ETC.
   x Jesus Christ - Pictures, illus-
    trations, etc.

JESUS CHRIST - PARABLES - SERMONS.
    BQT 885; BQT 3057

JESUS CHRIST - PARABLES - STUDY.

JESUS CHRIST - PASSION.
    BQT 920-945 (225.x91)
sa Cantus Passionis Domini Nostri
  Jesu Christi.
  Five Wounds, Devotion to.
  Holy Face.
  Holy Shroud.
  Holy Week.
  Jesus Christ - Agony.

232

JESUS CHRIST - PASSION -- Continued.
  sa Jesus Christ - Biography -
        Passion week.
     Jesus Christ - Relics of the
        Passion.
     Lent.
     Officium Passionis Domini Nostri
        Jesu Christi.
     Precious Blood.
     Veil of Veronica.
  x Jesus Christ - Death.
     Passion of Christ.

JESUS CHRIST - PASSION - ART.
  See   JESUS CHRIST - ART.

JESUS CHRIST - PASSION - DEVOTIONAL
  LITERATURE.
        BQT 2587

JESUS CHRIST - PASSION - DRAMA.   See
  JESUS CHRIST - DRAMA.
  PASSION-PLAYS.

JESUS CHRIST - PASSION - INSTRUMENTS.
        BQT 940-942
  sa Cross, Relics of the.
     Crown of thorns.
  x Instruments of the Passion.

JESUS CHRIST - PASSION - JUVENILE
  LITERATURE.

JESUS CHRIST - PASSION - MEDITATIONS.
        BQT 2587   (24x2.2)

JESUS CHRIST - PASSION - MUSIC.   See
  PASSION-MUSIC.

JESUS CHRIST - PASSION - PRAYER-
  BOOKS.
        BQT 2661
  sa Missa Passionis Domini Nostri
        Jesu Christi.
  xx Jesus Christ - Prayer-books.

JESUS CHRIST - PASSION - SERMONS.
        BQT 3055
  sa Good Friday - Sermons.
     Holy Week - Sermons.
     Sermons, Lenten.
  xx Jesus Christ - Sermons.

JESUS CHRIST - PATRIOTISM.

JESUS CHRIST - PERSON.   use Jesus Christ.
        BQT 701   (232)
  Here are entered theological
     treatises on the person of
     Christ.
  √ Instead of the broad LC heading
     "Jesus Christ - Person and
     offices" libraries may find it
     desirable in most instances to
     use the heading "Jesus Christ"
     without any subdivision.
  For works on the character of
     Christ see   Jesus Christ -
     Character.
  sa Hypostatic union.

JESUS CHRIST - PICTURES, ILLUSTRA-
  TIONS, ETC.   See
  JESUS CHRIST - ART.
  JESUS CHRIST - PARABLES - PICTURES,
     ILLUSTRATIONS, ETC.

JESUS CHRIST - POETRY.
        BQT 966   (245.x2)
  x Jesus Christ in poetry.
  xx Jesus Christ in literature.
     Religion in literature.
     Religion in poetry.

JESUS CHRIST - POPULAR WORKS.
        BQT 686

JESUS CHRIST - PRAYER-BOOKS.
        BQT 2657-2670
  sa Eucharist - Prayer-books.
     Jesus Christ - Biography -
        Prayer-books.
     Jesus Christ - Passion -
        Prayer-books.
     Sacred Heart - Prayer-books.

JESUS CHRIST - PRAYERS.
        BQT 895
  sa Lord's Prayer.
  xx Bible - Prayers.

JESUS CHRIST - PREACHING.

JESUS CHRIST - PREACHING AT NAZARETH.
  x Jesus Christ - Rejection at
     Nazareth.

JESUS CHRIST - PRECIOUS BLOOD. See
PRECIOUS BLOOD.

JESUS CHRIST - PRECIOUS BLOOD, RELICS
OF THE. See
PRECIOUS BLOOD, RELICS OF THE.

JESUS CHRIST - PRE-EXISTENCE.

JESUS CHRIST - PRESENTATION.
BQT 846
sa Candlemas.
x Presentation of Jesus Christ.

JESUS CHRIST - PRIESTHOOD.
BQT 1121   (232.x7)

JESUS CHRIST - PROPHECIES.
BQT 877
"Here are entered works dealing
with prophecies made by Jesus
Christ. For works dealing with
prophecies concerning Jesus
Christ see Messiah - Prophecies." LC
sa Typology (Theology)
x Prophecies, Biblical.
xx Bible - Prophecies.
Prophecies.

JESUS CHRIST - PSYCHIATRY.

JESUS CHRIST - PSYCHOLOGY.
BQT 819

JESUS CHRIST - RATIONALISTIC
INTERPRETATIONS.
BQT 697

JESUS CHRIST - REDEMPTION. See
REDEMPTION.

JESUS CHRIST - REJECTION AT
NAZARETH. See   JESUS CHRIST -
PREACHING AT NAZARETH.

JESUS CHRIST - RELICS OF THE
PASSION.
sa Holy Coat.
Holy Shroud.
x Relics of the Passion.
xx Jesus Christ - Passion.

JESUS CHRIST - RESURRECTION.
BQT 947   (23x9.21)
sa Easter.
x Resurrection of Christ.
xx Easter.
Resurrection.

JESUS CHRIST - RESURRECTION -
CONTROVERSIAL LITERATURE.

JESUS CHRIST - RESURRECTION -
HISTORY OF DOCTRINES.

JESUS CHRIST - RESURRECTION -
JUVENILE LITERATURE.

JESUS CHRIST - RESURRECTION -
MEDITATIONS.

JESUS CHRIST - RESURRECTION -
SERMONS.
BQT 3057
xx Easter - Sermons.
Jesus Christ - Sermons.

JESUS CHRIST - ROSICRUCIAN
INTERPRETATIONS.
BQT 697

JESUS CHRIST - ROYAL OFFICE. See
JESUS CHRIST - KINGSHIP.

JESUS CHRIST - SACRED HEART. See
SACRED HEART.

JESUS CHRIST - SACRIFICE. See
MASS.

JESUS CHRIST - SECOND ADVENT. See
SECOND ADVENT.

JESUS CHRIST - SERMON ON THE MOUNT.
See   SERMON OF THE MOUNT.

JESUS CHRIST - SERMONS.
BQT 685
sa Jesus Christ - Biography -
Sermons.
Jesus Christ - Feasts - Sermons.
Jesus Christ - Passion - Sermons.
Jesus Christ - Resurrection -
Sermons.
Jesus Christ - Seven last words -
Sermons.

JESUS CHRIST - SEVEN LAST WORDS.
    BQT 934
    x Jesus Christ - Last words.
    Seven last words.

JESUS CHRIST - SEVEN LAST WORDS -
    DEVOTIONAL LITERATURE.

JESUS CHRIST - SEVEN LAST WORDS -
    MEDITATIONS.
    BQT 2587

JESUS CHRIST - SEVEN LAST WORDS -
    SERMONS.
    BQT 934; [BQT 3055.5]
    xx Jesus Christ - Sermons.

JESUS CHRIST - SIGNIFICANCE.

JESUS CHRIST - SIMILITUDES.
    BQT 881-893

JESUS CHRIST - SINLESSNESS.
    BQT 981
    x Sinlessness of Christ.

JESUS CHRIST - SOCIAL TEACHINGS.
    BS 2417

JESUS CHRIST - SPIRITUALISTIC
    INTERPRETATIONS.

JESUS CHRIST - TEACHING METHODS.
    BQT 902

JESUS CHRIST - TEACHINGS.
    BS 2415-2417
    x Teachings of Jesus.

JESUS CHRIST - TEMPTATION.
    BQT 865
    x Jesus Christ - Forty days in
       the wilderness.
    Temptation of Christ.

JESUS CHRIST - THEOSOPHICAL
    INTERPRETATIONS.
    BQT 697

JESUS CHRIST - TITLES.   See
    JESUS CHRIST - NAME.

JESUS CHRIST - TOMB.   See
    HOLY SEPULCHER.

JESUS CHRIST - TRANSFIGURATION.
    BQT 909   (232.x6)
    sa Missa in Transfiguratione Domini
       Nostri Jesu Christi.
    x Transfiguration of Christ.

JESUS CHRIST - TRANSFIXION.
    BQT 931
    x Transfixion of Christ.
    xx Jesus Christ - Crucifixion.

JESUS CHRIST - TRIAL.
    BQT 923

JESUS CHRIST - TYPOLOGY.
    BQT 782
    xx Typology (Theology)

JESUS CHRIST - VIRGIN BIRTH.   See
    VIRGIN BIRTH.

JESUS CHRIST - WORDS.
    BQT 820

JESUS CHRIST IN ART.   See
    JESUS CHRIST - ART.

JESUS CHRIST IN LITERATURE.
    BQT 965-969
    sa Jesus Christ - Drama.
    Jesus Christ - Fiction.
    Jesus Christ - Poetry.
    xx God in literature.

JESUS CHRIST IN MUSIC.
    x Jesus Christ - Music.

JESUS CHRIST IN POETRY.   See
    JESUS CHRIST - POETRY.

JESUS CHRIST IN THE LITURGY.
    BQT 4043
    x Liturgy - Jesus Christ.

JESUS CHRIST IN THE SACRAMENTS.
    xx Mystical Body of Christ.

JESUS CHRIST THE KING, FEAST OF.
    BQT 4245
    x Christ the King, Feast of.
    Feast of Jesus Christ the King.
    Kingship of Christ, Feast of the.
    xx Jesus Christ - Kingship.

JESUS CHRIST THE KING, MASS OF. See
MISSA DOMINI NOSTRI JESU CHRISTI
REGIS.

JESUS CHRIST THE KING, OFFICE OF. See
OFFICIUM DOMINI NOSTRI JESU CHRISTI
REGIS.

JEUNESSE OUVRIERE CHRETIENNE. See
JOCISTES.

JEWISH APOLOGETICS. See
JUDAISM - APOLOGETICS.

JEWISH ASCETICISM. See
ASCETICISM - JUDAISM.

JEWISH CHANT. See
CHANT (JEWISH)

JEWISH CHRISTIAN SCIENCE. See
JEWISH SCIENCE.

JEWISH CHRISTIANS.
sa Missions - Jews.

JEWISH CHRISTIANS - EARLY CHURCH.
xx Church history - Primitive and
early church.

JEWISH CONVERTS TO CHRISTIANITY. See
JEWS - CONVERTS TO CHRISTIANITY.

JEWISH COSTUME. See
COSTUME, JEWISH.

JEWISH DAY OF ATONEMENT. See
YOM KIPPUR.

JEWISH HOLY WAR. See
HOLY WAR, JEWISH.

JEWISH LAW.
BQV 1502-1525
References as in LC.

JEWISH LITURGICAL MUSIC. See
SYNAGOGUE MUSIC.

JEWISH MISSIONS. See
MISSIONS - JEWS.

JEWISH MONASTICISM. See
MONASTICISM, JEWISH.

JEWISH - NEW-YEAR. See
ROSH HA-SHANAH.

JEWISH PARABLES. See
PARABLES, JEWISH.

JEWISH PENTECOST. See
SHAVU'OTH (FEAST OF WEEKS)

JEWISH PREACHING. See
PREACHING, JEWISH.

JEWISH PRIESTS. See
PRIESTS, JEWISH.

JEWISH SCIENCE.
BM 729.J
"Here are entered works dealing
with a movement that, negatively,
seeks to counteract Christian
science with a Jewish counter-
part and, positively, reveals to
the Jew the sources of health,
serenity, and peace of mind
within his own faith." LC
References as in LC.

JEWISH SECTS.
BM 175
sa Conservative Judaism.
Essenes.
Hasidism.
Karaites.
Pharisees.
Qumran community.
Reconstructionist Judaism.
Reform Judaism.
Sabbathaians.
Sadducees.
Zadokites.
Zealots (Jewish party)
x Jews - Sects.
Sects, Jewish.

JEWISH THEOLOGY.
BM 600
"Here are entered systematic works
on the doctrines and dogmas of
the Jewish religion. Works dealing with Jewish faith and practice
are entered under the heading
Judaism." LC

JEWISH THEOLOGY -- Continued.
  sa Judaism.
     also special headings with "Jewish
       theology" added in parenthesis,
       e.g., Freedom (Jewish theology).
  x Theology, Jewish.
  xx Judaism.

JEWS.
  Classification and references as
    in LC.

JEWS - CONVERSION TO CHRISTIANITY.
     BV 4922
  "Here are entered works dealing
    theoretically with the conversion
    of Jews to Christianity." LC
  sa Jews - Converts to Christianity.
  xx Missions - Jews.

JEWS - CONVERTS TO CHRISTIANITY.
  x Jewish converts to Christianity.
  xx Jews - Conversion to Christianity.

JEWS - DICTIONARIES AND ENCYCLOPEDIAS.
     DS 102.8
  sa Judaism - Dictionaries.
  xx Judaism - Dictionaries.

JEWS - HYMNS.
     BM 679
  References as in LC.

JEWS - LAW. See
  JEWISH LAW.
  JEWS - LEGAL STATUS, LAWS, ETC.

JEWS - MISSIONS. See
  MISSIONS - JEWS [for Christian
    missions to the Jews]
  PROSELYTES AND PROSELYTING, JEWISH
    [for Jewish efforts to gain
    adherents]

JEWS - PERSECUTIONS.
  sa Refugees, Jewish.

JEWS - PRAYER-BOOKS.
     BM 665

JEWS - PRIESTS. See
  PRIESTS, JEWISH.

JEWS - RELIGION. See
  JUDAISM.

JEWS - RELIGIOUS EDUCATION. See
  RELIGIOUS EDUCATION, JEWISH.

JEWS - RESTORATION.
     BS 649.J
  "Here are entered works dealing
    with the belief - whether held
    by Jews or by Christians - that
    in fulfillment of Biblical
    prophecy, the Jews would some
    day return to Palestine, and
    thereby also meet a requirement
    for the realization of eschato-
    logical expectations." LC
  sa Jews - Diaspora.
     Messianic era (Judaism)
     Zionism.
  xx Zionism.

JEWS - RITES AND CEREMONIES.
     BM 700-720
  References as in LC.

JEWS - RITUAL. See
  JEWS - SOCIAL LIFE AND CUSTOMS.
  JEWS. LITURGY AND RITUAL.

JEWS - SECTS. See
  JEWISH SECTS.

JEWS - ZIONISM. See
  ZIONISM.

  Other subdivisions under Jews as
    in LC.

          ################

JEWS. LITURGY AND RITUAL.
     BM 660-675
  sa Chant (Jewish)
     Cultus, Jewish.
     Piyutim.
     Synagogue music.
  x Jews - Ritual.
  xx Synagogue music.

  Subdivisions under "Jews. Liturgy
    and ritual" as in LC.

          ################

JEWS AND CATHOLIC CHURCH. See
CATHOLIC CHURCH AND JEWS.

JEWS AND CHRISTIANITY. See
CHRISTIANITY AND OTHER RELIGIONS -
JUDAISM.

JEWS AND FREEMASONS. See
FREEMASONS AND JEWS.

JIHAD.
BP 176.J
References as in LC.

JOB, BOOK OF. See
BIBLE. O.T. JOB.

JOCISTES.
BQT 3589
sa Young Christian Workers.
x Jeunesse ouvriere chretienne.

JOEL, BOOK OF. See
BIBLE. O.T. JOEL.

JOHANNINE LITERATURE (BIBLE). See
BIBLE. N.T. JOHANNINE LITERATURE.

JOHANNITERORDEN. See
ORDER OF ST. JOHN OF JERUSALEM
(EVANGELICAL)

JOHN, SAINT, EPISTLES OF. See
BIBLE. N.T. EPISTLES OF JOHN.

JOHN, SAINT, GOSPEL OF. See
BIBLE. N.T. JOHN.

JOHN THE BAPTIST'S DAY.
BQT 4234   (23x5.31)
x St. John the Baptist's Day.

JOINDER OF ISSUE (CANON LAW)

JONAH, BOOK OF. See
BIBLE. O.T. JONAS.

JONAS, BOOK OF. See
BIBLE. O.T. JONAS.

JOSEPH, SAINT.
BQT 1097-1101
x Saint Joseph.

JOSEPH, SAINT - BIOGRAPHY.
BQT 1097   (23x3.8)

JOSEPH, SAINT - BIOGRAPHY -
SOURCES, BIBLICAL.

JOSEPH, SAINT - CULTUS.

JOSEPH, SAINT - DEVOTIONAL
LITERATURE.
BQT 2599

JOSEPH, SAINT - FICTION.

JOSEPH, SAINT - LEGENDS.

JOSEPH, SAINT - MEDITATIONS.
BQT 2599   (24x2.9)

JOSEPH, SAINT - NOVENAS. See
NOVENAS - ST. JOSEPH.

JOSEPH, SAINT - PERIODICALS.

JOSEPH, SAINT - POETRY.

JOSEPH, SAINT - PRAYER-BOOKS.
BQT 2681   (24x3.3; 24x8.73)
sa March devotions.
Missa Sancti Joseph.

JOSEPH, SAINT - PRAYER-BOOKS,
ENGLISH, [FRENCH, GERMAN, ETC.]

JOSEPH, SAINT - SERMONS.
[BQT 3077]

JOSEPH, SAINT - THEOLOGY.
BQT 1097

JOSEPH, SAINT, FEAST OF.
BQT 4234
x Feast of St. Joseph.

JOSEPH, SAINT, LITANY OF. See
LITANY OF ST. JOSEPH.

JOSEPHINISM.
BQT 120; BQT 369 (Theology)
BQX 987; BQX 1547; BQX 1946
(Church history)

JOSEPHISM. See JOSEPHINISM.

JOSHUA, BOOK OF. See
BIBLE. O.T. JOSUE.

JOSUE, BOOK OF. See
BIBLE. O.T. JOSUE.

✓ Journal writing

JOURNALISM, RELIGIOUS.
    x Religious journalism.
    xx Advertising - Churches.
       Religious literature -
         Authorship.
       Religious newspapers and
         periodicals.

JOY.
        BJ 1480-1486 (Ethics)
        BQT 1220 (Fruits of the Holy
          Spirit)
        BQT 1793; BQT 2375 (Virtues)
    sa Happiness.
       Pleasure.
    xx Emotions.

JUBILATE DEO OMNIS TERRA, SERVITE
DOMINO (MUSIC). See
PSALMS (MUSIC) - 99th PSALM.

JUBILEE INDULGENCES.
        BQT 1399
    sa Holy Year.

JUBILEE SERMONS.
        BQT 3089
    x Sermons, Jubilee.

JUBILEE YEAR. See
HOLY YEAR.

✓ JUDAISM.
    "Here are entered works on
      Jewish faith and practice in
      which the main stream of ortho-
      dox Judaism is treated and no
      cleavage is stressed.
    "Systematic works on the doctrine
      and dogmas of Judaism are entered
      under the heading Jewish theology.
    "Polemic works limited to any one
      of the sects, schisms, or
      cleavages within Judaism are
      entered under the name of such
      a movement, e.g., Hasidism,
      Jewish Science, Reform Judaism."
      LC

JUDAISM -- Continued.
    sa Jewish theology.
    Other references as in LC.

JUDAISM - APOLOGETIC WORKS.
        BM 648
    "Here are entered works defending
      the Jewish religion and Judaism
      in general." LC
    References as in LC.

JUDAISM - ASCETICISM. See
ASCETICISM - JUDAISM.

JUDAISM - CONTROVERSIAL LITERATURE.
        BM 585
        BT 1120 (Christian apologetics)
        BP 173.J (Mohammedan apolo-
          getics)
    "Here are entered works against
      the Jewish religion." LC

JUDAISM - DICTIONARIES.
    sa Jews - Dictionaries and encyclo-
       pedias.
    xx Jews - Dictionaries and encyclo-
       pedias.

JUDAISM - HISTORY.
        BM 150-198

JUDAISM - HISTORY - ANCIENT PERIOD.
    xx Palestine - History - To 70 A.D.

JUDAISM - HISTORY - POST-EXILIC
PERIOD.
    xx Palestine - History - To 70 A.D.

JUDAISM - HISTORY - TALMUDIC PERIOD.

JUDAISM - HISTORY - MIDDLE AGES.

JUDAISM - HISTORY - MODERN PERIOD.

JUDAISM - INFLUENCE.

JUDAISM - PICTURES, ILLUSTRATIONS, ETC.

JUDAISM - RECONSTRUCTIONIST MOVEMENT.
  See RECONSTRUCTIONIST JUDAISM.

JUDAISM - RELATIONS - CHRISTIANITY.
    BM 535

    Other subdivisions under Judaism
    as in LC.

JUDAISM, CONSERVATIVE. See
    CONSERVATIVE JUDAISM.

JUDAISM, REFORM. See
    REFORM JUDAISM.

JUDAISM AND COMMUNISM. See
    COMMUNISM AND JUDAISM.

JUDAISM AND LABOR.
    References as in LC.

JUDAISM AND SOCIAL PROBLEMS.
    HN 40.J
    x Religion and social problems.
      Social problems and Judaism.

JUDAISM AND SOCIALISM. See
    SOCIALISM AND JUDAISM.

JUDAISM AND ZIONISM. See
    ZIONISM AND JUDAISM.

JUDAISM IN LITERATURE.
    xx Jews in literature.
      Religion in literature.

JUDE, SAINT, CATHOLIC EPISTLE OF. See
    BIBLE. N.T. JUDE.

JUDGES (CANON LAW)
    xx Ecclesiastical courts.

JUDGES, BOOK OF. See
    BIBLE. O.T. JUDGES.

JUDGMENT, LAST. See JUDGMENT DAY.

JUDGMENT DAY.
    BQT 1467   (236.x93)
  sa Second advent.
   x Day of Judgment.
    Judgment, Last.
    Last judgment.
  xx End of the world.
    Eschatology.
    Future life.
    Second advent.

JUDGMENT DAY - ART.
    BQT 5902
    xx Christian art.

JUDGMENT DAY - BIBLICAL TEACHING.
    sa Day of Jehovah.

JUDGMENT DAY - EARLY WORKS TO 1800.

JUDGMENT DAY - MEDITATIONS.
    BQT 2610

JUDGMENT DAY - SERMONS.

JUDGMENTS (CANON LAW)
    xx Trials, Ecclesiastical.

JUDICIAL ASSISTANCE (CANON LAW)

JUDICIAL CERTAINTY (CANON LAW)

JUDICIAL CONFESSION. See
    CONFESSION, JUDICIAL.

JUDICIAL DISCRETION (CANON LAW)
    BQV230 1577

JUDICIAL POWER (CANON LAW)

JUDICIAL SENTENCE (CANON LAW)
    BQV230 1868-1877
    xx Civil procedure (Canon law)

JUDITH, BOOK OF. See
    BIBLE. O.T. JUDITH.

JULY DEVOTIONS.
    BQT 4495
    xx Devotions, Popular.

JUNE DEVOTIONS.
    BQT 4495
    xx Devotions, Popular.

JURISDICTION (CANON LAW)
    sa Appeal as from abuse.
      Bishops (Canon law)
      Delegation of powers (Canon
      law)
      Privilegium fori.
    xx Bishops (Canon law)
      Ecclesiastical courts.

JURISDICTION, TERRITORIAL (CANON LAW)

JURISTIC PERSONS (CANON LAW)

JUS AD REM (CANON LAW)

JUS PRIMARIUM PRECUM.
  xx Church and state.

JUS REFORMANDI.
  xx Church and state.

√JUSTICE.
       BQT 1821; BQT 1942-1949
         (Moral theology)   (24x1.651)
         JC 578 (Political theory)
         GN 493 (Primitive)
  sa Divine law.
     Gratitude.
     Natural law.
  xx Conduct of life.
     Moral theology.

JUSTICE (VIRTUE)
       BQT 1210; BQT 1789   (24x1.52)
  sa Observance (Virtue)
  xx Virtues, Moral.

JUSTICE, ORIGINAL.
       BQT 634   (231.x71)
  Here are entered works on the state
   of Adam and Eve before the fall.
  sa Fall of man.
     Sin, Original.
   x Original justice.
     Primitive justice.
  xx Man (Theology)
     Paradise.

JUSTIFICATION.
       BQT 1126-1220   (234.12)
  sa Faith.
     Good works (Theology)
  xx Good works (Theology)
     Salvation.

JUSTIFICATION - BIBLICAL TEACHING.

JUSTIFICATION - HISTORY OF DOCTRINES.

JUSTIFICATION - HISTORY OF DOCTRINES -
  EARLY CHURCH.

JUSTIFICATION - HISTORY OF DOCTRINES -
  MIDDLE AGES.

JUSTIFICATION - HISTORY OF DOCTRINES -
  MODERN PERIOD.

JUSTIFICATION - HISTORY OF DOCTRINES -
  16th, [17th, etc.] CENTURY.

JUVENILE LITERATURE, CATHOLIC. See
CHILDREN'S LITERATURE - CATHOLIC
AUTHORS.

KANONES (LITURGY)
       BQT 5255
  "Kanon in the Byzantine Divine
   Office is a rhythmical composition consisting of 2, 3, 4 or 9
   odes, divided into troparia,
   having a certain relation to the
   scriptural canticles." AT
  xx Byzantine rite - Hymns.

KARAITES.
       BM 175.K
  xx Jewish sects.

KARMATHIANS.
       BP 195
   x Carmathians.
     Quarmathians.

KATCINAS.
  xx Indians of North America -
     Religion and mythology.

KENOSIS.
       BQT 731
   x Jesus Christ - Kenosis.
  xx Incarnation.

KERYGMATIC THEOLOGY.
       BQT 17
  Here are entered works on the
   study of theology which is
   oriented to the preaching and
   teaching of the Christian
   message.
  xx Religious education.

KHLYSTY.
[BQX 6157]; BX 9798
xx Sects, Russian.
Skoptsi.

KINDNESS.
sa Mercy.

KINDNESS (THEOLOGY)
BQT 1220
x Benignity (Theology)
xx Fruits of the Holy Spirit.
Love (Theology)

KINGDOM OF GOD.
BQT 317
sa God - Fatherhood.
x Jesus Christ - Kingdom.
xx Children of God.
Church.

KINGDOM OF GOD - BIBLICAL TEACHING.
sa Day of Jehovah.

KINGDOM OF GOD - HISTORY OF
DOCTRINES.

KINGDOM OF GOD - SERMONS.
[BQT 3089]

KINGS, BOOKS OF. See
BIBLE. O.T. KINGS.

KINGS AND RULERS - BIBLICAL
TEACHING.
BS 680
JC 381
xx Political science - Biblical
teaching.

KINGS AND RULERS - RITES AND
CEREMONIES.

KINGS AND RULERS (IN RELIGION,
FOLKLORE, ETC.)
xx Theocracy.

KING'S SON, MARRIAGE OF THE. See
MARRIAGE OF THE KING'S SON (PARABLE)

KINGSHIP OF CHRIST. See
JESUS CHRIST - KINGSHIP.

KINGSHIP OF CHRIST, FEAST OF THE.
See JESUS CHRIST THE KING,
FEAST OF.

KISS OF PEACE.
BQT 4078

KNEELING (POSTURE IN WORSHIP). See
POSTURE IN WORSHIP.

KNIGHTS HOSPITALLERS OF ST. JOHN OF
JERUSALEM. See KNIGHTS OF MALTA.

KNIGHTS OF MALTA. (Geog. subdiv.)
CR 4715-4731
BQX 7505.M
Known under various names succes-
sively, namely: 1113-1309 as
Knights Hospitallers of St.
John of Jerusalem, or Order of
St. John of Jerusalem; 1309-1522
as Knights of Rhodes; 1523-1798
as Knights of Malta. They are
still called Knights of Malta,
though no longer residing on
Malta. Their official name at
present is Sovereign Military
Order of St. John of Jerusalem,
with headquarters in Rome.
x Hospitallers of St. John of
Jerusalem, Order of.
Jerusalem, Order of the Knights
of St. John of.
Knights Hospitallers of St.
John of Jerusalem.
Knights of Rhodes.
Knights of St. John of Jerusalem.
Malta, Knights of.
Order of Malta.
Order of St. John of Jerusalem.
Ordo Fratrum Hospitaliorum
Hierosolymitanorum.
Ordo Militiae Sancti Joannis
Baptistae Hospitalis Hiero-
solymitani.
Sovereign Military Order of St.
John of Jerusalem.
xx Military religious orders.

KNIGHTS OF MALTA - ARMS AND ARMOR.

KNIGHTS OF MALTA - BIBLIOGRAPHY.

KNIGHTS OF MALTA - BIOGRAPHY.

KNIGHTS OF MALTA - COINS. See
COINS.

KNIGHTS OF MALTA - DIRECTORIES.

KNIGHTS OF MALTA - DRAMA.

KNIGHTS OF MALTA - EXHIBITIONS.

KNIGHTS OF MALTA - GOVERNMENT.

KNIGHTS OF MALTA - HERALDRY.

KNIGHTS OF MALTA - HISTORY.

KNIGHTS OF MALTA - HISTORY -
SOURCES.

KNIGHTS OF MALTA - HISTORY -
1113-1309.

KNIGHTS OF MALTA - HISTORY -
1309-1522.
sa Rhodes - Siege, 1480.
Rhodes - Siege, 1522.

KNIGHTS OF MALTA - HISTORY -
1523-1798.
sa Malta - Siege, 1565.
Malta - Siege, 1798.

KNIGHTS OF MALTA - HISTORY -
1798-

KNIGHTS OF MALTA - HISTORY -
20th CENTURY.

KNIGHTS OF MALTA - HISTORY,
MILITARY.

KNIGHTS OF MALTA - HISTORY,
NAVAL.

KNIGHTS OF MALTA - HOSPITALS,
CHARITIES, ETC.

KNIGHTS OF MALTA - MEDALS. See
MEDALS.

KNIGHTS OF MALTA - MISSIONS.

KNIGHTS OF MALTA - MONUMENTS.

KNIGHTS OF MALTA - NUMISMATICS. See
NUMISMATICS.

KNIGHTS OF MALTA - ORGANIZATION.

KNIGHTS OF MALTA - PERIODICALS.

KNIGHTS OF MALTA - POPULAR WORKS.

KNIGHTS OF MALTA - PROFESSION. See
PROFESSION, RELIGIOUS - KNIGHTS
OF MALTA.

KNIGHTS OF MALTA - RELIGIOUS LIFE.

KNIGHTS OF MALTA - SEALS.

KNIGHTS OF MALTA - SONGS AND MUSIC.

#################

KNIGHTS OF MALTA - AUSTRIA,
[BELGIUM, CANADA, ETC.]

#################

KNIGHTS OF MALTA. ASSOCIATION
BELGE, [ASSOCIATION FRANCAISE,
ASSOCIAZIONE MISSIONARIA, ETC.]

KNIGHTS OF MALTA. COMMANDERIES.

KNIGHTS OF MALTA. COMMANDERIES.
DINMORE, ENGLAND, [PAILHES, FRANCE;
ETC.]

KNIGHTS OF MALTA. GENERAL CONVENTION,
[place, date]

KNIGHTS OF MALTA. GRAND MASTER.

KNIGHTS OF MALTA. GRAND MASTER,
[date and name]

KNIGHTS OF MALTA. GRAND PRIORY.

KNIGHTS OF MALTA. GRAND PRIORY.
ENGLAND, [FRANCE, ETC.]

KNIGHTS OF MALTA. LANGUE.

KNIGHTS OF MALTA. LANGUE. ENGLISH,
[GERMAN, ETC.]

KNIGHTS OF MALTA. LITURGY AND
RITUAL.
BQT 4841-4849

KNIGHTS OF MALTA. NAVY.

KNIGHTS OF MALTA. STATUTA.

################

KNIGHTS OF RHODES. See
KNIGHTS OF MALTA.

KNIGHTS OF ST. JOHN OF JERUSALEM.
See KNIGHTS OF MALTA.

KNIGHTS TEMPLARS (MILITARY RELIGIOUS
ORDER). See TEMPLARS.

KNOWLEDGE, THEORY OF (RELIGION)
BQT 239-243
sa Belief and doubt.
Faith.
God - Knowableness.
Illumination of intellect.
xx Religion - Philosophy.

KNOWLEDGE OF GOD. See
GOD - FOREKNOWLEDGE.
GOD - KNOWABLENESS.
GOD - OMNISCIENCE.

KOHELET, BOOK OF. See
BIBLE. O.T. ECCLESIASTES.

KONKO (SECT)
xx Shinto sects.

KONVENTIKELPLAKATET, 1726.
xx Church and state in Sweden.

KORAN.
BP 100-127 (297)
References as in LC.

KORAN - THEOLOGY.
BP 132
xx Mohammedan theology.

Other subdivisions as in LC.

KORAN AS LITERATURE.
BP 130.8
xx Religious literature.

KOREA - CHURCH HISTORY.
BQX 3401-3419

KOREAN WAR, 1950-1953 - RELIGIOUS
ASPECTS.

KULTURKAMPF.
DD 118
BQX 1948 (Church history)
xx Catholic Church - Germany.
Church and state in Germany.

KUMRAN COMMUNITY. See
QUMRAN COMMUNITY.

KYRIALE.
BQT 4301-4303 (783.22)
A liturgical book containing
selections from the Graduale,
that is, the chanted parts of
the Ordinary of the Mass, such
as, the Kyrie, Gloria, etc.
x Ordinarium Missae (Chant)
xx Graduale.
Mass - Music.
Ordinarium Missae.

KYRIALE - ACCOMPANIMENT.

KYRIE ELEISON.

LABARUM.
xx Jesus Christ - Monograms.

LABOR AND RELIGION. See
RELIGION AND· LABOR.

LABOR AND THE CHURCH. See
CHURCH AND LABOR.

LABOR DAY MASS.
x Church and labor.

LABOR UNIONS, CATHOLIC. See
TRADE -UNIONS, CATHOLIC.

LAITY.   (Geog. subdiv.)
         BQT 361 (Relation to hierarchy)
             (23x9.21)
         BQT 3523-3527 (Catholic action)
             (24x8.5)
         BQT 2271-2289 (State of life)
             (24x1.8)
      sa Catholic action.
         Catholic social action.
         Confraternities.
         Men in church work.
         Secular institutes.
         Third orders.
       x Apostolate, Lay.
         Lay apostolate.
         Laymen.
      xx Apostolate.
         Vocation.

LAITY - BIBLICAL TEACHING.

LAITY - BIBLIOGRAPHY.

LAITY - BIOGRAPHY.
         BQX 8271-8279

LAITY - PAPAL TEACHING.

LAITY - SPIRITUAL LIFE.

LAITY (CANON LAW)
         BQV230 682-725   (348.x39)
      xx Persons (Canon law)

LAITY (CANON LAW, ORTHODOX EASTERN)

LAITY AND CLERGY. See
    CLERGY AND LAITY.

LAMAISM.
         BL 1485   (294.32)
      References as in LC.

LAMAIST MONASTERIES. See
    MONASTERIES, LAMAIST.

LAMAIST MONASTICISM. See
    MONASTICISM, LAMAIST.

LAMB OF GOD.
    x Jesus Christ - Lamb of God.
    xx Jesus Christ - Name.

LAMBETH CONFERENCE.
         BR 759
    sa Lambeth Quadrilateral.

LAMBETH QUADRILATERAL.
    x Chicago-Lambeth Quadrilateral.
    xx Anglican Communion - Relations.
       Christian union.
       Lambeth Conference.

LAMENTATIONS OF JEREMIAS. See
    BIBLE. O.T. LAMENTATIONS.

LAMPETIANS. See MESSALIANS.

LANCE, HOLY. See HOLY LANCE.

LAND - TAXATION.
    sa Church property - Taxation.
    Other references as in LC.

LANGUAGE, LITURGICAL. See
    LITURGICAL LANGUAGE.

LANGUAGE AND RELIGION. See
    RELIGION AND LANGUAGE.

LANGUAGE QUESTION IN THE CHURCH.
       (Geog. subdiv., Direct)
    sa Bible - Publication and dis-
         tribution.
       Bible - Versions.
       Latin language - Church Latin.
       Liturgical language.
     x Language - Religious aspects.
    xx Bible - Publication and dis-
         tribution.
       Bible - Versions.
       Languages - Religious aspects.
       Religion and language.
       Religious literature.

LANGUAGES - RELIGIOUS ASPECTS.
    sa Bible - Language, style.
       Bible - Versions.
       Greek language, Biblica.
       Language question in the church.
       Latin language - Church Latin.

LANGUAGES - RELIGIOUS ASPECTS -- Continued.
  sa Liturgical language.
    Religion and language.
   x Biblical languages.
    Ecclesiastical languages.
    Languages, Biblical.
    Languages, Ecclesiastical.

LANGUAGES, BIBLICAL. See
  LANGUAGES - RELIGIOUS ASPECTS.

LANGUAGES, ECCLESIASTICAL. See
  LANGUAGES - RELIGIOUS ASPECTS.

LAPSED CATHOLICS. See
  CATHOLICS, LAPSED.

LARCENY (CANON LAW)

LA SALETTE, FRANCE (SHRINE)
    BQT 1075   (23x3.61)
    [BQX 1818] (274.4)
   x Notre Dame de La Salette (Shrine)
    Our Lady of La Salette (Shrine)

LAST JUDGMENT. See
  JUDGMENT DAY.

LAST SACRAMENTS. See
  EXTREME UNCTION.
  VIATICUM.

LAST SUPPER.
    BQT 916   (225.x91)
   x Jesus Christ - Last Supper.
    Supper, Last.
   xx Eucharist.

LAST THINGS. See ESCHATOLOGY.

LATERAN COUNCIL, 1st, 1123.
    BQX 697   (26x2.31)
    BQV 12 (Documents)

LATERAN COUNCIL, 2d, 1139.
    BQX 703   (26x2.32)
    BQV 12 (Documents)

LATERAN COUNCIL, 3d, 1179.
    BQX 714   (26x2.33)
    BQV 12 (Documents)

LATERAN COUNCIL, 4th, 1215.
    BQX 727   (26x2.34)
    BQV 12 (Documents)

LATERAN COUNCIL, 5th, 1512-1517.
    BQX 910   (26x2.41)
    BQV 12 (Documents)

LATERAN PACT, 1929. See
  CONCORDAT OF 1929 (ITALY)

LATIN CHRISTIAN LITERATURE. See
  CHRISTIAN LITERATURE - LATIN
  AUTHORS.

LATIN FATHERS OF THE CHURCH. See
  FATHERS OF THE CHURCH, LATIN.

LATIN KINGDOM OF JERUSALEM. See
  JERUSALEM - HISTORY - LATIN
  KINGDOM, 1099-1244.

LATIN LANGUAGE - CHURCH LATIN.
  sa Liturgical language - Latin.
   x Church Latin.
    Ecclesiastical Latin.
    Latin language, Ecclesiastical.
   xx Language question in the church.
    Languages - Religious aspects.
    Liturgical language - Latin.

LATIN LANGUAGE - CHURCH LATIN -
  COMPOSITION AND EXERCISES.

LATIN LANGUAGE - CHURCH LATIN -
  GLOSSARIES, VOCABULARIES, ETC.

LATIN LANGUAGE - CHURCH LATIN -
  GRAMMAR.

LATIN LANGUAGE - LITURGICAL USE. See
  LITURGICAL LANGUAGE - LATIN.

LATIN LANGUAGE, ECCLESIASTICAL. See
  LATIN LANGUAGE - CHURCH LATIN.

LATIN RITE. See LITURGY.

LATTER-DAY SAINTS. See
  MORMONS AND MORMONISM.

LATTER RAIN MOVEMENT. See
  PENTECOSTAL CHURCHES.

246

LAUDA, ANIMA MEA, DOMINUM (MUSIC). See
PSALMS (MUSIC) - 145th PSALM.

LAUDA, JERUSALEM, DOMINUM (MUSIC). See
PSALMS (MUSIC) - 147th PSALM.

LAUDATE DOMINUM IN SANCTIS EIUS (MUSIC).
See PSALMS (MUSIC) - 150th PSALM.

LAUDATE DOMINUM OMNES GENTES (MUSIC).
See PSALMS (MUSIC) - 116th PSALM.

LAUDATE, PUERI, DOMINUM (MUSIC). See
PSALMS (MUSIC) - 112th PSALM.

LAUDES. See ACCLAMATIONS (LITURGY)

LAW - PAPAL STATES.
x Papal States - Law.

LAW (THEOLOGY)
BQT 1831-1959   (24x1.x3)
BS 639
"Here are entered works on law as a
theological concept." LC
sa Law and gospel.
Neonomianism.
x Bible - Law.
xx Law and gospel.

LAW (THEOLOGY) - BIBLICAL TEACHING.

LAW (THEOLOGY) - HISTORY OF
DOCTRINES.

LAW, CHURCH. See
CANON LAW.
ECCLESIASTICAL LAW.

LAW, DIVINE. See DIVINE LAW.

LAW, ECCLESIASTICAL. See
ECCLESIASTICAL LAW.

LAW, MOSAIC. See
JEWISH LAW.

LAW, NATURAL. See
NATURAL LAW.

LAW AND GOSPEL.
BT 85
"Here are entered works dealing
with the theological concept
of law in its relation to the
gospel." LC
sa Freedom (Theology)
Law (Theology)
Neonomianism.
x Gospel and law.

LAW AND RELIGION. See
RELIGION AND LAW.

LAW AND THE BIBLE. See
BIBLE AND LAW.

LAW REPORTS, DIGESTS, ETC. -
CATHOLIC CHURCH.

LAWYERS (CANON LAW)
BQV230 1655-1666   (348.x5)
xx Trials, Ecclesiastical.

LAXISM. See PROBABILISM.

LAY APOSTOLATE. See
CATHOLIC ACTION.
LAITY.

LAY BROTHERS.
BQX 6838; BQX 6901-7774
(271.x1)
Here are entered works dealing
with members of a religious
order who are occupied chiefly
with manual labor and the
material affairs of a monastery
or religious community, as distinct from the choir monks and
those who receive holy orders.
They are also known as Converse
Brothers or Conversi. Cf. note
under Brothers.
sa Brothers.
also subdivision "Lay Brothers"
under names of religious com-
munities, e.g., Benedictines.
Lay Brothers; Jesuits. Lay
Brothers.

✓Leadership 150

LAY BROTHERS -- Continued.
  x Brotherhoods, Religious.
    Brothers, Converse.
    Brothers, Lay.
    Converse Brothers.
  xx Brothers.
    Religious orders.

LAY BROTHERS - BIOGRAPHY.

LAY BROTHERS - DEVOTIONAL LITERATURE.

LAY BROTHERS - MEDITATIONS.
      BQT 2555

LAY BROTHERS - PRAYER-BOOKS.
      BQT 2626

LAY BROTHERS - VOCATION.

LAY BROTHERS (CANON LAW)
      BQV230 564-565   (348.x37)
  xx Religious orders (Canon law)

LAY CONFESSION.
  "An humble accusation of one's
    sins to a lay person (a) as an
    exercise of humility and for the
    purpose of receiving direction
    from a prudent person or (b)
    when dying without the ministra-
    tion of a priest available." AT
  xx Confession.

LAY MISSIONARIES. See
  MISSIONARIES, LAY.

LAY TEACHERS, CATHOLIC. See
  CATHOLIC EDUCATION - LAY TEACHERS.

LAYING-ON OF HANDS. See
  IMPOSITION OF HANDS.

LAYMEN. See LAITY.

LAYMEN'S RETREAT MOVEMENT.
      BQT 2548
  xx Retreats for men.

LAZARUS AND DIVES (PARABLE). See
  DIVES AND LAZARUS (PARABLE)

LEARNING AND SCHOLARSHIP - CATHOLIC
  CHURCH. See CATHOLIC LEARNING
  AND SCHOLARSHIP.

LECTIONARIUM.
      BQT 4247; BQT 4297-4298
      (26x5.2)
  "A book containing the epistles
    and gospels for mass." AT
  sa Epistolarium.
    Evangeliarium.
    Plenarium.
  x Epistles, Liturgical.
    Gospels, Liturgical.
    Lectionary (Mass)
    Lessons (Mass)
  xx Bible. N.T. Epistles and
    Gospels, Liturgical.

LECTIONARIUM DIVINI OFFICII.
      BQT 4387
  "A book containing the lessons
    appointed to be read at matins,
    either those extracted from the
    breviary or those proper to a
    particular place or body of
    persons." AT
  x Lectionary (Divine office)
    Lessons (Breviary)

LECTIONARY (DIVINE OFFICE). See
  LECTIONARIUM DIVINI OFFICII.

LECTIONARY (MASS). See
  LECTIONARIUM.

LECTORS (HOLY ORDER). See
  MINOR ORDERS.

LEGAL ETHICS, CATHOLIC.

LEGAL MAXIMS (CANON LAW)

LEGAL RESPONSIBILITY (CANON LAW)
  sa Duress (Canon law)
    Guilt (Canon law)
    Ignorance (Canon law)
  xx Persons (Canon law)

LEGATES, PAPAL.
      BQV230 265-270   (348.x325)
  sa Delegates, Apostolic.
    Nuncios, Papal.

248

LEGATES, PAPAL -- Continued.
    x Papal legates.
    xx Ambassadors.
        Delegates, Apostolic.
        Diplomatic and consular service.
        Diplomats.
        Holy See - Diplomatic service.
        Nuncios, Papal.

LEGENDARIUM.
        BQT 4268
    A liturgical book containing
        readings from the lives of the
        saints for use at Matins.

LEGENDS, CHRISTIAN.
        BQX 91
    sa subdivision "Legends" under
        special topics, e.g., Mary,
        Blessed Virgin - Legends.
    x Christian legends.
    xx Homiletical illustrations.
        Saints.

LEGION OF DECENCY.
        BQT 3429

LEGISLATION (CANON LAW)
        BQV230 8-24
    sa Promulgation (Canon law)
    xx Canon law - Interpretation and
        construction.

LEGISLATIVE BODIES - CHAPLAINS'
    PRAYERS.
    x Chaplains' prayers.
    xx Chaplains.

LEGISLATIVE BODIES (CANON LAW)
        BQV230 7
    xx Catholic Church - Government.

LEGITIMACY (CANON LAW). See
    ILLEGITIMACY (CANON LAW)

LEGITIMATION OF CHILDREN (CANON LAW)

LEGITIME (CANON LAW)
    xx Inheritance and succession
        (Canon law)

LEITURGIKON.
        BQT 5243
    A liturgical book of the Byzantine
        Rite containing the prayers for
        the priest at the Divine Liturgy
        (Mass). The prayers are selected
        from the Euchologion.

LENT.
        BQT 4222   (264.x5)
    sa Ash Wednesday.
        Easter.
        Holy Week.
        Passiontide.
        Septuagesima.
        Shrovetide.
        Stations, Roman.
    x Quadragesima.
    xx Ash Wednesday.
        Church year.
        Easter season.
        Fast days.
        Jesus Christ - Passion.

LENT - DEVOTIONAL LITERATURE.

LENT - HISTORY.

LENT - LITURGY.
        BQT 4222
    sa Gospels, Lenten.

LENT - MEDITATIONS.
        [BQT 2606.4]

LENT - PASTORAL LETTERS.

LENT - PRAYER-BOOKS.
        [BQT 2649]

LENT - SERMONS.
        BQT 2995   (252.x53)
    Here are entered sermons ex-
        plaining the meaning of lent.
    For series of sermons planned to
        be given during the lenten
        season see Sermons, Lenten.
    sa Sermons, Lenten.
    x Lenten sermons.
    xx Sermons, Lenten.

LENTEN GOSPELS. See
    GOSPELS, LENTEN.

LENTEN MENUS.
TX 739; with recipes, TX 837
x Fast-day menus.

LENTEN SERMONS. See
LENT - SERMONS.
SERMONS, LENTEN.

LEONINE SACRAMENTARY. See
SACRAMENTARIUM LEONIANUM.

LESION (CANON LAW)

LESSONS (BREVIARY). See
LECTIONARIUM DIVINI OFFICII.

LESSONS (MASS). See
EPISTOLARIUM.
LECTIONARIUM.

LETTERS, PAPAL.
BQV 2-8   (26x3)
sa Briefs, Papal.
Bulls, Papal.
Encyclicals, Papal.
x Papal letters.
Popes - Letters.
xx Canon law.
Documents, Papal.

LETTERS, PASTORAL. See
PASTORAL LETTERS.

LETTISH CATHOLICS. See
CATHOLICS, LETTISH.

LEVAVI OCULOS MEOS IN MONTES (MUSIC).
See PSALMS (MUSIC) - 120th PSALM.

LEVITICUS, BOOK OF. See
BIBLE. O.T. LEVITICUS.

LIABILITY (CANON LAW)

LIBATIONS.
References as in LC.

LIBEL AND SLANDER.   (Geog. subdiv.)
References as in LC.

LIBEL AND SLANDER (CANON LAW)
BQV230 2355

LIBEL AND SLANDER (ETHICS). See
SLANDER.

LIBER COMITIS. See COMES.

LIBER GRADUALIS. See GRADUALE.

LIBER ORDINARIUS. See
ORDINARIUM.

LIBER PASSIONARIUS. See
PASSIONARIUM.

LIBER PONTIFICALIS.
BQ 6119.P6-7   (280.x5)

LIBER PROMISSIONUM. See
PROFESSION, RELIGIOUS.

LIBER USUALIS.
BQT 4653   (783.83)
"A liturgical book containing
the proper Masses and all the
hours except Matins and Lauds
for all Sundays of the year
and for feasts which may dis-
place the Sunday, together
with the chant." AT
xx Graduale.

LIBERA ME, DOMINE (MUSIC)

LIBERAL JUDAISM. See
REFORM JUDAISM.

LIBERALISM (RELIGION)
BQX 1034; BQX 1073; BQX 1798
(Church history)
BQT 123 (Theology)   (24x1.x09)

LIBERALISM (RELIGION) - CONTROVERSIAL
LITERATURE.

✓ LIBERATION THEOLOGY (230)

LIBERTY (THEOLOGY). See   x Theology of Liberation
FREEDOM (THEOLOGY)

LIBERTY, RELIGIOUS. See
RELIGIOUS LIBERTY.

LIBERTY OF CONSCIENCE.
      BQV 325
      BV 741
  sa Dissenters.
     Free thought.
     Persecution.
     Public opinion.
     Religious liberty.
   x Intolerance.
  xx Church and state.
     Conscience.
     Persecution.
     Religious liberty.
     Toleration.

LIBERTY OF SPEECH IN THE CHURCH.
      BV 740
   x Freedom of speech in the church.
     Authority (Religion)
     Church - Authority.
     Heresy.
     Toleration.

LIBERTY OF THE WILL. See
  FREE WILL AND DETERMINISM.

LIBRARIES, BENEDICTINE, [CAPUCHIN,
  JESUIT, ETC.]
   x Benedictine, [Capuchin,
     Jesuit, etc.] libraries.
  xx Monastic libraries.

LIBRARIES, CATHOLIC.
  sa Libraries, Church.
     Monastic libraries.
     Theological libraries.
   x Catholic libraries.
  xx Theological libraries.

LIBRARIES, CHURCH.
      BQT 3344   (027.23)
  sa Libraries, Sunday-school.
   x Church libraries.
     Churches - Libraries.
     Libraries, Parish.
     Parish libraries.
  xx Libraries, Catholic.
     Libraries, Sunday-school.

LIBRARIES, MARIAN. See
  MARIAN LIBRARIES.

LIBRARIES, MONASTIC. See
  MONASTIC LIBRARIES.

LIBRARIES, PARISH. See
  LIBRARIES, CHURCH.

LIBRARIES, SEMINARY. See
  THEOLOGICAL LIBRARIES.

LIBRARIES, SUNDAY-SCHOOL.
      Z 675
  sa Libraries, Church.
     Sunday-school literature.
   x Sunday-school libraries.
  xx Libraries, Church.
     Sunday-school literature.

LIBRARIES, THEOLOGICAL. See
  THEOLOGICAL LIBRARIES.

LIFE - BIBLICAL TEACHING.
  sa Christian life - Biblical
     teaching.

LIFE - MORAL AND RELIGIOUS ASPECTS.
      BQT 1902-1925

LIFE, BOOK OF. See
  BOOK OF LIFE.

LIFE, SPIRITUAL. See
  SPIRITUAL LIFE.

LIFE AFTER DEATH. See
  FUTURE LIFE.
  IMMORTALITY.

LIFE OF CHRIST. See
  JESUS CHRIST - BIOGRAPHY.

LIGHT, INNER. See INNER LIGHT.

LIGHTS, FEAST OF. See
  HANUKKAH (FEAST OF LIGHTS)

LIGHTS, LITURGICAL. See
  CANDLES AND LIGHTS.

LIGHTS AND CANDLES. See
  CANDLES AND LIGHTS.

LIMBO.
      BQT 1558-1563   (236.7)
  xx Infant salvation.

LIQUOR PROBLEM.
  sa Alcoholism and religion.

LIS PENDENS (CANON LAW)
  xx Actions and defenses (Canon law)
    Civil procedure (Canon law)

LITANIES.
    BQT 4089; BQT 4250; BQT 4493
      (24x8.7)

LITANIES (MUSIC)
    M 2P79.L55

LITANY OF LORETO. See
  LITANY OF OUR LADY.

LITANY OF OUR LADY.
    BQT 4493 (24x8.72)
  x Litany of Loreto.
    Loreto, Litany of.
    Mary, Blessed Virgin - Litany.
  xx Mary, Blessed Virgin - Prayer-
    books.

LITANY OF OUR LADY - DEVOTIONAL
  LITERATURE.

LITANY OF OUR LADY - MEDITATIONS.
    BQT 2598

LITANY OF OUR LADY - POETRY.

LITANY OF OUR LADY - SERMONS.
    BQT 3060
  xx Mary, Blessed Virgin - Sermons.

LITANY OF ST. JOSEPH.
    BQT 4493 (24x8.73)
  x Joseph, Saint, Litany of.

LITANY OF THE HOLY FACE.
    BQT 4493 (24x8.7)
  x Holy Face, Litany of the.

LITANY OF THE HOLY INFANCY.
    BQT 4493
  x Holy Infancy, Litany of the.
  xx Holy Childhood.

LITANY OF THE HOLY NAME.
    BQT 4493 (24x8.71)
  x Holy Name, Litany of the.

LITANY OF THE SACRED HEART.
    BQT 4493 (24x8.71)
  x Sacred Heart, Litany of the.

LITANY OF THE SAINTS.
    BQT 4493 (24x8.71)
  x Saints, Litany of the.

LITERATURE, APOCALYPTIC. See
APOCALYPTIC LITERATURE.

LITERATURE, CATHOLIC. See
CATHOLIC LITERATURE.

LITERATURE, CHRISTIAN. See
CHRISTIAN LITERATURE.

LITERATURE, DEVOTIONAL. See
DEVOTIONAL LITERATURE.

LITERATURE, IMMORAL.
    BQT 1935
    HQ 471
    PN 49
  sa Literature and morals.
  x Immoral literature.
  xx Literature and morals.
  Other references as in LC.

LITERATURE, RELIGIOUS. See
RELIGIOUS LITERATURE.

LITERATURE AND LITURGY. See
LITURGY AND LITERATURE.

LITERATURE AND MORALS.
    PN 49
    BQT 1866
  sa Books and reading - Moral
    aspects.
    Children's literature - Moral
    and religious aspects.
    Literature, Immoral.
  x Morals and literature.
  xx Literature, Immoral.
    Religion in literature.

LITERATURE AND RELIGION. See
RELIGION AND LITERATURE.

LITHUANIA - CHURCH HISTORY.
    BQX 2691-2699

LITIS CONTESTATIO (CANON LAW)
BQV230 1726-1731

LITTLE OFFICE OF THE BLESSED VIRGIN.
See OFFICIUM PARVUM BEATAE
MARIAE VIRGINIS.

LITURGICAL ACCLAMATIONS. See
ACCLAMATIONS (LITURGY)

LITURGICAL APOSTOLATE. See
LITURGICAL MOVEMENT.

LITURGICAL ART. See
CHRISTIAN ART.

LITURGICAL BOOKS.
BQT 4241-4483 (26x5)
sa names of liturgical books, e.g.,
Breviarium, Missale, etc.
x Books, Liturgical.

LITURGICAL BOOKS - BIBLIOGRAPHY.

LITURGICAL BOOKS - HISTORY.

LITURGICAL CANDLES. See
CANDLES AND LIGHTS.

LITURGICAL COLORS. See
COLORS, LITURGICAL.

LITURGICAL DRAMA.
BQ 5151-5167
sa Mysteries and miracle-plays.
x Drama, Liturgical.
xx Bible plays.
Drama, Medieval.
Mysteries and miracle-plays.
Religious drama.

LITURGICAL ENGLISH. See
LITURGICAL LANGUAGE - ENGLISH.

LITURGICAL HYMNS. See
HYMNS, LITURGICAL.

LITURGICAL LANGUAGE.
BQT 4058-4066
"Here are entered works on the
language or languages used in
the liturgy of the church. Subdivided, if necessary, by the

LITURGICAL LANGUAGE -- Continued.
name of any particular language
involved, e.g., Liturgical language - English." LC
x Language, Liturgical.
Liturgy - Language.
xx Language question in the church.
Languages - Religious aspects.

LITURGICAL LANGUAGE - DICTIONARIES.

LITURGICAL LANGUAGE - ENGLISH.
x English language - Liturgical use.
Liturgical English.

LITURGICAL LANGUAGE - LATIN.
sa Latin language - Church Latin.
x Latin language - Liturgical use.
Liturgical Latin.
xx Latin language - Church Latin.

LITURGICAL LANGUAGE - SLAVIC.
sa Church Slavic language.
x Slavic language - Liturgical use.
xx Church Slavic language.

LITURGICAL LATIN. See
LITURGICAL LANGUAGE - LATIN.

LITURGICAL LAW.
BQV230 1255-1321 (348.x415)
sa Christian art (Canon law)
Church music (Canon law)
x Liturgy - Laws.
xx Rites and ceremonies (Catholic)

LITURGICAL LAW - COLLECTIONS.

LITURGICAL LIFE.
BQT 4048
xx Christian life.
Spiritual life.

LITURGICAL LIGHTS. See
CANDLES AND LIGHTS.

LITURGICAL MOVEMENT. (Geog. subdiv.)
BQT 4131
"The activity of the Western church
which seeks to restore intelli-
gent participation, first, in
the sacrifice of the mass, then,
in the other offices of the

LITURGICAL MOVEMENT -- Continued.
   church (as distinguished from
   popular devotions) as the prin-
   cipal and ordinary way of common
   prayer of the faithful at large."
   AT
  sa Liturgy - History - Modern
     period.
   x Apostolate, Liturgical.
    Liturgical apostolate.

LITURGICAL MOVEMENT - ANGLICAN
  COMMUNION.
   x Anglican Communion - Liturgical
    apostolate.

LITURGICAL MOVEMENT - PROTESTANT
  CHURCHES.
   x Protestant Churches - Liturgical
    movement.

LITURGICAL MUSIC. See
  CHURCH MUSIC.

LITURGICAL POSTURE. See
  POSTURE IN WORSHIP.

LITURGICAL PRAYER. See
  LITURGY.

LITURGICAL SEQUENCES. See
  SEQUENCES (LITURGY)

LITURGICAL SERMONS. See
  LITURGY - SERMONS.
  SERMONS, LITURGICAL.

LITURGICAL VESTMENTS. See
  CHURCH VESTMENTS.

LITURGICAL WEEK. See
  LITURGY - CONGRESSES.

LITURGICAL YEAR. See
  CHURCH YEAR.

LITURGICS. See
  LITURGY - STUDY AND TEACHING.

LITURGIES. See
  LITURGY.
  LITURGY - COLLECTIONS.

LITURGIOLOGY. See
  LITURGY - METHODOLOGY.

LITURGY.
    BQT 4001-6278   (264-26x5)
  "The forms of prayer, acts and
  ceremonies used in the public
  and official worship of the
  church, principally in the
  offering of the eucharistic
  sacrifice, the singing of the
  divine office and the administration of the sacraments, and
  the use thereof. This must be
  distinguished from the public
  use of popular devotions." AT
  The term is here used to stand
   for the liturgy of the Latin
   Rite. For the liturgy of the
   Eastern Churches, see Eastern
   Churches. Liturgy and ritual.
  sa Chant.
    Christian art.
    Church music.
    Church year.
    Devotions, Popular.
    Divine office.
    Feasts, Ecclesiastical.
    Mass.
    Rites and ceremonies (Catholic)
    Rites and uses.
    Sacraments (Liturgy)
    also names of sacraments, e.g.,
     Baptism (Liturgy) and sub-
     division "Liturgy and ritual"
     under names of churches and
     rites, e.g., Church of England.
     Liturgy and ritual; Mozarabic
     Rite. Liturgy and ritual.
  x Catholic Church. Liturgy and
    ritual.
    Catholic Church - Liturgy.
    Latin Rite.
    Liturgical prayer.
    Liturgies.
    Prayer, Liturgical.
  xx Church music.
    Church year.
    Religion.
    Rites and ceremonies (Catholic)
    Theology.
    Worship.

LITURGY - ADDRESSES, ESSAYS, LECTURES.
[BQT 4038]; BQT 4144
(264.x04)

LITURGY - BIBLIOGRAPHY.
BQT 4001
Z 7813   (016.264)

LITURGY - BIOGRAPHY.
BQT 4019

LITURGY - CALENDAR. See
CHURCH CALENDAR.

LITURGY - CASES.
BQT 4152

LITURGY - CATECHISMS, QUESTION-BOOKS.
BQT 4037

LITURGY - COLLECTED WORKS.
BQT 4006-4008

LITURGY - COLLECTED WORKS - EARLY
CHURCH.

LITURGY - COLLECTED WORKS - MIDDLE
AGES.

LITURGY - COLLECTED WORKS - MODERN
PERIOD.

LITURGY - COLLECTIONS.
BQT 4005-4008   (264.x08)
x Liturgies.

LITURGY - CONGRESSES.
BQT 4003; BQT 4119
(264.x06)
x Liturgical week.
Week, Liturgical.

Liturgy – CULTURAL ADAPTATION
See
LITURGY + CULTURE

LITURGY - DICTIONARIES.
BQT 4009   (264.x03)

LITURGY - GLOSSARIES, VOCABULARIES,
ETC.

LITURGY - HANDBOOKS, MANUALS, ETC.
BQT 4146
sa Rites and ceremonies (Catholic) -
Handbooks, manuals, etc.

LITURGY - HISTORY.   (Geog. subdiv.,
Indirect)
BQT 4021-4031; BQT 4121-4140
(264.x09)
xx Rites and ceremonies (Catholic) -
History.

LITURGY - HISTORY - EARLY CHURCH.
BQT 4026; BQT 4125
xx Church history - Primitive and
early church.
Church orders, Ancient.

LITURGY - HISTORY - MIDDLE AGES.
BQT 4028; BQT 4127

LITURGY - HISTORY - MODERN PERIOD.
BQT 4031; BQT 4129-4131
sa Liturgical movement.

LITURGY - JESUS CHRIST. See
JESUS CHRIST IN THE LITURGY.

LITURGY - LANGUAGE. See
LITURGICAL LANGUAGE.

LITURGY - LAWS. See
LITURGICAL LAW.

LITURGY - MANUSCRIPTS.

LITURGY - MARY, BLESSED VIRGIN. See
MARY, BLESSED VIRGIN, IN THE LITURGY.

LITURGY - MEDITATIONS.
BQT 2606
sa Church year - Meditations.

LITURGY - METHODOLOGY.
BQT 4011-4015
x Liturgiology.

LITURGY - MYSTERY PRINCIPLE.
BQT 4049
x Mysterium (Liturgy)

LITURGY - PAPAL TEACHING.
[BQT 4036]

LITURGY - PARAPHRASES.

LITURGY - PARTICIPATION.
sa Mass - Participation.
x Participation in the liturgy.

LITURGY - PERIODICALS.
  BQT 4002   (264.x05)

LITURGY - POPULAR WORKS.
  BQT 4037; BQT 4143

LITURGY - SAINTS. See
  SAINTS IN THE LITURGY.

LITURGY - SERMONS.
  [BQT 4038]
  Here are entered works explaining,
    through sermons, the meaning of
    the liturgy in all its phases.
  For collections of sermons pre-
    pared from a liturgical view-
    point see Sermons, Liturgical.
  sa Rites and ceremonies (Catholic) -
    Sermons.
    Sermons, Liturgical.
  x Liturgical sermons.
  xx Sermons, Liturgical.

LITURGY - SOURCES.
  BQT 4005-4008

LITURGY - STUDY AND TEACHING.
  BQT 4016   (264.x07)
  x Liturgics.

LITURGY - STUDY CLUBS.
  [BQT 4016.5]

LITURGY - TEXTBOOKS.
  BQT 4034-4035; BQT 4146-4149
    (264.x02)

LITURGY - TEXTBOOKS - 19th CENTURY.

LITURGY - TEXTBOOKS - 20th CENTURY.

        #################

LITURGY. CHURCH OF ENGLAND. See
  CHURCH OF ENGLAND. LITURGY AND
  RITUAL.

LITURGY. EASTERN CHURCHES. See
  EASTERN CHURCHES. LITURGY AND
  RITUAL.

        #################

LITURGY (CANON LAW). See
  LITURGICAL LAW.

LITURGY AND ART.
  BQT 4069; BQT 5669
  x Art and liturgy.

LITURGY AND BIBLE.
  BQT 4064
  x Bible and liturgy.

LITURGY AND CATECHETICS.
  x Catechetics and liturgy.
LITURGY and CULTURE
LITURGY AND DRAMA.
  sa Religious drama.
  x Drama and liturgy.
  xx Religious drama.

LITURGY AND EDUCATION.
  [BQT 4070]
  x Education and liturgy.

LITURGY AND LITERATURE.
  x Literature and liturgy.
  xx Religion and literature.

LITURGY AND MISSIONS.
  [BQT 4070]
  x Missions and liturgy.

LITURGY AND PREACHING. See
  PREACHING AND LITURGY.

LITURGY AND SOCIOLOGY.
  BQT 4048
  x Sociology and liturgy.
  xx Religion and sociology.

LITURGY AND THEOLOGY.
  x Theology and liturgy.

LITURGY OF ST. BASIL.
  x St. Basil, Liturgy of.
  xx Byzantine Rite. Liturgy and
    ritual.

LITURGY OF ST. JAMES.
  x St. James, Liturgy of.
  xx Byzantine Rite. Liturgy and
    ritual.

LITURGY OF ST. JOHN CHRYSOSTOM.
    x St. John Chrysostom, Liturgy of.
    xx Byzantine Rite. Liturgy and
        ritual.

LITURGY OF ST. MARK.
    x St. Mark, Liturgy of.
    xx Alexandrian Rite.

LITURGY OF THE PRESANCTIFIED.
    x Presanctified, Liturgy of the.
    xx Byzantine Rite. Liturgy and
        ritual.

LOCAL CHURCH COUNCILS.
      BV 626
    x Church councils, Local.
      Federations, Local church.
    xx Christian union.
      Church polity.
      Church work.
      Coundils and synods.
      Ecumenical movement.
      Sects.

LOCI THEOLOCI.
      BQT 248
    By this term are understood the
      sources (fontes theologici) for
      theological doctrines. The
      chief sources are the Bible and
      tradition.
    sa Tradition (Theology)
    xx Rule of faith.
      Theology - Methodology.

LOGOS.
      BQT 721   (232.x32)
    sa Alogi.
      Memra (The word)
    x Jesus Christ - Logos doctrine.
    xx Jesus Christ.

LOLLARDS.
      BQT 95
      BQX 2049   (289.9)
    x Wyclifites.
    xx Sects, Medieval.

✔ Loneliness

LORD, DAY OF THE. See
  DAY OF JEHOVAH.

LORD'S DAY. See
  SABBATH.
  SUNDAY.

LORD'S PRAYER.
      BQT 897   (226.x7)
      BQT 2695 (Devotions)
        (24x7.11)
    x Our Father.
      Pater noster.
    xx Bible - Prayers.
      Jesus Christ - Prayers.
      Prayers.

LORD'S PRAYER - COMMENTARIES.

LORD'S PRAYER - DEVOTIONAL
  LITERATURE.

LORD'S PRAYER - JUVENILE
  LITERATURE.

LORD'S PRAYER - MEDITATIONS.
  [BQT 2610.5]

LORD'S PRAYER - PICTURES,
  ILLUSTRATIONS, ETC.

LORD'S PRAYER - POETRY.

LORD'S PRAYER - SERMONS.
      BQT 3089

LORD'S SUPPER.
      BV 823-828 (General)
      BX 5149.C5 (Church of
        England)
    Here are entered works dealing
      with the eucharistic liturgy
      in the various Protestant
      churches. Works dealing with
      the eucharistic liturgy in the
      Catholic sense are entered
      under Eucharist.
    Subdivisions and references as
      in LC.

LORETO, LITANY OF. See
  LITANY OF OUR LADY.

LORRAINE - CHURCH HISTORY.
  [BQX 1820]

LORRAINE, CROSS OF. See
  CROSS OF LORRAINE.

LOSS OF CONSCIOUSNESS.
  sa Use of reason.
  xx Use of reason.
  Other references as in LC.

LOST SHEEP (PARABLE)

LOST TRIBES OF ISRAEL.
     DS 131
  References as in LC.

LOUISETS.
     BX 4737
     BQX 1783
  sa Nonjurors, French Catholic.
   x Incommunicants.
     La Petite Eglise.
  xx Catholic Church - France.
     Concordat of 1801 (France)
     Nonjurors, French Catholic.

LOURDES (SHRINE)
     BQT 1067-1071   (23x3.62)
   x Notre Dame de Lourdes (Shrine)
     Our Lady of Lourdes (Shrine)

LOVE (THEOLOGY)
     BQT 1203 (Dogmatic theology)
       (24x1.51)
     BQT 1783-1785 (Moral theology)
     BQT 2191 (Asceticism)
  Here are entered works on the love
    which man accords God; also
    general works on the theological
    virtue of charity or love.
  For works dealing specifically with
    love of neighbor see Charity.
  sa Desire for God.
     God - Love.
     Kindness (Theology)
   x God - Lovableness.
     God - Worship and love.
     Love of God.
  xx Perfection, Christian.
     Virtues, Theological.

LOVE (THEOLOGY) - BIBLICAL TEACHING.

LOVE (THEOLOGY) - DEVOTIONAL
  LITERATURE.

LOVE (THEOLOGY) - EARLY WORKS TO 1800.

LOVE (THEOLOGY) - HISTORY OF DOCTRINES.

LOVE (THEOLOGY) - MEDITATIONS.
     [BQT 2610.5]

LOVE (THEOLOGY) - POPULAR WORKS.

LOVE (THEOLOGY) - SERMONS.

LOVE, MYSTIC.
     BQT 2477
   x Mystic love.

LOVE, PERFECT. See
  PERFECTION, CHRISTIAN.

LOVE FEASTS.
  "Here are entered works dealing
    with modern religious services
    in imitation of the historic
    agape." LC
  sa Agape.
  xx Agape.
     Methodist Church.
     Sacred meals.

LOVE OF GOD. See
  LOVE (THEOLOGY)

LOVE OF NEIGHBOR. See
  CHARITY.

LOW MASS.
     BQT 4159
   x Mass, Low.
     Mass, Private.
     Private mass.

LOW MASS - RITES AND CEREMONIES.
     BQT 4334
  xx Mass - Rites and ceremonies.

LUCERNARIUM.
     BQT 4175
  "A primitive evening office, the
    parent of Vespers, at which all
    the lamps of the church were
    lit and a hymn sung." AT
  xx Vespers.

LUKE, SAINT, GOSPEL OF. See
    BIBLE. N.T. LUKE.

LUST.
       BQT 1813
    xx Capital sins.
       Chastity.

✓ LUTHERAN CHURCH.
       BX 8001-8080   (284.1)

LUTHERAN CHURCH - CLERGY.
    x Clergy - Lutheran Church.

LUTHERAN CHURCH - CONTROVERSIAL
    LITERATURE.

LUTHERAN CHURCH - DOCTRINE.
    x Theology - Lutheran Church.

LUTHERAN CHURCH. LITURGY AND RITUAL.

    Other subdivisions under Lutheran
      Church as in LC.

LUTHERANS, COLORED. See
    LUTHERANS, NEGRO.

LUTHERANS, NEGRO.
       BX 8060.N
    References as in LC.

LUTHERANS, DANISH, [POLISH, ETC.]
    "Here are entered works on
      Lutherans living outside their
      native country but using their
      native language in church
      services." LC
    x Danish, [Polish, etc.] Lutherans.

LUXEMBURG (GRAND DUCHY) - CHURCH
    HISTORY.
       BQX 2711-2719

LYING. See
    TRUTHFULNESS AND FALSEHOOD.

LYONS, COUNCIL OF, 1st, 1245.
       BQX 733   (26x2.35)

LYONS, COUNCIL OF, 2d, 1274.
       BQX 739   (26x2.36)
    xx Catholic Church and reunion -
      History.

MACCABEES.
    x Asmoneans.
      Hasmonaeans.
    xx Jews - History - 586 B.C. -
      70 A.D.

MACCABEES, 1-2 BOOKS OF. See
    BIBLE. O.T. 1-2 MACHABEES.

MACCABEES, FEAST OF THE. See
    HANUKKAH (FEAST OF LIGHTS)

MACHABEES, 1-2 BOOKS OF. See
    BIBLE. O.T. 1-2 MACHABEES.

MACHABEES, THIRD BOOK OF (APO-
    CRYPHAL)
       BS 1821-1825

MACHABEES, FOURTH BOOK OF (APO-
    CRYPHAL)
       BS 1821-1825

MADONNA. See
    MARY, BLESSED VIRGIN - ART.

MAESTRO DI CAMERA.
       BQX 169

MAGGID (CABALA)
    References as in LC.

MAGI.
       BQT 845
    xx Epiphany.

MAGI - ART.
       BQT 5858
    xx Christian art.
      Jesus Christ - Art.

MAGI - DRAMA.

MAGI - FICTION.

MAGI - SERMONS.

✓ MAGISTERIUM ECCLESIAE. ~~See~~
    CHURCH - TEACHING ~~OFFICE~~ authority

MAGNIFICAT.
       BQT 2695
    x Canticle of Our Lady.

MAGNIFICAT - SERMONS.

MAGNIFICAT (MUSIC)
M 1113

MAHDISM.
BP 1666.93
xx Eschatology, Mohammedan.
Mohammedanism.

MAHOMMEDANISM. See
MOHAMMEDANISM.

MAJOR ORDERS.
BQT 354 (23x7.6)
sa Deacons.
Ordination.
Subdeacons.
x Orders, Major.
xx Clergy.
Deacons.
Ordination.
Priesthood.
Subdeacons.

MAJOR PROPHETS. See
BIBLE. O.T. MAJOR PROPHETS.

MAJORITIES (CANON LAW)
xx Election law (Canon law)

MALABAR - CHURCH HISTORY.
BQX 5632-5659; BQX 6481-6539
sa St. Thomas Christians.

MALABAR JACOBITE CHURCH.
x Jacobite Church, Malabar.
Nestorian Malabar Church.

MALABAR JACOBITE CHURCH - HISTORY.
BQX 5407-5429

MALABAR JACOBITE CHURCH - LAW.
BQV 1347-1348

MALABAR JACOBITE CHURCH. LITURGY
AND RITUAL.
BQT 5407-5429

MALABAR RITE.
x Syro-Malabar Rite.

MALABAR RITE - CANON LAW.
BQV 1258-1270

MALABAR RITE - HISTORY.
BQX 6491-6510

MALABAR RITE. LITURGY AND RITUAL.
BQT 5441-5449

MALABAR RITES.
BQX 6481-6488
"Here are entered works dealing
with the controversy concerning
the participation of Christian
converts in the native rites
and ceremonies of Malabar." LC
sa Chinese rites.
xx Chinese rites.

MALACHI, BOOK OF. See
BIBLE. O.T. MALACHIAS.

MALACHIAS, BOOK OF. See
BIBLE. O.T. MALACHIAS.

MALANKARA RITE.

MALANKARA RITE - CANON LAW.
BQV 1187.3-.5

MALANKARA RITE - HISTORY.
BQX 5652-5659

MALANKARA RITE. LITURGY AND
RITUAL.
BQT 5165-5170

MALANKARESE MONASTICISM. See
MONASTICISM, MALANKARESE.

MALEDICTION. See
BLESSING AND CURSING.

MALICIOUS PROSECUTION (CANON LAW)

MALTA, KNIGHTS OF. See
KNIGHTS OF MALTA.

MAN (JEWISH THEOLOGY)

MAN (THEOLOGY)
BQT 618-643 (231.x7)
sa Bible - Ethnology.
Desire for God.
Evolution.

MAN (THEOLOGY) -- Continued.
  sa Fall of man.
     Humanism, Religious.
     Image of God.
     Justice, Original.
     Personality.
     Physical education and training -
       Moral and religious aspects.
     Pure nature.
     Sin.
     Soul.
     Vocation - Biblical teaching.
   x Anthropology, Theological.
     Man, Doctrine of.
     Theological anthropology.
  xx Dogmatic theology.

MAN (THEOLOGY) - BIBLICAL TEACHING.
    [BQT 618.5]
   x Anthropology, Biblical.
     Bible - Anthropology.
     Biblical anthropology.

MAN (THEOLOGY) - EARLY WORKS TO 1800.

MAN (THEOLOGY) - HISTORY OF DOCTRINES.
  sa Pelagianism.

MAN (THEOLOGY) - HISTORY OF DOCTRINES -
  EARLY CHURCH.

MAN (THEOLOGY) - HISTORY OF DOCTRINES -
  MIDDLE AGES.

MAN (THEOLOGY) - MEDITATIONS.

MAN (THEOLOGY) - PAPAL TEACHING.

MAN (THEOLOGY) - SERMONS.

MAN, DOCTRINE OF. See
  MAN (THEOLOGY)

MAN, FALL OF. See
  FALL OF MAN.

MAN BORN BLIND (MIRACLE). See
  HEALING OF THE MAN BORN BLIND
  (MIRACLE)

MANDAEANS.
  x Christians of St. John.
    Disciples of St. John.
  xx Gnosticism.

MANDATUM.
    BQT 4223
  Here are entered works on the
  ceremony of the washing of feet
  on Maundy Thursday.
  xx Maundy Thursday.
    Washing of feet.

MANGER IN CHRISTIAN ART AND TRADITION.
  See CRIB IN CHRISTIAN ART AND
  TRADITION.

MANICHAEISM.
    BQT 72   (273.x21)
    BQX 297 (Church history)
  xx Dualism (Theology)
    Heresies and heretics - Early
     church.

MANIFESTATION OF CONSCIENCE. See
  CONSCIENCE, MANIFESTATION OF.

MANNA.
    BS 1245

MANNERS AND CUSTOMS.
  xx Rites and ceremonies.
  Other references as in LC.

MANUALE.
    BQT 4273.M3
  A collection of prayers and directives for the sacraments, visitations, blessings, etc. A pre-
  decessor of the Rituale.
  xx Rituale.

MARCH DEVOTIONS.
    BQT 4495
  xx Devotions, Popular.
    Joseph, Saint - Prayer-books.

MARCIANITES. See MESSALIANS.

MARIAN CONGRESS. See
  MARY, BLESSED VIRGIN - CONGRESSES.

MARIAN LIBRARIES.
   x Libraries, Marian.

MARIAN YEAR.
     BQT 2679
   For special Marian Years add date.
   x Mary, Blessed Virgin - Marian
     Year.
   xx Indulgences.

MARIOLATRY. See
   MARY, BLESSED VIRGIN - CULTUS -
   CONTROVERSIAL LITERATURE.

MARIOLOGY. See
   MARY, BLESSED VIRGIN.

MARK, SAINT, GOSPEL OF. See
   BIBLE. N.T. MARK.

MARKS OF THE CHURCH. See
   CHURCH - MARKS.

MARONITE RITE.
   x Syro-Maronite Rite.

MARONITE RITE - BIOGRAPHY.

MARONITE RITE - CANON LAW.
     BQV 1171-1177   (348.x7)

MARONITE RITE - CHURCH MUSIC. See
   CHURCH MUSIC - MARONITE RITE.

MARONITE RITE - HISTORY.
     BQX 5611-5622   (28x2.8)

MARONITE RITE. LITURGY AND RITUAL.
     BQT 5150-5164   (264.x73)

MARONITE RITE. LITURGY AND RITUAL -
   MASS.
   x Mass - Maronite Rite.

MARPRELATE CONTROVERSY.
     BR 757; BQX 2076   (285.9)
   xx Church of England.

MARRIAGE.   (Geog. subdiv., Indirect)
     HQ 503-1057   (173.1)
     GN 480 (Ethnology)
     GR 465 (Folklore)   (392.5)
     BQT 1423-1437; BQT 2073 (Sacra-
       ment)   (23x7.7; 24x1.97)

MARRIAGE.
   References as in LC, with the
     following additional reference.
   sa Conjugal state.

X MARRIAGE - ANNULMENT.   *see Annulment*
   sa Divorce.
   x Annulment of marriage.
     Nullity of marriage.
   xx Marriage - Dissolution.

MARRIAGE - ANNULMENT (CANON LAW)
     BQV230 1118-1132
   sa Defender of the marriage bond.
   xx Divorce (Canon law)
     Matrimonial actions (Canon law)
     Nullity (Canon law)

MARRIAGE - ANNULMENT (CHURCH OF
   ENGLAND)

MARRIAGE - BIBLICAL TEACHING.

MARRIAGE - BIOGRAPHY.

MARRIAGE - CASES.

MARRIAGE - CASES (CANON LAW)
     BQV230 1960-1992   (348.x54)
   xx Trials, Ecclesiastical (Marriage)

MARRIAGE - CATECHISMS, QUESTION-BOOKS.

MARRIAGE - DISPENSATIONS.
   x Dispensations for marriage.

MARRIAGE - DISPENSATIONS (CANON LAW)

MARRIAGE - DISSOLUTION.
   sa Death - Proof and certification.
     Divorce.
     Marriage - Annulment.
     Marriage - Indissolubility.
     Pauline privilege.
     Separation (Law)
   x Dissolution of marriage.
   xx Divorce.
     Marriage - Indissolubility.

MARRIAGE - DISSOLUTION (CANON LAW)
     BQV230 1118-1127
   xx Divorce (Canon law)

MARRIAGE - IMPEDIMENTS.   (Geog.
  subdiv., Direct)
    x Impediments to marriage.

MARRIAGE - IMPEDIMENTS (CANON LAW)
        BQV230 1035-1080   (348.x427)
  sa Abduction (Canon law)
     Adoption (Canon law)
     Affinity (Canon law)
     Consanguinity (Canon law)
     Crime and criminals (Canon law)
     Disparity of cult.
     Dispensations (Canon law)
     Impotence (Canon law)
     Marriage - Validation (Canon
       law)
     Marriage, Mixed.
     Mixed religion.
     Ordination (Canon law)
     Rape (Canon law)
     Vows (Canon law)
  xx Impediments (Canon law)
     Marriage (Canon law)

MARRIAGE - IMPEDIMENTS (CANON LAW,
  EASTERN)

MARRIAGE - INDISSOLUBILITY.
        BQT 1426
        BQV230 1013
  sa Marriage - Dissolution.
   x Indissolubility of marriage.
     Marriage - Unity.
  xx Marriage - Dissolution.

MARRIAGE - INSTRUCTION AND STUDY.
  sa Marriage instructions.

MARRIAGE - MEDITATIONS.
        [BQT 2608.7]

MARRIAGE - PAPAL TEACHING.

MARRIAGE - POPULAR WORKS.

MARRIAGE - SERMONS.
        BQT 3001
   x Marriage sermons.
     Sermons, Marriage.
  xx Occasional sermons.

MARRIAGE - STATISTICS.

MARRIAGE - UNITY. See
  MARRIAGE - INDISSOLUBILITY.

MARRIAGE - VALIDATION.
     [BQT 1435]

MARRIAGE - VALIDATION (CANON LAW)
        BQV230 1133-1141
  sa Sanatio in radice.
  xx Marriage - Impediments (Canon
     law)

################

MARRIAGE - CHURCH OF ENGLAND,
  [LUTHERAN CHURCH, ORTHODOX
  EASTERN CHURCH, ETC.]

################

MARRIAGE (CANON LAW)
        BQV230 1143   (348.x427)
  sa Adultery (Canon law)
     Banns of marriage.
     Betrothal (Canon law)
     Bigamy (Canon law)
     Clandestinity (Canon law)
     Consent (Canon law)
     Divorce (Canon law)
     Domicile (Canon law)
     Marriage - Impediments.
     Matrimonial actions (Canon law)
     Minors (Canon law)
     Parents (Canon law)
     Pauline privilege.
     Separation (Canon law)
     Trials, Ecclesiastical (Marriage)
  xx Irregularities.
     Marriage law.
     Sacraments (Canon law)

MARRIAGE (CANON LAW) - HISTORY.

MARRIAGE (CANON LAW, ORIENTAL)

MARRIAGE (CANON LAW, ORIENTAL -
  BULGARIAN)

MARRIAGE (CANON LAW, ORIENTAL -
  MELKITE)

MARRIAGE (CANON LAW, ORTHODOX
  EASTERN)

MARRIAGE (LITURGY)
      BQT 4453   (264.x63)
  xx Sacraments (Liturgy)

MARRIAGE (LITURGY) - HISTORY.

MARRIAGE (SACRAMENT)
      BQT 1423-1437 (Dogmatic theology)
        (23x7.7)
      BQT 2073 (Moral theology)
        (24x1.97)

MARRIAGE (SACRAMENT) - EFFICACY.

MARRIAGE (SACRAMENT) - HISTORY OF
  DOCTRINES.

MARRIAGE (SACRAMENT) - MINISTER.

MARRIAGE, COMPANIONATE.
      HQ 734-743
  x Companionate marriage.

MARRIAGE, INTERRACIAL. See
  MISCEGENATION.

MARRIAGE, MIXED.   (Geog. subdiv.)
      BQT 1432
      BQV230 1060-1064 (Canon law)
        (348.x427)
  Here are entered works dealing
    with marriages between Catholics
    and non-Catholics. For works
    dealing with marriages between
    persons of different races see
    Miscegenation.
  sa Disparity of cult.
    Mixed religion.
  x Intermarriage.
    Mixed marriage.
  xx Marriage - Impediments (Canon
      law)
    Miscegenation.

MARRIAGE, MIXED - PROMISES.

MARRIAGE, MIXED - SERMONS.
      BQT 3065
  x Marriage sermons.
    Sermons, Marriage.

MARRIAGE, PROMISE OF. See
  BETROTHAL.

MARRIAGE BOND, DEFENDER OF THE. See
  DEFENDER OF THE MARRIAGE BOND.

MARRIAGE COUNSELING.
      BQT 3535
  References as in LC.

MARRIAGE CUSTOMS AND RITES.
  xx Rites and ceremonies.
  Other references as in LC.

MARRIAGE IN CANA (MIRACLE)
  x Cana, Marriage in.
    Wedding in Cana.

MARRIAGE OF THE KING'S SON (PARABLE)
  x Kings's son, Marriage of the.
    Wedding garment (Parable)

MARRIAGE INSTRUCTIONS.
      BQT 1437
  Here are entered works containing
    the required instructions to be
    given to parties contemplating
    a Catholic marriage.
  xx Marriage - Instruction and
    study.

MARRIAGE INVESTIGATION (CANON LAW)

MARRIAGE LAW.   (Geog. subdiv.,
  Direct)
      HQ 1011-1019   (347.6)
  References as in LC, with the
    following additional reference.
  sa Marriage (Canon law)

MARRIAGE OF CLERGY.
      BQT 2299
  x Clergy - Marriage.
  xx Celibacy.

MARRIAGE OF CONSCIENCE.
      BQV230 1104-1107
  "A marriage celebrated without
    banns before a priest and
    witnesses who are bound to
    secrecy." AT
  x Conscience, Marriage of.

MARRIAGE PROPOSALS (CANON LAW)

MARRIAGE REGISTERS. See
    REGISTERS OF BIRTHS, ETC.

MARRIAGE SERMONS. See
    MARRIAGE - SERMONS.
    MARRIAGE, MIXED - SERMONS.

MARRIAGE SERVICE.
      BQT 4453
    x Rites and ceremonies, Marriage.

MARTIN, SAINT, CLOAK OF. See
    ST. MARTIN'S CLOAK.

MARTYRDOM.
      BQT 1580
      BQX 211-214; BQX 268-269
        (History)
  sa Baptism of blood.
    Heroic virtue.
    Martyrs.
  x Baptism, Second.
    Second baptism.
  xx Asceticism.
    Death.
    Martyrs.
    Persecution.
    Suffering.
    Witness bearing (Christianity)

MARTYRIA.
      BQT 5929
  Here are entered works dealing
    with churches and chapels dedi-
    cated to a martyr.
  xx Church architecture.
    Sepulchral monuments.
    Shrines.

MARTYROLOGIUM.
      BQT 4263; BQT 4431   (26x5.4)
      BQX 8218
  "A list for every day of the year
    of martyrs and other saints
    whose feasts or commemorations
    occur on each day, generally
    with a brief note about each
    individual." AT
  sa Menologium.
    Passionarium.
  x Martyrology.
  xx Martyrs.
    Saints.

MARTYROLOGIUM - BIBLIOGRAPHY.

MARTYROLOGIUM - HISTORY.

MARTYROLOGIUM. ENGLISH, [FRENCH,
    GERMAN, ETC.]

MARTYROLOGIUM. AUGUSTINIAN,
    [BENEDICTINE, CISTERCIAN, ETC.]

MARTYROLOGIUM ROMANUM.
      BQT 4431
    x Roman Martyrology.

MARTYROLOGY. See MARTYROLOGIUM.

MARTYRS.   (Geog. subdiv.,
      BQX 211-214
      BQX 8211-8538 (Biography)
      BQX 268-269 (Early church)
  sa Martyrdom.
    Martyrologium.
    Refugees, Religious.
    Saints.
  xx Christian biography.
    Church history.
    Heroes.
    Martyrdom.
    Persecution.
    Religious orders.
    Saints.

MARTYRS - CULTUS.
      BQT 1581   (23x5.2)
  x Martyrs - Veneration.
    Veneration of martyrs.
  xx Saints - Cultus.

MARTYRS - LEGENDS.
  sa Theban Legion.

MARTYRS - MEDITATIONS.
      BQT 2603

MARTYRS - PRAYER-BOOKS.
      BQT 2687

MARTYRS - SERMONS.
      BQT 3089

MARTYRS - VENERATION. See
    MARTYRS - CULTUS.

################

MARTYRS, BENEDICTINE, [DOMINICAN,
JESUIT, ETC.]
   x Benedictine, [Dominican,
      Jesuit, etc.] martyrs.

###################

✓ MARY, BLESSED VIRGIN.
      BQT 1000-1093   (23x3)
  sa Ave Maria.
   x Blessed Virgin Mary.
     Mariology.
     Virgin Mary, Blessed.
  xx Dogmatic theology.
     Jesus Christ.

MARY, BLESSED VIRGIN - ADDRESSES,
ESSAYS, LECTURES.
      BQT 1009; BQT 1049

MARY, BLESSED VIRGIN - ANNUNCIATION.
  See ANNUNCIATION.

⌐ MARY, BLESSED VIRGIN - APPARITIONS
AND MIRACLES.
      BQT 1061-1075   (23x3.6)
   x Mary, Blessed Virgin - Miracles.
  xx Apparitions.
     Miracles.

MARY, BLESSED VIRGIN - ART.
      BQT 5881-5887   (264.x64)
  sa Annunciation - Art.
     Immaculate Conception - Art.
   x Madonna.
     Mary, Blessed Virgin - Icono-
       graphy.
     Mary, Blessed Virgin, in art.
  xx Christian art.
     Jesus Christ - Art.

MARY, BLESSED VIRGIN - ASSUMPTION.
  See ASSUMPTION.

MARY, BLESSED VIRGIN - BIBLICAL
TEACHING.
      BQT 1013
  xx Mary, Blessed Virgin - History
     of doctrines.

MARY, BLESSED VIRGIN - BIBLIOGRAPHY.
      BQT 1000
      Z 8552   (016.23x3)

MARY, BLESSED VIRGIN - BIBLIOGRAPHY -
CATALOGS.

MARY, BLESSED VIRGIN - BIOGRAPHY.
      BQT 1042-1059   (23x3.5)

MARY, BLESSED VIRGIN - BIOGRAPHY -
APOCRYPHAL AND LEGENDARY LITERA-
TURE.
      BQT 1044

MARY, BLESSED VIRGIN - BIOGRAPHY -
JUVENILE LITERATURE.
      BQT 1048

MARY, BLESSED VIRGIN - BIOGRAPHY -
MEDITATIONS.
      BQT 2597

MARY, BLESSED VIRGIN - BIOGRAPHY -
MOTION PICTURES.

MARY, BLESSED VIRGIN - BIOGRAPHY -
SERMONS.
      BQT 1049

MARY, BLESSED VIRGIN - BIOGRAPHY -
SOURCES.
      BQT 1044

MARY, BLESSED VIRGIN - BIOGRAPHY -
SOURCES, BIBLICAL.
      BQT 1042

MARY, BLESSED VIRGIN - CALENDAR.
  xx Saints - Calendar.

MARY, BLESSED VIRGIN - CATECHISMS,
QUESTION-BOOKS.

MARY, BLESSED VIRGIN - COLLECTED
WORKS.
      BQT 1005-1006

MARY, BLESSED VIRGIN - COLLECTED
WORKS - EARLY CHURCH.

MARY, BLESSED VIRGIN - COLLECTED
WORKS - MIDDLE AGES.

MARY, BLESSED VIRGIN - COLLECTED
WORKS - 16th, [17th, etc.]
CENTURY.

MARY, BLESSED VIRGIN - COLLECTIONS.
    BQT 1003

MARY, BLESSED VIRGIN - CONFRATERNITIES.
        BQT 2810-2814   (24x8.8)
    sa names of individual confrater-
        nities, e.g., Sodality of the
        Blessed Virgin Mary.
    x Mary, Blessed Virgin - Sodalities.
    xx Confraternities.

MARY, BLESSED VIRGIN - CONGRESSES.
    BQT 1002
    x Marian Congresses.

MARY, BLESSED VIRGIN - CONTROVERSIAL
LITERATURE.
    [BQT 1095]

MARY, BLESSED VIRGIN - CO-REDEMPTION.
See CO-REDEMPTION.

MARY, BLESSED VIRGIN - CULTUS.
    (Geog. subdiv., Direct)
        BQT 1038   (23x3.7)
        [BQT 1039] (By country)
    sa Mary, Blessed Virgin - Prayer-
        books.
        Mary, Blessed Virgin, in the
        liturgy.

    x Hyperdulia.
        Mary, Blessed Virgin - Invocation.
        Mary, Blessed Virgin - Veneration.
    xx Saints - Cultus.

MARY, BLESSED VIRGIN - CULTUS -
CONTROVERSIAL LITERATURE.
    x Mariolatry.

MARY, BLESSED VIRGIN - CULTUS -
SERMONS.
    xx Mary, Blessed Virgin - Sermons.

MARY, BLESSED VIRGIN - DEATH.
    BQT 1058
    xx Assumption.

MARY, BLESSED VIRGIN - DEVOTIONAL
LITERATURE.
    BQT 2597

MARY, BLESSED VIRGIN - DICTIONARIES.
    [BQT 1004]

MARY, BLESSED VIRGIN - DOLORS. See
SORROWS OF OUR LADY.

MARY, BLESSED VIRGIN - DRAMA.
    BQT 1087
    xx Mary, Blessed Virgin, in
        literature.

MARY, BLESSED VIRGIN - EARLY
WORKS TO 1800.

MARY, BLESSED VIRGIN - EASTERN
CHURCHES. See
EASTERN CHURCHES - MARIOLOGY.

MARY, BLESSED VIRGIN - EXAMPLE.

MARY, BLESSED VIRGIN - FEASTS.
        BQT 4249-4230   (23x3.72)
    sa names of individual feasts,
        e.g., Assumption, Feast of
        the.
    xx Feasts, Ecclesiastical.

MARY, BLESSED VIRGIN - FEASTS -
SERMONS.
    BQT 3060
    xx Mary, Blessed Virgin - Sermons.

MARY, BLESSED VIRGIN - FICTION.
    BQT 1089
    xx Mary, Blessed Virgin, in
        literature.

MARY, BLESSED VIRGIN - HISTORY OF
DOCTRINES.   (Geog. subdiv.)
    BQT 1012-1016
    sa Mary, Blessed Virgin - Biblical
        teaching.
    xx Mary, Blessed Virgin - Theology.

MARY, BLESSED VIRGIN - HISTORY OF
DOCTRINES - EARLY CHURCH.

MARY, BLESSED VIRGIN - HISTORY OF
DOCTRINES - MIDDLE AGES.
    BQT 1014

MARY, BLESSED VIRGIN - HISTORY OF
DOCTRINES - MODERN PERIOD.
BQT 1016

MARY, BLESSED VIRGIN - HISTORY OF
DOCTRINES - 16th, [17th, etc.]
CENTURY.
BQT 1016

MARY, BLESSED VIRGIN - HOLINESS.
BQT 1093

MARY, BLESSED VIRGIN - HUMILITY.
BQT 1093

MARY, BLESSED VIRGIN - HYMNS.
BQT 1086; BQT 4681-4689
(245)

MARY, BLESSED VIRGIN - HYMNS,
ENGLISH, [FRENCH, GERMAN, ETC.]

MARY, BLESSED VIRGIN - ICONOGRAPHY.
See MARY, BLESSED VIRGIN - ART.

MARY, BLESSED VIRGIN - IMMACULATE
CONCEPTION. See
IMMACULATE CONCEPTION.

MARY, BLESSED VIRGIN - IMMACULATE
HEART. See
IMMACULATE HEART OF MARY.

MARY, BLESSED VIRGIN - INVOCATION.
See MARY, BLESSED VIRGIN - CULTUS.

MARY, BLESSED VIRGIN - JUVENILE
LITERATURE.
BQT 1007

MARY, BLESSED VIRGIN - LEGENDS.
BQT 1044
xx Saints - Legends.

MARY, BLESSED VIRGIN - LITANY. See
LITANY OF OUR LADY.

MARY, BLESSED VIRGIN - MARIAN YEAR.
See MARIAN YEAR.

MARY, BLESSED VIRGIN - MAY DEVOTIONS.
See MAY DEVOTIONS.

MARY, BLESSED VIRGIN - MEDIATION.
BQT 1032
sa Co-redemption.
xx Co-redemption.
Mary, Blessed Virgin - Cultus.

MARY, BLESSED VIRGIN - MEDITATIONS.
BQT 2597-2598   (24x2.4)

MARY, BLESSED VIRGIN - MIRACLES.
See MARY, BLESSED VIRGIN - APPARI-
TIONS AND MIRACLES.

MARY, BLESSED VIRGIN - MOHAMMEDAN
INTERPRETATIONS.
BQT 1093

MARY, BLESSED VIRGIN - MOTHERHOOD.
BQT 1005-1011
Here are entered works on the
Blessed Virgin as the Mother of
Jesus Christ, who was God and
man.
x Mother of God.
xx Mary, Blessed Virgin - Theology.

MARY, BLESSED VIRGIN - MOTHERHOOD -
PRAYER-BOOKS.
BQT 2679
sa Missa Maternitatis Beatae Mariae
Virginis.

MARY, BLESSED VIRGIN - MOTHERHOOD -
SERMONS.

MARY, BLESSED VIRGIN - MOTHERHOOD
(SPIRITUAL)
BQT 1034
Here are entered works on the
Blessed Virgin as the Mother
of men.
xx Co-redemption.
Mary, Blessed Virgin - Offices.

MARY, BLESSED VIRGIN - MUSIC. See
MARY, BLESSED VIRGIN, IN MUSIC.

MARY, BLESSED VIRGIN - NAME. See
MARY, BLESSED VIRGIN - TITLES.

MARY, BLESSED VIRGIN - NOVENAS. See
NOVENAS - BLESSED VIRGIN MARY.

MARY, BLESSED VIRGIN - OFFICES.
    BQT 1030-1034
 sa Mary, Blessed Virgin - Mediation.
   Mary, Blessed Virgin - Mother-
    hood (Spiritual)

MARY, BLESSED VIRGIN - PAPAL TEACHING.

MARY, BLESSED VIRGIN - PERIODICALS.
    BQT 1001

MARY, BLESSED VIRGIN - POETRY.
    BQT 1085
 sa Rosary - Poetry.
 x Mary, Blessed Virgin, in poetry.
 xx Mary, Blessed Virgin, in
    literature.

MARY, BLESSED VIRGIN - POPULAR WORKS.
    BQT 1007

MARY, BLESSED VIRGIN - PRAYER-BOOKS.
    BQT 2673-2679   (24x3.2)
 sa Franciscan Crown.
   Horae Beatae Mariae Virginis.
   May devotions.
   Missa Beatae Mariae Virginis.
   Officium Parvum Beatae Mariae
    Virginis.
   Rosary.
   also subdivision "Prayer-books"
    under special titles of Mary
    (e.g., Immaculate Heart of
    Mary - Prayer-books) and
    names of Marian devotions
    (e.g., Our Lady of Fatima,
    Devotion to)
 xx Mary, Blessed Virgin - Cultus.

MARY, BLESSED VIRGIN - PRAYER-BOOKS,
ENGLISH, [FRENCH, GERMAN, ETC.]

MARY, BLESSED VIRGIN - PREROGATIVES.
    BQT 1020-1034
 sa Immaculate Conception.
   Mary, Blessed Virgin - Queen-
    ship.
   Mary, Blessed Virgin - Virgin-
    ity.

MARY, BLESSED VIRGIN - PRESENTATION,
FEAST OF THE. See
PRESENTATION OF THE BLESSED VIRGIN
MARY, FEAST OF THE.

MARY, BLESSED VIRGIN - PRIESTHOOD.
    BQT 1034

MARY, BLESSED VIRGIN - PROTESTANT
INTERPRETATIONS.

MARY, BLESSED VIRGIN - PURIFICATION.
    BQT 846
 sa Candlemas.
   Missa in Purificatione Beatae
    Mariae Virginis.
 x Purification of the Blessed
    Virgin Mary.

MARY, BLESSED VIRGIN - QUEENSHIP.
    BQT 1034
 xx Mary, Blessed Virgin -
    Prerogatives.

MARY, BLESSED VIRGIN - ROSARY. See
ROSARY.

MARY, BLESSED VIRGIN - SACRED HEART.
See IMMACULATE HEART OF MARY.

MARY, BLESSED VIRGIN - SERMONS.
    BQT 1049; BQT 3060
    (252.x22)
 sa Litany of Our Lady - Sermons.
   Mary, Blessed Virgin - Bio-
    graphy - Sermons.
   Mary, Blessed Virgin - Cultus -
    Sermons.
   Mary, Blessed Virgin - Feasts -
    Sermons.
   May devotions - Sermons.
   Rosary - Sermons.

MARY, BLESSED VIRGIN - SHRINES.
    BQT 1061-1075   (23x3.61)
 sa names of individual shrines,
    e.g., Fatima, Portugal (Shrine);
    Lourdes (Shrine)
 xx Shrines.

MARY, BLESSED VIRGIN - SINLESSNESS.
    BQT 1022
 x Sinlessness of Our Lady.
 xx Immaculate Conception.

MARY, BLESSED VIRGIN - SODALITIES.
See MARY, BLESSED VIRGIN - CON-
FRATERNITIES.

MARY, BLESSED VIRGIN - SORROWS. See
  SORROWS OF OUR LADY.

MARY, BLESSED VIRGIN - SYMBOLISM.

MARY, BLESSED VIRGIN - THEOLOGY.
     BQT 1012
  sa Mary, Blessed Virgin - History
     of doctrines.
     Mary, Blessed Virgin - Motherhood.

MARY, BLESSED VIRGIN - TITLES.
     BQT 1030-1034; BQT 1079
     BQT 2679 (Devotions)
     BQT 2598 (Meditations)
  sa Help of Christians.
     Star of the sea.
  x Mary, Blessed Virgin - Name.

MARY, BLESSED VIRGIN - TOMB.

MARY, BLESSED VIRGIN - TYPOLOGY.
     BQT 1043
  xx Typology (Theology)

MARY, BLESSED VIRGIN - VENERATION. See
  MARY, BLESSED VIRGIN - CULTUS.

MARY, BLESSED VIRGIN - VIRGINITY.
     BQT 1027   (23x3.4)
  sa Jesus Christ - Brethren.
  xx Mary, Blessed Virgin - Pre-
     rogatives.
     Virgin birth.

MARY, BLESSED VIRGIN - VISITATION.
  See VISITATION FESTIVAL.

MARY, BLESSED VIRGIN - WORDS.

MARY, BLESSED VIRGIN - YEARBOOKS.
     BQT 1001

MARY, BLESSED VIRGIN, AND EDUCATION.

MARY, BLESSED VIRGIN, AND MISSIONS.
     BQT 1093

MARY, BLESSED VIRGIN, AND RELIGIOUS
  ORDERS.
     BQT 1093
  x Religious orders - Mary, Blessed
     Virgin.

MARY, BLESSED VIRGIN, AND RELIGIOUS
  ORDERS - BENEDICTINES, [FRANCIS-
  CANS, ETC.]

MARY, BLESSED VIRGIN, AND THE CHURCH.
     BQT 1034

MARY, BLESSED VIRGIN, HOURS OF THE.
  See HORAE BEATAE MARIAE VIRGINIS.

MARY, BLESSED VIRGIN, IN ART. See
  MARY, BLESSED VIRGIN - ART.

MARY, BLESSED VIRGIN, IN LITERATURE.
     BQT 1083-1089
  sa Mary, Blessed Virgin - Drama.
     Mary, Blessed Virgin - Fiction.
     Mary, Blessed Virgin - Poetry.
  xx Religion in literature.

MARY, BLESSED VIRGIN, IN MUSIC.
     BQT 1093
  x Mary, Blessed Virgin - Music.

MARY, BLESSED VIRGIN, IN POETRY. See
  MARY, BLESSED VIRGIN - POETRY.

MARY, BLESSED VIRGIN, IN THE LITURGY.
  sa Assumption - Liturgy.
  x Liturgy - Mary, Blessed Virgin.
  xx Mary, Blessed Virgin - Cultus.

MARY, BLESSED VIRGIN, LITTLE OFFICE
  OF THE. See
  OFFICIUM PARVUM BEATAE MARIAE VIRGINIS.

MARY, BLESSED VIRGIN, MASS OF THE. See
  MISSA BEATAE MARIAE VIRGINIS.

MASONS (SECRET ORDER). See
  FREEMASONS.

MASS. See Eucharist
     BQT 1318-1336 (Theology)
     (23x7.31)
     BQT 4071-4079; BQT 4154-4167
     (Liturgy)   (264.x61)
  Here are entered works on the
     Eucharist considered as a sacri-
     fice. Cf. note under Eucharist.
  sa Communion, Holy.
     Consecration at mass.
     Eucharist.

MASS -- Continued.
  sa Introits.
     Missale.
     Prefaces (Liturgy)
     Propers.
     Sacrifice.
     Transubstantiation.
  x Eucharistic liturgy.
     Mass (Liturgy)
     Sacrifice of the mass.
  xx Communion, Holy.
     Dogmatic theology.
     Eucharist.
     Jesus Christ.
     Liturgy.
     Sacraments (Liturgy)
     Transubstantiation.

MASS - ADDRESSES, ESSAYS, LECTURES.

MASS - BIBLIOGRAPHY.
     BQT 1318

MASS - CANON. See
  CANON OF THE MASS.

MASS - CATECHISMS, QUESTION-BOOKS.
     BQT 3197

MASS - CELEBRATION.
    [BQT 4334.5]
     BQV230 820-823   (348.x42)
  Here are entered works on the
    place, time, and other circum-
    stances for celebrating Mass.
    For works regulating the actions
    and words at Mass see Mass -
    Rites and ceremonies.
  sa Bination.
     Concelebration.

MASS - CEREMONIES. See
  MASS - RITES AND CEREMONIES.

MASS - CONTROVERSIAL LITERATURE.

MASS - DRAMA.

MASS - EARLY WORKS TO 1800.

MASS - FILMSTRIPS.

MASS - HISTORY.
     BQT 4154-4161   (264.x61)

MASS - HISTORY - EARLY CHURCH.
     BQT 4156

MASS - HISTORY - MIDDLE AGES.
     BQT 4161

MASS - HISTORY - MODERN PERIOD.

MASS - HISTORY - 16th, [17th,
  etc.] CENTURY.

MASS - INSTRUCTION AND STUDY.
     BQT 3197
  x Mass - Manuals of instruction.

MASS - JUVENILE LITERATURE.
     BQT 1320

MASS - MANUALS OF INSTRUCTION. See
  MASS - INSTRUCTION AND STUDY.

MASS - MEDITATIONS.
     BQT 2589

MASS - MUSIC.
  sa Graduale.
     Kyriale.
     Masses.
     Offertories.
     Sequences (Liturgy)

MASS - PARTICIPATION.
  xx Liturgy - Participation.

MASS - PICTURES, ILLUSTRATIONS, ETC.

MASS - POETRY.

MASS - POPULAR WORKS.
     BQT 1320

MASS - PRAYER-BOOKS.
     BQT 2669
  sa Missals.
     Prayers before and after
      Mass.

MASS - PRAYER-BOOKS, ENGLISH,
  [FRENCH, GERMAN, ETC.]

MASS - RITES AND CEREMONIES.
    BQT 4331-4351 (264.x61)
 sa High Mass - Rites and cere-
    monies.
   Low Mass - Rites and cere-
    monies.
   Pontifical Mass - Rites and
    ceremonies.
  x Mass - Ceremonies.
   Mass - Rubrics.
   Mass (Liturgy)
   Missale - Rubrics.

MASS - RUBRICS. See
 MASS - RITES AND CEREMONIES.

MASS - SERMONS.
    BQT 1320 (252.x54)
 sa Eucharist - Sermons.

MASS - STUDY AND TEACHING.
    BQT 4165

MASS - SYMBOLISM.
    BQT 4167

    ################

MASS - AMBROSIAN RITE. See
 AMBROSIAN RITE - MASS.

MASS - BYZANTINE RITE. See
 BYZANTINE RITE. LITURGY AND
 RITUAL - DIVINE LITURGY.

MASS - MARONITE RITE. See
 MARONITE RITE. LITURGY AND
 RITUAL - MASS.

MASS - MOZARABIC RITE. See
 MOZARABIC RITE - MASS.

    ################

MASS (CANON LAW)
    BQV230 802-844 (348.x42)
 sa Celebret.
   Church attendance (Canon law)
   Eucharist (Canon law)
   Mass intentions.
   Mass stipends.
 xx Eucharist (Canon law)

MASS (LITURGY) See
 MASS.
 MASS - RITES AND CEREMONIES.

MASS (MUSIC)
 sa Organ mass.

MASS, CONSECRATION AT. See
 CONSECRATION AT MASS.

MASS, CONVENTUAL.
 "The daily community Mass which
  must be said or sung in all
  conventual churches of regulars
  who are bound to the public
  recitation of the Divine Office."
  AT
 x Conventual mass.
 xx Divine office.
   Religious orders.

MASS, DIALOGUE.
    BQT 4163
 x Dialogue mass.
   Missa recitata.

MASS, EVENING.
 x Evening mass.

MASS, EVENING (CANON LAW)
    BQV230 821

MASS, FOUNDATION. See
 FOUNDATION MASS.

MASS, GREGORIAN. See
 GREGORIAN MASS.

MASS, HIGH. See HIGH MASS.

MASS, LOW. See LOW MASS.

MASS, NUPTIAL.
    BQT 4453
 sa Missa pro Sponso et Sponsa.
 x Nuptial mass.
   Wedding mass.

MASS, NUPTIAL (CANON LAW)

MASS, PAPAL.
 x Papal mass.

MASS, PONTIFICAL. See
  PONTIFICAL MASS.

MASS, PRIVATE. See LOW MASS.

MASS, RED. See RED MASS.

MASS, REQUIEM.
      BQT 4456
  sa Missa pro defunctis.
   x Black mass.
     Dead, Mass for the.
     Mass for the dead.
     Requiem mass.

MASS, VOTIVE. See VOTIVE MASS.

MASS FACING THE PEOPLE.
      [BQT 4332.5]

MASS FOR THE DEAD. See
  MASS, REQUIEM.

MASS FOR THE PEOPLE.
      BQV230 466   (348.x36)
  "A mass which canon law requires
     to be applied by pastors for
     the faithful under their care."
     AT
   x Missa pro populo.
  xx Mass intentions.
     Pastors.

MASS INTENTIONS.
      BQV230 809   (348.x42)
  sa Foundation mass.
     Gregorian mass.
     Mass for the people.
   x Intentions, Mass.
  xx Mass (Canon law)

MASS OF ...
  Texts for single masses in honor
     of Our Lord, the Blessed Virgin
     Mary, the saints, etc., are
     entered under the Latin form
     "Missa ..."

MASS OF ALL SOULS' DAY. See
  MISSA IN COMMEMORATIONE OMNIUM
  FIDELIUM DEFUNCTORUM.

MASS OF JESUS CHRIST THE KING. See
  MISSA DOMINI NOSTRI JESU CHRISTI
  REGIS.

MASS OF OUR LADY, HELP OF CHRISTIANS.
  See MISSA BEATAE MARIAE VIRGINIS
  AUXILIUM CHRISTIANORUM.

MASS OF OUR LADY OF GUADALUPE, [OF
  MOUNT CARMEL, OF PERPETUAL HELP,
  ETC.]. See MISSA BEATAE MARIAE
  VIRGINIS DE GUADALUPE, [DE MONTE
  CARMELO, DE PERPETUO SUCCURSU,
  ETC.]

MASS OF OUR LADY OF LOURDES. See
  MISSA DE APPARITIONE BEATAE MARIAE
  VIRGINIS IMMACULATAE.

MASS OF OUR LADY OF THE MIRACULOUS
  MEDAL. See MISSA BEATAE MARIAE
  VIRGINIS IMMACULATAE A SACRO
  NUMISMATE.

MASS OF OUR LADY OF THE SACRED HEART.
  See MISSA BEATAE MARIAE VIRGINIS
  A SACRO CORDE JESU.

MASS OF SAINT AGNES, [BARBARA,
  CECILIA, ETC.]. See MISSA SANCTAE
  AGNETIS, [BARBARAE, CAECILIAE,
  ETC.]

MASS OF SAINT ANTHONY OF PADUA,
  [BENEDICT, COSMAS AND DAMIAN, ETC.].
  See MISSA SANCTI ANTONII DE PADUA,
  [BENEDICTI, COSMAE ET DAMIANI, ETC.]

MASS OF THE ANNUNCIATION. See
  MISSA IN ANNUNTIATIONE BEATAE
  MARIAE VIRGINIS.

MASS OF THE ASSUMPTION. See
  MISSA IN ASSUMPTIONE BEATAE
  MARIAE VIRGINIS.

MASS OF THE BLESSED SACRAMENT. See
  MISSA DE SANCTISSIMO EUCHARISTIAE
  SACRAMENTO.

MASS OF THE CATECHUMENS.
    BQT 4074
Here are entered works dealing
    with the part of the Mass from
    the beginning to the offertory.
    In the early centuries of
    Christianity the catechumens
    attended only this part of the
    Mass.
x Catechumens, Mass of the.

MASS OF THE FAITHFUL.
    BQT 4075
"That part of the Mass from the
    offertory to the end, the
    sacrifice proper ..." AT
sa Canon of the mass.
    Ordinarium Missae.

MASS OF THE FINDING OF THE CROSS.
See MISSA IN INVENTIONE SANCTAE
CRUCIS.

MASS OF THE FIVE WOUNDS. See
    MISSA SACRORUM QUINQUE VULNERUM.

MASS OF THE HOLY CROSS. See
    MISSA DE SANCTA CRUCE.

MASS OF THE HOLY SPIRIT. See
    MISSA DE SPIRITU SANCTO.

MASS OF THE IMMACULATE CONCEPTION.
    See MISSA IN CONCEPTIONE IMMACU-
    LATA BEATAE MARIAE VIRGINIS.

MASS OF THE IMMACULATE HEART OF MARY.
    See MISSA IMMACULATI CORDIS BEATAE
    MARIAE VIRGINIS.

MASS OF THE MATERNITY OF THE BLESSED
    VIRGIN MARY. See MISSA MATERNITA-
    TIS BEATAE MARIAE VIRGINIS.

MASS OF THE PASSION OF JESUS CHRIST.
    See MISSA PASSIONIS DOMINI NOSTRI
    JESU CHRISTI.

MASS OF THE PRECIOUS BLOOD. See
    MISSA PRETIOSISSIMI SANGUINIS
    DOMINI NOSTRI JESU CHRISTI.

MASS OF THE PRESANCTIFIED. See
    GOOD FRIDAY.

MASS OF THE PURIFICATION. See
    MISSA IN PURIFICATIONE BEATAE
    MARIAE VIRGINIS.

MASS OF THE SACRED HEART. See
    MISSA SACRATISSIMI CORDIS JESU.

MASS OF THE SEVEN DOLORS OF MARY.
    See MISSA SEPTEM DOLORUM BEATAE
    MARIAE VIRGINIS.

MASS OF THE TRANSFIGURATION. See
    MISSA IN TRANSFIGURATIONE DOMINI
    NOSTRI JESU CHRISTI.

MASS OF THE VISITATION OF OUR LADY.
    See MISSA IN VISITATIONE BEATAE
    MARIAE VIRGINIS.

MASS STIPENDS.
    BQV230 824-844   (348.x42)
x Stipends, Mass.
xx Fees, Ecclesiastical.
    Mass (Canon law)
    Offerings.

MASS WINE. See
    WINE - LITURGICAL USE.

MASSACRE OF THE INNOCENTS. See
    HOLY INNOCENTS, MASSACRE OF THE.

MASSALIANS. See MESSALIANS.

MASS-BOOK. See MISSALE.

MASSES.
    M 2010-2017
sa Propers (Music)
    Requiems.
x Ordinarium Missae (Music)
xx Mass - Music.
    Sacred vocal music.
    Other subdivisions as in LC.

MASSES, INSTRUMENTAL. See
    ORGAN MASSES.

MASSES, ORGAN. See ORGAN MASSES.

MASSES (UNISON)
    M 2011

MASTER OF CEREMONIES.

MASTER OF CEREMONIES - HANDBOOKS,
  MANUALS, ETC.
    BQT 4344
    xx Rites and ceremonies (Catholic) -
       Handbooks, manuals, etc.

MASTER OF NOVICES.
    BQT 2327
  "A novice master or mistress is
  an experienced religious
  appointed by the superior of
  a monastery or institute, to
  supervise the training of the
  novices." AT
  x Mistress of novices.
    Novice masters.
    Novice mistresses.
  xx Novitiate.
    Superiors, Religious.

MASTER OF NOVICES (CANON LAW)
    BQV230 559
  xx Superiors, Religious (Canon
    law)

MATER ECCLESIA. See
  CHURCH - MOTHERHOOD.

MATERIALISM. (Philosophic theory)
    BD 331 (Metaphysics)
    B 825 (Philosophic systems,
      General)   (146)
    B 851-4695 (Philosophic
      systems, Special, local)
  Here are entered works dealing
  with the philosophical theory
  that we can know nothing but
  matter and that the human mind
  is but a function of an organized material substance.
  sa Dualism.
    Idealism.
    Monism.
    Realism.

MATERIALISM -- Continued.
  xx Animism.
    Dualism.
    Idealism.
    Monism.
    Philosophy.
    Positivism.
    Realism.

MATERIALISM (THEOLOGY)
    [BQT 123]
  Here are entered works dealing
  with the views and practices
  which stress material values
  over against spiritual values,
  seeking material development
  and comfort in a measure in-
  compatible with the moderated
  detachment from physical
  things as taught by Christianity.
  sa Secularism.
    Spirituality.
  xx Secularism.
    Wealth, Ethics of.
  x Consumerism

MATERIALISM (THEOLOGY) - SERMONS.
    BQT 3089

MATINS.
    BQT 4175
  sa Invitatorium.
    Matutinale.
  xx Divine office.
    Vigils (Liturgy)

MATRIMONIAL ACTIONS (CANON LAW)
  sa Defender of the marriage bond.
    Divorce suits (Canon law)
    Marriage - Annulment (Canon law)
    Separation (Canon law)
  xx Civil procedure (Canon law)
    Marriage (Canon law)

MATRIMONY. See MARRIAGE.

MATTHEW, SAINT, GOSPEL OF. See
  BIBLE. N.T. MATTHEW.

MATUTINALE.
     BQT 4265; BQT 4380
A liturgical book containing the
  prayers and readings for Matins.
  x Horae Matutinales.
  xx Breviarium.
     Matins.

MAUNDY THURSDAY.
     BQT 916; BQT 4223   (264.x52)
  sa Mandatum.
  x Holy Thursday.
  xx Holy Week.

MAURISTS. See
  BENEDICTINES. CONGREGATIONS. ST.
  MAUR.

MAY DEVOTIONS.
     BQT 2675; BQT 4495   (24x8.72)
  x Mary, Blessed Virgin - May
     devotions.
  xx Devotions, Popular.
     Mary, Blessed Virgin - Prayer-
     books.

MAY DEVOTIONS - PAPAL TEACHING.

MAY DEVOTIONS - SERMONS.
     BQT 3060
  xx Mary, Blessed Virgin - Sermons.

MECHITARISTS.
     BQX 5709
  x Benedictines, Mechitarist.
  xx Benedictines.

MEDAL OF ST. BENEDICT.
     BQT 4522
  x Benedict, Saint, Medal of.
  xx Medals, Devotional.

MEDALS, DEVOTIONAL.
     BQT 4522 (Sacramentals)
     BQT 6028 (Christian art)
  sa Medal of St. Benedict.
     Miraculous Medal.
  x Devotional medals.
     Medals, Religious.
     Religious medals.

MEDALS, RELIGIOUS. See
  MEDALS, DEVOTIONAL.

MEDICAL MISSIONS. See
  MISSIONS, MEDICAL.

MEDICINE, CLERICAL. See
  PASTORAL MEDICINE.

MEDICINE, PASTORAL. See
  PASTORAL MEDICINE.

MEDICINE AND CANON LAW. See
  CANON LAW AND MEDICINE.

MEDICINE AND RELIGION.
     BQT 3493; BL 65
  sa Psychiatry and religion.
  x Religion and medicine.
  xx Pastoral medicine.

MEDICINE AND RELIGION - PAPAL
  TEACHING.

MEDIEVAL SECTS. See
  SECTS, MEDIEVAL.

✓MEDITATION.
     BQT 2259-2264   (24x7.11)
  "Here are entered works on the
     nature of meditation or mental
     prayer as a form and method of
     promoting the spiritual life.
     For works that contain solely
     meditations see Meditations."
  LC
  sa Contemplation.

  xx Prayer, Mental.

MEDITATION (BUDDHISM)
     BL 1478.6

MEDITATION (HINDUISM)

✓MEDITATIONS.
     BQT 2514-2610   (24x2)
  "Here are entered works containing
     thoughts or reflections on spir-
     itual truths. Meditations in-
     tended for use in 'spiritual
     exercises' or 'retreats' receive
     the additional subject entry
     Retreats. For works on the nature
     of meditation see Meditation."
  LC

MEDITATIONS -- Continued.
  sa Devotional literature (Daily
    readings)
    Retreats.
    also subdivision "Meditations"
     under such entries as Eucha-
     rist, Jesus Christ - Passion,
     Priests, etc.
  xx Devotional literature.

MEDITATIONS, ENGLISH, [FRENCH,
  GERMAN, ETC.]
    [BQT 2534-2544]

MEDITATIONS, ENGLISH, FRENCH,
  GERMAN, ETC.] - TRANSLATIONS FROM
  FRENCH, [GERMAN, LATIN, ETC.]

MEDITATIONS, ENGLISH, FRENCH,
  GERMAN, ETC.] - TRANSLATIONS INTO
  FRENCH, [GERMAN, ITALIAN, ETC.]

MEDIUMS.
    BV 1281
  References as in LC supplement
  1956-58.

MEETING-HOUSES, FRIEND. See
  CHURCHES, FRIEND.

MELCHISEDECHIANS.
    [BQT 49]
  xx Heresies and heretics - Early
    church.
    Trinity - History of doctrines.

MELKITE RITE. See
  BYZANTINE RITE, MELKITE.

MEMORIAL OF RITES. See
  MEMORIALE RITUUM.

MEMORIALE RITUUM.
    BQT 4435
  "A liturgical book compiled by
  Pope Benedict XIII in 1725 for
  use in parish churches wherein,
  on account of lack of sacred
  ministers, certain ceremonies
  cannot be carried out according
  to the rubrics: namely, those
  of Candlemas, Ash Wednesday,
  Palm Sunday and the last three
  days of holy week." AT
  x Memorial of Rites.

MEMRA (THE WORD)
  xx God - Name.
    Logos.

MEN - PRAYER-BOOKS.
    BQT 2637

MEN - PRAYER-BOOKS - ENGLISH,
  [FRENCH, GERMAN, ETC.]

MEN - RELIGIOUS LIFE.
    BQT 2283
  sa Retreats for men.

MEN - SERMONS.
    BQT 3015

MEN IN CHURCH WORK.
  sa Church work with men.
  xx Church work with men.
    Laity.

MENAION.
    BQT 5253
  "A liturgical book of the Byzantine
  rite in 12 or 6 volumes, one for
  each month or two months, beginning with September. It contains the proper parts of the
  Divine Office for all immovable
  feasts." AT

MENDICANT ORDERS.
    BQX 6821; BQX 6838   (271)
  "The name includes not only
  Dominicans, Franciscans, Carmelites and Augustinians, but is
  now also accorded to Trinitarians,
  Mercedarians, Servites, Hierony-
  mites, Minims, Brothers of St.
  John-of-God, and Order of Penance."
  AT
  sa Friars.
    Religious orders.
  xx Religious orders.

MENNONITES.
    BX 8101-8143   (289.7)
  References and subdivisions as
  in LC.

MENOLOGION.
    BQT 5242
  A liturgical book of the Byzantine
  Rite, containing the lives of

MENOLOGION -- Continued.
    the saints in their daily order
    throughout the year.
    xx Martyrologium.

MENSURATION IN THE BIBLE.
    x Bible - Mensuration.

MENTAL ILLNESS (CANON LAW)
    sa Insanity (Canon law)

MENTAL PRAYER. See
    PRAYER, MENTAL.

MENTALLY HANDICAPPED CHILDREN,
    CHURCH WORK WITH. See
    CHURCH WORK WITH MENTALLY HANDI-
    CAPPED CHILDREN.

MERCERSBURG THEOLOGY.
        BX 9571
    References as in LC.

MERCHANT SEAMEN - CHARITIES. See
    MERCHANT SEAMEN - MISSIONS AND
    CHARITIES.

MERCHANT SEAMEN - MISSIONS AND
    CHARITIES.
        BQT 3282-3289
        BQT 3668-3699 (Charities)
    x Merchant seamen - Charities.
    Missions, Seamen's.
    Seamen's missions.
    xx Charities.

MERCY.
        BQT 1793
    xx Kindness.

MERCY - SERMONS.
        BQT 3089

MERCY OF GOD. See
    GOD - MERCY.

MERCY SEAT. See
    ARK OF THE COVENANT.

MERIT (JEWISH THEOLOGY)
        BM 645
    References as in LC supplement
    1959-60.

MERIT (THEOLOGY)
        BQT 1193   (234.13)
    Here are entered works on the
    right to reward, which by divine
    ordinance is due to a good and
    supernatural work done for
    God's sake.
    sa Reward (Theology)
    xx Grace (Theology)
    Reward (Theology)

MESSALIANS.
        BQT 50   (273.x2)
    x Adelphians.
    Enthusiasts (Messalians)
    Euchites.
    Lampetians.
    Marcianites.
    Massalians.
    xx Asceticism - History - Early
    church.
    Dogmatic theology - History -
    Early church.
    Heresies and heretics - Early
    church.
    Mysticism - History - Early
    church.
    Prayer - History.

MESSIAH.
        BL 475 (Comparative religion)
        (291.61)
        BQT 744-746 (Theology)
        BM 615 (Judaism)
    sa Jesus Christ.
    Messianic era (Judaism)
    Pseudo-Messiahs.
    xx Jesus Christ - Messiahship.
    Judaism.

MESSIAH - ART.
        BQT 5876

MESSIAH - COMPARATIVE STUDIES.
        BL 475

MESSIAH - LEGENDS.
    xx Messianic era (Judaism)

MESSIAH - PROPHECIES.
        BQT 746
    x Bible - Prophecies - Messiah.
    xx Prophecies.

MESSIAH - SERMONS.

MESSIAHS, FALSE. See
  PSEUDO-MESSIAHS.

MESSIANIC ERA (JUDAISM)
  sa Messiah - Legends.
  xx Eschatology, Jewish.
     Jews - Restoration.
     Messiah

MESSIANIC PSALMS. See
  BIBLE. O.T. PSALMS, MESSIANIC.

METAMORPHOSIS (IN RELIGION,
  FOLKLORE, ETC.)
       BL 325.M
  References as in LC.

METHODISM.
       BX 8201-8495
  xx Dissenters.

METHODIST CHURCH.
       BX 8201-8495
  sa Love feasts.
  Subdivisions as in LC.

METHODIST CHURCHES. See
  CHURCHES, METHODIST.

METHODIST EPISCOPAL CHURCH.
       BX 8380-8389   (287.6)
  Subdivisions as in LC.

METHODIST EPISCOPAL CHURCH, SOUTH.
       BX 8390-8399

METHODISTS.
       BX 8201-8495

METHODISTS, GERMAN, [SWEDISH, ETC.]

METHODISTS, NEGRO.
       BX 8435-8473
  References as in LC.

METHODISTS IN GERMANY, [MARYLAND,
  THE U.S., ETC.]

MEXICO - CHURCH HISTORY.
       BQX 4171-4247   (277.2)

MEXICO - CHURCH HISTORY - EARLY
  PERIOD TO 1821.

MEXICO - CHURCH HISTORY - 1821-

MEXICO - CHURCH HISTORY - 20th
  CENTURY.

MEXICO - RELIGION.

MICAH, BOOK OF. See
  BIBLE. O.T. MICHEAS.

MICHEAS, BOOK OF. See
  BIBLE. O.T. MICHEAS.

MIDRASH.
       BM 511-518
  References as in LC.

MID-WEEK SERVICES. See
  CHURCH-NIGHT SERVICES.

MIGRANTS, CHURCH WORK WITH. See
  CHURCH WORK WITH MIGRANTS.

MILITARY CHAPLAINS. See
  CHAPLAINS, MILITARY.

MILITARY ORDINARIATE.
  x Military vicariate.

MILITARY ORDINARIATE (CANADA)
       BQX 4161

MILITARY ORDINARIATE (NETHERLANDS)
       BQX 2334

MILITARY ORDINARIATE (U.S.)
       BQX 4583

MILITARY RELIGIOUS ORDERS.
       BQX 663
       BQX 6838
  sa Hospitallers.
     Knights of Malta.
     Templars.
     Teutonic Knights.
   x Religious orders, Military.
  xx Crusades.
     Religious orders.

MILITARY RELIGIOUS ORDERS - INSIGNIA.
CR 4653; CR 4705

MILITARY VICARIATE. See
MILITARY ORDINARIATE.

MILLENIUM.
BQT 51; BQT 1471 (236.x95)
sa Second advent.
x Chiliasm.
xx Eschatology.
Future life.
Jesus Christ.
Second advent.

MILLENIUM - HISTORY OF DOCTRINES.

MINISTER OF A SACRAMENT. See
SACRAMENTS - MINISTER.

MINISTERS AS AUTHORS. See
CLERGYMEN AS AUTHORS.

MINISTERS OF THE GOSPEL. See
CLERGY.

MINISTRY. ~~See~~
xx CLERGY.
xx PASTORAL THEOLOGY.

MINISTRY, COUNTRY. See
RURAL CLERGY.

Ministry to the sick
x Sick, Church work with
Church work with the sick

MINISTRY, URBAN. See
CITY CLERGY.

MINOR BASILICAS.
xx Basilicas.

MINOR CANONS, CATHEDRAL, COLLEGIATE, ETC.
A vicar choral is "a clerical or lay assistant in the choir or a cathedral or collegiate church. The title seems to be now extinct in the Catholic Church."
AT
x Canons, Minor.
Choral vicars.
Priest vicars.
Vicars, Priest.
Vicars choral.

MINOR CANONS, CATHEDRAL, COLLEGIATE, ETC. -- Continued.
xx Cathedrals.
Chapters, Cathedral, collegiate, etc.
Clergy.

MINOR ORDERS.
BQT 358; BQT 1413 (23x7.6)
sa Ordination.
x Acolytes (Holy order)
Door-keepers (Holy order)
Exorcists (Holy order)
Lectors (Holy order)
Orders, Minor.
Ostiaries (Holy order)
xx Clergy.
Ordination.

MINOR PROPHETS. See
BIBLE. O.T. MINOR PROPHETS.

MINOR SEMINARIES. See
THEOLOGICAL SEMINARIES, MINOR.

MINORESSES. See POOR CLARES.

MINORITES. See FRANCISCANS.

MINORS (CANON LAW)
x Children (Canon law)
xx Parent and child (Canon law)
Marriage (Canon law)

MIRACLE-PLAYS. See
MYSTERIES AND MIRACLE-PLAYS.

MIRACLES.
BQT 556 (Theology)
(23x9.12)
BQT 2483 (Mysticism)
sa Eucharist - Miracles.
Holy wells.
Jesus Christ - Miracles.
Mary, Blessed Virgin - Apparitions and miracles.
Revelation.
Shrines.
Stigmatization.
Supernatural.
also individual miracles, e.g., Healing of the man born blind (Miracle); Healing of the nobleman's son (Miracle)

280

MIRACLES -- Continued.
  x ~~Bible - Miracles.~~
    ~~Divine healing.~~
  xx Apparitions.
    Christianity.
    Church history.
    Faith-cure.
    Mysticism.
    Psychology, Religious.
    Relics and reliquaries.
    Shrines.
    Supernatural.

MIRACLES OF CHRIST. See
  JESUS CHRIST - MIRACLES.

MIRACULOUS MEDAL.
    [BQT 1093]
  sa Missa Beatae Mariae Virginis
    Immaculatae a Sacro Numismate.
  x Medal, Miraculous.
  xx Medals, Devotional.

MISCEGENATION.
    GN 237
    E 185.62 (Negroes in the U.S.)
    "Here are entered works on marriage
    between persons of different
    races, especially between whites
    and Negroes in the United States,
    and on the resulting mixture of
    hybridity." LC
  sa Marriage, Mixed.
  x Interracial marriage.
    Marriage, Interracial.
  Other references as in LC.

MISERERE MEI, DEUS. See
  BIBLE. O.T. PSALMS L.

MISERERE MEI, DEUS (MUSIC). See
  PSALMS (MUSIC) - 50th PSALM.

MISERERE MEI, DEUS, MISERERI
  MEI (MUSIC). See
  PSALMS (MUSIC) - 56th PSALM.

MISSA ...
  Texts for single masses in honor
    of Our Lord, the Blessed Virgin
    Mary, the saints, etc., are
    entered under the heading be-

MISSA ... -- Continued.
    ginning with Missa, as seen in
    the entries immediately follow-
    ing.
    Commentaries on such single masses
    are entered under the same
    heading.

MISSA BEATAE MARIAE VIRGINIS.
    BQT 4321
  x Mary, Blessed Virgin, Mass
    of the.
  xx Mary, Blessed Virgin - Prayer-
    books.

MISSA BEATAE MARIAE VIRGINIS A SACRO
  CORDE JESU.
    BQT 4321
  x Mass of Our Lady of the Sacred
    Heart.
    Our Lady of the Sacred Heart,
    Mass of.

MISSA BEATAE MARIAE VIRGINIS
  AUXILIUM CHRISTIANORUM.
    BQT 4321
  x Mass of Our Lady, Help of
    Christians.
  xx Help of Christians.

MISSA BEATAE MARIAE VIRGINIS DE
  GUADALUPE, [DE MONTE CARMELO,
  DE PERPETUO SUCCURSU, ETC.]
    BQT 4321
  x Mass of Our Lady of Guadalupe,
    [of Mount Carmel, of Perpetual
    Help, etc.]

MISSA BEATAE MARIAE VIRGINIS
  IMMACULATAE A SACRO NUMISMATE.
    BQT 4321
  x Mass of Our Lady of the Miracu-
    lous Medal.
  xx Miraculous Medal.

MISSA DE APPARITIONE BEATAE MARIAE
  VIRGINIS IMMACULATAE.
    BQT 4321
  x Mass of Our Lady of Lourdes.
    Our Lady of Lourdes, Mass of.

MISSA DE SANCTA CRUCE.
    [BQT 4320]
    x Holy Cross, Mass of the.
    Mass of the Holy Cross.

MISSA DE SANCTISSIMO EUCHARISTIAE
   SACRAMENTO.
    [BQT 4320]
    x Blessed Sacrament, Mass of the.
    Mass of the Blessed Sacrament.
   xx Eucharist - Prayer-books.

MISSA DE SPIRITU SANCTO.
    BQT 4328
    x Mass of the Holy Spirit.
   xx Holy Spirit - Prayer-books.

MISSA DOMINI NOSTRI JESU CHRISTI
   REGIS.
    [BQT 4320]
    x Jesus Christ the King, Mass of.
    Mass of Jesus Christ the King.

MISSA IMMACULATI CORDIS BEATAE
   MARIAE VIRGINIS.
    BQT 4321
    x Immaculate Heart of Mary, Mass
      of the.
    Mass of the Immaculate Heart
      of Mary.

MISSA IN ANNUNTIATIONE BEATAE
   MARIAE VIRGINIS.
    BQT 4321
    x Annunciation, Mass of the.
    Mass of the Annunciation.

MISSA IN ASSUMPTIONE BEATAE MARIAE
   VIRGINIS.
    BQT 4321
    x Assumption, Mass of the.
    Mass of the Assumption.

MISSA IN COMMEMORATIONE OMNIUM
   FIDELIUM DEFUNCTORUM.
    BQT 4322
    x All Souls' Day Mass.
    Mass of All Souls' Day.

MISSA IN CONCEPTIONE IMMACULATA
   BEATAE MARIAE VIRGINIS.
    BQT 4321
    x Immaculate Conception, Mass
      of the.
    Mass of the Immaculate Con-
      ception.

MISSA IN INVENTIONE SANCTAE CRUCIS.
    [BQT 4320]
    x Mass of the Finding of the Cross.
   xx Cross, Finding of the.

MISSA IN NATIVITATE DOMINI NOSTRI
   JESU CHRISTI.
    [BQT 4320]
    x Christmas Mass.

MISSA IN PURIFICATIONE BEATAE
   MARIAE VIRGINIS.
    BQT 4321
    x Mass of the Purification.
   xx Candlemas.
    Mary, Blessed Virgin - Purifi-
      cation.

MISSA IN SABBATO SANCTO.
    BQT 4326
   Here are entered some older texts
    of the Holy Saturday Mass.
    x Holy Saturday Mass.
   xx Ordo Sabbati Sancti.

MISSA IN TRANSFIGURATIONE DOMINI
   NOSTRI JESU CHRISTI.
    [BQT 4320]
    x Mass of the Transfiguration.
   xx Jesus Christ - Transfiguration.

MISSA IN VISITATIONE BEATAE MARIAE
   VIRGINIS.
    BQT 4321
    x Mass of the Visitation of Our
      Lady.
   xx Visitation Festival.

MISSA MATERNITATIS BEATAE MARIAE
   VIRGINIS.
    BQT 4321
    x Mass of the Maternity of the
      Blessed Virgin.
   xx Mary, Blessed Virgin - Prayer-
      books.

MISSA PASSIONIS DOMINI NOSTRI JESU
   CHRISTI.
    [BQT 4320]
    x Mass of the Passion of Jesus
      Christ.
   xx Jesus Christ - Passion -
      Prayer-books.

MISSA PRETIOSISSIMI SANGUINIS DOMINI
  NOSTRI JESU CHRISTI.
        [BQT 4320]
    x Mass of the Precious Blood.
      Precious Blood, Mass of the.

MISSA PRO DEFUNCTIS.
        BQT 4322
    xx Mass, Requiem.
       Missale.
       Prayers for the dead.

MISSA PRO POPULO. See
  MASS FOR THE PEOPLE.

MISSA PRO SPONSO ET SPONSA.
        BQT 4324
    x Wedding Mass.
    xx Mass, Nuptial.

MISSA RECITATA. See
  MASS, DIALOGUE.

MISSA SACRATISSIMI CORDIS JESU.
        [BQT 4320]
    x Mass of the Sacred Heart.
      Sacred Heart, Mass of the.

MISSA SACRORUM QUINQUE VULNERUM.
        [BQT 4320]
    x Mass of the Five Wounds.
    xx Five Wounds, Devotion to.

MISSA SANCTAE AGNETIS, [BARBARAE,
  CAECILIAE, ETC.]
        BQT 4328
    x Mass of Saint Agnes, [Barbara,
      Cecilia, etc.]

MISSA SANCTI ANTONII DE PADUA,
  [BENEDICTI, COSMAE ET DAMIANI,
  ETC.]
        BQT 4328
    x Mass of Saint Anthony of Padua,
      [Benedict, Cosmas and Damian,
      etc.]

MISSA SEPTEM DOLORUM BEATAE MARIAE
  VIRGINIS.
        BQT 4321
    x Mass of the Seven Dolors of
      Mary.
      Sorrows of Our Lady, Mass of
      the.

MISSALE.
        BQT 4245; BQT 4291-4328
          (26x5.1)
    "The liturgical book which contains
      all the prayers necessary to
      enable a priest to celebrate
      Mass throughout the year; each
      use of the Latin Rite has its own
      proper Missal, the 'Missale roma-
      num' being easily the most widely
      used." AT
    Cf. note under Missals.
    sa Commune sanctorum.
       Ordinarium Missae.
       Sacramentarium.
       also entries beginning with
         Missa.
     x Mass-book.
    xx Mass.

MISSALE - ART.
        ND 3375

MISSALE - BIBLIOGRAPHY.

MISSALE - COMMENTARIES.
        BQT 4166

MISSALE - HISTORY.
        [BQT 4329]

MISSALE - MANUSCRIPTS.
        Z 113Z

MISSALE - MANUSCRIPTS - FACSIMILES.

MISSALE - MEDITATIONS.
        BQT 2606

MISSALE - RUBRICS. See
  MASS - RITES AND CEREMONIES.

        ################

MISSALE. BENEDICTINE, [CARMELITE,
  DOMINICAN, ETC.]
        BQT 4700-4907

        ################

MISSALE AMBROSIANUM.
        BQT 4913
    xx Ambrosian Rite - Mass.

MISSALE PLENARIUM.
   BQT 4245
   Another name for Missale when the
   Missal first became a complete
   (plenarium) compilation of texts.
   xx Plenarium.

MISSALE ROMANUM [with date of pub-
   lication]
   BQT 4291-4328
   x Roman Missal.

MISSALE ROMANUM. ENGLISH, [FRENCH,
   GERMAN, ETC.]
   BQT 4293-4294

MISSALS.
   BQT 4293
   Here are entered popular editions
   of the Missal, for which the
   main entry is under editor,
   translator, or title.
   Critical works on the official
   Missal, as, bibliographies,
   commentaries, histories, manuscripts, etc., are entered under
   Missale.
   xx Mass - Prayer-books.
   Prayer-books.

MISSALS, ENGLISH, [FRENCH, GERMAN,
   ETC.]

MISSIOLOGY. See
   MISSIONS - THEORY.

MISSION ART. See
   MISSIONS AND ART.

MISSION EDUCATION.
   BQT 3248
   Here is entered literature dealing with educational work done
   at home for the missions, such as
   giving publicity to, arousing
   interest in, and encouraging
   support for the missions.
   sa Missionaries - Education.
   Missions - Educational work.
   xx Missions - Sermons.

MISSION FEAST.

MISSION INDIANS OF CALIFORNIA. See
   INDIANS OF NORTH AMERICA - CALI-
   FORNIA.

MISSION LAW. See
   MISSIONS (CANON LAW)

MISSION LITERATURE. See
   MISSIONS - BIBLIOGRAPHY.

MISSION METHODS. See
   APOLOGETICS, MISSIONARY.

MISSION SCIENCE. See
   MISSIONS - THEORY.

MISSION SERMONS. See
   MISSIONS - SERMONS.
   PARISH MISSIONS - SERMONS.
   SERMONS, MISSION.

MISSIONARIES.
   BQT 3244-3245
   x Missions - Biography.
   xx Christian biography.
   Missions.

MISSIONARIES - BIBLIOGRAPHY.

MISSIONARIES - CORRESPONDENCE,
   REMINISCENCES, ETC.

MISSIONARIES - EDUCATION.
   BQT 3251
   xx Mission education.

MISSIONARIES - MEDITATIONS.

MISSIONARIES - RETREATS. See
   RETREATS FOR MISSIONARIES.

MISSIONARIES - SPIRITUAL LIFE.

MISSIONARIES - VOCATION.
   x Vocation, Missionary.
   xx Vocation, Ecclesiastical.

MISSIONARIES - VOYAGES AND TRAVELS.
   See VOYAGES AND TRAVELS, MISSIONARY.

MISSIONARIES, BELGIAN, [FRENCH,
   GERMAN, ETC.]

MISSIONARIES, LAY.
        BQT 3229
    x Lay missionaries.
    xx Catholic action.

MISSIONARIES, NEGRO.
    x Negro missionaries.

MISSIONARIES, WOMEN.
        BQT 3244-3245
    "Here are entered biographical
    works on women missionaries.
    For the work of women in
    promoting missions see Women
    in missionary work." LC
    Cf. note under Religious orders
    of women - Missions.
    sa Religious orders of women -
        Missions.
    x Missions - Biography.
    xx Women as missionaries.

MISSIONARIES AS SCIENTISTS.

MISSIONARY APOLOGETICS. See
    APOLOGETICS, MISSIONARY.

MISSIONARY PLAYS.
        BV 2086
        BQT 3229
    x Missions - Dramas.
    xx Religious drama.

MISSIONARY RELIGIOUS ORDERS. See
    RELIGIOUS ORDERS, MISSIONARY.

MISSIONARY STORIES.
    x Missions - Stories.
    xx Children's stories.

MISSIONARY TRAVELS. See
    VOYAGES AND TRAVELS, MISSIONARY.

MISSIONS.   (Geog. subdiv., Direct)
        BQT 3203-3299   (266)
    sa Indians of Central America,
        [Mexico, North America, South
        America] - Missions.
        Language question in the church.
        Missionaries.
        Spanish missions of California,
        [New Mexico, Texas, etc.]
        also subdivision "Missions" under
        names of churches, denominations,

MISSIONS -- Continued.
        religious orders, etc. (e.g.,
        Church of England - Missions;
        Lutheran Church - Missions;
        Jesuits - Missions)
    x Catholic Church - Missions.
    xx Apostolate.
        Catholic Church - History.
        Christianity.
        Church - Teaching office.
        Church history.
        Pastoral theology.
        Social service, Catholic.

MISSIONS - ADDRESSES, ESSAYS,
    LECTURES.

MISSIONS - AGRICULTURAL WORK.
        S 532
        BQT 3263
    x Agricultural work of missions.
    xx Agricultural education.
        Missions - Educational work.

MISSIONS - ALMANACS, YEARBOOKS, ETC.
        BQT 3211
        AY 81.R6-7
    x Missions - Yearbooks.
    xx Almanacs, Catholic.

MISSIONS - ATLASES. See
    MISSIONS - GEOGRAPHY - MAPS.

MISSIONS - BIBLICAL TEACHING.
        BQT 3229
        BV 2073

MISSIONS - BIBLIOGRAPHY.
        [BQT 3201]
        Z 7817   (016.266)
    x Mission literature.

MISSIONS - BIOGRAPHY. See
    MISSIONARIES.
    MISSIONARIES, WOMEN.

MISSIONS - CATECHISMS, QUESTION-BOOKS.

MISSIONS - CHRONOLOGY. See
    MISSIONS - HISTORY - CHRONOLOGY.

MISSIONS - CONGRESSES.
        BQT 3205-3206   (266.x06)

MISSIONS - CONTROVERSIAL LITERATURE.

MISSIONS - COOPERATIVE MOVEMENT.
   (Geog. subdiv., Direct)
   xx Ecumenical movement.

MISSIONS - DICTIONARIES.
      BQT 3211

MISSIONS - DIRECTORIES.
      BQT 3211

MISSIONS - DRAMA. See
   MISSIONARY PLAYS.

MISSIONS - EARLY WORKS TO 1800.

MISSIONS - EDUCATIONAL WORK.
      BQT 3263
   sa Missions - Agricultural work.
      Missions - Industrial work.
   x Educational missions.
   xx Church and education.
      Mission education.

MISSIONS - EXERCISES, RECITATIONS,
ETC.

MISSIONS - EXHIBITIONS AND MUSEUMS.
      BQT 3205-3206   (266.x06)
   x Missions - Museums.

MISSIONS - FICTION.
   x Missions - Stories.

MISSIONS - FINANCE.

MISSIONS - GEOGRAPHY.
   xx Ecclesiastical geography.
      Religion and geography.

MISSIONS - GEOGRAPHY - DICTIONARIES.

MISSIONS - GEOGRAPHY - MAPS.
      BQX 34
   x Missions - Atlases.
      Missions - Maps.

MISSIONS - HISTORY.
      BQT 3231-3236   (266.x09)

MISSIONS - HISTORY - CHRONOLOGY.
   x Missions - Chronology.

MISSIONS - HISTORY - EARLY PERIOD.
      BQT 3233
   xx Church history - Primitive and
      early church.

MISSIONS - HISTORY - MIDDLE AGES.
      BQT 3234
   xx Church history - Middle Ages.

MISSIONS - HISTORY - MODERN PERIOD.
      BQT 3236
   xx Church history - Modern period.

MISSIONS - HISTORY - 16th CENTURY.

MISSIONS - HISTORY - 17th CENTURY.

MISSIONS - HISTORY - 18th CENTURY.

MISSIONS - HISTORY - 19th CENTURY.

MISSIONS - HISTORY - 20th CENTURY.

MISSIONS - HYMNS.
   x Hymns, Mission.

MISSIONS - INDUSTRIAL WORK.
      BQT 3263
   x Industrial missions.
   xx Missions - Educational work.
      Technical education.

MISSIONS - INFLUENCE.
      BQT 3255-3259
   Here are entered works dealing
      with the impact of the missions
      upon civilization, society, and
      politics.

MISSIONS - JUVENILE LITERATURE.
      BQT 3225

MISSIONS - MAPS. See
   MISSIONS - GEOGRAPHY - MAPS.

MISSIONS - MUSIC.

MISSIONS - MUSEUMS. See
   MISSIONS - EXHIBITIONS AND
MUSEUMS.

MISSIONS - PAPAL TEACHING.
      BQT 3229

MISSIONS - PERIODICALS.
    BQT 3203   (266.x05)

MISSIONS - PERSONAL NARRATIVES.

MISSIONS - PICTURES, ILLUSTRATIONS,
ETC.
  xx Catholic Church - Pictures,
     illustrations, etc.

MISSIONS - POETRY.

MISSIONS - POPULAR WORKS.
    BQT 3225

MISSIONS - PRAYER-BOOKS.
    BQT 2648

MISSIONS - PRAYER-BOOKS - ENGLISH,
[FRENCH, GERMAN, ETC.]

MISSIONS - RURAL WORK.
  x Missions, Rural.
    Rural missions.

MISSIONS - SERMONS.
    BQT 3224
  Here are entered works containing
    sermons on the missions and on
    missionary work.
  For works consisting of sermons
    to be delivered in the mission
    field see Sermons, Mission.
  sa Mission education.
    Sermons, Mission.
  x Mission sermons.
  xx Mission education.
    Sermons, Mission.

MISSIONS - SOCIAL WORK.
    BQT 3259

MISSIONS - SOCIETIES.
    BQT 3209   (266.x06)

MISSIONS - STATISTICS.
    BQT 3211

MISSIONS - STORIES. See
  MISSIONARY STORIES.
  MISSIONS - FICTION.

MISSIONS - STUDY AND TEACHING.

MISSIONS - STUDY AND TEACHING
(ELEMENTARY)

MISSIONS - STUDY AND TEACHING
(SECONDARY)

MISSIONS - THEORY.
    BQT 3221-3222   (266.x01)
  x Missiology.
    Mission science.

MISSIONS - YEARBOOKS. See
  MISSIONS - ALMANACS, YEARBOOKS, ETC.

################

MISSIONS - AFRICA, [BRAZIL,
CHINA, ETC.]

################

The following group of subdivisions
  indicates missions to the respective people or bodies.

MISSIONS - BLIND.
  sa Blind, Bibles for the.
  xx Blind.

MISSIONS - BUDDHISTS.
  x Buddhist missions.

MISSIONS - CHILDREN.
    BQT 3282
  x Children - Missions.

MISSIONS - EASTERN CHURCHES.
    BQX 5433; BQX 5454
  Here is entered literature dealing
    with missionary work of the
    Western or Latin Church among
    the Orthodox or Separated Eastern
    Churches. For material about
    missionary work carried on by
    the Eastern Churches see Eastern
    Churches - Missions.
  sa Religious orders - Missions -
    Eastern Churches.

MISSIONS - EMIGRANTS.
   [BQT 3286]
    x Emigration and immigration -
     Missions.
  xx Church work with migrants.

MISSIONS - INDIANS. See
  INDIANS - MISSIONS.
  INDIANS OF CENTRAL AMERICA -
   MISSIONS.
  INDIANS OF MEXICO - MISSIONS.
  INDIANS OF NORTH AMERICA -
   MISSIONS.
  INDIANS OF SOUTH AMERICA -
   MISSIONS.
  also subdivision "Missions" under
   names of tribes, e.g., Dakota
   Indians - Missions.

MISSIONS - JEWS.
   BQT 3293
  Here are entered works dealing
   with the missionary efforts of
   the Catholic Church among the
   Jews.
  sa Jews - Conversion to Christian-
    ity.
  x Jewish missions.
  xx Jewish Christians.

MISSIONS - LEPERS.
   BQT 3275 (266.x3)
  xx Leprosy.

MISSIONS - MOHAMMEDANS.
   BQT 3291
  Here are entered works dealing
   with the spread of Christianity
   among Mohammedans.
  For works dealing with the spread
   of Mohammedanism see Mohammedanism - Missions.

MISSIONS - NEGROES
   BQT 3287
   BQX 4337 (U.S.) (266.x73)
  x Missions, Negro.
   Negro missions.
   Negroes - Missions.

################

MISSIONS (CANON LAW)
   BQV 234-235
  sa Native clergy (Canon law)
   Quasi-parishes (Canon law)
  x Mission law.

MISSIONS, CITY. See
  CITY MISSIONS.

MISSIONS, FOREIGN.
   BQT 3203-3299
   BQX 951-958
   BQX 5433-5435
  sa Native clergy.
  x Foreign missions.

MISSIONS, FOREIGN - BIBLIOGRAPHY.

MISSIONS, FOREIGN - DIRECTORIES.

MISSIONS, FOREIGN - SOCIETIES, ETC.

MISSIONS, HOME.
   BQX 4368 (U.S.)
  x Church extension.
   Home mission.

MISSIONS, INDIAN. See
  INDIANS - MISSIONS; etc., as
   under MISSIONS - INDIANS.

MISSIONS, INNER. See
  INNER MISSIONS.

MISSIONS, INSTITUTIONAL. See
  INSTITUTIONAL MISSIONS.

MISSIONS, MEDICAL. (Geog. subdiv.,
  Direct)
   BQT 3273
  sa Zenana missions.
  x Medical missions.
  xx Medicine.

MISSIONS, NEGRO. See
  MISSIONS - NEGRO.

MISSIONS, PARISH. See
  PARISH MISSIONS.

MISSIONS, PAROCHIAL. See
  PARISH MISSIONS.

MISSIONS, POPULAR. See
  PARISH MISSIONS.

MISSIONS, PROTESTANT. See
  PROTESTANT CHURCHES - MISSIONS.

MISSIONS, RURAL. See
  MISSIONS - RURAL WORK.

MISSIONS, SEAMEN'S. See
  MERCHANT SEAMEN - MISSIONS AND
  CHARITIES.

################

MISSIONS, AMERICAN, [BELGIAN,
  FRENCH, ETC.]
      BQT 3239
  Here are entered works dealing
    with missions sent out from
    special countries. For works
    dealing with missions in
    foreign countries see country
    subdivision under Missions,
    e.g., Missions - America;
    Missions - China; etc.
  x American, [Belgian, French,
    etc.] missions.

################

MISSIONS, AUGUSTINIAN, [BENEDICTINE,
  FRANCISCAN, ETC.] See
  AUGUSTINIANS - MISSIONS.
  BENEDICTINES - MISSIONS.
  etc.

################

MISSIONS AND ART.
      BQT 3229
  x Art, Mission.
    Mission art.

MISSIONS AND CULTURE.

MISSIONS IN LITERATURE.
  xx Religion in literature.

MISSIONS AND LITURGY. See
  LITURGY AND MISSIONS.

MISTAKE (CANON LAW)
  x Error (Canon law)

MISTRESS OF NOVICES. See
  MASTER OF NOVICES.

MITHRAISM.
      BL 1585
  sa Zoroastrianism.

MIXED LIFE.
      BQT 2203
  Here are entered works on that
    form of the spiritual life in
    which the active life is super-
    added to the contemplative, as
    exemplified in certain religious
    orders.
  xx Active life.
    Christian life.
    Contemplative life.
    Perfection, Christian.
    Religious life.
    Spiritual life.

MIXED MARRIAGE. See
  MARRIAGE, MIXED.

MIXED RELIGION.
      BQV230 1061
  "A prohibiting impediment of
    marriage which arises when one
    party is a Catholic and the
    other is a baptized non-
    Catholic." AT
  x Religion, Mixed.
  xx Marriage - Impediments (Canon
    law)
    Marriage, Mixed.

MODERN ASSYRIANS. See
  ASSYRIANS, MODERN.

MODERN RELIGIONS. See
  RELIGIONS, MODERN.

MODERNISM.
      BQT 123 (Theology)
      BQX 1071   (273.8x1)
  Here are entered works on a move-
    ment, originating in the late
    nineteenth century, which affects

MODERNISM -- Continued.
a preference for what is modern
and a disregard for what is ancient and medieval. Pope Pius X
described it as a "Synthesis of
all heresies." Founded in agnosticism and the theory of immun-
ence, Modernism proceeds to de-
molish dogmas, the sacraments,
the authenticity of the Scriptures, ecclesiastical authority
and discipline.
sa Agnosticism.
   Americanism (Catholic con-
      troversy)
xx Agnosticism.
   Revelation.

MODERNISM - CHURCH OF ENGLAND.
x Church of England - Modernism.

MODERNIST-FUNDAMENTALIST CONTROVERSY.
   BT 78
"Here are entered works on the
controversy among Protestants in
the 20th century over liberal and
conservative interpretations of
Christianity, as well as declara-
tive statements of the position
taken by fundamentalists. For
statements of the modernist
position see Modernism." LC
References as in LC.

MODES, MUSICAL (CHANT). See
CHANT - MODES AND TONES.

MODESTY.
xx Chastity.

MOHAMMEDAN CONVERTS. See
CONVERTS, MOHAMMEDAN.

MOHAMMEDAN ESCHATOLOGY. See
ESCHATOLOGY, MOHAMMEDAN.

MOHAMMEDAN HERESIES AND HERETICS. See
HERESIES AND HERETICS, MOHAMMEDAN.

MOHAMMEDAN HYMNS. See
HYMNS, MOHAMMEDAN.

MOHAMMEDAN MONASTICISM. See
MONASTICISM, MOHAMMEDAN.

MOHAMMEDAN SECTS.
   BP 195   (297)
sa Heresies and heretics, Mohammedan.
Other references as in LC.

MOHAMMEDAN SERMONS.
   BP 25; BP 165
x Sermons, Mohammedan.

MOHAMMEDAN SERMONS, ARABIC.

MOHAMMEDAN THEOLOGY.
   BP 166
sa Fate and fatalism (Mohammedanism)
   Koran - Theology.

MOHAMMEDANISM.   (Geog. subdiv.,
   Direct)
   BP 1-195   (297)
sa Druses.
   Mahdism.
Other references as in LC.

MOHAMMEDANISM - MISSIONS.
Here are entered works dealing
with the spread of Mohammedanism.
For works dealing with the spread
of Christianity among Mohammedans
see Missions - Mohammedans.

Other subdivisions under Mohammedanism as in LC.

MOHAMMEDANS.
References and subdivisions as
in LC.

MOHAMMEDANS - RELIGIOUS EDUCATION.
See RELIGIOUS EDUCATION, MOHAMMEDAN.

MOLINISM.
   BQT 114; BQT 1129   (273.x72)
"The system proposed by Luis de
Molina (1535-1600) and developed
by other Jesuit theologians, to
solve the problem of reconciling
the freedom of man's will with the
efficacy of divine grace." AT
xx Grace (Theology)

MONACHISM. See MONASTICISM.

MONARCHIANISM.
        BQT 49; BQT 583
    xx Heresies and heretics - Early
        church.
        Trinity - History of doctrines.

MONASTERIES.   (Geog. subdiv.,
    Indirect)
        BQT 5928; NA 4850 (Architec-
            ture)   (726.7)
        BQX 6801-8043 (Church his-
            tory)   (271)
    A monastery is "the fixed abode of
    a community of monks, canons reg-
    ular or nuns; the name is extended
    to include houses of friars and
    certain more recent congregations,
    e.g., Passionists, Redemptorists,
    but never of Jesuits." AT
    Here are entered works on religious
    houses in general.
    sa Abbeys.
        Chantries.
        Convents.
        Enclosure (Monasticism)
        Priories.
        Religious orders.
        Secularization.
     x Cloisters.
        Religious houses.
    xx Abbeys.
        Catholic institutions.
        Church property.
        Convents.
        Religious orders.

MONASTERIES - ANNIVERSARY SERMONS. See
    ANNIVERSARY SERMONS - MONASTERIES.

MONASTERIES (CANON LAW)
        BQV230 492-498
    xx Religious orders (Canon law)

MONASTERIES, BUDDHIST.   (Geog. subdiv.,
    Indirect)
     x Buddhist monasteries.
    xx Monasticism, Buddhist.

MONASTERIES, DOUBLE. See
    DOUBLE MONASTERIES.

MONASTERIES, LAMAIST.   (Geog. subdiv.,
    Indirect)
     x Lamaist monasteries.
    xx Monasticism, Lamaist.

MONASTIC ARCHIVES. See
    ARCHIVES, MONASTIC.

MONASTIC BREVIARY. See
    BREVIARIUM. BENEDICTINE, [CIS-
    TERCIAN, ETC.]

MONASTIC CONFRATERNITIES. See
    RELIGIOUS ORDERS - CONFRATERNITIES.

MONASTIC LIBRARIES.   (Geog. subdiv.,
    Indirect)
        BQ 105   (027.672)
    sa Libraries, Benedictine, [Capu-
        chin, etc.]
     x Libraries, Monastic.
    xx Libraries, Catholic.

MONASTIC LIFE. See MONASTICISM.

MONASTIC LIFE FOR WOMEN. See
    NUNS.

MONASTIC ORDERS. See
    MONASTICISM.

MONASTIC PROFESSION. See
    PROFESSION, RELIGIOUS.

MONASTIC RITES AND CEREMONIES. See
    RELIGIOUS ORDERS - RITES AND
    CEREMONIES.
    RELIGIOUS ORDERS FOR WOMEN - RITES
    AND CEREMONIES.

MONASTIC SCHOOLS.   (Geog. subdiv.,
    Indirect)
    sa Subdivision "Education" under
        names of religious orders,
        e.g., Benedictines - Educa-
        tion.
     x Schools, Monastic.
    xx Religious orders - Education.

MONASTIC VOCATION. See
    VOCATION, RELIGIOUS.
    VOCATION, RELIGIOUS, FOR WOMEN.

MONASTICISM.   (Geog. subdiv.)
      [BQT 2305] (Asceticism)
      BQX 6838   (271)
   Here are entered works treating
      specifically of monastic life
      (ancient and modern) as distin-
      guished from the religious ob-
      servance of canons regular,
      friars and the later orders and
      congregations which stress the
      active over against the contem-
      plative life.
   "The essence of monasticism is the
      formation of a community of monks,
      bound to live together until
      death, under rule, in common
      life, in the monastery of their
      profession, as a religious family,
      leading a life not of marked aus-
      terity but devoted to the service
      of God ... Monasticism is known
      in all the great religions, e.g.,
      Moslem, Confucian, Buddhist, with
      the notable exception of Judaism."
      AT
   sa Abbots.
      Contemplative life.
      Nuns.
      Religious life.
      Religious orders.
      also names of monastic orders,
         e.g., Camaldolese, Carthusians,
         Trappists, etc.
    x Monachism.
      Monastic life.
      Monastic orders.
      Monks.
      Orders, Monastic.
   xx Religious life.
      Religious orders.

MONASTICISM - HISTORY.

MONASTICISM - HISTORY - EARLY PERIOD.

MONASTICISM - HISTORY - MIDDLE AGES.

MONASTICISM - HISTORY - MODERN PERIOD.

MONASTICISM - HISTORY - 20th CENTURY.

MONASTICISM, BUDDHIST.
      BL 1478
   sa Monasteries, Buddhist.
    x Buddhist monasticism.
      Religious orders, Buddhist.

MONASTICISM, COPTIC.
         BQX 5509 (Monophysite)
         BQX 5519 (Catholic)
    x Coptic monasticism.

MONASTICISM, EASTERN.
         BQX 5549; BQX 6402-6405;
            BQX 6801-6825
    x Eastern Churches - Monasticism.

MONASTICISM, ETHIOPIC.
      BQX 5545
    x Ethiopic monasticism.

MONASTICISM, IRISH.
      BQX 2210
   Here are entered works on Celtic
      or Irish monasticism, notably
      that fostered by St. Columban,
      which flourished not only in
      Ireland but also spread to the
      European continent.
   sa Culdees.
      Schottenklöster.
    x Celtic monasticism.
      Irish monasticism.
   xx Ireland - Church history.
      Religious orders - Ireland.

MONASTICISM, IRISH - MISSIONS.
      BQX 2218-2219

MONASTICISM, JEWISH.
      BM 175
   sa Essenes.
      Qumran community.
    x Jewish monasticism.

MONASTICISM, LAMAIST.
   sa Monasteries, Lamaist.
    x Lamaist monasticism.

MONASTICISM, MALANKARESE.
      BQX 5659
    x Malankarese monasticism.

MONASTICISM, MOHAMMEDAN.   (Geog.
   subdiv., Indirect)
      x Mohammedan monasticism.

MONASTICISM, ORTHODOX EASTERN.
      BQX 5901-5910
      x Orthodox Eastern monasticism.

MONASTICISM, TAOIST.
      x Taoist monasticism.

MONIALES ORDINIS SANCTI BENEDICTI.
   See BENEDICTINE NUNS.

MONISM.
   Classifications and references
      as in LC.

MONKS. See MONASTICISM.

MONOLITHIC CHURCHES.   See
   CAVE CHURCHES.

MONOPHYSITES.
      BQT 66   (273.x4)
   sa Eutychians.
      Schism, Acacian, 484-519.
   xx Heresies and heretics - Early
      church.
      Jesus Christ - History of
         doctrines.

MONOTHEISM.
      BL 221   (291.14)
   xx Polytheism.
      Trinity - History of doctrines.

MONOTHELISM.
      BQT 67
   A seventh century heresy which
      affirmed that there was but one
      will and one operation in the
      person of Christ.
   xx Heresies and heretics - Early
      church.
      Jesus Christ - History of
         doctrines.

MONSTRANCES.
      BQT 4358
   x Ostensorium.
   xx Sacred vessels.

MONTANISM.
      BQT 50   (273.x1)
   xx Asceticism - History - Early
      church.
      Heresies and heretics - Early
      church.

MONTE CASSINO (BENEDICTINE ABBEY) -
   SIEGE, 1944.
   xx World War, 1939-1945 - Campaigns -
      Italy.

MOON (IN RELIGION, FOLK-LORE, ETC.)

MOON WORSHIP.
      BL 438
   References as in LC.

MORAL DOUBT. See
   DOUBT (CANON LAW)

MORAL EDUCATION.
      LC 251-318   (377)
      LC 2751 (Negro)
   sa Religious education.
    x Character education.
      Education, Ethical.
      Education, Moral.
      Ethical education.
      Morals.
   xx Catholic education.
      Education.
      Ethics.
      Religious education.

MORAL PERSONS. See
   CORPORATIONS, ECCLESIASTICAL.

MORAL PHILOSOPHY. See ETHICS.

MORAL SERMONS. See
   MORAL THEOLOGY - SERMONS.

✔ MORAL THEOLOGY.
      BQT 1703-2073   (24x1)
   "The science of human acts con-
      sidered in the light of man's
      supernatural destiny." AT
   sa Canon law.
      Casuistry.
      Christian life.
      Commandments, Ten.

MORAL THEOLOGY -- Continued.
  sa Commandments of the Church.
     Conduct of life.
     Confession.
     Ethics.
     Human acts.
     Justice.
     Natural law.
     Pastoral medicine.
     Pastoral theology.
     Probabilism.
     Sacraments.
     Sin.
     Virtues, Moral.
   x Catholic Church - Discipline.
     Catholic ethics.
     Ethics, Catholic.
     Morals.
     Theology, Moral.
  xx Canon law.
     Church discipline.
     Conduct of life.
     Ethics.
     Natural law.
     Theology.

MORAL THEOLOGY - BIBLICAL TEACHING.
  See BIBLE - ETHICS.

MORAL THEOLOGY - BIBLIOGRAPHY.
     [BQT 1701]

MORAL THEOLOGY - CATECHISMS,
  QUESTION-BOOKS.
     BQT 1720

MORAL THEOLOGY - COLLECTED WORKS.
     BQT 1714-1716   (24x1.x08)

MORAL THEOLOGY - COLLECTED WORKS -
  EARLY CHURCH.

MORAL THEOLOGY - COLLECTED WORKS -
  MIDDLE AGES.

MORAL THEOLOGY - COLLECTED WORKS -
  16th CENTURY.

MORAL THEOLOGY - COLLECTED WORKS -
  17th CENTURY.

MORAL THEOLOGY - COLLECTED WORKS -
  18th CENTURY.

MORAL THEOLOGY - COLLECTED WORKS -
  19th CENTURY.

MORAL THEOLOGY - COLLECTED WORKS -
  20th CENTURY.

MORAL THEOLOGY - COLLECTIONS.
     BQT 1703

MORAL THEOLOGY - DICTIONARIES.
     [BQT 1704]

MORAL THEOLOGY - HANDBOOKS,
  MANUALS, ETC.
     BQT 1717   (24x1.x02)

MORAL THEOLOGY - HISTORY.   (Geog.
  subdiv., Indirect)
     BQT 1705   (24x1.x09)

MORAL THEOLOGY - HISTORY - EARLY
  CHURCH.
     [BQT 1707]
  xx Church history - Primitive and
     early church.

MORAL THEOLOGY - HISTORY - MIDDLE
  AGES.
     [BQT 1708]

MORAL THEOLOGY - HISTORY - MODERN
  PERIOD.
     [BQT 1709]

MORAL THEOLOGY - JUVENILE LITERATURE.
     BQT 1719

MORAL THEOLOGY - METHODOLOGY.

MORAL THEOLOGY - MISCELLANEA.

MORAL THEOLOGY - PERIODICALS.
     [BQT 1702]

MORAL THEOLOGY - POPULAR WORKS.
     BQT 1718

MORAL THEOLOGY - SERMONS.
   x Moral sermons.
     Sermons, Moral.

MORAL THEOLOGY - STUDY AND TEACHING.

MORAL THEOLOGY - TEXTBOOKS.
      BQT 1717   (24x1.x02)

MORAL THEOLOGY - TEXTBOOKS -
   17th CENTURY.

MORAL THEOLOGY - TEXTBOOKS -
   18th CENTURY.

MORAL THEOLOGY - TEXTBOOKS -
   1800-1870.

MORAL THEOLOGY - TEXTBOOKS -
   1871-1917.

MORAL THEOLOGY - TEXTBOOKS -
   1918-

MORAL THEOLOGY AND ASCETICISM. See
   ASCETICISM AND MORAL THEOLOGY.

MORAL THEOLOGY AND CANON LAW. See
   CANON LAW AND MORAL THEOLOGY.

MORAL VIRTUES. See
   VIRTUES, MORAL.

MORALITIES.
     PN 1771
     BQ 5151-5167
  sa Drama, Medieval.
    Mysteries and miracle-plays.
   x Morality plays.
    Plays, Medieval.
  xx Drama, Medieval.
    Mysteries and miracle-plays.
    Religious drama.
    Theater.

MORALITY PLAYS. See
   MORALITIES.

MORALS. See
   CONDUCT OF LIFE.
   ETHICS.
   MORAL CONDITIONS.
   MORAL EDUCATION.
   MORAL THEOLOGY.

MORALS AND ART. See
   ART AND MORALS.

MORALS AND LITERATURE. See
   LITERATURE AND MORALS.

MORALS AND MUSIC. See
   MUSIC AND MORALS.

MORALS AND THE STATE. See
   STATE AND MORALS.

MORALS AND WAR. See
   WAR AND MORALS.

MORAVIAN CHURCH.   (Geog. subdiv.)
     BX 5783
   sa Love feasts.
   Subdivisions as in LC.

MORAVIANS.
     BX 8551-8593
   Explanatory note, references and
    subdivisions as in LC.

MORAVIANS IN NORTH CAROLINA,
[PENNSYLVANIA, ETC.]

MORMON CHURCHES. See
   CHURCHES, MORMON.

MORMONS AND MORMONISM.
     BX 8601-8695
     HQ 994 (Polygamy)
   References and subdivisions as
   in LC.

MORTAL SIN. See SIN, MORTAL.

MORTAGES (CANON LAW)
     BQV230 1541   (348.x46)

MORTALITY.
  xx Death.
   Other references as in LC.

MORTIFICATION.
     BQT 2221
   x Self-denial.
  xx Penance (Virtue)
    Perfection, Christian.
    Sacrifice, Spirit of.
    Temptation.

MOSAIC LAW. See JEWISH LAW.

MOSAICS.
 xx Christian art.
  Church decoration and ornament.
 Other references as in LC.

MOSLEMS. See MOHAMMEDANS.

MOTAZILITES.
 xx Mohammedan sects.

MOTET.
  BQT 4596 (738.4)
 xx Church music.
  Part-song.

MOTHER-GODDESSES.
  BL 325.M
 sa Sekhmet (Egyptian Deity)
 x Goddesses, Mother.
 xx Gods.

MOTHER OF GOD. See
MARY, BLESSED VIRGIN - MOTHERHOOD.

MOTHERS.
  BQT 2281 (Christian family)
  HQ 759 (Sociology) (173.5)
 sa Love, Maternal.
  Parents.
 xx Family.
  Family, Christian.
  Parents.
  Woman.

MOTHERS - BIBLICAL TEACHING. See
WOMEN IN THE BIBLE.

MOTHERS - PRAYER-BOOKS.
  BQT 2648

MOTHERS - RELIGIOUS LIFE.
  BQT 2281

MOTHERS - SERMONS.
  BQT 3019

MOTHER'S DAY SERMONS.
  BQX 3089
 x Sermons, Mother's Day.

MOTHERS GENERAL.
 xx Religious orders of women.
  Superiors, Religious.

MOTU PROPRIO.
  BQV230 45-46
  BQV 2-8 (Documents) (26x3)
 "A rescript drawn up and issued by
  the pope on his own initiative,
  without the advice of others,
  and personally signed by him."
 AT
 sa Rescripts, Papal.

MOUNTAINS (IN RELIGION, FOLK-LORE,
ETC.)
 x Sacred mountains.

MOVEMENT, ECUMENICAL. See
ECUMENICAL MOVEMENT.

MOVING-PICTURES - MORAL AND
RELIGIOUS ASPECTS.
  PN 1995.3
 sa Moving-pictures and Catholic
  Church.
 x Moving-pictures and religion.

MOVING-PICTURES - PLOTS, THEMES,
ETC. - RELIGION.
 x Moving-pictures and religion.
  Religious films.

MOVING-PICTURES, RELIGIOUS.
 x Religious moving-pictures.
 xx Religious drama.

MOVING-PICTURES AND CATHOLIC CHURCH.
 x Catholic Church and moving-
  pictures.
  Church and moving-pictures,
  Catholic.
 xx Moving-pictures - Moral and
  religious aspects.

MOVING-PICTURES AND RELIGION. See
MOVING-PICTURES - MORAL AND
 RELIGIOUS ASPECTS.
MOVING-PICTURES - PLOTS, THEMES,
 ETC. - RELIGION.

MOVING-PICTURES IN CHURCH WORK.
  BV 1643
 xx Church work.
  Religious education - Audi-
  visual aids.

MOZARABIC CHANT.
BQT 4928
x Chant, Mozarabic.
xx Chant.

MOZARABIC RITE.
BQT 4921-4929   (264.x82)
x Gothic Rite.
Spanish Rite.
Visigothic Rite.

MOZARABIC RITE - DIVINE OFFICE.
x Divine Office - Mozarabic Rite.

MOZARABIC RITE - MASS.
x Mass - Mozarabic Rite.

MUHAMMEDANS. See MOHAMMEDANS.

MURET, BATTLE OF, 1213.
DC 611.L3
xx Albigenses.

MURRONE, HERMITS OF. See
CELESTINES (BENEDICTINE)

MUSIC - DISCOGRAPHY.
sa Chant - Discography.

MUSIC - MANUSCRIPTS.
sa Chant - Manuscripts.
Other references as in LC.

MUSIC - SUNDAY-SCHOOLS. See
SUNDAY-SCHOOLS - HYMNS.

MUSIC - THEORY - MEDIEVAL.
sa Chant - Instruction and
study - To 1800.

MUSIC, CHURCH. See CHURCH MUSIC.

MUSIC, SACRED. See CHURCH MUSIC.

MUSIC AND MORALS.
ML 3920
x Morals and music.
Songs - Moral aspects.
Other references as in LC.

MUSIC IN CHURCHES.
ML 3001
sa Music in synagogues.
Religion and music.
xx Church music.
Religion and music.

MUSIC IN RELIGION. See
RELIGION AND MUSIC.

MUSIC IN SYNAGOGUES.
References as in LC.

MUSICAL INSTRUMENTS (CHURCH MUSIC)
BQT 4607-4609
x Instruments, Musical (Church
music)

MUSICAL METER AND RHYTHM (CHURCH
MUSIC)
BQT 4591
sa Chant - Rhythm.
x Rhythm (Church music)

MUSICAL NOTATION (CHURCH MUSIC)
BQT 4592

MUSICIANS (CHURCH MUSIC)
x Church music - Biography.

MYSTERIES, RELIGIOUS.
BL 610 (Comparative religion)
HS 491 (Freemasonry and
ancient mysteries)
sa Cultus.
Eleusinian mysteries.
Oracles.
x Religious mysteries.
xx Religion.
Rites and ceremonies.

MYSTERIES AND MIRACLE-PLAYS.
PN 1761-1766 (History and
criticism)
sa Bible plays.
Drama, Medieval.
Liturgical drama.
Moralities.
x Bible - Drama.
Miracle-plays.
Plays, Medieval.

MYSTERIES AND MIRACLE-PLAYS -- Continued.
   xx Drama, Medieval.
      Easter - Drama.
      Liturgical drama.
      Moralities.
      Pageants.
      Passion-plays.
      Religious drama.
      Theater.

MYSTERIUM (LITURGY). See
  LITURGY - MYSTERY PRINCIPLE.

MYSTERY.
   xx Revelation.

MYSTIC LOVE. See LOVE, MYSTIC.

MYSTIC PRAYER. See
  CONTEMPLATION.

MYSTIC SUFFERING. See
  SUFFERING, MYSTIC.

MYSTIC UNION. See MYSTICAL UNION.

MYSTICAL BODY OF CHRIST.
     BQT 320-323; BQT 775-778
  "The members of the church are
   bound together and to Christ,
   their head, into a spiritual
   though real body by the supernatural life of grace received
   in baptism." AT
  sa Church.
     Jesus Christ in the sacraments.
     Mystical union.
     Priesthood, Universal.
   x Corpus Christi mysticum.
     Jesus Christ - Mystical Body.
   xx Church.

MYSTICAL BODY OF CHRIST - PAPAL
  TEACHING.

MYSTICAL BODY OF CHRIST - POPULAR
  WORKS.

MYSTICAL THEOLOGY.
  Some Catholic libraries may prefer
   to use the heading "Mystical
   theology" for Catholic mysticism,
   and the heading "Mysticism" for
   works on mysticism in general.

MYSTICAL UNION.
     [BQT 2464]
  "Here are entered works dealing
   with the indwelling of the
   Triune God, or of any person of
   the Trinity, in the hearts of
   believers and, conversely,
   works dealing with the union
   between man and the Triune God,
   especially between men and
   Jesus Christ." LC
  For works dealing with the Church
   as the mystical body of Christ
   see Mystical Body of Christ.
  sa Adoption (Theology)
     Children of God.
   x God and man, Mystical union of.
     Mystic union.
     Unio mystica.
     Union, Mystical.
     Union with Christ.
   xx Contemplation.
     Immanence of God.
     Mystical Body of Christ.
     Mysticism.
     Perfection, Christian.
     Religion (Virtue)
     Theology.

MYSTICAL UNION - HISTORY OF
DOCTRINES.

MYSTICISM. (Geog. subdiv.)
     BQT 2403-2497 (24x9)
  "Experimental knowledge of God's
   presence, in which the soul has,
   as a great reality, a sense of
   contact with Him. It is the
   same as passive contemplation
   or mystical union." AT
  sa Asceticism.
     Contemplation.
     Ecstasy.
     Enthusiasm.
     Miracles.
     Mystical union.
     Prayer, Mental.
     Prophecies.
     Revelation, Private.
     Spiritual life.
     Stigmatization.
     Visions.
   x Theology, Mystical.

MYSTICISM -- Continued.
  xx Asceticism.
    Perfection, Christian.
    Philosophy.
    Spiritual life.
    Theology.

MYSTICISM - BIBLICAL TEACHING.

MYSTICISM - BIBLIOGRAPHY.
    [BQT 2401]

MYSTICISM - BIOGRAPHY.
    BQT 2455
    x Mystics.

MYSTICISM - CATECHISMS, QUESTION-
  BOOKS.
  sa Spiritual life - Catechisms,
    question-books.

MYSTICISM - COLLECTED WORKS.
    BQT 2406-2430

MYSTICISM - COLLECTIONS.
    BQT 2403   (24x9.08)

MYSTICISM - COMPARATIVE STUDIES.
    BL 625

MYSTICISM - DICTIONARIES.

MYSTICISM - HISTORY.
    BQT 2449-2457   (24x9.09)
  Here are entered works on the history of mysticism and of mystical
  theology, subdivided by period,
  e.g., Grabmann, Martin. Mittel-
  alterliches Geistesleben; Abhand-
  lungen zur Geschichte der Scho-
  lastik und Mystik (MYSTICISM -
  HISTORY - MIDDLE AGES).
  Individual mystical treatises (not
  history) are entered under Mysticism with direct period subdivision, e.g., Suso, Heinrich,
  1300-1366. Little book of
  eternal wisdom (MYSTICISM -
  MIDDLE AGES).

MYSTICISM - HISTORY - EARLY CHURCH.
  sa Messalians.
  xx Church history - Primitive and
    early church.

MYSTICISM - HISTORY - MIDDLE AGES.
  sa Alumbrados.
    Beghards.
    Beguines.
    Brethren and Sisters of the
      Free Spirit.
    Fraticelli.
    Humiliati.
    Illuminati.
  xx Church history - Middle Ages.

MYSTICISM - HISTORY - MODERN PERIOD.

MYSTICISM - HISTORY - 19th CENTURY.

MYSTICISM - HISTORY - 20th CENTURY.

MYSTICISM - PERIODICALS.
    [BQT 2402)

MYSTICISM - POPULAR WORKS.
    BQT 2437

MYSTICISM - PSYCHOLOGY.
    BQT 2443

MYSTICISM - SELECTIONS.

MYSTICISM - TERMINOLOGY.

################

MYSTICISM - EARLY CHURCH.
  Cf. note under Mysticism - History.
  Books in this category, and the
    following periodic subdivisions,
    may be distributed in various
    parts of the classification
    schedule.

MYSTICISM - MIDDLE AGES.

MYSTICISM - MODERN PERIOD.

MYSTICISM - 16th CENTURY.

MYSTICISM - 17th CENTURY.

MYSTICISM - 18th CENTURY.

MYSTICISM - 19th CENTURY.

MYSTICISM - 20th CENTURY.

################

MYSTICISM - EASTERN CHURCHES.
BQX 5443
x Eastern Churches - Mysticism.

MYSTICISM - ORTHODOX EASTERN CHURCH.
BQX 5881
sa Hesychasm.
x Orthodox Eastern Church -
Mysticism.

MYSTICISM - PROTESTANT CHURCHES.
[BQT 2439]
x Protestant Churches - Mysticism.

MYSTICISM - BRAHMANISM, [HINDUISM,
JUDAISM, ETC.]

################

MYSTICISM IN LITERATURE.
PN 49
PR 145; PR 585.M (English
literature)
sa Occultism in literature.
xx Occultism in literature.

MYSTICS. See
MYSTICISM - BIOGRAPHY.

MYTHOLOGY.
BL 300-315 (Comparative
(291)
sa Demythologization.
Other references and subdivisions
as in LC.

MYTHOLOGY AND THE BIBLE. See
BIBLE AND MYTHOLOGY.

NAGUALISM.
GN 470
References as in LC.

NAHUM, BOOK OF. See
BIBLE. O.T. NAHUM.

NAILS, HOLY. See HOLY NAILS.

NAMEDAYS.
[BQT 4053]
xx Birthdays.
Feasts, Ecclesiastical.
Patron saints.

NAMES, BIBLICAL. See
BIBLE - NAMES.

NAMES, CHRISTIAN. See
NAMES, PERSONAL.

NAMES, PERSONAL. (Geog. subdiv.)
CS 2300-2389 (929.4)
sa Anonyms and pseudonyms.
Nicknames.
Patron saints.
Saints - Names.
also subdivision "Name" under
names of persons and, in
theology, under names of
Deity, namely, God, Holy
Spirit, Jesus Christ.
x Baptismal names.
Christian names.
Forenames.
Names, Christian.
Personal names.
Surnames.

NANTES, EDICT OF. See
EDICT OF NANTES.

NATIONAL COUNCILS. See
PLENARY COUNCILS.

NATIONAL PARISHES. See
PARISHES, NATIONAL.

NATIONALISM AND RELIGION. (Geog.
subdiv., Indirect)
BQT 3454; BQX 943; BQX 1073
"Here are entered works dealing
with the influence of nationalism upon religion, and with the
question as to which shall be
the dominant principle in the
life of the individual and of
the nation; included also is
the theory that a nation should
be a unit in its religious as
well as in its political life."
LC
sa Church and state.
Religion and language.
Religion and state.
Theocracy.
x Religion and nationalism.

300

NATIONALISM AND RELIGION -- Continued.
 xx Church and state.
    Religion and state.
    Theocracy.

NATIVE CLERGY.
      BQT 3253
  x Clergy, Indigenous.
    Clergy, Native.
    Indigenous clergy.
 xx Missions, Foreign.

NATIVE CLERGY (CANON LAW)
 xx Clergy (Canon law)
    Missions (Canon law)

NATIVISM.
      BQX 4383
  "Here are entered works dealing
   with the policy of favoring the
   native inhabitant of a country
   as against the immigrant. In
   American history this policy
   developed a peculiar antagonism
   toward the Catholic Church
   rather than toward any particular
   alien group." LC
 sa American Party.
    Ku Klux Klan (1915-   )
 xx U.S. - Foreign population.

NATIVITY OF CHRIST. See
  JESUS CHRIST - NATIVITY.

NATURAL HISTORY, BIBLICAL. See
  BIBLE - NATURAL HISTORY.

NATURAL LAW.
      BQT 1843 (Moral theology)
        (24x1.x31)
      JC 571-609 (Political science)
        (340.1)
 sa Divine law.
    Ethics.
    International law.
    Jurisprudence.
    Law - Philosophy.
    Moral theology.
    Political science.
  x Law, Natural.
 xx Ethics.
    Justice.
    Moral theology.

NATURAL LAW AND CANON LAW. See
  CANON LAW AND NATURAL LAW.

NATURAL THEOLOGY.
      BL 175-190   (210)
  "The science which has God for
   its object and is pursued by
   the natural light of human
   reason." AT
 sa God.
    Philosophy of nature.
  x Theodicy.
    Theology, Natural.
 xx Apologetics.
    Dogmatic theology.
    God.
    God - Existence.
    Philosophy.
    Philosophy of nature.
    Religion.
    Religion and science.
    Theology.

NATURALISM.
      B 828.2
      BL 2700-2790
      BQT 123
  References as in LC, with the
   following additional reference.
 xx Revelation.

NATURE - RELIGIOUS INTERPRETATIONS.
 xx Bible - Natural history.
    Bible and science.
    Philosophy of nature.
    Religion and science.

NATURE (IN RELIGION, FOLK-LORE, ETC.)
  References as in LC.

NATURE IN THE BIBLE.
      BS 660-667
 xx Bible - Natural history.

NATURE-WORSHIP.
      BL 435   (291.212)
  References as in LC.

NAVAL CHAPLAINS. See
  CHAPLAINS, MILITARY.

NAVARRESE SAINTS. See
  SAINTS, NAVARRESE.

NAZARITE (JUDAISM)

NEDERLANDSE HERVORMDE KERK.
References and subdivisions
as in LC.

NEGRO BAPTISTS. See
BAPTISTS, NEGRO.

NEGRO CATHOLICS. See
CATHOLICS, NEGRO.

NEGRO DISCIPLES OF CHRIST. See
DISCIPLES OF CHRIST, NEGRO.

NEGRO LUTHERANS. See
LUTHERANS, NEGRO.

NEGRO METHODISTS. See
METHODISTS, NEGRO.

NEGRO MISSIONARIES. See
MISSIONARIES, NEGRO.

NEGRO MISSIONS. See
MISSIONS - NEGROES.

NEGRO PRIESTS. See
PRIESTS, NEGRO.

NEGRO RACE - RELIGION.
sa Negroes - Religion.
xx Negroes - Religion.

NEGROES - MISSIONS. See
MISSIONS - NEGROES.

NEGROES - RELIGION.
References as in LC.

NEHEMIAS, BOOK OF. See
BIBLE. O.T. 2 ESDRAS.

NEONOMIANISM.
xx Antinomianism.
Arminianism.
Calvinism.
Law (Theology)
Law and gospel.

NEO-ORTHODOXY.
"Here are entered works dealing
with a mid-twentieth century
trend in Christian theology
which emphasizes the transcendence of God, the sin of man,
and justification by faith.
It represents the more conservative point of view that
results from the theology of
Karl Barth, and is opposed by
the liberal point of view." LC
xx Dialectical theology.

NEOPHYTES. See CONVERTS.

NEOPLATONISM.
B 517; B 645
sa Alexandrian school.
xx Alexandrian school.
Church history - Primitive and
early church.
Philosophy, Early Christian.

NEO-SCHOLASTICISM.
B 839
Here are entered works dealing
with the movement, begun in the
middle of the nineteenth century,
to bring scholastic philosophy
up to date, particularly by
keeping it in touch with contemporary scientific research.
x Philosophy, Scholastic.
Theology, Scholastic.
xx Philosophy, Modern.
Scholasticism.
Thomism.

NEPHITES.
sa Book of Mormons.
Indians - Origin.
Mormons and Mormonism.

NESTORIAN CHURCH.
x Chaldean Church.
East Syrian Church.
Syrian Church, East.

NESTORIAN CHURCH - HISTORY.
BQX 6431-6459   (273.x4)

302

NESTORIAN CHURCH - LAW.
BQV 1351-1254   (348.x7)

NESTORIAN CHURCH. LITURGY AND
RITUAL.
BQT 5407-5429

NESTORIAN MALABAR CHURCH. See
MALABAR JACOBITE CHURCH.

NESTORIAN MONASTICISM. See
MONASTICISM, NESTORIAN.

NESTORIANS.
BQT 68
BQX 6433
sa Assyrians, Modern.
xx Adoptionism.
Assyrians, Modern.
Heresies and heretics - Early
church.
Jesus Christ - History of
doctrines.

NESTORIANS IN CHINA.

NETHERLANDS - CHURCH HISTORY.
BQX 2322-2334   (274.92)

NETHERLANDS - CHURCH HISTORY -
MIDDLE AGES.

NETHERLANDS - CHURCH HISTORY -
1523-1648.

NETHERLANDS - CHURCH HISTORY -
1648-

NETHERLANDS - CHURCH HISTORY -
20th CENTURY.

NEUMES.
BQT 4592   (781.24)
xx Chant.
Other classifications and
references as in LC.

NEW DEVOTION. See
DEVOTIO MODERNA.

NEW ENGLAND THEOLOGY.
BX 7250
x Theology, New England.
xx Calvinism.
Congregationalism.

NEW JERUSALEM CHURCH.
BX 8701-8749   (289.4)
x Church of the New Jerusalem.
Swedenborgianism.
Subdivisions as in LC.

NEW TESTAMENT. See BIBLE. N.T.

NEW TESTAMENT GREEK. See
GREEK LANGUAGE, BIBLICAL.

NEW THOUGHT.
BF 638-645
References as in LC.

NEW YEAR, JEWISH. See
ROSH HA-SHANAH.

NEW YEAR SERMONS.
x Sermons, New Year.
xx Occasional sermons.

NEW YEAR'S EVE.

NEW YEAR'S EVE SERMONS.
BQT 3009
x Sermons, New Year's Eve.

NEWMAN CLUB.
BQT 3653
xx Catholic education.
Church work with students.

NEWSPAPERS, CATHOLIC. See
CATHOLIC NEWSPAPERS.

NICAEA, COUNCIL OF, 325.
BQX 402   (26x2.21)
BQV 12 (Documents)

NICAEA, COUNCIL OF, 787.
BQX 556
BQV 12 (Documents)

NICENE-CONSTANTINOPOLITAN CREED.
BQT 149
x Constantinopolitan Creed.

NICENE CREED.
BQT 147   (238.1)
sa Nicaea, Council of, 325.
xx Creeds.
Filioque controversy.

NICENE CREED (MUSIC). See
   CREDO (MUSIC)

NIHILIANISM.
      BQT 86
   x Nihilism (Theology)
   xx God.
      Jesus Christ - History of
         doctrines.
      Sects, Medieval.

NIHILISM.
      BX 914-917
   References as in LC.

NIHILISM (PHILOSOPHY)

NIHILISM (THEOLOGY). See
   NIHILIANISM.

NINE FIRST FRIDAYS. See
   FIRST FRIDAY DEVOTIONS.

NIRVANA.
      BL 1475.N
   sa Annihilationism.

NISI DOMINUS AEDIFICAVERIT
   DOMUM (MUSIC). See
   PSALMS (MUSIC) - 126th PSALM.

NO-POPERY RIOTS, 1780. See
   GORDON RIOTS, 1780.

NOAH'S ARK.
   xx Deluge.

NOBILITY, PAPAL.   (Geog. subdiv.,
   Indirect)
         CR 5547-5577 (Orders,
            decorations, etc.)
   x Papal nobility.

NOBLEMAN'S SON (MIRACLE). See
   HEALING OF THE NOBLEMAN'S SON
   (MIRACLE)

NON-CATHOLICS.
   Here are entered works about non-
   Catholics insofar as they are
   subject to or exempt from the
   laws of the Catholic Church.
   The term non-Catholics includes

NON-CATHOLICS -- Continued.
   non-baptized persons as well as
   baptized persons who adhere to
   heretical forms of Christianity.
   sa Apostasy.
      Communicatio in sacris.
      Heresies and heretics.
      Infidels.
      Paganism.
      Protestants.
      Retreats for non-Catholics.
      Salvation outside the Church.
      Schism.
   xx Catholic Church.
      Catholics, Lapsed.

NON-CATHOLICS - DEVOTIONAL
   LITERATURE.
      BQT 3573

NON-CATHOLICS (CANON LAW)
      BQV230 12
      BQV230 1099
      BQV230 1325
      BQV230 1350

NON CHURCH-AFFILIATED PEOPLE.
   (Geog. subdiv., Direct)
   xx Church and social problems.
      Irreligion.
      Religion and sociology.

NONJURORS.
      BX 5087   (274.2)
   xx Church of England.

NONJURORS, ENGLISH CATHOLIC.
      DA 499
   x Catholic nonjurors, English.
      English Catholic nonjurors.

NONJURORS, FRENCH CATHOLIC.
      BQX 1783
   sa Louisets.
   x Catholic nonjurors, French.
      French Catholic nonjurors.
   xx Catholic Church - France.
      Catholics in France.
      France - History - Revolution -
         Religious history.
      Louisets.

NORITO. See SHINTO PRAYERS.

NORWAY - CHURCH HISTORY.
        BQX 2732-2738   (274.81)

NOSAIRIANS.
        BP 195.N   (297)
    References as in LC.

NOSSA SENHORA DA FATIMA (SHRINE). See
    FATIMA, PORTUGAL (SHRINE)

NOTARIES (CANON LAW)
    xx Chancellors, Diocesan.

NOTRE DAME DE LA SALETTE (SHRINE).
    See LA SALETTE, FRANCE (SHRINE)

NOTRE DAME DE LOURDES (SHRINE). See
    LOURDES (SHRINE)

NOVATIONISTS.
        BQT 50
    xx Asceticism - History - Early
        church.
        Heresies and heretics - Early
        church.

NOVEMBER DEVOTIONS.
        BQT 4495
    xx Devotions, Popular.
        Prayers for the dead.

NOVENAS.
        BQT 4494   (24x8.7)
    xx Devotions, Popular.

NOVENAS - ALL SOULS' DAY.
    x All Souls' Day - Novenas.

NOVENAS - BLESSED VIRGIN MARY.
    x Mary, Blessed Virgin - Novenas.

NOVENAS - SACRED HEART.
    x Sacred Heart - Novenas.

NOVENAS - SACRED HEARTS.
    x Sacred Hearts - Novenas.

NOVENAS - ST. JOSEPH.
    x Joseph, Saint - Novenas.

NOVENAS - SERMONS.

NOVICE MASTERS. See
    MASTER OF NOVICES.

NOVICE MISTRESSES. See
    MASTER OF NOVICES.

NOVICES. See NOVITIATE.

NOVICIATE. See NOVITIATE.

NOVITIATE.
        BQT 2327
    sa Master of novices.
        Postulancy.
    x Novices.
        Noviciate.
    xx Religious life.

NOVITIATE - BENEDICTINES, [CARME-
    LITES, ETC.]

NOVITIATE (CANON LAW)
        BQV230 542-571   (348.x57)
    xx Religious orders (Canon law)
    Nuclear Warfare   x Atomic warfare
NUESTRA SENORA DE GUADALUPE (SHRINE),
    MEXICO. See GUADALUPE, MEXICO
    (SHRINE)

NUESTRA SENORA DE GUADALUPE (SHRINE),
    SPAIN. See GUADALUPE, SPAIN
    (SHRINE)

NULLITY (CANON LAW)
        BQV230 11
    sa Actions and defenses (Canon
        law)
        Ignorance (Canon law)
        Marriage - Annulment (Canon
        law)

NULLITY OF MARRIAGE. See
    MARRIAGE - ANNULMENT.

NUMBERS, BOOK OF. See
    BIBLE. O.T. NUMBERS.

NUMINOUS, THE. See
    HOLY, THE.

NUMISMATICS.
        CJ (general)
        BQT 6028 (Religious art)
        BQX 67 (Christian archaeology)
    References and subdivisions as
        in LC.

NUNC DIMITTIS.
    BQT 2695
  x Canticle of Simeon.
    Simeon, Canticle of.

NUNCIATURE CONTROVERSY. See
  NUNCIOS, PAPAL.

NUNCIOS, PAPAL.
    BQV230 265-270   (348.x324)
  sa Legates, Papal.
  x Nunciature controversy.
    Nuntios, Papal.
    Papal nuncios.
  xx Ambassadors.
    Diplomats.
    Holy See - Diplomatic service.
    Legates, Papal.

NUNNERIES. See CONVENTS.

NUNS.
    BQX 6842
  Here are entered works on cloistered
    religious orders of women dedi-
    cated to the contemplative life.
  sa Abbesses.
    Contemplative life.
    Convents.
    Religious orders of women.
    also names of orders of nuns,
      e.g., Benedictine Nuns,
      Carmelite Nuns, Poor Clares,
      etc.
  x Monastic life for women.
    Women in religion.
  xx Monasticism.
    Religious life for women.
    Religious orders of women.

NUNS - RETREATS. See
  RETREATS FOR NUNS.

NUNS (CANON LAW)
    BQV230 488,7   (348.x37)
  xx Religious orders of women
    (Canon law)

NUNS IN LITERATURE.
  xx Women in literature.

NUNTIONS, PAPAL. See
  NUNCIOS, PAPAL.

NUPTIAL MASS. See MASS, NUPTIAL.

NURSES AND NURSING.
    BQT 2011 (Moral obligations)
    BQT 3685 (Church work)
  Other classifications and refer-
    ences as in LC.

NURSES AND NURSING - PRAYER-BOOKS.
    BQT 2648

NURSES AND NURSING - RETREATS. See
  RETREATS FOR NURSES.

O ANTIPHONS.
    BQT 4221
  x Greater antiphons.
  xx Advent.

OATHS (CANON LAW)
    BQV230 1316-1321   (348.x415)
  xx Vows (Canon law)

OBADIAH, BOOK OF. See
  BIBLE. O.T. ABDIAS.

OBEDIENCE.
    BQT 1892-1895   (24x1.62)
  xx Conduct of life.
    Evangelical counsels.

OBEDIENCE (CANON LAW)

OBEDIENCE (VOW)
    BQT 2314   (24x7.16)
  xx Vows.

OBLATES.
    BQX 6838
  Here are entered works dealing
    with members, men or women, of
    certain religious communities,
    who have offered themselves to
    the service of God without be-
    coming professed monks or sis-
    ters of the community. They may
    or may not live with the monas-
    tic community.
  More recently the term also applies
    to certain congregations of pro-
    fessed religious, men or women,
    in the accepted sense of religious
    community, e.g., Oblates of Mary
    Immaculate, Oblate Sisters of the
    Assumption.

OBLATES -- Continued.
  sa Third orders.
    also subdivision "Oblates" under
     the names of some religious orders,
     e.g., Benedictines. Oblates.
  xx Religious orders.
    Third orders.

OBLATES OF ST. BENEDICT. See
  BENEDICTINES. OBLATES.

OBLATIONS. See OFFERINGS.

OBSEQUIES. See
  FUNERAL RITES AND CEREMONIES.

OBSERVANCE (VIRTUE)
    BQT 1793
  Observance is a special virtue
    annexed to justice "whereby
    worship and honor are paid to
    persons in positions of
    dignity." Summa theol. II,
    II, q.102, a.1.
  xx Justice (Virtue)

OBSESSION.
    BF 1555 (Occultism)   (133.4)
    BQT 666; BQT 2491
  sa Demonomania.
  xx Demonomania.

OCCASIONAL SERMONS.
    [BQT 3000]   (252.x5)
  Here are entered works containing
    a collection of sermons preached
    on special days or for special
    occasions, e.g., anniversaries,
    dedications, festivals, funerals,
    First Mass, etc. Works con-
    taining sermons of one kind only
    are entered under the specific
    subject, e.g., Confirmation -
    Sermons; Funeral sermons; etc.
  sa Anniversary sermons.
    Baccalaureate addresses.
    Church dedication - Sermons.
    Confirmation - Sermons.
    Election sermons.
    Farewell sermons.
    First Communion sermons.
    First Mass sermons.
    Funeral sermons.

OCCASIONAL SERMONS -- Continued.
  sa Marriage - Sermons.
    New Year sermons.
    Ordination sermons.
    Thanksgiving sermons.
  x Sermons, Occasional.
    Sermons for special occasions.

OCCASIONALISM.
  xx God.
  Other references as in LC supple-
    ment 1956-58.

OCCASIONARII.
    BQT 1734

OCCASIONS FOR SIN.
    BQT 1805
  x Sin, Occasions for.
  xx Temptation.

OCCULT SCIENCES.
    BF 1405-1999   (133)
  References as in LC.

OCCULTISM IN LITERATURE.
  sa Mysticism in literature.
    Supernatural in literature.
  xx Mysticism in literature.
    Supernatural in literature.

OCTATEUCH (BIBLE). See
  BIBLE. O.T. OCTATEUCH.

OCTAVARIUM ROMANUM.
    BQT 4388
  xx Breviarium.

OCTAVES (LITURGY)
    [BQT 4217]

OCTOBER DEVOTIONS.
    BQT 4495
  xx Devotions, Popular.
    Rosary.

OECUMENICAL COUNCILS. See
  COUNCILS AND SYNODS, ECUMENICAL.

OFFENSES AGAINST RELIGION.
  sa Apostasy.
    Blasphemy.
    Heresy.

OFFENSES AGAINST RELIGION -- Continued.
  sa Insubordination (Canon law)
     Sacrilege.
     Simony.
   x Crimes, Religious.
     Crimes against religion.
     Religion, Crimes against.
     Religion, Offenses against.
  xx Criminal law.

OFFENSES AGAINST RELIGION (CANON LAW)
     BQV230 2320-2329

OFFERINGS.
  Here are entered works on bread,
    wine, candles and other vegetable
    and lifeless things, formerly
    offered in kind by the people
    of various religions and by
    Catholics especially at Mass.
  sa Mass stipends.
   x Oblations.
  xx Sacrifice.

OFFERINGS (JUDAISM)

OFFERINGS, VOTIVE. See
  VOTIVE OFFERINGS.

OFFERTORIES.
  "Here are entered works on the
    place of the offertory in the
    mass of the Catholic Church,
    and on the music accompanying
    it; also general works of an
    inclusive nature." LC
   x Offertory.
  xx Mass - Music.

OFFERTORIES - ANGLICAN COMMUNION,
  [LUTHERAN CHURCH, ETC.]

OFFERTORIES (CHANT)
     BQT 4629
  xx Antiphonal chant.

OFFERTORIES (MUSIC)
     BQT 4667
     M 2079; M 2099
  xx Propers (Music)

OFFERTORY. See OFFERTORIES.

OFFICE, DIVINE. See
  DIVINE OFFICE.

OFFICE FOR THE DEAD. See
  OFFICIUM PRO DEFUNCTIS.

OFFICE OF ALL SOULS' DAY. See
  OFFICIUM IN COMMEMORATIONE
  OMNIUM FIDELIUM DEFUNCTORUM.

OFFICE OF JESUS CHRIST THE KING.
  See OFFICIUM DOMINI NOSTRI JESU
  CHRISTI REGIS.

OFFICE OF OUR LADY OF THE SACRED
  HEART. See OFFICIUM BEATAE MARIAE
  VIRGINIS A SACRO CORDE JESU.

OFFICE OF SAINT AGATHA, [GERTRUDE,
  HEDWIG, ETC.]. See
  OFFICIUM SANCTAE AGATHAE, [GER-
  TRUDIS, HEDWIGIS, ETC.]

OFFICE OF SAINT BARNABAS, [BRUNO,
  DAMASUS, ETC.]. See
  OFFICIUM SANCTI BARNABAE, [BRU-
  NONIS, DAMASI, ETC.]

OFFICE OF THE BLESSED VIRGIN, LITTLE.
  See OFFICIUM PARVUM BEATAE MARIAE
  VIRGINIS.

OFFICE OF THE IMMACULATE CONCEPTION.
  See OFFICIUM IN CONCEPTIONE IMMA-
  CULATA BEATAE MARIAE VIRGINIS.

OFFICE OF THE MOST BLESSED SACRAMENT.
  See OFFICIUM DE SANCTISSIMO SACRA-
  MENTO.

OFFICE OF THE SACRED HEART. See
  OFFICIUM SACRATISSIMI CORDIS JESU.

OFFICES, ECCLESIASTICAL.
     BQV230 145-195   (348.x31)
  sa Election law (Canon law)
   x Ecclesiastical office.
  xx Clergy (Canon law)

OFFICIA PROPRIA.
     BQT 4399
  A collection of texts of the
    divine office proper to locali-

308

OFFICIA PROPRIA -- Continued.
  ties. Subdivided by religious order
  (e.g., Officia propria. Augustinian), by abbey (e.g., Officia
  propria. Montecassino (Benedictine
  abbey)), by diocese (e.g., Officia
  propria. Ratisbon (Diocese)), by
  cathedral (e.g., Officia propria.
  Canterbury (Cathedral)).
  xx Breviarium.

OFFICIUM ...
  Single divine office texts in
  honor of Our Lord, the Blessed
  Virgin Mary, the saints, etc.,
  are entered under the heading
  beginning with Officium, as in
  the following entries.

OFFICIUM BEATAE MARIAE VIRGINIS A
  SACRO CORDE JESU.
    BQT 4397
  x Office of Our Lady of the Sacred
    Heart.
    Our Lady of the Sacred Heart,
    Office of.

OFFICIUM CORPORIS CHRISTI.
    BQT 4395
  xx Corpus Christi festival.

OFFICIUM DE SANCTISSIMO SACRAMENTO.
    BQT 4395
  x Blessed Sacrament, Office of the.
    Office of the Blessed Sacrament.

OFFICIUM DOMINI NOSTRI JESU CHRISTI
  REGIS.
    BQT 4395
  x Jesus Christ the King, Office of.
    Office of Jesus Christ the King.

OFFICIUM HEBDOMADAE SANCTAE.
    BQT 4391-4392   (26x5.9)
  A name given to the book contain-
    ing all the liturgical prayers
    for Holy Week.
  sa Ordo Hebdomadae Sanctae.
  x Holy Week Office.
  xx Holy Week.

OFFICIUM HEBDOMADAE SANCTAE.   ENGLISH,
  [FRENCH, GERMAN, ETC.]

OFFICIUM IN COMMEMORATIONE OMNIUM
  FIDELIUM DEFUNCTORUM.
    BQT 4398
  x All Souls' Day Office.
    Office of All Souls' Day.

OFFICIUM IN CONCEPTIONE IMMACULATA
  BEATAE MARIAE VIRGINIS.
    BQT 4397
  x Immaculate Conception, Office
    of the.
    Office of the Immaculate Con-
    ception.

OFFICIUM IN EPIPHANIA DOMINI NOSTRI
  JESU CHRISTI.
    BQT 4395
  xx Epiphany.

OFFICIUM IN NATIVITATE DOMINI NOSTRI
  JESU CHRISTI.
    BQT 4395
  xx Christmas service.

OFFICIUM PARVUM BEATAE MARIAE
  VIRGINIS.
    BQT 4401-4409   (24x8.72)
  x Little Office of the Blessed
    Virgin.
    Mary, Blessed Virgin, Little
    Office of the.
  xx Mary, Blessed Virgin - Prayer-
    books.

OFFICIUM PARVUM BEATAE MARIAE
  VIRGINIS - COMMENTARIES.
    BQT 4409

OFFICIUM PARVUM BEATAE MARIAE
  VIRGINIS. ENGLISH, [FRENCH,
  GERMAN, ETC.]

OFFICIUM PASCHATIS.
    BQT 4395
  x Easter Office.

OFFICIUM PASSIONIS DOMINI NOSTRI
  JESUS CHRISTI.
    BQT 4395
  x Passion of Christ, Office of
    the.
  xx Jesus Christ - Passion.

OFFICIUM PENTECOSTES.
[BQT 4396]
xx Pentecost festival.

OFFICIUM PRO DEFUNCTIS.
BQT 4411-4419
x Dead, Office for the.
Office for the dead.
xx Breviarium.
Prayers for the dead.

OFFICIUM PRO DEFUNCTIS. BENEDICTINE,
[CISTERCIAN, ETC.]
BQT 4736; BQT 4766; etc.

OFFICIUM SACRATISSIMI CORDIS JESU.
BQT 4395
x Office of the Sacred Heart.
Sacred Heart, Office of the.

OFFICIUM SANCTAE AGATHAE, [GERTRUDIS,
HEDWIGIS, ETC.]
BQT 4398
x Office of Saint Agatha, [Ger-
trude, Hedwig, etc.]

OFFICIUM SANCTI BARNABAE, [BRUNONIS,
DAMASI, ETC.]
BQT 4398
x Office of Saint Barnabas,
[Bruno, Damasus, etc.]

OIL, HOLY. See HOLY OILS.

O-KEE-PA (RELIGIOUS CEREMONY)
E 99.M (Mandan Indians)
xx Indians of North America -
Dances.

OKTOECHOS.
BQT 5254
A liturgical book of the Byzantine
Rite for the Divine Office (and
the less variable parts of the
Mass) from the first Sunday after
Pentecost till the 10th Sunday
before Easter.

OLD AGE - RELIGIOUS LIFE.

OLD CATHOLIC CHURCH.
BX 4751-4793
xx Jansenists.

OLD CATHOLICISM.
BX 4751-4793   (284.81)
x Catholicism, Old.
Christian Catholicism.

OLD CHURCH SLAVIC LANGUAGE. See
CHURCH SLAVIC LANGUAGE.

OLD SLOVENIAN LANGUAGE. See
CHURCH SLAVIC LANGUAGE.

OLD TESTAMENT. See BIBLE. O.T.

OLIVETANS.
BQX 7103
x Benedictines, Olivetan.
xx Benedictines.

OMNES GENTES, PLAUDITE MANIBUS (MUSIC).
See PSALMS (MUSIC) - 46th PSALM.

ONTOLOGISM.
BQT 529
"A philosophical system according
to which God is the principle
and the means of our knowledge."
AT
sa Pantheism.
xx God.
Theism.

ORATIONS (LITURGY). See
COLLECTS.

ORATORIES.
BQT 5926   (726.41)
xx Chapels.
Churches.

ORATORIES (CANON LAW)
BQV230 1188-1196   (348.x413)
xx Churches (Canon law)
Sacred places (Canon law)

ORDEN DER RITTER DES HOSPITALS ST.
MARIEN DES DEUTSCHEN HAUSES. See
TEUTONIC KNIGHTS.

ORDER OF CITEAUX. See
CISTERCIANS.

ORDER OF FRIARS MINOR. See
FRANCISCANS.

310

ORDER OF FRIARS MINOR CAPUCHIN. See
CAPUCHINS.

ORDER OF FRIARS PREACHERS. See
DOMINICANS.

ORDER OF MALTA. See
KNIGHTS OF MALTA.

ORDER OF OUR LADY OF MOUNT CARMEL.
See CARMELITES.

ORDER OF ST. AUGUSTINE. See
AUGUSTINIANS.

ORDER OF ST. BASIL THE GREAT. See
BASILIANS.

ORDER OF ST. BENEDICT. See
BENEDICTINES.

ORDER OF ST. CLARE. See
POOR CLARES.

ORDER OF ST. JOHN OF JERUSALEM.
See KNIGHTS OF MALTA.

ORDER OF ST. JOHN OF JERUSALEM (ANGLI-
CAN)
x English Order of St. John of
Jerusalem.

ORDER OF ST. JOHN OF JERUSALEM (EVAN-
GELICAL)
x Evangelical Order of St. John
of Jerusalem.
Johanniterorden.

ORDERS, ANGLICAN. See
ANGLICAN ORDERS.

ORDERS, HOLY. See ORDINATION.

ORDERS, MAJOR. See MAJOR ORDERS.

ORDERS, MINOR. See MINOR ORDERS.

ORDERS, MONASTIC. See
MONASTICISM.

ORDERS, RELIGIOUS. See
RELIGIOUS ORDERS.

ORDERS OF KNIGHTHOOD AND CHIVALRY,
PAPAL.
BQX 172
x Papal orders of knighthood and
chivalry.

ORDINALE.
BQT 4273
"A form of prayers and ceremonies
for the conferring of Holy
Orders." AT

ORDINARIES.
BQV230 198   (348.x31)
xx Persons (Canon law)

ORDINARIUM.
BQT 4273
A liturgical book of the Middle
Ages, containing regulations
for church services. It is the
forerunner of the modern Rituale
and Caeremoniale.
sa Rituale.
x Liber Ordinarius.

ORDINARIUM MISSAE.
BQT 4254
By this term is understood that
section of the Missal which com-
prises the unchanging part of
the Mass, including the entire
canon.
sa Canon Missae.
Kyriale.
x Ordinary of the Mass.
xx Mass of the Faithful.
Missale.

ORDINARIUM MISSAE (CHANT). See
KYRIALE.

ORDINARIUM MISSAE (MUSIC). See
MASSES.

ORDINARY OF THE MASS. See
ORDINARIUM MISSAE.

ORDINATION.
BQT 1413-1415   (23x7.6)
sa Bishops.
Deacons.
Major orders.

ORDINATION -- Continued.
  sa Minor orders.
    Priests.
    Subdeacons.
   x Holy orders.
    Orders, Holy.
  xx Clergy.
    Major orders.
    Minor orders.
    Priesthood.
    Sacraments.

ORDINATION - CATECHISMS, QUESTION-
  BOOKS.

ORDINATION - HANDBOOKS, MANUALS,
  ETC.
      BQT 1415

ORDINATION - HISTORY.

ORDINATION - IMPEDIMENTS.
      BQV230 983-991
  sa Irregularities.
   x Impediments to ordination.
  xx Impediments (Canon law)

ORDINATION - MEDITATIONS.
    [BQT 2608.2]

ORDINATION - SERMONS. See
  ORDINATION SERMONS.

ORDINATION (CANON LAW)
      BQV230 948-1011   (348.x426)
  sa Incardination (Canon law)
    Irregularities.
    Trials, Ecclesiastical (Ordina-
      tion)
  xx Clergy (Canon law)
    Marriage - Impediments (Canon
      law)
    Sacraments (Canon law)

ORDINATION (CANON LAW) - HISTORY.

ORDINATION (LITURGY)
      BQT 4448-4451
  xx Sacraments (Liturgy)

ORDINATION SERMONS.
      BQT 3004
  sa First Mass sermons.
   x Ordination - Sermons.
    Sermons, Ordination.
  xx Occasional sermons.

ORDO CANONICORUM REGULARIUM SANCTI
  AUGUSTINI. See
  AUGUSTINIAN CANONS.

ORDO CARTUSIANORUM. See
  CARTHUSIANS.

ORDO DIVINI OFFICII [with name of
  diocese or of religious order]
      BQT 4281-4287
   x Directorium.

ORDO FRATRUM BEATISSIMAE VIRGINIS
  MARIAE DE MONTE CARMELO. See
  CARMELITES.

ORDO FRATRUM CARMELITARUM. See
  CARMELITES.

ORDO FRATRUM CARMELITARUM DISCAL-
  CEATORUM. See
  CARMELITES, DISCALCED.

ORDO FRATRUM EREMITARUM SANCTI
  AUGUSTINI. See AUGUSTINIANS.

ORDO FRATRUM HOSPITALIORUM HIERO-
  SOLYMITANORUM. See
  KNIGHTS OF MALTA.

ORDO FRATRUM MINORUM. See
  FRANCISCANS.

ORDO FRATRUM MINORUM CAPUCCINORUM.
  See CAPUCHINS.

ORDO FRATRUM PRAEDICATORUM. See
  DOMINICANS.

ORDO HEBDOMADAE SANCTAE.
      BQT 4326; [BQT 4391.3]
  The name of the text for the
    Masses of Holy Week as revised
    by Pope Pius XII and first
    published in 1956.

312

ORDO HEBDOMADAE SANCTAE -- Continued.
sa Ordo Sabbati Sancti.
xx Holy Week.
    Officium Hebdomadae Sanctae.

ORDO MILITIAE SANCTI JOANNIS BAPTISTAE
HOSPITALIS HIEROSOLYMITANI. See
KNIGHTS OF MALTA.

ORDO ROMANUS.
    BQT 4271
The name of a collection of rubrics
  and directions for the carrying
  out of sacred ceremonies according to the use of the Latin Church
  from the 7th to the 15th century.

ORDO SABBATI SANCTI.
    [BQT 4391.6]
The name of the text used for the
  new Easter vigil service, first
  published in 1951.
sa Missa in Sabbato Sancto.
xx Easter Vigil.
    Holy Saturday.
    Ordo Hebdomadae Sanctae.

ORDO SANCTAE CLARAE. See
POOR CLARES.

ORDO SANCTI BASILII MAGNI. See
BASILIANS.

ORDO SANCTI BENEDICTI. See
BENEDICTINES.

ORDRE DE CHARTREUX. See
CARTHUSIANS.

ORGAN, BLESSING OF.
    BQT 4522
x Blessing of organ.

ORGAN MASS.
    ML 647
xx Mass (Music)

ORGAN MASSES.
    M 14.3
x Instrumental masses.
  Masses, Instrumental.
  Masses, Organ.

ORIENTAL CANON LAW. See
CODEX JURIS CANONICI ORIENTALIS.
EASTERN CHURCHES - CANON LAW.

ORIENTAL CHURCH, CONGREGATION FOR
THE. See CONGREGATIO PRO
ECCLESIA ORIENTALI.

ORIENTAL CHURCHES. See
EASTERN CHURCHES.

ORIENTATION (RELIGION)
    BL 619
xx Symbolism, Christian.
Other references as in LC.

ORIENTATION OF CHURCHES.
    [BQT 5914.5]
x Churches - Orientation.
xx Church architecture.
   Symbolism, Christian.

ORIGINAL JUSTICE. See
JUSTICE, ORIGINAL.

ORIGINAL SIN. See
SIN, ORIGINAL.

ORTHODOX EASTERN CHURCH.   (Geog.
subdiv., Direct)
Here are entered works dealing
  with those Eastern Churches
  which follow the Byzantine Rite
  in various languages, but
  acknowledge no allegiance to
  the Pope.
sa Byzantine Rite.
x Eastern Orthodox Church.
  Greek Church.
  Holy Orthodox Eastern Catholic
    and Apostolic Church.
xx Byzantine Rite.

ORTHODOX EASTERN CHURCH - ASCETICISM.
See ASCETICISM - ORTHODOX EASTERN
CHURCH.

ORTHODOX EASTERN CHURCH - BIBLIOGRAPHY.

ORTHODOX EASTERN CHURCH - CATECHISMS.
    BQX 5877

ORTHODOX EASTERN CHURCH - CHURCH MUSIC.
See CHURCH MUSIC - ORTHODOX EASTERN
CHURCH.

ORTHODOX EASTERN CHURCH - CONFESSION.
See CONFESSION - ORTHODOX EASTERN
CHURCH.

ORTHODOX EASTERN CHURCH - CONVERTS.
See CONVERTS, ORTHODOX EASTERN.

ORTHODOX EASTERN CHURCH - GOVERNMENT.

ORTHODOX EASTERN CHURCH - HERESIES
AND HERETICS. See
HERESIES AND HERETICS - ORTHODOX
EASTERN CHURCH.

ORTHODOX EASTERN CHURCH - HISTORY.
      BQX 5801-6189   (28x1.1)
sa Schism - Eastern and Western
      Church.

ORTHODOX EASTERN CHURCH - HYMNS.

ORTHODOX EASTERN CHURCH - LAW.
      BQV 1360-1484   (348.x7)

ORTHODOX EASTERN CHURCH - MEMBERSHIP.

ORTHODOX EASTERN CHURCH - MISSIONS.

ORTHODOX EASTERN CHURCH - MYSTICISM.
See MYSTICISM - ORTHODOX EASTERN
CHURCH.

ORTHODOX EASTERN CHURCH - PERIODICALS.

ORTHODOX EASTERN CHURCH - POPULAR
DEVOTIONS.
      BQT 5236

ORTHODOX EASTERN CHURCH - PRAYER-
BOOKS.
      BQX 5896

ORTHODOX EASTERN CHURCH - RELATIONS -
CATHOLIC CHURCH.
      BQX 5890
sa Schism - Eastern and Western
      Church.
      Schism, Acacian, 484-519.

ORTHODOX EASTERN CHURCH - SAINTS.
      BQX 5898
x Saints - Orthodox Eastern Church.

ORTHODOX EASTERN CHURCH - SERMONS.
      BQX 5885

ORTHODOX EASTERN CHURCH - THEOLOGY.
      BQX 5876-5914

ORTHODOX EASTERN CHURCH - YEARBOOKS.

################

ORTHODOX EASTERN CHURCH. LITURGY AND
RITUAL.
      BQT 5232-5347   (264.x76)

################

ORTHODOX EASTERN CHURCH, ALBANIAN.
x Albanian Orthodox Church.

ORTHODOX EASTERN CHURCH, ALBANIAN -
HISTORY.
      BQX 5921-5927

ORTHODOX EASTERN CHURCH, ALBANIAN -
LAW.
      BQV 1391-1394

ORTHODOX EASTERN CHURCH, ALBANIAN.
LITURGY AND RITUAL.
      BQT 5262-5263

ORTHODOX EASTERN CHURCH, BULGARIAN.
x Bulgarian Orthodox Church.

ORTHODOX EASTERN CHURCH, BULGARIAN -
HISTORY.
      BQX 5931-5939   (28x1.1)

ORTHODOX EASTERN CHURCH, BULGARIAN -
LAW.
      BQV 1396-1399   (348.x7)

ORTHODOX EASTERN CHURCH, BULGARIAN.
LITURGY AND RITUAL.
      BQT 5270-5271   (264.x76)

ORTHODOX EASTERN CHURCH, GREEK.
x Greek Orthodox Church.

ORTHODOX EASTERN CHURCH, GREEK -
HISTORY.
BQX 2991-2997

ORTHODOX EASTERN CHURCH, GREEK -
LAW.
BQV 1421-1424

ORTHODOX EASTERN CHURCH, GREEK.
LITURGY AND RITUAL.
BQT 5294-5295

ORTHODOX EASTERN CHURCH, RUMANIAN.
x Rumanian Orthodox Church.

ORTHODOX EASTERN CHURCH, RUMANIAN -
HISTORY.
BQX 6021-6029   (28x1.1)

ORTHODOX EASTERN CHURCH, RUMANIAN -
LAW.
BQV 1431-1440   (348.x7)

ORTHODOX EASTERN CHURCH, RUMANIAN.
LITURGY AND RITUAL.
BQT 5302-5303   (264.x76)

ORTHODOX EASTERN CHURCH, RUSSIAN.
sa Sects, Russian.
x Russian Church.

ORTHODOX EASTERN CHURCH, RUSSIAN -
HISTORY.
BQX 6031-6149   (28x1.1)

ORTHODOX EASTERN CHURCH, RUSSIAN -
LAW.
BQV 1441-1470   (348.x7)

ORTHODOX EASTERN CHURCH, RUSSIAN -
RELATIONS - CATHOLIC CHURCH,
[CHURCH OF ENGLAND, ETC.]

ORTHODOX EASTERN CHURCH, RUSSIAN -
THEOLOGY.
BQX 6125

ORTHODOX EASTERN CHURCH, RUSSIAN.
LITURGY AND RITUAL.
BQT 5306-5307   (264.x76)

ORTHODOX EASTERN CHURCH SERBIAN.
x Serbian Orthodox Church.

ORTHODOX EASTERN CHURCH, SERBIAN -
HISTORY.
BQX 6161-6179   (28x1.1)

ORTHODOX EASTERN CHURCH, SERBIAN -
LAW.
BQV 1471-1481   (348.x7)

ORTHODOX EASTERN CHURCH, SERBIAN.
LITURGY AND RITUAL.
BQT 5342-5343   (264.x76)

ORTHODOX EASTERN CHURCHES. See
EASTERN CHURCHES, ORTHODOX.

ORTHODOX EASTERN MONASTICISM. See
MONASTICISM, ORTHODOX EASTERN.

OSEE, BOOK OF. See
BIBLE. O.T. OSEE.

OSTENSORIUM. See MONSTRANCE.

OSTIARIES (HOLY ORDERS). See
MINOR ORDERS.

OUR FATHER. See
LORD'S PRAYER.

OUR LADY HELP OF CHRISTIANS. See
HELP OF CHRISTIANS.

OUR LADY OF FATIMA (SHRINE). See
FATIMA, PORTUGAL (SHRINE)

OUR LADY OF FATIMA, DEVOTION TO.
BQT 2598
BQT 2679

OUR LADY OF FATIMA, NOVENA TO. See
NOVENAS - OUR LADY OF FATIMA.

OUR LADY OF GUADALUPE (SHRINE), MEXICO.
See GUADALUPE, MEXICO (SHRINE)

OUR LADY OF GUADALUPE (SHRINE), SPAIN.
See GUADALUPE, SPAIN (SHRINE)

OUR LADY OF GUADALUPE, DEVOTION TO.
BQT 2598
BQT 2679

OUR LADY OF GUADALUPE, FEAST OF.
BQT 4230
x Feast of Our Lady of Guadalupe.

OUR LADY OF GUADALUPE, MASS OF. See
MISSA BEATAE MARIAE VIRGINIS DE
GUADALUPE.

OUR LADY OF LA SALETTE (SHRINE). See
LA SALETTE, FRANCE (SHRINE)

OUR LADY OF LOURDES (SHRINE). See
LOURDES (SHRINE)

OUR LADY OF LOURDES, DEVOTION TO.
BQT 2598
BQT 2679

OUR LADY OF LOURDES, FEAST OF.
BQT 4230
x Feast of Our Lady of Lourdes.

OUR LADY OF LOURDES, MASS OF. See
MISSA DE APPARITIONE BEATAE MARIAE
VIRGINIS IMMACULATAE.

OUR LADY OF MOUNT CARMEL, FEAST OF.
BQT 4230
x Feast of Our Lady of Mount
Carmel.
Mount Carmel, Feast of Our
Lady of.

OUR LADY OF MOUNT CARMEL, ORDER OF.
See CARMELITES.

OUR LADY OF THE BLESSED SACRAMENT.
BQT 2679
x Blessed Sacrament, Our Lady
of the.

OUR LADY OF THE SACRED HEART.
BQT 2679
x Sacred Heart, Our Lady of the.

OUR LADY OF THE SACRED HEART -
DEVOTIONAL LITERATURE.

OUR LADY OF THE SACRED HEART -
MEDITATIONS.
BQT 2598

OUR LADY OF THE SACRED HEART -
PRAYER-BOOKS.
BQT 2679

OUR LADY OF THE SACRED HEART,
FEAST OF.
BQT 4230
x Feast of Our Lady of the
Sacred Heart.

OUR LADY OF THE SACRED HEART,
MASS OF. See
MISSA BEATAE MARIAE VIRGINIS
A SACRO CORDE JESU.

OUR LADY OF THE SACRED HEART,
NOVENA TO. See
NOVENAS - OUR LADY OF THE
SACRED HEART.

OUR LADY OF THE SACRED HEART,
OFFICE OF. See
OFFICIUM BEATAE MARIAE VIRGINIS
A SACRO CORDE JESU.

OXFORD MOVEMENT.
BQX 2093   (270.x81)
sa Anglo-Catholicism.
x Tractarianism.
xx Church of England.

PAGANISM.
BL   (290)
BQX 291-299 (Church history)
BQ 68 (Paganism and Christian
literature)
BQT 44 (Paganism and theology)
sa Civilization, Pagan.
x Heathenism.
xx Christianity and other religions.
Infidels.
Non-Catholics.
Religions.

PAGANISM AND CHRISTIANITY. See
CHRISTIANITY AND PAGANISM.

PAGANISM IN LITERATURE.

PAINTING, RELIGIOUS.
BQT 6042-6218
x Religious painting.
xx Christian era.

316

PALATINI.
By this term are understood high
officials of the papal court
from the 4th to the 11th century. Their Latin name was
"judices palatini."
xx Papal court.

PALEOGRAPHY, MUSICAL.
sa Chant - Manuscripts.
Other references as in LC.
Palestine see Holy Land
PALESTINE - CHURCH HISTORY.
BQX 3445-3447
BQX 5570-5577

PALESTINE - HISTORY - TO A.D. 70.
sa Bible - History of Biblical
events.
Bible - History of contemporary
events.
Judaism - History - Ancient
period.

PALESTINE - RELIGION.
BL 1670-1672

PALESTINE (PATRIARCHATE)
BQX 3445

PALLIUM.
BQT 4365 (Church vestments)
BQV230 275-279 (Canon law)
(348.x324)
xx Archbishops (Canon law)
Church vestments.

PALM SUNDAY.
BQT 4223   (264.x52)
xx Holy Week.

PALM SUNDAY - SERMONS.
[BQT 2995.4]

PAMPHLETS, CATHOLIC. See
CATHOLIC PAMPHLETS.

PAN (DEITY)
BL 820.P

PANTHEISM.
BL (Comparative religion)
BQT 529 (Theology)

PANTHEISM -- Continued.
sa Amalricians.
Deism.
Polytheism.
Theism.
xx God.
Ontologism.
Philosophy.
Religion.
Theism.

PAPACY. See
HOLY SEE.
POPES.

PAPAL BLESSING.
BQT 4474
x Blessing, Papal.

PAPAL BRIEFS. See
BRIEFS, PAPAL.

PAPAL BULLS. See
BULLS, PAPAL.

PAPAL CEREMONIAL. See
CAEREMONIALE ROMANUM.

PAPAL CEREMONIES, CONGREGATION OF.
See CONGREGATIO CAEREMONIALIS.

PAPAL CHAMBERLAINS.
x Chamberlains, Papal.

PAPAL COINS. See
COINS, PAPAL.

PAPAL CONCLAVES. See
POPES - ELECTION.

PAPAL COURT.
BQX 169-171
sa Curia Romana.
Palatini.
x Court, Papal.
Popes - Court.
xx Curia Romana.

PAPAL DECORATIONS OF HONOR. See
DECORATIONS OF HONOR, PAPAL.

PAPAL DOCUMENTS. See
DOCUMENTS, PAPAL.

PAPAL ELECTIONS. See
  POPES - ELECTIONS.

PAPAL ENCYCLICALS. See
  ENCYCLICALS, PAPAL.

PAPAL GUARDS.
      UA 749.5
      BQX 169
    x Guards, Papal.

PAPAL INFALLIBILITY. See
  POPES - INFALLIBILITY.

PAPAL LEGATES. See
  LEGATES, PAPAL.

PAPAL LETTERS. See
  LETTERS, PAPAL.

PAPAL MASS. See
  MASS, PAPAL.

PAPAL NOBILITY. See
  NOBILITY, PAPAL.

PAPAL NUNCIOS. See
  NUNCIOS, PAPAL.

PAPAL ORDERS OF KNIGHTHOOD AND
  CHIVALRY. See
  ORDERS OF KNIGHTHOOD AND
  CHIVALRY, PAPAL.

PAPAL PROTECTION. See
  PROTECTION, PAPAL.

PAPAL RESCRIPTS. See
  RESCRIPTS, PAPAL.

PAPAL SCHISM. See
  SCHISM, THE GREAT WESTERN,
  1378-1417.

PAPAL SECRETARY OF STATE. See
  SECRETARIA STATUS (PAPAL)

PAPAL STATES.
      BQX 124-127; BQX 757
    Here are entered works dealing
      with the temporal domains of the
      Pope which began with the Peace
      of Constantine and ceased to

PAPAL STATES -- Continued.
      exist when they were seized by
      Italy in 1870. By the Treaty of
      the Lateran in 1929 the temporal
      sovereignty of the Pope is rec-
      ognized in respect to Vatican
      City.
    sa Patrimony of St. Peter.
      Vatican City.
    x States of the Church.

PAPAL STATES - ECONOMIC CONDITIONS.

PAPAL STATES - FOREIGN RELATIONS.
  Subdivided by country, e.g., Papal
    States - Foreign relations -
    U.S. (with duplicate entry under
    U.S. - Foreign relations - Papal
    States)

PAPAL STATES - HISTORY.

PAPAL STATES - HISTORY - MIDDLE AGES.

PAPAL STATES - HISTORY - MODERN
  PERIOD.

PAPAL STATES - HISTORY - 1815-1870.

PAPAL STATES - HISTORY - 1870-1929.

PAPAL STATES - LAW. See
  LAW - PAPAL STATES.

PAPAL STATES - POLITICS AND
  GOVERNMENT.

################

PAPAL STATES. ARMY.

PAPAL STATES. LAWS, STATUTES, ETC.

PAPAL STATES. NAVY.

################

PAPAL TAXATION. See
  TAXATION, PAPAL.

PAPAL TIARA. See
  TIARA, PAPAL.

318

PAPAL UNIFORMS. See
    UNIFORMS, PAPAL.

PARABLES.
        BQ 278
    "Here are entered collections of
    parables and works on the nature
    of parables." LC
    sa Allegories.
        Bible - Parables.
        Fables.
        Jesus Christ - Parables.
        also names of parables, e.g.,
            Pearl of Great Price (Parable);
            The Sower (Parable)
    x Stories.
    xx Allegories.
        Fables.

PARABLES, BIBLICAL. See
    BIBLE - PARABLES.
    JESUS CHRIST - PARABLES.

PARABLES, BUDDHIST.
    x Buddhist parables.

PARABLES, CHRISTIAN. See
    BIBLE - PARABLES.
    JESUS CHRIST - PARABLES.

PARABLES, CONFUCIAN.
    x Confucian parables.

PARABLES, HASIDIC.
    x Hasidic parables.
    xx Hasidism.
        Parables, Jewish.

PARABLES, JEWISH.
    sa Bible. O.T. - Parables.
        Parables, Hasidic.
    x Jewish parables.

PARACLETE. See HOLY SPIRIT.

PARADISE.
        BQT 1541-1551   (236.6)
    sa Eden.
        Heaven.
        Justice, Original.
    xx Fall of man.
        Heaven.

PARADISE IN ART.
    xx Christian art.

PARAGUAY - CHURCH HISTORY.
    BQX 4891-4899

PARALIPOMENON, BOOKS OF. See
    BIBLE. O.T. PARALIPOMENON.

PARALITURGY.
    [BQT 4057]
    A form of devotional exercises
    based on liturgical forms, not
    considered worship in the strict
    sense.
✔ PARENT + Child see PARENTING
PARENT AND CHILD (CANON LAW)
    BQV230 99
    sa Minors (Canon law)
    xx Guardian and ward (Canon law)

✔ PARENTS ING
        BQT 1894 (Duties)
        BQT 2279 (Christian family)
    sa Family, Christian.
        Fathers.
        Husband and wife.
        Mothers.
    xx Family Christian.
        Fathers.
        Mothers.
    x Parent + Child; Child + Parent
PARENTS - PRAYER-BOOKS.
    BQT 2648

PARENTS - SERMONS.
    BQT 3001

PARENTS (CANON LAW)
    xx Marriage (Canon law)
        Persons (Canon law)

PARISH ADMINISTRATION.
    BQT 3304-3373
    xx Pastoral theology.

PARISH ARCHIVES. See
    ARCHIVES, PARISH.

PARISH HOUSES.
    xx Churches.

PARISH LIBRARIES. See
   LIBRARIES, CHURCH.

PARISH MISSIONS.
     BQT 3031-3047　(252.x52)
  "Here are entered works dealing
   with those special periods of
   revival in a parish when
   missioners come in and conduct
   a series of sermons, instructions,
   and other religious exercises.
   As the institution originated
   in the Catholic Church, subdivision by denomination is
   necessary only when such missions
   have been adopted by another
   denomination.
  "If the mission is limited to work
   with children an additional
   entry is made under the heading
   Church work with children." LC
  sa Convert making.
   x Missions, Parish.
     Missions, Parochial.
     Parochial missions.
     Popular missions.
   xx Pastoral theology.

PARISH MISSIONS - HANDBOOKS,
  MANUALS, ETC.

PARISH MISSIONS - SERMONS.
     BQT 3034-3047
   x Mission sermons.
   xx Sermons, Mission.

PARISH REGISTERS. See
  REGISTERS OF BIRTHS, ETC.

PARISH SCHOOLS. See
  CHURCH SCHOOLS.

PARISH SOCIETIES. See
  CONFRATERNITIES.

PARISH VICARS. See
  VICARS, PAROCHIAL.

PARISHES.　(Geog. subdiv., Direct)
     BQT 3304-3373　254
  sa Parsonages.
  xx Clergy.
    Corporations, Ecclesiastical.
    Pastoral theology.

PARISHES - ANNIVERSARY SERMONS. See
  ANNIVERSARY SERMONS - PARISHES.

PARISHES - FINANCE.
     BQT 3311-3321
  xx Church finance.

PARISHES - HISTORY.

PARISHES - CHURCH OF ENGLAND, [ETC.]

PARISHES (CANON LAW)
     BQV230 216　(348.x36)
  sa Quasi-parishes (Canon law)
    Vicars, Parochial.
  xx Benefices, Ecclesiastical (Canon
    law)
    Clergy (Canon law)
    Dioceses (Canon law)
    Pastors.

PARISHES (CANON LAW, ORTHODOX
EASTERN)

PARISHES, NATIONAL.
     BQT 3359
  x National parishes.

PAROCHIAL MISSIONS. See
  PARISH MISSIONS.

PAROCHIAL SCHOOLS. See
  CHURCH SCHOOLS.

PAROCHIAL VICARS. See
  VICARS, PAROCHIAL.

PAROUSIA. See SECOND ADVENT.

PARESES.
     BL 1500-1590
  References as in LC.

PARSONAGES.
   x Deaneries (Buildings)
    Rectories (Buildings)
    Vicarages (Buildings)
  xx Church lands.
    Church property.
    Churches.
    Clergy.
    Parishes.

320

PARTICIPATION IN NON-CATHOLIC
   WORSHIP. See
COMMUNICATIO IN SACRIS.

PARTICIPATION IN THE LITURGY. See
LITURGY - PARTICIPATION.

PARTICULAR EXAMEN.
      BQT 2216
   xx Conscience, Examination of.
      Perfection, Christian.

PARTIES TO ACTION (CANON LAW)

PASCHAL CANDLE.
      [BQT 4224.2]
   xx Candles and lights.
      Easter vigil.

PASCHAL PRECEPT. See
EASTER DUTY.

PASCHAL VIGIL. See
EASTER VIGIL.

PASSION MUSIC.
    x Jesus Christ - Passion - Music.
   xx Passion-plays.
      Religious drama.

PASSION MUSIC - HISTORY AND
   CRITICISM.
   xx Church music.
      Oratorio.

PASSION MUSIC - TO 1800.

PASSION OF CHRIST, OFFICE OF THE.
   See OFFICIUM PASSIONIS DOMINI
   NOSTRI JESU CHRISTI.

PASSION OF JESUS CHRIST. See
   JESUS CHRIST - PASSION.

PASSION-PLAYS.
      PN 3203-3299   (792.1)
      BQ 5157.P   (244.x2)
   sa Mysteries and miracle-plays.
      Passion music.
    x Jesus Christ - Passion - Drama.
      Plays, Medieval.

PASSION-PLAYS -- Continued.
   xx Drama, Medieval.
      Jesus Christ - Drama.
      Religious drama.
      Theater.

PASSIONARIUM.
      BQT 4268
   A liturgical book of the Middle
   Ages containing readings for
   the second nocturn of the
   Divine Office on feasts of
   saints.
    x Liber Passionarius.
   xx Martyrologium.

PASSIONS. See EMOTIONS.

PASSIONTIDE.
      [BQT 4222.5]
   "The period from Passion Sunday to
      Holy Saturday morning." AT
   sa Holy Week.
   xx Lent.

PASSOVER.
      BM 675.P
   References as in LC.

PASSOVER SERMONS.
    x Sermons, Passover.
   xx Sermons, Jewish.

PASTORAL CONFERENCES. See
   CLERGY CONFERENCES.

X PASTORAL COUNSELING. *see Counselling*
      BQT 2931-2941
   sa Pastoral psychology.
    x Counseling, Pastoral.
      Cure of souls.
   xx Church work.
      Pastoral theology.

PASTORAL EPISTLES. See
   BIBLE. N.T. PASTORAL EPISTLES.

PASTORAL LETTERS.   (Geog. subdiv.,
   Indirect)
    x Catholic Church - Pastoral
      letters.
      Letters, Pastoral.

PASTORAL MEDICINE.
BQT 2932-2934   (25x5)
Here are entered works dealing
with the correct moral application of physiology, hygiene and
pathology to clergymen and their
subjects.
sa Clergy and medicine.
Medicine and religion.
Pastoral psychology.
x Clerical medicine.
Medicine, Clerical.
Medicine, Pastoral.
xx Moral theology.
Pastoral theology.

PASTORAL PRAYERS.
"Here are entered works containing
the formal or general prayers
used in public worship." LC
x Prayers, Pastoral.
Prayers, Pulpit.
Pulpit prayers.
xx Public worship.

PASTORAL PSYCHOLOGY.
BQT 2933
"Here are entered works dealing
with the application by the
clergymen of modern psychology,
psychiatry, and psychotherapy
to the spiritual problems of
the individual." LC
sa Psychiatric social work.
Scruples.
x Clerical psychology.
Psychology, Clerical.
Psychology, Pastoral.
xx Casuistry.
Church work.
Pastoral counseling.
Pastoral medicine.
Pastoral theology.
Psychiatric social work.
Psychology, Religious.
Therapeutics, Suggestive.

PASTORAL THEOLOGY.
BQT 2903-3699   (25x4)
"That branch of theology which
deals with the care of souls.
It takes the teaching of dog-
matic, moral and ascetical

PASTORAL THEOLOGY -- Continued.
theology and the rules of canon
law and applies them to the
everyday work of the parochial
clergy in all its aspects." AT
sa Catechetics.
Catholic action.
Clergy.
Clergy and social problems.
Confraternities.
Convert making.
Missions.
Parish administration.
Parish missions.
Parishes.
Pastoral counseling.
Pastoral medicine.
Pastoral psychology.
Pastors.
Preaching.
Priesthood.
Religious surveys.
Sick-calls.
Social service, Catholic.
Sociology, Religious.
Visitations (Church work)
x Care of souls.
Cure of souls.
Ministry.
Theology, Pastoral.
xx Asceticism.
Canon law.
Clergy.
Moral theology.
Theology.

PASTORAL THEOLOGY - ADDRESSES,
ESSAYS, LECTURES.
BQT 2917

PASTORAL THEOLOGY - ANECDOTES,
FACETIAE, SATIRE, ETC.
BQT 2924   (25x4.04)
x Clergy - Anecdotes, facetiae,
satire, etc.
xx Religion - Anecdotes, facetiae,
satire, etc.

PASTORAL THEOLOGY - BIBLIOGRAPHY.
[BQT 2901]
Z 7820   (016.25x4)

PASTORAL THEOLOGY - BIOGRAPHY.

PASTORAL THEOLOGY - COLLECTED WORKS.

PASTORAL THEOLOGY - CONGRESSES.
[BQT 2904]

PASTORAL THEOLOGY - EARLY WORKS TO
1800.

PASTORAL THEOLOGY - FICTION.

PASTORAL THEOLOGY - HANDBOOKS,
MANUALS, ETC.
BQT 2915   (25x4.02)
sa Clergy - Handbooks, manuals,
etc.

PASTORAL THEOLOGY - HISTORY.
BQT 2910

PASTORAL THEOLOGY - HISTORY -
EARLY CHURCH.

PASTORAL THEOLOGY - HISTORY -
MIDDLE AGES.

PASTORAL THEOLOGY - HISTORY -
MODERN PERIOD.

PASTORAL THEOLOGY - METHODOLOGY.
BQT 2908

PASTORAL THEOLOGY - PERIODICALS.
BQT 2903   (25x4.05)

PASTORAL THEOLOGY - PERSONAL
NARRATIVES.

PASTORAL THEOLOGY - POPULAR WORKS.
BQT 2924

PASTORAL THEOLOGY - SOCIETIES, ETC.
BQT 2904

PASTORAL THEOLOGY - TEXTBOOKS.
BQT 2912-2913

PASTORAL THEOLOGY - TEXTBOOKS -
19th CENTURY.

PASTORAL THEOLOGY - TEXTBOOKS -
20th CENTURY.

################

PASTORAL THEOLOGY - CHURCH OF
ENGLAND, [LUTHERAN CHURCH, ETC.]

################

PASTORAL THEOLOGY (JUDAISM)
References as in LC supplement 1956-58.

PASTORAL VISITATIONS. See
VISITATIONS (CHURCH WORK)

PASTORS.
BQV230 451-470   (348.x36)
sa Mass for the people.
Parishes (Canon law)
Vicars, Parochial.
x Curates.
Rectors.
xx Clergy (Canon law)
Pastoral theology.
Persons (Canon law)

PASTORS - REMOVAL.
BQV230 2147-2161   (348.x59)
x Removal of pastors.
xx Clergy - Deposition.

PASTORS - RESIDENCE. See
CLERGY - RESIDENCE.

PASTORS, ASSISTANT. See
ASSISTANT PASTORS.

PATARIA. See PATARINES.

PATARINES.
BQX 503; BQX 2595
BQX 5933 (Eastern Church)
x Pataria.
xx Celibacy.
Milan - History - To 1535.

PATER NOSTER. See
LORD'S PRAYER.

PATIENCE.
BQT 1793   (24x1.52)
xx Conduct of life.

PATRIARCHS (BIBLE)
  BS 573
  "Here are entered works on the
    patriarchs of the Old Testa-
    ment. For works on the later
    ecclesiastical hierarchies
    known as patriarchates and on
    their dignitaries see Patri-
    archs and patriarchate." LC
  xx Bible - Biography.

PATRIARCHS (BIBLE) - JUVENILE
  LITERATURE.

PATRIARCHS AND PATRIARCHATE.
  BQX 5413
  Cf. note under Patriarchs (Bible)
  xx Bishops.

PATRIMONY OF ST. PETER.
  "The land and other property with
    which the see of Rome was en-
    dowed after the Peace of Constan-
    tine. After the States of the
    Church were definitely estab-
    lished in the 8th century, the
    name was sometimes applied to
    them in general, and to the
    duchy of Rome, coterminous with
    the province of Latio and the
    last territory left to Pope
    Pius up to 1870, in particular."
    AT
  xx Papal States.

PATRISTICS. See
  FATHERS OF THE CHURCH.

PATROLOGY. See
  FATHERS OF THE CHURCH.

PATRON SAINTS.
  BQX 8227
  sa Namedays.
  x Saints, Patron.
  xx Feasts, Ecclesiastical.
    Names, Personal.
    Saints.

PATRON SAINTS - PRAYER-BOOKS.
  BQT 2687

PATRON SAINTS - SERMONS.

PATRONAGE, ECCLESIASTICAL.   (Geog.
  subdiv., Indirect)
  x Ecclesiastical patronage.
  xx Benefices, Ecclesiastical.
    Church and state.
    Church property.

PATRONAGE, ECCLESIASTICAL (CANON LAW)

PAUL, SAINT, EPISTLES. See
  BIBLE. N.T. EPISTLES OF PAUL.

PAULICIANS.
  BQT 72
  xx Heresies and heretics - Early
    church.

PAULINE PRIVILEGE.
  BQT 1430
  BQV230 1120-1127   (348.x427)
  "If of two unbaptized persons
    united in a consummated marriage
    one is converted to the faith
    and the other will neither be
    converted nor live in peace with
    the Christian, the marriage may
    be completely dissolved." AT
  xx Divorce (Canon law)
    Marriage - Dissolution.
    Marriage (Canon law)

PAX (OSCULATORY)

PAYMENT (CANON LAW)

✓ PEACE.   261
  Classifications and references as
    in LC, with the following
    additional reference.
  sa Catholic Church and peace.

PEACE - BIBLICAL TEACHING.
  BS 680
  x Bible and peace.
  xx Peace (Theology)
    War and religion.

PEACE - PAPAL TEACHING.

PEACE (THEOLOGY)
  BQT 1918
  sa Peace - Biblical teaching.

PEACE (THEOLOGY) - MEDITATIONS.
  [BQT 2610.5]

PEACE, PRAYERS FOR. See
PRAYERS FOR PEACE.

PEARL OF GREAT PRICE (PARABLE)

PECULIUM.
xx Religious orders (Canon law)

PELAGIANISM.
          BQT 75 (General)   (273.x41)
          BQT 636 (Doctrine of creation)
          BQT 1143 (Doctrine of grace)
sa Semi-Pelagianism.
xx Grace (Theology)
   Heresies and heretics - Early
      church.
   Man (Theology) - History of
      doctrines.
   Semi-Pelagianism.

PENALTIES, ECCLESIASTICAL.
          BQV230 2214-2414   (348.x6)
sa Censures, Ecclesiastical.
   Ignorance (Canon law)
   Infamy (Canon law)
   Precept (Canon law)
 x Ecclesiastical penalties.
   Punishment (Canon law)
xx Canon law.

✓ PENANCE.
          BQT 1364-1401; BQT 2058
             (23x7.4)
sa Absolution.
   Confession.
   Conscience, Examination of.
   Contrition.
   Indulgences.
   Penitentials.
   Power of the keys.
   Repentence.
   Satisfaction.
   Seal of confession.
xx Absolution.
 x Confession.
   Forgiveness of sin.
   Repentence.
   Sacraments.
 x Reconciliation

PENANCE - CATECHISMS, QUESTION-BOOKS.
          BQT 3197

PENANCE - CONTROVERSIAL LITERATURE.

PENANCE - DEVOTIONAL LITERATURE.
          [BQT 2608.4]

PENANCE - EARLY WORKS.

PENANCE - EFFICACY.
          BQT 1384

PENANCE - HISTORY.
          BQT 1364-1365.
xx Auricular confession.

PENANCE - HISTORY - EARLY CHURCH.

PENANCE - HISTORY - MIDDLE AGES.

PENANCE - HISTORY - MODERN PERIOD.

PENANCE - HISTORY - 16th, [17th,
   etc.] CENTURY.

PENANCE - MEDIEVAL WORKS.

PENANCE - MINISTER.
          [BQT 1472]

PENANCE - POPULAR WORKS.

PENANCE - RESERVED CASES. See
RESERVED CASES.

PENANCE - SERMONS.

PENANCE (CANON LAW)
          BQV230 870-936   (348.x42)
sa Absolution (Canon law)
   Confessors (Canon law)
xx Sacraments (Canon law)

PENANCE (CANON LAW) - HISTORY.

PENANCE (VIRTUE)
          BQT 2221
sa Fast days.
   Fasting.
   Flagellants and flagellation.
   Impenitence.
   Mortification.
   Penitents.
   Pilgrims and pilgrimages.
xx Asceticism.
   Perfection, Christian.

PENANCE (VIRTUE) - SERMONS.

PENITENCE. See REPENTANCE.

PENITENTIAL BOOKS. See
    PENITENTIALS.

PENITENTIAL DISCIPLINE.
        BQT 1365
    sa Satisfaction.
    x Discipline, Penitential.

PENITENTIAL PSALMS. See
    BIBLE. O.T. PSALMS, PENITENTIAL.

PENITENTIALS.
        BQT 4446
    x Penitential books.
    xx Penance.

PENITENTIARIES.
    Penitentiaries are a college of
        priests drawn from the mendicant
        orders and assigned to the
        basilicas of St. Peter, St. John
        Lateran and St. Mary Major in
        Rome to hear the confession of
        anyone at any time, having wide
        powers to absolve from reserved
        sins.
    xx Reserved cases.

PENITENTS.
        BQT 2705
    xx Penance (Virtue)

PENNANTS, CHURCH. See
    CHURCH PENNANTS.

PENSIONS (CANON LAW)
        BQV230 1429   (348.x45)
    xx Benefices, Ecclesiastical.
        (Canon law)

PENSIONS, ECCLESIASTICAL. See
    CLERGY - SALARIES, PENSIONS, ETC.

PENTATEUCH (BIBLE). See
    BIBLE. O.T. PENTATEUCH.

PENTECOST.
        BQT 597
    xx Holy Spirit.

PENTECOST - DRAMA.

PENTECOST - SERMONS.
    sa Pentecost season - Sermons.

PENTECOST FESTIVAL.
        [BQT 4224.5]   (264.x5)
        BM 695.P (Jewish)
    sa Officium Pentecostes.
        Shavu'oth (Feast of Weeks)
    x Feast of Pentecost.
        Whitsunday.

PENTECOST SEASON.
        [BQT 4224.5]
    xx Church year.
        Eastern season.

PENTECOST SEASON - MEDITATIONS.
        [BQT 2606.7]

PENTECOST SEASON - SERMONS.
        [BQT 2996.5]
    xx Pentecost - Sermons.

PENTECOSTAL CHURCHES.   (Geog.
    subdiv., Indirect)
    Scope note and references as
        in LC.

PENTEKOSTARION.
        BQT 5254
    A liturgical book of the Byzantine
        Rite for the Divine Office from
        Easter to Pentecost.

PEPIN, DONATION OF. See
    DONATION OF PEPIN.

PERFECT LOVE. See
    PERFECTION, CHRISTIAN.

PERFECTION, CHRISTIAN.
        BQT 2190-2396   (24x7.02)
    sa Active life.
        Asceticism.
        Charity.
        Contemplative life.
        Evangelical counsels.
        Illuminative way to perfection.
        Imitation of the saints.
        Imperfections (Theology)
        Intention.
        Jesus Christ - Example.

326

PERFECTION, CHRISTIAN -- Continued.
  sa Love (Theology)
      Mixed life.
      Mortification.
      Mystical union.
      Mysticism.
      Particular examen.
      Penance (Virtue)
      Prayer.
      Presence of God, Practice of.
      Purgative way to perfection.
      Sacrifice, Spirit of.
      Spiritual direction.
      State of perfection.
      Unitive way to perfection.
      Vocation.
      Wealth, Ethics of.
   x Christian perfection.
      Love, Perfect.
      Perfect love.
  xx Asceticism.
      Grace, Habitual.
      Spiritual life.

PERFECTION, CHRISTIAN - BIBLICAL
  TEACHING.

PERFECTION, CHRISTIAN - HISTORY OF
  DOCTRINES.

PERFECTION, CHRISTIAN - PAPAL
  TEACHING.

PERFECTION, RELIGIOUS. See
  RELIGIOUS LIFE.

PERFECTION, STATE OF. See
  STATE OF PERFECTION.

PERIODICALS, CATHOLIC. See
  CATHOLIC PERIODICALS.

PERPETUAL ADORATION.
      BQT 2589 (24x8.71)
   x Adoration, Perpetual.
  xx Adoration of the Blessed
      Sacrament.
      Devotions, Popular.
      Eucharist - Cultus.

PERSECUTION. (Geog. subdiv.)
      BQX 211-218
  sa Acta Martyrum.
      Anti-Catholic polemic.

PERSECUTION -- Continued.
  sa Dragonades.
      Inquisition.
      Jews - Persecution.
      Liberty of conscience.
      Martyrdom.
      Martyrs.
      Massacres.
      Proscriptions.
      Refugees, Religious.
      Religious liberty.
   x Church history - Persecution.
  xx Church history.
      Inquisition.
      Liberty of conscience.
      Religious liberty.

PERSECUTION - EARLY CHURCH.
      BQX 255-268 (270.1)
  xx Church history - Primitive
      and early church.

PERSECUTION - EARLY CHURCH - FICTION.

PERSECUTION - MIDDLE AGES.

PERSECUTION - MODERN PERIOD.
      BQX 781-796; BQX 985
      (270.5)

PERSECUTION - 16th CENTURY.

PERSECUTION - 17th CENTURY.

PERSECUTION - 18th CENTURY.

PERSECUTION - 19th CENTURY.

PERSECUTION - 20th CENTURY.

      ################

PERSECUTION - GERMANY.
      BQX 1113-1116

PERSECUTION - RUSSIA.
      BQX 6066

      ################

PERSEVERANCE (THEOLOGY)
      BQT 1165 (24x7.13)
  sa Sanctification.
  xx Grace, Habitual.

PERSEVERANCE (THEOLOGY) - SERMONS.
Persnal DEVELOPMENT:
PERSONAL GOD. See
  GOD - PERSONALITY.

PERSONAL INJURIES (CANON LAW)
     BQV230 2350-2359

PERSONALITY. *Identity, Persnal*
        BD 331 (Ontology)
        BG 698 (Psychology)
        BQT 631 (Theology)
        (231.x73)
  References as in LC, with the
    following additional reference.
  xx Man (Theology)

PERSONS (CANON LAW)
        BQV230 87-725   (348.x3)
  sa Abbesses (Canon law)
     Abbots (Canon law)
     Abbots nullius (Canon law)
     Administrators apostolic.
     Age (Canon law)
     Archbishops (Canon law)
     Bishops (Canon law)
     Cardinals (Canon law)
     Chancellors, Diocesan.
     Chaplains (Canon law)
     Chapters, Cathedral, collegiate,
       etc.
     Clergy (Canon law)
     Coadjutor bishops (Canon law)
     Confessors (Canon law)
     Consultors, Diocesan.
     Domicile (Canon law)
     Election law (Canon law)
     Laity (Canon law)
     Legal responsibility (Canon
       law)
     Ordinaries.
     Parents (Canon law)
     Pastors.
     Popes (Canon law)
     Precedence, Ecclesiastical
       (Canon law)
     Prelates.
     Priests (Canon law)
     Protonotaries apostolic.
     Religious orders (Canon law)
     Religious persons (Canon law)
     Superiors, Religious (Canon
       law)

PERSONS (CANON LAW) -- Continued.
  sa Vicars apostolic.
     Vicars capitular.
     Vicars forane.
     Vicars general.
   x Ecclesiastical persons.
  xx Canon law.

PERSONS (CANON LAW, EASTERN)
  xx Eastern Churches - Canon law.

PERSONS (INTERNATIONAL LAW)
     JX 4000-4081
  sa Holy See (International law)
  Other references as in LC.

PERSONS, RELIGIOUS. See
  RELIGIOUS PERSONS.

PETER, SAINT, CHAINS OF. See
  ST. PETER'S CHAINS.

PETER, SAINT, CHAIR OF. See
  ST. PETER'S CHAIR.

PETER, SAINT, EPISTLES OF. See
  BIBLE. N.T. EPISTLES OF PETER.

PETER'S PENCE.
  xx Catholic Church - Finance.

LA PETITE EGLISE. See LOUISETS.

PEWS AND PEW RIGHTS.
  xx Church finance.
     Church property.
     Church support.

PHARISEES.
        BM 175.P   290
  sa Qumran community.
     Zealots (Jewish party)
  xx Jewish sects.

PHILEMON, EPISTLE TO. See
  BIBLE. N.T. PHILEMON.

PHILIPPIANS, EPISTLE TO THE. See
  BIBLE. N.T. PHILIPPIANS.

PHILISTINES.
     DS 90   (939.45)

PHILOSOPHY, EARLY CHRISTIAN.
      B 630-708
  sa Neoplatonism.
    Scholasticism.
   x Christian philosophy, Early.
    Early Christian philosophy.
  xx Philosophy and religion.
    Scholasticism.

PHILOSOPHY, SCHOLASTIC. See
NEO-SCHOLASTICISM.
SCHOLASTICISM.

PHILOSOPHY AND RELIGION.
      BL 51; BQT 236 (General)
       (215)
      B 56 (Philosophy)
  sa Personalism.
    Philosophy, Early Christian.
    Theology and philosophy.
   x Religion and philosophy.

PHILOSOPHY AND THEOLOGY. See
THEOLOGY AND PHILOSOPHY.

PHILOSOPHY OF NATURE.
  sa Natural theology.
    Nature - Religious interpretations.
  xx Natural theology.

PHILOSOPHY OF RELIGION. See
RELIGION - PHILOSOPHY.

PHOCIAN SCHISM. See
SCHISM, PHOCIAN.

PHONORECORDS - CATALOGS. See
CHANT - DISCOGRAPHY.

PHONORECORDS IN MISSIONARY WORK.
    BQT 3229

PHYLACTERIES.
  References as in LC.

PHYSICAL EDUCATION AND TRAINING -
MORAL ASPECTS.
  xx Man (Theology)

PHYSICIANS - RELIGIOUS LIFE.
    [BQT 2289]

PHYSIOLOGY - MORAL AND RELIGIOUS
ASPECTS.

PIAE CAUSAE. See
PIOUS FOUNDATIONS.

PICTURE BIBLES. See
BIBLE - PICTURE BIBLES.

PIETA.
  xx Jesus Christ - Art.

PIETISM. (Geog. subdiv.,
Indirect)
    BQT 125 (273.x72)

PIETY.
    BQT 1862 (24x1.52)
  xx Religion (Virtue)

PIETY - BIBLICAL TEACHING.

PILGRIMS AND PILGRIMAGES. (Geog.
subdiv., Direct)
    BQT 4496
  sa Holy wells.
    Processions, Ecclesiastical.
    Saints.
    Shrines.
  xx Penance (Virtue)
    Shrines.

PILGRIMS AND PILGRIMAGES, AMERICAN,
[FRENCH, SWISS, ETC.]

PILLAR SAINTS. See STYLITES.

PILLARS OF MOHAMMEDANISM.
    BP 176
  References as in LC supplement 1961.

PIOUS ASSOCIATIONS. See
CONFRATERNITIES.

PIOUS FOUNDATIONS.
  sa Foundation mass.
   x Foundations, Pious.
  xx Corporations, Ecclesiastical.

PISA, COUNCIL OF, 1409.
    BQX 815

PIYUTIM.
    BM 670.P
  References as in LC.

PLACE (CANON LAW)

PLACES, SACRED. See
SACRED PLACES.

PLACITUM REGIUM.
x Exequatur.
Regium placet.
xx Church and state.

PLAIN CHANT. See CHANT.

PLAINSONG. See CHANT.

PLAYS, BIBLE. See BIBLE PLAYS.

PLAYS, CHRISTMAS. See
CHRISTMAS PLAYS.

PLAYS, MEDIEVAL. See
CARNIVAL PLAYS.
CHRISTMAS PLAYS, MEDIEVAL.
DRAMA, MEDIEVAL.
MORALITIES.
MYSTERIES AND MIRACLE-PLAYS.
PASSION-PLAYS.

PLEADING (CANON LAW)

PLEASURE.
BF 515 (Psychology)
BJ 1480-1486 (Ethics)
sa Happiness.
xx Happiness.
Joy.
Other references as in LC.

PLENARIUM.
BQT 4254
An ancient liturgical book which
contained the Scriptural readings from the Mass, sometimes
the Epistles, sometimes the
Epistles and Gospels in full
(plene), in contrast to the
Comes which indicated only the
first words.
sa Missale Plenarium.
xx Comes.
Evangeliarium.
Lectionarium.

PLENARY COUNCILS.
BQV230 281-292 (General)
(26x2.6)
BQV 341-1020 (Local)
(26x2.61)
"A council of the ecclesiastical
authorities, i.e., residential
archbishops and bishops, administrators of dioceses and vicars
capitular, abbots and prelates
nullius, vicars and prefects
apostolic, of a given territory,
usually a kingdom, state or
nation ... presided over by a
legate of the Holy See." AT
The individual plenary councils
since the Council of Trent are
entered under the name of the
place where the council was
held, followed by the designation "Plenary council of" and
date. Make a reference from the
country or the region represented
by the council (e.g., Baltimore,
Plenary Council of, 2d, 1866.
Refer from: Catholic Church. U.S.
Plenary Council. 2d, Baltimore,
1866).
The individual national councils
and general synods of the early
church and the Middle Ages,
prior to the Council of Trent,
are entered under the name of the
place (e.g., Toledo, Council of,
3d, 589; Elvira, Synod of, ca.300).
x Councils and synods, National.
Councils and synods, Plenary.
National councils.

PNEUMATOLOGY (THEOLOGY)
xx Holy Spirit.
Spirit.

POENITENTIARIA APOSTOLICA.
BQV230 258 (348.x33)
BQV 71-74 (Documents)
(348.x15)
x Sacred Penitentiary.

POETRY, CATHOLIC. See
CATHOLIC POETRY.

330

POETRY, CHRISTIAN. See
CHRISTIAN POETRY.

POETRY, RELIGIOUS. See
RELIGIOUS POETRY.

POETRY AND RELIGION. See
RELIGION AND POETRY.

POETS.
sa Hymn writers.
Other references as in LC.

POETS, CATHOLIC. See
CATHOLIC POETS.

POLAND - CHURCH HISTORY.
BQX 2742-2787   (274.38)

POLAND - CHURCH HISTORY - EARLY
PERIOD TO 1517.

POLAND - CHURCH HISTORY - 1517-1648.

POLAND - CHURCH HISTORY - 1648-

POLAND - CHURCH HISTORY - 20th
CENTURY.

POLAND - CHURCH HISTORY - 1945-

POLEMIC, ANTI-CATHOLIC. See
ANTI-CATHOLIC POLEMIC.

POLEMIC, ANTI-PROTESTANT. See
ANTI-PROTESTANT POLEMIC.

POLEMICS (THEOLOGY). See
APOLOGETICS.

POLISH LITERATURE - CATHOLIC AUTHORS.

✓ POLITICAL SCIENCE - BIBLICAL
TEACHING.
BS 680
sa Kings and rulers - Biblical
teaching.
xx Christianity and politics.

POLITICS AND CHRISTIANITY. See
CHRISTIANITY AND POLITICS.

Politics - Biblical

POLITY, ECCLESIASTICAL. See
CHURCH POLITY.

POLYGLOT BIBLES. See
BIBLE - VERSIONS, POLYGLOT.

POLYPHONIC CHANT.
BQT 4634
x Chant, Polyphonic.

POLYPHONIC CHURCH MUSIC.
BQT 4531-4609   (783.4)
x Church music, Polyphonic.

POLYTHEISM.
BL 355   (291.14)
sa Monotheism.
xx God.
Pantheism.
Religions.
Theism.

PONTIFICAL INSIGNIA. See
INSIGNIA, PONTIFICAL.

PONTIFICAL MASS.
x Mass, Pontifical.

PONTIFICAL MASS - RITES AND
CEREMONIES.
BQT 4333
xx Mass - Rites and ceremonies.

PONTIFICAL SERVICE.
[BQT 4333.2]
sa Caeremoniale Episcoporum.
Pontificale Romanum.
x Rites and ceremonies, Pontifical.

PONTIFICAL SERVICE - HANDBOOKS,
MANUALS, ETC.

PONTIFICALE ROMANUM.
BQT 4436   (26x5.7)
"A liturgical book containing
the prayers and ceremonies of
certain rites ordinarily reserved to a bishop." AT
x Roman Pontifical.
xx Benedictionale.
Pontifical service.

PONTIFICALE ROMANUM - COMMENTARIES.

POOR, CHURCH WORK WITH THE. See
   CHURCH WORK WITH THE POOR.

POOR CLARES.   (Geog. subdiv., Direct)
      BQX 7903.P6   (271.9)
   x Clares, Poor.
      Clarisses.
      Franciscans. Second order.
      Minoresses.
      Order of St. Clare.
      Ordo Sanctae Clarae.
      Sisters of St. Clare.

POOR LAWS (CANON LAW)

POOR SOULS IN PURGATORY. See
   PURGATORY.

POOR SOULS IN PURGATORY, PRAYERS
   FOR THE. See
   PRAYERS FOR THE DEAD.

POPES.
      BQT 365-373 (Ecclesiology)
         (23x9.3)
      BQX 101-137; BQX 321-1097
      (Church history)   (922.21)
   sa Antipopes.
      Documents, Papal.
      Holy See.
      Power of the keys.
      Tiara, Papal.
      also the subdivision "Papal
         teaching" under such specific
         headings as Catholic action,
         Liturgy, Marriage, Religious
         orders, etc.
   x Catholic Church. Pope.
      Papacy.
   xx Apostolic succession.
      Catholic Church - Government.
      Catholic Church - History.
      Church history.
      Holy See.

POPES - ANECDOTES.

POPES - AUTHORITY. See
   POPES - INFALLIBILITY.
   POPES - PRIMACY.

POPES - BIBLIOGRAPHY.
   BQX 104

POPES - BIO-BIBLIOGRAPHY.

POPES - BIOGRAPHY.
   BQX 101-104 (Collected)
      (922.21)
   BQX 321-1097 (Individual)
   xx Christian biography.

POPES - BRIEFS. See
   BRIEFS, PAPAL.

POPES - BULLS. See
   BULLS, PAPAL.

POPES - CHRONOLOGY.
   BQX 43

POPES - CORONATION.

POPES - COSTUME.

POPES - COURT. See
   PAPAL COURT.

POPES - ELECTION.
   BQX 110 (General)
   BQV230 160-178 (Canon
      law)   (348.x322)
   BQT 4437.6 (Ceremonial)
   sa Popes - Renunciation.
   x Conclaves, Papal.
      Elections, Papal.
      Papal conclaves.
      Papal elections.
   xx Election law (Canon law)

POPES - ENCYCLICALS. See
   ENCYCLICALS, PAPAL.

POPES - HERALDRY.
   CR 1115
   xx Heraldry, Sacred.

POPES - HISTORY.
   BQX 101-1097

POPES - HISTORY - ADDRESSES,
   ESSAYS, LECTURES.

POPES - HISTORY - BIBLIOGRAPHY.

POPES - HISTORY - ERRORS, INVEN-
TIONS, ETC.
        BX 958
        BQX 87

POPES - HISTORY - SOURCES.

        ################

POPES - HISTORY - EARLY CHURCH.

POPES - HISTORY - MIDDLE AGES.

POPES - HISTORY - 1309-1378.
        BQX 761
    x Avignon, Popes at.
        Babylonian Captivity, Papal.

POPES - HISTORY - MODERN PERIOD.

POPES - HISTORY - 16th CENTURY.

POPES - HISTORY - 17th CENTURY.

POPES - HISTORY - 18th CENTURY.

POPES - HISTORY - 19th CENTURY.

POPES - HISTORY - 1870-1929.
    sa Roman Question.

POPES - HISTORY - 20th CENTURY.

POPES - HISTORY - 1929-

        ################

POPES - INFALLIBILITY. *See INFALLIBILITY*
        BQT 366-373
    x Infallibility of the pope.
        Papal infallibility.
        Popes - Authority.
    xx Authority (Religion)
        Church - Infallibility.
        Ultramontanism.

POPES - INFALLIBILITY - CONTRO-
VERSIAL LITERATURE.
        [BQT 368]

POPES - INFALLIBILITY - SERMONS.

POPES - LEGENDS.
        BQX 173

POPES - LETTERS. See
    LETTERS, PAPAL.

POPES - MEDALS.
        CJ 6205.P

POPES - MONUMENTS.

POPES - POPULAR WORKS.

POPES - PORTRAITS.

POPES - PRIMACY.
        BQT 365
    sa Bishops.
        Conciliar theory.
        Councils and synods.
        Febronianism.
    x Popes - Authority.
        Popes - Supremacy.
        Primacy of the pope.
        Supremacy of the pope.
    xx Bishops.
        Church - Apostolicity.
        Church - Foundation.
        Councils and synods.

POPES - PRIMACY - SEDES.

POPES - PRIMACY - SERMONS.

POPES - RENUNCIATION.
    xx Popes - Election.

POPES - RESIDENCE.

POPES - RITES AND CEREMONIES.
    sa Caeremoniale Romanum.

POPES - SERMONS.
        BQT 3089
    Here are entered sermons about
    the Pope.

POPES - SUPREMACY. See
    POPES - PRIMACY.

POPES - TEMPORAL POWER.
        BQX 115-137   (27x2.2)
    sa Church and state.
        Donation of Pepin.

333

POPES - TEMPORAL POWER -- Continued.
  sa Italian Question, 1848-1870.
     Roman Question.
   x Temporal power of the pope.
  xx Church and state.
     Church history - Middle Ages.
     Roman Question.

POPES - TOMB.
     BQT 6038

POPES - VACANCY OF THE HOLY SEE. See
  VACANCY OF THE HOLY SEE.

POPES - VOYAGES AND TRAVELS.
     BX 958.V
  xx Voyages and travels.

POPES (CANON LAW)
     BQV230 218-221   (348.x322)
  xx Persons (Canon law)

POPULAR DEVOTIONS. See
  DEVOTIONS, POPULAR.

POPULAR MISSIONS. See
  PARISH MISSIONS.

PORTIUNCULA INDULGENCE.
  xx Indulgences.

PORTUGAL - CHURCH HISTORY.
     BQX 2791-2822   (274.69)

PORTUGAL - CHURCH HISTORY - EARLY
  PERIOD.

PORTUGAL - CHURCH HISTORY - MIDDLE
  AGES.

PORTUGAL - CHURCH HISTORY - MODERN
  PERIOD.

PORTUGAL - CHURCH HISTORY - 1801-

PORTUGAL - CHURCH HISTORY - 20th
  CENTURY.

POSITIVE THEOLOGY. See
  THEOLOGY - METHODOLOGY.

POSITIVISM.
     B 831 (General)   (146)
     B 851-4695 (Special, local)
  References as in LC.

POSSESSION (CANON LAW)
     BQV230 1693-1700   (348.x5)
  sa Adverse possession (Canon law)

POSSESSION, DEMONIAC. See
  DEMONIAC POSSESSION.

POSTULANCY.
  xx Novitiate.
     Religious orders.

POSTULANCY (CANON LAW)
     BQV230 539-541

POSTURE, LITURGICAL. See
  POSTURE IN WORSHIP.

POSTURE IN WORSHIP.
     BQT 4518
  sa Genuflexion.
   x Bowing of the head (Posture
     in worship)
     Kneeling (Posture in worship)
     Liturgical posture.
     Posture, Liturgical.
     Prostration (Posture in
     worship)
     Sitting (Posture in worship)
     Standing (Posture in worship)
     Worship, Posture in.
  xx Cultus.
     Rites and ceremonies.
     Worship.

THE POUNDS (PARABLE). See
  THE TALENTS (PARABLE)

POVERTY.
     HV 1-4630   (339.1)
  References as in LC.

POVERTY - BIBLICAL TEACHING.
     see Poverty
POVERTY (VIRTUE)
     BQT 2389
     see Poverty

POVERTY (VOW)
     BQT 2312   (24x1.83)
  xx Vows.

POWER OF THE KEYS.
BQT 1371
This expression denotes the complete ecclesiastical authority
of orders, jurisdiction and
doctrine possessed by St. Peter
and his successors and all members of the hierarchy in their
degree. It generally refers
only to the power of absolution
in confession.
x Binding and loosing.
xx Absolution.
Penance.
Popes.

PRAGMATIC SANCTION OF BOURGES. See
PRAGMATIC SANCTION OF CHARLES VII,
1438.

PRAGMATIC SANCTION OF CHARLES V, 1549.
BQV 396

PRAGMATIC SANCTION OF CHARLES VI, 1713.
BQV 396
DB 69.3
JN 1625

PRAGMATIC SANCTION OF CHARLES VII, 1438.
BQV 386
x Pragmatic Sanction of Bourges.
xx Gallicanism.

PRAGMATIC SANCTIONS.
BQV 306
xx Church and state.

PRAGUE, INFANT JESUS OF (STATUE). See
INFANT JESUS OF PRAGUE (STATUE)

√ PRAYER.
BQT 2241-2264   (24x7.11)
sa Devotion.
Divine office.
Prayer-books.
Prayers.
x Prayer, Vocal.
Vocal prayer.

xx Asceticism.
Christian life.
Good works (Theology)

PRAYER -- Continued.
sa Perfection, Christian.
Prayers.
Worship.

PRAYER - BIBLICAL TEACHING.
x Bible and prayer.
xx Bible - Prayers.

PRAYER - CATECHISMS, QUESTION-BOOKS.

PRAYER - CONFRATERNITIES.
BQT 2814
xx Confraternities.

PRAYER - EARLY WORKS TO 1800.

PRAYER - HISTORY.
sa Messalians.

PRAYER - JUVENILE LITERATURE.

PRAYER - POPULAR WORKS.
BQT 2245

PRAYER - PSYCHOLOGY.
BV 225
x Psychology of prayer.
xx Psychology, Religious.

PRAYER - SERMONS.

PRAYER - STUDY AND TEACHING.
BQT 2247

PRAYER (BANTU RELIGION)

PRAYER (GREEK RELIGION)

PRAYER (HINDUISM)
BL 1475.P

PRAYER (JUDAISM)

PRAYER (ROMAN RELIGION)

PRAYER (SIKHISM)

PRAYER, LITURGICAL. See
LITURGY.

PRAYER, MENTAL.
   BQT 2259-2264; BQT 2468
      (24x9.1)
By this term are understood "all
   kinds of prayer other than vocal,
   including meditation, affective
   prayer, and contemplation." AT
sa Contemplation.
   Meditation.
 x Mental prayer.
xx Contemplation.
   Mysticism.

PRAYER, MYSTIC. See
CONTEMPLATION.

PRAYER, VOCAL. See PRAYER.

PRAYER BOOK. CHURCH OF ENGLAND. See
CHURCH OF ENGLAND. BOOK OF COMMON
PRAYER.

PRAYER-BOOKS.
   BQT 2611-2697   (24x3)
sa Breviarium.
   Diurnale.
   Missale.
   Primer (Prayer-book)
   also subdivision "Prayer-books"
      under names of churches (e.g.,
      Lutheran Church - Prayer-books)
      and under names of religious
      mysteries and saints (e.g.,
      Eucharist - Prayer-books;
      Joseph, Saint - Prayer-books)
 x Books of prayer.
   Catholic Church - Prayer-books.
xx Devotional literature.
   Devotions, Popular.
   Prayer.
   Prayers.

PRAYER-BOOKS - BIBLIOGRAPHY.

PRAYER-BOOKS, ENGLISH, [GERMAN,
LATIN, ETC.]
   BQT 2611-2619

PRAYER-BOOKS FOR CHILDREN. See
CHILDREN - PRAYER-BOOKS.

PRAYER IN ART.
 xx Art.

PRAYER-MEETINGS.
   sa Church-night services.
   xx Public worship.

PRAYER OF AZARIAS. See
   BIBLE. O.T. DANIEL. chap. III,
   24-25.

PRAYER OF MANASSES.
   BS 1811-1815
    x Bible. O.T. Apocrypha. Prayer
      of Manasses.

PRAYERS.
   BQT 2611-2697   (24x3) 242
   BQT 4089
   BQT 4503-4506
   BQT 4498
sa Acclamations (Liturgy)
   Ave Maria.
   Collects.
   Grace at meals.
   Indulgences.
   Litanies.
   Lord's Prayer.
   Prayer.
   Prayer-books.
   Responses (Liturgy)
   Rosary.
   also subdivision "Prayers"
      under special subjects,
      e.g., Schools - Prayers;
      Sunday-schools - Prayers.
xx Devotions, Popular.
   Prayer.
   Sacramentals.

################

PRAYERS, ENGLISH, [FRENCH,
GERMAN, ETC.]
   BQT 2611-2619

################

PRAYERS, ALTAR. See
ALTAR PRAYERS.

PRAYERS, ASSYRO-BABYLONIAN. See
ASSYRO-BABYLONIAN PRAYERS.

PRAYERS, EJACULATORY. See
EJACULATIONS.

336

PRAYERS, FAMILY. See
FAMILY - PRAYER-BOOKS.

PRAYERS, HINDU. See
HINDUISM - PRAYER-BOOKS.

PRAYERS, MEDIEVAL.

PRAYERS, PASTORAL. See
PASTORAL PRAYERS.

PRAYERS, PULPIT. See
PASTORAL PRAYERS.

PRAYERS, SHINTO. See
SHINTO PRAYERS.

PRAYERS, TABLE. See
GRACE AT MEALS.

PRAYERS BEFORE AND AFTER MASS.
x Preces ante et post missam.
xx Mass - Prayer-books.
Priests - Prayer-books.

PRAYERS FOR PEACE.
x Peace, Prayers for.

PRAYERS FOR THE DEAD.
BQT 2691; BQT 4055 (Devo-
tions) (24x3.6)
BQT 1537 (Theology)
(236.x53)
sa Missa pro defunctis.
November devotions.
Officium pro defunctis.
x Dead, Prayers for the.
Poor souls in purgatory,
Prayers for the.
xx Devotions, Popular.
Purgatory - Prayer-books.

PRAYERS FOR THE DEAD - ANGLICAN
COMMUNION.

PRAYERS FOR THE SICK.
BQT 4455 (24x3.7)
x Sick, Prayers for the.
xx Sick - Prayer-books.

PRAZSKE JEZULATKO. See
INFANT JESUS OF PRAGUE (STATUE)

PREACHERS, ORDER OF. See
DOMINICANS.

PREACHING.
BQT 2952-2968 (251)
sa Homiletical illustrations.
Homiletics.
Sermons.
x Sacred oratory.
xx Church - Teaching office.
Election.
Homiletics.
Pastoral theology.
Sermons.

PREACHING - AUDIENCE.
BQT 2968

PREACHING - HISTORY. (Geog.
subdiv., Indirect)
BQT 2954-2956 (251)

PREACHING - HISTORY - EARLY CHURCH.

PREACHING - HISTORY - MIDDLE AGES.

PREACHING - HISTORY - MODERN PERIOD.

PREACHING (CANON LAW)
BQV230 1337-1358 (348.x44)

PREACHING, EXTEMPORANEOUS.
x Extemporaneous preaching.

PREACHING, JEWISH.
BM 730
x Jewish preaching.

PREACHING AND THE LITURGY.
x Liturgy and preaching.

PREACHING FRIARS. See
DOMINICANS.

PREBENDS.
xx Benefices, Ecclesiastical
(Canon law)

PRECEDENCE, ECCLESIASTICAL.

PRECEDENCE, ECCLESIASTICAL (CANON
LAW)
BQV230 106 (348.x3)
xx Persons (Canon law)

PRECEPT (CANON LAW)
BQV230 24; BQV230 2310
By precept in Canon law is understood
a command given to a single person
by his ecclesiastical superior.
x Canonical precept.
xx Church discipline (Canon law)
Penalties, Ecclesiastical.

PRECEPTS, SIX HUNDRED AND THIRTEEN.
See COMMANDMENTS, SIX HUNDRED
AND THIRTEEN.

PRECEPTS OF THE CHURCH. See
COMMANDMENTS OF THE CHURCH.

PRECES ANTE ET POST MISSAM. See
PRAYERS BEFORE AND AFTER MASS.

PRECIOUS BLOOD.
[BQT 718.5]
x Blood of Jesus.
Jesus Christ - Precious blood.
xx Jesus Christ - Humanity.
Jesus Christ - Passion.

PRECIOUS BLOOD - ART.
BQT 5876

PRECIOUS BLOOD - CONFRATERNITIES.
xx Confraternities.

PRECIOUS BLOOD - DEVOTIONAL
LITERATURE.

PRECIOUS BLOOD - MEDITATIONS.
BQT 2593

PRECIOUS BLOOD - PRAYER-BOOKS.
BQT 2670   (24x8.71)

PRECIOUS BLOOD - SERMONS.
BQT 3057

PRECIOUS BLOOD, FEAST OF THE.
BQT 4225
x Feast of the Precious Blood.

PRECIOUS BLOOD, MASS OF THE. See
MISSA PRETIOSISSIMI SANGUINIS
DOMINI JESU CHRISTI.

PRECIOUS BLOOD, RELICS OF THE.
BQT 942
x Jesus Christ - Precious Blood,
Relics of.
xx Jesus Christ - Relics of the
Passion.

PREDESTINATION.
BQT 547; BQT 1135-1148
(231.x18)
sa Book of life.
Election (Theology)
Free will and determinism.
God - Foreknowledge.
Necessity (Philosophy)
Reprobation.
xx Calvinism.
Dogmatic theology.
Election (Theology)
Fate and fatalism.
Grace (Theology)
Infant baptism.

PREDESTINATION (MOHAMMEDANISM)
xx Mohammedanism.

PREDICADORES. See DOMINICANS.

PREFACES (LITURGY)
sa Exultet (Preface)
xx Mass.

PREFECTS APOSTOLIC. See
VICARS APOSTOLIC.

PREJUDICES AND ANTIPATHIES (RELIGION)
BQT 245
x Antipathies and prejudices
(Religion)

PRELATES.
BQV230 110   (348.x324)
sa Abbots.
Archbishops.
Bishops. ·
Cardinals.
Protonotaries apostolic.
Vicars apostolic.
xx Curia Romana.
Persons (Canon law)

338

PREMONSTRATENSIAN SAINTS. See
SAINTS, PREMONSTRATENSIAN.

PRE-REFORMATION. See
REFORMATION - EARLY MOVEMENTS.

PRESANCTIFIED, LITURGY OF THE. See
LITURGY OF THE PRESANCTIFIED.

PRESANCTIFIED, MASS OF THE. See
GOOD FRIDAY.

PRESBYTERATE. See
PRIESTHOOD.

PRESBYTERIAN CHURCH. (Geog.
subdiv., Direct)
BX 8901-9225 (285)
xx Church of Scotland.
Subdivisions as in LC.

PRESBYTERIAN CHURCH IN THE U.S.
BX 8950-8968
"Commonly known as the Presbyterian
Church South." LC
x Presbyterian Church South.
Subdivisions as in LC.

PRESBYTERIAN CHURCH IN THE U.S.
(GENERAL)
"Here are entered works on the
Presbyterian Church in the entire
United States not limited to the
'Presbyterian Church in the U.S.,
the corporate name of southern
Presbyterianism." LC

PRESBYTERIAN CHURCH IN THE U.S.A.
BX 8950-8958

PRESBYTERIAN CHURCH OF ENGLAND.
BX 9052-9058
Subdivisions as in LC.

PRESBYTERIAN CHURCH SOUTH. See
PRESBYTERIAN CHURCH IN THE U.S.

PRESBYTERIAN THEOLOGICAL SEMINARIES.
See THEOLOGICAL SEMINARIES, PRES-
BYTERIAN.

PRESBYTERIANISM.
BX 8901-9225
References as in LC.

PRESBYTERIANS.

PRESBYTERIANS, NEGRO.
References as in LC.

PRESBYTERIANS IN DELAWARE,
[IRELAND, ETC.]

PRESBYTERIANS, GERMAN, [HUNGARIAN,
ITALIAN, ETC.]
"Here are entered works on Presbyterians living outside of
Germany, [Hungary, etc.] but
using the German, [Hungarian,
etc.] language in their church
services." LC.
x German, [Hungarian, etc.] Presbyterians.

PRESCHOOL EDUCATION, CATHOLIC. See
CATHOLIC EDUCATION, PRESCHOOL.

PRESCRIPTION (CANON LAW)
BQV230 1509-1512 (348.x46)
sa Bona fides (Canon law)
xx Church property (Canon law)

PRESENCE OF GOD, PRACTICE OF.
BQT 2230
xx God - Omnipresence.
Immanence of God.
Perfection, Christian.
Recollection (Spiritual)

PRESENTATION OF JESUS CHRIST. See
JESUS CHRIST - PRESENTATION.

PRESENTATION OF JESUS CHRIST, FEAST
OF. See CANDLEMAS.

PRESENTATION OF THE BLESSED VIRGIN
MARY, FEAST OF THE.
BQT 4230 (23x3.72)
x Feast of the Presentation of
the Blessed Virgin Mary.
Mary, Blessed Virgin - Presentation, Feast of the.

Presiders' See Celebrants

PRESS, CATHOLIC. See
CATHOLIC PRESS.

PRESUMPTIONS (CANON LAW)
BQV230 1825-1828   (348.x5)
BQV230 1082 (Marriage)
xx Evidence (Canon law)
Fictions (Canon law)

PRIDE AND VANITY.
BJ 1535.P   (179.8)
BQT 1813   (24x1.44)
sa Humility.
x Vanity.
xx Capital sins.
Conduct of life.

PRIEST-WORKER MOVEMENT.
[BQT 3416.5]
xx Catholic Church and social
problems.
Church and labor.

PRIESTESSES. See PRIESTS.

PRIESTHOOD.
BQT 355; BQT 1419   (23x7.6)
BQT 2293-2299 (State of life)
(24x8.3)
sa Major orders.
Ordination.
x Presbyterate.
xx Apostolate.
Apostolic succession.
Clergy.
Ordination.
Pastoral theology.

PRIESTHOOD - BIBLICAL TEACHING.

PRIESTHOOD - BIBLIOGRAPHY.

PRIESTHOOD - CONTROVERSIAL LITERATURE.

PRIESTHOOD - HISTORY.

PRIESTHOOD - HISTORY - EARLY CHURCH.

PRIESTHOOD - HISTORY - MIDDLE AGES.

PRIESTHOOD - HISTORY - MODERN PERIOD.

PRIESTHOOD - PAPAL TEACHING.

PRIESTHOOD - SERMONS.
BQT 3055

PRIESTHOOD, COMMON. See
PRIESTHOOD, UNIVERSAL.

PRIESTHOOD, UNIVERSAL.
BQT 361
Here are entered works on the
distinction between ordained
priests and all members of the
Church as participating in the
one priesthood of Christ through
the ministry of the ordained
priests.
x Common priesthood.
Priesthood, Common.
Universal priesthood.
xx Mystical Body of Christ.

PRIESTS.
sa Celebrants.
x Priestesses.
xx Clergy.

PRIESTS - ADDRESSES, SERMONS, ETC.
BQT 3013
Here are entered addresses and
sermons given to priests.
x Priests - Sermons.

PRIESTS - ANNIVERSARY SERMONS. See
ANNIVERSARY SERMONS - PRIESTS.

PRIESTS - BIOGRAPHY.
BQX 8261   (922)
xx Catholic Church - Biography.
Christian biography.

PRIESTS - BOOKS AND READING. See
CLERGY - BOOKS AND READING.

PRIESTS - CONFRATERNITIES.
Here are entered works on societies
of diocesan or secular priests
associated for mutual cooperation
in the pursuit of a specific
object of religion or charity
by means of prayer, example and
counsel.
xx Religious orders.

PRIESTS - CORRESPONDENCE, REMINISCENCES, ETC.

PRIESTS - EDUCATION. See CLERGY - EDUCATION.

PRIESTS - FICTION.
BQT 2299

PRIESTS - FUNERAL SERVICES.

PRIESTS - MEDITATIONS.
BQT 2551   (24x2.6)

PRIESTS - PERIODICALS. See CLERGY - PERIODICALS.

PRIESTS - PRAYER-BOOKS.
BQT 2621   (24x3.12)
sa Prayers before and after mass.

PRIESTS - RETREATS. See RETREATS FOR CLERGY.
RETREATS FOR RELIGIOUS.

PRIESTS - SERMONS. See PRIESTS - ADDRESSES, SERMONS, ETC.

PRIESTS - SPIRITUAL LIFE.
BQT 2293

PRIESTS - VOCATION.
BQT 2294
x Sacerdotal vocation.
Vocation, Sacerdotal.
xx Clergy - Vocation.
Vocation, Ecclesiastical.

PRIESTS - VOCATION (CANON LAW)
BQV230 1353

PRIESTS (CANON LAW)

PRIESTS, BUDDHIST.
x Buddhist priests.

PRIESTS, COLORED. See PRIESTS, NEGRO.

PRIESTS, EGYPTIAN.
x Egyptian priests.

PRIESTS, GREEK.
x Greek priests.

PRIESTS, ITALIAN.
x Italian priests.

PRIESTS, JEWISH.
BM 652
sa Hallah.
Zadokites.
x Jewish priests.

PRIESTS, NEGRO.
x Colored priests.
Negro priests.
Priests, Colored.
xx Catholics, Negro.

PRIESTS, ROMAN.
Here are entered works dealing with the priests of the religion of ancient pagan Rome.
x Roman priests.

PRIESTS AND CATHOLIC ACTION.

PRIESTS AND SOCIAL PROBLEMS. See CLERGY AND SOCIAL PROBLEMS.

PRIESTS AS AUTHORS. See CLERGYMEN AS AUTHORS.

PRIESTS IN LITERATURE. See CLERGY IN LITERATURE.

PRIMACY OF THE POPE. See POPES - PRIMACY.

PRIMATES (ECCLESIASTIC)
sa Exarchs.
xx Bishops.
Exarchs.

PRIME.
BQT 4175
"That portion of the Divine Office assigned to the first hour (Prima hora) i.e., about 6 a.m., the approximate time of its recital in monastic churches." AT
xx Divine Office.

PRIMER (PRAYER-BOOK)
BQT 4278
"The generic name of a type of prayer book in ordinary use by the laity in England before the

PRIMER (PRAYER-BOOK) -- Continued.
Reformation ... The contents
varied, but always contained as
a nucleus the Little Office of
Our Lady, Office of the Dead,
Penitential and Gradual Psalms,
Pater, Ave, Credo, and Litany."
AT
  x Prymer (Prayer-book)
  xx Prayer-books.

PRIMITIVE BAPTISTS.
      BX 6380-6389
  Subdivisions as in LC.

PRIMITIVE CHRISTIANITY. See
  CHURCH HISTORY - PRIMITIVE AND
  EARLY CHURCH.

PRIMITIVE JUSTICE. See
  JUSTICE, ORIGINAL.

PRIMITIVE RELIGION. See
  RELIGION, PRIMITIVE.

PRIORIES.
  sa Abbeys.
  xx Catholic institutions.
     Convents.
     Monasteries.

PRIORS, CLAUSTRAL.
  A claustral prior is "the
     second-in-command of an abbey
     of monks or canons regular,
     sometimes called the dean."
     AT
  x Claustral priors.
  xx Superiors, Religious.

PRISCILLIANISTS.
      BQT 72
  xx Gnosticism.
     Heresies and heresy - Early
        church.

PRISON CHAPLAINS. See
  CHAPLAINS, PRISON.

PRISONERS, CHURCH WORK WITH. See
  CHURCH WORK WITH PRISONERS.

PRISONS - MISSIONS AND CHARITIES.
      BQT 3698

PRISONS - RELIGIOUS LIFE.
  xx Chaplains, Prison.

PRIVATE MASS. See
  LOW MASS.

PRIVATE SCHOOLS - RELIGIOUS LIFE.
  "Here are entered works that deal
     with the attitude towards and
     treatment of religion in private
     schools." LC

PRIVILEGE (CANON LAW)
      BQV230 63-79 (General)
         (348.x24)
      BQV230 613-625 (Religious)
         (348.x37)
  sa Exemption (Canon law)
     Immunity, Ecclesiastical.
     Indults.
     Privilegium fori.
  xx Religious orders (Canon law)

PRIVILEGED ALTARS. See
  ALTARS, PRIVILEGED.

PRIVILEGIUM CLERICALE. See
  PRIVILEGIUM FORI.

PRIVILEGIUM FORI.   (Geog. subdiv.,
  Direct)
  Here are entered works dealing
     with the exemption of clerics
     from lay courts, whether civil
     or criminal, unless with per-
     mission of the proper ecclesias-
     tical authority.
  x Benefit of clergy.
     Clergy, Privilege of.
     Privilegium clericale.
  xx Ecclesiastical courts.
     Immunity, Ecclesiastical.
     Jurisdiction (Canon law)
     Privilege (Canon law)

PROBABILIORISM. See
  PROBABILISM.

342

PROBABILISM.
        BQT 1763   (24x1.21)
    sa Doubt (Canon law)
      x Aequiprobabilism.
        Equiprobabilism.
        Laxism.
        Probabiliorism.
        Tuitiorism.
     xx Casuistry.
        Moral theology.

PROBLEM CHILDREN, CHURCH WORK WITH.
    See   CHURCH WORK WITH PROBLEM
    CHILDREN.

PROCEDURE (CANON LAW)
    sa Appellate procedure (Canon law)
       Civil procedure (Canon law)
       Criminal procedure (Canon law)

PROCEDURE (CANON LAW, ANGLICAN)

PROCEDURE (CANON LAW, EASTERN)

PROCESS (CANON LAW)
✓ *Process theology see Theology, Process*
PROCESSION OF THE BLESSED SACRAMENT.
        BQT 4458
      x Blessed Sacrament, Procession
           of the.
     xx Eucharist.

PROCESSION OF THE HOLY SPIRIT.   See
    HOLY SPIRIT - PROCESSION.

PROCESSIONALE.
        BQT 4273

PROCESSIONS, ECCLESIASTICAL.
    (Geog. subdiv., Direct)
        BQT 4089; BQT 4458
      x Ecclesiastical processions.
     xx Pilgrims and pilgrimages.
        Rites and ceremonies (Catholic)

PROCESSIONS, ECCLESIASTICAL (CANON
    LAW)
        BQV230 1290-1295   (348.x415)

PROCURATORS (CANON LAW)
     xx Agency (Canon law)

PRODIGAL SON (PARABLE)
        BQT 888   (226.x6)

PRODIGAL SON (PARABLE) - ART.
        BQT 5889   (246.x66)

PRODIGAL SON (PARABLE) - DRAMA.

PRODIGAL SON (PARABLE) - FICTION.

PRODIGAL SON (PARABLE) - MEDITATIONS.

PRODIGAL SON (PARABLE) - SERMONS.
        BQT 3089

PRODIGAL SON (PARABLE) - SONGS AND
    MUSIC.

PROFESSION, CHOICE OF. See
    VOCATIONAL GUIDANCE.

PROFESSION, MONASTIC. See
    PROFESSION, RELIGIOUS.

PROFESSION, RELIGIOUS.
    [BQT 2328]
        BQT 4465 (texts)
    "A contract whereby a novice freely
    gives himself or herself, by the
    taking of vows, to the religious
    life in a community approved by
    the church." AT
      x Liber promissionum.
        Monastic profession.
        Profession, Monastic.
        Religious profession.
     xx Initiation (in religion, folk-
           lore, etc.)
        Religious life.
        Vows.

PROFESSION, RELIGIOUS - ANNIVERSARY
    SERMONS. See ANNIVERSARY SERMONS -
    RELIGIOUS PROFESSION.

PROFESSION, RELIGIOUS - HISTORY.

PROFESSION, RELIGIOUS - SERMONS.
        BQT 3009

PROFESSION, RELIGIOUS - BENEDICTINES,
    [CISTERCIANS, FRANCISCANS, ETC.]

PROFESSION, RELIGIOUS (CANON LAW)
        BQV230 572   (348.x37)

PROFESSION OF FAITH.
"Here are entered works limited
in their scope to the formal
profession of faith required of
the Catholic clergy, involving
acceptance of the teachings of
the church." LC
x Faith, Profession of.
xx Church - Teaching office.
Creeds - Subscription.
Witness bearing (Christianity)

PROFESSION OF FAITH (CANON LAW)
BQV230 1406-1408   (348.x44)
xx Clergy (Canon law)

PROHIBITED BOOKS.
BQT 1992-1994   (24x1.7)
sa Blasphemy.
Censorship.
Condemned books.
Expurgated books.
Index librorum prohibitorum.
Liberty of the press.
x Books, Forbidden.
Books, Prohibited.
Forbidden books.
xx Blasphemy.
Books and reading - Moral
aspects.
Condemned books.
Expurgated books.

PROHIBITED BOOKS (CANON LAW)
BQV230 1384-1405   (348.x443)
xx Censorship (Canon law)

PROHIBITED SOCIETIES. See
CONDEMNED SOCIETIES.

PROMOTOR JUSTITIAE. See
PROMOTORS OF JUSTICE (CANON LAW)

PROMOTORS OF JUSTICE (CANON LAW)
BQV230 1586   (348.x5)
"Here are entered works dealing
with those Catholic diocesan
officials whose duty it is to
represent and defend the authority and law of the church in all
ecclesiastical trials except
those dealing with the sacraments
of holy order and marriage." LC

PROMOTORS OF JUSTICE (CANON LAW) --
Continued.
sa Defender of the marriage bond.
x Promotor justitiae.
xx Defender of the marriage bond.

PROMULGATION (CANON LAW)
xx Legislation (Canon law)

PRONES.
xx Sermons.

PROOF (CANON LAW) See
EVIDENCE (CANON LAW)

PROPAGANDA, CATHOLIC. See
CATHOLIC PROPAGANDA.

PROPAGANDA, RELIGIOUS. See
RELIGIOUS PROPAGANDA.

PROPAGATION OF THE FAITH, CONGREGA-
TION OF THE. See
CONGREGATIO DE PROPAGANDA FIDE.

PROPERS.
BQT 4319

PROPERS - SERMONS.

PROPERS (MUSIC)
M 2148.2
sa Graduals (Music)
Introits (Music)
Offertories (Music)
Sequences (Music)
xx Masses.

PROPERTY (CANON LAW)
sa Things (Canon law)
xx Things (Canon law)

PROPERTY, CHURCH. See
CHURCH PROPERTY.

PROPERTY TAX.
sa Church property - Taxation.
Other references as in LC.

PROPHECIES.
        BQT 273 (Criteria of revelation)
          (23x9.12)
        BQT 2483 (Mysticism)
        BF 1783-1815 (Occultism)
          (133.3)
  sa Apocalyptic literature.
     Astrology.
     Bible - Prophecies.
     Divination.
     Fortune-telling.
     Jesus Christ - Prophecies.
     Oracles.
  xx Divination.
     Mysticism.
     Occult sciences.
     Supernatural.

PROPHECIES, BIBLICAL. See
  BIBLE - PROPHECIES.
  BIBLE. O.T. - PROPHECIES.
  BIBLE. N.T. - PROPHECIES.
  JESUS CHRIST - PROPHECIES.
  and subdivision "Prophecies" under
    certain Biblical books, e.g.,
    Bible. O.T. Isaias - Pro-
    phecies.

PROPHETS.
        BS 1505; BS 1560 (Bible: bio-
          graphy)
        BS 1501-1675 (Bible: pro-
          phetic books) (224)
        BF 1783-1815 (Occultism)
  sa Sibyls.
  xx Bible - Biography.

PROPHETS, BOOKS OF THE. See
  BIBLE. O.T. PROPHETS.

PROPHETS, MAJOR. See
  BIBLE. O.T. MAJOR PROPHETS.

PROPHETS, MINOR. See
  BIBLE. O.T. MINOR PROPHETS.

PROPOSED RELIGIONS. See
  RELIGIONS (PROPOSED, UNIVERSAL,
  ETC.)

PROROGATION (CANON LAW)
  xx Civil procedure (Canon law)

PROSE (LITURGY). See
  SEQUENCES (LITURGY)

PROSELYTES AND PROSELYTING, JEWISH.
  xx Judaism.

PROSPHORA.
  The name for the altar bread of
    the Byzantine Rite.
  xx Altar breads.

PROSTRATION (POSTURE IN WORSHIP)
  See POSTURE IN WORSHIP.

PROTECTION, PAPAL.
        BQX 493
  "Here are entered works dealing
    with the protection granted by
    the popes during the Middle
    Ages to monasteries and also to
    dioceses and churches." LC
  x Papal protection.

PROTESTANT CHURCH ORDERS. See
  CHURCH ORDERS, PROTESTANT.

PROTESTANT CHURCHES.   (Geog.
  subdiv., Indirect)
        BX 4800-9890   (283.288)
  sa Protestantism.
    also names of churches, e.g.,
      Lutheran Church; Methodist
      Episcopal Church; etc.
  xx Church history.
    Protestantism.

PROTESTANT CHURCHES - DOCTRINE. See
  PROTESTANTISM.

PROTESTANT CHURCHES - EDUCATION.

PROTESTANT CHURCHES - GOVERNMENT.

PROTESTANT CHURCHES - LITURGICAL
  MOVEMENT. See
  LITURGICAL MOVEMENT - PROTESTANT
  CHURCHES.

PROTESTANT CHURCHES - MISSIONS.
  x Missions, Protestant.

PROTESTANT CHURCHES - MISSIONS -
  EASTERN CHURCHES.
        BQX 5433

PROTESTANT CHURCHES - MYSTICISM. See
MYSTICISM - PROTESTANT CHURCHES.

PROTESTANT CHURCHES - RELATIONS.

PROTESTANT CHURCHES - RELATIONS -
CATHOLIC CHURCH.

PROTESTANT CHURCHES - RELATIONS -
ORTHODOX EASTERN CHURCH.

PROTESTANT CHURCHES - RELATIONS -
ORTHODOX EASTERN CHURCH, RUSSIAN.

################

PROTESTANT CHURCHES. LITURGY AND
RITUAL.

################

PROTESTANT EPISCOPAL CHURCH IN
THE U.S.A.
BX 5800-5995 (283)
"Established in 1789. For works
dealing with the English Church
in America during the colonial
period, see Church of England in
America." LC
x Episcopal Church.
Subdivisions as in LC.

PROTESTANT EPISCOPAL CHURCHES. See
CHURCHES, ANGLICAN.

PROTESTANT FRANCISCANS. See
FRANCISCANS. THIRD ORDER (PRO-
TESTANT)

PROTESTANT REFORMATION. See
REFORMATION.

PROTESTANT RELIGIOUS ORDERS. See
RELIGIOUS ORDERS, PROTESTANT.
RELIGIOUS ORDERS OF WOMEN, PRO-
TESTANT.

PROTESTANT THEOLOGY. See
PROTESTANTISM.

PROTESTANT THIRD ORDERS. See
THIRD ORDERS (PROTESTANT)

PROTESTANTISM. (Geog. subdiv.)
BX 4800-4983 (284)
BQT 130-135 (History of
Protestant theology)
Here are entered works on the
principles and theory of
Protestantism.
sa Protestant Churches.
Reformation.
x Protestant Churches - Doctrine.
Protestant theology.
Theology, Protestant.
xx Christianity.
Church history.
Protestant Churches.
Reformation.

PROTESTANTISM - ADDRESSES, ESSAYS,
LECTURES.

PROTESTANTISM - BIBLIOGRAPHY.

PROTESTANTISM - COLLECTED WORKS.

PROTESTANTISM - CONTROVERSIAL
LITERATURE.
sa Anti-Protestant polemic.

PROTESTANTISM - DICTIONARIES.

PROTESTANTISM - HISTORIOGRAPHY.

PROTESTANTISM - HISTORY.
BX 4804-4807
xx Church history - Modern period.

PROTESTANTISM - PICTURES, ILLUSTRA-
TIONS, ETC.

PROTESTANTISM - SERMONS.

PROTESTANTISM, EVANGELICAL. See
EVANGELICALISM.

PROTESTANTS.
xx Non-Catholics.

PROTESTANTS IN CANADA, [GERMANY,
UNITED STATES, ETC.]

PROTHESIS.
BQT 5965
"The part of the sanctuary of a
church of the Byzantine rite to
the north of the altar, and the
table therein at which takes
place the office of the Prothesis
or proskomide." AT

PROTONOTARIES APOSTOLIC.
x Apostolic protonotaries.
xx Persons (Canon law)
Prelates.

PROVERBS, BOOK OF. See
BIBLE. O.T. PROVERBS.

PROVIDENCE, DIVINE.
BQT 612   (231.x17)
x Divine providence.
God - Providence.
Providence and government of
God.
Theodicy.
xx Dogmatic theology.
God.
Good and evil.

PROVIDENCE, DIVINE - DEVOTIONAL
LITERATURE.

PROVIDENCE, DIVINE - EARLY WORKS
TO 1800.

PROVIDENCE, DIVINE - HISTORY OF
DOCTRINES.

PROVIDENCE, DIVINE - JUVENILE
LITERATURE.

PROVIDENCE, DIVINE - MEDITATIONS.
BQT 2581

PROVIDENCE, DIVINE - SERMONS.
BQT 3089

PROVIDENCE AND GOVERNMENT OF GOD.
See PROVIDENCE, DIVINE.

PROVINCIAL COUNCILS. See
COUNCILS AND SYNODS, PROVINCIAL.

PRUDENCE.
BQT 1211; BQT 1789
xx Virtues, Moral.

PRYMER (PRAYER BOOK). See
PRIMER (PRAYER-BOOK)

PSALMODY.
[BQT 4605]
"Here are entered works on the
singing of Psalms in public
worship." LC
sa Bible. O.T. Psalms.
Church music.
Hymns.
xx Church music.
Hebrew poetry.
Hymns.

PSALMS. See
BIBLE. O.T. PSALMS.
PSALTERIUM.

PSALMS (MUSIC)
M 2079
Individual psalms by number.
For Catholic-Protestant numbering
of the psalms see Bible. O.T.
Psalms (p. 47).
sa Introits (Music)
x Bible. O.T. Psalms - Music.
xx Psalterium.
Sacred vocal music.

PSALMS (MUSIC) - 1st PSALM.
x Beatus vir, qui non abiit in
consilio impiorum (Music)

PSALMS (MUSIC) - 2d PSALM.
x Quare fremuerent gentes (Music)

PSALMS (MUSIC) - 4th PSALM.
x Cum invocarem, exaudivit me
Deus (Music)

PSALMS (MUSIC) - 6th PSALM.
x Domine, ne in furore tuo arguas
me (Music)

PSALMS (MUSIC) - 8th PSALM.
x Domine, Dominus noster (Psalm)

PSALMS (MUSIC) - 9th PSALM.
    x Confitebor tibi Domine in toto
      corde meo, narrabo (Music)

PSALMS (MUSIC) - 11th PSALM.
    x Salvum me fac, Domine (Music)

PSALMS (MUSIC) - 26th PSALM.
    x Dominus illuminatio mea, et
      salus mea (Music)

PSALMS (MUSIC) - 30th PSALM.
    x In Te, Domine, speravi (Music)

PSALMS (MUSIC) - 32d PSALM.
    x Exultate, justi, in Domino (Music)

PSALMS (MUSIC) - 35th PSALM.
    x Dixit injustus ut delinquat in
      semetipso (Music)

PSALMS (MUSIC) - 38th PSALM.
    x Dixi, Costodiam vias meas (Music)

PSALMS (MUSIC) - 45th PSALM.
    x Deus noster refugium et
      virtus (Music)

PSALMS (MUSIC) - 46th PSALM.
    x Omnes gentes, plaudite mani-
      bus (Music)

PSALMS (MUSIC) - 50th PSALM.
    x Miserere mei, Deus (Music)

PSALMS (MUSIC) - 53d PSALM.
    x Deus, in nomine tuo salvum me
      fac (Music)

PSALMS (MUSIC) - 56th PSALM.
    x Miserere mei, Deus, misereri
      mei (Music)

PSALMS (MUSIC) - 66th PSALM.
    x Deus misereatur nostri (Music)

PSALMS (MUSIC) - 68th PSALM.
    x Salvum me fac, Deus (Music)

PSALMS (MUSIC) - 69th PSALM.
    x Deus, in adjutorium meum
      intende (Music)

PSALMS (MUSIC) - 79th PSALM.
    x Qui regis Israel, intende (Music)

PSALMS (MUSIC) - 83d PSALM.
    x Quam dilecta tabernacula
      tua (Music)

PSALMS (MUSIC) - 85th PSALM.
    x Inclina, Domine, aurem
      tuam (Music)

PSALMS (MUSIC) - 90th PSALM.
    x Qui habitat in adjutorio
      Altissimi (Music)

PSALMS (MUSIC) - 94th PSALM.
    sa Invitatorium.
    x Venite, exultemus Domino (Music)

PSALMS (MUSIC) - 95th PSALM.
    x Cantate Domino canticum novum,
      cantate Domino (Music)

PSALMS (MUSIC) - 99th PSALM.
    x Jubilate Deo omnis terra,
      servite Domino (Music)

PSALMS (MUSIC) - 101st PSALM.
    x Domine, exaudi orationem mean,
      et clamor meus ad te veniat
      (Music)

PSALMS (MUSIC) - 102d PSALM.
    x Benedic, anima mea Domino et
      omnia quae intra me sunt
      (Music)

PSALMS (MUSIC) - 103d PSALM.
    x Benedic, anima mea Domino,
      Domine Deus meus (Music)

PSALMS (MUSIC) - 109th PSALM.
    x Dixit Dominus Domino meo (Music)

PSALMS (MUSIC) - 111th PSALM.
    x Beatus vir, qui timet Dominum
      (Music)

PSALMS (MUSIC) - 112th PSALM.
    x Laudate pueri, Dominum (Music)

PSALMS (MUSIC) - 113th PSALM.
    x In exitu Israel de Egypto (Music)

PSALMS (MUSIC) - 116th PSALM.
  x Laudate Dominum omnes
      gentes (Music)

PSALMS (MUSIC) - 118th PSALM.
  x Beati immaculati in via (Music)

PSALMS (MUSIC) - 119th PSALM.
  x Ad Dominum cum tribularer
     clamavi (Music)

PSALMS (MUSIC) - 120th PSALM.
  x Levavi oculos meos in
     montes (Music)

PSALMS (MUSIC) - 126th PSALM.
  x Nisi Dominus aedificaverit
     domum (Music)

PSALMS (MUSIC) - 128th PSALM.
  x Saepe expugnaverunt me (Music)

PSALMS (MUSIC) - 129th PSALM.
  x De profundis (Music)

PSALMS (MUSIC) - 135th PSALM.
  x Confitemini Domino quoniam bonus,
    quoniam in aeternum misercordia
    ejus (Music)

PSALMS (MUSIC) - 137th PSALM.
  x Confitebor tibi Domine in toto
    corde meo quoniam audisti
    verba oris mei (Music)

PSALMS (MUSIC) - 142d PSALM.
  x Domine, exaudi orationem meam,
    auribus percipe obsecrationem
    meam (Music)

PSALMS (MUSIC) - 143d PSALM.
  x Benedictus Dominus, Deus
    meus (Music)

PSALMS (MUSIC) - 144th PSALM.
  x Exalatabo te, Deus meus,
    rex (Music)

PSALMS (MUSIC) - 145th PSALM.
  x Lauda, anima mea, Dominum
    (Music)

PSALMS (MUSIC) - 147th PSALM.
  x Lauda, Jerusalem, Dominum (Music)

PSALMS (MUSIC) - 150th PSALM.
  x Laudate Dominum in sanctis
    ejus (Music)

PSALMS, GRADUAL. See
  BIBLE. O.T. PSALMS, GRADUAL.

PSALMS, MESSIANIC. See
  BIBLE. O.T. PSALMS, MESSIANIC.

PSALMS, PENITENTIAL. See
  BIBLE. O.T. PSALMS, PENITENTIAL.

PSALTER. See PSALTERIUM.

PSALTERIUM.
    BQT 4261; BQT 4379   (26x5.9)
  "That portion of the Breviary
   which contains the psalms
   arranged as they are to be said
   in the divine office during the
   course of the week." AT
  sa Psalms (Music)
   x Psalms.
    Psalter.
  xx Bible. O.T. Psalms.
    Breviarium.

PSALTERIUM - ART.
    ND 3357

PSALTERIUM - COMMENTARIES. See
  BIBLE. O.T. PSALMS - COMMENTARIES.

PSALTERIUM - DICTIONARIES.

PSALTERIUM - MANUSCRIPTS.
    Z 113 Z

PSALTERIUM - MANUSCRIPTS - FACSIMILES.

      ################

PSALTERIUM. ENGLISH, [FRENCH,
  GERMAN, ETC.]

      ################

PSALTERIUM MOZARABICUM.

PSEUDEPIGRAPHA (O.T.). See
   APOCRYPHAL BOOKS (O.T.)

PSEUDEPIGRAPHA (N.T.). See
   APOCRYPHAL BOOKS (N.T.)

PSEUDO-MESSIAHS.
      BM 752
   x False Messiahs.
   Messiahs, False.
   xx Jews - Biography.
   Messiah.

PSYCHIATRY AND PASTORAL THEOLOGY.

PSYCHIATRY AND RELIGION.
   x Religion and psychiatry.
   xx Medicine and religion.

PSYCHOLOGY, BIBLICAL. See
   BIBLE - PSYCHOLOGY.

PSYCHOLOGY, CLERICAL. See
   PASTORAL PSYCHOLOGY.

PSYCHOLOGY, PASTORAL. See
   PASTORAL PSYCHOLOGY.

PSYCHOLOGY, RELIGIOUS.
      BQT 245   (291.12)
   sa Asceticism and psychology.
   Confession - Psychology.
   Conversion - Psychology.
   Discernment of spirits.
   Enthusiasm.
   Maggid (Cabala)
   Miracles.
   Pastoral psychology.
   Prayer - Psychology.
   Psychology, Applied.
   Religion and geography.
   Saints.
   Salvation - Psychology.
   Stigmatization.
   x Psychology and religion.
   Religion - Psychology.
   Religion and psychology.
   Religious psychology.
   xx Asceticism.
   Religion.

PSYCHOLOGY, RELIGIOUS - PERIODICALS.

PSYCHOLOGY AND ASCETICISM. See
   ASCETICISM AND PSYCHOLOGY.

PSYCHOLOGY AND RELIGION. See
   PSYCHOLOGY, RELIGIOUS.

PSYCHOLOGY OF PRAYER. See
   PRAYER - PSYCHOLOGY.

PUBLIC LAW (CANON LAW). See
   CANON LAW.
   CATHOLIC CHURCH - GOVERNMENT.

PUBLIC POLICY (CANON LAW)

PUBLIC RELATIONS - CHURCHES.
   sa Advertising - Churches.
   Religious propaganda.
   x Churches - Public relations.
   xx Advertising - Churches.
   Church work.

PUBLIC WORSHIP.
      BV 5-25   (291.x3)
   sa Church-night services.
   Pastoral prayers.
   Prayer-meetings.
   Sunday evening services.
   xx Church attendance.
   Worship.

PULPIT PRAYERS. See
   PASTORAL PRAYERS.

PULPITS.
      BQT 5947   (726.592)
   xx Church furniture.

PUNISHMENT.
   sa Future punishment.
   Other references as in LC.

PUNISHMENT (CANON LAW). See
   PENALTIES, ECCLESIASTICAL.

PUNISHMENT, ETERNAL. See
   HELL.

350

PURE NATURE.
BQT 633
"The condition in which man would
be had God never given him any
gifts beyond those due to human
nature ..." AT
x Status naturae purae.
xx Man (Theology)

PURGATIVE WAY TO PERFECTION.
BQT 2206
xx Perfection, Christian.

PURGATORY.
BQT 1533-1539   (236.5)
sa All Souls' Day.
Future life.
Future punishment.
Heroic act of charity.
Indulgences.
x Church suffering.
Poor souls in purgatory.
xx Eschatology.
Future life.
Future punishment.
Indulgences.

PURGATORY - ART.
BQT 5905

PURGATORY - CONTROVERSIAL LITERATURE.
BQT 1539

PURGATORY - DEVOTIONAL LITERATURE.

PURGATORY - MEDITATIONS.

PURGATORY - PRAYER-BOOKS.
BQT 2691
sa Prayers for the dead.

PURGATORY - SERMONS.
BQT 3089
sa All Souls' Day sermons.
xx All Souls' Day sermons.

PURIFICATION OF THE BLESSED VIRGIN
MARY. See MARY, BLESSED VIRGIN -
PURIFICATION.

PURIM (FEAST OF ESTHER)
BM 695.P
x Esther, Feast of.
Feast of Esther.

PURITANS.
BX 9301-9359   (274.2)
F 67 (Massachusetts)
F 7 (New England)
References as in LC.

PURITY.
[BQT 2383]
Here are entered works dealing
with that condition of innocence
which is preserved by abstinence
from sin of any kind.
sa Chastity.

QUADRAGESIMA. See LENT.

QUAESTIONES DISPUTATAE.
Here are entered works about re-
gulated disputations conducted
by medieval scholastics as a
part of a university education.
xx Theology - Disputations.

QUAESTIONES QUODLIBETALES.
Here are entered works about
medieval university disputations
on various topics.
x Quodlibeta.

QUAKERS. See
FRIENDS, SOCIETY OF.

QUAM DILECTA TABERNACULA TUA (MUSIC).
See PSALMS (MUSIC) - 83d PSALM.

QUARE FREMUERENT GENTES (MUSIC). See
PSALMS (MUSIC) - 2d PSALM.

QUARTODECIMANS.
BV 55
References as in LC.

QUASI-DOMICILE (CANON LAW)
BQV230 90-95
xx Domicile (Canon law)

QUASI-PARISHES (CANON LAW)
BQV230 216
xx Parishes (Canon law)
Missions (Canon law)

QUASI-RELIGIOUS SOCIETIES.
    BQX 6838
  sa Secular institutes.
   x Religious orders without vows.
     Societies living in common
       without vows.
  xx Religious orders.

QUASI-RELIGIOUS SOCIETIES (CANON LAW)
    BQV230 673-681

QUESTIONS AND ANSWERS - BIBLE. See
  BIBLE - EXAMINATIONS, QUESTIONS, ETC.

QUESTIONS AND ANSWERS - CATHOLIC
  CHURCH.
    BQT 221

QUESTIONS AND ANSWERS - THEOLOGY.
   x Christianity - Questions and
       answers.
     Theology - Questions and
       answers.

QUI HABITAT IN ADJUTORIO ALTISSIMI
  (MUSIC). See
  PSALMS (MUSIC) - 90th PSALM.

QUI REGIS ISRAEL, INTENDE (MUSIC).
  See PSALMS (MUSIC) - 79th PSALM.

QUIETISM.
    BQT 125   (24x9.2)
    BQT 2461 (Mysticism)
    BQX 991 (History)

QUINQUENNIAL REPORTS OF BISHOPS.
  See BISHOPS - QUINQUENNIAL REPORTS.

QUMRAN COMMUNITY.
    BM 175
   x Kumran community.
  xx Essenes.
     Jewish sects.
     Monasticism, Jewish.
     Pharisees.

QUMRAN SCROLLS. See
  DEAD SEA SCROLLS.

QUODLIBETA. See
  QUAESTIONES QUODLIBETALES.

RABBINICAL COURTS.   (Geog. subdiv.,
  Direct)
   x Courts, Rabbinical.
  xx Courts, Jewish.

RABBINICAL LITERATURE.
  References as in LC supplement
  1956-58.

RABBINICAL SEMINARIES.   (Geog.
  subdiv., Indirect)
  References as in LC.

RABBIS.   (Geog. subdiv., Direct)
  References as in LC.

RABBIS - INSTALLATION. See
  INSTALLATION (RABBIS)

RABBIS - ORDINATION. See
  SEMIKHAH.

RACE PROBLEMS.
  sa Integrated churches.
  Other references as in LC.

RADIO IN RELIGION.
    BQT 3618
   x Religion and radio.
     Religious broadcasting.
  xx Church work.

RADIO SERMONS.
    BQT 3007
   x Sermons, Radio.

RANSOM CAPTIVES.
    BQX 673
  sa Mercedarians.
     Trinitarians.
     Vincentians.
   x Captives, Ransom of.
  xx Slavery and the Church.

RANTERS.
  xx Antinomianism.

RAPE (CANON LAW)
    BQV230 2354 (Criminal law)
      (348.x6)
    BQV230 1074 (Marriage impedi-
      ment)   (348.x427)
  xx Crime and criminals (Canon law)
     Marriage - Impediments.

RASKOLNIKS.
    BQX 6154
    BX 601
xx Sects, Russian.

RATING OF CLERGYMEN. See
CLERGY, RATING OF.

RATIONALISM.
    BD 181 (Epistemology)
    B 833 (Philosophy: general)
        (149.7)
    B 851-4695 (Philosophy:
        special, local)
    BQT 123 (Theology)   (211)
sa Agnosticism.
    Atheism.
    Belief and doubt.
    Deism.
    Indifferentism (Religion)
    Irreligion.
    Theism.
xx Agnosticism.
    Atheism.
    Belief and doubt.
    Christianity - Controversial
        literature.
    Deism.
    Modernism.

RATISBON, DIET OF, 1532.
    DD 184
x Diet of Ratisbon, 1532.

RATISBON, DIET OF, 1653-1654.
x Diet of Ratisbon, 1653-1654.

READERS AND SPEAKERS, CATHOLIC. See
CATHOLIC READERS AND SPEAKERS.

REAL PRESENCE. See
TRANSUBSTANTIATION.
REALITY
REASON, USE OF. See
USE OF REASON.

REASON AND FAITH. See
FAITH AND REASON.

RECAPITULATION.
    BQT 1119
Here are entered works on the
    theory that all things in

RECAPITULATION -- Continued.
    heaven and on earth, are
    harmoniously united in Jesus
    Christ who is both creator
    and redeemer.
x Anakephalaiosis.
xx Eschatology.
    Jesus Christ.

RECIDIVISTS (MORAL THEOLOGY)
    BQT 1734   (24x1.941)
Recipes   x Cookery
RECLUSES.
    BQT 6838
sa Anchoresses.
xx Hermits.
    Religious orders.

RECOGNITION, HEAVENLY. See
HEAVENLY RECOGNITION.

RECOLLECTION (SPIRITUAL).
    BQT 2230
sa Detachment.
    Presence of God, Practice of.
xx Spirituality.

RECOLLECTS. See RECOLLETS.

RECOLLETS (AUGUSTINIAN)
    BQX 7003   (271.x1)
x Augustinian Recollets.

RECOLLETS (FRANCISCAN)
x Franciscan Recollets.
xx Franciscans.

Reconciliation see Penance

RECONSTRUCTIONIST JUDAISM.
x Judaism - Reconstructionist
    movement.
xx Jewish sects.

RECTORIES (BUILDINGS). See
PARSONAGES.

RECTORS. See PASTORS.

RECUSANTS. See
CATHOLICS IN ENGLAND.
CATHOLICS IN LANCASHIRE, ENGLAND,
and in other English counties.

RED CROSS (SYMBOL)
  xx Crosses.

RED MASS.
    [BQT 4328]
    "A votive Mass of the Holy Ghost;
    in England, particularly one
    celebrated for the benefit of
    the judges, counsel and solici-
    tors of the Supreme Court of
    Judicature at the beginning of
    the legal year or Michaelmas
    Term." AT
    x Mass, Red.

RED MASS SERMONS.
      BQT 3009

RED SCAPULAR OF THE PASSION. See
  SCAPULAR OF THE PASSION (RED)

∟ REDEMPTION.
        BQT 1117-1123   (232.x7)
    sa Atonement.
       Co-redemption.
       Salvation.
     x Jesus Christ - Redemption.
       Soteriology.
    xx Dogmatic theology.
       Jesus Christ.

REDEMPTION - BIBLICAL TEACHING.

REDEMPTION - COMPARATIVE STUDIES.

REDEMPTION - HISTORY OF DOCTRINES.

REDEMPTION - SERMONS.

REDEMPTION OF THE FIRST-BORN.
      BM 720.R
    References as in LC.

REFORM, CHURCH. See
  CHURCH REFORM.

REFORM JUDAISM.   (Geog. subdiv.,
  Direct)
    x Judaism - Reform movement.
      Judaism, Reform.
      Liberal Judaism.
    xx Jewish sects.

REFORMATION.   (Geog. subdiv.,
  Indirect)
      BQX 831-920   (270.6)
      D 220-234
    sa Anabaptists.
       Calvinism.
       Counter-Reformation.
       Europe - History - 1517-1648.
       Peasants' War, 1524-1525.
       Protestantism.
       Sacramentarians.
       Schmalkaldic League, 1530-1547.
       Sixteenth century.
       Trent, Council of, 1545-1563.
       also names of religious sects,
         e.g., Huguenots; Hussites;
         Waldenses.
     x Church history - Reformation.
       Reformation - History.
       Protestant Reformation.
    xx Catholic Church - History.
       Christianity.
       Church history.
       Church history - Modern
         period.
       Church reform.
       Counter-Reformation.
       Protestantism.
       Sixteenth century.

REFORMATION - ANNIVERSARIES, ETC.

REFORMATION - BIBLIOGRAPHY.

REFORMATION - BIOGRAPHY.
      BQX 887-888

REFORMATION - CAUSES.
      BQX 841-849

REFORMATION - DRAMA.

REFORMATION - EARLY MOVEMENTS.
    "Here are entered works descrip-
    tive of reform movements pre-
    ceding the Reformation." LC
    x Pre-Reformation.
    xx Church history - Middle Ages.
       Sects, Medieval.

REFORMATION - FICTION.

REFORMATION - HISTORY. See
REFORMATION.

REFORMATION - POETRY.

REFORMATION - SATIRE.

REFORMATION - SOURCES.

################

REFORMATION - ENGLAND.
    BQX 2055-2079   (274.205)
  x Great Britain - Church history -
    Reformation.

REFORMATION - GERMANY.
    BR 295-430
    BQX 1921-1939
    DD 176-189
  sa Augsburg Confession.
  x Germany - Church history -
    Reformation.

REFORMATION - IRELAND.
    [BQX 2236]

REFORMATION - NETHERLANDS.
    BQX 2329

REFORMATION - SCOTLAND.
    BQX 2167
    DA 784

REFORMATION - SPAIN.
    BQX 2941

REFORMATION - SWITZERLAND.
    BQX 3035

################

REFORMED CHURCH.
    BX 9401-9595   (284.1)
  sa Arminians.
    Calvinism.
    Zwinglianism.
  Subdivisions as in LC.

REFORMED CHURCH - RELIGIOUS ORDERS.

REFORMED CHURCH IN AMERICA.
    BX 9501-9543   (285.1)
  Scope note and subdivisions
    as in LC.

REFORMED CHURCH IN THE UNITED STATES.
    BX 9551-9593
  Explanatory note and references
    as in LC.

REFORMED EPISCOPAL CHURCH.
    BX 6051-6093   (283)

REFORMED PRESBYTERIAN CHURCH.
  Scope note and references as in
    LC supplement 1959-60.

REFORMED PRESBYTERIAN CHURCH IN
NORTH AMERICA.
    BX 8990-8993   (285.5)

REFORMERS.
  xx Christian biography.

REFORMERS - ANNIVERSARIES, ETC.

REFORMERS - PORTRAITS.

REFUGEES, RELIGIOUS.
  sa names of groups and individuals,
    e.g., Dukhobors; Huguenots;
    Roger Williams.
  x Religious refugees.
  xx Martyrs.
    Persecution.

REGENERATION (THEOLOGY)
    BQT 1170   (234.4)
  xx Baptism.
    Conversion.
    Grace, Habitual.
    Repentance.
    Salvation.

REGISTERS OF BIRTHS, ETC.   (Geog.
  subdiv., Direct)
  sa Church work - Forms, blanks,
    etc.
  x Births, Registers.
    Church registers.
    Deaths, Registers.
    Marriage registers.
    Parish registers.

REGISTERS OF BIRTHS, ETC. (CANON LAW)
    BQV230 470
  xx Church census.

REGIUM PLACET. See
  PLACITUM REGIUM.

REINCARNATION.
    BL 515   (129.4)
    BP 573.R (Theology)
  References as in LC.

RELEASED TIME (RELIGIOUS EDUCATION)
    BQX 4360

RELICS AND RELIQUARIES.
    BQT 1586   (23x5.22)
    BQT 4462; BQT 4522

  sa Custodials.
    Images, Veneration of.
    Miracles.
    Saints.
    Shrines.
   x Reliquaries.
  xx Christian antiquities.
    Christian art.
    Images, Veneration of.
    Saints.
    Shrines.

RELICS AND RELIQUARIES (CANON LAW)
    BQV230 1281-1289   (348.x43)

RELICS OF THE CROSS. See
  CROSS, RELICS OF THE.

RELICS OF THE PASSION. See
  JESUS CHRIST - RELICS OF THE
  PASSION.

RELIGION.
    BL 48-50   (201)
  Here are entered works on religion
    as a science or system of beliefs
    and practices having reference to
    man's relation to God.
  Cf. note under Religion (Virtue)
  sa Agnosticism.
    Apologetics.
    Asceticism.
    Atheism.
    Belief and doubt.

RELIGION -- Continued.
  sa Catechetics.
    Cultus.
    Deism.
    Dogmatic theology.
    Faith.
    Fetishism.
    God.
    Irreligion.
    Liturgy.
    Mysteries, Religious.
    Mysticism.
    Mythology.
    Natural theology.
    Pantheism.
    Positivism.
    Psychology, Religious.
    Rationalism.
    Religions.
    Revelation.
    Sacrifice.
    Satanism.
    Skepticism.
    Spiritual life.
    Supernatural.
    Theism.
    Theology.
    also subdivision "Religion"
      or "Religion and mythology"
      under names of countries,
      races, peoples, etc. (e.g.,
      France - Religion; Germanic
      tribes - Religion; Indians -
      Religion and mythology) and
      headings beginning with the
      word "Religious."
  xx God.
    Religions.
    Theology.

RELIGION - ADDRESSES, ESSAYS,
  LECTURES.

RELIGION - ANECDOTES, FACETIAE,
  SATIRE, ETC..
    BQT 2831   (244.x7)
  sa Pastoral theology - Anecdotes,
    facetiae, satire, etc.
  x Anecdotes, Religious.

RELIGION - BIBLIOGRAPHY.
    Z 7751-7850   (016.2)

RELIGION - CONTROVERSIAL LITERATURE.

RELIGION - DICTIONARIES.
BL 31   (203)

RELIGION - EXHIBITIONS AND MUSEUMS.
BL 45-46
sa subdivision "Exhibitions and
museums" under Catholic Church
and under names of denominations, e.g., Baptists - Exhibitions and museums.
x Religion - Museums.

RELIGION - HISTORIOGRAPHY.
BR 138

RELIGION - HISTORY.

RELIGION - MUSEUMS. See
RELIGION - EXHIBITIONS AND MUSEUMS.

RELIGION - PERIODICALS.
BL 1-9   (205)

RELIGION - PHILOSOPHY.
BL 51   (201)
sa Knowledge, Theory of (Religion)
x Philosophy of religion.
xx Philosophy and religion.

RELIGION - PSYCHOLOGY. See
PSYCHOLOGY, RELIGIOUS.

RELIGION - SOCIETIES.
BL 11-19   (206)

RELIGION - STORY-TELLING. See
STORY-TELLING - RELIGION.

RELIGION - STUDY AND TEACHING.
"Here are entered works treating
the study and teaching of religion and religious as a science.
Works dealing with religious
instruction in schools and
private life are entered under
Religious education. Works
dealing with the scientific and
professional study of the
Christian religion are entered
under Theology - Study and
teaching." LC

RELIGION (VIRTUE)
BQT 1862   (24x1.61)
Here are entered works on religion
considered as a virtue by which
men exhibit due worship and
reverence to God.
sa Adoration.
Blasphemy.
Devotion.
Idols and images - Worship.
Mystical union.
Piety.
Sacrilege.
Superstition.
Worship.

RELIGION (VIRTUE) - SERMONS.
BQT 3089

RELIGION, ASSYRO-BABYLONIAN. See
ASSYRO-BABYLONIAN RELIGION.

RELIGION, COMPARATIVE. See
RELIGIONS.

RELIGION, CRIMES AGAINST. See
OFFENSES AGAINST RELIGION.

RELIGION, MIXED. See
MIXED RELIGION.

RELIGION, PRIMITIVE.
BL 370
GN 470-474 (Ethnology)
References as in LC.

RELIGION, PROPOSED. See
RELIGIONS (PROPOSED, UNIVERSAL,
ETC.)

RELIGION AND ALCOHOLISM. See
ALCOHOLISM AND RELIGION.

RELIGION AND ARCHITECTURE. See
ARCHITECTURE AND RELIGION.

RELIGION AND ART. See
ART AND RELIGION.

RELIGION AND ASTRONAUTICS.
BL 254
x Astronautics and religion.
xx Religion and science.
Other references as in LC supplement 1959-60.

RELIGION AND COMMUNISM. See
COMMUNISM AND RELIGION.

RELIGION AND EDUCATION. See
CATHOLIC EDUCATION.
CHURCH AND EDUCATION.

RELIGION AND ETHICS.
        BJ 47
    sa Buddhist ethics.
        Ethics.
        Ethics, Jewish.
        Mohammedan ethics.
        Moral theology.
    x Ethics and religion.

RELIGION AND GEOGRAPHY.
        BL 65.G
    sa Ecclesiastical geography.
        Missions - Geography.
        Orientation (Religion)
    x Geography and religion.
    xx Man - Influence and
        environment.
        Psychology, Religious.
        Religion, Primitive.
        Religion and science.

RELIGION AND GEOLOGY. See
BIBLE AND GEOLOGY.

RELIGION AND LABOR.
    sa Church and labor.
    x Labor and religion.
    xx Christianity and economics.

RELIGION AND LANGUAGE.
    sa Language question in the church.
    x Language and religion.
    xx Languages - Religious aspects.
        Nationalism and religion.

RELIGION AND LAW.
        BL 65.L
    sa subdivision "Religious aspects"
        under the law of different
        jurisdictions, e.g., Law -
        Great Britain - Religious
        aspects.
    x Christianity and law.
        Law - Religious aspects.
        Law and Christianity.
        Law and religion.

RELIGION AND LITERATURE.
    sa Liturgy and literature.
        Religion and poetry.
    x Literature and religion.

RELIGION AND MEDICINE. See
MEDICINE AND RELIGION.

RELIGION AND MUSIC.
    sa Church music.
        Music in churches.
        Music in synagogues.
    x Music and religion.
        Music in religion.
    xx Church music.
        Music in churches.
        Music in synagogues.

RELIGION AND NATIONALISM. See
NATIONALISM AND RELIGION.

RELIGION AND PHILOSOPHY. See
PHILOSOPHY AND RELIGION.

RELIGION AND POETRY.
        PN 1077
    x Poetry and religion.
    xx Religion and literature.
        Religion in poetry.

RELIGION AND POLITICS. See
CHRISTIANITY AND POLITICS.

RELIGION AND PSYCHIATRY. See
PSYCHIATRY AND RELIGION.

RELIGION AND PSYCHOLOGY. See
PSYCHOLOGY, RELIGIOUS.

RELIGION AND RADIO. See
RADIO IN RELIGION.

RELIGION AND SCIENCE.
        BL 240-265
        BQT 237
    sa Apologetics.
        Bible and science.
        Buddhism and science.
        Catholic Church and science.
        Christianity - Evidences.
        Creation.
        Evolution.

358

RELIGION AND SCIENCE -- Continued.
  sa Faith and reason.
    Man - Origin.
    Natural theology.
    Nature - Religious inter-
      pretations.
    Religion and astronautics.
    Religion and geography.
    Theology and science.
  x Christianity and science.
    Church and science.
    Geology and religion.
    Science and religion.
  xx Evolution.
    Natural theology.

RELIGION AND SCIENCE - HISTORY OF
  CONTROVERSY.   (Geog. subdiv., Direct)
    BL 245

################

RELIGION AND SCIENCE - EARLY WORKS
  TO 1800.

RELIGION AND SCIENCE - 1801-1859.

RELIGION AND SCIENCE - 1860-1899.

RELIGION AND SCIENCE - 1900-1925.
  sa Modernist-fundamentalist
    controversy.

RELIGION AND SCIENCE - 1926-1945.

RELIGION AND SCIENCE - 1946-

################

RELIGION AND SEX. See
  SEX AND RELIGION.

RELIGION AND SOCIAL PROBLEMS. See
  BUDDHISM AND SOCIAL PROBLEMS.
  CATHOLIC CHURCH AND SOCIAL PROBLEMS.
  CHURCH AND SOCIAL PROBLEMS.
  JUDAISM AND SOCIAL PROBLEMS.
  RELIGION AND SOCIOLOGY.

RELIGION AND SOCIOLOGY.
    BL 60
  "Here are entered general and
    comparative works not limited

RELIGION AND SOCIOLOGY -- Continued.
  to the Christian religion. For
  works so limited, see Sociology,
  Christian, and related subjects
  referred to under that heading."
  LC
  sa Buddhism and social problems.
    Church and social problems.
    Liturgy and sociology.
    Non church-affiliated people.
  x Religion and social problems.
    Sociology and religion.
  xx Sociology, Religious.

RELIGION AND STATE.   (Geog. subdiv.,
  Direct)
    BL 65.S
  sa Church and state.
    Mohammedanism and state.
    Nationalism and religion.
  x State and religion.
  xx Church and state.
    Nationalism and religion.

RELIGION AND TEMPERANCE. See
  TEMPERANCE AND RELIGION.

RELIGION AND WAR. See
  WAR AND RELIGION.

RELIGION IN DRAMA.
  xx Drama.
    Religion in literature.

RELIGION IN LITERATURE.
    PN 49 (General)
    PS 166; PS 310.R (American)
    PR 145; PR 508.R (English)
  sa Bible in literature.
    Fiction - Moral and religious
      aspects.
    God in literature.
    Gods in literature.
    Jesus Christ - Drama.
    Jesus Christ - Fiction.
    Jesus Christ - Poetry.
    Literature and morals.
    Mary, Blessed Virgin, in
      literature.
    Missions in literature.
    Religion in drama.
    Religion in poetry.
    Religious poetry.
    Theater - Moral and religious
      aspects.

RELIGION IN POETRY.
  sa Jesus Christ - Poetry.
     Religion and poetry.
  xx Religion in literature.

RELIGION OF HUMANITY. See
  POSITIVISM.

RELIGION OF THE FUTURE. See
  RELIGIONS (PROPOSED, UNIVERSAL,
  ETC.)

RELIGIONS.
      BL-BX   (280-299)
  sa Babism.
     Bahaism.
     Brahmanism.
     Buddha and Buddhism.
     Christianity.
     Confucius and Confucianism.
     Druids and druidism.
     Druses.
     Fetishism.
     Fire-worshipers.
     Gnosticism.
     Gods.
     Hinduism.
     Humanism, Religious.
     Jains.
     Judaism.
     Lamaism.
     Mandaeans.
     Mohammedanism.
     Mythology.
     Nagualism.
     Paganism.
     Parsees.
     Polytheism.
     Positivism.
     Religion.
     Sects.
     Shamanism.
     Shinto.
     Spiritualism.
     Taoism.
     Theosophy.
     Yezidis.
     Zoroastrianism.
   x Comparative religion.
     Denominations, Religious.
     Religion, Comparative.
     Religions, Comparative.
     Religious denominations.

RELIGIONS -- Continued.
  xx Civilization.
     Gods.
     Religion.

RELIGIONS - BIBLIOGRAPHY.
    [BL 30]
     Z 7751-7860   (016.2)

RELIGIONS - BIOGRAPHY.

RELIGIONS - CLASSIFICATION.
     BL 350-385   (291.14)

RELIGIONS - CONGRESSES.
     BL 21

RELIGIONS - HISTORY.

RELIGIONS - PICTURES, ILLUSTRA-
    TIONS, ETC.

RELIGIONS (PROPOSED, UNIVERSAL, ETC.)
     BL 390
  "Here are entered works advocating
    or proposing a universal or
    world religion." LC
   x Proposed religions.
     Religion, Proposed.
     Religion, Universal.
     Religion of the future.
     Religions, Universal.
     Universal religion.

RELIGIONS, COMPARATIVE. See
  RELIGIONS.

RELIGIONS, MODERN.
     BL 98
   x Modern religions.
     Religions, Non-christian
RELIGIONS, UNIVERSAL. See   x Non-Christian
  RELIGIONS (PROPOSED, UNIVERSAL,   Religions
  ETC.)

RELIGIOUS, CONGREGATION OF. See
  CONGREGATIO DE RELIGIOSIS.

360

RELIGIOUS ART. See
    CATHEDRALS.
    CHRISTIAN ART.
    CHURCH ARCHITECTURE.
    IDOLS AND IMAGES.
    MOSQUES.
    TEMPLES.
    sa Art, Buddhist; Art, Gothic;
        Art Medieval; etc., and
        the headings referred to
        under these subjects.

RELIGIOUS BEQUESTS. See
    CHARITABLE BEQUESTS.

RELIGIOUS BIOGRAPHY.
    sa Christian biography.
    xx Christian biography.

RELIGIOUS BROADCASTING. See
    RADIO IN RELIGION.

RELIGIOUS CEREMONIES. See
    RITES AND CEREMONIES.

RELIGIOUS CONFESSORS. See
    CONFESSORS FOR RELIGIOUS.
    CONFESSORS FOR SISTERS.

RELIGIOUS CONGREGATIONS. See
    RELIGIOUS ORDERS.

RELIGIOUS CONVERSION. See
    CONVERSION.

RELIGIOUS CORPORATIONS. See
    CORPORATIONS, ECCLESIASTICAL.

RELIGIOUS DENOMINATIONS. See
    RELIGIONS.
    SECTS.
    also names of churches and sects.

RELIGIOUS DRAMA.
        PN 1880
        BQ 5151-5167; BQ 5261-5267
        (244.x2)
    sa Christmas plays.
       Christmas plays, Medieval.
       Church and theater.
       Easter - Drama.

RELIGIOUS DRAMA -- Continued.
    sa Liturgy and drama.
       Missionary plays.
       Moralities.
       Moving-pictures, Religious.
       Mysteries and miracle-plays.
       Passion music.
       Passion-plays.
     x Drama, Liturgical.
       Drama, Religious.
       Liturgical drama.
    xx Church music.
       Drama.
       Liturgy and drama.
       Religious literature.

RELIGIOUS DRAMA - HISTORY AND
    CRITICISM.

RELIGIOUS DRAMA - PRESENTATION, ETC.

RELIGIOUS DRAMA, ENGLISH, [ITALIAN,
    SPANISH, ETC.]

RELIGIOUS EDUCATION.   (Geog.
    subdiv., Indirect)
        BV 1471-1490   (377)
        BQT 3103-3197   (25x3)
    "Here are entered works on the
     history and theory of religious
     education, also works dealing
     with instruction in religion in
     schools and private life." LC
    Cf. note under Church and education.
    sa Bible - Study.
       Bible in the schools.
       Catechetical sermons.
       Church and college.
       Church and education.
       Church schools.
       Directors of religious
         education.
       Kerygmatic theology.
       Moral education.
       Sunday-schools.
       Theological seminaries.
       Theology - Study and teaching.
     x Christian doctrine.
       Christian education.
       Education, Christian.
       Education, Ethical.
       Education, Religious.

RELIGIOUS EDUCATION -- Continued.
  xx Catholic education.
     Christian life.
     Church - Teaching office.
     Education.
     Moral education.
     Theology - Study and teaching.

RELIGIOUS EDUCATION - ADDRESSES,
  ESSAYS, LECTURES.

RELIGIOUS EDUCATION - AUDIO-VISUAL
  AIDS.
     BQT 3193
  sa Church work - Audio-visual aids.
     Moving-pictures in church work.

RELIGIOUS EDUCATION - BIBLIOGRAPHY.
    [BQT 3101]
    Z 7849

RELIGIOUS EDUCATION - CONGRESSES.

RELIGIOUS EDUCATION - CURRICULA.

RELIGIOUS EDUCATION - HISTORY.
    BQT 3106-3107   (26x3.09)

RELIGIOUS EDUCATION - HOME TRAINING.
    BQT 3115
  sa Family, Christian.

RELIGIOUS EDUCATION - LAW AND
  LEGISLATION. (Geog. subdiv.,
  Direct)
  xx Church and state.

RELIGIOUS EDUCATION - PERIODICALS.

RELIGIOUS EDUCATION - PSYCHOLOGY.

RELIGIOUS EDUCATION - SERMONS.
    BQT 3112

RELIGIOUS EDUCATION - SOCIETIES.
    BQT 3103

RELIGIOUS EDUCATION - STORIES. See
  BIBLE STORIES.
  CATECHISM STORIES.

RELIGIOUS EDUCATION - STUDY AND
  TEACHING.
  "Here are entered works dealing
    with religious education as a
    subject for study in the
    curriculum for the training
    of clergymen, and of directors
    and professors of religious
    education." LC

RELIGIOUS EDUCATION - STUDY CLUBS.
    BQT 3591
  x Study clubs, Religious.

RELIGIOUS EDUCATION - TEACHER
  TRAINING.

RELIGIOUS EDUCATION - TEACHERS'
  MANUALS. See
  RELIGIOUS EDUCATION - TEXTBOOKS.

RELIGIOUS EDUCATION - TEACHING
  METHODS.
    BQT 3148-3154
  sa Catechetics.

RELIGIOUS EDUCATION - TEXTBOOKS.
    BQT 3161-3197
  sa Bible - Study - Textbooks.
    Catechisms.
    Sunday-schools - Manuals,
     textbooks, etc.
  x Religious education - Teachers'
    manuals.
  xx Catechisms.

RELIGIOUS EDUCATION - TEXTBOOKS FOR
  ADOLESCENTS.
    BQT 3173-3179

RELIGIOUS EDUCATION - TEXTBOOKS FOR
  ADULTS.
    BQT 3183-3189

RELIGIOUS EDUCATION - TEXTBOOKS FOR
  CHILDREN.
    BQT 3163-3169

RELIGIOUS EDUCATION - TEXTBOOKS FOR
  COLLEGIANS.
    BQT 3183-3189

362

RELIGIOUS EDUCATION - TEXTBOOKS FOR
  YOUNG PEOPLE.
      BQT 3173-3189

RELIGIOUS EDUCATION (CANON LAW)
      BQV230 1372-1383

RELIGIOUS EDUCATION, JEWISH.
      x Jews - Religious education.

RELIGIOUS EDUCATION, MOHAMMEDAN.
      x Mohammedans - Religious education.

RELIGIOUS EDUCATION OF ADOLESCENTS.
      BQT 3138

RELIGIOUS EDUCATION OF ADULTS.
      BQT 3143

RELIGIOUS EDUCATION OF CHILDREN.
      BQT 3135-3136
      x Children - Religious education.
      Education of children, Religious.

RELIGIOUS EDUCATION OF CHILDREN,
  JEWISH.
      BM 103

RELIGIOUS EDUCATION OF CHILDREN,
  MOHAMMEDAN.
      BP 44

RELIGIOUS EDUCATION OF PRE-SCHOOL
  CHILDREN.
      BQT 3135

RELIGIOUS EDUCATION OF ~~YOUNG PEOPLE~~ Adolescents.
      BQT 3140-3142

RELIGIOUS EDUCATION SCHOOLS. See
  VACATION SCHOOLS, RELIGIOUS.

RELIGIOUS FESTIVALS. See
  FEASTS, ECCLESIASTICAL.

RELIGIOUS FILMS. See
  MOVING-PICTURES - PLOTS, THEMES,
  ETC. - RELIGION.

RELIGIOUS FREEDOM. See
  RELIGIOUS LIBERTY.

RELIGIOUS HISTORY. See
  CHURCH HISTORY.
  also subdivision "Church history"
    under names of countries,
    cities, etc.; and names of
    denominations, sects, churches,
    councils, etc.

RELIGIOUS HOUSES. See
  CONVENTS.
  MONASTERIES.

RELIGIOUS HUMANISM. See
  HUMANISM, RELIGIOUS.

RELIGIOUS INDIFFERENCE. See
  INDIFFERENTISM (RELIGION)

RELIGIOUS INSTITUTES. See
  RELIGIOUS ORDERS.

RELIGIOUS INSTRUCTION. See
  CATECHETICS.
  RELIGIOUS EDUCATION.

RELIGIOUS JOURNALISM. See
  JOURNALISM, RELIGIOUS.

RELIGIOUS LAW AND LEGISLATION.
  (Geog. subdiv., Direct)
  "Here are entered works on law
    and legislation on matters of
    religion in non-Christian
    countries. For the same in
    Christian countries see
    Ecclesiastical law." LC

RELIGIOUS LEGACIES. See
  CHARITABLE BEQUESTS.

RELIGIOUS LIBERTY.   (Geog.
  subdiv., Direct)
      BV 741   (261.7)
      BQV 294; BQV 325
  sa Blasphemy.
     Church and state.
     Liberty of conscience.
     Persecution.
     Sunday legislation.
  x Freedom of religion.
     Freedom of worship.
     Intolerance.
     Liberty, Religious.
     Religious freedom.

RELIGIOUS LIBERTY -- Continued.
  xx Church and state.
    Civil rights.
    Free thought.
    Liberty.
    Liberty of conscience.
    Persecution.
    Personality (Law)
    Toleration.

RELIGIOUS LIBERTY (INTERNATIONAL
LAW)
  xx International law.
    Minorities.

✓ RELIGIOUS LIFE.
    BQT 2300-2359   (24x7.3)
  Here are entered works dealing
    with the principles of the
    religious life, that is, works
    on religious asceticism or
    religious perfection. Cf. note
    under Religious orders.
  As a subdivision under classes
    of persons and institutions the
    heading "Religious life" is
    employed in a broader sense,
    namely, insofar as religion
    affects the life of people and
    of institutions (e.g., Chil-
    dren - Religious life; Prisons -
    Religious life; Young men -
    Religious life). Cf. note under
    Christian life.
  For works emphasizing the asceti-
    cal peculiarity of individual
    religious communities use the
    subdivision "Spiritual life",
    e.g., Benedictines - Spiritual
    life; Franciscans - Spiritual
    life.
  sa Asceticism.
    Celibacy.
    Chapters of faults.
    Contemplative life.
    Evangelical counsels.
    Mixed life.
    Monasticism.
    Novitiate.
    Profession, Religious.
    Religious orders.
    Retreats for religious.
    Superiors, Religious.
    Vows.

RELIGIOUS LIFE -- Continued.
  x Perfection, Religious.
    Religious orders - Spiritual
    life.
    Religious perfection.

  xx Asceticism.
    Monasticism.
    Religious orders.
    State of perfection.

RELIGIOUS LIFE - ADDRESSES, ESSAYS,
LECTURES.

RELIGIOUS LIFE - BIBLICAL TEACHING.
    [BQT 2328]

RELIGIOUS LIFE - PAPAL TEACHING.
    [BQT 2328]

       ################

RELIGIOUS LIFE - EARLY CHURCH.
  xx Church history - Primitive
    and early church.

RELIGIOUS LIFE - MIDDLE AGES.
  xx Church history - Middle Ages.

RELIGIOUS LIFE - MODERN PERIOD.
  xx Church history - Modern period.

RELIGIOUS LIFE - 20th CENTURY.

       ################

RELIGIOUS LIFE FOR WOMEN.
    [BQT 2345]
  sa Nuns.
    Religious orders of women.
    Retreats for sisters.
  x Religious orders of women -
    Spiritual life.
    Sisters.
  xx Religious orders of women.

RELIGIOUS LIFE FOR WOMEN - EARLY
CHURCH.

RELIGIOUS LITERATURE.
  sa Bible as literature.
    Catholic literature.
    Christian literature, Early.

364

RELIGIOUS LITERATURE -- Continued.
  sa Devotional literature.
     Koran as literature.
     Language question in the
       church.
     Religious drama.
     Religious poetry.
     Sacred books.
   x Literature, Religious.

RELIGIOUS LITERATURE - AUTHORSHIP.
  sa Journalism, Religious.
   x Religious writing.

RELIGIOUS LITERATURE - BIBLIOGRAPHY.

RELIGIOUS LITERATURE - HISTORY AND
  CRITICISM.

RELIGIOUS LITERATURE - PUBLICATION
  AND DISTRIBUTION.
  sa Bible - Publication and dis-
     tribution.
  xx Booksellers and bookselling -
     Colportage, subscription
     trade, etc.

RELIGIOUS LITERATURE - SELECTIONS.

RELIGIOUS LITERATURE - TRANSLATIONS
  INTO CHINESE, [JAPANESE, ETC.]

RELIGIOUS LITERATURE, FRENCH,
  [GERMAN, LATIN, ETC.]

RELIGIOUS LITERATURE, JEWISH.
  References as in LC supple-
     ment 1961.

RELIGIOUS MEDALS. See
  MEDALS, DEVOTIONAL.

RELIGIOUS MOVING-PICTURES. See
  MOVING-PICTURES, RELIGIOUS.

RELIGIOUS MUSIC. See
  CHURCH MUSIC.

RELIGIOUS MYSTERIES. See
  MYSTERIES, RELIGIOUS.

RELIGIOUS NEWSPAPERS AND PERIODICALS.
  (Geog. subdiv., Direct)
  sa Catholic newspapers.
     Catholic periodicals.
     Journalism, Religious.
   x Religious periodicals.

RELIGIOUS ORDERS.   (Geog. subdiv.,
  Indirect)
       BQT 2303-2359 (Asceticism)
       BQX 6801-8043 (History)
       (271)
  Here are entered works on the re-
     ligious orders insofar as the
     books regard rather the external
     expression of the religious life
     as seen in its foundations and
     activities.
  Works dealing with the inner or
     ascetical aspect of the reli-
     gious orders, that is, with re-
     ligious perfection or the prin-
     ciples of the religious life,
     are entered under the heading
     "Religious life".
  sa Abbots.
     Brothers.
     Canons regular.
     Cardinal protectors.
     Convents.
     Corporations, Ecclesiastical.
     Double monasteries.
     Friars.
     Hermits.
     Hospitallers.
     Inclusi.
     Lay brothers.
     Martyrs.
     Mass, Conventual.
     Mendicant orders.
     Military religious orders.
     Monasteries.
     Monasticism.
     Oblates.
     Postulancy.
     Priests - Confraternities.
     Quasi-religious societies.
     Recluses.
     Religious life.
     Religious persons.
     Saints.

RELIGIOUS ORDERS -- Continued.
  sa Secular institutes.
     Third orders.
     also names of religious orders,
        e.g., Augustinians; Brothers
        of the Christian Schools;
        Carmelites; etc.
   x Congregations, Religious.
     Institutes, Religious.
     Orders, Religious.
     Religious congregations.
     Religious institutes.
     Religious societies.
     Societies, Religious.
  xx Catholic Church - Government.
     Catholic Church - History.
     Christian biography.
     Church history.
     Church property.
     Civilization, Medieval.
     Clergy.
     Corporations, Ecclesiastical.
     Friars.
     Mendicant orders.
     Middle Ages - History.
     Monasteries.
     Monasticism.
     Religious life.

RELIGIOUS ORDERS - ADDRESSES,
  ESSAYS, LECTURES.

RELIGIOUS ORDERS - ANECDOTES.

RELIGIOUS ORDERS - ARCHITECTURE.
     BQT 5909

RELIGIOUS ORDERS - ARCHIVES. See
  ARCHIVES, MONASTIC.

RELIGIOUS ORDERS - ART.

RELIGIOUS ORDERS - BIBLIOGRAPHY.
     BQX 6801
     Z 7839   (016.271)

RELIGIOUS ORDERS - BIOGRAPHY.
     BQX 6851
  sa Religious orders - Personal
     narratives.
  xx Catholic Church - Biography.
     Christian biography.

RELIGIOUS ORDERS - BIOGRAPHY -
  SERMONS.

RELIGIOUS ORDERS - CATECHISMS,
  QUESTION-BOOKS.

RELIGIOUS ORDERS - CHARITIES. See
  RELIGIOUS ORDERS - HOSPITALS,
  CHARITIES, ETC.

RELIGIOUS ORDERS - COLLECTED WORKS.

RELIGIOUS ORDERS - COMMON LIFE.
     BQT 2323
   x Common life (Religious orders)

RELIGIOUS ORDERS - CONFESSORS. See
  CONFESSORS FOR RELIGIOUS.

RELIGIOUS ORDERS - CONFRATERNITIES.
   x Confraternities, Monastic.
     Monastic confraternities.

RELIGIOUS ORDERS - CONGRESSES.
     [BQX 6803]

RELIGIOUS ORDERS - CONTROVERSIAL
  LITERATURE.

RELIGIOUS ORDERS - CORRESPONDENCE,
  REMINISCENCES, ETC.

RELIGIOUS ORDERS - CUSTOMS. See
  RELIGIOUS ORDERS - RITES AND
  CEREMONIES.

RELIGIOUS ORDERS - DEVOTIONAL
  LITERATURE.

RELIGIOUS ORDERS - DICTIONARIES.
     BQX 6805

RELIGIOUS ORDERS - DIETARY RULES.

RELIGIOUS ORDERS - DIRECTORIES.
     BQX 6805

RELIGIOUS ORDERS - DRAMA.

RELIGIOUS ORDERS - EDUCATION.
  sa Monastic schools.
     Religious orders, Teaching.

RELIGIOUS ORDERS - FICTION.

RELIGIOUS ORDERS - FINANCE.

RELIGIOUS ORDERS - GOVERNMENT.
        BQV230 499-537   (348.x37)

RELIGIOUS ORDERS - HABIT.
    sa Clergy - Costume.
        Scapulars.
     x Ecclesiastical costume.
        Habit, Monastic.
    xx Church vestments.
        Clergy - Costume.

RELIGIOUS ORDERS - HERALDRY.
    xx Heraldry, Sacred.

RELIGIOUS ORDERS - HISTORY.
        BQX 6801-8043   (271)

RELIGIOUS ORDERS - HISTORY - EARLY
    PERIOD.
        BQX 6812-6817
    sa Girovagues.
        Sarabites.
    xx Church history - Primitive
        and early church.

RELIGIOUS ORDERS - HISTORY - MIDDLE
    AGES.
        BQX 6821
    xx Church history - Middle Ages.

RELIGIOUS ORDERS - HISTORY - MODERN
    PERIOD.
        BQX 6825
    xx Church history - Modern period.

RELIGIOUS ORDERS - HISTORY - 16th
    CENTURY.

RELIGIOUS ORDERS - HISTORY - 17th
    CENTURY.

RELIGIOUS ORDERS - HISTORY - 18th
    CENTURY.

RELIGIOUS ORDERS - HISTORY - 19th
    CENTURY.

RELIGIOUS ORDERS - HISTORY - 20th
    CENTURY.

RELIGIOUS ORDERS - HOSPITALS,
    CHARITIES, ETC.
        BQT 3659
    x Religious orders - Charities.

RELIGIOUS ORDERS - HUMOR, CARICATURES,
    ETC.

RELIGIOUS ORDERS - IMPEDIMENTS.
        BQV230 542; BQV230 586
    xx Religious orders (Canon law)

RELIGIOUS ORDERS - INFLUENCE.

RELIGIOUS ORDERS - JUVENILE
    LITERATURE.

RELIGIOUS ORDERS - LEGENDS.

RELIGIOUS ORDERS - MARY, BLESSED
    VIRGIN. See MARY, BLESSED VIRGIN,
    AND RELIGIOUS ORDERS.

RELIGIOUS ORDERS - MEDITATIONS.
        BQT 2554-2556

RELIGIOUS ORDERS - MISCELLANEA.

RELIGIOUS ORDERS - MISSIONS.
    sa Religious orders, Missionary.
        also subdivision "Missions"
        under names of particular
        religious orders, e.g., Fran-
        ciscans - Missions; Jesuits -
        Missions.

RELIGIOUS ORDERS - MISSIONS -
    EASTERN CHURCHES.
        BQX 5454
    xx Missions - Eastern Churches.

RELIGIOUS ORDERS - MISSIONS -
    PERIODICALS.

RELIGIOUS ORDERS - MOVING-PICTURES.

RELIGIOUS ORDERS - PERIODICALS.
        [BQX 6802]

RELIGIOUS ORDERS - PERSONAL
    NARRATIVES.
    xx Religious orders - Biography.

RELIGIOUS ORDERS - PICTURES,
    ILLUSTRATIONS, ETC.

RELIGIOUS ORDERS - POETRY.

RELIGIOUS ORDERS - POPULAR WORKS.

RELIGIOUS ORDERS - PRAYER-BOOKS.
        BQT 2624-2629

RELIGIOUS ORDERS - PROPERTY.

RELIGIOUS ORDERS - PROPERTY (CANON
    LAW)

RELIGIOUS ORDERS - RECRUITING.
    See also subdivision "Recruiting"
        under names of religious orders,
        e.g., Franciscans - Recruiting.
    xx Vocation, Religious.

RELIGIOUS ORDERS - RETREATS. See
    RETREATS FOR RELIGIOUS.

RELIGIOUS ORDERS - RITES AND
    CEREMONIES.
        BQT 4700-4907
        x Monastic rites and ceremonies.
        Rites and ceremonies, Monastic.

RELIGIOUS ORDERS - RULES.
        BQX 6861-6862
        See also names of individual
        religious orders with sub-
        division "Rules."

RELIGIOUS ORDERS - SERMONS.
        BQT 2306; BQT 3014

RELIGIOUS ORDERS - SOCIAL ASPECTS.

RELIGIOUS ORDERS - SPIRITUAL LIFE.
    See RELIGIOUS LIFE.

RELIGIOUS ORDERS - SUPPRESSION.
        [BQX 842]

RELIGIOUS ORDERS - SUPPRESSION -
    AUSTRIA.
        BQX 1554

RELIGIOUS ORDERS - SUPPRESSION -
    ENGLAND.
        BQX 2062

RELIGIOUS ORDERS - SUPPRESSION -
    FRANCE.
        BQX 1784

RELIGIOUS ORDERS - SUPPRESSION -
    GERMANY.
        BQX 1927; BQX 1964

RELIGIOUS ORDERS - SUPPRESSION -
    PORTUGAL.
        BQX 2801

RELIGIOUS ORDERS - SUPPRESSION -
    SPAIN.
        BQX 2964

RELIGIOUS ORDERS - SUPPRESSION -
    SWEDEN.
        BQX 3017

RELIGIOUS ORDERS - SUPPRESSION -
    SWITZERLAND.
        BQX 3042

RELIGIOUS ORDERS - TAXATION.

RELIGIOUS ORDERS - VOCATION. See
    VOCATION, RELIGIOUS.

RELIGIOUS ORDERS - VOWS. See
    VOWS.

################

RELIGIOUS ORDERS - AUSTRIA,
    [BAVARIA, ENGLAND, ETC.]

RELIGIOUS ORDERS - IRELAND.
        BQX 2210
        sa Monasticism, Irish.
        xx Monasticism, Irish.

################

RELIGIOUS ORDERS (CANON LAW)
        BQV230 487-681   (348.x37)
        sa Dismissal of religious.

RELIGIOUS ORDERS (CANON LAW) -- Continued.
  sa Exclaustration.
     Exemption (Canon law)
     Lay brothers (Canon law)
     Monasteries (Canon law)
     Novitiate (Canon law)
     Peculium.
     Privileges (Canon law)
     Religious orders - Impediments.
     Religious orders of women
       (Canon law)
     Secularization (Canon law)
     Spiritual directors (Canon
       law)
     Superiors, Religious (Canon
       law)
     Third orders (Canon law)
     Trials, Ecclesiastical (Reli-
       gious)
     Visitations, Ecclesiastical
       (Canon law)
     Vocation, Religious (Canon law)
     Vows (Canon law)
  xx Canon law.
     Persons (Canon law)
     Religious orders of women
       (Canon law)

RELIGIOUS ORDERS (CANON LAW) -
  HISTORY.
    BQV 200.M2

RELIGIOUS ORDERS (CANON LAW,
  EASTERN)
  xx Eastern Churches - Canon law.

RELIGIOUS ORDERS (CANON LAW,
  ORTHODOX EASTERN)

RELIGIOUS ORDERS, ANGLICAN.
    BX 5183-5185
  x Anglican religious orders.

RELIGIOUS ORDERS, BUDDHIST. See
  MONASTICISM, BUDDHIST.

RELIGIOUS ORDERS, DIOCESAN.
  x Diocesan religious orders.

RELIGIOUS ORDERS, EASTERN. See
  MONASTICISM, EASTERN.

RELIGIOUS ORDERS, EPISCOPALIAN.
    BX 5970-5974
  x Episcopalian religious orders.

RELIGIOUS ORDERS, HOSPITAL. See
  HOSPITALLERS.

RELIGIOUS ORDERS, IRISH. See
  MONASTICISM, IRISH.

RELIGIOUS ORDERS, MILITARY. See
  MILITARY RELIGIOUS ORDERS.

RELIGIOUS ORDERS, MISSIONARY.
    BQX 6838
  x Missionary religious orders.
  xx Religious orders - Missions.

RELIGIOUS ORDERS, PROTESTANT.
    BV 4410-4422
  x Protestant religious orders.

RELIGIOUS ORDERS, TEACHING.
    BQX 6838
  x Teaching religious orders.
  xx Religious orders - Education.

RELIGIOUS ORDERS OF WOMEN.　(Geog.
  subdiv., Indirect)
    [BQT 2345] (Asceticism)
    BQX 6841-6842; BQX 7801-8043
    (271.9)
  Some libraries, particularly those
  with smaller collections or with
  only current English titles in
  the collection, may prefer to
  use the heading "Sisterhoods"
  instead of "Religious orders of
  women." This decision should be
  made according to local preference, adapting the subdivisions
  given below to the changed choice
  of heading. Libraries whose
  collections include many foreign
  titles, and perhaps older titles,
  are likely to find the heading
  "Religious orders of women" more
  suitable.
  sa Abbesses.
    Anchoresses.
    Beguinages.
    Canonesses.
    Convents.
    Mothers general.

369

RELIGIOUS ORDERS OF WOMEN -- Continued.
  sa Nuns.
    Religious life for women.
    sa names of religious orders of
      women, e.g., Brigidines;
      Daughters of Charity of St.
      Vincent de Paul; Sisters of
      Mercy; etc.
   x Sisterhoods.
    Sisters.
    Women in religion.
  xx Nuns.
    Religious life for women.

RELIGIOUS ORDERS OF WOMEN -
  BIBLIOGRAPHY.

RELIGIOUS ORDERS OF WOMEN -
  BIOGRAPHY.

RELIGIOUS ORDERS OF WOMEN -
  CATECHISMS, QUESTION-BOOKS.

RELIGIOUS ORDERS OF WOMEN -
  CHAPLAINS. See
  CHAPLAINS FOR SISTERS.

RELIGIOUS ORDERS OF WOMEN -
  CHARITIES. See
  RELIGIOUS ORDERS OF WOMEN -
    HOSPITALS, CHARITIES, ETC.

RELIGIOUS ORDERS OF WOMEN -
  CONFESSORS. See
  CONFESSORS FOR SISTERS.

RELIGIOUS ORDERS OF WOMEN -
  CONGRESSES.

RELIGIOUS ORDERS OF WOMEN -
  CORRESPONDENCE, REMINISCENCES, ETC.

RELIGIOUS ORDERS OF WOMEN -
  DEVOTIONAL LITERATURE.

RELIGIOUS ORDERS OF WOMEN -
  DIRECTORIES.

RELIGIOUS ORDERS OF WOMEN -
  DRAMA.

RELIGIOUS ORDERS OF WOMEN -
  EDUCATION.

RELIGIOUS ORDERS OF WOMEN -
  GOVERNMENT.

RELIGIOUS ORDERS OF WOMEN -
  HISTORY.

RELIGIOUS ORDERS OF WOMEN -
  HOSPITALS, CHARITIES, ETC.
   x Religious orders of women -
    Charities.

RELIGIOUS ORDERS OF WOMEN -
  MEDITATIONS.
    BQT 2556

RELIGIOUS ORDERS OF WOMEN -
  MISSIONS.
  Here is entered literature on the
    work in the missions of religious
    orders of women, particularly
    since the sixteenth century.
  xx Missionaries, Women.
    Women in missionary work.

RELIGIOUS ORDERS OF WOMEN -
  PERIODICALS.

RELIGIOUS ORDERS OF WOMEN -
  PERSONAL NARRATIVES.

RELIGIOUS ORDERS OF WOMEN -
  POETRY.

RELIGIOUS ORDERS OF WOMEN -
  PRAYER-BOOKS.

RELIGIOUS ORDERS OF WOMEN -
  RETREATS. See
  RETREATS FOR SISTERS.

RELIGIOUS ORDERS OF WOMEN -
  RITES AND CEREMONIES.
   x Monastic rites and ceremonies.
    Rites and ceremonies, Monastic.

RELIGIOUS ORDERS OF WOMEN -
  RULES.
    [BQX 6862.5]

RELIGIOUS ORDERS OF WOMEN -
  SERMONS.
      BQT 3014

RELIGIOUS ORDERS OF WOMEN -
  SOCIAL ASPECTS.

RELIGIOUS ORDERS OF WOMEN -
  SPIRITUAL LIFE. See
  RELIGIOUS LIFE OF WOMEN.

RELIGIOUS ORDERS OF WOMEN -
  VOCATION. See
  VOCATION, RELIGIOUS, FOR WOMEN.

RELIGIOUS ORDERS OF WOMEN -
  VOWS. See VOWS.

RELIGIOUS ORDERS OF WOMEN (CANON LAW)
      BQV230 487-681   (348.x37)
  sa Chaplains for sisters (Canon
        law)
     Dowry (Canon law)
     Nuns (Canon law)
     Religious orders (Canon law)
     Superiors, Religious (Canon
        law)
  xx Religious orders (Canon law)

RELIGIOUS ORDERS OF WOMEN, ANGLICAN.
      BX 5185
  x Anglican religious orders.

RELIGIOUS ORDERS OF WOMEN, PROTESTANT.
      BV 4422
  x Protestant religious orders.

RELIGIOUS ORDERS WITHOUT VOWS. See
  QUASI-RELIGIOUS SOCIETIES.

RELIGIOUS PAINTING. See ART, CHRISTIAN
  PAINTING, RELIGIOUS.

RELIGIOUS PEACE OF AUGSBURG. See
  AUGSBURG, RELIGIOUS PEACE OF.

RELIGIOUS PERFECTION. See
  RELIGIOUS LIFE.

RELIGIOUS PERIODICALS. See
  RELIGION - PERIODICALS.
  RELIGIOUS NEWSPAPERS AND PERIODICALS.

RELIGIOUS PERSONS.
  By this term are understood
    those persons who are members
    of religious orders.
  x Persons, Religious.
  xx Religious orders.

RELIGIOUS PERSONS (CANON LAW)
      BQV230 487-681
  sa Trials, Ecclesiastical (Persons)
  xx Persons (Canon law)

RELIGIOUS POETRY.
      PN 6110.R; BQ 5081 (General
        collections)
      BQ 265-268 (History and
        criticism)   (245)
  sa Carols.
     Christian poetry.
     Hymns.
  x Poetry, Religious.
  xx Religion in literature.
     Religious literature.

RELIGIOUS POETRY, ENGLISH,
  [FRENCH, GERMAN, ETC.]

RELIGIOUS POETRY, HEBREW.
  sa Azharot.
     Piyutim.
  xx Hebrew poetry.

RELIGIOUS PROFESSION. See
  PROFESSION, RELIGIOUS.

RELIGIOUS PROPAGANDA.
      BV 653
  x Propaganda, Religious.
  xx Public relations - Churches.

RELIGIOUS PSYCHOLOGY. See
  PSYCHOLOGY, RELIGIOUS.

RELIGIOUS REFUGEES. See
  REFUGEES, RELIGIOUS.

RELIGIOUS RITES. See
  RITES AND CEREMONIES.

RELIGIOUS SCULPTURE. See
  SCULPTURE, RELIGIOUS.

RELIGIOUS SOCIAL WORK. See
  CHURCH CHARITIES.

RELIGIOUS SOCIETIES. See
  CONFRATERNITIES.
  RELIGIOUS ORDERS.

RELIGIOUS SOCIOLOGY. See
  SOCIOLOGY, RELIGIOUS.

RELIGIOUS SUPERIORS. See
  SUPERIORS, RELIGIOUS.

RELIGIOUS SURVEYS.   (Geog. subdiv.,
  Direct)
      BQT 3309
  sa Church statistics.
   x Surveys, Religious.
  xx Pastoral theology.
     Sociology, Religious.

RELIGIOUS TELEVISION. See
  TELEVISION IN RELIGION.

RELIGIOUS THOUGHT.   (Geog. subdiv., Indirect)

RELIGIOUS THOUGHT - ANCIENT PERIOD.
  xx Church history - Primitive
     and early church.

RELIGIOUS THOUGHT - MIDDLE AGES.
  xx Church history - Middle Ages.

RELIGIOUS THOUGHT - MODERN PERIOD.
  xx Church history - Modern
     period.

RELIGIOUS THOUGHT - 16th CENTURY.

RELIGIOUS THOUGHT - 17th CENTURY.

RELIGIOUS THOUGHT - 18th CENTURY.

RELIGIOUS THOUGHT - 19th CENTURY.

RELIGIOUS THOUGHT - 20th CENTURY.

RELIGIOUS VACATION SCHOOLS. See
  VACATION SCHOOLS, RELIGIOUS.

RELIGIOUS VOCATION. See
  VOCATION, RELIGIOUS.

RELIGIOUS WRITING. See
  RELIGIOUS LITERATURE - AUTHORSHIP.

RELIGIOUS ZIONISM.
      DS 150.R3-39
  References as in LC supple-
    ment 1956-58.

RELIQUARIES. See
  RELICS AND RELIQUARIES.

REMONSTRANTS.
      BQT 1145   (284.9)
  xx Arminianism.

REMOVAL OF PASTORS. See
  PASTORS - REMOVAL.

RENAISSANCE.
      BQX 797
      BQX 882
      BQX 936
  Other classifications and
    references as in LC.

RENAISSANCE CHURCH ARCHITECTURE.
  See CHURCH ARCHITECTURE,
  RENAISSANCE. *Renewal, Church see Church Reform*

RENUNCIATION (CANON LAW)
      BQV230 184-191   (348.x31)
  sa Clergy - Deposition.
  xx Benefices, Ecclesiastical
       (Canon law)
     Clergy - Deposition.

REPARATION (CANON LAW)
  xx Alienation (Canon law)
     Damages (Canon law)

REPARATION (THEOLOGY) See
  SATISFACTION.

REPENTANCE.
      BQT 1170; BQT 1375   (234.5)
  sa Attrition.
     Contrition.
     Penance.
     Regeneration (Theology)
   x Penitence.
  xx Contrition.
     Conversion.
     Dogmatic theology.

REPENTANCE -- Continued.
  sa Forgiveness of sin.
     Grace, Habitual.
     Penance.
     Salvation.
     Sin.

REPENTANCE - HISTORY OF DOCTRINES.

REPENTANCE (JUDAISM)

REPROBATION.
     BQT 1135
  xx Damned.
     Predestination.

REQUIEM MASS. See
  MASS, REQUIEM.

REQUIEMS.
     M 2010-2011; M 2013-2014
  xx Funeral music.
     Sacred vocal music.
  Subdivisions as in LC.

REREDOS. See ALTARPIECES.

RES (CANON LAW). See
  THINGS (CANON LAW)

RESCRIPTS (CANON LAW)

RESCRIPTS, PAPAL.
     BQV230 36-62
      BQV 2-8 (Documents)   (26x3)
  sa Briefs, Papal.
     Bulls, Papal.
     Motu proprio.
  x Papal rescripts.
  xx Documents, Papal.

RESERVATION OF THE EUCHARIST. See
  EUCHARIST - RESERVATION.

RESERVED CASES.
     BQV230 893-900 (Canon law)
      (348.x42)
     BQT 1391 (Theology)
      (23x7.4)
  sa Absolution (Canon law)
     Penitentiaries.
  x Cases, Reserved.
     Penance - Reserved cases.
  xx Censures, Ecclesiastical.

RESIDENCE, CLERICAL. See
  CLERGY - RESIDENCE.

RESIGNATION.
     BQT 1793   (24x7.5)

RESPONSES (LITURGY)
     BQT 4319; BQT 4421
     BQT 4599 (Church music)
  sa Acclamations (Liturgy)
     Responsorium.
     also names of individual
      responses, e.g., Amen.
  xx Acclamations (Liturgy)
     Divine office.
     Prayers.

RESPONSIBILITY.
     BQT 1754
  sa Duty.
     Free will and determinism.
     Ignorance, Invincible.
  xx Guilt.
     Free will and determinism.

RESPONSORIUM.
     BQT 4262.5
  A liturgical book containing
  versicles and responses sung
  after each lesson at Matins
  and at other parts of the
  Divine Office.
  xx Responses (Liturgy)

REST OF ESTHER. See
  BIBLE. O.T. ESTHER.

RESTITUTIO IN INTEGRUM (CANON LAW)
     BQV230 1689   (348.x5)
  xx Contracts (Canon law)

RESTITUTION.
     BQT 1946

RESTITUTION (CANON LAW)
  xx Damages (Canon law)

RESTORATIONISM.
  "Here are entered works that deal
    with the belief that all men,
    including sinners who die un-
    repentant, will be saved as a
    consequence of the restitution

RESTORATIONISM -- Continued.
    of all things to the control
    of God." LC
  sa Universalism.

RESURRECTION.
    BL 505 (Comparative religion)
    BQT 1465 (Theology)   (236.8)
  sa Future life.
    Jesus Christ - Resurrection.
  x Body, Resurrection of the.
  xx Dogmatic theology.
    Eschatology.
    Future life.

RESURRECTION - ART.

RESURRECTION - BIBLICAL TEACHING.

RESURRECTION - EARLY WORKS TO 1800.

RESURRECTION - HISTORY OF DOCTRINE.

RESURRECTION - SERMONS.

RESURRECTION (EGYPTIAN RELIGION)

RESURRECTION (JUDAISM)

RESURRECTION OF CHRIST. See
  JESUS CHRIST - RESURRECTION.

RETALIATION - BIBLICAL TEACHING.

RETREATS.
    BQT 2549-2573   (24x8.9)
  "Here are entered works dealing
    with periods of retirement for
    the purpose of meditation and
    spiritual development." LC
  x Exercises, Spiritual.
    Spiritual exercises.
  xx Meditations.
    Spiritual life.

RETREATS - CONGRESSES, CONFERENCES,
  ETC.

RETREATS - HISTORY.

RETREATS FOR BOYS. See
  RETREATS FOR CHILDREN.
  RETREATS FOR YOUNG MEN.

RETREATS FOR CHILDREN.
    BQT 2570   (24x8.95)
  x Boys - Retreats.
    Children - Retreats.
    Girls - Retreats.
    Retreats for boys.
    Retreats for girls.
  xx Children - Religious life.
    Youth - Religious life.

RETREATS FOR CLERGY.
    BQT 2551   (24x8.92)
  sa Retreats for religious.
    Retreats for seminarians.
  x Clerical retreats.
    Priests - Retreats.
    Retreats for priests.

RETREATS FOR GIRLS. See
  RETREATS FOR CHILDREN.
  RETREATS FOR YOUNG WOMEN.

RETREATS FOR LAYMEN. See
  RETREATS FOR MEN.
  RETREATS FOR YOUNG MEN.

RETREATS FOR MARRIED MEN. See
  RETREATS FOR MEN.

RETREATS FOR MARRIED WOMEN. See
  RETREATS FOR WOMEN.

RETREATS FOR MEN.
    BQT 2558   (24x8.95)
  sa Laymen's retreat movement.
  x Retreats for laymen.
    Retreats for married men.
  xx Men - Religious life.
    Retreats for young men.

RETREATS FOR MISSIONARIES.
    [BQT 2551.3]
  x Missionaries - Retreats.

RETREATS FOR NON-CATHOLICS.
    BQT 2573
  xx Non-Catholics.

RETREATS FOR NUNS. See
  RETREATS FOR SISTERS.

RETREATS FOR NURSES.
    BQT 2573   (26x8.95)
  x Nurses and nursing - Retreats.

374

RETREATS FOR PRIESTS. See
  RETREATS FOR CLERGY.

RETREATS FOR RELIGIOUS.
      BQT 2554   (24x8.93)
  sa Retreats for Benedictines,
      [Franciscans, Jesuits, etc.]
     Retreats for sisters.
   x Priests - Retreats.
     Religious orders - Retreats.
  xx Religious life.
     Retreats for clergy.
     Retreats for sisters.

RETREATS FOR SEMINARIANS.
      [BQT 2551.2]
   x Seminarians - Retreats.
  xx Retreats for clergy.

RETREATS FOR SISTERS.
      BQT 2556   (24x8.93)
  sa Retreats for religious.
   x Nuns - Retreats.
     Religious orders of women -
       Retreats.
     Retreats for nuns.
  xx Religious life for women.
     Retreats for religious.

RETREATS FOR WOMEN.
      BQT 2560   (24x8.95)
   x Retreats for married women.
     Women - Retreats.
  xx Retreats for young women.
     Woman - Religious life.

RETREATS FOR WORKINGMEN.
      BQT 2573
   x Workingmen's retreats.

RETREATS FOR YOUNG MEN.
      BQT 2566   (24x8.95)
  sa Retreats for men.
   x Boys - Retreats.
     Retreats for boys.
     Retreats for laymen.
     Young men - Retreats.
  xx Boys - Religious life.
     Young men - Religious life.
     Youth - Religious life.

RETREATS FOR YOUNG WOMEN.
      BQT 2568   (24x8.95)
  sa Retreats for women.
   x Girls - Retreats.
     Retreats for girls.
     Young women - Retreats.
  xx Girls - Religious life.
     Young women - Religious life.
     Youth - Religious life.

RETREATS FOR BENEDICTINES,
  [FRANCISCANS, JESUITS, ETC.]

RETRIBUTION. See
  REWARD (THEOLOGY)

RETROACTIVE LAWS (CANON LAW)

REUNION OF CHRISTENDOM. See
  CATHOLIC CHURCH AND REUNION.
  CHRISTIAN UNION.

✓ REVELATION.
      BQT 264-289   (23x9.6)
      BQT 236 (Reason and
        revelation)
      BQT 19 (Mystic revelation)
  sa Dogma.
     Fideism.
     Mystery.
     Naturalism.
  xx Bible - Inspiration.
     Dogmatic theology.
     Faith.
     Inspiration.
     Miracles.
     Modernism.
     Religion.
     Supernatural.
     Theophanies.
     Tradition (Theology)

REVELATION - BIBLICAL TEACHING.

REVELATION - EARLY WORKS TO 1800.

REVELATION - HISTORY OF DOCTRINES.

REVELATION - SERMONS.

REVELATION (HINDUISM)

REVELATION (JEWISH THEOLOGY)

REVELATION, BOOK OF. See
  BIBLE. N.T. APOCALYPSE.

REVELATION OF SINAI.
  x Sinai revelation.
  xx Commandments, Ten.

REVELATIONS, PRIVATE.
      BQT 2483   (24x9.1)
  xx Faith.
     Mysticism.

REVERENCE.

REVISIONIST ZIONISM.   (Geog.
  subdiv., Direct)
  References as in LC.

REVIVAL, EVANGELICAL. See
  EVANGELICAL REVIVAL.

REVIVALISTS. See
  EVANGELISTS.

REVIVALS.   (Geog. subdiv., Direct)
      BV 3750-3797
  References as in LC.

REVOLUTIONS.
      BQT 1915 (Moral theology)
  Other classifications and
    references as in LC.

REWARD (THEOLOGY)
      BQT 1514
  sa Merit (Theology)
  x Retribution.
  xx Future life.
     Good works (Theology)

REWARD (THEOLOGY) - BIBLICAL
  TEACHING.

REWARD (THEOLOGY) - EARLY WORKS
  TO 1800.

REWARD (THEOLOGY) - SERMONS.

RHYTHM (CHURCH MUSIC) See
  CHANT - RHYTHM.
  MUSICAL METER AND RHYTHM (CHURCH
    MUSIC)

RIGHT OF ASYLUM. See
  ASYLUM, RIGHT OF.

RING OF THE FISHERMAN.
  xx Seals (Numismatics)

RITES, CHINESE. See
  CHINESE RITES.

RITES, CONGREGATION OF. See
  CONGREGATIO SACRORUM RITUUM.

RITES AND CEREMONIES.   (Geog.
  subdiv., Indirect)
      BV 170-199 (Comparative
        religion) (291.38)
      GN (Primitive religion)
      GT (Manners and customs)
  sa Coronations.
     Cultus.
     Funeral rites and ceremonies.
     Manners and customs.
     Marriage customs and rites.
     Mysteries, Religious.
     Posture in worship.
     Secret societies.
   x Ceremonies.
     Religious ceremonies.
     Religious rites.
     Ritual (Ceremonies)
  xx Ritualism.

RITES AND CEREMONIES - INDIANS.
  See subdivision "Rites and cere-
    monies" under Indians.

RITES AND CEREMONIES - JEWS. See
  JEWS - RITES AND CEREMONIES.

RITES AND CEREMONIES (CATHOLIC)
      BQT 4331-4351   (264.x6)
  This term is here used to signify
    the actions and words used in
    divine worship of the Catholic
    Church and in the administration
    of the sacraments, and the rules
    laid down to govern the actions
    and words, ordinarily called rubrics.
  sa Caeremoniale.
     Canonization.
     Church etiquette.
     Liturgical law.

RITES AND CEREMONIES (CATHOLIC) --
Continued.
sa Liturgy.
Processions, Ecclesiastical.
Rituale.
also subdivision "Rites and
ceremonies" under such headings
as Divine Office and Mass.
x Catholic Church - Ceremonies and
practices.
Catholic Church - Liturgy.
Ecclesiastical rites and ceremonies.
Rubrics (Liturgy)
xx Liturgy.

RITES AND CEREMONIES (CATHOLIC) -
DICTIONARIES.

RITES AND CEREMONIES (CATHOLIC) -
HANDBOOKS, MANUALS, ETC.
BQT 4441
sa Altar boys - Handbooks, manuals,
etc.
Master of ceremonies - Handbooks,
manuals, etc.
Sacristans - Handbooks, manuals,
etc.
xx Liturgy - Handbooks, manuals, etc.

RITES AND CEREMONIES (CATHOLIC) -
HISTORY.
sa Liturgy - History.

RITES AND CEREMONIES (CATHOLIC) -
POPULAR WORKS.

RITES AND CEREMONIES (CATHOLIC) -
SERMONS.
BQT 3089
xx Liturgy - Sermons.

RITES AND CEREMONIES (CATHOLIC) -
TEXTBOOKS.
BQT 4332

RITES AND CEREMONIES, FUNERAL. See
FUNERAL RITES AND CEREMONIES.

RITES AND CEREMONIES, MARRIAGE. See
MARRIAGE SERVICE.

RITES AND CEREMONIES, MONASTIC. See
RELIGIOUS ORDERS - RITES AND
CEREMONIES.
RELIGIOUS ORDERS OF WOMEN - RITES
AND CEREMONIES.

RITES AND CEREMONIES, PONTIFICAL.
See PONTIFICAL SERVICE.

RITES AND USES.
BQT 4136-4139; BQT 4703-4949
(264.x82)
Here are entered collective works
on liturgical groups or families
of the Latin Rite, such as,
Ambrosian Rite, Sarum Rite,
Slavonic Rite, etc.
x Uses (Liturgy)
xx Liturgy.

RITES AND USES - BIBLIOGRAPHY.

RITUAL (BOOK) See RITUALE.

RITUAL (CEREMONIES) See
RITES AND CEREMONIES.

RITUALE.
BQT 4273   (26x5.6)
"A book containing the prayers
and ceremonies for the administration of the sacraments,
blessings, etc." AT
sa Manuale.
x Ritual (Book)
xx Benedictionale.
Ordinarium.
Rites and ceremonies (Catholic)

RITUALE ROMANUM.
BQT 4434
sa Collectio Rituum.
x Roman Ritual.

RITUALISM.
BV 180   (291.x37)
BX 5123 (Church of England)
sa Rites and ceremonies.

ROCK CHURCHES. See
CAVE CHURCHES.

ROCOCO CHURCH ARCHITECTURE. See
CHURCH ARCHITECTURE, ROCOCO.

ROGATION DAYS.
BQT 4236
xx Feasts, Ecclesiastical.

ROMAN BREVIARY. See
BREVIARIUM ROMANUM.

ROMAN CATECHISM. See
CATECHISMUS ROMANUS.

ROMAN CATHOLIC CHURCH. See
CATHOLIC CHURCH.

ROMAN CEREMONIAL. See
CAEREMONIALE ROMANUM.

ROMAN CHURCH ARCHITECTURE. See
CHURCH ARCHITECTURE, ROMAN.

ROMAN CONGREGATIONS. See
CONGREGATIONS, ROMAN.

ROMAN CURIA. See
CURIA ROMANA.

ROMAN GRADUAL. See
GRADUALE ROMANUM.

ROMAN LAW AND CANON LAW. See
CANON LAW AND ROMAN LAW.

ROMAN MARTYROLOGY. See
MARTYROLOGIUM ROMANUM.

ROMAN MISSAL. See
MISSALE ROMANUM.

ROMAN PONTIFICAL. See
PONTIFICALE ROMANUM.

ROMAN PRIESTS. See
PRIESTS, ROMAN.

ROMAN QUESTION.
BQX 132-137   (27x2.6)
Here are entered works dealing
with the matters at issue between the Holy See and the
civil government of Italy
consequent upon the seizure of

ROMAN QUESTION -- Continued.
Rome by the Piedmontese in 1870
and terminated by the Treaty of
the Lateran in 1929.
sa Italian Question, 1848-1870.
Popes - Temporal power.
xx Holy See - Relations (diplomatic) with Italy.
Popes - History - 1870-1929.
Popes - Temporal power.

ROMAN RITUAL. See
RITUALE ROMANUM.

ROMAN ROTA. See
ROMANA ROTA.

ROMAN STATIONS. See
STATIONS, ROMAN.

ROMAN TRIBUNALS. See
CURIA ROMANA.

ROMANA ROTA.
BQV230 259   (348.x33)
BQV 75-78 (Documents)
(348.x15)
x Roman Rota.
Rota Romana.

ROMANESQUE CHURCH ARCHITECTURE. See
CHURCH ARCHITECTURE, ROMANESQUE.

ROMANS, EPISTLE TO THE. See
BIBLE. N.T. ROMANS.

ROME - RELIGION.
DG 121-135

ROME (CITY) - CHURCH HISTORY.

ROME (CITY) - CHURCHES.
BQX 2536-2537 (Church
History)
BQT 5681-5683 (Ecclesias-
tical art)

ROME (CITY) - RELIGIOUS AND
ECCLESIASTICAL INSTITUTIONS.

ROME (CITY). SAN PIETRO IN VATICANO
(BASILICA). See VATICAN CITY.
SAN PIETRO (BASILICA)

ROSARY. 242
        BQT 2677; BQT 4487; BQT 4522
        (24x8.72)
    sa Crosier indulgence.
       October devotions.
     x Mary, Blessed Virgin - Rosary.
    xx Beads.
       Devotions, Popular.
       Mary, Blessed Virgin - Prayer-
          books.
       Prayers.

ROSARY - BIBLIOGRAPHY.

ROSARY - EARLY WORKS TO 1800.

ROSARY - HISTORY.

ROSARY - JUVENILE LITERATURE.

ROSARY - MEDITATIONS.
        [BQT 2610.5]

ROSARY - MOVING-PICTURES.

ROSARY - POETRY.
    xx Mary, Blessed Virgin - Poetry.

ROSARY - SERMONS.
        BQT 3089
    xx Mary, Blessed Virgin - Sermons.

ROSARY, SERAPHIC. See
    FRANCISCAN CROWN.

ROSH HA-SHANAH.
        BM 695.N
     x Jewish New-Year.
       New-Year, Jewish.

ROSICRUCIANS.
    Classifications and references
       as in LC.

ROTA ROMANA. See
    ROMANA ROTA.

ROYAL SUPREMACY (CHURCH OF ENGLAND)
        BX 5157

RUBRICS (LITURGY) See
    RITES AND CEREMONIES (CATHOLIC)

RULE OF FAITH.
        BQT 248-254; BQT 101
        (23x9.53)
    Here are entered works on the
       standard or norm which enables
       members of the Church to de-
       termine what they must believe.
    sa Loci theologici.
     x Faith, Rule of.
    xx Church - Teaching office.
       Creeds.
       Dogma.
       Faith.
       Tradition (Theology)

RULES, RELIGIOUS. See
    RELIGIOUS ORDERS - RULES.

RUMANIA - CHURCH HISTORY.
        BQX 2927-2849   (274.98)

RUMANIA - CHURCH HISTORY - EARLY
    PERIOD TO 1697.

RUMANIA - CHURCH HISTORY - 1698-

RUMANIA - CHURCH HISTORY - 20th
    CENTURY.

RUMANIAN CATHOLIC RITE. See
    BYZANTINE RITE, RUMANIAN.

RUMANIAN ORTHODOX CHURCH. See
    ORTHODOX EASTERN CHURCH, RUMANIAN.

RURAL BISHOPS. See
    CHOREPISCOPI.

RURAL CHAPTERS.
    "Here are entered works dealing
       with the medieval country
       clergy placed under the juris-
       diction of the rural dean or
       archdeacon." LC
     x Chapters, Rural.
    xx Archdeacons.
       Chapters, Cathedral, collegiate,
          etc.
       Dioceses.
       Rural deans.

RURAL CHURCH ARCHITECTURE. See
    CHURCH ARCHITECTURE, RURAL.

RURAL CHURCHES.   (Geog. subdiv.,
  Indirect)
      BQT 3354; BV 638
  sa Community churches.
     Federated churches.
     Missions - Rural church.
     Rural clergy.
     Suburban churches.
   x Village churches.
  xx Rural clergy.
     Suburban churches.

RURAL CLERGY.   (Geog. subdiv.,
  Indirect)
  sa Rural churches.
   x Clergy, Country.
     Clergy, Rural.
     Country clergy.
     Country ministry.
     Ministry, Country.
  xx Church work.
     Rural churches.

RURAL CLERGY - SALARIES, PENSIONS,
  ETC.

RURAL DEANS.
  sa Rural chapters.
     Vicars forane.
   x Deans, Rural.
  xx Bishops.
     Dioceses.

RURAL LIFE, CATHOLIC. See
  SOCIOLOGY, RURAL (CATHOLIC)

RURAL MISSIONS. See
  MISSIONS - RURAL WORK.

RURAL SCHOOLS, CATHOLIC.
   x Catholic rural schools.
  xx Catholic education.
     Church schools.

RUSSIA - CHURCH HISTORY.
      BQX 6041-6150   (274.7)

RUSSIA - CHURCH HISTORY - 989-1589.
      BQX 6052-6054

RUSSIA - CHURCH HISTORY - 1589-1720.
      BQX 6057-6058

RUSSIA - CHURCH HISTORY - 1721-1917.
      BQX 6060

RUSSIA - CHURCH HISTORY - 1917-
      BQX 6063-6078

RUSSIA - RELIGION.
      BR 933

RUSSIA - RELIGION - 1917-
      BR 936

RUSSIA, COMMISSIO PRO. See
  COMMISSIO PRO RUSSIA.

RUSSIAN CATHOLIC RITE. See
  BYZANTINE RITE, RUSSIAN.

RUSSIAN CHRISTIAN LITERATURE. See
  CHRISTIAN LITERATURE - RUSSIAN
  AUTHORS.

RUSSIAN CHURCH. See
  ORTHODOX EASTERN CHURCH, RUSSIAN.

RUSSIAN SECTS. See
  SECTS, RUSSIAN.

RUTH, BOOK OF. See
  BIBLE. O.T. RUTH.

RUTHENIAN CATHOLIC RITE. See
  BYZANTINE RITE, RUTHENIAN.

SABBATARIANS.
  sa Seventh-day Adventists.
     Seventh-day Baptists.

SABBATH.
      BV 110-115   (291.x36)
      BM 685 (Judaism)
  sa Sunday.
   x Lord's Day.
  xx Judaism.

SABBATH - BIBLICAL TEACHING.

SABBATH (JEWISH LAW)
  References as in LC supple-
    ment 1957-61.

SABBATH LEGISLATION.   (Geog. subdiv.,
  Direct)
  References as in LC supple-
    ment 1959-60.

380

SABBATHAIANS.
BM 199.S
x Shabbathaians.
xx Cabala.
Jewish sects.

SABBATICAL YEAR (JUDAISM)
BM 720.S
xx Agricultural laws and legislation (Jewish law)
Land tenure - Law.

SABELLIANISM.
BQT 49; BQT 583   (273.x22)
xx Heresies and heretics - Early
church.
Trinity - History of doctrines.

SACER ORDO CISTERCIENSIS. See
CISTERCIANS.

SACERDOTAL VOCATION. See
PRIESTS - VOCATION.

SACRAMENT, BLESSED. See
EUCHARIST.

SACRAMENT HOUSES.
BQT 5959   (729.912)
xx Aumbries.
Church decoration and
ornament.
Church furniture.

SACRAMENTAL CHARACTER. See
CHARACTER (SACRAMENTS)

SACRAMENTALS.
BQT 1447; BQT 4501-4526
(23x7.8; 24x8.6)
sa Blessings.
Exorcism.
Holy oils.
Prayers.
also names of sacramentals,
e.g., Holy water, Scapulars,
etc.
xx Grace (Theology)
Sacraments.

SACRAMENTALS (CANON LAW)
BQV230 1144-1153   (348.x43)
xx Sacraments (Canon law)

SACRAMENTARIANS.
"Here are entered works dealing
primarily with the 16th century
application of the term "sacramentarians" to Zwingli and
others who denied the real
presence in the Lord's Supper,
stating instead that the com-
municant receives the sacrament of the body and blood of
Christ, i.e., the sacramental
symbols of them.
"In a wider sense the term was
applied to those who deviated
from the accepted teachings of
the sacraments." LC
sa Enthusiasm.
Reformation.
Sacraments - History of
doctrines.

SACRAMENTARIUM.
BQT 4244   (25x5.21)
"The first complete liturgical
book known in the Latin rite.
It contained the celebrant's
part of the mass and also the
services for other sacraments
which are now in the Rituale
and Pontificale." AT
x Sacramentary.
xx Missale.

SACRAMENTARIUM - BIBLIOGRAPHY.

SACRAMENTARIUM - CONCORDANCES.

SACRAMENTARIUM - HISTORY.

SACRAMENTARIUM AMBROSIUM.

SACRAMENTARIUM GALLICANUM.
x Gallican Sacramentary.

SACRAMENTARIUM GELASIANUM.
x Gelasian Sacramentary.

SACRAMENTARIUM GREGORIANUM.
x Gregorian Sacramentary.

SACRAMENTARIUM LEONIANUM.
x Leonine Sacramentary.

SACRAMENTARY. See SACRAMENTARIUM.

✓SACRAMENTS.   265
        BQT 1233-1437; BQT 2041-2073
  sa Baptism.
     Confirmation.
     Eucharist.
     Extreme Unction.
     Marriage.
     Ordination.
     Penance.
     Sacramentals.
  xx Dogmatic theology.
     Grace (Theology)
     Moral theology.
     Theology.

SACRAMENTS - ADDRESSES, ESSAYS,
   LECTURES.
        BQT 1238

SACRAMENTS - BIBLICAL TEACHING.

SACRAMENTS - CHARACTER. See
   CHARACTER (SACRAMENTS)

SACRAMENTS - CATECHISMS, QUESTION-
   BOOKS.

SACRAMENTS - EARLY WORKS TO 1800.

SACRAMENTS - EFFICACY.
        BQT 1244
  sa Donatists.

SACRAMENTS - HISTORY.
  sa Sacramentarians.

SACRAMENTS - HISTORY - SOURCES.

SACRAMENTS - HISTORY - EARLY PERIOD.

SACRAMENTS - HISTORY - MIDDLE AGES.

SACRAMENTS - HISTORY - MODERN PERIOD.

SACRAMENTS - HISTORY - 20th CENTURY.

SACRAMENTS - MEDITATIONS.
        BQT 2608   (24x2.9)

SACRAMENTS - MINISTER.
        BQT 1245
   x Minister of a sacrament.

SACRAMENTS - POPULAR WORKS.

SACRAMENTS - SERMONS.

SACRAMENTS - TYPOLOGY.

SACRAMENTS - VALIDITY.

        ################

SACRAMENTS - ANGLICAN COMMUNION.
        BX 5148-5149

SACRAMENTS - EASTERN CHURCHES.
        BQX 5443

SACRAMENTS - LUTHERAN CHURCH.
        BX 8072-8080

SACRAMENTS - METHODIST CHURCH.
        BX 8330-8332

SACRAMENTS - ORTHODOX EASTERN CHURCH.
        BQX 5881

        ################

SACRAMENTS (CANON LAW)
        BQV230 731-1153   (348.x42)
  sa Baptism (Canon law)
     Confirmation (Canon law)
     Eucharist (Canon law)
     Extreme Unction (Canon law)   Anointing of
     Marriage (Canon law)   the sick
     Ordination (Canon law)
     Penance (Canon law)
     Sacramentals (Canon law)
  xx Canon law.
     Things (Canon law)

SACRAMENTS (CANON LAW, EASTERN)
        BQV 1120

SACRAMENTS (LITURGY)
        BQT 4087-4088; BQT 4443-4453
          (264.x63)
  sa Baptism (Liturgy)
     Confirmation (Liturgy)

382

SACRAMENTS (LITURGY) -- Continued..
  sa Eucharist.
    Extreme Unction (Liturgy)
    Marriage (Liturgy)
    Mass.
    Ordination (Liturgy)
  xx Liturgy.

SACRAMENTS (MORAL THEOLOGY)
    BQT 2041-2073

SACRAMENTS, CONGREGATION OF THE.
  See CONGREGATIO DE DISCIPLINA
  SACRAMENTORUM.

Sacraments of Initiation

SACRED ART. See
CHRISTIAN ART.

*x Initiation
Sacraments*

√SACRED BOOKS.
    BL 7071   (291.8)
  sa names of individual books, e.g.,
    Avesta, Bible, Koran, Vedas;
    also subdivision "Sacred
    books" under names of religions,
    e.g., Buddha and Buddhism -
    Sacred books.
   x Books, Sacred.
    Sacred literatures.
  xx Religious literature.

SACRED BOOKS - CATALOGING. See
  CATALOGING OF SACRED BOOKS.

SACRED CANTATAS. See
  CANTATAS, SACRED.

SACRED CHORUSES. See
  CHORUSES, SACRED.

SACRED GROVES.
    BL 583
  References as in LC.

SACRED HEART.
    BQT 718   (232.x44)
   x Heart of Jesus.
    Jesus Christ - Sacred Heart.
  xx Jesus Christ - Humanity.
    Sacred Hearts.

SACRED HEART - ART.
    BQT 5876

SACRED HEART - BIBLICAL TEACHING.

SACRED HEART - BIBLIOGRAPHY.

SACRED HEART - CONFRATERNITIES.
    BQT 2814

SACRED HEART - CULTUS.   (Geog.
  subdiv., Direct)
    [BQT 718.2]

SACRED HEART - CULTUS - BIBLIO-
  GRAPHY.

SACRED HEART - CULTUS - HISTORY.

SACRED HEART - CULTUS - HISTORY -
  EARLY CHURCH.

SACRED HEART - CULTUS - HISTORY -
  MIDDLE AGES.

SACRED HEART - CULTUS - HISTORY -
  MODERN PERIOD.

SACRED HEART - CULTUS - EASTERN
  CHURCHES.

SACRED HEART - DEVOTIONAL
  LITERATURE.
    BQT 2591

SACRED HEART - ENTHRONEMENT.
   x Enthronement of the Sacred
    Heart.

SACRED HEART - HYMNS.
    BQT 4681-4689   (245)

SACRED HEART - MEDITATIONS.
    BQT 2591   (24x2.2)

SACRED HEART - NOVENAS. See
  NOVENAS - SACRED HEART.

SACRED HEART - PAPAL TEACHING.

SACRED HEART - PERIODICALS.

SACRED HEART - POETRY.

SACRED HEART - PRAYER-BOOKS.
    BQT 2663   (24x8.71)

SACRED HEART - PROMISES.

SACRED HEART - SERMONS.
  BQT 3056 (252.x21)

SACRED HEART - THEOLOGY.
  BQT 718

SACRED HEART, FEAST OF THE.
  BQT 4225
  x Feast of the Sacred Heart.

SACRED HEART, LITANY OF THE. See
 LITANY OF THE SACRED HEART.

SACRED HEART, MASS OF THE. See
 MISSA SACRATISSIMI CORDIS JESU.

SACRED HEART, NOVENA OF THE. See
 NOVENAS - SACRED HEART.

SACRED HEART, OFFICE OF THE. See
 OFFICIUM SACRATISSIMI CORDIS JESU.

SACRED HEART OF MARY. See
 IMMACULATE HEART OF MARY.

SACRED HEARTS.
 sa Immaculate Heart of Mary.
  Sacred Heart.
 x Jesus and Mary, Sacred Hearts
  of.

SACRED HEARTS - DEVOTIONAL
 LITERATURE.

SACRED HEARTS - MEDITATIONS.
  [BQT 2591.2]

SACRED HEARTS - NOVENAS. See
 NOVENAS - SACRED HEARTS.

SACRED HEARTS - PRAYER-BOOKS.
  [BQT 2663.2]

SACRED LITERATURES. See
 SACRED BOOKS.

SACRED MEALS.
  BL 619.S
 sa Agape.
  Love feasts.
  Other references as in LC.

SACRED MOUNTAINS. See
 MOUNTAINS (IN RELIGION, FOLK-LORE,
 ETC.

SACRED MUSIC. See
 CHURCH MUSIC.

SACRED NUMBERS. See
 SYMBOLISM OF NUMBERS.

SACRED ORATORY. See
 PREACHING.

SACRED PENITENTIARY. See
 POENTENTIARIA APOSTOLICA.

SACRED PLACES.
  BL 580-586 (291.35)
  BQT 4525-4526
 sa Shrines.
 x Holy places.
  Places, Sacred.

SACRED PLACES (CANON LAW)
  BQV230 1154-1242 (348.x413)
 sa Altars (Canon law)
  Cathedrals (Canon law)
  Cemeteries (Canon law)
  Chapels (Canon law)
  Churches (Canon law)
  Oratories (Canon law)
 xx Canon law.
  Things (Canon law)

SACRED SCIENCES.
 sa Bible.
  Canon law.
  Church history.
  Theology.
 x Sciences, Sacred.

SACRED SCRIPTURE. See BIBLE.

SACRED SONGS.
  Subdivisions as in LC.

SACRED THINGS. See
 THINGS (CANON LAW)

SACRED VESSELS.
  BQT 4358; BQT 6026 (264.4)
  BQT 4481 (Consecration of)
 sa Chalices.
  Custodials.
  Monstrances.

384

SACRED VESSELS -- Continued.
  x Altar vessels.
    Vessels, Sacred.
  xx Church furniture.
    Church plate.

SACRED VESSELS (CANON LAW)

SACRED VOCAL MUSIC.
  "Here are entered collections of
  miscellaneous sacred vocal compositions. Works on sacred
  music are entered under the
  headings Church music and Synagogue music - History and
  criticism." LC
  sa Advent music.
    Amens (Music)
    Antiphons (Music)
    Chant.
    Epiphany music.
    Holy-week music.
    Masses.

SACRIFICE.
    BQT 1321 (General)
    BQT 1117 (Christology)
    (232.x7)
    BL 570 (Comparative religion)
    (291.x34)
  sa Atonement.
    Cultus.
    Libations.
    Offerings.
    Votive offerings.
  xx Dogmatic theology.
    Ethnology.
    Mass.
    Religion.
    Religion, Primitive.
    Worship.

SACRIFICE - HISTORY.

SACRIFICE - SERMONS.

SACRIFICE, SPIRIT OF.
    [BQT 2220]
  sa Mortification.
  xx Perfection, Christian.

SACRIFICE OF THE MASS. See
  MASS.

SACRILEGE.
    BQT 1866 (24x1.61)
  x Church desecration.
    Desecration.
  xx Blasphemy.
    Offenses against religion.
    Religion (Virtue)

SACRILEGE (CANON LAW)

SACRISTANS.
  "Here are entered works dealing
  with church officials, sometimes
  in holy orders, in charge of the
  sacred vessels, vestments, etc.
  Works on church officials who
  take care of church buildings in
  general are entered under Sextons."
  LC supplement 1961.
  sa Sextons.
  xx Church vestments.
    Janitors.
    Sextons.

SACRISTANS - HANDBOOKS, MANUALS, ETC.
    BQT 4346
  xx Rites and ceremonies (Catholic) -
    Handbooks, manuals, etc.

SADDUCCEES.
    BM 175.S
  xx Jewish sects.

SAEPE EXPUGNAVERUNT ME (MUSIC). See
  PSALMS (MUSIC) - 128th PSALM.

SAINT (THE WORD)

ST. AUGUSTINE, CANONESSES REGULAR OF.
  See AUGUSTINIAN CANONESSES.

ST. AUGUSTINE, CANONS REGULAR OF.
  See AUGUSTINIAN CANONS.

ST. AUGUSTINE, ORDER OF. See
  AUGUSTINIANS.

ST. BARTHOLOMEW'S DAY, MASSACRE OF,
  1572.
    BQX 1773 (274.402)
  sa Huguenots in France.
  x Bartholomew, Saint, Massacre of.

ST. BASIL, LITURGY OF. See
  LITURGY OF ST. BASIL.

ST. BASIL THE GREAT, ORDER OF. See
  BASILIANS.

ST. BENEDICT, MEDAL OF. See
  MEDAL OF ST. BENEDICT.

ST. BENEDICT, ORDER OF. See
  BENEDICTINES.

ST. BENEDICT, SISTERS OF THE ORDER
  OF. See
  BENEDICTINE SISTERS.

ST. DOMINIC, ORDER OF. See
  DOMINICANS.

ST. FRANCIS, ORDER OF. See
  FRANCISCANS.

ST. JAMES, LITURGY OF. See
  LITURGY OF ST. JAMES.

ST. JOHN CHRYSOSTOM, LITURGY OF. See
  LITURGY OF ST. JOHN CHRYSOSTOM.

ST. JOHN THE BAPTIST'S DAY. See
  JOHN THE BAPTIST'S DAY.

ST. JOSEPH. See JOSEPH, SAINT.

ST. JOSEPH, SCAPULAR OF. See
  SCAPULAR OF ST. JOSEPH.

ST. JOSEPH, SISTERS OF. See
  SISTERS OF ST. JOSEPH.

ST. MARK, LITURGY OF. See
  LITURGY OF ST. MARK.

ST. MARTIN'S CLOAK.
    BQT 2603
  x Cloak of St. Martin.
    Martin, Saint, Cloak of.

ST. NICHOLAS DAY.
  sa Santa Claus.
  xx Santa Claus.

ST. PATRICK'S DAY.

ST. PATRICK'S DAY SERMONS.

ST. PETER'S BASILICA, VATICAN CITY.
  See VATICAN CITY. SAN PIETRO
  (BASILICA)

ST. PETER'S CHAINS.
    BQT 2603
  x Chains of St. Peter.
    Peter, Saint, Chains of.

ST. PETER'S CHAIR.
    BQT 4234
  x Cathedra Petri.
    Chair of Peter.
    Peter, Saint, Chair of.

ST. THOMAS CHRISTIANS.
    BQX 6481-6488
  x Christians of St. Thomas.
  xx Malabar - Church history.

ST. WALBURGA'S OIL.
    BQT 2689
  x Walburga, Saint, Oil of.

SAINTS. (Geog. subdiv., Direct)
    BQT 1573-1589 (23x5) *(Lives - 920)*
  sa All Saints' Day. *(Calendar 264)*
    Apostles.
    Blessed.
    Doctors of the church.
    Fathers of the church.
    Glory (Theology)
    Hagiography.
    Hermits.
    Heroic virtue.
    Legends, Christian.
    Martyrologium.
    Martyrs.
    Patron saints.
    Relics and reliquaries.
    Shrines.
    Stigmatization.
  xx Blessed.
    Christian biography.
    Devotional literature.
    Fathers of the church.
    Feasts, Ecclesiastical.
    Martyrs.
    Pilgrims and pilgrimages.
    Psychology, Religious.
    Relics and reliquaries.
    Religious orders.

SAINTS - ANECDOTES, FACETIAE,
SATIRE, ETC.

SAINTS - ART.
BQT 5894-5895   (246.x65)
sa Apostles - Art.
Christian art.
Evangelists (Bible) - Art.
Saints - Symbolism.
x Saints - Iconography.
xx Christian art.

SAINTS - BIBLIOGRAPHY.
[BQT 1571]
Z 7844   (016.244x9)

SAINTS - BIOGRAPHY.
BQX 8211-8358   (244.x9)

SAINTS - BIOGRAPHY - JUVENILE
LITERATURE.

SAINTS - CALENDAR.
BQT 4233   (23x5.31)
"Here are entered works limited
to lists of saints arranged
chronologically by the days on
which they are commemorated."
LC
sa Mary, Blessed Virgin - Calendar.
x Heortology.

SAINTS - CANONIZATION. See
CANONIZATION.

SAINTS - COMMEMORATION.
x Commemoration of saints.
xx Saints - Cultus.

SAINTS - CONTROVERSIAL LITERATURE.

SAINTS - CULTUS.   (Geog. subdiv.)
BQT 1581; BQT 2196   (23x5.2)
sa Images, Veneration of.
Martyrs - Cultus.
Mary, Blessed Virgin - Cultus.
Saints - Commemoration.
x Dulia.
Saints - Invocation.
Saints - Veneration.
xx Images, Veneration of.
Shrines.

SAINTS - DICTIONARIES.
BQX 8215

SAINTS - DRAMA.

SAINTS - EARLY CHURCH.

SAINTS - EXAMPLE.

SAINTS - FEASTS. See
FEASTS, ECCLESIASTICAL.

SAINTS - FICTION.

SAINTS - ICONOGRAPHY. See
SAINTS - ART.

SAINTS - INVOCATION. See
SAINTS - CULTUS.

SAINTS - JUVENILE LITERATURE.
BQX 8208

SAINTS - LEGENDS.
sa Mary, Blessed Virgin -
Legends.

SAINTS - MEDITATIONS.
BQT 2602-2603   (24x2.9)

SAINTS - MIDDLE AGES.

SAINTS - NAMES.
xx Names, Personal.

SAINTS - PICTORIAL WORKS.

SAINTS - POETRY.

SAINTS - POPULAR WORKS.
BQX 8207

SAINTS - PRAYER-BOOKS.
BQT 2687-2689

SAINTS - PRAYER-BOOKS - ENGLISH,
[FRENCH, GERMAN, ETC.]

SAINTS - SERMONS.
[BQT 2992.5]
sa Feasts, Ecclesiastical - Sermons.
xx Feasts, Ecclesiastical - Sermons.

SAINTS - SYMBOLISM.
     BQT 5844
  xx Saints - Art.
     Symbolism, Christian.

SAINTS - TRANSLATION.
     BQT 1586
  Here are entered works on the
    transferring of a saint's
    relics from one place to
    another.

SAINTS - VENERATION. See
  SAINTS - CULTUS.

       ################

SAINTS - EASTERN CHURCHES. See
  EASTERN CHURCHES - SAINTS.

SAINTS - ORTHODOX EASTERN CHURCH.
  See ORTHODOX EASTERN CHURCH -
  SAINTS.

       ################

SAINTS, BIBLICAL.
     BS 579; BS 2448
     BQX 8227
  x Biblical saints.
  xx Bible - Biography.

SAINTS, COMMUNION OF. See
  COMMUNION OF SAINTS.

SAINTS, IMITATION OF THE. See
  IMITATION OF THE SAINTS.

SAINTS, JUVENILE.
  x Juvenile saints.

SAINTS, LITANY OF THE. See
  LITANY OF THE SAINTS.

SAINTS, PATRON. See
  PATRON SAINTS.

SAINTS, PILLAR. See
  STYLITES.

SAINTS, WOMEN.
     BQX 8221   (244.x9)
  x Women saints.

       ################

SAINTS, AUGUSTINIAN.
  x Augustinian saints.
  xx Augustinians - Biography.

SAINTS, BENEDICTINE.
  x Benedictine saints.
  xx Benedictines - Biography.

SAINTS, BRETON.
  x Breton saints.
  xx Saints, French.

SAINTS, CARMELITE.
  x Carmelite saints.
  xx Carmelites - Biography.

SAINTS, DOMINICAN.
  x Dominican saints.
  xx Dominicans - Biography.

SAINTS, FRANCISCAN.
  x Franciscan saints.
  xx Franciscans - Biography

SAINTS, FRENCH.
  sa Saints, Breton.
  x French saints.

SAINTS, HINDU.
     BL 2003
  x Hindu saints.
  xx Hinduism.

SAINTS, IRISH.
  x Irish saints.

SAINTS, JESUIT.
  sa Martyrs, Jesuit.
  x Jesuit saints.
  xx Jesuits - Biography.

SAINTS, MOHAMMEDAN.
  x Mohammedan saints.

SAINTS, NAVARRESE.
  x Navarrese saints.
  xx Saints, Spanish.

SAINTS, PREMONSTRATENSIAN.
x Premonstratensian saints.

SAINTS, SPANISH.
sa Saints, Navarrese.
x Spanish saints.

################

SAINTS IN THE LITURGY.
BQT 4053
x Liturgy - Saints.

SALVATION.
BQT 1105-1220   (234)
sa Atonement.
Grace (Theology)
Infant salvation.
Justification.
Regeneration (Theology)
Repentance.
Salvation outside the church.
Sanctification.
Sin.
x Soteriology.
xx Conversion.
Covenants (Theology)
Dogmatic theology.
Faith.
Future life.
Jesus Christ.
Redemption.
Universalism.

SALVATION - BIBLICAL TEACHING.
BQT 1111

SALVATION - COMPARATIVE STUDIES.

SALVATION - HISTORY OF DOCTRINES.

SALVATION - HISTORY OF DOCTRINES -
EARLY CHURCH.

SALVATION - HISTORY OF DOCTRINES -
MIDDLE AGES.

SALVATION - HISTORY OF DOCTRINES -
MODERN PERIOD.

SALVATION - HISTORY OF DOCTRINES -
16th, [17th, etc.] CENTURY.

SALVATION - POPULAR WORKS.

SALVATION - PSYCHOLOGY.
xx Psychology, Religious.

SALVATION - SERMONS.
BQT 1109
BQT 3089   (252.3)

SALVATION - STUDY AND TEACHING.

SALVATION (BRAHMANISM)
BL 1215

SALVATION (GERMANIC RELIGION)
xx Germanic tribes - Religion.

SALVATION (HINDUISM)
xx Hinduism.

SALVATION (JUDAISM)
xx Judaism.

SALVATION ARMY.
Classifications and references
as in LC.

SALVATION OUTSIDE THE CHURCH.
BQT 316
sa Universalism.
x Catholic Church and salvation.
Extra ecclesiam nulla salus.
xx Church.
Non-Catholics.
Universalism.

SALVE REGINA.
BQT 2695

SALVE REGINA (MUSIC)
BQT 4682
M 2079.L79

SALVUM ME FAC, DEUS (MUSIC) See
PSALMS (MUSIC) - 68th PSALM.

SALVUM ME FAC, DOMINE (MUSIC) See
PSALMS (MUSIC) - 11th PSALM.

SAMARITAN WOMAN (BIBLICAL CHARACTER)
BS 2520

SAMARITAN WOMAN (BIBLICAL CHARACTER) -
ART.
BQT 5893

SAMARITAN WOMAN (BIBLICAL CHARACTER) -
DRAMA.

SAMARITAN WOMAN (BIBLICAL CHARACTER) -
FILMSTRIPS.

SAMARITAN WOMAN (BIBLICAL CHARACTER) -
SERMONS.
BQT 3089

SAMARITANS.
DS 129   (22x9.78)

SAMUEL, BOOKS OF. See
BIBLE. O.T. 1-2 KINGS.

SANATIO IN RADICE.
BQV230 1138-1141
xx Marriage - Validation (Canon
law)

SANCTI COLUMNARES. See
STYLITES.

SANCTIFICATION.
BQT 1192; BQT 1579
sa Good works (Theology)
Imitation of the saints.
x Sanctity.
xx Christian life.
Dogmatic theology.
Faith.
Grace, Habitual.
Holiness.
Perseverance (Theology)
Salvation.
Spiritual life.

SANCTIFICATION - HISTORY OF
DOCTRINES.

SANCTIFYING GRACE. See
GRACE, HABITUAL.

SANCTITY. See
HOLINESS.
SANCTIFICATION.

SANCTORALE.
BQT 4273
"The part of the Breviary or
Missal containing the proper
offices of the saints." AT

SANCTUARY (LAW) See
ASYLUM, RIGHT OF.

SANCTUS (THE WORD)

SANTA CLAUS.
GT 4985
sa St. Nicholas' Day.
xx St. Nicholas' Day.

SARABITES.
xx Religious orders - History -
Early period.

SARCOPHAGI.
BQX 68 (Christian archae-
ology)   (236.5)
NB (Sculpture)
References as in LC.

SARDICA, COUNCIL OF, 343.
BQX 405

SARUM RITE.
BQT 4139   (264.x82)

SATAN. See DEVIL.

SATANISM.
BL 480 (Comparative reli-
gion)
BF 1546-1561 (Occult
sciences)   (133.42)
BQT 2461
sa Demoniac possession.
Occult sciences.
x Black Mass (Satanism)
Diabolism.
xx Demoniac possession.
Demonology.
Devil.
Devil-worship.
Religion.

SATISFACTION.
      BQT 1378   (23x7.4)
   "The act by which the sinner
      endeavors to make reparation
      to God for offenses committed
      against Him by undergoing
      some form of punishment." AT
   sa Atonement.
    x Reparation (Theology)
   xx Atonement.
      Penance.
      Penitential discipline.
      Sin.

SATISFACTION - HISTORY OF DOCTRINES.

SAVOYARD MISSIONARIES. See
   MISSIONARIES, SAVOYARD.

SCANDAL.
      BQT 1786   (24x1.51)

SCANDINAVIA - RELIGION.

SCAPULAR OF MOUNT CARMEL.
      BQT 4522
    x Brown scapular.

SCAPULAR OF ST. JOSEPH.
    x St. Joseph, Scapular of.

SCAPULAR OF THE PASSION (BLACK)
      BQT 4522
    x Black scapular of the Passion.

SCAPULAR OF THE PASSION (RED)
      BQT 4522
    x Red scapular of the Passion.

SCAPULARS.
      BQT 4522   (23x7.8)
   xx Church vestments.
      Indulgences.
      Religious orders - Habit.

SCHISM.
      BQT 332 (Apologetics)
      BQT 36 (History of theology)
   sa Heresy.
   xx Apostasy.
      Catholics, Lapsed.
      Irenics.
      Non-Catholics.

SCHISM - EASTERN AND WESTERN CHURCH.
      BQX 5828   (270.3)
   sa Schism, Acacian, 484-519.
    x Eastern Schism.
      Great Schism.
      Greco-Roman Schism.
      Schism - Greek and Latin church.
      Schism - Latin and Greek church.
   xx Catholic Church - History.
      Catholic Church - Relations -
         Orthodox Eastern Church.
      Orthodox Eastern Church -
         History.
      Orthodox Eastern Church - Rela-
         tions - Catholic Church.

SCHISM - GREEK AND LATIN CHURCH. See
   SCHISM - EASTERN AND WESTERN CHURCH.
   SCHISM, ACACIAN, 484-519.

SCHISM - LATIN AND GREEK CHURCH. See
   SCHISM - EASTERN AND WESTERN CHURCH.
   SCHISM, ACACIAN, 484-519.

SCHISM, ACACIAN, 484-519.
    x Acacian Schism.
      Greco-Roman Schism.
      Schism - Greek and Latin Church.
      Schism - Latin and Greek Church.
   xx Catholic Church - Relations -
         Orthodox Eastern Church.
      Church history - Primitive and
         early church.
      Monophysites.
      Orthodox Eastern Church - Rela-
         tions - Catholic Church.
      Schism - Eastern and Western
         Church.

SCHISM, THE GREAT WESTERN, 1378-1417.
      BQX 766   (270.5)
    x Great Schism.
      Great Western Schism.
      Western Schism.
   xx Church history - Middle Ages.

SCHISM, PHOCIAN.
      BQX 5744
    x Phocian Schism.
   xx Photius, Patriarch of Con-
         stantinople, ca. 820-891.

SCHISMATIC EASTERN CHURCHES. See
EASTERN CHURCHES, ORTHODOX.

SCHOLASTICISM.
       B 839 (General and modern)
       B 734 (Medieval)
       BD 125 (Metaphysics)
       B 851-4695 (Special, local)
       BQT 81-103 (Theology)
       BQX 670 (Church history)
        (270.4)
  "The philosophy that flourished
  during the Middle Ages and
  which is personified in the
  Dominican St. Thomas Aquinas.
  It is the philosophy of the
  Fathers reduced to a grand
  synthesis and presented in a
  didactic form." AT
sa Individuation.
  Neo-scholasticism.
  Philosophy, Early Christian.
  Philosophy, Medieval.
  Theology and philosophy.
  Thomism.
  Universals (Philosophy)
 x Philosophy, Scholastic
  Theology, Scholastic.
xx Philosophy, Early Christian.
  Philosophy, Medieval.

SCHOLASTICISM - BIBLIOGRAPHY.

SCHOLASTICISM - CONGRESSES.

SCHOLASTICISM - DICTIONARIES,
  INDEXES, ETC.

SCHOLASTICISM - HISTORY.

SCHOLASTICISM - PERIODICALS.

SCHOLASTICISM - SOCIETIES.

SCHOLIA.
 xx Bible - Commentaries.
  Fathers of the church.

SCHOOL CHAPLAINS. See
CHAPLAINS, SCHOOL.

SCHOOL SONG-BOOKS, CATHOLIC.
  x Catholic school song-books.
 xx Song-books, Catholic.

SCHOOLS - PRAYERS.

SCHOOLS, DENOMINATIONAL. See
CHURCH SCHOOLS.

SCHOOLS, MONASTIC. See
MONASTIC SCHOOLS.

SCHOOLS, PAROCHIAL. See
CHURCH SCHOOLS.

SCHOTTENKLÖSTER.
  Here are entered works on
  monastic foundations established on the European con-
  tinent, particularly in Germany, by Irish and Scottish
  missionaries.
  x Scottish monasteries.
 xx Monasticism, Irish.

SCIENCE AND BUDDHISM. See
BUDDHISM AND SCIENCE.

SCIENCE AND RELIGION. See
RELIGION AND SCIENCE.

SCIENCE AND THE BIBLE. See
BIBLE AND SCIENCE.

SCIENCE AND THE CATHOLIC CHURCH.
  See CATHOLIC CHURCH AND SCIENCE.

SCIENCE AND THEOLOGY. See
THEOLOGY AND SCIENCE.

SCIENCES, SACRED. See
SACRED SCIENCES.

SCIENTISTS, CATHOLIC.
  "Works mainly biographical are
  entered here. Works on the
  attainments of Catholics as
  scientists are entered under
  the heading Catholics as
  scientists." LC
sa Catholics as scientists.
 x Catholic scientists.
xx Catholic Church and science.

SCOTISM.
      BQT 82
  xx Scholasticism.

SCOTISM - BIBLIOGRAPHY.

SCOTLAND - CHURCH HISTORY.
      BQX 2151-2187   (274.1)

SCOTLAND - CHURCH HISTORY - EARLY
  PERIOD TO 1577.

SCOTLAND - CHURCH HISTORY - 1577-

SCOTLAND - CHURCH HISTORY - 19th
  CENTURY.

SCOTLAND - CHURCH HISTORY - 20th
  CENTURY.

SCOTTISH MISSIONS. See
  MISSIONS, SCOTTISH.

SCOTTISH MONASTERIES. See
  SCHOTTENKLOSTER.

SCREENS (CHURCH DECORATION)
      BQT 5945; BQT 6025
  sa Altarpieces.
  x Altar screens.
  xx Christian art.
    Church decoration and ornament.
    Church furniture.

SCRIBES, JEWISH.
      BM 652
  "Here are entered works dealing
  with the Jewish functionaries
  engaged in the transcription of
  Jewish religious documents, such
  as the Torah, phylacteries,
  mezuzah." LC

SCRIPTURES, HOLY. See BIBLE.

SCRUPLES.
      BQT 1765; BQT 2239
        (24x1.x2; 24x7.51)
  xx Conscience, Examination of.
    Pastoral psychology.
    Spiritual direction.

SCULPTURE, RELIGIOUS.
      BQT 5991-6038
  x Religious sculpture.
  xx Christian art.

SEA IN THE BIBLE.
  sa Fishing in the Bible..
  xx Sea in literature.

SEAL OF CONFESSION.
      BQT 1385   (23x7.4)
  x Confession, Seal of.
  xx Penance.

SEALS (CHRISTMAS, ETC.)
  x Christmas seals.
    Easter seals.

SEALS (NUMISMATICS)
      CD 5001-6471   (727)
      BQX 67 (Christian archae-
        ology)   9246.5)
  References as in LC.

SEAMEN - PRAYER-BOOKS.
      BQT 2573

SEAMEN - RELIGIOUS LIFE.
  xx Armed forces - Religious life.

SEAMEN'S MISSIONS. See
  MERCHANT SEAMEN - MISSIONS AND
  CHARITIES.

SECOND ADVENT.
      BQT 1469   (236.x93)
  sa Judgment-day.
    Millenium.
  x Jesus Christ - Second coming.
    Parousia.
    Second coming of Christ.
  xx Advent.
    Eschatology.
    Jesus Christ.
    Judgment-day.
    Millennium.

SECOND ADVENTISTS. See
  ADVENTISTS.

SECOND BAPTISM. See
  MARTYRDOM.

SECOND COMING OF CHRIST. See
  SECOND ADVENT.

SECONDARY EDUCATION, CATHOLIC. See
  CATHOLIC EDUCATION, SECONDARY.

SECRET DISCIPLINE. See
  DISCIPLINE OF THE SECRET.

SECRET SOCIETIES.
  xx Rites and ceremonies.
  Other references as in LC.

SECRET SOCIETIES AND CATHOLIC CHURCH.
      HS 164
      BQT 1895
  sa Freemasons and Catholic Church.
   x Catholic Church and secret
      societies.

SECRETARIA BREVIUM AD PRINCIPES.
      BQV 95-96

SECRETARIA LITTERARUM LATINARUM.
      BQV 98

SECRETARIA STATUS (PAPAL)
      BQV 91-94
    x Papal Secretary of State.

SECRETARIES, CHURCH. See
  CHURCH SECRETARIES.

SECTS.   (Geog. subdiv., Indirect)
      BR 157
      BQT 130; BT 990 (Creeds)
  See note under Heresies and
    heretics.
  sa Dissenters.
      Local church councils.
      Unionism (Religion)
      also names of churches and
        sects.
   x Christian sects.
      Denominations, Religious.
      Religious denominations.
      Sects, Christian.
      Sects, Modern.
  xx Apostasy.
      Church history.
      Church history - Modern
        period.

SECTS -- Continued.
  xx Dogmatic theology - History -
        Modern period.
      Heresies and heretics - Modern
        period.
      Religions.

SECTS - NAMES.
  sa Friends, Society of.
      also similar headings.

SECTS - NETHERLANDS.
  sa Zwijndrechtsche Nieuwlichters.

SECTS, BUDDHIST. See
  BUDDHIST SECTS.

SECTS, CHRISTIAN. See
  SECTS.

SECTS, HINDU. See
  HINDU SECTS.

SECTS, JAINA. See
  JAINA SECTS.

SECTS, JEWISH. See
  JEWISH SECTS.

SECTS, MEDIEVAL.
      BQ 5286 (Collections)
      BQT 86-103 (History)
  sa Adamites.
      Albigenses.
      Bogomiles.
      Cathari.
      Circumcellions.
      Flagellants (Sect)
      Lollards.
      Nihilianism.
      Reformation - Early movements.
      Waldenses.
   x Medieval sects.
  xx Church history - Middle Ages.
      Dogmatic theology - History -
        Middle Ages.
      Heresies and heretics - Middle
        Ages.

SECTS, MODERN. See SECTS.

SECTS, MOHAMMEDAN. See
  MOHAMMEDAN SECTS.

SECTS, RUSSIAN.
    BQX 6152-6157
  sa Dukhobors.
    Klysty.
    Raskolniks.
    Skoptsi.
    Stundists.
   x Russian sects.
  xx Orthodox Eastern Church,
    Russian.

SECTS, SHINTO. See
  SHINTO SECTS.

SECULAR CANONS. See
  CANONS SECULAR.

SECULAR INSTITUTES. (Geog. subdiv.)
    BQX 6836
   x Institutes, Secular.
  xx Laity.
    Quasi-religious societies.
    Religious orders.

SECULAR INSTITUTES - BIBLIOGRAPHY.

SECULAR INSTITUTES (CANON LAW)
    [BQV230 681.5]

SECULARISM.
    BQT 123
  "The teaching that the foundation
   of morality, duty, and religion
   is to be sought in nature alone."
   AT
  sa Agnosticism.
    Anti-clericalism.
    Civilization, Secular.
    Spirituality.
    Supernatural.
  xx Irreligion.
    Materialism (Theology)

SECULARISM - CONTROVERSIAL
  LITERATURE.

SECULARIZATION.
  "Here are entered works on the
   enforced transfer or alienation of territory from ecclesiastical to civil rulers, and
   of the transfer of property,

SECULARIZATION -- Continued.
   especially monastic, from
   ecclesiastical to government
   or other secular ownership,
   use, or control." LC
   x Impropriation.
  xx Church and state.
    Church property.
    Convents.
    Monasteries.

SECULARIZATION (CANON LAW)
    BQV230 638-642   (348.x37)
  "The act by which a religious is
   permanently separated from his
   order or congregation and
   released from his religious
   vows." AT
  xx Indults.
    Religious orders (Canon law)

SEDUCTION.
    BQT 1936
  References as in LC.

SEDUCTION (CANON LAW)
  sa Solicitation (Canon law)

SEE, HOLY. See HOLY SEE.

SEGREGATION - RELIGIOUS ASPECTS.

SEKHMET (EGYPTIAN DEITY)
  xx Mother-goddesses.

SELF-DENIAL. See
  MORTIFICATION.

SELF-EXAMINATION. See
  CONSCIENCE, EXAMINATION OF.

SELFIRATH PERIOD.
  References as in LC.

SEMI-ARIANISM. See
  ARIANISM.

SEMI-PELAGIANISM.
    BQT 75 (General)   (273.x41)
    BQT 1143
  sa Pelagianism.
  xx Election (Theology)
    Grace (Theology)

SEMI-PELAGIANISM -- Continued.
   xx Heresies and heretics - Early
       church.
     Pelagianism.

SEMIKHAH.
    x Ordination (Jewish law)
     Rabbis - Ordination.
    xx Jewish law.

SEMINARIANS.
       BQT 2295-2296
    xx Theological seminaries.
     Theology - Study and teaching.

SEMINARIANS - BOOKS AND READING.

SEMINARIANS - CORRESPONDENCE,
   REMINISCENCES, ETC.

SEMINARIANS - MEDITATIONS.
     [BQT 2551.2]

SEMINARIANS - PRAYER-BOOKS.
     BQT 2622

SEMINARIANS - RETREATS. See
   RETREATS FOR SEMINARIANS.

SEMINARIANS - SERMONS.
     [BQT 3013.5]

SEMINARIANS - SPIRITUAL LIFE.

SEMINARIES, RABBINICAL. See
   RABBINICAL SEMINARIES.

SEMINARIES, THEOLOGICAL. See
   THEOLOGICAL SEMINARIES.

SEMINARY AND UNIVERSITY STUDIES,
   CONGREGATION OF. See
   CONGREGATIO DE SEMINARIIS ET
   UNIVERSITATIBUS STUDIORUM.

SEMINARY LIBRARIES. See
   THEOLOGICAL LIBRARIES.

SEPARATE BAPTISTS.
   xx Baptists.

SEPARATED EASTERN CHURCHES. See
   EASTERN CHURCHES, ORTHODOX.

SEPARATION (CANON LAW)
   sa Divorce (Canon law)
   xx Divorce (Canon law)
     Marriage (Canon law)
     Matrimonial actions (Canon
     law)

SEPARATION OF POWERS (CANON LAW)

SEPTUAGESIMA.
     [BQT 4221.8]
   xx Church year.
     Lent.

SEPTUAGINT.
   For texts of the Septuagint see
     Bible. O.T. Greek. [date].
     Septuagint.
   For books about the Septuagint see
     BIBLE. O.T. GREEK. VERSIONS -
     SEPTUAGINT.

SEPULCHER, EASTER. See
   EASTER SEPULCHER.

SEPULCHER, HOLY. See
   HOLY SEPULCHER.

SEPULCHRAL MONUMENTS.
     BQT 5929-5930; BQT 6038
   References as in LC, with the
     following additional reference.
   sa Martyria.

SEQUENCES (LITURGY)
      BQ 5087 (Critical studies)
      BQT 4253; BQT 4309-4311 (Texts)
   sa names of sequences, e.g., Dies
     irae; Stabat mater; etc.
   x Liturgical sequences.
     Prose (Liturgy)
   xx Church music.
     Hymns, Liturgical.

SEQUENCES (MUSIC)
   sa names of sequences, e.g., Dies
     irae (Music)
   xx Hymns.
     Propers (Music)

SERAPHIC ROSARY. See
   FRANCISCAN CROWN.

SERAPHIM. See
ANGELS.

SERBIAN CHURCH SLAVIC LANGUAGE. See
CHURCH SLAVIC LANGUAGE.

SERBIAN ORTHODOX CHURCH. See
ORTHODOX EASTERN CHURCH, SERBIAN.

√ SERMON ON THE MOUNT.
BQT 891
sa Beatitudes.
x Jesus Christ - Sermon on the
Mount.

SERMON ON THE MOUNT - MEDITATIONS.
BQT 2593

SERMON ON THE MOUNT - PICTURES,
ILLUSTRATIONS, ETC.

SERMON ON THE MOUNT - SERMONS.
BQT 3057

√ SERMONS.
Here are entered collections of
sermons by two or more authors.
The collected sermons of one
author generally fall under a
language heading, e.g., Sermons,
English; Sermons, French; etc.
For works about the art and science
of preaching see Homiletics.
sa Homiletics.
Preaching.
Prones.
also kinds of sermons listed
below, and subdivision "Sermons" under special topics,
e.g., Death - Sermons; Mass -
Sermons; etc.
x Homilies.
Sermons - Collections.
xx Homiletics.
Preaching.

SERMONS - COLLECTIONS. See
SERMONS.

SERMONS - COPYRIGHT. See
COPYRIGHT - LECTURES, SERMONS, ETC.

SERMONS - ILLUSTRATIONS. See
HOMILETICAL ILLUSTRATIONS.

SERMONS - OUTLINES.
BQT 2961   (252.x02)

SERMONS - TEXTS FOR SERMONS.

################

SERMONS - CHURCH OF ENGLAND,
[ORTHODOX EASTERN CHURCH,
ETC.]. See
CHURCH OF ENGLAND, [ORTHODOX
EASTERN CHURCH, ETC.] - SERMONS.

################

SERMONS, ENGLISH, [FRENCH,
GERMAN, ETC.]
BQT 2981-2989

SERMONS, ENGLISH - MIDDLE
ENGLISH (1100-1500)
xx English literature - Middle
English (1100-1500)

SERMONS, ENGLISH - TRANSLATIONS
FROM GERMAN, [HUNGARIAN, LATIN,
ETC.]

SERMONS, ENGLISH - TRANSLATIONS
INTO FRENCH, [GERMAN, ITALIAN,
ETC.]

SERMONS, LATIN - BIBLIOGRAPHY.

################

SERMONS, ADVENT. See
ADVENT SERMONS.

SERMONS, ANNIVERSARY. See
ANNIVERSARY SERMONS.

SERMONS, APOLOGETICAL. See
APOLOGETICS - SERMONS.

SERMONS, BACCALAUREATE. See
BACCALAUREATE ADDRESSES.

SERMONS, BUDDHIST. See
BUDDHIST SERMONS.

SERMONS, CANONIZATION. See
  CANONIZATION SERMONS.

SERMONS, CATECHETICAL. See
  CATECHETICAL SERMONS.

SERMONS, CHRISTMAS. See
  CHRISTMAS SERMONS.

SERMONS, CHURCH DEDICATION. See
  CHURCH DEDICATION - SERMONS.

SERMONS, CHURCH YEAR.
    BQT 2991   (252.x1)
  Here are entered sermons planned
    to be delivered during the
    course of the church year, as
    for all Sundays and feasts of
    the liturgical cycles.
  For sermons on the meaning of
    the church year itself see
    Church year - Sermons.
  sa Church year - Sermons.
  x Church year sermons.

SERMONS, COLLEGE. See
  UNIVERSITIES AND COLLEGES -
  SERMONS.

SERMONS, COMMUNION. See
  COMMUNION, FREQUENT - SERMONS.
  COMMUNION, HOLY - SERMONS.
  EUCHARIST - SERMONS.
  FIRST COMMUNION SERMONS.

SERMONS, CONFIRMATION. See
  CONFIRMATION - SERMONS.

SERMONS, COURT. See
  COURT SERMONS.

SERMONS, DOCTRINAL. See
  DOGMATIC THEOLOGY - SERMONS.

SERMONS, EASTER. See
  EASTER - SERMONS.

SERMONS, ELECTION. See
  ELECTION SERMONS.

SERMONS, EXECUTION. See
  EXECUTION SERMONS.

SERMONS, FAREWELL. See
  FAREWELL SERMONS.

SERMONS, FAST-DAY. See
  FAST DAYS - SERMONS.

SERMONS, FESTIVAL. See
  FEASTS, ECCLESIASTICAL - SERMONS.

SERMONS, FIRST COMMUNION. See
  FIRST COMMUNION SERMONS.

SERMONS, FUNERAL. See
  FUNERAL SERMONS.

SERMONS, GOOD FRIDAY. See
  GOOD FRIDAY - SERMONS.

SERMONS, GRADUATION. See
  BACCALAUREATE ADDRESSES.

SERMONS, HOLY-WEEK. See
  HOLY WEEK - SERMONS.

SERMONS, INSTALLATION. See
  INSTALLATION SERMONS.

SERMONS, JEWISH.
  sa Bar Mitzvah sermons.
    Hadran.
    High Holy Day sermons.
    Passover sermons.
    Rosh ha-shanah sermons.
    Synagogue dedication sermons.

SERMONS, LENTEN.
    BQT 2995   (252.x53)
  Here are entered sermons planned
    to be given during the lenten
    season. They usually consist
    of sermon courses for the
    duration of lent and may treat
    of various topics, e.g.,
    Passion and death of Christ,
    Seven last words of Christ,
    Sacraments, Sin, etc.
  For sermons or instructions on
    the meaning of lent as such
    see Lent - Sermons.
  sa Lent - Sermons.
  x Lenten sermons.
  xx Jesus Christ - Passion - Sermons.
    Lent - Sermons.

SERMONS, LENTEN - OUTLINES.

SERMONS, LITURGICAL.
  Here are entered collections of
    sermons liturgical in spirit.
  For sermons explaining the
    meaning of the liturgy see
    Liturgy - Sermons.
  sa Liturgy - Sermons.
   x Liturgical sermons.
  xx Liturgy - Sermons.

SERMONS, MARRIAGE. See
  MARRIAGE - SERMONS.
  MARRIAGE, MIXED - SERMONS.

SERMONS, MEDIEVAL.

SERMONS, MISSION.
        BQT 3009
  Here are entered works containing
    sermons for the use of mission-
    aries laboring in the mission
    fields.
  For works containing sermons
    about the missions and about
    missionary work see Missions -
    Sermons.
  sa Missions - Sermons.
    Parish missions - Sermons.
   x Mission sermons.
  xx Missions - Sermons.
    Parish missions.

SERMONS, MOHAMMEDAN. See
  MOHAMMEDAN SERMONS.

SERMONS, MORAL. See
  MORAL THEOLOGY - SERMONS.

SERMONS, MOTHER'S DAY. See
  MOTHER'S DAY SERMONS.

SERMONS, NEW YEAR. See
  NEW YEAR SERMONS.

SERMONS, NEW YEAR'S EVE. See
  NEW YEAR'S EVE SERMONS.

SERMONS, OCCASIONAL. See
  OCCASIONAL SERMONS.

SERMONS, PASSOVER. See
  PASSOVER SERMONS.

SERMONS, RADIO. See
  RADIO SERMONS.

SERMONS, TRIDUUM. See
  TRIDUUM SERMONS.

SERMONS, UNIVERSITY. See
  UNIVERSITIES AND COLLEGES -
  SERMONS.

SERMONS, VISITATION. See
  VISITATION SERMONS.

SERMONS FOR CHILDREN. See
  CHILDREN'S SERMONS.

SERMONS FOR SPECIAL OCCASIONS. See
  OCCASIONAL SERMONS.

SERPENT (IN PARADISE)
        BS 1238
  xx Devil.
    Fall of man.

SERPENT-WORSHIP.
  sa Brazen Serpent.
    Tree of life.
   x Snake-worship.

SERPENTS (IN RELIGION, FOLK-LORE, ETC.)
   x Snakes (in religion, folk-lore,
     etc.)

SERVANT OF JEHOVAH.
   x Jahweh, Servant of.
    Jehovah, Servant of.
  xx Jesus Christ - Name.

SERVERS. See ALTAR BOYS.

SERVICES, DEDICATION. See
  DEDICATION SERVICES.

SERVILE WORK.
        BQT 1887
  "Servile work consists of labour
    that is principally bodily,
    manual or mechanical, its actual

SERVILE WORK -- Continued.
    denotation depending on tradi-
    tional usage and the common
    estimation of men." AT
    x Work, Servile.
    xx Sunday.

SEVEN DOLORS OF MARY. See
    SORROWS OF OUR LADY.

SEVEN GIFTS OF THE HOLY SPIRIT. See
    GIFTS OF THE HOLY SPIRIT.

SEVEN LAST WORDS. See
    JESUS CHRIST - SEVEN LAST WORDS.

SEVEN REDUCTIONS, WAR OF THE,
    1754-1756.
    x Jesuit War, 1754-1756 (South
        America)
      War of the Seven Reductions,
        1754-1756.

SEVEN SLEEPERS OF EPHESUS.
    BQX 269
    x Ephesus, Seven Sleepers of.

SEVEN SORROWS OF OUR LADY. See
    SORROWS OF OUR LADY.

SEVENTH-DAY ADVENTISTS.   (Geog.
    subdiv., Direct)
    BX 6150-6154
    References as in LC.

SEVENTH-DAY ADVENTISTS, NEGRO.
    References as in LC.

SEVENTH-DAY BAPTISTS.   (Geog.
    subdiv., Direct)

SEX AND RELIGION.
    HQ 61
    References as in LC.

SEX INSTRUCTION.
    BQT 1934
    HQ 56
    References as in LC.

SEXTONS.
    sa Sacristans.
    xx Sacristans.
    Cf. note under Sacristans.
  x Sexual abuse
SEXUAL ETHICS.
    HQ 31
    BQT 1932-1938 (Moral
        theology)   (24x1.64)
    References as in LC.

SHABBATHAIANS. See
    SABBATHAIANS.

SHABU'OTH. See
    SHAVU'OTH (FEAST OF WEEKS)

SHAKERS.
    BX 9751-9793   (289.8)
    Subdivisions as in LC.

SHAMANISM.
    BL 2370.S
    References as in LC.

SHAVU'OTH (FEAST OF WEEKS)
    BM 695.S
    sa Sefirah period.
    x Feast of weeks.
      Jewish Pentecost.
      Shabu'oth.
      Shevuoth.
    xx Pentecost festival.
      Three festivals.

SHEVUOTH. See
    SHAVU'OTH (FEAST OF WEEKS)

SHIITES.
    BP 195.S   (297)
    xx Mohammedan sects.

SHIN (SECT)
    BL 1442.S
    xx Buddhist sects.

SHINTO.
    BL 2220   (299.56)
    References as in LC.

SHINTO PRAYERS.
    x Norito.
      Prayers, Shinto.

400

SHINTO SHRINES.
        BL 2211.S

SHIP MODELS (CHURCH DECORATION)
    xx Christian art.
        Church decoration and ornament.

SHORT STORIES, CATHOLIC.
    x Catholic short stories.
        Stories, Catholic.
    xx Catholic fiction.
        Catholic literature.

SHRINES.   (Geog. subdiv., Direct)
        BQT 4525-4526
        BQX 70
    sa Martyria.
        Mary, Blessed Virgin - Shrines.
        Miracles.
        Pilgrims and pilgrimages.
        Relics and reliquaries.
        Saints - Cultus.
        Tombs.
    xx Cultus.
        Miracles.
        Pilgrims and pilgrimages.
        Relics and reliquaries.
        Saints.

SHRINES, BUDDHIST. See
    BUDDHIST SHRINES.

SHRINES, JAINA. See
    JAINA SHRINES.

SHROUD, HOLY. See
    HOLY SHROUD.

SHROVETIDE.
        GT 4995
    x Fastnacht.
    xx Carnival.
        Lent.

SICK.
    Classifications and references
        as in LC.

SICK - DEVOTIONAL LITERATURE.

SICK - MEDITATIONS.
        BQT 2573

SICK - PRAYER-BOOKS.
        BQT 2648
    sa Prayers for the sick.

SICK (CANON LAW)

SICK, CHURCH WORK WITH THE. See
    CHURCH WORK WITH THE SICK.
        Ministry to the Sick

SICK, PRAYERS FOR THE. See
    PRAYERS FOR THE SICK.

SICK-CALLS.
        BQT 2935; BQT 4455   (25x5)
    xx Church work with the sick.
        Pastoral theology.

SIGN OF THE CROSS. See
    CROSS, SIGN OF THE.

SIGNATURA APOSTOLICA.
        BQV230 259
        BQV 79-82 (Documents)
    x Apostolic Signatura.

SIKHS.
    Classifications and references
        as in LC.

SILENCE.
        BQT 1793

SILENCE - MEDITATIONS.
        [BQT 2610.5]

SILENCE (CANON LAW)
    xx Consent (Canon law)
        Declaration of intention
        (Canon law)

SIMEON, CANTICLE OF. See
    NUNC DIMITTIS.

SIMHAT TORAH.
        BM 695.S
    References as in LC.

SIMONY.
        BQX 503 (Church history)
        BQT 1866 (Moral theology)
        (24x1.61)
    xx Offenses against religion.

SIMPLICITY.
BQT 1793

SIMULATION (CANON LAW)
sa Dolus (Canon law)
xx Contracts (Canon law)
Declaration of intention
(Canon law)

SIMULTANEUM. (Geog. subdiv.,
Direct)
"Here are entered works on the
simultaneous use of churches,
schools, cemeteries, etc., in
Europe for the exercise of
religion by congregations of
differing creed. It is not to
be equated with the American
federated church where joint
worship is involved." LC
References as in LC.

SIN.
BQT 1803-1816   (24x1.4)
sa Atonement.
Fall of man.
Free will and determinism.
Guilt.
Repentance.
Satisfaction.
Temptation.
Vice.
xx Confession.
Dogmatic theology.
Good and evil.
Guilt.
Human acts.
Man (Theology)
Moral theology.
Salvation.

SIN - BIBLICAL TEACHING.

SIN - HISTORY OF DOCTRINES.

SIN - HISTORY OF DOCTRINES -
EARLY CHURCH.

SIN - HISTORY OF DOCTRINES -
MIDDLE AGES.

SIN - HISTORY OF DOCTRINES -
MODERN PERIOD.

SIN - HISTORY OF DOCTRINES -
16th, [17th, etc.] CENTURY.

SIN - JEWISH INTERPRETATION.
xx Judaism.

SIN - MEDITATIONS.

SIN - PSYCHOLOGY.

SIN - SERMONS.
BQT 3089

SIN (ASSYRO-BABYLONIAN RELIGION)
xx Assyro-Babylonian religion.

SIN, FORGIVENESS OF. See
FORGIVENESS OF SIN.

SIN, MORTAL.
BQT 1807   (24x1.41)
x Mortal sin.

SIN, MORTAL - SERMONS.
BQT 3089

SIN, OCCASIONS FOR. See
OCCASIONS FOR SIN.

SIN, ORIGINAL.
BQT 641-643   (231.x72)
sa Concupiscence.
Fall of man.
x Original sin.
xx Fall of man.
Justice, Original.

SIN, ORIGINAL - HISTORY OF DOCTRINES.

SIN, VENIAL.
BQT 1809   (24x1.41)
x Venial sin.

SIN AGAINST THE HOLY SPIRIT.
BQT 1816
x Sin, Unpardonable.
Unpardonable sin.

SINAI REVELATION. See
REVELATION ON SINAI.

402

SINGLE PEOPLE - RELIGIOUS LIFE.
      BQT 2273

SINGLE PEOPLE, CHURCH WORK WITH. See
   CHURCH WORK WITH SINGLE PEOPLE.

SINLESSNESS OF CHRIST. See
   JESUS CHRIST - SINLESSNESS.

SINLESSNESS OF OUR LADY. See
   MARY, BLESSED VIRGIN - SINLESSNESS.

SINS, CAPITAL. See
   CAPITAL SINS.

SINS, DEADLY. See
   CAPITAL SINS.

SIRACH, BOOK OF. See
   BIBLE. O.T. ECCLESIASTICUS.

SISTERHOODS. See
   RELIGIOUS ORDERS OF WOMEN.
   See also note under Religious
      orders of women.

SISTERS. See
   RELIGIOUS LIFE FOR WOMEN.
   RELIGIOUS ORDERS OF WOMEN.

SISTERS OF CHARITY.
      BQX 7849-7877
   x Charity, Sisters of.

SISTERS OF ST. CLARE. See
   POOR CLARES.

SISTERS OF ST. JOSEPH.
      BQX 7953-7965
   x St. Joseph, Sisters of.

SISTERS OF THE ORDER OF ST.
   BENEDICT. See
   BENEDICTINE SISTERS.

SISTERS OF THE ORDER OF ST.
   DOMINIC. See
   DOMINICAN SISTERS.

SITTING (POSTURE IN WORSHIP) See
   POSTURE IN WORSHIP.

SKEPTICISM.
   Classifications and references
      as in LC.

SKOPTSI.
      [BQX 6157]
      BX 9798
   sa Khlysty.
   xx Sects, Russian.

SLANDER.
      BJ 1535.J (Ethics)   (177.3)
   x Detraction.
      Libel and slander (Ethics)

SLANDER (LAW) See
   LIBEL AND SLANDER.

SLAVERY AND THE CHURCH.
      HT 910-921
      BQX 478 (Church history)
   sa Ransom of captives.
   x Church and slavery.
   xx Church and social problems.

SLAVERY IN THE BIBLE.
      HT 915
   xx Slavery (Jewish law)
      Slavery and slaves in
         literature.

SLAVERY IN THE TALMUD.
   xx Slavery (Jewish law)
      Slavery and slaves in
         literature.

SLAVIC LANGUAGE - LITURGICAL USE.
      See LITURGICAL LANGUAGE - SLAVIC.

SLAVONIC USE.
      BQT 4931-4949
   x Glagolitic liturgy.

SLAVS - CHURCH HISTORY.
      BQX 5764-5796

SLOTH.
      BQT 1813
   xx Capital sins.

SLOVENIAN LANGUAGE (OLD). See
   CHURCH SLAVIC LANGUAGE.

SNAKE-WORSHIP. See
  SERPENT-WORSHIP.

SNAKES (IN RELIGION, FOLK-LORE, ETC.)
  See SERPENTS (IN RELIGION, FOLK-LORE,
  ETC.)

SOCIAL ACTION, CATHOLIC. See
  CATHOLIC SOCIAL ACTION.

SOCIAL ENCYCLICALS. See
  CATHOLIC CHURCH AND SOCIAL
  PROBLEMS - PAPAL TEACHING.

SOCIAL JUSTICE. See
  CATHOLIC CHURCH AND SOCIAL PROBLEMS.
  SOCIOLOGY, CHRISTIAN.
  ↳Social Problems
SOCIAL PROBLEMS - SERMONS.

SOCIAL PROBLEMS AND BUDDHISM. See
  BUDDHISM AND SOCIAL PROBLEMS.

SOCIAL PROBLEMS AND JUDAISM. See
  JUDAISM AND SOCIAL PROBLEMS.

SOCIAL PROBLEMS AND THE CHURCH. See
  CHURCH AND SOCIAL PROBLEMS.

SOCIAL SERVICE, CATHOLIC.
      BQT 3403-3653
  Protestant literature on welfare
    work is entered under Church
    work. Cf. note under that
    heading.
  sa Catholic Church - Charities.
    Catholic Church and social
      problems.
    Hospitallers.
    Missions
   x Catholic social service.
    Social work, Catholic.
  xx Catholic Church - Charities.
    Charity.
    Pastoral theology.

SOCIAL SURVEYS.
  xx Sociology, Religious.
  Other references as in LC.
  ↳Social Theology   x 261
SOCIAL WORK, CATHOLIC. See   x Theology, Social
  SOCIAL SERVICE, CATHOLIC.

SOCIALISM, CHRISTIAN.
      HX 51-54   (335.7)
      BQT 3445
  sa Christianity and economics.
    Church and social problems.
   x Christian socialism.
  xx Christian democracy.
    Christianity.
    Christianity and economics.
    Church and social problems.

SOCIALISM AND CATHOLIC CHURCH.
      HX 536   (335.7)
      BQT 3445
  sa Communism and Catholic Church.
    Communism and religion.
   x Catholic Church and socialism.
  xx Communism and religion.

SOCIALISM AND JUDAISM.
   x Judaism and socialism.

SOCIALISM AND RELIGION.
  sa Christianity and economics.

SOCIETAS JESU. See JESUITS.

SOCIETIES, CATHOLIC. See
  CATHOLIC SOCIETIES.

SOCIETIES, CHURCH. See
  CHURCH SOCIETIES.

SOCIETIES, CONDEMNED. See
  CONDEMNED SOCIETIES.

SOCIETIES, FORBIDDEN. See
  CONDEMNED SOCIETIES.

SOCIETIES, RELIGIOUS. See
  CONFRATERNITIES.
  RELIGIOUS ORDERS.

SOCIETIES LIVING IN COMMON WITHOUT
  VOWS. See
  QUASI-RELIGIOUS SOCIETIES.

SOCIETY OF JESUS. See JESUITS.

SOCINIANISM.
      BQT 583; BQT 1146   (273.x7)
  sa Arianism.
    Jesus Christ - Divinity.

404

SOCINIANISM -- Continued.
 sa Trinity.
    Unitarianism.
 xx Arianism.
    Jesus Christ - Divinity.
    Trinity.
    Unitarianism.

SOCIOLOGY, BIBLICAL.
    BS 670
    "Here are entered works on social
    ideas, institutions, and teach-
    ings of the Bible as distinct
    from the social ideas, institu-
    tions and teachings developed
    by post-Biblical Judaism and
    Christianity." LC
 sa Bible - Economics.
    Bible - Ethics.
    Sociology, Christian.
    Sociology, Jewish.
  x Bible - Sociology.
    Sociology, Christian - Biblical
       teaching.
 xx Bible - Ethics.
    Sociology, Christian.
    Sociology, Jewish.

SOCIOLOGY, CHRISTIAN.   (Geog. sub-
    div., Indirect)
       BQT 3403-3653
    "Here are entered works on social
    theory from a Christian point of
    view. The relationship of this
    heading to Church and social
    problems is that of abstract to
    concrete, of theory to practice,
    and works to which these headings
    are appropriate are classified
    respectively in theology or
    social reform. Works covering
    both aspects are entered under
    the one heading which more
    nearly expresses the primary
    interest of the work." LC
 sa Catholic action.
    Catholic Church and social
       problems.
    Catholic social action.
    Christianity and economics.
    Church and industry.
    Church and social problems.

SOCIOLOGY, CHRISTIAN -- Continued.
 sa Social ethics.
    Sociology, Biblical.
    Sociology, Religious.
    Sociology, Rural (Catholic)
    Wealth, Ethics.
  x Christian sociology.
    Social justice.
    Sociology, Christian - Modern
       period.
 xx Christianity and economics.
    Social ethics.
    Social problems.
    Sociology, Biblical.

SOCIOLOGY, CHRISTIAN - BIBLICAL
    TEACHING. See
    SOCIOLOGY, BIBLICAL.

SOCIOLOGY, CHRISTIAN - CATECHISMS,
    QUESTION-BOOKS.

SOCIOLOGY, CHRISTIAN - COLLECTIONS.
    BQT 3405

SOCIOLOGY, CHRISTIAN - CONGRESSES.
    [BQT 3404]

SOCIOLOGY, CHRISTIAN - HISTORY.

SOCIOLOGY, CHRISTIAN - PAPAL
    TEACHING.
    [BQT 3415.3]

SOCIOLOGY, CHRISTIAN - PERIODICALS.
    BQT 3403

SOCIOLOGY, CHRISTIAN - SERMONS.

SOCIOLOGY, CHRISTIAN - SOCIETIES.
    BQT 3516

SOCIOLOGY, CHRISTIAN - YEARBOOKS.

      ################

SOCIOLOGY, CHRISTIAN - EARLY PERIOD.

SOCIOLOGY, CHRISTIAN - MIDDLE AGES.

SOCIOLOGY, CHRISTIAN - MODERN PERIOD.
    See SOCIOLOGY, CHRISTIAN.

      ################

SOCIOLOGY, RELIGIOUS.   (Geog.
  subdiv., Indirect)
        BL 60
  sa Religion and sociology.
     Religious surveys.
     Social surveys.
   x Religious sociology.
  xx Pastoral theology.
     Sociology, Christian.

SOCIOLOGY, RURAL (CATHOLIC)
        BQT 3447
   x Catholic Church and rural
       sociology.
     Catholic rural life.
     Rural life, Catholic.
  xx Catholic Church and social
       problems.
     Sociology, Christian.

SOCIOLOGY AND LITURGY. See
  LITURGY AND SOCIOLOGY.

SOCIOLOGY AND RELIGION. See
  RELIGION AND SOCIOLOGY.

SODALITIES. See
  CONFRATERNITIES.

SODOMY.   (Geog. subdiv., Direct)
        HQ 79
        BQT 1937 (Moral theology)
  References as in LC.

SOLDIERS - PRAYER-BOOKS.
  xx Armed forces - Prayer-books.

SOLDIERS - RELIGIOUS LIFE.
        BQT 2289
  xx Armed forces - Religious life.

SOLEMN LEAGUE AND COVENANT.
   x Covenants (Church history)

SOLICITATION (CANON LAW)
        BQV230 904
  xx Confessors (Canon law)
     Seduction (Canon law)

SOLOMON, SONG OF. See
  BIBLE. O.T. CANTICLE OF
  CANTICLES.

SOLOMON, WISDOM OF. See
  BIBLE. O.T. WISDOM.

SON OF MAN.
  xx Jesus Christ - Name.

SONG OF SOLOMON. See
  BIBLE. O.T. CANTICLE OF
  CANTICLES.

SONG OF THE THREE CHILDREN. See
  BIBLE. O.T. DANIEL. chap. III,
  57-90

SONG-BOOKS, CATHOLIC.
  sa School song-books, Catholic.
   x Catholic song-books.

SONG-BOOKS, SUNDAY-SCHOOL. See
  SUNDAY-SCHOOLS - HYMNS.

SONGS - MORAL ASPECTS. See
  MUSIC AND MORALS.

SONGS OF DEGREES. See
  BIBLE. O.T. PSALMS, GRADUAL.

SONS OF GOD.
        BS 1238

SOPHONIAS, BOOK OF. See
  BIBLE. O.T. SOPHONIAS.

SORORES ORDINIS SANCTI BENEDICTI.
  See BENEDICTINE SISTERS.

SORROW.
        BJ 1487
   x Grief.
  xx Suffering.

SORROW FOR SIN. See
  CONTRITION.

SORROWS OF OUR LADY.
   x Dolors of Our Lady.
     Mary, Blessed Virgin - Dolors.
     Mary, Blessed Virgin - Sorrows.
     Seven dolors of Mary.
     Seven sorrows of Our Lady.

SORROWS OF OUR LADY - DEVOTIONAL
  LITERATURE.

SORROWS OF OUR LADY - MEDITATIONS.
    BQT 2598

SORROWS OF OUR LADY - PRAYER-BOOKS.
    BQT 2679

SORROWS OF OUR LADY - SERMONS.
    BQT 3060

SORROWS OF OUR LADY, FEAST OF THE.
    BQT 4230
    x Feast of the Seven Dolors of
        Mary.

SORROWS OF OUR LADY, MASS OF THE.
    See MISSA SEPTEM DOLORUM BEATAE
    MARIAE VIRGINIS.

SOTERIOLOGY. See
    REDEMPTION.
    SALVATION.

SOUL.
        BL 290 (Comparative religion)
        (291.x22)
        BQT 625-629 (Dogmatic theol-
            ogy) (231.x73)
        BD 420-428 (Philosophy)
    sa Animism.
        Future life.
        Immortality.
        Personality.
        Pre-existence.
        Psychology.
        Reincarnation.
        Spirit.
        Spiritual life.
        Transmigration.
    xx Animism.
        Future life.
        Immortality.
        Man (Theology)
        Personality.
        Philosophy.
        Spirit.
        Spirituality.

SOUL - SERMONS.
    BQT 3089

SOUL - THEOLOGY.

SOUL OF CHRIST (PRAYER). See
    ANIMA CHRISTI.

SOUTH AMERICA - CHURCH HISTORY.
    BQX 4701-4931   (278)

SOUTH AMERICA - CHURCH HISTORY -
    EARLY PERIOD TO 1800.

SOUTH AMERICA - CHURCH HISTORY -
    1801-

SOUTH AMERICA - CHURCH HISTORY -
    20th CENTURY.

SOVEREIGN MILITARY ORDER OF ST.
    JOHN OF JERUSALEM. See
    KNIGHTS OF MALTA.

THE SOWER (PARABLE)
    BQT 888   (226.x6)

SPAIN - CHURCH HISTORY.
    BQX 2871-2991   (274.6)

SPAIN - CHURCH HISTORY - EARLY
    PERIOD TO 711.

SPAIN - CHURCH HISTORY - 711-1469.

SPAIN - CHURCH HISTORY - 1469-1665.

SPAIN - CHURCH HISTORY - 1665-

SPAIN - CHURCH HISTORY - 19th
    CENTURY.

SPAIN - CHURCH HISTORY - 20th
    CENTURY.

SPAIN - RELIGION.
    BR 1023
    BQX 2891

SPANISH INQUISITION. See
    INQUISITION - SPAIN.

SPANISH MISSIONS OF CALIFORNIA.
    BQX 4378 (History)
    BQT 5985-5986 (Church
        architecture)
    "Here is entered literature deal-
        ing chiefly with the old Span-

SPANISH MISSIONS OF CALIFORNIA --
Continued.
ish mission buildings of California. For material of organized missionary activities
in California see Missions -
California." LC
xx Missions.

SPANISH MISSIONS OF GEORGIA.
xx Missions.

SPANISH MISSIONS OF NEW MEXICO.
xx Missions.

SPANISH MISSIONS OF TEXAS.
xx Missions.

SPANISH MISSIONS OF THE U.S.
xx Missions.

SPANISH RITE. See
MOZARABIC RITE.

SPANISH SAINTS. See
SAINTS, SPANISH.

SPEAKING WITH TONGUES. See
GLOSSOLALIA.

SPEECHES, ADDRESSES, ETC., CATHOLIC.
See CATHOLIC SPEECHES, ADDRESSES,
ETC.

SPINSTERS - RELIGIOUS LIFE.
BQT 2273

SPIRES, DIET OF, 1526.
x Diet of Spires, 1526.

SPIRIT.
sa Consciousness.
Mind and body.
Pneumatology (Theology)
Soul.
Spirits.
Spiritualism.
xx Soul.
Spirits.
Spiritualism.

SPIRIT, HOLY. See HOLY SPIRIT.

SPIRITISM. See SPIRITUALISM.

SPIRITS.
sa Angels.
Apparitions.
Demonology.
Ghosts.
Mediums.
Spirit.
Spiritualism.
Witchcraft.

SPIRITS, DISCERNMENT OF. See
DISCERNMENT OF SPIRITS.

SPIRITUAL COMMUNION. See
COMMUNION, SPIRITUAL.

SPIRITUAL DIRECTION.
BQT 2236   (24x8.1)
sa Conscience, Manifestation of.
Scruples.
x Direction, Spiritual.
xx Perfection, Christian.

SPIRITUAL DIRECTORS.
"Here are entered works dealing
with the officials in charge
of the spiritual life in monastic and other ecclesiastical
institutions and organizations."
LC
x Directors, Spiritual.
xx Clergy.
Confessors.
Spiritual life.

SPIRITUAL DIRECTORS (CANON LAW)
BQV230 588
BQV230 1358
xx Religious orders (Canon law)
Theological seminaries (Canon
law)

SPIRITUAL EXERCISES. See
RETREATS.

SPIRITUAL EXERCISES OF ST. IGNATIUS.
See IGNATIUS LOYOLA, SAINT. EXER-
CITIA SPIRITUALIA.

SPIRITUAL LIFE.
BQT 2102-2497   (24x7-24x9)
Here are entered works on the
supernatural or inner life, also
called the life of the soul,
which brings men closer to God.
sa Asceticism.
   Christian life.
   Devotional literature.
   Faith.
   Liturgical life.
   Mixed life.
   Mysticism.
   Perfection, Christian.
   Retreats.
   Sanctification.
   Spiritual directors.
   Spirituality.
 x Life, Spiritual.
xx Asceticism.
   Christian life.
   Conduct of life.
   Grace (Theology)
   Mysticism.
   Religion.
   Soul.
   Spirituality.
   Virtue.
   Virtues, Infused.

SPIRITUAL LIFE - ADDRESSES,
SERMONS, ETC.

SPIRITUAL LIFE - BIBLICAL TEACHING.
BQT 2164

SPIRITUAL LIFE - CATECHISMS,
QUESTION-BOOKS.
sa Asceticism - Catechisms,
   question-books.
   Mysticism - Catechisms,
   question-books.

SPIRITUAL LIFE - POETRY.

SPIRITUAL LIFE - POPULAR WORKS.
BQT 2188

SPIRITUAL READING. See
DEVOTIONAL LITERATURE.

SPIRITUAL WORKS OF MERCY.
BQT 2393-2396
 x Works of mercy, Spiritual.
xx Good works (Theology)

SPIRITUALISM.
BQT 1866 (Moral theology)
Other classifications and
references as in LC.

SPIRITUALITY.
Here are entered works dealing
with spiritual values or
spiritual-mindedness in the
broad sense, as opposed, namely,
to materialism or secularism
in religion, philosophy,
literature, and the arts.
sa Recollection (Spiritual)
   Soul.
   Spiritual life.
xx Materialism (Theology)
   Secularism.
   Spiritual life.

SPOLIATION (CANON LAW)
xx Church property (Canon law)

SPONSORS.
 x Godfathers.
   Godmothers.
xx Baptism.

SPOUSES. See
HUSBAND AND WIFE.

STABAT MATER.
BQT 4314

STABAT MATER (MUSIC)
BQT 4682
M 2079.L82

STAFF, PASTORAL.
BQT 5846
 x Crosier.
   Crozier.
xx Bishops.
   Christian antiquities.
   Christian art.
   Church vestments.

STALLS, CHOIR. See
  CHOIR-STALLS.

STANDING (POSTURE IN WORSHIP) See
  POSTURE IN WORSHIP.

STAR OF THE SEA.
      BQT 2698
    x Stella maris.
    xx Mary, Blessed Virgin - Titles.

STARS (IN RELIGION, FOLK-LORE, ETC.)

STATE AND CHURCH. See
  CHURCH AND STATE.

STATE AND MORALS.
      JC 516
    x Moral and the State.

STATE AND RELIGION. See
  RELIGION AND STATE.

STATE OF PERFECTION.
  "A technical term in canon law,
    denoting that the Church
    officially recognizes certain
    modes of life as stable condi-
    tions in which perfection is
    either acquired or presupposed ...
    Two states of perfection are
    definitely admitted: the religious
    life and the episcopal office."
    AT
  sa Episcopacy.
     Religious life.
    x Perfection, State of.
    xx Perfection, Christian.

STATES OF THE CHURCH. See
  PAPAL STATES.

STATIONS, ROMAN.
      BQT 4157
    x Roman stations.
    xx Fast days.
       Lent.

STATIONS OF THE CROSS.
      BQT 4489 (Devotions)
        (24x8.71)
    x Cross, Stations of the.
       Way of the Cross.
    xx Devotions, Popular.

STATIONS OF THE CROSS - ART.
      BQT 5959

STATIONS OF THE CROSS - DEVOTIONAL
  LITERATURE.

STATIONS OF THE CROSS - DRAMA.

STATIONS OF THE CROSS - HISTORY.

STATIONS OF THE CROSS - MEDITATIONS.
  [BQT 2587.5]

STATIONS OF THE CROSS - POETRY.

STATIONS OF THE CROSS - SERMONS.
      BQT 3089

STATIONS OF THE CROSS, ENGLISH,
  [FRENCH, GERMAN, ETC.]

STATISTICS, CHURCH. See
  CHURCH STATISTICS.

STATUES.
  References as in LC.

STATUS NATURAE PURAE. See
  PURE NATURE.

STEALING.
      BQT 1945
    x Theft.
  Other references as in LC.

STELLA MARIS. See
  STAR OF THE SEA.

STERILIZATION, SEXUAL - MORAL
  ASPECTS.
      BQT 1910

STEWARDSHIP, CHRISTIAN.

STEWARDSHIP, CHRISTIAN - BIBLICAL
  TEACHING.

STIGMATISTS.

STIGMATIZATION.
      BQT 2485   (24x9.3)
    xx Miracles.
       Mysticism.
       Psychology, Religious.
       Saints.

STIPENDS, MASS. See
MASS STIPENDS.

STOLE FEES. See
FEES, ECCLESIASTICAL.

STORIES, BIBLE. See
BIBLE STORIES.

STORIES, CATECHISM. See
CATECHISM STORIES.

STORIES, CATHOLIC. See
CATHOLIC FICTION.
SHORT STORIES, CATHOLIC.

STORIES, FIRST COMMUNION. See
FIRST COMMUNION STORIES.

STORY-TELLING - RELIGION.
BQT 3150
sa Bible stories.
Catechism stories.
x Religion - Story-telling.

STRIKES AND LOCKOUTS - MORAL
ASPECTS.
BQT 1948

STUDENTS - HYMNALS.
BQT 4683-4689

STUDENTS - PRAYER-BOOKS.
BQT 2648

STUDENTS - RELIGIOUS LIFE.
BQT 3652-3653

STUDENTS - SERMONS.
BQT 3019
xx Universities and colleges -
Sermons.

STUDENTS, CATHOLIC. (Geog.
subdiv., Direct)
x Catholic students.
xx Catholic education.

STUDENTS, CHURCH WORK WITH. See
CHURCH WORK WITH STUDENTS.

STUDY CLUBS, RELIGIOUS. See
RELIGIOUS EDUCATION - STUDY CLUBS.

STUNDISTS.
[BQX 6157]
xx Sects, Russian.

STYLITES.
x Pillar Saints.
Saints, Pillar.
Sancti Columnares.

SUBDEACONS.
BQT 356; BQT 1417   (23x7.6)
sa Major orders.
Ordination.
xx Major orders.

SUBJECT HEADINGS - CATHOLIC
LITERATURE.
x Catholic literature - Subject
headings.

SUBJECT HEADINGS - THEOLOGY.
Z 695.1   (025.3)
x Theology - Subject headings.

SUBSISTENCE (PHILOSOPHY) See
HYPOSTASIS.

SUBURBAN CHURCHES.
BV 637.7
BQT 3359
sa City churches.
Rural churches.
x Churches, Suburban.
xx Church work.
City churches.
Rural churches.

✓ SUFFERING.
BQT 568; BQT 2223
sa Good and evil.
Joy.
Martyrdom.
Pain.
Sorrow.
xx Good and evil.

SUFFERING - BIBLICAL TEACHING.

SUFFERING - DEVOTIONAL LITERATURE.

SUFFERING - EARLY WORKS TO 1800.

SUFFERING - MEDITATIONS.
    [BQT 2610.5]

SUFFERING - SERMONS.
    BQT 3089

SUFFERING (JUDAISM)

SUFFERING, MYSTIC.
    BQT 2485
  sa Victim souls.
  x Mystic suffering.

SUICIDE.
    BV 6543-6548
    RA 1136 (Medical jurisprudence)
    BQT 1904 (Moral theology)
  Subdivisions as in LC.

SUKKOTH.
  x Feast of Tabernacles.
    Tabernacles, Feast of.
  xx Three Festivals.

SUMMARY PROCEEDINGS (CANON LAW)

SUMMONS (CANON LAW)
    BQV 1711
  xx Civil procedure (Canon law)

SUNDAY.
    BQT 4214 (Liturgy)   (264.x1)
    BQT 1882-1887 (Moral
      theology)   (24x1.61)
  sa Sabbath.
    Servile work.
    Sunday-legislation.
  x Lord's Day.
  xx Sabbath.
    Sunday-legislation.

SUNDAY EVENING SERVICES.
  x Sunday night services.
  xx Public worship.

SUNDAY-LEGISLATION.   (Geog.
  subdiv., Indirect)
  Classifications and references
    as in LC.

SUNDAY NIGHT SERVICES. See
  SUNDAY EVENING SERVICES.

SUNDAY-SCHOOL CONVENTIONS.
  References as in LC supple-
    ment 1956-58.

SUNDAY-SCHOOL INSTITUTES.
  References as in LC supple-
    ment 1956-58.

SUNDAY-SCHOOL LIBRARIES. See
  LIBRARIES, SUNDAY-SCHOOL.

SUNDAY-SCHOOL LITERATURE.
  Classifications and references
    as in LC.

SUNDAY-SCHOOL VISITATIONS. See
  VISITATIONS (RELIGIOUS EDUCATION)

SUNDAY-SCHOOLS.
    BQT 3125   (258)
  sa Bible - Study.
    Sunday-school literature.
  xx Church work.
    Religious education.
    Schools.

SUNDAY-SCHOOLS - DIRECTORIES.

SUNDAY-SCHOOLS - EXERCISES,
  RECITATIONS, ETC.

SUNDAY-SCHOOLS - HYMNS.
  x Music - Sunday-schools.
    Song-books, Sunday-school.
    Sunday-schools - Music.
  xx Children's songs.
    Hymns.

SUNDAY-SCHOOLS - MANUALS,
  TEXTBOOKS, ETC.
  xx Religious education -
    Textbooks.

SUNDAY-SCHOOLS - MUSIC. See
  SUNDAY-SCHOOLS - HYMNS.

SUNDAY-SCHOOLS - PERIODICALS.

SUNDAY-SCHOOLS - PRAYERS.

411

SUNDAY-SCHOOLS - QUESTION-BOOKS.
   sa Bible - Catechisms, question-
       books.
      Catechisms.
   xx Bible - Catechisms, question-
       books.
      Bible - Study - Textbooks.

SUNDAY-SCHOOLS - RECORDS.

SUNDAY-SCHOOLS - SOCIETIES, ETC.

SUN-WORSHIP.
   References as in LC.

SUPER-EGO.
   xx Conscience.
   Other references as in LC.

SUPERIORS, RELIGIOUS.
      BQT 2351
   sa Abbesses.
      Abbots.
      Master of novices.
      Mothers general.
      Priors, Claustral.
   x Religious superiors.
   xx Religious life.

SUPERIORS, RELIGIOUS (CANON LAW)
      BQV230 499-517   (348.x37)
   sa Abbesses (Canon law)
      Abbots (Canon law)
      Conscience, Manifestation of
       (Canon law)
      Master of novices (Canon law)
   xx Persons (Canon law)
      Religious orders (Canon law)
      Religious orders of women
       (Canon law)

SUPERNATURAL.
      BF 1001-1999   (133)
      BL 100 (Comparative religion)
       (291.62)
      BQT 556; BQT 620 (Theology)
       (231.x71)
      GR 500 (Folk-lore)   (398.4)
   sa Divination.
      Inspiration.
      Miracles.
      Occult sciences.

SUPERNATURAL -- Continued.
   sa Prophecies.
      Psychical research.
      Revelation.
      Spiritualism.
      Superstition.
   xx Miracles.
      Religion.
      Secularism.

SUPERNATURAL IN LITERATURE.
      PN 56.S
   sa Fantastic fiction.
      Occultism in literature.
      Shakespeare, William -
       Supernatural element.
      Supernatural in moving-pictures.
   xx Fantastic fiction.
      Occultism in literature.

SUPERNATURAL IN MOVING-PICTURES.
      PN 1995.9
   xx Supernatural in literature.

SUPERNATURAL VIRTUES. See
   VIRTUES, INFUSED.

SUPERSTITION.
      BR 135
      BF 1001-1999 (Occult
       sciences)   (133)
      AZ 999 (Popular delusions)
      BQT 1866 (Religion)
       (24x1.61)
   xx Religion (Virtue)
   Other references as in LC.

SUPPER, LAST. See
   LAST SUPPER.

SUPPER, PARABLE OF. See
   GREAT SUPPER (PARABLE)

SUPPRESSION OF RELIGIOUS ORDERS. See
   RELIGIOUS ORDERS - SUPPRESSION.

SUPPRESSION OF THE JESUITS. See
   JESUITS - SUPPRESSION.

SUPREMACY OF THE POPE. See
   POPES - PRIMACY.

SURNAMES. See
    NAMES, PERSONAL.

SURVEYS, RELIGIOUS. See
    RELIGIOUS SURVEYS.

SUSANNA, HISTORY OF. See
    BIBLE. O.T. DANIEL. chap. XIII.

SUSPENSION (CANON LAW)
        BQV230 2278-2285   (348.x6)
    xx Censures, Ecclesiastical.
        Clergy (Canon law)

SWEARING.
        BJ 1535.P   (179.5)
        GT 3080 (Manners and customs)
        BQT 1874 (Moral theology)
            (24x1.61)
    "Here are entered works on profane
    language. Works on judicial or
    official oaths are entered under
    Oaths. Works on blasphemy in
    the legal and theological sense,
    'maliciously reviling God or
    religion' are entered under
    Blasphemy." LC
    x Cursing.

SWEDEN - CHURCH HISTORY.
        BQX 3001-3019   (274.85)

SWEDEN - CHURCH HISTORY - EARLY
    PERIOD TO 1527.

SWEDEN - CHURCH HISTORY - 1528-

SWEDEN - CHURCH HISTORY - 20th
    CENTURY.

SWEDEN - RELIGION.
        BR 1013
        BQX 3017

SWEDENBORGIANISM. See
    NEW JERUSALEM CHURCH.

SWITZERLAND - CHURCH HISTORY.
        BQX 3021-3049

SWITZERLAND - CHURCH HISTORY -
    EARLY PERIOD TO 1291.

SWITZERLAND - CHURCH HISTORY -
    1292-1522.

SWITZERLAND - CHURCH HISTORY -
    1522-1648.

SWITZERLAND - CHURCH HISTORY -
    1648-

SWITZERLAND - CHURCH HISTORY -
    20th CENTURY.

SWITZERLAND - RELIGION.
        BR 1033
        BQX 3046

SYLVESTRINES.
        BQX 7104
    x Benedictines, Sylvestrine.
    xx Benedictines.

SYMBOLICS. See CREEDS.

SYMBOLICS, COMPARATIVE. See
    CREEDS - COMPARATIVE STUDIES.

SYMBOLISM, CHRISTIAN.
        BQT 5821-5909   (246.x6)
    sa Christian art.
        Orientation (Religion)
        Orientation of churches.
        Saints - Symbolism.
    x Christian symbolism.
    xx Christian art.

SYMBOLS (RELIGION) See
    CREEDS.

SYNAGOGUE ARCHITECTURE.
    Classification and references
        as in LC.

SYNAGOGUE DEDICATION SERMONS.
        BM 744.6
    xx Sermons, Jewish.

SYNAGOGUE MUSIC.
    sa Jews. Liturgy and ritual.
    xx Jews. Liturgy and ritual.
    Other references and subdivisions
        as in LC.

SYNAGOGUE SEATING.
References as in LC supplement 1961.

SYNAGOGUES.
Classifications and references
as in LC.

SYNAXIS.
BQT 4026
"Any gathering together for divine
worship, but particularly that
of the earliest Christians,
whether for the holy eucharist
or for the prayers, praises and
readings from which has developed
the divine office or both
together." AT
xx Worship - History - Early church.

SYNCRETISTIC CONTROVERSY.
BX 8020 (Lutheranism)
References as in LC.

SYNDICALISM, CATHOLIC.
x Catholic syndicalism.
xx Catholic Church and social
problems.
Trade-unions, Catholic.

SYNODS. See
COUNCILS AND SYNODS.

SYNODS, BUDDHIST. See
BUDDHIST COUNCILS AND SYNODS.

SYRIA - CHURCH HISTORY.
BQX 3545-3547

SYRIAC FATHERS OF THE CHURCH. See
FATHERS OF THE CHURCH, SYRIAC.

SYRIAN CHURCH, EAST. See
NESTORIAN CHURCH.

SYRIAN CULTUS. See
CULTUS, SYRIAN.

SYRIAN RITE.

SYRIAN RITE - CANON LAW.
BQV 1181-1187

SYRIAN RITE - HISTORY.
BQX 5601-5609

SYRIAN RITE. LITURGY AND RITUAL.
BQT 5130-5149

SYRIAN RITE, EAST. See
CHALDEAN RITE.

SYRO-CHALDEAN RITE. See
CHALDEAN RITE.

SYRO-MALABAR RITE. See
MALABAR RITE.

SYRO-MARONITE RITE. See
MARONITE RITE.

TABERNACLE.
BM 654 (221.93)
Here are entered works on the
Jewish tabernacle of the
Old Testament.
References as in LC.

TABERNACLES.
BQT 4359 (264.x4)

TABERNACLES, FEAST OF THE. See
SUKKOTH.

TABLE BLESSINGS. See
GRACE AT MEALS.

TABLE PRAYERS. See
GRACE AT MEALS.

THE TALENTS (PARABLE)
BQT 888 (226.x6)
x The pounds (Parable)

TALMUD.
BM 500-509 (22x9.2)
References and subdivisions
as in LC.

TALMUD TORAHS.
References as in LC.

TANTRISM.
BL 1480
sa Baptism (Hinduism)

TANTRISM, BUDDHIST.
BL 1495.T

TAOISM.   (Geog. subdiv., Direct)
        BL 1900-1940   (299.51)
    References as in LC.

TAOIST MONASTICISM. See
    MONASTICISM, TAOIST.

THE TARES (PARABLE)

TAXATION, PAPAL.
    x Papal taxation.
    xx Catholic Church - Finance.

TE DEUM.
        BQT 2695
        M 2079.L9

TEACHERS, CATHOLIC.
    sa Catholic education - Lay
        teachers.
        Educators, Catholic.
    x Catholic teachers.
    xx Catholic education.
        Educators, Catholic.

TEACHING OF THE TWELVE APOSTLES.
        BQ 1300-1312   (280.x1)
    x Didache.
        Doctrina apostolorum.

TEACHING ~~OFFICE~~ OF THE CHURCH. See
    CHURCH - TEACHING ~~OFFICE~~. authority

TEACHING RELIGIOUS ORDERS. See
    RELIGIOUS ORDERS, TEACHING.

TEACHINGS OF JESUS. See
    JESUS CHRIST - TEACHINGS.
Teen age see ADOLESENCE
TELEVISION IN RELIGION.
        BQT 3618
    x Religious television.
    xx Church work.
        Television broadcasting.

TEMPERANCE.
        HV 5001-5720   (178)
        BQT 1905 (Moral theology)
        (24x1.52)
    "Here are entered general works
        on the temperance question,
        including books on the temperance

TEMPERANCE -- Continued.
        movement, popular and con-
        troversial works, and fic-
        tion." LC
    sa Alcoholism and religion.
    Other references as in LC.

TEMPERANCE - ADDRESSES, ESSAYS,
    LECTURES.
    x Temperance - Sermons.

TEMPERANCE - BIBLICAL TEACHING.
    x Bible and temperance.
        Temperance in the Bible.

TEMPERANCE - MORAL AND RELIGIOUS
    ASPECTS.
        BQT 1905   (24x1.63)

TEMPERANCE - SERMONS. See
    TEMPERANCE - ADDRESSES, ESSAYS,
    LECTURES.

    Other subdivisions under
    Temperance as in LC.

TEMPERANCE (VIRTUE)
        BQT 1212; BQT 1789   (24x1.52)
    Here are entered works dealing
        with temperance considered in
        a broader meaning, namely, as
        a virtue which enables human
        beings to control their natural
        appetite for any sensual
        pleasure.
    sa Abstinence.
        Chastity.
        Gluttony.
    xx Virtues, Moral.

TEMPERANCE AND RELIGION.
    x Religion and temperance.

TEMPERANCE IN THE BIBLE. See
    TEMPERANCE - BIBLICAL TEACHING.

TEMPLARS.
        CR 4746-4755 (Chivalry)
        BQX 663; BQX 768; BQX 1753;
        BQX 7756 (Church history)
    sa Freemasons.
        Knights Templars.

416

TEMPLARS -- Continued.
   x Knights Templars (Military
      religious order)
  xx Crusades.
    Military religious orders.

TEMPLE OF JERUSALEM. See
  JERUSALEM. TEMPLE.

TEMPLES.   (Geog. subdiv., Indirect)
  Classifications, references, and
    subdivisions as in LC.

TEMPORAL POWER OF BISHOPS. See
  BISHOPS - TEMPORAL POWER.

TEMPORAL POWER OF THE POPE. See
  POPES - TEMPORAL POWER.

TEMPTATION.
     BQT 7805   (24x1.x11)
     BQT 2239 (Asceticism)
  sa Mortification.
    Occasions for sin.
  xx Sin.

TEMPTATION OF CHRIST. See
  JESUS CHRIST - TEMPTATION.

TEN COMMANDMENTS. See
  COMMANDMENTS, TEN.

TEN LOST TRIBES OF ISRAEL. See
  LOST TRIBES OF ISRAEL.

TEN VIRGINS (PARABLE)
     BQT 888   (226.x6)
  x Virgins, Ten (Parable)

TEN VIRGINS (PARABLE) - SERMONS.
     BQT 3089

TENEBRAE.
     BQT 4392   (264.x52)
  "A name given to the special
    matins and lauds of Maundy
    Thursday, Good Friday and
    Holy Saturday." AT
  xx Holy Week.
    Officium Hebdomadae Sanctae.

TENRI (SECT)
  References as in LC.

TERTIARIES. See THIRD ORDERS.

TESTAMENT, NEW. See
  BIBLE. N.T.

TESTAMENT, OLD. See
  BIBLE. O.T.

TESTIMONY (CANON LAW) See
  EVIDENCE (CANON LAW)

TEUTONIC KNIGHTS.
     CR 4759-5775 (Chivalry)
     BQX 663; BQX 7757 (Church
      history)
     DD 491-558 (History)
  x Deutscher Ritter-orden.
    Orden der Ritter des Hospitals
      St. Marien des Deutschenhauses.
    Teutonic Order.

TEUTONIC KNIGHTS. LITURGY AND
  RITUAL.
     BQT 4881-4889

TEUTONIC ORDER. See
  TEUTONIC KNIGHTS.

THANKFULNESS. See GRATITUDE.

THANKSGIVING SERMONS.
  xx Occasional sermons.

THEATER - MORAL AND RELIGIOUS
  ASPECTS.
     PN 2047-2051
  xx Art and morals.
    Religion in literature.

THEATER AND CATHOLIC CHURCH.
  x Catholic Church and theater.

THEATER AND CHURCH. See
  CHURCH AND THEATER.

THEBAN LEGION.
  xx Martyrs - Legends.

THEFT. See STEALING.

417

THEISM.
        BQT 514 (Dogmatic theology)
          (231)
        BL 200 (Natural theology)
          (211)
        BL 2700-2790 (Rationalism)
  sa Atheism.
     Christianity.
     Deism.
     God.
     Ontologism.
     Pantheism.
     Polytheism.
  xx Atheism.
     Christianity.
     Deism.
     God.
     Pantheism.
     Philosophy.
     Rationalism.
     Religion.
     Theology.

THEOCRACY.
        JC 20-89
  sa Kings and rulers (in religion,
     folk-lore, etc.)
     Nationalism and religion.
     War and religion.
  xx Church and state.
     God.
     Nationalism and religion.

THEODICY. See
   GOOD AND EVIL.
   NATURAL THEOLOGY.
   PROVIDENCE, DIVINE.

THEOLOGIANS.
  sa Doctors of the church.
   x Theology - Biography.
  xx Bible - Study - Biography.
     Christian biography.
     Clergy.

THEOLOGIANS, AMERICAN, [FRENCH,
  GERMAN, ETC.]

THEOLOGIANS, CAPUCHIN, [DOMINICAN,
  FRANCISCAN, ETC.]
   x Capuchin, [Dominican, Franciscan,
     etc.] theologians.

THEOLOGICAL ANTHROPOLOGY. See
  MAN (THEOLOGY)

THEOLOGICAL EDUCATION. See
  RELIGIOUS EDUCATION.
  THEOLOGY - STUDY AND TEACHING.
  THEOLOGICAL SEMINARIES.

THEOLOGICAL LIBRARIES.
        BQ 105
        Z 675.T
  sa Libraries, Catholic.
   x Libraries, Seminary.
     Libraries, Theological.
     Seminary libraries.
  xx Libraries, Catholic.

THEOLOGICAL SEMINARIES.   (Geog.
  subdiv., Indirect)
  sa Seminarians.
   x Seminaries, Theological.
     Theological education.
  xx Catholic institutions.
     Church - Teaching office.
     Clergy - Education.
     Corporations, Ecclesiastical.
     Religious education.
     Theology - Study and teaching.

THEOLOGICAL SEMINARIES - CURRICULA.
        BQX 197

THEOLOGICAL SEMINARIES - SERMONS.
  xx Universities and colleges -
     Sermons.

THEOLOGICAL SEMINARIES (CANON LAW)
        BQV230 1352-1371
  sa Spiritual directors (Canon law)

THEOLOGICAL SEMINARIES (CANON LAW,
  ORTHODOX EASTERN)

THEOLOGICAL SEMINARIES, MINOR.
   x Minor seminaries.

THEOLOGICAL SEMINARIES, BAPTIST,
  [LUTHERAN, PRESBYTERIAN, ETC.]
  References as in LC.

THEOLOGICAL VIRTUES. See
  VIRTUES, THEOLOGICAL.

418

THEOLOGY.
    BQT   (230-269)
    "The science which treats of God
      and the things of God." AT
sa Asceticism.
    Atheism.
    Bible.
    Canon law.
    Christianity.
    Deism.
    Dogmatic theology.
    God.
    Liturgy.
    Moral theology.
    Mysticism.
    Natural theology.
    Pastoral theology.
    Religion.
    Sacraments.
    Theism.
    Worship.
xx Christianity.
    God.
    Religion.
    Sacred sciences.

THEOLOGY - ADDRESSES, ESSAYS,
  LECTURES.

THEOLOGY - BIBLIOGRAPHY.
    BQT 2
    Z 7751-7860   (016.23)
    x Dogmatic theology - Bibliography.

THEOLOGY - BIBLIOGRAPHY - BEST
  BOOKS. See
  BIBLIOGRAPHY - BEST BOOKS -
  THEOLOGY.

THEOLOGY - BIOGRAPHY. See
  THEOLOGIANS.

THEOLOGY - CATALOGING. See
  CATALOGING OF THEOLOGY.

THEOLOGY - COLLECTED WORKS.
  Here are entered the collected
    works of individual theologians.
    Cf. note under Catholic Church -
    Collected works.

THEOLOGY - COLLECTED WORKS - EARLY
  CHURCH.
    BQ 1006-6286

THEOLOGY - COLLECTED WORKS - MIDDLE
  AGES.
    BQ 6301-6999

THEOLOGY - COLLECTED WORKS - MODERN
  PERIOD.
    BQ 7003-7499

THEOLOGY - COLLECTED WORKS - 16th
  CENTURY.

THEOLOGY - COLLECTED WORKS - 17th
  CENTURY.

THEOLOGY - COLLECTED WORKS - 18th
  CENTURY.

THEOLOGY - COLLECTED WORKS - 19th
  CENTURY.

THEOLOGY - COLLECTED WORKS - 20th
  CENTURY.

THEOLOGY - COLLECTIONS.
    BQT 184
    BQ 302-379
  Here are entered collections of
    works by several authors cover-
    ing all branches of theology.

THEOLOGY - CONGRESSES.
    [BQT 4]

THEOLOGY - DICTIONARIES.
    BQT 6-7   (203)
  sa Questions and answers -
    Theology.
  x Dogmatic theology - Dictionaries.

THEOLOGY - DICTIONARIES - FRENCH,
  [GERMAN, LATIN, ETC.]

THEOLOGY - DISPUTATIONS.
  sa Quaestiones disputatae.
  x Disputations, Theological.

THEOLOGY - HANDBOOKS, MANUALS, ETC.
    BQT 185

THEOLOGY - HISTORY.   (Geog. subdiv.)
     BQT 31-137
  sa Heresies and heretics.

THEOLOGY - HISTORY - BIBLIOGRAPHY.

THEOLOGY - HISTORY - SOURCES.

     #################

THEOLOGY - HISTORY - EARLY PERIOD.
     BQT 39-77

THEOLOGY - HISTORY - MIDDLE AGES.
     BQT 81-103

THEOLOGY - HISTORY - 12th CENTURY.

THEOLOGY - HISTORY - 13th CENTURY.

THEOLOGY - HISTORY - MODERN PERIOD.
     BQT 108-128

THEOLOGY - HISTORY - 16th CENTURY.

THEOLOGY - HISTORY - 17th CENTURY.

THEOLOGY - HISTORY - 18th CENTURY.

THEOLOGY - HISTORY - 19th CENTURY.

THEOLOGY - HISTORY - 20th CENTURY.

     ################

THEOLOGY - INTRODUCTIONS.
     BQT 11
  x Dogmatic theology - Intro-
    ductions.
    Theology - Propaedeutics.

THEOLOGY - METHODOLOGY.
     BQT 11
  "The method of deriving the truths
   of revelation and the dogmas of
   faith from the loci theologici,
   without proceeding to the refu-
   tation of the adversaries of
   the faith." AT
  sa Apologetics - Methodology.
    Dialectical theology.
    Intuition (Theology)
    Loci theologici.

THEOLOGY - METHODOLOGY -- Continued.
  x Dogmatic theology - Methodology.
    Positive theology.
    Theology, Positive.

THEOLOGY - NATURE.
     BQT 11

THEOLOGY - PERIODICALS.
     BQT 3   (205)
  x Dogmatic theology - Periodicals.

THEOLOGY - POPULAR WORKS.
     BQT 186

THEOLOGY - PROPAEDEUTICS. See
  THEOLOGY - INTRODUCTIONS.

THEOLOGY - QUESTIONS AND ANSWERS.
  See QUESTIONS AND ANSWERS -
  THEOLOGY.

THEOLOGY - RESEARCH.

THEOLOGY - SOCIETIES.

THEOLOGY - SOURCES.
  x Dogmatic theology - Sources.

THEOLOGY - SOURCES, BIBLICAL.
     BQT 207; BQT 251

THEOLOGY - STUDY AND TEACHING.
     BQX 197
  sa Catechetics.
    Church and education.
    Religious education.
    Seminarians.
    Theological seminaries.
  x Theological education.
  xx Church and education.
    Religious education.

THEOLOGY - STUDY AND TEACHING -
  HISTORY.
     [BQT 20]; BQT 137

THEOLOGY - SUBJECT HEADINGS. See
  SUBJECT HEADINGS - THEOLOGY.

THEOLOGY - TERMINOLOGY.

THEOLOGY - TEXTBOOKS.
     BQT 185

420

THEOLOGY - TEXTBOOKS - MIDDLE AGES.

THEOLOGY - TEXTBOOKS - 16th CENTURY.

THEOLOGY - TEXTBOOKS - 17th CENTURY.

THEOLOGY - TEXTBOOKS - 18th CENTURY.

THEOLOGY - TEXTBOOKS - 19th CENTURY.

THEOLOGY - TEXTBOOKS - 20th CENTURY.

THEOLOGY - YEARBOOKS.

################

THEOLOGY - EASTERN CHURCHES. See
    EASTERN CHURCHES - THEOLOGY.

THEOLOGY - LUTHERAN CHURCH. See
    LUTHERAN CHURCH - DOCTRINE.

################

THEOLOGY, ANGLICAN. See
    CHURCH OF ENGLAND - DOCTRINE.

THEOLOGY, ASCETICAL. See
    ASCETICISM.

THEOLOGY, BIBLICAL. See
    BIBLE - THEOLOGY.

THEOLOGY, BIBLICAL (O.T.). See
    BIBLE. O.T. - THEOLOGY.

THEOLOGY, BIBLICAL (N.T.). See
    BIBLE. N.T. - THEOLOGY.

THEOLOGY, COMPARATIVE.
    [BQT 187]
    sa Apologetics - Debates.
       Creeds - Comparative studies.
     x Comparative theology.
    xx Creeds - Comparative studies.

THEOLOGY, COVENANT. See
    COVENANTS (THEOLOGY)

THEOLOGY, CRISIS. See
    DIALECTICAL THEOLOGY.

THEOLOGY, DIALECTICAL. See
    DIALECTICAL THEOLOGY.

THEOLOGY, DISPENSATIONAL. See
    DISPENSATIONALISM.

THEOLOGY, DOCTRINAL. See
    DOGMATIC THEOLOGY.

THEOLOGY, DOGMATIC. See
    DOGMATIC THEOLOGY.

THEOLOGY, FEDERAL. See
    COVENANTS (THEOLOGY)

THEOLOGY, FUNDAMENTAL. See
    APOLOGETICS.

THEOLOGY, JEWISH. See
    JEWISH THEOLOGY.

THEOLOGY, MORAL. See
    MORAL THEOLOGY.

THEOLOGY, MYSTICAL. See
    MYSTICISM.

THEOLOGY, NATURAL. See
    NATURAL THEOLOGY.

THEOLOGY, NEW ENGLAND. See
    NEW ENGLAND THEOLOGY.

THEOLOGY, PASTORAL. See
    PASTORAL THEOLOGY.

THEOLOGY, POSITIVE. See
    THEOLOGY - METHODOLOGY.
    THEOLOGY, PROCESS

THEOLOGY, PROTESTANT. See
    PROTESTANTISM.

THEOLOGY, SCHOLASTIC. See
    NEO-SCHOLASTICISM.
    SCHOLASTICISM.
    Theology, Social see Social Theology

THEOLOGY AND CANON LAW. See
    CANON LAW AND THEOLOGY.

THEOLOGY AND HISTORY.
    BQT 22
  x History and theology.
  xx History - Philosophy.

THEOLOGY AND LITURGY. See
LITURGY AND THEOLOGY.

THEOLOGY AND PHILOSOPHY.
    [BQT 23]
  x Philosophy and theology.
  xx Philosophy and religion.
    Scholasticism.

THEOLOGY AND SCIENCE.
    BQT 26
  x Science and theology.
  xx Religion and science.

Theology of Liberation see Liberation Theology

THEOPHANIES.
    BQT 128
    BQT 517
  sa Apparitions.
    Incarnation.
    Jesus Christ - Appearances.
    Revelation.
    Visions.

THEOSOPHISTS.

THEOSOPHY.
    BP 500-585   (212)
  References and subdivisions
    as in LC.

THERAPEUTICS, SUGGESTIVE.
  sa Pastoral psychology.
  Other references as in LC.

THESSALONIANS, EPISTLES TO THE. See
BIBLE. N.T. THESSALONIANS.

THINGS (CANON LAW)
    BQV230 726-1551
  sa Benefices, Ecclesiastical
    (Canon law)
    Property (Canon law)
    Sacraments (Canon law)
    Sacred places (Canon law)
  x Res (Canon law)
    Sacred things.
  xx Canon law.
    Property (Canon law)

THIRD ORDER SECULAR OF ST. FRANCIS.
  See FRANCISCANS. THIRD ORDER.

THIRD ORDERS.
    BQX 6838
  Third orders are either secular
  or regular. The members of a
  third order secular are laymen
  and women who live in the world
  and pursue the ordinary avoca-
  tions of secular life. They
  constitute a true religious order
  since they complete a novitiate
  and follow a rule. In place of
  vows they make but a solemn
  promise.
  The members of a third order regular leave the world and follow
  their rule under the ordinary
  simple vows of religion in
  community. The latter are
  mainly sisterhoods.
  Individual third orders are entered under their own name if
  they have one (e.g., Sisters of
  the Third Order of St. Francis
  of the Perpetual Adoration),
  otherwise under the name of the
  first order to which they belong,
  with subdivision "Third order"
  (e.g., Dominicans. Third Order).
  A list of third orders can be
  found in the New Catholic Dictionary.
  sa Oblates.
  x Tertiaries.
  xx Christian life.
    Laity.
    Oblates.
    Religious orders.

THIRD ORDERS - BIBLIOGRAPHY.

THIRD ORDERS - DEVOTIONAL LITERATURE.

THIRD ORDERS - SERMONS.

THIRD ORDERS (CANON LAW)
    BQV230 702-706   (24x8.82)
  xx Religious orders (Canon law)

THIRD ORDERS (PROTESTANT)
  x Protestant third orders.

THIRTY-NINE ARTICLES. See
CHURCH OF ENGLAND. ARTICLES OF
RELIGION.

THIRTY-YEARS' WAR, 1618-1648.
D 251-271   (940.24)
xx Counter-Reformation.
Other references as in LC.

THOMAS AQUINAS, SAINT, 1225?-1274.
BQ 6821-6935   (280.x6)
Omit dates when used with
subdivisions.

THOMAS AQUINAS, SAINT - ADDRESSES,
ESSAYS, LECTURES.

THOMAS AQUINAS, SAINT - AESTHETICS.
BQ 6898
x subdivision "Art".

THOMAS AQUINAS, SAINT - ANGELS
(THEOLOGY)
BQ 6911

THOMAS AQUINAS, SAINT - ANNIVER-
SARIES [with date].
BQ 6869

THOMAS AQUINAS, SAINT - ANTHRO-
POLOGY.
BQ 6899.4
xx subdivision "Man (theology")

THOMAS AQUINAS, SAINT - ART. See
THOMAS AQUINAS, SAINT - AESTHETICS.
THOMAS AQUINAS, SAINT, IN ART.

THOMAS AQUINAS, SAINT - ASCETICISM.
BQ 6918

THOMAS AQUINAS, SAINT - ASTRONOMY.
BQ 6899.2

THOMAS AQUINAS, SAINT - AUTHORSHIP.
BQ 6881

THOMAS AQUINAS, SAINT - BIBLICAL
SCHOLARSHIP.
BQ 6919
sa subdivision "Sources - Bible".

THOMAS AQUINAS, SAINT - BIBLIOGRAPHY.
BQ 6867
x subdivision "Editions".

THOMAS AQUINAS, SAINT - BIOGRAPHY.
BQ 6870

THOMAS AQUINAS, SAINT - BIOLOGY.
BQ 6899.4

THOMAS AQUINAS, SAINT - CAUSATION
(METAPHYSICS)
BQ 6891

THOMAS AQUINAS, SAINT - CHARACTER.
BQ 6872
x subdivision "Personality".

THOMAS AQUINAS, SAINT - CHRISTOLOGY.
BQ 6905

THOMAS AQUINAS, SAINT - CHRONOLOGY
OF WORKS.
BQ 6875

THOMAS AQUINAS, SAINT - CHURCH (THE-
ORY). See subdivision "Ecclesiology".

THOMAS AQUINAS, SAINT - CIVILIZATION,
PHILOSOPHY OF. See subdivision
"Philosophy of civilization".

THOMAS AQUINAS, SAINT - CONCORDANCES.
BQ 6879

THOMAS AQUINAS, SAINT - COSMOLOGY.
BQ 6899.3

THOMAS AQUINAS, SAINT - CREATION.
BQ 6906

THOMAS AQUINAS, SAINT - CRITICISM,
TEXTUAL.
BQ 6875-6879

THOMAS AQUINAS, SAINT - CRITICISM
AND INTERPRETATION.
BQ 6867-6935

THOMAS AQUINAS, SAINT - CULTUS.
BQ 6872
sa subdivision "Relics".

THOMAS AQUINAS, SAINT - DEVOTIONAL
  LITERATURE.
      [BQ 6871.5]

THOMAS AQUINAS, SAINT - DICTIONARIES,
  INDEXES, ETC.
      BQ 6879

THOMAS AQUINAS, SAINT - DRAMA.
      [BQ 6874.2]
  xx Thomas Aquinas, Saint, in
      literature.

THOMAS AQUINAS, SAINT - ECCLESIOLOGY.
  x subdivision "Church (theory)".

THOMAS AQUINAS, SAINT - ECONOMICS.
      BQ 6899

THOMAS AQUINAS, SAINT - EDITIONS.
  See subdivision "Bibliography".

THOMAS AQUINAS, SAINT - EDUCATION.
      BQ 6870
  x subdivision "Learning".

THOMAS AQUINAS, SAINT - EDUCATION
  (THEORY)
      BQ 6879
  x subdivision "Pedagogy".

THOMAS AQUINAS, SAINT - EPISTEMOLOGY.
      BQ 6892
  x subdivision "Knowledge, Theory of".

THOMAS AQUINAS, SAINT - ESCHATOLOGY.
      BQ 6915

THOMAS AQUINAS, SAINT - ETHICS.
      BQ 6893
  xx subdivision "Moral theology".

THOMAS AQUINAS, SAINT - EVOLUTION
  THEORY.
      BQ 6899.9

THOMAS AQUINAS, SAINT - FAITH.
      BQ 6914

THOMAS AQUINAS, SAINT - FICTION.
      BQ 6874
  xx Thomas Aquinas, Saint, in
      literature.

THOMAS AQUINAS, SAINT - FREE WILL.
      BQ 6906

THOMAS AQUINAS, SAINT - GOD (THEOLOGY)
      BQ 6904
  sa subdivision "Natural theology".

THOMAS AQUINAS, SAINT - GRACE.
      BQ 6913

THOMAS AQUINAS, SAINT - HISTORY,
  PHILOSOPHY OF. See subdivision
  "Philosophy of history".

THOMAS AQUINAS, SAINT - HOMILETICS.
      BQ 6920

THOMAS AQUINAS, SAINT - ICONOGRAPHY.
      BQ 6873

THOMAS AQUINAS, SAINT - INFLUENCE.
      BQ 6927

THOMAS AQUINAS, SAINT - JURIS-
  PRUDENCE.
      BQ 6899.2

THOMAS AQUINAS, SAINT - JUVENILE
  LITERATURE.
      BQ 6871

THOMAS AQUINAS, SAINT - KNOWLEDGE,
  THEORY OF. See subdivision
  "Epistemology".

THOMAS AQUINAS, SAINT - LANGUAGE,
  STYLE, ETC.
      BQ 6878
  x subdivision "Style".

THOMAS AQUINAS, SAINT - LEARNING.
  See subdivision "Education".

THOMAS AQUINAS, SAINT - LITURGY.
      BQ 6920

THOMAS AQUINAS, SAINT - LOGIC.
      BQ 6894

THOMAS AQUINAS, SAINT - MAN (THE-
  OLOGY)
      BQ 6907
  sa subdivision "Anthropology".

THOMAS AQUINAS, SAINT - MANUSCRIPTS.
    BQ 6821

THOMAS AQUINAS, SAINT - MARIOLOGY.
    BQ 6910

THOMAS AQUINAS, SAINT - MASS (THEORY)
    BQ 6920

THOMAS AQUINAS, SAINT - METAPHYSICS.
    BQ 6891
  x subdivision "Ontology".

THOMAS AQUINAS, SAINT - METHODOLOGY.
    BQ 6881

THOMAS AQUINAS, SAINT - MIRACLES
  (THEORY)
    BQ 6906

THOMAS AQUINAS, SAINT - MORAL
  THEOLOGY.
    BQ 6917
  sa subdivision "Ethics".

THOMAS AQUINAS, SAINT - MYSTICAL
  BODY OF CHRIST.
    BQ 6920

THOMAS AQUINAS, SAINT - MYSTICISM.
    BQ 6918

THOMAS AQUINAS, SAINT - NATURAL LAW.
    BQ 6893

THOMAS AQUINAS, SAINT - NATURAL
  THEOLOGY.
    BQ 6896
  x subdivision "Theodicy".
  xx subdivision "God (theology)".

THOMAS AQUINAS, SAINT - ONTOLOGY.
  See subdivision "Metaphysics".

THOMAS AQUINAS, SAINT - PEACE.
  See subdivision "War and peace".

THOMAS AQUINAS, SAINT - PEDAGOGY.
  See subdivision "Education (theory)".

THOMAS AQUINAS, SAINT - PERIODICALS.
  See subdivision "Societies,
  periodicals, etc."

THOMAS AQUINAS, SAINT - PERSONALITY.
  See subdivision "Character".

THOMAS AQUINAS, SAINT - PHILOSOPHY.
    BQ 6889-6899
  xx Thomism.

THOMAS AQUINAS, SAINT - PHILOSOPHY
  OF CIVILIZATION.
    BQ 6899.2
  x subdivision "Civilization,
    Philosophy of".

THOMAS AQUINAS, SAINT - PHILOSOPHY
  OF HISTORY.
    BQ 6899.9
  x subdivision "History, Philosophy
    of".

THOMAS AQUINAS, SAINT - PHYSICS.
    BQ 6899.3

THOMAS AQUINAS, SAINT - POLITICAL
  SCIENCE.
    BQ 6899.2

THOMAS AQUINAS, SAINT - PRAYER-BOOKS.
    BQT 2603   (24x3.5)

THOMAS AQUINAS, SAINT - PROVIDENCE.
    BQ 6906
  x subdivision "Theodicy".

THOMAS AQUINAS, SAINT - PSYCHOLOGY.
    BQ 6895

THOMAS AQUINAS, SAINT - REDEMPTION.
  See subdivision "Soteriology".

THOMAS AQUINAS, SAINT - RELICS.
    BQ 6872
  xx subdivision "Cultus".

THOMAS AQUINAS, SAINT - RELIGIOUS
  LIFE (THEORY)
    BQ 6920

THOMAS AQUINAS, SAINT - SACRAMENTS.
    BQ 6909

THOMAS AQUINAS, SAINT - SACRAMENTS -
    BAPTISM.

THOMAS AQUINAS, SAINT - SACRAMENTS -
    CONFIRMATION.

THOMAS AQUINAS, SAINT - SACRAMENTS -
    EXTREME UNCTION.

THOMAS AQUINAS, SAINT - SACRAMENTS -
    MARRIAGE.

THOMAS AQUINAS, SAINT - SACRAMENTS -
    ORDINATION.

THOMAS AQUINAS, SAINT - SACRAMENTS -
    PENANCE.

THOMAS AQUINAS, SAINT - SALVATION.
   See subdivision "Soteriology:.

THOMAS AQUINAS, SAINT - SCIENCE.
    BQ 6899.3

THOMAS AQUINAS, SAINT - SECRETARIES.

THOMAS AQUINAS, SAINT - SIN (THEORY)
    BQ 6917

THOMAS AQUINAS, SAINT - SIN, ORIGINAL.
    BQ 6907

THOMAS AQUINAS, SAINT - SLAVERY.
    BQ 6899.2

THOMAS AQUINAS, SAINT - SOCIAL ETHICS.
    BQ 6899

THOMAS AQUINAS, SAINT - SOCIETIES,
   PERIODICALS, ETC.
    BQ 6868-6869
   x subdivision "Periodicals".

THOMAS AQUINAS, SAINT - SOCIOLOGY.
    BQ 6908
   x subdivisions "Redemption" and
    "Salvation".

THOMAS AQUINAS, SAINT - SOUL (THEORY)
    BQ 6895

THOMAS AQUINAS, SAINT - SOURCES.
    BQ 6882-6886

THOMAS AQUINAS, SAINT - SOURCES -
   ARISTOTLE, [PLATO, ST. AUGUSTINE,
   ETC.]
    BQ 6884

THOMAS AQUINAS, SAINT - SOURCES -
   BIBLE.
    BQ 6883
   xx subdivision "Biblical
    scholarship".

THOMAS AQUINAS, SAINT - SOURCES -
   FATHERS OF THE CHURCH.
    BQ 6886

THOMAS AQUINAS, SAINT - STUDY.
    BQ 6935

THOMAS AQUINAS, SAINT - STYLE.
   See subdivision "Language, style,
   etc.

THOMAS AQUINAS, SAINT - THEODICY.
   See subdivisions "Natural theology"
   and "Providence".

THOMAS AQUINAS, SAINT - THEOLOGY.
    BQ 6901-6920
   xx Thomism.

THOMAS AQUINAS, SAINT - TRINITY.
    BQ 6904

THOMAS AQUINAS, SAINT - VIRTUE.
    BQ 6917

THOMAS AQUINAS, SAINT - WAR AND
   PEACE.
    BQ 6893
   x subdivision "Peace".

THOMAS AQUINAS, SAINT, IN ART.
    BQ 6873
   x subdivision "Art".

THOMAS AQUINAS, SAINT, IN
   LITERATURE.
    BQ 6873
   sa subdivisions "Drama" and
    "Fiction".

426

THOMISM.
BQ 6929-6935
"The system of philosophy and
theology of St. Thomas Aquinas,
held by numerous Catholic
schools of thought and in particular by Dominicans." AT
sa Neo-scholasticism.
Thomas Aquinas, Saint - Philosophy.
Thomas Aquinas, Saint - Theology.
xx Scholasticism.

THOMISM - BIBLIOGRAPHY.

THOMISM - COLLECTIONS.

THOMISM - PERIODICALS.

THORNS, CROWN OF. See
CROWN OF THORNS.

THREE (THE NUMBER)
sa Trinities.
Other references as in LC.

THREE CHAPTERS (CHRISTOLOGICAL
CONTROVERSY)
BQT 75

THREE FESTIVALS.
BM 693
sa Passover.
Shavuo'th (Feast of Weeks)
Sukkoth.

THREE "HAIL MARYS".
A devotion instituted by Pia
Societas sub titulo "Saluta-
tionis Angelicae ter repititae",
around 1900.
x Capuchins - Popular devotions -
Three "Hail Marys".
Hail Marys, Three.
Tres "Ave Maria".

THREE HOURS.
BQT 4491   (24x8.71)
x Tre ore.
xx Devotions, Popular.
Good Friday.

THURIFERS.
BQT 4345
xx Altar boys.

TIARA, PAPAL.
CR 4480
x Papal tiara.
xx Crowns.
Popes.

TIME (CANON LAW)
BQV230 31-35   (348.x23)

TIMOTHY, SAINT, EPISTLE TO. See
BIBLE. O.T. TIMOTHY.

TITHES.   (Geog. subdiv., Direct)
HJ 2281-2287   (336.279254)
BV 771; BQT 3314 (Church
finance)   (24x1.81)
BX 5165 (Church of England)
sa Annates.
Church tax.
Easter dues.
x First fruits.
xx Annates.
Church finance.
Church tax.
Fees, Ecclesiastical.
Taxation.

TITHES - JEWS.
References as in LC.

TITHES (CANON LAW)
BQV230 1502   (348.x46)

TITHES (JEWISH LAW)
References as in LC.

TITULAR CHURCHES.
x Churches, Titular.

TITULAR DIOCESES.
x Dioceses, Titular.

TITUS, EPISTLE TO. See
BIBLE. N.T. TITUS.

TOBIAS, BOOK OF. See
BIBLE. O.T. TOBIAS.

TOBIT, BOOK OF. See
  BIBLE. O.T. TOBIAS.

TOLEDO, COUNCIL OF, 11th, 675.

TOLERATION.
        BQV 325
  sa Liberty of conscience.
     Liberty of speech in the
       church.
     Religious liberty.
     Teaching, Freedom of.
   x Intolerance.
  xx Indifferentism (Religion)

TOLERATION - SERMONS.

TOLERATION (CANON LAW)
        BQV 294

TOMBS.   (Geog. subdiv.)
        NA 6120-6199 (Architecture)
        BQT 5929 (Church archi-
          tecture)   (726.82)
  sa Catacombs.
  Other references as in LC.

TONGUES, GIFT OF. See
  GLOSSOLALIA.

TONSURE.
  xx Clergy.

TORAH. See TALMUD.

TOTEMISM.
  Classifications and references
    as in LC.

TOWER OF BABEL.
        BS 1238
   x Babel, Tower of.

TOWERS.
        NA 2930 (Architecture)
        BQT 5934 (Church archi-
          tecture)   (725.97)
  References as in LC.

TOWN CHURCHES. See
  CITY CHURCHES.

TRACTARIANISM. See
  OXFORD MOVEMENT.

TRADE-UNIONS, CATHOLIC.
        HD 6481
  sa Syndicalism, Catholic.
   x Catholic labor unions.
     Catholic trade-unions.
     Christian labor unions.
     Labor unions, Catholic.
  xx Catholic Church and social
       problems.
     Christian democracy.
     Trade-unions.

TRADE-UNIONS, CATHOLIC - CONGRESSES.

TRADITION (JUDAISM)
   x Oral law (Judaism)
     Oral tradition (Judaism)

TRADITION (MOHAMMEDANISM) See
  HADITH.

TRADITION (THEOLOGY)
        BQT 253-254   (23x9.5)
  "The sum of revealed doctrine
   which has not been committed to
   Sacred Scripture (though it may
   have appeared in uninspired
   writing) but which has been
   handed down by a series of
   legitimate shepherds of the
   Church from age to age." AT
  sa Revelation.
     Rule of faith.
     Traditionalism (Theology)
  xx Authority (Religion)
     Loci theologici.

TRADITIONALISM (THEOLOGY)
        BQT 123
  "The teaching of those who main-
   tained that by reason alone man
   could not arrive at the truths
   of natural religion." AT
  sa Fideism.
  xx Fideism.
     Tradition (Theology)

428

TRANSCENDENCE OF GOD.
   x Divine transcendence.
     God - Transcendence.
   xx Christianity - Philosophy.
     Immanence of God.

TRANSFIGURATION OF CHRIST. See
   JESUS CHRIST - TRANSFIGURATION.

TRANSFIXION OF CHRIST. See
   JESUS CHRIST - TRANSFIXION.

TRANSLATION TO HEAVEN.
   xx Death.
     Future life.

TRANSPLANTATION (PHYSIOLOGY) -
   MORAL ASPECTS.

TRANSUBSTANTIATION.
     BQT 1326   (23x7.3)
   "The mode by which, according
   to the infallible teaching of
   the church, Christ's presence
   in the eucharist is brought
   about." AT
   sa Eucharist.
     Mass.
   x Eucharist - Real presence.
     Real presence.
   xx Dogmatic theology.
     Mass.

TRANSUBSTANTIATION - SERMONS.

TRAPPISTINES.   (Geog. subdiv.,
   Direct)
     BQX 7880   (271.9)
   x Cistercian Nuns, Reformed.

TRAPPISTS.   (Geog. subdiv.,
   Direct)
     BQX 7279   (271.x1)
   sa Cistercians.
   xx Benedictines.
     Cistercians.

TRAPPISTS - BIBLIOGRAPHY.

TRAPPISTS - BIOGRAPHY.

TRAPPISTS - CANON LAW.

TRAPPISTS - CONTROVERSIAL
   LITERATURE.

TRAPPISTS - HISTORY.

TRAPPISTS - MEDITATIONS.

TRAPPISTS - MISSIONS.

TRAPPISTS - RULES.

TRAPPISTS - SPIRITUAL LIFE.

    ################

TRAPPISTS. LAY BROTHERS.

TRAPPISTS. LITURGY AND RITUAL.
   See CISTERCIANS. LITURGY AND
   RITUAL.

TRAPPISTS. OBLATES.

    ################

TRAVELERS - PRAYER-BOOKS.
     BQT 2648

TRAVELERS (CANON LAW)
     BQV230 14

TRE ORE. See THREE HOURS.

TREE OF KNOWLEDGE. See
   TREE OF LIFE.

TREE OF LIFE.
   x Tree of knowledge.
   xx Eden.
     Serpent-worship.

TREE-WORSHIP.
     BL 444   (291.2123)
   References as in LC.

TRENT, COUNCIL OF, 1545-1563.
     BQX 875-878 (Church
       history)   (270.6)
     BQT 108 (Theology)
     BQV 12 (Documents)   (26x2.42)
   sa Counter-Reformation.
   x Council of Trent.
   xx Counter-Reformation.
     Reformation.

TRENT, COUNCIL OF. CATECHISM. See
CATECHISMUS ROMANUS.

TRES "AVE MARIA". See
THREE "HAIL MARYS".

TRIADS (RELIGION) See
TRINITIES.

TRIAL PRACTICE (CANON LAW)

TRIALS, ECCLESIASTICAL.
BQV230 1552-2194 (348.x5)
sa Actions and defenses (Canon
law)
Appellate procedure (Canon
law)
Auditors (Canon law)
Civil procedure (Canon law)
Confession, Judicial (Canon
law)
Contumacy (Canon law)
Criminal procedure (Canon law)
Denunciation (Canon law)
Judgments (Canon law)
Lawyers (Canon law)
Litis contestatio (Canon law)
Witnesses (Canon law)
x Canonical trials.
Ecclesiastical trials.
xx Canon law.
Crime and criminals (Canon
law)

TRIALS, ECCLESIASTICAL (BISHOPS)
xx Bishops (Canon law)

TRIALS, ECCLESIASTICAL (CLERGY)
xx Clergy (Canon law)

TRIALS, ECCLESIASTICAL (EASTERN
CHURCHES)
BQV 1120

TRIALS, ECCLESIASTICAL (MARRIAGE)
BQV230 1960-1992 (348.x54)
sa Marriage - Cases.
xx Marriage (Canon law)

TRIALS, ECCLESIASTICAL (ORDINATION)
BQV230 1993-1998 (348.x59)
xx Ordination (Canon law)

TRIALS, ECCLESIASTICAL (RELIGIOUS)
xx Religious orders (Canon law)
Religious persons (Canon law)

TRIBUNALS, ECCLESIASTICAL. See
ECCLESIASTICAL COURTS.

TRIBUNALS, ROMAN. See
CURIA ROMANA.

TRIDUUM SERMONS.
x Sermons, Triduum.

TRINITIES.
BL 474
sa Triads (Literature)
Trinity.
x Triads (Religion)
xx Three (The number)
Trinity.

TRINITY.
BQT 572-599 (231.x2)
sa God.
God - Personality.
Holy Spirit.
Jesus Christ.
Socinianism.
Trinities.
Tritheism.
Unitarianism.
x Blessed Trinity.
Holy Trinity.
xx Dogmatic theology.
God.
Holy Spirit.
Jesus Christ.
Jesus Christ - Divinity.
Socinianism.
Trinities.
Unitarianism.

TRINITY - ART.
BQT 5851 (246.x64)
xx God - Art.

TRINITY - CULTUS.

TRINITY - EARLY WORKS TO 1800.

TRINITY - HISTORY OF DOCTRINES.
  sa Adoptianism.
    Antitrinitarians.
    Arianism.
    Athanasianism.
    Melchisedechians.
    Monarchianism.
    Monotheism.
    Sabellianism.

TRINITY - HISTORY OF DOCTRINES -
  EARLY CHURCH.

TRINITY - HISTORY OF DOCTRINES -
  MIDDLE AGES.

TRINITY - HISTORY OF DOCTRINES -
  MODERN PERIOD.

TRINITY - HISTORY OF DOCTRINES -
  16th, [17th, etc.] CENTURY.

TRINITY - MEDITATIONS.
    BQT 2580

TRINITY - POETRY.

TRINITY - POPULAR WORKS.
    BQT 573

TRINITY - PRAYER-BOOKS.
    BQT 2652   (24x3.7)

TRINITY - PROCESSION.
    BQT 577-579
  sa Holy Spirit - Procession.

TRINITY - SERMONS.

TRITHEISM.
    BQT 583
  xx Trinity.

TROPARION.
    BQT 5255
  "A generic name for the short
    hymns of the Byzantine Rite."
    AT
  xx Byzantine Rite - Hymns.

TROPARIUM.
    BQT 4251   (26x5.9)
  A collection of interpolated
    verses at divine services,
    e.g., at the Kyrie, etc.

TROPES (CHANT)
    BQT 4629

TRUCE OF GOD.
    BQX 475
  References as in LC.

✓ TRUST IN GOD.   230
    BQT 1793
    BQT 2366
  sa Faith.
  x Confidence in God.

TRUST IN GOD (MOHAMMEDANISM)
  xx God (Mohammedanism)

TRUSTEEISM.
    BQX 4394
  xx Catholic Church - U.S. -
    History - 1783-1865.

TRUTH.
  Classifications and references
    as in LC.

TRUTHFULNESS AND FALSEHOOD.
    BJ 1420-1428 (Ethics)
    BQT 1952-1957 (Theology)
      (24x1.66)
  sa Honesty.
  x Falsehood.
    Lying.
  xx Conduct of life.
    Honesty.
    Truth.

TUTIORISM. See
  PROBABILISM.

TWELFTH DAY. See EPIPHANY.

TWELFTH NIGHT. See EPIPHANY.

TWELVE TRIBES OF ISRAEL.
  x Israel, Twelve tribes of.
  xx Jews - History - To 586 B.C.
    Lost tribes of Israel.

TYPES, BIBLICAL. See
   TYPOLOGY (THEOLOGY)

TYPIKON.
      BQT 5242
   "The calendar and rubrics of the
      Byzantine Rite, corresponding
      to the Latin Ordo." Lynn

TYPOLOGY (THEOLOGY)
      BS 478   (220.6)
      BQT 690

   sa Church - Typology.
      Eucharist - Typology.
      Jesus Christ - Typology.
      Mary, Blessed Virgin -
         Typology.
    x Bible - Typology.
      Types, Biblical.
   xx Covenants (Theology)
      Jesus Christ - Prophecies.

UKRAINIAN CATHOLIC RITE. See
   BYZANTINE RITE, RUTHENIAN.

ULTRAMONTANISM.
      BQX 987 (Church history)
      BQT 371 (Theology)
   As used by modern non-Catholic
      controversialists, this term is
      used to describe the supposed
      exaggeration of papal preroga-
      tives.
   sa Popes - Infallibility.
      Vatican Council, 1st, 1869-1870.
   xx Anti-Catholic polemic.

UNBELIEF.
      BQT 242   (23x9.52)

UNBELIEF - SERMONS.

UNCTION. See ANOINTINGS.

UNCTION, EXTREME. See
   EXTREME UNCTION.

UNIATE EASTERN CHURCHES. See
   EASTERN CHURCHES, CATHOLIC.

UNIFORMS, PAPAL.
      GT 975
    x Papal uniforms.

UNIO MYSTICA. See
   MYSTICAL UNION.

UNION, CHRISTIAN. See
   CHRISTIAN UNION.

UNION, HYPOSTATIC. See
   HYPOSTATIC UNION.

UNION, MYSTICAL. See
   MYSTICAL UNION.

UNION CHURCHES. See
   COMMUNITY CHURCHES.

UNION WITH CHRIST. See
   MYSTICAL UNION.

UNIONISM (RELIGION)
   "Here are entered works -- from
      or descriptive of a Lutheran
      point of view -- dealing with
      joint worship and work among
      adherents of church bodies not
      united in doctrine.
   "Works dealing with the same
      problem but from or descriptive
      of a Catholic point of view are
      entered under the heading Com-
      municatio in sacris." LC
   sa Communicatio in sacris.
      Simultaneum.
   xx Christian union.
      Communicatio in sacris.
      Indifferentism (Religion)
      Lutheran Church - Discipline.
      Sects.
      Syncretistic controversy.

UNITARIAN CHURCHES.
      BX 9801-9869   (288)
   Subdivisions as in LC.

UNITARIANISM.
      BX 9801-9869   (288)

   sa Arianism.
      Humanism, Religious.
      Jesus Christ - Divinity.
      Socinianism.
      Trinity.

UNITARIANISM -- Continued.
  xx Congregationalism.
    Jesus Christ - Divinity.
    Socinianism.
    Trinity.

UNITARIANS.

UNITAS FRATRUM. See
  MORAVIANS.

UNITED AMERICAN FREEWILL BAPTISTS.
    BX 6370-6379

UNITED BRETHREN. See
  MORAVIANS.

UNITED BRETHREN IN CHRIST.   (Geog.
  subdiv., Direct)
    BX 9875-9876   (284.6)

UNITED CHURCH OF CANADA.
    BX 9881-9883

UNITED LUTHERAN CHURCH IN AMERICA.
    BX 8048

UNITED PRESBYTERIAN CHURCH OF
  NORTH AMERICA.
    BX 8980-8988   (285.4)

Unity, Church   see Church-Unity

U.S. - CHURCH HISTORY.
    BQX 3202-4584

U.S. - CHURCH HISTORY - EARLY
  PERIOD TO 1783.

U.S. - CHURCH HISTORY - COLONIAL
  PERIOD.

U.S. - CHURCH HISTORY - 1783-1865.

U.S. - CHURCH HISTORY - 19th CENTURY.

U.S. - CHURCH HISTORY - 1865-1900.

U.S. - CHURCH HISTORY - 20th CENTURY.

U.S. - FOREIGN POPULATION.
    E 184
  sa Nativism.
  Other references as in LC.

U.S. - HISTORY - REVOLUTION -
  RELIGIOUS ASPECTS.
    E 209

U.S. - HISTORY - CIVIL WAR -
  RELIGIOUS ASPECTS.
    E 540 (Churches and the war)
    E 635 (Religion in the army)

U.S. - RELIGION.
    BR 513-569
    BQX 4361

U.S. - RELIGION - 19th CENTURY.

U.S. - RELIGION - 20th CENTURY.

UNITIVE WAY TO PERFECTION.
    BQT 2208
  xx Perfection, Christian.

UNIVERSAL PRIESTHOOD. See
  PRIESTHOOD, UNIVERSAL.

UNIVERSAL RELIGION. See
  RELIGIONS (PROPOSED, UNIVERSAL,
  ETC.)

UNIVERSALISM.
    BQT 1114; BQT 1527
    BX 9901-9969   (289.1)
  sa Future punishment.
    Salvation.
    Salvation outside the church.
  xx Future punishment.
    Restorationism.
    Salvation outside the church.

UNIVERSE, DESTRUCTION OF.
    BQ 991
    [BQT 1461]
  x Destruction of the universe.
  xx Cosmogony.
    End of the world.
    Eschatology.
    Future life.

UNIVERSITIES AND COLLEGES - CHAPEL
  EXERCISES.

UNIVERSITIES AND COLLEGES - CHAPLAINS.
  See CHAPLAINS, UNIVERSITY AND
  COLLEGE.

UNIVERSITIES AND COLLEGES - RELIGION.
    BQT 3652-3655
 sa subdivision "Religion" under
    names of individual univer-
    sities and colleges.
 xx Church and college.

UNIVERSITIES AND COLLEGES - SERMONS.
    BQT 3009
    BV 4310
 sa Students - Sermons.
    Theological seminaries - Sermons.
  x College sermons.
    Sermons, College.
    Sermons, University.

UNIVERSITIES AND COLLEGES (CANON LAW)
 xx Educational law and legislation
    (Canon law)

UNIVERSITIES AND COLLEGES, CATHOLIC.
    LC 487
  x Catholic universities and
    colleges.
 xx Catholic education, Higher.
    Catholic institutions.
    Church schools.

UNIVERSITIES AND COLLEGES, CATHOLIC -
  CURRICULA.

UNIVERSITIES AND COLLEGES, CATHOLIC -
  DIRECTORIES.

UNIVERSITIES AND COLLEGES, CATHOLIC -
  RELIGION.

UNIVERSITIES AND COLLEGES, CATHOLIC -
  SERMONS.

UNIVERSITIES AND COLLEGES, CATHOLIC
  (CANON LAW)
    BQV230 1376-1380
 xx Catholic education (Canon law)

UNIVERSITY CHAPLAINS. See
  CHAPLAINS, UNIVERSITY AND COLLEGE.

UNIVERSITY SERMONS. See
  UNIVERSITIES AND COLLEGES -
  SERMONS.

UNJUST JUDGE (PARABLE)
    BQT 888   (226.x6)
  x Importunate widow (Parable)

UNJUST STEWARD (PARABLE)
    BQT 888   (226.x6)

UNPARDONABLE SIN. See
  SIN AGAINST THE HOLY SPIRIT.

URBAN CHURCHES. See
  CITY CHURCHES.

URBAN CLERGY. See
  CITY CLERGY.

URBAN MINISTRY. See
  CITY CLERGY.

URIM AND THUMMIM.
  References as in LC supple-
    ment 1959-60.

USE OF REASON.
 sa Loss of consciousness.
  x Reason, Use of.
 xx Free will and determinism.
    Insanity.
    Loss of consciousness.

USE OF REASON (CANON LAW)
 xx Insanity (Canon law)

USES (LITURGY) See
  RITES AND USES.

USURY (CANON LAW) See
  INTEREST AND USURY (CANON LAW)

VACANCY OF THE HOLY SEE.
  x Holy See, Vacancy of the.
    Popes - Vacancy of the
    Holy See.

VACATION BIBLE SCHOOLS. See
  VACATION SCHOOLS, RELIGIOUS.

VACATION CHURCH SCHOOLS. See
  VACATION SCHOOLS, RELIGIOUS.

VACATION SCHOOLS, CATHOLIC.
   x Catholic vacation schools.
   xx Catholic education.

VACATION SCHOOLS, RELIGIOUS.
     BQT 3127
   x Church camps.
    Church vacation schools.
    Religious vacation schools.
    Vacation Bible schools.
    Vacation church schools.
   xx Church schools.

VACATION SCHOOLS, RELIGIOUS -
   EXERCISES, RECITATIONS, ETC.

VACATION SCHOOLS, RELIGIOUS -
   TEACHERS' MANUALS.

VACATION SCHOOLS, RELIGIOUS -
   TEXTBOOKS.

VALENTINIANS.
     BQT 48
   xx Jesus Christ - History of
     doctrines.

VALLUMBROSIANS.
     BQX 7105
   x Benedictines, Vallumbrosian.
   xx Benedictines.

VANITY. See
   PRIDE AND VANITY.

VATICAN.
     BQT 5806
   By this term is meant the Vatican
   palace as the center of the
   administrative activities of
   the Pope. For the organization
   and administration of the papal
   court and household see Curia
   Romana.

VATICAN CITY.
     BQX 141-143
   "The area of Rome recognized by
   the Treaty of the Lateran as
   constituting the territorial
   extent of the temporal sovereignty of the holy see." AT
   xx Papal States.

VATICAN CITY. SAN PIETRO (BASILICA)
     BQT 5683 (Church architecture)
     NA 5620 (Architecture)
     BQX 68 (Christian archaeology)
     BQX 141 (Church history)
   x Rome (City). San Pietro in
     Vaticano (Basilica)
    St. Peter's Basilica, Vatican
    City.
    San Pietro (Basilica), Vatican
    City.

VATICAN CITY (VICARIATE)
     BQX 2539

VATICAN COUNCIL, 1st, 1869-1870.
     BQT 127   282. A14 1870
     BQX 1057   (26x2.43)
     BQV 12 (Documents)
   xx Ultramontanism.

VATICAN COUNCIL, 2d, 1962-65
     [BQX 1134] 282. A15
     BQV 12 (Documents)

VEIL OF VERONICA.
     BQT 942
   x Veronica, Veil of.
   xx Holy face.
    Jesus Christ - Passion.

VENERATION OF IMAGES. See
   IMAGES, VENERATION OF.

VENERATION OF MARTYRS. See
   MARTYRS - CULTUS.

VENERATION OF SAINTS. See
   SAINTS - CULTUS.

VENI CREATOR SPIRITUS.
     BQT 4393   (245.x1)
     M 2079.L92
   xx Holy Spirit - Prayer-books.

VENI SANCTE SPIRITUS.
     BQT 4315   (245.x1)
     M 2079.L94
   xx Holy Spirit - Prayer-books.

VENITE EXULTEMUS DOMINO (INVITATORY)
See INVITATORIUM.

VENITE EXULTEMUS DOMINO (MUSIC)
See PSALMS (MUSIC) - 94th PSALM.

VENIAL SIN. See
SIN, VENIAL.

VERONICA, VEIL OF. See
VEIL OF VERONICA.

VESPERALE.
BQT 4382   (783.24)
"A book containing the text and
chant for the office of Vespers
throughout the year." AT
xx Breviarium.
Vespers.

VESPERS.
BQT 4175
"The evening hour of the divine
office and, with Lauds, the
most solemn." AT
sa Church-night services.
Evening-service music.
Lucernarium.
Vesperale.
xx Church-night services.
Divine Office.
Evening-service music.

VESSELS, SACRED. See
SACRED VESSELS.

VESTMENTS. See   (246)
CHURCH VESTMENTS.

VIATICUM.
BQT 1349
By this term is meant "holy
communion given to those in
danger of death." AT
x Last sacraments.
xx Communion, Holy.

VICARAGES (BUILDINGS) See
PARSONAGES.

VICARS, COADJUTOR.
BQV230 475
x Coadjutor vicars.
xx Vicars, Parochial.

VICARS, PAROCHIAL.
BQV230 471-478   (348.x36)
sa Assistant pastors.
Vicars, Coadjutor.
x Curates.
Parish vicars.
Parochial vicars.
xx Clergy.
Parishes (Canon law)
Pastors.

VICARS APOSTOLIC.   (Geog.
subdiv., Indirect)
BQV230 293-311   (348.x3)
sa Bishops.
x Apostolic prefects.
Apostolic vicars.
Prefects apostolic.
xx Bishops.
Persons (Canon law)
Prelates.

VICARS CAPITULAR.
BQV230 429-444   (348.x3)
sa Administrators apostolic.
Chapters, Cathedral,
collegiate, etc.
x Capitular vicars.
xx Administrators apostolic.
Bishops (Canon law)
Chapters, Cathedral,
collegiate, etc.
Dioceses (Canon law)
Persons (Canon law)

VICARS CHORAL. See
MINOR CANONS, CATHEDRAL, COL-
LEGIATE, ETC.

VICARS DELEGATE.
BQV230 196-210
xx Delegation of powers (Canon
law)

VICARS FORANE.
BQV230 445-450   (348.x3)
xx Persons (Canon law)
Rural deans.

VICARS-GENERAL.
    BQV230 366-371   (348.x35)
xx Bishops.
   Curia, Diocesan.
   Deans.
   Persons (Canon law)

VICE.
    BJ 1518-1695 (Ethics)   (170)
    [BQT 1797-1798] (Moral theology)
sa Crime and criminals.
   Degeneration.
   Imperfections (Theology)
   also special vices, e.g.,
      Opium habit; Prostitution;
      etc.
xx Crime and criminals.
   Defective and delinquent
      classes.
   Sin.
   Virtue.

VICE - SERMONS.
    [BQT 3072.5]

VICTIM SOULS.
    BQT 2485
    "A soul, chosen by God and de-
    liberately corresponding with
    the divine will, who freely
    sacrifices himself, his health,
    happiness, etc., and suffers,
    after the example of the cruci-
    fied Christ, for the advantage
    of the church and the good of
    others in general or of a par-
    ticular person." AT
xx Suffering, Mystic.

VIENNA, CONCORDAT OF, 1448. See
CONCORDAT OF VIENNA, 1448.

VIENNE, COUNCIL OF, 1311-1312.
    BQX 802
    x Council of Vienne, 1311-1312.

VIGIL OF EASTER. See
EASTER VIGIL.

VIGILS (LITURGY)
    BQT 4236
sa Matins.
xx Feasts, Ecclesiastical.

VILLAGE CHURCHES. See
RURAL CHURCHES.

✓ VIOLENCE
VIOLENCE (CANON LAW) See
DURESS (CANON LAW)

VIRGIN BIRTH.
    BQT 841
sa Mary, Blessed Virgin -
   Virginity.
   x Jesus Christ - Virgin birth.

VIRGIN BIRTH (MYTHOLOGY)

VIRGIN MARY, BLESSED. See
MARY, BLESSED VIRGIN.

VIRGINITY.
    BQT 1933   (23x7.7)
sa Celibacy.
   Chastity.

VIRGINS, CONSECRATION OF. See
CONSECRATION OF VIRGINS.

VIRGINS, TEN (PARABLE) See
TEN VIRGINS (PARABLE)

VIRTUE.
    BQT 1196-1212; BQT 1777-1793
    (24x1.5)
    BJ 1518-1533 (Ethics)
sa Character.
   Ethics.
   Habit.
   Imperfections (Theology)
   Spiritual life.
   Vice.
   Worth.
xx Conduct of life.
   Habit.
   Human acts.

VIRTUE - BIBLICAL TEACHING.

VIRTUE - BIBLIOGRAPHY.

VIRTUE - DEVOTIONAL LITERATURE.

VIRTUE - HISTORY OF DOCTRINES.

VIRTUE - MEDITATIONS.
    [BQT 2610.5]

VIRTUE - SERMONS.

VIRTUE - STUDY AND TEACHING.
    BQT 3197

VIRTUE, HEROIC. See
  HEROIC VIRTUE.

VIRTUES, CARDINAL. See
  VIRTUES, MORAL.

VIRTUES, INFUSED.
  sa Habit.
     Spiritual life.
     Virtues, Moral.
     Virtues, Theological.
   x Infused virtues.
     Supernatural virtues.
     Virtues, Supernatural.
  xx Grace (Theology)

VIRTUES, MORAL.
    BQT 1207-1212 (Dogmatic
        theology)
    BQT 1789-1793 (Moral
        theology)   (24x1.52)
  sa Fortitude.
     Justice (Virtue)
     Prudence.
     Temperance (Virtue)
   x Cardinal virtues.
     Moral virtues.
     Virtues, Cardinal.
  xx Grace, Habitual.
     Moral theology.
     Virtues, Infused.

VIRTUES, SUPERNATURAL. See
  VIRTUES, INFUSED.

VIRTUES, THEOLOGICAL.
    BQT 1196-1203 (Dogmatic
        theology)
    BQT 1780-1786 (Moral
        theology)   (24x1.51)
  sa Faith.
     Hope.
     Love (Theology)
   x Theological virtues.
  xx Grace, Habitual.
     Virtues, Infused.

VIRTUES, THEOLOGICAL - BIBLICAL
  TEACHING.

VIRTUES, THEOLOGICAL - DEVOTIONAL
  LITERATURE.

VIRTUES, THEOLOGICAL - SERMONS.

VIRTUES IN ART.
    BQT 5909   (246.66)

VIRTUES IN LITERATURE.

VISIGOTHIC RITE. See
  MOZARABIC RITE.

VISION, BEATIFIC. See
  BEATIFIC VISION.

VISIONS.
    BF 1815 (Occult sciences)
    BQT 2483 (Mysticism)
  sa Apparitions.
     Dreams.
     Hallucinations and illusions.
  xx Apparitions.
     Mysticism.
     Theophanies.

VISIT AD LIMINA.
    BQV230 341   (348.x35)
  The full term is Visit ad limina
     apostolorum. It is "a visit to
     the thresholds of the Apostles
     Peter and Paul, i.e., to their
     tombs and to their living
     representative, the pope, which
     must be made, personally if
     possible, by every archbishop
     and bishop-in-ordinary in the
     Latin rite, once every five
     years if from Europe and once
     every ten years if from else-
     where." AT
   x Ad limina apostolorum.
  xx Bishops (Canon law)
     Visitations, Ecclesiastical
        (Canon law)

438

VISITATION FESTIVAL.
BQT 4230
sa Missa in Visitatione Beatae
Mariae Virginis.
xx Mary, Blessed Virgin - Visitation.

VISITATION SERMONS.
x Sermons, Visitation.
xx Visitations, Ecclesiastical.

VISITATIONS (CHURCH WORK)
sa Canvassing (Church work)
x Pastoral visitations.
Visitations, Pastoral.
xx Canvassing (Church work)
Church work.
Pastoral theology.

VISITATIONS (RELIGIOUS EDUCATION)
x Sunday-school visitations.
Visitations, Sunday-school.
xx Canvassing (Church work)
Evangelistic work.

VISITATIONS, ECCLESIASTICAL.
(Geog. subdiv., Direct)
[BQT 4442]
sa Visitation sermons.
x Ecclesiastical visitations.

VISITATIONS, ECCLESIASTICAL (CANON
LAW)
sa Visit ad limina.
Visitors apostolic.
xx Dioceses (Canon law)
Religious orders (Canon law)

VISITATIONS, PASTORAL. See
VISITATIONS (CHURCH WORK)

VISITATIONS, SUNDAY-SCHOOL. See
VISITATIONS (RELIGIOUS EDUCATION)

VISITORS APOSTOLIC.
x Apostolic visitors.
xx Visitations, Ecclesiastical
(Canon law)

VOCAL MUSIC.   (Geog. subdiv.,
Indirect)
sa Hymns.
Other references as in LC.

VOCAL PRAYER. See
PRAYER.

VOCATION.
BQT [2266]-2309   (24x8.3)
This term is here used to mean
the circumstances in which
every man has to pass his life
on earth, because our lives are
under the care of God's providence.
sa Family, Christian.
Laity.
Professions.
Vocational guidance.
also subdivision "Vocation"
under particular states of
life, e.g., Clergy - Vocation;
Missionaries - Vocation.
x Calling.
xx Duty.
Occupations.
Perfection, Christian.
Work.

VOCATION - ADDRESSES, SERMONS, ETC.

VOCATION - BIBLICAL TEACHING.
xx Man (Theology)

VOCATION - CATECHISMS, QUESTION-BOOKS.

VOCATION, CHOICE OF. See
VOCATIONAL GUIDANCE.

VOCATION, ECCLESIASTICAL.
[BQT 2292]
Here are entered works on ecclesias-
tical vocation in general. Works
on vocations to more specific
states are entered the respective
specific heading, e.g., Vocation,
Religious; Missionaries - Voca-
tion; Priests - Vocation; etc.
sa Brothers - Vocation.
Clergy - Vocation.
Missionaries - Vocation.
Priests - Vocation.
Vocation, Religious.
Vocation, Religious, for
women.

VOCATION, ECCLESIASTICAL - BIBLIO-
GRAPHY.

VOCATION, ECCLESIASTICAL (CANON LAW)
BQV230 1353

VOCATION, MISSIONARY. See
MISSIONARIES - VOCATION.

VOCATION, RELIGIOUS.
BQT 2309
sa Religious orders - Recruiting.
x Monastic vocation.
Religious orders - Vocation.
Religious vocation.
xx Vocation, Ecclesiastical.

VOCATION, RELIGIOUS (CANON LAW)
BQV230 538
xx Religious orders (Canon law)

VOCATION, RELIGIOUS, FOR WOMEN.
BQT 2309; [BQT 2345]
x Religious orders for women -
Vocation.
xx Vocation, Ecclesiastical.

VOCATION, SACERDOTAL. See
PRIESTS - VOCATION.

VOCATIONAL GUIDANCE.
References as in LC.

VOTIVE MASS.
BQT 4321-4328
"A Mass differing from that of
the feast or office of the day,
celebrated for a special intention as directed by authority
or because the circumstances
require it (e.g., a nuptial or
exequial Mass) or simply at the
choice of the priest." AT
x Mass, Votive.

VOTIVE OFFERINGS.
x Offerings, Votive.
xx Sacrifice.

VOWS.
BQT 2311-2314 (Religious
perfection)
BQT 1876-1878 (Moral theology)
(24x1.83)
BQT 4465-4469 (Liturgy)

VOWS -- Continued.
sa Chastity (Vow)
Obedience (Vow)
Poverty (Vow)
Profession, Religious.
x Religious orders - Vows.
Religious orders for women -
Vows.
xx Evangelical counsels.
Religious life.

VOWS - MEDITATIONS.

VOWS - SERMONS.
BQT 3089

VOWS (CANON LAW)
BQV230 1307-1317   (348.x37)
sa Oaths (Canon law)
xx Marriage - Impediments (Canon
law)
Religious orders (Canon law)

VOYAGES AND TRAVEL, MISSIONARY.
x Missionaries - Voyages and
travel.

VULGATE.
For texts of the Vulgate see
Bible. Latin. [date]. Vulgate.
BS 75
Bible. O.T. Latin. [date]. Vulgate.
BS 775
Bible. N.T. Latin. [date]. Vulgate.
BS 1975
For books about the Vulgate see
BIBLE. LATIN - VERSIONS - VULGATE.
BS 85
BIBLE. O.T. LATIN - VERSIONS -
VULGATE.
BS 785
BIBLE. N.T. LATIN - VERSIONS -
VULGATE.
BS 1985

VULGATE COMMISSION. See
COMMISSIO VULGATAE EMENDANDAE.

WAHABIS.
BP 195.W   (297)
xx Mohammedan sects.

440

WALBURGA, SAINT, OIL OF. See
ST. WALBURGA'S OIL.

WALDENSES.
        BQT 92   (284.4)
   xx Albigenses.
      Sects, Medieval.

WALDENSES IN SOUTH AMERICA,
   [THE U.S., ETC.]

WAR - MORAL ASPECTS. See
   WAR AND CRIME.
   WAR AND MORALS.
   WAR AND RELIGION.

WAR AND CHRISTIANITY. See
   WAR AND RELIGION.

WAR AND MORALS.
        BQT 1911-1918
   sa War and crime.
      War and religion.
      also subdivision "Moral
         aspects" under names of
         wars, e.g., World War,
         1939-1945 - Moral aspects.
    x Morals and war.
      War - Moral aspects.
   xx War and religion.

WAR AND RELIGION.
        BQT 1911-1918
   sa Catholic Church and war.
      Conscientious objectors.
      European War, 1914-1918 -
         Catholic Church.
      European War, 1914-1918 -
         Religious aspects.
      Jihad.
      Pacifism.
      Peace - Biblical teaching.
      War and morals.
      World War, 1939-1945 -
         Catholic Church.
      World War, 1939-1945 -
         Friends, Society of.
      also subdivision "Religious
         aspects" under names of
         wars, e.g., World War,
         1939-1945 - Religious
         aspects.

WAR AND RELIGION -- Continued.
    x Christianity and war.
      Church and war.
      Religion and war.
      War - Moral aspects.
      War and Christianity.
      War and the church.
   xx Theocracy.
      War and morals.

WAR AND RELIGION - BIBLICAL
   TEACHING.

WAR AND RELIGION - PAPAL
   TEACHING.

WAR AND THE CHURCH. See
   WAR AND RELIGION.

WAR OF THE SEVEN REDUCTIONS,
   1754-1756. See
   WAR OF THE SEVEN REDUCTIONS,
   1754-1756.

WASHING OF THE FEET.
        BQT 4474
   Here are entered works in general
      on the practice and ceremony of
      the washing of feet.
   sa Mandatum.
    x Feet, Washing of.
      Foot, Washing of.

WATER (IN RELIGION, FOLK-LORE, ETC.)
   References as in LC.

WATER, BAPTISMAL. See
   BAPTISMAL WATER.

WATER, BLESSED. See
   HOLY WATER.

WATER, HOLY. See
   HOLY WATER.

WAY OF THE CROSS. See
   STATIONS OF THE CROSS.

WEALTH, ETHICS OF.
        BQT 3435
        HB 835
   sa Avarice.
      Business ethics.

WEALTH, ETHICS OF -- Continued.
  sa Christianity and economics.
    Materialism (Theology)
  x Ethics of wealth.
  xx Business ethics.
    Ethics.
    Honesty.
    Luxury.
    Perfection, Christian.
    Social ethics.
    Sociology, Christian.

WEDDING. See
  MARRIAGE.
  MARRIAGE CUSTOMS AND RITES.
  MARRIAGE SERVICE.

WEDDING GARMENT (PARABLE) See
  MARRIAGE OF THE KING'S SON (PARABLE)

WEDDING IN CANA. See
  MARRIAGE IN CANA (MIRACLE)

WEDDING MASS. See
  MASS, NUPTIAL.
  MISSA PRO SPONSO ET SPONSA.

WEEK, LITURGICAL. See
  LITURGY - CONGRESSES.

WEEK-DAY CHURCH SCHOOLS.
  BV 1580-1583

WEEK-NIGHT SERVICES. See
  CHURCH-NIGHT SERVICES.

WELFARE WORK IN INDUSTRY.
  sa Chaplains, Industrial.
  Other references as in LC.

WELLS, HOLY. See
  HOLY WELLS.

WESTERN SCHISM. See
  SCHISM, THE GREAT WESTERN,
  1378-1417.

WHITE FRIARS. See
  CARMELITES.

WHITE MONKS. See
  CISTERCIANS.

WHITSUNDAY. See
  PENTECOST FESTIVAL.

WIDOWS - RELIGIOUS LIFE.
  [BQT 2289]

WIDOWS (CANON LAW)
  BQV230 1142

WILL.
    BQT 2373-2375 (Asceticism)
  Other classifications and
    references as in LC.

WILLS. (Geog. subdiv., Direct)
    BQT 1947 (Moral theology)
  References as in LC.

WILLS (CANON LAW)
    BQV230 1513-1517 (348.x46)
  sa Inheritance and succession
    (Canon law)
  xx Church property (Canon law)
    Inheritance and succession
    (Canon law)

WINE - LITURGICAL USE.
    BQV230 815
  x Altar wine.
    Mass wine.
  xx Eucharist - Elements.

WISDOM, BOOK OF. See
  BIBLE. O.T. WISDOM.

WISDOM LITERATURE (BIBLE) See
  BIBLE. O.T. WISDOM LITERATURE.

WISDOM OF SOLOMON. See
  BIBLE. O.T. WISDOM.

✓ WIT AND HUMOR, ~~CATHOLIC. See~~
  ~~CATHOLIC WIT AND HUMOR.~~
    x Humor

WITCHCRAFT.
  References as in LC.

WITNESS BEARING (CHRISTIANITY)
  sa Martyrdom.
    Profession of faith.

442

WITNESSES (CANON LAW)
 BQV230 1754-1791 (348.x5)
 sa Evidence (Canon law)
 Evidence, Expert (Canon law)
 xx Trials, Ecclesiastical.

WITNESSES OF JEHOVAH. See
 JEHOVAH'S WITNESSES.

WOMAN - BIBLICAL TEACHING. See
 WOMEN IN THE BIBLE.

WOMAN - PRAYER-BOOKS.

WOMAN - RELIGIOUS LIFE.
 BQT 2284
 sa Retreats for women.
 xx Women and religion.

WOMAN - RETREATS. See
 RETREATS FOR WOMEN.

WOMAN - SERMONS.
 BQT 3016

WOMEN AND RELIGION.
 BL 458; BQT 618 (Religion)
 HQ 1393 (Sociology)
 "Here are entered works on the
 mutual relationship of women
 and religion, and on the
 position of women in the
 various religions." LC
 sa Woman - Religious life.
 Women in Buddhism.
 Women in Christianity.
 Women in church work.
 Women in Hinduism.
 Women in Mohammedanism.
 Women in the Bible.
 Women in the Koran.
 Women in the Talmud.
 x Women in religion.

WOMEN AS MISSIONARIES.
 sa Missionaries, Women.
 Women in missionary work.

WOMEN IN BUDDHISM.
 xx Buddha and Buddhism.
 Women and religion.

WOMEN IN CHRISTIANITY. *see Women in the church*
 xx Women and religion.

WOMEN IN CHRISTIANITY - PAPAL
 TEACHING.

✓ WOMEN IN THE CHURCH ~~WORK~~. *253* *Christianity*
 BV 4415 *x Women in*
 xx Women and religion.

WOMEN IN HINDUISM.
 BL 2015.W
 References as in LC.

WOMEN IN LITERATURE.
 sa Nuns in literature.
 Other references as in LC.

WOMEN IN MISSIONARY WORK.
 BV 2610
 "Here are entered works dealing
 with the work of women in
 promoting missions. For
 biographical works on women
 missionaries see Missionaries,
 Women." LC
 sa Religious orders of women -
 Missions.
 xx Women as missionaries.

WOMEN IN MOHAMMEDANISM.
 References as in LC supplement 1959-60.

WOMEN IN RELIGION. See
 CONVENTS.
 NUNS.
 RELIGIOUS ORDERS OF WOMEN.
 WOMEN AND RELIGION.

✓ WOMEN IN THE BIBLE. *220, 221, 225*
 BS 575
 sa Women in the Talmud.
 x Bible - Women.
 Mothers - Biblical teaching.
 Woman - Biblical teaching.
 xx Women and religion.

WOMEN IN THE KORAN.
 BP 134.W
 References as in LC.

WOMEN IN THE TALMUD.
BM 509.W
References as in LC.

WOMEN SAINTS. See
SAINTS, WOMEN.

WORK.
BF 481 (Psychology)
BJ 1498 (Ethics)
sa Benedictines and work.
Bocation.
Other references as in LC.

WORK, SERVILE. See
SERVILE WORK.

WORKINGMEN - DEVOTIONAL LITERATURE.
BQT 2573

WORKINGMEN - PRAYER-BOOKS.
BQT 2648

WORKINGMEN - RELIGIOUS LIFE.
BQT 2573

WORKINGMEN'S RETREATS. See
RETREATS FOR WORKINGMEN.

WORKS OF MERCY, CORPORAL. See
CORPORAL WORKS OF MERCY.

WORKS OF MERCY, SPIRITUAL. See
SPIRITUAL WORKS OF MERCY.

WORLD, END OF THE. See
END OF THE WORLD.

WORLD WAR, 1939-1945 - CATHOLIC
CHURCH.
D 810.C
BQX 1111 (Church history)
xx War and religion.

WORLD WAR, 1939-1945 - CHURCHES. See
WORLD WAR, 1939-1945 - RELIGIOUS
ASPECTS.
WORLD WAR, 1939-1945 - WAR WORK -
CHURCHES.

WORLD WAR, 1939-1945 - RELIGIOUS
ASPECTS.
D 744.2
sa World War, 1939-1945 - War
work - Churches.
x World War, 1939-1945 -
Churches.
xx War and religion.

WORLD WAR, 1939-1945 - WAR WORK -
CHURCHES.
x World War, 1939-1945 -
Churches.
xx World War, 1939-1945 -
Religious aspects.

WORLD WAR, 1939-1945 - WAR WORK -
CATHOLIC CHURCH, [METHODIST
CHURCH, SALVATION ARMY, ETC.]

WORMS, CONCORDAT OF, 1122. See
CONCORDAT OF WORMS, 1122.

WORMS, DIET OF, 1521.
x Diet of Worms, 1521.

WORSHIP.
BV 2-25 (Christian)
(217)
BL 550-620 (Comparative
religion) (291.x3)
BM 656-658 (Judaism)
BQT 1862-1878 (Commandment
of God) (241.x6)
BQT 4021-4031 (Liturgy)
GN 470-474 (Primitive)
sa Adoration.
Ancestor-worship.
Animal-worship.
Church attendance.
Cultus.
Devil-worship.
Fetishism.
Fire-worshipers.
Idols and images - Worship.
Liturgy.
Moon-worship.

444

WORSHIP -- Continued.
  sa Nature-worship.
     Orientation (Religion)
     Phallicism.
     Posture in worship.
     Prayer.
     Public worship.
     Responsive worship.
     Sacrifice.
     Serpent-worship.
     Sun-worship.
     Tree-worship.
   x God - Worship and love.
  xx Religion (Virtue)
     Theology.

WORSHIP - FILMSTRIPS.

WORSHIP - HISTORY.

WORSHIP - HISTORY - PRIMITIVE
  TIMES.
        GN 473

WORSHIP - HISTORY - OLD
  TESTAMENT.
        BS 680

WORSHIP - HISTORY - EARLY
  CHURCH.
        BQT 4026
        BV 6
  sa Synaxis.

WORSHIP - HISTORY - MIDDLE
  AGES.
        BQT 4028
        BV 7

WORSHIP - HISTORY - MODERN
  PERIOD.
        BQT 4031
        BV 8

WORSHIP (RELIGIOUS EDUCATION)
        BV 1522

WORSHIP, COMMUNICATION IN. See
   COMMUNICATIO IN SACRIS.

WORSHIP, POSTURE IN. See
   POSTURE IN WORSHIP.

WORSHIP PROGRAMS.
   References as in LC.

WOUNDS OF CHRIST, DEVOTION TO. See
   FIVE WOUNDS, DEVOTION TO.

WRATH.
   xx Anger.

WRATH OF GOD. See
   ANGER OF GOD.

WYCLIFITES. See
   LOLLARDS.

YAHVEH. See
   JAHVE.

YAHVEH, DAY OF. See
   DAY OF JEHOVAH.

YAHVEH, SERVANT OF. See
   SERVANT OF JEHOVAH.

YEAR, CHRISTIAN. See
   CHURCH YEAR.

✔ YEAR, CHURCH. See
   CHURCH YEAR.

YEAR, HOLY. See
   HOLY YEAR.

YEAR, JUBILEE. See
   HOLY YEAR.

YEAR, LITURGICAL. See
   CHURCH YEAR.

YEAR, MARIAN. See
   MARIAN YEAR.

YEARBOOKS, CATHOLIC. See
   CATHOLIC CHURCH - YEARBOOKS.

YEZIDIS.
BL 1595
xx Devil-worship.
Religions.

YOM KIPPUR.
BM 695.A8
BM 675.A8 (Liturgical form)
References as in LC.

YOUNG CHRISTIAN WORKERS.
BQT 3589
xx Jocistes.

YOUNG MEN - MEDITATIONS.
BQT 2566

YOUNG MEN - PRAYER-BOOKS.
BQT 2638

YOUNG MEN - RELIGIOUS LIFE.
BQT 2283
sa Retreats for young men.
xx Youth - Religious life.

YOUNG MEN - RETREATS. See
RETREATS FOR YOUNG MEN.

YOUNG MEN - SERMONS.
BQT 3015

YOUNG MEN'S CHRISTIAN ASSOCIATIONS.
BV 1000-1220
Subdivisions as in LC.

YOUNG WOMEN - MEDITATIONS.
BQT 2568

YOUNG WOMEN - PRAYER-BOOKS.
BQT 2640

YOUNG WOMEN - RELIGIOUS LIFE.
BQT 2284
sa Retreats for young women.
xx Youth - Religious life.

YOUNG WOMEN - RETREATS. See
RETREATS FOR YOUNG WOMEN.

YOUNG WOMEN - SERMONS.
BQT 3016

YOUNG WOMEN'S CHRISTIAN ASSOCIATIONS.
BV 1300-1393
Subdivisions as in LC.

YOUTH - MEDITATIONS.
BQT 2564

YOUTH - PRAYER-BOOKS.
BQT 2638

YOUTH - RELIGIOUS LIFE.
BQT 2282-2287
sa Boys - Religious life.
Girls - Religious life.
Retreats for children.
Retreats for young men.
Retreats for young women.
Young men - Religious life.
Young women - Religious life.

YOUTH - SERMONS.
BQT 3015-3017

YOUTH, CHURCH WORK WITH. See
CHURCH WORK WITH YOUTH.

YOUTH, JEWISH - RELIGIOUS LIFE.

YOUTH MOVEMENT, CATHOLIC. See
CATHOLIC YOUTH MOVEMENT.

YUGOSLAVIA - CHURCH HISTORY.
BQX 2672-2690
BQX 6301-6308 (Orthodox
Church)

ZACHARIAS, BOOK OF. See
BIBLE. O.T. ZACHARIAS.

ZADKOKITES.
BM 175.Z
xx Jewish sects.
Priests, Jewish.

ZAIDITES.
BP 195.Z   (297)
xx Mohammedan sects.

ZEALOTS (JEWISH PARTY)
  xx Jewish sects.
  Other references as in LC.

ZECHARIAH, BOOK OF. See
  BIBLE. O.T. ZACHARIAS.

ZEN (SECT)
      BL 1442.Z
  xx Buddhist sects.

ZENANA MISSIONS.
  xx Missions, Medical.

ZEPHANIAH, BOOK OF. See
  BIBLE. O.T. SOPHONIAS.

ZIONISM.   (Geog. subdiv., Direct)
      DS 149   (296)
  Scope note and references
    as in LC.

ZIONISM, GENERAL. See
  GENERAL ZIONISM.

ZIONISM AND JUDAISM.
  References as in LC.

ZIONISTS.
  Subdivisions as in LC.

ZOOLATRY. See
  ANIMAL-WORSHIP.

ZOOLOGY OF THE BIBLE. See
  BIBLE - NATURAL HISTORY.

ZOROASTRIANISM.
      BL 1500-1590   (295)
  References as in LC.

ZWINGLIANISM.
      BR 345-346   (284.2)
  sa Calvinism.
  xx Calvinism.
    Reformed Church.

APPENDIX

NAMES OF SAINTS

At the request of catalogers and librarians in Catholic libraries a list of names of saints with cross references from variant forms of the name, English, vernacular and Latin, was published as an appendix to the third edition of Catholic Subject Headings. The list was so well received that it was repeated in expanded form in the fourth edition, and is again included in further expanded form in the fifth edition, with but slight changes.

The original list was based on the findings and conclusions of a study made by one of the library science students at the Catholic University of America. The student had accepted an assignment to make a study of the forms for names of saints in a catalog where the names had been established according to ALA rules and Library of Congress practice.[1] The investigation was prompted by a twofold experience: the annoying lack of uniformity in the files, and the difficulty encountered by both catalogers and users in locating entries. The findings of the study disclosed that the practical application of ALA rule 47 (Saints) with its exceptions, besides ignoring usage, is in large measure an arbitrary procedure, especially in regard to medieval and modern saints, producing great diversity and many inconsistencies.

A comparison with the practice of leading libraries in other countries, and with the practice of European and American bibliographic and reference tools, indicates that usage in a particular country is the basic norm for establishing names of saints. The British Museum, for example, enters all saints, ancient, medieval and modern, according to English usage (e.g., Jerome, Saint; Francis of Assisi, Saint; Philip Neri, Saint) and achieves accessibility and uniformity. Similarly, the Bibliothèque Nationale enters saints according to French usage, with direct approach and uniformity in the entries.

Accessibility and direct approach, consistency and uniformity, and simplicity would seem to be the desirable criteria for devising rules governing name entries. With this in mind, the following basic procedure is suggested, according to which the list of saints' names submitted below is constructed:
    1) Enter saints under forename.
    2) The name is established according to English usage.
    3) Make references from the various forms in use.

Saints are thus entered under forename according to the accepted form of the name in this country. The entry will, consequently, be in English. A foreign form, either Latin or vernacular, is used only when that is accepted usage in this country. Examples:
        Jerome, Saint.
        Caesarius, Saint.
        Maria Goretti, Saint.

1. Sister Mary Julia Burkart, S.C.M.M. Forms of Saints' Names in the Public Catalog of the Catholic University of America Library. A Dissertation Submitted to the Catholic University of America in Partial Fulfillment of the Requirements for the Degree of Master of Science in Library Science. 1953.

It will then be necessary to outline methods for differentiating saints bearing the same forename, which is again done according to common usage in referring to them, as follows:

1) Forename followed by an epithet usually associated with the name (attributive, place of origin, etc.). Examples:

    Albert the Great, Saint.
    Catherine of Siena, Saint.
    John of the Cross, Saint.

2) Forename followed by surname (this is the practice for many modern saints). Examples:

    Frances Cabrini, Saint.
    John Berchmans, Saint.

3) The title of office is added (in English) after the designation "Saint" when neither of the foregoing provisions applies, or whenever it is desirable to do so for ready identification. The title of office is always added for popes and for sovereigns. Examples:

    Augustine, Saint, Abp. of Canterbury.
    Augustine, Saint, Bp. of Hippo.
    Benedict, Saint, Abbot of Monte Cassino.
    Gregory VII, Saint, Pope.
    Louis IX, Saint, King of France.

The foregoing procedure and directives are not new discoveries. They merely revert to well established practice, which practice is in turn based on expressed or implied directives. Clearly formulated methods of procedure, in substance identical with the above summarized procedure, can be found in the Vatican Norme (rule 60), in Attwater's Dictionary of Saints, and in The Book of Saints by the Ramsgate Benedictines. The method outlined above is also a logical development of rule 23 in Cutter's Rules for a Dictionary Catalogue, which says: "Put under Christian or forename ... b. Persons canonized." It is interesting to note that the British Museum, which enters all saints under forename, in the new edition of its printed catalog is changing the entries for two sixteenth-century personalities, both canonized in 1935, to forename entries, though it had a long list of titles arranged under each surname form, as both were voluminous authors. The new forms of entry read: John Fisher, Saint, and Thomas More, Saint (with reference from More, Sir Thomas).

Because of the great span of history covered by the Christian saints, with the same names recurring in different centuries, and because much of the literature consists of biographical studies, it is considered useful to add the dates of birth and death, even if only approximate, in the heading.

This list is not intended to be an exhaustive list of saints' names. It includes those names more likely to come within the average cataloger's experience while processing books. Additional names can be found as needed in the various dictionaries and encyclopedias listed below, also in the British Museum Catalogue of Printed Books and in the current British National Bibliography. A comprehensive new encyclopedia of the saints, projected in ten folio volumes, of which two volumes have been published to date, entitled Bibliotheca Sanctorum (text in

Italian), is another of the inspirations of the late Pope John XXIII. It will include all names ever considered as saints, with the appropriate information and
guidance under each name, also variant forms of the name, truly an encyclopedia
for its purpose. An English edition is in the planning.

References

In addition to the theological encyclopedias listed in front of this work,
the following publications are specifically useful for establishing the English
form of saints' name and for determining variant forms in other languages.

Acta sanctorum quotquot toto orbe coluntur vel a catholicis scriptoribus cele-
    brantur, quae ex latinis et graecis aliarumque gentium antiquis monumentis
    collegit, digessit, notis illustravit Joannes Bollandus, Societatis Jesu ...
    Editio novissima, curante Joanne Carnandet. Parisiis, V. Palme, 1863-
    (67 vols. have been published to date)
Attwater, Donald. A dictionary of the saints. New and rev. ed. London, Burns
    & Oates, 1958.
Baring-Gould, Sabine. The lives of the saints ... New and rev. ed. 16 v.
    Edinburgh, J. Grant, 1914.
Baudot, J. L., O.S.B. Vies des saints et des bienheureux selon l'ordre du calen-
    drier, avec l'historiques des fêtes, par les rr. pp. Baudot et Chaussin,
    O.S.B. 13 v. Paris, Letouzey et Ané, 1935-59.
Bibliotheca sanctorum [dal] Istituto Giovanni XXIII nella Pontificia Università
    Lateranense. Roma, 1961-
The Book of saints; a dictionary of the servants of God canonized by the Catholic
    Church: extracted from the Roman & other martyrologies. Compiled by the
    Benedictine monks of St. Augustine's Abbey, Ramsgate. 4th ed., rev. and enl.
    New York, Macmillan, 1947.
Butler, Alban. Lives of the saints. Edited, revised and supplemented by Herbert
    Thurston, S.J., and Donald Attwater. 4 v. New York, Kenedy, 1956.
Coulson, John, ed. The saints; a concise biographical dictionary. With an in-
    troduction by C. C. Martindale, S. J. London, Burns & Oates; New York,
    Hawthorn Books, 1958.
Holweck, F. G. A biographical dictionary of the saints, with a general introduc-
    tion on hagiology. St. Louis, Herder, 1924. (This is by far the most com-
    prehensive of the single-volume dictionaries of the saints, though other
    later publications are at times more accurate)

Adalbert, Saint, Abp. of Prague,
    956(ca.)-997.
  x Adalbertus, Saint, Abp. of Prague.
  x Voitech, Saint, Abp. of Prague.

Adalbertus, Saint, Abp. of Prague. See
  Adalbert, Saint, Abp. of Prague,
  956(ca.)-997.

Adalheida, Saint. See
  Adelaide, Saint, 931-999.

Adam (Biblical character)
  x Adamus (Biblical character)

Adamus (Biblical character) See
  Adam (Biblical character)

Adelaide, Saint, 931-999.
  x Adalheida, Saint.
  x Adelheid, Saint.

Adelheid, Saint. See
  Adelhaide, Saint, 931-999.

Ado, Saint, Abp. of Vienne,
    800(ca.)-875.
  x Adon, Saint, Abp. of Vienne.

Adon, Saint, Abp. of Vienne. See
  Ado, Saint, Abp. of Vienne,
  800(ca.)-875.

Aegidius, Saint. See
  Giles, Saint, d. ca. 725.

Aelred, Saint, 1109?-1166.
  x Aelredus, Saint.
  x Ailred, Saint.
  x Ethelred, Saint.
  x Ethilredus, Saint.

Aelredus, Saint. See
  Aelred, Saint, 1109?-1166.

Aemilian, Saint. See
  Emilian, Saint, d. 574.

Agatha, Saint, 3d century.

Agnes, Saint, 3d century.

Agnes de Assisio, Saint. See
  Agnes of Assisi, Saint, d. 1253.

Agnes de Monte-Politiano, Saint. See
  Agnes of Montepulciano, Saint,
  1268(ca.)-1317.

Agnes of Assisi, Saint, d. 1253.
  x Agnes de Assisio, Saint.
  x Agnese di Assisi, Saint.

Agnes of Montepulciano, Saint,
    1268(c .)-1317.
  x Agnes de Monte-Politiano, Saint.
  x Agnese da Montepulciano, Saint.
  x Inés de Monte Pulciano.
  x Segni, Agnese de'.

Agnese da Montepulciano, Saint. See
  Agnes of Montepulciano, Saint,
  1268(ca.)-1317.

Agnese di Assisi, Saint. See
  Agnes of Assisi, Saint, d. 1253.

Ailred, Saint. See
  Aelred, Saint, 1109?-1166.

Alacoque, Margaret Mary, Saint. See
  Margaret Mary Alacoque, Saint,
  1647-1690.

Albert the Great, Saint, 1193-1280.
  x Albertus Magnus, Saint.

Albertus Magnus, Saint. See
  Albert the Great, Saint, 1193-1280.

Alcantara, Peter of, Saint. See
  Peter of Alcantara, Saint, 1499-
  1562.

Alcimus Ecdicius Avitus, Saint. See
  Avitus, Alcimus Ecdicius, Saint,
  d. 518.

Aldhelm, Saint, Bp. of Sherborne,
    640-709
  x Aldhelmus, Saint, Bp. of Sher-
    borne.
  x Ealdhelm, Saint, Bp. of Sher-
    borne.

Aldhelmus, Saint, Bp. of Sherborne.
See   Aldhelm, Saint, Bp. of Sherborne, 640-709.

Alfonso Maria de' Liguori, Saint. See
Alphonsus Liguori, Saint, 1696-1787.

Alonso Rodriguez, Saint. See
Alphonsus Rodriguez, Saint,
1532-1617.

Aloysius Gonzaga, Saint, 1568-1591.
x Gonzaga, Aloysius, Saint.
x Gonzaga, Luigi, Saint.
x Luigi Gonzaga, Saint.

Alphonsus Liguori, Saint, 1696-1787.
x Alfonso Maria de' Liguori, Saint.
x Liguori, Alfonso Maria de', Saint.

Alphonsus Rodriguez, Saint, 1532-1617.
x Alonso Rodriguez, Saint.
x Rodriguez, Alonso, Saint.

Amadeus, Saint, Bp. of Lausanne,
ca. 1110-1159.
x Amédée, Saint, Bp. of Lausanne.

Amandus, Saint, 7th century.

Amarinus, Saint, d. 674.
x Marinus, Saint.

Ambrose, Saint, Bp. of Milan, 340-397.
x Ambrosius, Saint, Bp. of Milan.

Ambrosius, Saint, Bp. of Milan. See
Ambrose, Saint, Bp. of Milan, 340-
397.

Amédée, Saint, Bp. of Lausanne. See
Amadeus, Saint, Bp. of Lausanne,
ca. 1110-1159.

Anastasius I, Saint, Pope, d. 401.

Anastasius I, Saint, Patriarch of
Antioch, d. 599.

André Fournet, Saint. See
Andrew Fournet, Saint, 1752-1834.

Andrea Avellino, Saint. See
Andrew Avellino, Saint, 1521-1608.

Andreas, Saint, Apostle. See
Andrew, Saint, Apostle.

Andreas Avellino, Saint. See
Andrew Avellino, Saint, 1521-1608.

Andreas Bobola, Saint. See
Andrew Bobola, Saint, 1591?-1657.

Andreas Fournet, Saint. See
Andrew Fournet, Saint, 1752-1834.

Andrew, Saint, Apostle.
x Andreas, Saint, Apostle.

Andrew Avellino, Saint, 1521-1608.
x Andrea Avellino, Saint.
x Andreas Avellino, Saint.
x Avellino, Andrea, Saint.

Andrew Bobola, Saint, 1591?-1657.
x Andreas Bobola, Saint.
x Andrzej Bobola, Saint.
x Bobola, Andrew, Saint.

Andrew Fournet, Saint, 1752-1834.
x André Fournet, Saint.
x Andreas Fournet, Saint.
x Fournet, André Hubert, Saint.

Andrzej Bobola, Saint. See
Andrew Bobola, Saint, 1591?-1657.

Angela Merici, Saint, 1474-1540.
x Merici, Angela, Saint.

Angilbert, Saint, Abbot of St.
Riquier, d. 814.
x Angilbertus, Saint, Abbot of
St. Riquier.
x Engelbert, Saint, Abbot of
St. Riquier.
x Engelbertus, Saint, Abbot of
St. Riquier.
x Inglevert, Saint, Abbot of
St. Riquier.

Angilbertus, Saint, Abbot of St.
Riquier. See Angilbert, Saint,
Abbot of St. Riquier, d. 814.

Anna, Saint, Mother of the Blessed
Virgin Mary. See Anne, Saint,
Mother of the Blessed Virgin Mary.

Anne, Saint, Mother of the Blessed
   Virgin Mary.
   x Anna, Saint, Mother of the
      Blessed Virgin Mary.

Anschar, Saint. See
   Ansgar, Saint, Abp. of Hamburg
   and Bremen, 801-865.

Anselm, Saint, Abp. of Canterbury,
   1033-1109.
   x Anselmus, Saint, Abp. of
      Canterbury.

Anselm, Saint, Bp. of Lucca, d. 1086.
   x Anselmo, Saint, Bp. of Lucca.
   x Anselmus, Saint, Bp. of Lucca.

Anselmo, Saint, Bp. of Lucca. See
   Anselm, Saint, Bp. of Lucca, d. 1086.

Anselmus, Saint, Abp. of Canterbury.
   See Anselm, Saint, Abp. of Canterbury, 1033-1109.

Anselmus, Saint, Bp. of Lucca. See
   Anselm, Saint, Bp. of Lucca, d. 1086.

Ansgar, Saint, Abp. of Hamburg and
      Bremen, 801-865.
   x Anschar, Saint.
   x Ansgarius, Saint.
   x Anskar, Saint.

Ansgarius, Saint. See
   Ansgar, Saint, Abp. of Hamburg and
   Bremen, 801-865.

Anskar, Saint. See
   Ansgar, Saint, Abp. of Hamburg and
   Bremen, 801-865.

Anthony, Saint, 251?-356?
   x Anthony of the Desert, Saint.
   x Antonius Magnus, Saint.

Anthony Claret, Saint, 1807-1870.
   x Antonio María Claret y Clará,
      Saint.
   x Antonius Maria Claret, Saint.
   x Claret y Clará, Antonio María,
      Saint.

Anthony Gianelli, Saint, 1789-1846.
   x Antonio Maria Gianelli, Saint.
   x Antonius Maria Gianelli, Saint.
   x Gianelli, Antonio Maria, Saint.

Anthony of Padua, Saint, 1195-1231.
   x Antonio de Padova, Saint.
   x Antonio de Lisboa, Saint.
   x Antonius de Padua, Saint.
   x Antony of Padua, Saint.

Anthony of the Desert, Saint. See
   Anthony, Saint, 251?-356?

Anthony Zaccaria, Saint, 1502-1539.
   x Antonio Maria Zaccaria, Saint.
   x Antonius Maria Zaccaria, Saint.
   x Zaccaria, Antonio Maria, Saint.

Antonino Pierozzi, Saint. See
   Antoninus, Saint, Abp. of Florence,
   1389-1459.

Antoninus, Saint, Abp. of Florence,
   1389-1459.
   x Antonino Pierozzi, Saint.
   x Pierozzi, Antonino, Saint.

Antoninus, Saint, of Placentia,
   4th century.

Antoninus, Saint, Abbot of Sorrento,
   d. 830.

Antonio de Padova, Saint. See
   Anthony of Padua, Saint, 1195-1231.

Antonio de Lisboa, Saint. See
   Anthony of Padua, Saint, 1195-1231.

Antonio María Claret y Clará, Saint.
   See Anthony Claret, Saint, 1807-1870.

Antonio Maria Gianelli, Saint. See
   Anthony Gianelli, Saint, 1789-1846.

Antonio Maria Zaccaria, Saint. See
   Anthony Zaccaria, Saint, 1502-1539.

Antonius de Padua, Saint. See
   Anthony of Padua, Saint, 1195-1231.

Antonius Magnus, Saint. See
   Anthony, Saint, 251?-356?

Antonius Maria Claret, Saint. See
   Anthony Claret, Saint, 1807-1870.

Antonius Maria Gianelli, Saint. See
   Anthony Gianelli, Saint, 1789-1846.

Antonius Maria Zaccaria, Saint. See
   Anthony Zaccaria, Saint, 1502-1539.

Antony of Padua, Saint. See
   Anthony of Padua, Saint, 1195-1231.

Apollonia, Saint, d. 249.

Aquinas, Thomas, Saint. See
   Thomas Aquinas, Saint, 1225?-1274.

Arrighi, Biagio. See
   Theophilus of Corte, Saint,
   1676-1740.

Athanasius, Saint, Patriarch of
   Alexandria, d. 373.

Attala, Saint, d. 741.

Audoenus, Saint. See
   Owen, Saint, Bp. of Rouen,
   ca. 609-ca. 683.

Audoin, Saint. See
   Owen, Saint, Bp. of Rouen,
   ca. 609-ca. 683.

Augustine, Saint, Abp. of Canterbury,
   d. 604.
   x Augustinus, Saint, Abp. of
     Canterbury.

Augustine, Saint, Bp. of Hippo.
   (354-430)
   x Augustinus, Saint, Bp. of Hippo.
   x Augustinus, Aurelius, Saint,
     Bp. of Hippo.

Augustinus, Saint, Abp. of Canterbury.
   See Augustine, Saint, Abp. of
   Canterbury, d. 604.

Augustinus, Saint, Bp. of Hippo. See
   Augustine, Saint, Bp. of Hippo,
   354-430.

Augustinus, Aurelius, Saint, Bp. of
   Hippo. See Augustine, Saint, Bp. of
   Hippo, 354-430.

Avellino, Andrea, Saint. See
   Andrew Avellino, Saint, 1521-1608.

Avitus, Saint, of Aurillac, d. 527.

Avitus, Saint, Abp. of Vienne. See
   Avitus, Alcimus Ecdicius, Saint,
   d. 518.

Avitus, Alcimus Ecdicius, Saint,
   d. 518.
   x Alcimus Ecdicius Avitus, Saint.
   x Avitus, Saint, Abp. of Vienne.

Baeda Venerabilis, Saint. See
   Bede the Venerable, Saint, 673-735.

Barat, Madeleine Louise Sophie, Saint.
   See Madeleine Sophie Barat, Saint,
   1779-1865.

Barbarigo, Gregorio, Saint. See
   Gregory Barbarigo, Saint, 1625-1697.

Barnabas, Saint, Apostle.

Bartholomaeus, Saint, Apostle. See
   Bartholomew, Saint, Apostle.

Bartholomew, Saint, Apostle.
   x Bartholomaeus, Saint, Apostle.

Bartolomea Capitanio, Saint, 1807-1833.
   x Capitanio, Bartolomea, Saint.

Basil, Saint, the Great, 330(ca.)-379.
   x Basilius, Saint, the Great.
   x Basilius Magnus, Saint.

Basilius, Saint, the Great. See
   Basil, Saint, the Great, 330(ca.)-
   379.

Basilius Magnus, Saint. See
    Basil, Saint, the Great, 330(ca.)-
    379.

Baudolinus, Saint, d. 730.

Baylon, Paschal, Saint. See
    Paschal Baylon, Saint, 1540-1592.

Becket, Thomas, Saint. See
    Thomas à Becket, Saint, Abp. of
    Canterbury, 1118?-1170.

Beda Venerabilis, Saint. See
    Bede the Venerable, Saint, 673-735.

Bede the Venerable, Saint, 673-735.
    x Baeda Venerabilis, Saint.
    x Beda Venerabilis, Saint.

Bellarmine, Robert, Saint. See
    Robert Bellarmine, Saint, 1542-1621.

Bellarmino, Roberto Francesco Romolo,
    Saint. See Robert Bellarmine,
    Saint, 1542-1621.

Beltrán, Luis, Saint. See
    Louis Bertrand, Saint, 1525-1581.

Benedetto il Moro, Saint. See
    Benedict the Moor, Saint, 1526-1589.

Benedict, Saint, of Aniane, d. 821.
    x Benedictus, Saint, of Aniane.

Benedict, Saint, Abbot of Monte
    Cassino, 480-547.
    x Benedict of Nursia, Saint.
    x Benedictus, Saint, Abbot of
      Monte Cassino.

Benedict, Saint, the Bridge Builder.
    See Bénézet, Saint, d. 1184.

Benedict Biscop, Saint, 628-(ca.)-
    689 or 690.
    x Benedictus Biscop, Saint.
    x Biscop, Benedict, Saint.

Benedict Joseph Labre, Saint,
    1748-1783.
    x Benedictus Josephus Labre, Saint.
    x Benoit Joseph Labre, Saint.
    x Labre, Benedict Joseph, Saint.

Benedict of Nursia, Saint. See
    Benedict, Saint, Abbot of Monte
    Cassino, 480-547.

Benedict the Moor, Saint, 1526-1589.
    x Benedetto il Moro, Saint.
    x Benedictus a S. Philadelpho.

Benedictus, Saint, of Aniane. See
    Benedict, Saint, of Aniane, d. 821.

Benedictus, Saint, Abbot of Monte
    Cassino. See Benedict, Saint,
    Abbot of Monte Cassino, 480-547.

Benedictus a S. Philadelpho. See
    Benedict the Moor, Saint, 1526-1589.

Benedictus Biscop, Saint. See
    Benedict Biscop, Saint, 628(ca.)-
    589 or 590.

Benedictus Fundator Pontis Avenioen-
    sis. See Benezet, Saint, d. 1184.

Benedictus Josephus Labre, Saint.
    See Benedict Joseph Labre, Saint,
    1748-1783.

Bénézet, Saint, d. 1184.
    x Benedict, Saint, the Bridge
      Builder.
    x Benedictus Fundator Pontis
      Avenionensis.

Benincasa, Caterina. See
    Catherine of Siena, Saint,
    1347-1380.

Benizi, Philip, Saint. See
    Philip Benizi, Saint, 1233-1285.

Benoit Joseph Labre, Saint. See
    Benedict Joseph Labre, Saint,
    1748-1783.

Berchmans, Jan, Saint. See
John Berchmans, Saint, 1599-1621.

Berchmans, John, Saint. See
John Berchmans, Saint, 1599-1621.

Bernadetta Soubirous, Saint. See
Bernadette Soubirous, Saint,
1844-1879.

Bernadette Soubirous, Saint.
1844-1879.
x Bernadetta Soubirous, Saint.
x Marie Bernard, Soeur.
x Soubirous, Bernadette, Saint.

Bernard of Clairvaux, Saint,
1091?-1153.
x Bernardus, Saint, of Clairvaux.

Bernard of Menthon, Saint, 923-1008.
x Bernardus Menthonensis, Saint.

Bernard Tolomei, Saint, 1272-1348.
x Bernardus Ptolomaeus, Saint.
x Ptolomaeus, Bernardus, Saint.
x Tolomei, Bernard, Saint.

Bernardine of Siena, Saint, 1380-1444.
x Bernardino da Siena, Saint.
x Bernardinus Senensis, Saint.

Bernardino da Siena, Saint. See
Bernardine of Siena, Saint,
1380-1444.

Bernardinus Senensis, Saint. See
Bernardine of Siena, Saint.
1380-1444.

Bernardone of Assisi, Francesco. See
Francis of Assisi, Saint, 1182-1226.

Bernardus, Saint, of Clairvaux. See
Bernard of Clairvaux, Saint,
1091?-1153.

Bernardus Menthonensis, Saint. See
Bernard of Menthon, Saint, 923-1008.

Bernardus Ptolomaeus, Saint. See
Bernard Tolomei, Saint, 1272-1348.

Bertilla Boscardin, Saint, 1888-1922.
x Boscardin, Bertilla, Saint.

Bertrand, Louis, Saint. See
Louis Bertrand, Saint, 1525-1581.

Bianchi, Francesco Saverio, Saint.
See Francis Xavier Bianchi, Saint,
1743-1815.

Bichier des Ages, Jeanne Elisabeth,
Saint. See Jeanne Elisabeth Bichier
des Ages, Saint, 1773-1838.

Billiart, Marie Rose Julie, Saint.
See Julia Billiart, Saint, 1751-
1816.

Bingen, Hildegard see Hildegard, Saint

Birgitta, Saint, of Sweden, 1303-1373.
x Bridget, Saint, of Sweden.
x Brigid, Saint, of Sweden.

Birndorfer, Johann Evangelist. See
Conrad of Parzham, Saint, 1818-
1894.

Biscop, Benedict, Saint. See
Benedict Biscop, Saint, 628(ca.)-
689 or 690.

Blasques Villacasten, Saint. See
Peter Baptist, Saint, 1545-1597.

Blessed Virgin, Mary. See
Mary, Blessed Virgin.

Bobola, Andrew, Saint. See
Andrew Bobola, Saint, 1591?-1657.

Boellet, Nicolette. See
Colette, Saint, 1381-1447.

Bonaventure, Saint. See
Bonaventure, Saint, 1221-1274.

Bonaventure, Saint, 1221-1274.
x Bonaventura, Saint.
x Fidanza, Giovanni.

Boniface I, Saint, Pope, d. 422.
x Bonifacius I, Saint, Pope.

Boniface IV, Saint, Pope, d. 615.
    x Bonifacius IV, Saint, Pope.

Boniface, Saint, Bp. of Lausanne,
    1181?-1260?
    x Boniface of Brussels, Saint.
    x Bonifacius, Saint, Bp. of
        Lausanne.

Boniface, Saint, Abp. of Mainz,
    680-755.
    x Bonifacius, Saint, Abp. of Mainz.
    x Winifried (Saint Boniface)

Boniface of Brussels, Saint. See
    Boniface, Saint, Bp. of Lausanne,
    1181?-1260?

Boniface of Querfurt, Saint, d. 1009.
    x Bonifacius of Querfurt, Saint.
    x Bruno of Querfurt, Saint.

Bonifacius I, Saint, Pope. See
    Boniface I, Saint, Pope, d. 422.

Bonifacius IV, Saint, Pope. See
    Boniface IV, Saint, Pope, d. 615.

Bonifacius, Saint, Bp. of Lausanne.
    See Boniface, Saint, Bp. of
    Lausanne, 1181?-1260?

Bonifacius, Saint, Abp. of Mainz. See
    Boniface, Saint, Abp. of Mainz,
    680-755.

Bonifacius of Querfurt, Saint. See
    Boniface of Querfurt, Saint, d. 1009.

Borgia, Francesco, Saint. See
    Francis Borgia, Saint, 1510-1672.

Borja, Francisco, Saint. See
    Francis Borgia, Saint, 1510-1572.

Borromeo, Charles, Saint. See
    Charles Borromeo, Saint, 1538-1584.

Boscardin, Bertilla, Saint. See
    Bertilla Boscardin, Saint, 1888-1922.

Bosco, Giovanni, Saint. See
    John Bosco, Saint, 1815-1888.

Bosco, John, Saint. See
    John Bosco, Saint, 1815-1888.

Brandanus, Saint. See
    Brendan, Saint, d. 577.

Brébeuf, Jean de, Saint. See
    John de Brébeuf, Saint, 1593-1649.

Brendan, Saint, d. 577.
    x Brandanus, Saint.
    x Brendanus, Saint.

Brendanus, Saint. See
    Brendan, Saint, d. 577.

Bride, Saint, of Ireland. See
    Brigid, Saint, of Ireland.

Bridget, Saint, of Ireland. See
    Brigid, Saint, of Ireland,
    ca.453-ca.524.

Bridget, Saint, of Sweden. See
    Birgitta, Saint, of Sweden,
    1303-1373.

Brigid, Saint, of Ireland, ca.453-
    ca.524.
    x Bride, Saint, of Ireland.
    x Bridget, Saint, of Ireland.
    x Brigida, Saint.

Brigid, Saint, of Sweden. See
    Birgitta, Saint, of Sweden,
    1303-1373.

Brigida, Saint. See
    Brigid, Saint, of Ireland,
    ca.453-ca.524.

Brito, João de, Saint. See
    John de Britto, Saint, 1647-1693.

Bruno, Saint, 1039(ca.)-1101.

Bruno, Saint, Abp. of Cologne,
    925-1054.

Bruno, Saint, Bp. of Segni, 1048-1123.
    x Bruno of Asti, Saint.

Bruno, Bp. of Toul. See
    Leo IX, Saint, Pope, 1002-1054.

Bruno of Asti, Saint. See
  Bruno, Saint, Bp. of Segni,
  1048-1123.

Bruno of Querfurt, Saint. See
  Boniface of Querfurt, Saint,
  d. 1009.

Bruno von Egisheim, Saint. See
  Leo IX, Saint, Pope, 1002-1054.

Bufalo, Gaspar del, Saint. See
  Gaspar del Bufalo, Saint, 1786-1837.

Bussa de Leoni, Francesca. See
  Frances of Rome, Saint, 1384-1440.

Cabrini, Frances Xavier, Saint. See
  Frances Cabrini, Saint, 1850-1917.

Caecilia, Saint. See
  Cecilia, Saint, 2d century.

Caesarius, Saint, Bp. of Arles,
  470?-543.

Cafasso, Giuseppe, Saint. See
  Joseph Cafasso, Saint, 1811-1860.

Cajetan, Saint, 1480-1547.
  x Cajetanus, Saint.
  x Gaetan, Saint.
  x Gaetano, Saint.

Cajetanus, Saint. See
  Cajetan, Saint, 1480-1547.

Calosinto, Carlo Gaetano. See
  John Joseph of the Cross, Saint,
  1654-1739.

Calybites, John, Saint. See
  John Calybites, Saint, d. ca. 450.

Camillus de Lellis, Saint, 1550-1614.
  x Lellis, Camillus de, Saint.

Canisius, Peter, Saint. See
  Peter Canisius, Saint, 1521-1597.

Capistran, John, Saint. See
  John Capistran, Saint, 1386-1456.

Capistrano, Giovanni di, Saint. See
  John Capistran, Saint, 1386-1456.

Capitanio, Bartolomea, Saint. See
  Bartolomea Capitanio, Saint,
  1807-1833.

Caracciolo, Francis, Saint. See
  Francis Caracciolo, Saint,
  1563-1608.

Carlo Borromeo, Saint. See
  Charles Borromeo, Saint, 1538-1584.

Carlo da Sezze, Saint. See
  Charles of Sezze, Saint, 1613-1670.

Carolus Borromaeus, Saint. See
  Charles Borromeo, Saint, 1538-1584.

Carolus de Sezze, Saint. See
  Charles of Sezze, Saint, 1613-1670.

Casanuova, Paolo Girolamo. See
  Leonard of Port Maurice, Saint,
  1676-1751.

Catalina de Tomás, Saint. See
  Catherine Tomás, Saint, 1533-1574.

Caterina da Bologna, Saint. See
  Catherine of Bologna, Saint,
  1413-1463.

Caterina da Genova, Saint. See
  Catherine of Genoa, Saint,
  1447-1510.

Caterina da Siena, Saint. See
  Catherine of Siena, Saint,
  1347-1380.

Caterina de' Ricci, Saint. See
  Catherine de' Ricci, Saint,
  1525-1590.

Catharina Alexandriae, Saint. See
  Catherine of Alexandria, Saint,
  4th century.

Catharina Bononiensis, Saint. See
  Catherine of Bologna, Saint,
  1413-1463.

Catharina de Genua, Saint. See
    Catherine of Genoa, Saint,
    1447-1510.

Catharina de Ricciis, Saint. See
    Catherine de' Ricci, Saint,
    1525-1590.

Catharina Labouré, Saint. See
    Catherine Labouré, Saint, 1806-1876.

Catharina Senensis, Saint. See
    Catherine of Siena, Saint,
    1347-1380.

Catharina Suecciae, Saint. See
    Catherine of Sweden, Saint,
    1331-1381.

Catharina Tomás, Saint. See
    Catherine Tomás, Saint, 1533-1574.

Catherine de' Ricci, Saint, 1525-1590.
    x Caterina de' Ricci, Saint.
    x Catharina de Ricciis, Saint.
    x Romola, Alessandra Lucrezia.

Catherine Labouré, Saint, 1806-1876.
    x Catharina Labouré, Saint.
    x Labouré, Catherine, Saint.

Catherine of Alexandria, Saint,
    4th century.
    x Catharina Alexandriae, Saint.

Catherine of Bologna, Saint, 1413-1463.
    x Caterina da Bologna, Saint.
    x Catharina Bononiensis, Saint.
    x Vigri-Mammolini, Caterina.

Catherine of Genoa, Saint, 1447-1510.
    x Caterina da Genova, Saint.
    x Catharina de Genua, Saint.
    x Fieschi-Adorno, Caterina.

Catherine of Siena, Saint, 1347-1380.
    x Benincasa, Caterina.
    x Caterina da Siena, Saint.
    x Catharina Senensis, Saint.

Catherine of Sweden, Saint, 1331-1381.
    x Catharina Suecciae, Saint.

Catherine Tomás, Saint, 1533-1574.
    x Catalina de Tomás, Saint.
    x Catharina Tomás, Saint.
    x Tomás, Catalina de, Saint.

Cecilia, Saint, 2d century.
    x Caecilia, Saint.

Celestine I, Saint, Pope, d. 432.
    x Coelestinus I, Saint, Pope.

Celestine V, Saint, Pope,
    1215(ca.)-1296.
    x Coelestinus V, Saint, Pope.
    x Peter Celestine, Saint.
    x Petrus Coelestinus, Saint.
    x Pietro di Morrone.

Chanel, Pierre Louis Marie, Saint.
    See Peter Chanel, Saint, 1803-1841.

Chantal, Jeanne Françoise (Frémiot)
    de Rabutin, Baronne de, Saint. See
    Jane Frances de Chantal, Saint,
    1572-1641.

Charles Borromeo, Saint, 1538-1584.
    x Borromeo, Charles, Saint.
    x Carlo Borromeo, Saint.
    x Carolus Borromaeus, Saint.

Charles of Sezze, Saint, 1613-1670.
    x Carlo da Sezze, Saint.
    x Carolus de Sezze, Saint.
    x Melchiori, Carlo.

Chiara d'Assisi, Saint. See
    Clare of Assisi, Saint, d. 1253.

Chiara da Montefalco, Saint. See
    Clare of Montefalco, Saint,
    ca. 1268-1308.

Christopher, Saint.
    x Christophorus, Saint.

Christophorus, Saint. See
    Christopher, Saint.

Chrysologus, Peter, Saint. See
    Peter Chrysologus, Saint,
    ca. 400-ca. 450.

Chrysostom, John, Saint. See
   John Chrysostom, Saint, d. 407.

Chrysostomus, Joannes, Saint. See
   John Chrysostom, Saint, d. 407.

Ciaran, Saint. See
   Kieran, Saint, d. ca. 530.

Ciudad, Juan. See
   John of God, Saint, 1495-1550.

Clara of Assisi, Saint. See
   Clare of Assisi, Saint, d. 1253.

Clara de Cruce, Saint. See
   Clare of Montefalco, Saint,
   ca. 1268-1308.

Clara de Monte Falcone, Saint. See
   Clare of Montefalco, Saint,
   ca. 1268-1308.

Clare of Assisi, Saint, d. 1253.
   x Chiara d'Assisi, Saint.
   x Clara de Assisi, Saint.

Clare of Montefalco, Saint,
      ca. 1268-1308.
   x Chiara da Montefalco, Saint.
   x Clara de Cruce, Saint.
   x Clara de Monte Falcone, Saint.
   x Clare of the Cross, Saint.

Clare of the Cross. See
   Clare of Montefalco, Saint,
   ca. 1268-1308.

Claret y Clará, Antonio Maria, Saint.
   See Anthony Claret, Saint, 1807-
   1870.

Claver, Peter, Saint. See
   Peter Claver, Saint, 1580-1654.

Clemens Maria Hofbauer, Saint. See
   Clement Hofbauer, Saint, 1751-1820.

Clemens Romanus. See
   Clement I, Saint, Pope, d. ca. 99.

Clement I, Saint, Pope, d. ca. 99.
   x Clemens Romanus.

Clement Hofbauer, Saint, 1751-1820.
   x Clemens Maria Hofbauer, Saint.
   x Hofbauer, Clement, Saint.
   x Klemens Maria Hofbauer, Saint.

Climacus, Joannes, Saint. See
   John Climacus, Saint, ca.525-ca.606.

Clotilda, Saint, Queen of the Franks.
   See Clotilde, Saint, Queen of the
   Franks, 475?-545.

Clotilde, Saint, Queen of the Franks,
      475?-545.
   x Clotilda, Saint, Queen of the
      Franks.

Coelestinus I, Saint, Pope. See
   Celestine I, Saint, Pope, d. 432.

Coelestinus V, Saint, Pope. See
   Celestine V, Saint, Pope,
   1215(ca.)-1296.

Colette, Saint, 1381-1447.
   x Boellet, Nicolette.

Colman, Saint, Bp. of Kilmacduagh,
      d. 632.
   x Colmanus, Saint, Bp. of
      Kilmacduagh.

Colman, Saint, Bp. of Lindisfarne,
      d. 676.
   x Colmanus, Saint, Bp. of
      Lindisfarne.

Colman, Saint, of Stocherau, d. 1012.
   x Colmanus, Saint, of Stocherau.

Colmanus, Saint, Bp. of Kilmacduagh.
   See Colman, Saint, Bp. of
   Kilmacduagh, d. 632.

Colmanus, Saint, Bp. of Lindisfarne.
   See Colman, Saint, Bp. of
   Lindisfarne, d. 676.

Colmanus, Saint, of Stocherau. See
   Colman, Saint, of Stocherau, d. 1012.

Columba, Saint, 521-597.
  x Columcille, Saint.
  x Columkille, Saint.

Columban, Saint, 543-615.
  x Columbanus, Saint, Abbot of
    Luxeuil and Bobbio.

Columbanus, Saint, Abbot of Luxeuil
  and Bobbio. See Columban, Saint,
  543-615.

Columcille, Saint. See
  Columba, Saint, 521-597.

Columkille, Saint. See
  Columba, Saint, 521-597.

Confalonieri, Corrado. See
  Conrad of Piacenza, 1290(ca.)-
  1351.

Conrad, Saint, Bp. of Constance,
    d. 975.
  x Conradus, Saint, Bp. of Constance.

Conrad of Parzham, Saint, 1818-1894.
  x Birndorfer, Johann Evangelist.
  x Conradus de Parzham, Saint.
  x Konrad von Parzham, Saint.

Conrad of Piacenza, Saint,
    1290(ca.)-1351.
  x Confalonieri, Corrado.
  x Conradus de Piacenza, Saint.
  x Corrado di Piacenza, Saint.

Conradus, Saint, Bp. of Constance.
  See Conrad, Saint, Bp. of
  Constance, d. 975.

Conradus de Parzham, Saint. See
  Conrad of Parzham, Saint, 1818-
  1894.

Conradus de Piacenza, Saint. See
  Conrad of Piacenza, Saint,
  1290(ca.)-1351.

Constabilis, Saint, Abbot of
  Cava, d. 1124.

Corrado di Piacenza, Saint. See
  Conrad of Piacenza, Saint,
  1290(ca.)-1351.

Cottolengo, Joseph Benedict, Saint.
  See Joseph Benedict Cottolengo,
  Saint, 1786-1842.

Cousin, Germaine, Saint. See
  Germaine Cousin, Saint, 1579-1601.

Cuthbert, Saint, 635-687.
  x Cuthbertus, Saint, Bp. of
    Lindisfarne.

Cuthbertus, Saint, Bp. of Lindisfarne.
  See Cuthbert, Saint, 635-687.

Cyprian, Saint, Bp. of Carthage,
    200(ca.)-258.
  x Cyprianus, Saint, Bp. of Carthage.

Cyprianus, Saint, Bp. of Carthage.
  See Cyprian, Saint, Bp. of
  Carthage, 200(ca.)-258.

Cyril, Saint, Patriarch of Alexandria,
    ca. 370-444.
  x Cyrillus, Saint, Patriarch of
    Alexandria.

Cyril, Saint, Bp. of Jerusalem,
    315(ca.)-386.
  x Cyrillus, Saint, Bp. of Jerusalem.

Cyril, Saint, of Thessalonica,
    827(ca.)-869.
  x Cyrillus, Saint, of Thessalonica.

Cyril, Saint, of Thurow, d. 1182.
  x Cyrillus, Saint, of Thurow.

Cyrillus, Saint, Patriarch of
  Alexandria. See Cyril, Saint,
  Patriarch of Alexandria, ca.370-444.

Cyrillus, Saint, Bp. of Jerusalem. See
  Cyril, Saint, Bp. of Jerusalem,
  315(ca.)-386.

Cyrillus, Saint, of Thessalonica.
See Cyril, Saint, of Thessalonica,
827(ca.)-869.

Cyrillus, Saint, of Thurow. See
Cyril, Saint, of Thurow, d. 1182.

Dadon, Saint. See
Owen, Saint, Bp. of Rouen,
ca. 609-ca. 683.

Damian, Peter, Saint. See
Peter Damian, Saint, 1007?-1072.

Damiani, Pietro, Saint. See
Peter Damian, Saint, 1007?-1072.

Danei, Paolo. See
Paul of the Cross, Saint, 1694-1775.

David, King of Israel.

David, Saint, 6th century.
x Dewi, Saint.

Davila y Ahumada, Teresa Sanchez
Cepeda. See Teresa of Avila,
Saint, 1515-1582.

Desa, Giuseppe. See
Joseph of Cupertino, Saint,
1603-1663.

De Sales, Francis, Saint. See
Francis de Sales, Saint, 1567-1622.

Desmaisières y Lopez de Dicastello
y Olmedo, María Micaela, vizcondesa
de Jorbalán. See Mary Michaela of
the Blessed Sacrament, Saint,
1809-1865.

Dewi, Saint. See
David, Saint, 6th century.

Di Rosa, Paolina. See
Maria Crocifissa Di Rosa, Saint,
1813-1855.

Divini, Pacifico, O.F.M. See
Pacificus of San Severino, Saint,
1653-1721.

Domenico Savio, Saint. See
Dominic Savio, Saint, 1842-1857.

Domingo de Guzman, Saint. See
Dominic, Saint, 1170-1221.

Domingo de Silos, Saint. See
Dominic of Silos, Saint, d. 1073.

✓ Dominic, Saint, 1170-1221.
x Domingo de Guzman, Saint.
x Dominicus Guzman, Saint.
x Guzman, Domingo de, Saint.

Dominic of Silos, Saint, d. 1073.
x Domingo de Silos, Saint.
x Dominicus de Silos, Saint.

Dominic Savio, Saint, 1842-1857.
x Domenico Savio, Saint.
x Dominicus Savio, Saint.
x Savio, Domenico, Saint.

Dominicus de Silos, Saint. See
Dominic of Silos, Saint, d. 1073.

Dominicus Guzman, Saint. See
Dominic, Saint, 1170-1221.

Dominicus Savio, Saint. See
Dominic Savio, Saint, 1842-1857.

Dorotheus, Saint, Archimandrite
of Gaza, 6th century.

Ealdhelm, Saint, Bp. of Sherborne.
See Aldhelm, Saint, Bp. of
Sherborne, 640-709.

Edmund, Saint, King of East Anglia,
841-870.
x Edmundus, Saint, King of East
Anglia.

Edmund, Saint, Abp. of Canterbury,
d. 1240.
x Edmund Rich, Saint, Abp. of
Canterbury.
x Edmundus Rich, Saint, Abp. of
Canterbury.

Edmund Rich, Saint, Abp. of Canterbury.
   See Edmund, Saint, Abp. of
   Canterbury, d. 1240.

Edmundus, Saint, King of East Anglia.
   See Edmund, Saint, King of East
   Anglia, 841-870.

Edmundus Rich, Saint. See
   Edmund, Saint, Abp. of Canterbury,
   d. 1240.

Eligius, Saint, ca. 590-660.
   x Eloi, Saint.

Elisabeth von Thüringen, Saint. See
   Elizabeth of Hungary, Saint,
   1207-1231.

Elizabeth Ann SETON, St.
   x Seton, Elizabeth Ann

Elizabeth of Hungary, Saint, 1207-1231.
   x Elisabeth von Thüringen, Saint.

Elizabeth of Portugal, Saint, 1271-
   1336.
   x Isabel, Saint.

Eloi, Saint. See
   Eligius, Saint, ca. 590-660.

Emilian, Saint, d. 574.
   x Aemilian, Saint.
   x Millán de la Cogolla, Saint.

Emilie de Vialar, Saint, 1797-1856.
   x Vialar, Emilie, Saint.

Emiliani, Jerome, Saint. See
   Jerome Emiliani, Saint, 1486-1537.

Emily de Rodat, Saint, 1787-1852.
   x Rodat, Marie Emilie de, Saint.

Engelbert, Saint, Abbot of St.
   Riquier. See Angilbert, Saint,
   Abbot of St. Riquier, d. 814.

Engelbert, Saint, Bp. of Cologne,
   1185(ca.)-1225.
   x Engelbertus, Saint, Bp. of
   Cologne.

Engelbertus, Saint, Bp. of Cologne,
   See Engelbert, Saint, Bp. of
   Cologne, 1185(ca.)-1225.

Engelbertus, Saint, Abbot of St.
   Riquier. See Angilbert, Saint,
   Abbot of St. Riquier, d. 814.

Ephraem Syrus. See
   Ephraem the Syrian, Saint,
   ca. 306-373.

Ephraem the Syrian, Saint, ca. 306-
   373.
   x Ephraem Syrus.

Epiphanius, Saint, Bp. of Constantia,
   ca. 315-403.

Ethelred, Saint. See
   Aelred, Saint, 1109?-1166.

Ethilredus, Saint. See
   Aelred, Saint, 1109?-1166.

Eudes, John, Saint. See
   John Eudes, Saint, 1601-1680.

Eve (Biblical character)
   x Eva (Biblical character)

Eva (Biblical character). See
   Eve (Biblical character)

Eymard, Pierre Julien, Saint. See
   Peter Julian Eymard, Saint,
   1811-1868.

Falconieri, Giuliana, Saint. See
   Juliana Falconieri, Saint,
   1270-1341.

Fara, Saint, ca. 595-657.

Felice da Cantalice, Saint. See
   Felix of Cantalice, Saint,
   1513-1587.

Felicitas, Saint, d. 202.

Felix III, Saint, Pope, d. 492.

Felix de Valois, Saint. See
   Felix of Valois, Saint, 1127-1212.

Felix of Cantalice, Saint, 1513-1587.
  x Felice da Cantalice, Saint.

Felix of Valois, Saint, 1127-1212.
  x Felix de Valois, Saint.

Ferrer, Vincent, Saint. See
  Vincent Ferrer, Saint, 1350(ca.)-
  1419.

Fidanza, Giovanni. See
  Bonaventure, Saint, 1221-1274.

Fieschi-Adorno, Caterina. See
  Catherine of Genoa, Saint,
  1447-1510.

Filippini, Lucia, Saint. See
  Lucy Filippini, Saint, 1672-1732.

Filippo Neri, Saint. See
  Philip Neri, Saint, 1515-1595.

Fisher, John, Saint. See
  John Fisher, Saint, 1469?-1535.

Fourier, Peter, Saint. See
  Peter Fourier, Saint, 1565-1640.

Fournet, André Hubert, Saint. See
  Andrew Fournet, Saint, 1752-1834.

Frances Cabrini, Saint, 1850-1917.
  x Cabrini, Frances Xavier, Saint.
  x Francesca Savario Cabrini, Saint.
  x Francisca Cabrini, Saint.

Frances of Rome, Saint, 1384-1440.
  x Bussa de Leoni, Francesca.
  x Francesca Romana, Saint.
  x Francisca Romana, Saint.

Francesca Romana, Saint. See
  Frances of Rome, Saint, 1384-1440.

Francesca Saverio Cabrini, Saint. See
  Frances Cabrini, Saint, 1850-1917.

Francesco Borgia, Saint. See
  Francis Borgia, Saint, 1510-1572.

Francesco Caracciolo, Saint. See
  Francis Caracciolo, Saint,
  1563-1608.

Francesco d'Assisi, Saint. See
  Francis of Assisi, Saint, 1182-1226.

Francesco de Geronimo, Saint. See
  Francis Jerome, Saint, 1642-1716.

Francesco de Paola, Saint. See
  Francis of Paula, Saint, 1416-1507.

Francesco di Girolamo, Saint. See
  Francis Jerome, Saint, 1642-1716.

Francesco di Pietro Bernardone. See
  Francis of Assisi, Saint, 1182-1226.

Francesco Saverio Bianchi, Saint.
  See Francis Xavier Bianchi, Saint,
  1743-1815.

Francis Borgia, Saint, 1510-1572.
  x Borgia, Francesco, Saint.
  x Borja, Francisco de, Saint.
  x Francesco Borgia, Saint.
  x Francisco de Borja, Saint.
  x Franciscus Borgia, Saint.

Francis Caracciolo, Saint, 1563-1608.
  x Caracciolo, Francis, Saint.
  x Francesco Caracciolo, Saint.
  x Franciscus Caracciolo, Saint.

Francis de Sales, Saint, 1567-1622.
  x De Sales, Francis, Saint.
  x Franciscus Salesius, Saint.
  x François de Sales, Saint.
  x Sales, Francis de, Saint.

Francis Jerome, Saint, 1642-1716.
  x Francesco de Geronimo, Saint.
  x Francesco di Girolamo, Saint.
  x Franciscus de Hieronymo, Saint.

Francis of Assisi, Saint, 1182-1226.
  x Bernardone of Assisi, Francesco.
  x Francesco d'Assisi, Saint.
  x Francesco di Pietro Bernardone.
  x Franciscus Assisiensis, Saint.

Francis of Paula, Saint, 1416-1507.
  x Francesco de Paola, Saint.
  x Franciscus de Paula, Saint.

Francis Solano, Saint, 1549-1610.
  x Francisco Solano, Saint.
  x Franciscus Solano, Saint.
  x Solano, Francis, Saint.

Franics Xavier, Saint, 1506-1552.
  x Francisco Xavier, Saint.
  x Franciscus Xaverius, Saint.
  x Xavier, Francis, Saint.

Francis Xavier Bianchi, Saint,
    1743-1815.
  x Bianchi, Francesco Saverio, Saint.
  x Francesco Saverio Bianchi, Saint.
  x Franciscus Xaverius Bianchi,
    Saint.

Francisca Cabrini, Saint. See
  Frances Cabrini, Saint, 1850-1917.

Francisca Romana, Saint. See
  Frances of Rome, Saint, 1384-1440.

Francisco de Borja, Saint. See
  Francis Borgia, Saint, 1510-1572.

Francisco Solano, Saint. See
  Francis Solano, Saint, 1549-1610.

Francisco Xavier, Saint. See
  Francis Xavier, Saint, 1506-1552.

Franciscus Assisiensis, Saint. See
  Francis of Assisi, Saint, 1182-1226.

Franciscus Borgia, Saint. See
  Francis Borgia, Saint, 1510-1572.

Franciscus Caracciolo, Saint. See
  Francis Caracciolo, Saint,
  1563-1608.

Franciscus de Hieronymo, Saint. See
  Francis Jerome, Saint, 1642-1716.

Franciscus de Paula, Saint. See
  Francis of Paula, Saint, 1416-1507.

Franciscus Salesius, Saint. See
  Francis de Sales, Saint,
  1567-1622.

Franciscus Solano, Saint. See
  Francis Solano, Saint, 1549-1610.

Franciscus Xaverius, Saint. See
  Francis Xavier, Saint, 1506-1552.

Franciscus Xaverius Bianchi, Saint.
  See Francis Xavier Bianchi,
  Saint, 1743-1815.

François de Sales, Saint. See
  Francis de Sales, Saint,
  1567-1622.

Frémiot, Jeanne Françoise. See
  Jane Frances de Chantal, Saint,
  1572-1641.

Gabriel, Saint, Archangel.

Gabriel of the Seven Dolors, Saint.
  See Gabriel Possenti, Saint,
  1838-1862.

Gabriel Possenti, Saint, 1838-1862.
  x Gabriel of the Seven Dolors,
    Saint.
  x Gabriele dell'Addolorata, Saint.
  x Possenti, Gabriel, Saint.

Gabriele dell'Addolorata, Saint.
  See Gabriel Possenti, Saint,
  1838-1862.

Gaetan, Saint. See
  Cajetan, Saint, 1480-1547.

Gaetano, Saint. See
  Cajetan, Saint, 1480-1547.

Galgani, Gemma, Saint. See
  Gemma Galgani, Saint, 1878-1903.

Gall, Saint, ca. 550-ca. 627.
  x Gallus, Saint.

Gallus, Saint. See
  Gall, Saint, ca. 550-ca. 627.

Garavito, Pedro. See
   Peter of Alcantara, Saint,
   1499-1562.

Garicoïts, Michael, Saint. See
   Michael Garicoïts, Saint,
   1797-1863.

Gaspar del Bufalo, Saint, 1786-1837.
   x Bufalo, Gaspar del, Saint.

Gemma Galgani, Saint, 1878-1903.
   x Galgani, Gemma, Saint.

Genevieve, Saint, 5th century.
   x Genovefa, Saint.

Gennaro, Saint. See
   Januarius, Saint, Bp. of
   Benevento, d. 305?

Genovefa, Saint. See
   Genevieve, Saint, 5th century.

George, Saint, d. 303.
   x Georgius, Saint.

Georgius, Saint. See
   George, Saint, d. 303.

Gerard Majella, Saint, 1726-1755.
   x Gerardus Majella, Saint.
   x Majella, Gerard, Saint.
   x Majela, Gerardo Maria, Saint.

Gerardus Majella, Saint. See
   Gerard Majella, Saint, 1726-1755.

Germain, Saint, Bp. of Auxerre. See
   Germanus, Saint, Bp. of Auxerre,
   378(ca.)-448.

Germain, Saint, Bp. of Paris. See
   Germanus, Saint, Bp. of Paris,
   496?-576.

Germaine Cousin, Saint, 1579-1601.
   x Germana Cousin, Saint.
   x Cousin, Germaine, Saint.

Germana Cousin, Saint. See
   Germaine Cousin, Saint, 1579-1601.

Germanus, Saint, Bp. of Auxerre,
   378(ca.)-448.
   x Germain, Saint, Bp. of Auxerre.

Germanus, Saint, Patriarch of
   Constantinople, 639(ca.)-733.

Germanus, Saint, Bp. of Paris,
   496?-576.
   x Germain, Saint, Bp. of Paris.

Gerosa, Vincenza, Saint. See
   Vincenza Gerosa, Saint.

Gertrud die Grosse, Saint. See
   Gertrude, Saint, the Great,
   1256-1302.

Gertrude, Saint, the Great, 1256-
   1302.
   x Gertrud die Grosse, Saint.
   x Gertrudis Magna, Saint.

Gertrude, Saint, of Nivelles,
   626-659.
   x Gertrudis, Saint, of Nivelles.

Gertrudis, Saint, of Nivelles. See
   Gertrude, Saint, of Nivelles,
   626-659.

Gertrudis Magna, Saint. See
   Gertrude, Saint, the Great,
   1256-1302.

Ghislieri, Michele. See
   Pius V, Saint, Pope, 1504-1572.

Gian Giuseppe della Croce, Saint.
   See John Joseph of the Cross,
   Saint, 1654-1739.

Gianelli, Antonio Maria, Saint. See
   Anthony Gianelli, Saint, 1789-1846.

Gilbert, Saint, 1083(?)-1189.
   x Gilbertus, Saint.

Gilbertus, Saint. See
   Gilbert, Saint, 1083(?)-1189.

Giles, Saint, d. ca. 725.
    x Aegidius, Saint.

Giovanni Battista de Rossi, Saint.
    See John Baptist de Rossi,
    Saint, 1698-1764.

Giovanni Bosco, Saint. See
    John Bosco, Saint, 1815-1888.

Giovanni di Capistrano, Saint. See
    John Capistran, Saint, 1386-1456.

Giovanni Gualberto, Saint. See
    John Gualbert, Saint, 995(ca.)-1073.

Giovanni Leonardi, Saint. See
    John Leonardi, Saint, 1541-1609.

Girolamo Emiliani, Saint. See
    Jerome Emiliani, Saint, 1486-1537.

Giuliana Falconieri, Saint. See
    Juliana Falconieri, Saint,
    1270-1341.

Giuliani, Veronica, Saint. See
    Veronica Giuliani, Saint, 1660-1727.

Giuseppe Benedetto Cottolengo, Saint.
    See Joseph Benedict Cottolengo,
    Saint, 1786-1842.

Giuseppe Cafasso, Saint. See
    Joseph Cafasso, Saint, 1811-1860.

Giuseppe da Leonessa, Saint. See
    Joseph of Leonessa, Saint,
    1556-1612.

Giuseppe de Copertino, Saint. See
    Joseph of Copertino, Saint,
    1603-1663.

Giuseppe Maria Pignatelli, Saint.
    See Joseph Pignatelli, Saint,
    1737-1811.

Giustiniani, Lorenzo, Saint. See
    Aloysius Gonzaga, Saint, 1568-1591.

Gonzaga, Aloysius, Saint. See
    Aloysius Gonzaga, Saint, 1568-1591.

Gonzaga, Luigi, Saint. See
    Aloysius Gonzaga, Saint, 1568-1591.

Goretti, Maria, Saint. See
    Maria Goretti, Saint, 1890-1902.

Gregorio Barbarigo, Saint. See
    Gregory Barbarigo, Saint,
    1625-1697.

Gregorius I, the Great, Saint, Pope.
    See Gregory I, the Great, Saint,
    Pope, 540(ca.)-604.

Gregorius VII, Saint, Pope. See
    Gregory VII, Saint, Pope,
    1015(ca.)-1085.

Gregorius, Saint, Bp. of Nyssa. See
    Gregory, Saint, Bp. of Nyssa,
    fl. 379-394.

Gregorius, Saint, Bp. of Tours. See
    Gregory, Saint, Bp. of Tours,
    538-594.

Gregorius Barbarigo, Saint. See
    Gregory Barbarigo, Saint, 1625-1697.

Gregorius Illuminator, Saint. See
    Gregory the Illuminator, Saint,
    240(ca.)-332(ca.)

Gregorius Nazianzenus, Saint, Patriarch
    of Constantinople. See Gregory of
    Nazianzus, Saint, ca. 329-390.

Gregorius Thaumaturgus, Saint, Bp. of
    Neocaesarea. See Gregory Thauma-
    turgus, Saint, ca. 213-275.

Gregory I, the Great, Saint, Pope,
    540(ca.)-604.
    x Gregorius I, the Great, Saint,
    Pope.

Gregory VII, Saint, Pope,
    1015(ca.)-1085.
    x Gregorius VII, Saint, Pope.
    x Hildebrand (Pope Gregory VII)

Gregory, Saint, Bp. of Nyssa,
    fl. 379-394.
    x Gregorius, Saint, Bp. of Nyssa.

Gregory, Saint, Bp. of Tours,
    538-594.
    x Gregorius, Saint, Bp. of Tours.

Gregory Barbarigo, Saint, 1625-1697.
    x Barbarigo, Gregorio, Saint.
    x Gregorio Barbarigo, Saint.
    x Gregorius Barbarigo, Saint.

Gregory of Nazianzus, Saint,
    ca. 329-390.
    x Gregorius Nazianzenus, Saint,
        Patriarch of Constantinople.

Gregory the Illuminator, Saint,
    240(ca.)-332(ca.)
    x Gregorius Illuminator, Saint.

Gregory Thaumaturgus, Saint,
    ca. 213-275.
    x Gregorius Thaumaturgus, Saint,
        Bp. of Neocaesarea.

Grignion de Montfort, Louis Marie,
    Saint. See Louis Grignion de
    Montfort, Saint, 1673-1716.

Guglielmo da Vercelli, Saint. See
    William of Vercelli, Saint,
    1085-1142.

Gulielmus Vercellensis, Saint. See
    William of Vercelli, Saint,
    1085-1142.

Guzman, Domingo de, Saint. See
    Dominic, Saint, 1170-1221.

Harding, Stephen, Saint. See
    Stephen Harding, Saint, d. 1134.

Hedwig, Saint, 1174-1243.
    x Hedwigis, Saint.
    x Jadwiga, Saint.

Hedwigis, Saint. See
    Hedwig, Saint, 1174-1243.

Helena, Saint, 246-326?

Hieronymus, Saint. See
    Jerome, Saint, ca. 340-420.

Hieronymus Emiliani, Saint. See
    Jerome Emiliani, Saint, 1486-1537.

Hilaire, Saint, Bp. of Poitiers. See
    Hilary, Saint, Bp. of Poitiers,
    d. 367.

Hilarion, Saint, ca. 291-372.

Hilarius, Saint, Pope. See
    Hilary, Saint, Pope, d. 468.

Hilarius, Saint, Bp. of Arles. See
    Hilary, Saint, Bp. of Arles, d. 449.

Hilarius, Saint, Bp. of Poitiers.
    See Hilary, Saint, Bp. of Poitiers,
    c. 367.

Hilary, Saint, Pope, d. 468.
    x Hilarius, Saint, Pope.

Hilary, Saint, Bp. of Arles, d. 449.
    x Hilarius, Saint, Bp. of Arles.

Hilary, Saint, Bp. of Poitiers,
    d. 367.
    x Hilaire, Saint, Bp. of Poitiers.
    x Hilarius, Saint, Bp. of Poitiers.

Hildebrand (Pope Gregory VII). See
    Gregory VII, Saint, Pope,
    1015(ca.)-1085.

Hildegard, Saint, 1098?-1179.
    x Hildegardis, Saint.
    x Binger, Hildegard

Hildegardis, Saint. See
    Hildegard, Saint, 1098?-1179.

Hofbauer, Clement, Saint. See
    Clement Hofbauer, Saint, 1751-1820.

Hubert, Saint, Bp. of Liege, d. 727.
    x Hubertus, Saint, Bp. of Liege.

Hubertus, Saint, Bp. of Liege. See
    Hubert, Saint, Bp. of Liege, d. 727.

Hugh, Saint, Bp. of Grenoble,
   1053-1132.
   x Hugo, Saint, Bp. of Grenoble.

Hugh, Saint, Bp. of Lincoln,
   1135?-1200.
   x Hugo, Saint, Bp. of Lincoln.

Hugo, Saint, Bp. of Grenoble. See
   Hugh, Saint, Bp. of Grenoble,
   1053-1132.

Hugo, Saint, Bp. of Lincoln. See
   Hugh, Saint, Bp. of Lincoln,
   1135?-1200.

Hyacinth, Saint, 1185-1257.
   x Hyacinthus, Saint.

Hyacinthus, Saint. See
   Hyacinth, Saint, 1185-1257.

Ignacio de Loyola, Saint. See
   Ignatius Loyola, Saint, 1491-1556.

Ignatius, Saint, Bp. of Antioch,
   1st century.

Ignatius a Laconi, Saint. See
   Ignatius of Laconi, Saint,
   1701-1781.

Ignatius Loyola, Saint, 1491-1556.
   x Ignacio de Loyola, Saint.
   x Iñigo de Loyola, Saint.
   x Loyola, Ignacio de, Saint.

Ignatius of Laconi, Saint, 1701-1781.
   x Ignatius a Laconi, Saint.
   x Ignazio da Laconi, Saint.

Ignazio da Laconi, Saint. See
   Ignatius of Laconi, Saint,
   1701-1781.

Ildephonsus, Saint, Abp. of Toledo,
   d. 667.

Inés de Monte Pulciano, Saint. See
   Agnes of Montepulciano, Saint,
   1268(ca.)-1317.

Inglevert, Saint, Abbot of St. Riquier.
   See Angilbert, Saint, Abbot of St.
   Riquier, d. 814.

Iñigo de Loyola, Saint. See
   Ignatius Loyola, Saint, 1491-1556.

Irenaeus, Saint, Bp. of Lyons,
   d. ca. 202.

Isaac Jogues, Saint, 1607-1646.
   x Jogues, Isaac, Saint.

Isabel, Saint. See
   Elizabeth of Portugal, Saint,
   1271-1336.

Isidore, Saint, Bp. of Seville,
   d. 636.
   x Isidorus, Saint, Bp. of Seville.

Isidorus, Saint, Bp. of Seville. See
   Isidore, Saint, Bp. of Seville,
   d. 636.

Ivo, Saint, Bp. of Chartres,
   ca. 1040-ca. 1116.

Jacob, the Patriarch.

Jacobus, Saint, Apostle, the Greater.
   See James, Saint, Apostle, the
   Greater.

Jacobus, Saint, Apostle, the Less.
   See James, Saint, Apostle, the
   Less.

Jacobus, Saint, Bp. of Nisibis. See
   James, Saint, Bp. of Nisibis,
   d. ca. 338.

Jadwiga, Saint. See
   Hedwig, Saint, 1174-1243.

James, Saint, Apostle, the Greater.
   x Jacobus, Saint, Apostle, the
   Greater.

James, Saint, Apostle, the Less.
   x Jacobus, Saint, Apostle, the
   Less.

James, Saint, Bp. of Nisibis,
    d. ca. 338.
  x Jacobus, Saint, Bp. of Nisibis.

Jan Berchmans, Saint. See
  John Berchmans, Saint, 1599-1621.

Jan of Nepomuk, Saint. See
  John Nepomucene, Saint,
  1330(ca.)-1383.

Jane Frances de Chantal, Saint,
    1572-1641.
  x Chantal, Jeanne Françoise (Frémiot)
    de Rabutin, baronne de, Saint.
  x Frémiot, Jeanne Françoise.
  x Jeanne Françoise de Chantal,
    Saint.
  x Joanna Francisca de Chantal,
    Saint.
  x Rabutin, Jeanne Françoise de,
    baronne de Chantal.

Jane of Valois, Saint, 1464-1505.
  x Jeanne, Saint, consort of
    Louis XII, King of France.
  x Jeanne de France, Saint.
  x Jeanne de Valois, Saint.
  x Joan of France, Saint.
  x Joan of Valois, Saint.
  x Joanna de Valois, Saint.

Januarius, Saint, Bp. of Benevento,
    d. 305?
  x Gennaro, Saint.

Jean Baptiste de La Salle, Saint.
  See John Baptist de La Salle,
  Saint, 1651-1719.

Jean Baptiste Marie Vianney, Saint.
  See John Baptist Vianney, Saint,
  1786-1859.

Jean de Brebeuf, Saint. See
  John de Brebeuf, Saint, 1593-1649.

Jean de Matha, Saint. See
  John of Matha, Saint, 1160-1213.

Jean Eudes, Saint. See
  John Eudes, Saint, 1601-1680.

Jean François Régis. See
  John Francis Régis, Saint,
  1597-1640.

Jeanne, Saint, consort of Louis
    XII, King of France. See
  Jane of Valois, Saint, 1464-1505.

Jeanne Antide Thouret, Saint. See
  Joan Antida Thouret, Saint,
  1765-1826.

Jeanne d'Arc, Saint. See
  Joan of Arc, Saint, 1412-1431.

Jeanne de France, Saint. See
  Jane of Valois, Saint, 1464-1505.

Jeanne de Lestonnac, Saint. See
  Joan de Lestonnac, Saint,
  1556-1640.

Jeanne de Valois, Saint. See
  Jane of Valois, Saint, 1464-1505.

Jeanne Elisabeth Bichier des Ages,
    Saint, 1773-1838.
  x Bichier des Ages, Jeanne
    Elisabeth, Saint.

Jeanne Françoise de Chantal, Saint.
  See Jane Frances de Chantal,
  Saint, 1572-1641.

Jerome, Saint, ca. 340-420.
  x Hieronymus, Saint.

Jerome Emiliani, Saint, 1486-1537.
  x Emiliani, Jerome, Saint.
  x Girolamo Emiliani, Saint.
  x Hieronymus Emiliani, Saint.

Joachim, Saint, Father of the
  Blessed Virgin Mary.

Joan Antida Thouret, Saint, 1765-1826.
  x Jeanne Antide Thouret, Saint.
  x Joanna Antida Thouret, Saint.
  x Thouret, Joan Antida, Saint.

Joan de Lestonnac, Saint, 1556-1640.
  x Jeanne de Lestonnac, Saint.
  x Joanna de Lestonnac, Saint.
  x Lestonnac, Jeanne de, Saint.

Joan of Arc, Saint, 1412-1431.
  x Jeanne d'Arc, Saint.
  x Joanna Arcensis, Saint.

Joan of France, Saint. See
  Jane of Valois, Saint, 1464-1505.

Joan of Valois, Saint. See
  Jane of Valois, Saint, 1464-1505.

Joanna Antida Thouret, Saint. See
  Joan Antida Thouret, Saint,
  1765-1826.

Joanna Arcensis, Saint. See
  Joan of Arc, Saint, 1412-1431.

Joanna de Lestonnac, Saint. See
  Joan de Lestonnac, Saint,
  1556-1640.

Joanna de Valois, Saint. See
  Jane of Valois, Saint, 1464-1505.

Joanna Francisca de Chantal, Saint.
  See Jane Frances de Chantal,
  Saint, 1572-1641.

Joannes, Saint, Apostle. See
  John, Saint, Apostle.

Joannes a Cruce, Saint. See
  John of the Cross, Saint,
  1542-1591.

Joannes Baptista, Saint. See
  John the Baptist, Saint.

Joannes Baptista de La Salle, Saint.
  See John Baptist de La Salle,
  Saint, 1651-1719.

Joannes Baptista de Rossi, Saint.
  See John Baptist de Rossi, Saint,
  1698-1764.

Joannes Baptista Vianney, Saint.
  See John Baptist Vianney, Saint,
  1786-1859.

Joannes Berchmans, Saint. See
  John Berchmans, Saint, 1599-1621.

Joannes Bosco, Saint. See
  John Bosco, Saint, 1815-1888.

Joannes Calybita, Saint. See
  John Calybites, Saint, d. ca. 450.

Joannes Chrysostomus, Saint. See
  John Chrysostom, Saint, d. 407.

Joannes Climacus, Saint. See
  John Climacus, Saint, ca. 525-
  ca. 606.

Joannes Damascenus, Saint. See
  John Damascene, Saint, 676?-749?

Joannes de Brébeuf, Saint. See
  John de Brébeuf, Saint, 1593-1649.

Joannes de Britto, Saint. See
  John de Britto, Saint, 1647-1693.

Joannes de Capistrano, Saint. See
  John Capistran, Saint, 1386-1456.

Joannes de Deo, Saint. See
  John of God, Saint, 1495-1550.

Joannes de Matha, Saint. See
  John of Matha, Saint, 1160-1213.

Joannes de Ribera, Saint. See
  John de Ribera, Saint, 1532-1611.

Joannes de Rubeis, Saint. See
  John Baptist de Rossi, Saint,
  1698-1764.

Joannes Ellemosynarius, Saint. See
  John the Almsgiver, Saint, Patriarch of Alexandria, d. 616?

Joannes Eudes, Saint. See
  John Eudes, Saint, 1601-1680.

Joannes Fisher, Saint. See
John Fisher, Saint, 1469?-1535.

Joannes Franciscus Régis, Saint.
See John Francis Régis, Saint,
1597-1640.

Joannes Gualbertus, Saint. See
John Gualbert, Saint, 995(ca.)-
1073.

Joannes Josephus a Cruce, Saint.
See John Joseph of the Cross,
Saint, 1654-1739.

Joannes Leonardi, Saint. See
John Leonardi, Saint, 1541-1609.

Joannes Nepomucenus, Saint. See
John Nepomucene, Saint,
1330(ca.)-1383.

Joannes Roffensis, Saint. See
John Fisher, Saint, 1469?-1535.

João de Brito, Saint. See
John de Britto, Saint, 1647-1693.

João de Deus, Saint. See
John of God, Saint, 1495-1550.

Joaquina de Vedruna, Saint,
1783-1854.
x Vedruna de Mas, Joaquina, Saint.

Job, the Patriarch.

Jogues, Isaac, Saint. See
Isaac Jogues, Saint, 1607-1646.

Johannes.
The references in this list are all
from the form "Joannes". According
to ecclesiastical tradition the
form "Johannes" is really more
correct.

John, Saint, Apostle.
x Joannes, Saint, Apostle.

John, Saint, the Baptist. See
John the Baptist, Saint.

John, Saint, Bp. of Rochester.
See John Fisher, Saint,
1469?-1535.

John Baptist de La Salle, Saint,
1651-1719.
x Jean Baptiste de La Salle, Saint.
x Joannes Baptista de La Salle,
Saint.
x La Salle, Jean Baptiste de,
Saint.

John Baptist de Rossi, Saint,
1698-1764.
x Giovanni Battista de Rossi,
Saint.
x Joannes Baptista de Rossi,
Saint.
x Joannes de Rubeis, Saint.
x Rossi, Giovanni Battista de,
Saint.

John Baptist Vianney, Saint,
1786-1859.
x Jean Baptiste Marie Vianney,
Saint.
x Joannes Baptista Vianney, Saint.
x Vianney, Jean Baptiste Marie,
Saint.

John Berchmans, Saint, 1599-1621.
x Berchmans, Jan, Saint.
x Berchmans, John, Saint.
x Jan Berchmans, Saint.
x Joannes Berchmans, Saint.

John Bosco, Saint, 1815-1888.
x Bosco, Giovanni, Saint.
x Bosco, John, Saint.
x Giovanni Bosco, Saint.
x Joannes Bosco, Saint.

John Calybites, Saint, d. ca. 450.
x Calybites, John, Saint.
x Joannes Calybita, Saint.

John Capistran, Saint, 1386-1456.
x Capistran, John, Saint.
x Capistrano, Giovanni di, Saint.
x Giovanni di Capistrano, Saint.
x Joannes de Capistrano, Saint.

John Chrysostom, Saint, d. 407.
  x Chrysostom, John, Saint.
  x Chrysostomus, Joannes, Saint.
  x Joannes Chrysostomus, Saint.

John Climacus, Saint, ca. 525-ca. 606.
  x Climacus, Joannes, Saint.
  x Joannes Climacus, Saint.

John Damascene, Saint, 676?-749?
  x Joannes Damascenus, Saint.

John de Brébeuf, Saint, 1593-1649.
  x Brébeuf, Jean de, Saint.
  x Jean de Brébeuf, Saint.
  x Joannes de Brébeuf, Saint.

John de Britto, Saint, 1647-1693.
  x Brito, João de, Saint.
  x Joannes de Britto, Saint.
  x João de Brito, Saint.
  x Pereira, João Heitor de Brito.

John de Ribera, Saint, 1532-1611.
  x Joannes de Ribera, Saint.
  x Juan de Ribera, Saint.
  x Ribera, Juan de, Saint.

John Eudes, Saint, 1601-1680.
  x Eudes, John, Saint.
  x Jean Eudes, Saint.
  x Joannes Eudes, Saint.

John Fisher, Saint, 1469?-1535.
  x Fisher, John, Saint.
  x Joannes Fisher, Saint.
  x Joannes Roffensis, Saint.
  x John, Saint, Bp. of Rochester.

John Francis Régis, Saint, 1597-1640.
  x Jean François Régis, Saint.
  x Joannes Franciscus Régis, Saint.
  x Régis, Jean François, Saint.

John Gualbert, Saint, 995(ca.)-1073.
  x Giovanni Gualberto, Saint.
  x Joannes Gualbertus, Saint.

John Joseph of the Cross, Saint,
    1654-1739.
  x Calosinto, Carlo Gaetano.
  x Gian Giuseppe della Croce,
    Saint.
  x Joannes Josephus a Cruce,
    Saint.

John Leonardi, Saint, 1541-1609.
  x Giovanni Leonardi, Saint.
  x Joannes Leonardi, Saint.
  x Leonardi, Giovanni, Saint.

John Nepomucene, Saint, 1330(ca.)-
    1383.
  x Jan of Nepomuk, Saint.
  x Joannes Nepomucenus, Saint.
  x Nepomuk, Jan of, Saint.

John of God, Saint, 1495-1550.
  x Ciudad, Juan.
  x Joannes de Deo, Saint.
  x João de Deus, Saint.
  x Juan de Dios, Saint.

John of Matha, Saint, 1160-1213.
  x Jean de Matha, Saint.
  x Joannes de Matha, Saint.

John of the Cross, Saint, 1542-1591.
  x Joannes a Cruce, Saint.
  x Juan de la Cruz, Saint.
  x Yepes, Juan.

John the Almsgiver, Saint, Patri-
    arch of Alexandria, d. 616?
  x Joannes Ellemosynarius, Saint.

John the Baptist, Saint.
  x Joannes Baptista, Saint.
  x John, Saint, the Baptist.

Josaphat, Saint, 1580-(ca.)-1623.
  x Kuncewic, Josaphat, Saint.

José de Colasanz, Saint. See
  Joseph Calasanctius, Saint,
  1556-1658.

José Oriol, Saint. See
  Joseph Oriol, Saint, 1650-1702.

Joseph, the Patriarch.
  x Josephus Patriarchus.

Joseph, Saint.
  x Joseph of Nazareth, Saint.
  x Josephus, Saint.

Joseph Benedict Cottolengo, Saint,
    1786-1842.
  x Cottolengo, Joseph Benedict,
    Saint.
  x Giuseppe Benedetto Cottolengo,
    Saint.
  x Josephus Benedictus Cottolengo,
    Saint.

Joseph Cafasso, Saint, 1811-1860.
  x Cafasso, Giuseppe, Saint.
  x Giuseppe Cafasso, Saint.
  x Josephus Cafasso, Saint.

Joseph Calasanctius, Saint,
    1556-1658.
  x José de Colasanz, Saint.
  x Josephus Calasanctius, Saint.

Joseph of Cupertino, Saint,
    1603-1663.
  x Desa, Giuseppe.
  x Giuseppe da Copertino, Saint.
  x Josephus a Cupertino, Saint.

Joseph of Leonessa, Saint, 1556-1612.
  x Giuseppe da Leonessa, Saint.
  x Josephus a Leonissa, Saint.

Joseph of Nazareth, Saint. See
  Joseph, Saint.

Joseph Oriol, Saint, 1650-1702.
  x José Oriol, Saint.
  x Josephus Oriol, Saint.
  x Oriol, José, Saint.

Joseph Pignatelli, Saint, 1737-1811.
  x Josephus Pignatelli, Saint.
  x Pignatelli, Giuseppe Maria,
    Saint.

Josephus, Saint. See
  Joseph, Saint.

Josephus a Leonissa, Saint. See
  Joseph of Leonessa, Saint,
  1556-1612.

Josephus a Cupertino, Saint. See
  Joseph of Cupertino, Saint,
  1603-1663.

Josephus Benedictus Cottolengo,
  Saint. See Joseph Benedict
  Cottolengo, Saint, 1786-1842.

Josephus Cafasso, Saint. See
  Joseph Cafasso, Saint, 1811-1860.

Josephus Calasanctius, Saint. See
  Joseph Calasanctius, Saint,
  1556-1658.

Josephus Oriol, Saint. See
  Joseph Oriol, Saint, 1650-1702.

Josephus Patriarchus. See
  Joseph, the Patriarch.

Josephus Pignatelli, Saint. See
  Joseph Pignatelli, Saint,
  1737-1811.

Juan de Dios, Saint. See
  John of God, Saint, 1495-1550.

Juan de la Cruz, Saint. See
  John of the Cross, Saint, 1542-1591.

Juan de Ribera, Saint. See
  John de Ribera, Saint, 1532-1611.

Judas, Saint, Apostle. See
  Jude, Saint, Apostle.

Jude, Saint, Apostle.
  x Judas, Saint, Apostle.

Julia Billiart, Saint, 1751-1816.
  x Billiart, Marie Rose Julie, Saint.

Juliana Falconieri, Saint, 1270-1341.
  x Falconieri, Giuliana, Saint.
  x Giuliana Falconieri, Saint.

Justin, Martyr, Saint, 100?-165?
   x Justinus, Martyr, Saint.

Justinianus, Laurentius, Saint. See
  Lawrence Justinian, Saint,
  1381-1435.

Justinus, Martyr, Saint. See
  Justin, Martyr, Saint, 100?-165?

✓ *Kempis, Thomas see Thomas a Kempis*

Kieran, Saint, d. ca. 530.
   x Ciaran, Saint.
   x Kieranus, Saint.
   x Kiernan, Saint.
   x Kyran, Saint.
   x Queranus, Saint.

Kieranus, Saint. See
  Kieran, Saint, d. ca. 530.

Kiernan, Saint. See
  Kieran, Saint, d. ca. 530.

Klaus, Bruder. See
  Nicholas of Flüe, Saint,
  1417-1487.

Klemens Maria Hofbauer, Saint.
  See Clement Hofbauer, Saint,
  1751-1820.

Kostka, Stanislaus, Saint. See
  Stanislaus Kostka, Saint,
  1550-1568.

Kuncewic, Josaphat, Saint. See
  Josaphat, Saint, 1590(ca.)-1623.

Kyran, Saint. See
  Kieran, Saint, d. ca. 530.

Labouré, Catherine, Saint. See
  Catherine Labouré, Saint,
  1806-1876.

Labre, Benedict Joseph, Saint. See
  Benedict Joseph Labre, Saint,
  1748-1783.

La Salle, Jean Baptiste de, Saint.
  See John Baptist de La Salle,
  Saint, 1651-1719.

Laurentius, Saint. See
  Lawrence, Saint, d. 258.

Laurentius a Brundusio, Saint. See
  Lawrence of Brindisi, Saint,
  1559-1619.

Laurentius Justinianus, Saint.
  See Lawrence Justinian, Saint,
  1381-1455.

Lawrence, Saint, d. 258.
   x Laurentius, Saint.

Lawrence Justinian, Saint, 1381-1455.
   x Giustiniani, Lorenzo, Saint.
   x Justinianus, Laurentius, Saint.
   x Laurentius Justinianus, Saint.
   x Lorenzo Giustiniani, Saint.

Lawrence of Brindisi, Saint,
  1559-1619.
   x Laurentius a Brundusio, Saint.
   x Lorenzo da Brindisi, Saint.
   x Rossi, Julius Caesar de.

Lazarus, Saint, 1st century.

Le Gras, Louise (de Marillac), Saint.
  See Louise de Marillac, Saint,
  1591-1660.

Lellis, Camillus de, Saint. See
  Camillus de Lellis, Saint,
  1550-1614.

Leo I, the Great, Saint, Pope, d. 461.

Leo IX, Saint, Pope, 1002-1054.
   x Bruno, Bp. of Toul.
   x Bruno von Geisheim, Saint.

Leonard of Port Maurice, Saint,
  1676-1751.
   x Casanuova, Paolo Girolamo.
   x Leonardo da Porto Maurizio,
     Saint.
   x Leonardus a Porto Mauritio,
     Saint.

Leonardi, Giovanni, Saint. See
  John Leonardi, Saint, 1541-1609.

Leonardo da Porto Maurizio, Saint.
See Leonard of Port Maurice,
Saint, 1676-1751.

Leonardus a Porto Mauritio, Saint.
See Leonard of Port Maurice,
Saint, 1676-1761.

Lestonnac, Jeanne de, Saint. See
Joan de Lestonnac, Saint,
1556-1640.

Lidwina, Saint, 1380-1433.
x Ludwina, Saint.
x Lydwina, Saint.

Liguori, Alfonso Maria de', Saint.
See Alphonsus Liguori, Saint,
1696-1787.

Lioba, Saint, 8th century.
x Liobgitha, Saint.

Liobgitha, Saint. See
Lioba, Saint, 8th century.

Liutgardis, Saint. See
Lutgarde, Saint, 1182-1246.

Lorenzo da Brindisi, Saint. See
Lawrence of Brindisi, Saint,
1559-1619.

Lorenzo Giustiniani, Saint. See
Lawrence Justinian, Saint,
1381-1455.

Louis IX, Saint, King of France,
1214-1270.
x Ludovicus IX, Saint, King of
France.

Louis, Saint, Bp. of Toulouse,
1274-1297.
x Louis of Anjou, Saint.
x Ludovicus, Saint, Bp. of
Toulouse.

Louis Bertrand, Saint, 1525-1581.
x Beltrán, Luis, Saint.
x Bertrand, Louis, Saint.
x Ludovicus Bertrandus, Saint.
x Luis Beltrán, Saint.

Louis Grignion de Montfort, Saint,
1673-1716.
x Grignion de Montfort, Louis
Marie, Saint.
x Ludovicus Grignion de Montfort,
Saint.
x Montfort, Louis Marie Grignion
de, Saint.

Louis of Anjou, Saint. See
Louis, Saint, Bp. of Toulouse,
1274-1297.

Louise de Marillac, Saint,
1591-1660.
x Le Gras, Louise (de Marillac),
Saint.
x Ludovica de Marillac, Saint.
x Marillac, Louise de, Saint.

Loyola, Ignacio de, Saint. See
Ignatius Loyola, Saint, 1491-1556.

Lucas, Saint, Evangelist. See
Luke, Saint, Evangelist.

Lucia, Saint. See
Lucy, Saint, d. ca. 304.

Lucia Filippini, Saint. See
Lucy Filippini, Saint, 1672-1732.

Lucian, Saint, of Antioch, d. 312.
x Lucianus, Saint.

Lucianus, Saint. See
Lucian, Saint, of Antioch, d. 312.

Lucy, Saint, d. ca. 304.
x Lucia, Saint.

Lucy Filippini, Saint, 1672-1732.
x Lucia Filippini, Saint.
x Filippini, Lucia, Saint.

Ludovica de Marillac, Saint.   See
  Louise de Marillac, Saint,
  1591-1660.

Ludovicus IX, Saint, King of France.
  See Louis IX, Saint, King of
  France, 1214-1270.

Ludovicus, Saint, Bp. of Toulouse.
  See Louis, Saint, Bp. of Toulouse,
  1274-1297.

Ludovicus Bertrandus, Saint. See
  Louis Bertrand, Saint, 1525-1581.

Ludovicus Grignion de Montfort, Saint.
  See Louis Grignion de Montfort,
  Saint, 1673-1716.

Ludwina, Saint. See
  Lidwina, Saint, 1380-1433.

Luigi Gonzaga, Saint. See
  Aloysius Gonzaga, Saint.

Luis Beltrán, Saint. See
  Louis Bertrand, Saint, 1525-1581.

Luke, Saint, Evangelist.
  x Lucas, Saint, Evangelist.

Lutgarde, Saint, 1182-1246.
  Liutgardis, Saint.

Lydwina, Saint. See
  Lidwina, Saint, 1380-1433.

Macarius, Saint, the Elder,
  4th century.

Machutus, Saint. See
  Malo, Saint, d. ca. 621.

Maclovius, Saint. See
  Malo, Saint, d. ca. 621.

Macrina, Saint, the Elder,
  4th century.

Macrina, Saint, the Younger,
  4th century.

Madeleine Sophie Barat, Saint,
  1779-1865.
  x Barat, Madeleine Louis Sophie,
    Saint.
  x Magdalena Sophia Barat, Saint.

Magdalena Sophia Barat, Saint. See
  Madeleine Sophie Barat, Saint,
  1779-1865.

Magdalene, Mary, Saint. See
  Mary Magdalene, Saint.

Majella, Gerard, Saint. See
  Gerard Majella, Saint, 1726-1755.

Malachias, Saint. See
  Malachy, Saint, 1094?-1148.

Malachy, Saint, 1094?-1148.
  x Malachias, Saint.
  x Maolmhaodhog ua Morgair, Saint.

Malo, Saint, d. ca. 621.
  x Machutus, Saint.
  x Maclovius, Saint.

Maolmhaodhog ua Morgair, Saint. See
  Malachy, Saint, 1094?-1148.

Marcus, Saint, Evangelist. See
  Mark, Saint, Evangelist.

Margaret, Saint, 3d century.
  x Margarita, Saint, 3d century.
  x Marina, Saint, of Antioch in
    Pisidia.

Margaret Mary Alacoque, Saint,
  1647-1690.
  x Alacoque, Margaret Mary, Saint.
  x Margarita Maria Alacoque, Saint.
  x Marguerite Marie Alacoque, Saint.

Margaret of Cortona, Saint, 1247-1297.
  x Margarita de Cortona, Saint.
  x Margherita da Cortona, Saint.

Margaret of Hungary, Saint, d. 1270.
  x Margarita Hungariae, Saint.

Margaret of Scotland, Saint,
   1045?-1093.
   x Margarita Scotiae, Saint.

Margarita, Saint, 3d century. See
   Margaret, Saint, 3d century.

Margarita de Cascia, Saint. See
   Rita, Saint, 1386-1456.

Margarita de Cortona, Saint. See
   Margaret of Cortona, Saint,
   1247-1297.

Margarita Hungariae. See
   Margaret of Hungary, Saint,
   d. 1270.

Margarita Maria Alacoque, Saint. See
   Margaret Mary Alacoque, Saint,
   1647-1690.

Margarita Scotiae, Saint. See
   Margaret of Scotland, Saint,
   1045?-1093.

Margherita da Cortona, Saint. See
   Margaret of Cortona, Saint,
   1247-1297.

Marguerite Marie Alacoque, Saint.
   See Margaret Mary Alacoque, Saint,
   1647-1690.

Maria, Saint, of Egypt. See
   Mary, Saint, of Egypt, 344-421.

Maria Crocifissa Di Rosa, Saint,
   1813-1855.
   x Di Rosa, Paolina.

Maria Domenica Mazzarello, Saint,
   1837-1881.
   x Mazzarello, Maria Domenica,
      Saint.

Maria Euphrasia Pelletier, Saint.
   See Mary Euphrasia Pelletier, Saint,
   1796-1868.

Maria Giuseppa Rossello, Saint,
   1811-1880.
   x Rossello, Maria Giuseppa, Saint.

Maria Goretti, Saint, 1890-1902.
   x Goretti, Maria, Saint.

Maria Maddalena de' Pazzi, Saint.
   See Mary Magdalene de' Pazzi,
   Saint, 1566-1607.

Maria Magdalena, Saint. See
   Mary Magdalene, Saint.

Maria Magdalena de Pazzis. See
   Mary Magdalene de' Pazzi, Saint,
   1566-1607.

Maria Magdalena Postel, Saint. See
   Mary Magdalene Postel, Saint,
   1756-1846.

María Micaela del Santísimo Sacramento, Saint. See Mary Michaela
   of the Blessed Sacrament, Saint,
   1809-1865.

Maria Virgo, Beata. See
   Mary, Blessed Virgin.

Marian of Quito, Saint. See
   Mariana de Paredes, Saint,
   1618-1645.

Mariana de Jesús, Saint. See
   Mariana de Paredes, Saint.
   1618-1645.

Mariana de Paredes, Saint, 1618-1645.
   x Marian of Quito, Saint.
   x Mariana de Jesús, Saint.
   x Paredes y Flores, Mariana de
      Jesús, Saint.

Marie Bernard, Soeur. See
   Bernadette Soubirous, Saint,
   1855-1879.

Marie de Sainte Eupharasie Pelletier,
   Saint. See Mary Euphrasie Pelletier, Saint, 1796-1868.

Marie Madeleine Postel, Saint. See
    Mary Magdalene Postel, Saint,
    1756-1846.

Marillac, Louise, Saint. See
    Louise de Marillac, Saint,
    1591-1660.

Marina, Saint, of Antioch in Pisidia.
    See Margaret, Saint, 3d century.

Marinus, Saint. See
    Amarinus, Saint, d. 674.

Mark, Saint, Evangelist.
    x Marcus, Saint, Evangelist.

Martha, Saint, 1st century.

Martin I, Saint, Pope, d. 655.
    x Martinus I, Saint, Pope.

Martin, Saint, Bp. of Tours,
    316(ca.)-397.
    x Martinus, Saint, Bp. of Tours.

Martin de Porres, Saint, 1579-1639.
    x Martinus de Porres, Saint.
    x Porres, Martin de, Saint.

Martin of Bracara, Saint. See
    Martin of Braga, Saint,
    520(ca.)-580.

Martin of Braga, Saint, 520(ca.)-580.
    x Martin of Bracara, Saint.
    x Martin of Dumio, Saint.
    x Martinus, Saint, Abp. of Braga.

Martin of Dumio, Saint. See
    Martin of Braga, Saint,
    520(ca.)-580.

Martin, Marie Françoise Thérèse.
    See Teresa of Lisieux, Saint,
    1873-1897.

Martinus I, Saint, Pope. See
    Martin I, Saint, Pope, d. 655.

Martinus, Saint, Abp. of Braga. See
    Martin of Braga, Saint,
    520(ca.)-580.

Martinus, Saint, Bp. of Tours. See
    Martin, Saint, Bp. of Tours,
    316(ca.)-397.

Martinus de Porres, Saint. See
    Martin de Porres, Saint, 1579-1639.

Mary, Blessed Virgin.
    x Blessed Virgin Mary.
    x Maria Virgo, Beata.
    x Virgin Mary, Blessed.

Mary, Saint, of Egypt, 344-421.
    x Maria, Saint, of Egypt.

Mary Euphrasia Pelletier, Saint,
    1796-1868.
    x Maria Euphrasia Pelletier,
      Saint.
    x Marie de Sainte Euphrasie
      Pelletier, Saint.
    x Pelletier, Marie de Sainte
      Euphrasie, Saint.

Mary Magdalene, Saint.
    x Magdalene, Mary, Saint.
    x Maria Magdalena, Saint.

Mary Magdalene de' Pazzi, Saint,
    1566-1607.
    x Maria Maddalena de' Pazzi, Saint.
    x Maria Magdalena de Pazzis, Saint.
    x Pazzi, Maria Maddalena de', Saint.

Mary Magdalene Postel, Saint.
    1756-1846.
    x Maria Magdalena Postel, Saint.
    x Marie Madeleine Postel, Saint.
    x Postel, Marie Madeleine, Saint.

Mary Michaela of the Blessed Sacra-
    ment, Saint, 1809-1865.
    x Desmaisieres y Lopez de Dicas-
      tello y Olmedo, María Micaela,
      vizcondesa de Jorbalan.
    x María Micaela del Santísimo
      Sacremento, Saint.

Mathias, Saint. Apostle. See
    Matthias, Saint, Apostle.

Matthaeus, Saint, Apostle. See
    Matthew, Saint, Apostle.

Matthaeus Tortus, pseud. See
    Robert Bellarmine, Saint,
    1542-1621.

Matthew, Saint, Apostle.
    x Matthaeus, Saint, Apostle.

Matthias, Saint, Apostle.
    x Mathias, Saint, Apostle.

Maurice, Saint, 3d century.
    x Mauritius, Saint.
    x Moritz, Saint.

Mauritius, Saint. See
    Maurice, Saint, 3d century.

Maximinus, Saint, Bp. of Aix,
    1st century.

Maximus, Saint, Bp. of Turin,
    fl. 451-465.

Mayela, Gerardo Maria, Saint. See
    Gerard Majella, Saint, 1726-1755.

Mazzarello, Maria Domenica, Saint.
    See Maria Domenica Mazzarello,
    Saint, 1837-1881.

Mechtilde, Saint, of Hackeborn,
    1241 or 2-1299?
    x Mechtildis, Saint.

Mechtildis, Saint. See
    Mechtilde, Saint, of Hackeborn,
    1241 or 2-1299?

Melania, Saint, the Younger,
    fl. 388-439.

Melchiori, Carlo. See
    Charles of Sezze, Saint,
    1613-1670.

Melito, Saint, Bp. of Sardis,
    2d century.

Merici, Angela, Saint. See
    Angela Merici, Saint, 1474-1540.

Michael, Saint, Archangel.

Michael Garicoïts, Saint, 1797-1863.
    x Garicoïts, Michel, Saint.
    x Michel Garicoïts, Saint.

Michel Garicoïts, Saint. See
    Michael Garicoïts, Saint,
    1797-1863.

Millán de la Cogolla, Saint. See
    Emilian, Saint, d. 574.

Monica, Saint, 333-387.

Montfort, Louis Marie Grignion de,
    Saint. See Louis Grignion de
    Montfort, Saint, 1673-1716.

More, Sir Thomas, Saint. See
    Thomas More, Saint, 1478-1535.

Moritz, Saint. See
    Maurice, Saint, 3d century.

Morus, Thomas, Saint. See
    Thomas More, Saint, 1478-1535.

Nepomuk, Jan of, Saint. See
    John Nepomucene, Saint,
    1330(ca.)-1383.

Neri, Philip, Saint. See
    Philip Neri, Saint, 1515-1595.

Nicholas I, the Great, Saint, Pope,
    d. 867.
    x Nicolaus I, the Great, Saint, Pope.

Nicholas, Saint, Bp. of Myra,
    4th century.
    x Nicaolaus, Saint, Bp. of Myra.

Nicholas of Flüe, Saint, 1417-1487.
  x Klaus, Bruder.
  x Nicolaus de Flüe, Saint.
  x Nikolaus von Flüe, Saint.

Nicolaus I, the Great, Saint, Pope.
  See Nicholas I, the Great, Saint,
  Pope, d. 867.

Nicolaus, Saint, Bp. of Myra. See
  Nicholas, Saint, Bp. of Myra,
  4th century.

Nicolaus de Flüe, Saint. See
  Nicholas of Flüe, Saint, 1417-1487.

Nolasco, Peter, Saint. See
  Peter Nolasco, Saint, ca. 1189-1258.

Norbert, Saint, Abp. of Magdeburg,
    1080-1134.
  x Norbertus, Saint, Abp. of
    Magdeburg.

Norbertus, Saint, Abp. of Magdeburg.
  See Norbert, Saint, Abp. of
  Magdeburg, 1080-1134.

Odilia, Saint, d. ca. 720.
  x Ottilia, Saint.

Odilo, Saint, Abbot of Cluny,
    962-1048.

Oriol, José, Saint. See
  Joseph Oriol, Saint, 1650-1702.

Ottilia, Saint. See
  Odilia, Saint, d. ca. 720.

Ouen, Saint. See
  Owen, Saint, Bp. of Rouen,
  ca. 609-ca. 683.

Owen, Saint, Bp. of Rouen,
    ca. 609-ca. 683.
  x Audoenus, Saint.
  x Audoin, Saint.
  x Dadon, Saint.
  x Ouen, Saint.

Pachomius, Saint, 4th century.

Pacifico de San Severino, Saint.
  See Pacificus of San Severino,
  Saint, 1653-1721.

Pacificus of San Severino, Saint,
    1653-1721.
  x Divini, Pacifico, O.F.M.
  x Pacifico de San Severino, Saint.

Pallotti, Vincent, Saint. See
  Vincent Pallotti, Saint,
  1795-1850.

Paolo della Croce, Saint. See
  Paul of the Cross, Saint,
  1694-1775.

Paredes y Flores, Mariana de Jesús,
  Saint. See Mariana de Paredes,
  Saint, 1618-1645.

Parenzo, Peter, Saint. See
  Peter Parenzo, Saint, d. 1199.

Paschal I, Saint, Pope, d. 824.
  x Paschalis I, Saint, Pope.

Paschal Baylón, Saint, 1540-1592.
  x Baylón, Paschal, Saint.
  x Paschalis Baylón, Saint.
  x Pascual Baylón, Saint.

Paschalis I, Saint, Pope. See
  Paschal I, Saint, Pope, d. 824.

Paschalis Baylón, Saint. See
  Paschal Baylón, Saint, 1540-1592.

Pascual Baylón, Saint. See
  Paschal Baylón, Saint, 1540-1592.

Patricius, Saint. See
  Patrick, Saint, 373?-463?

Patrick, Saint, 373?-463?
  x Patricius, Saint.

Paul, Saint, Apostle.
  x Paulus, Saint, Apostle.
  x Saul of Tarsus.

Paul, Saint, the Hermit, 4th century.
  x Paulus, Saint, the Hermit.

Paul of the Cross, Saint, 1694-1775.
  x Danei, Paolo.
  x Paolo della Croce, Saint.
  x Paulus a Cruce, Saint.

Paula, Saint, 374-404.

Paulinus, Saint, Bp. of Nola,
    353-431.

Paulinus II, Saint, Patriarch of
    Aquileia, d. 802.
  x Paulinus Aquileiensis, Saint.

Paulus, Saint, Apostle. See
  Paul, Saint, Apostle.

Paulus, Saint, the Hermit. See
  Paul, Saint, the Hermit,
  4th century.

Paulus a Cruce, Saint. See
  Paul of the Cross, Saint,
  1694-1775.

Pazzi, Maria Maddelena de', Saint.
  See Mary Magdalene de' Pazzi,
  Saint, 1566-1607.

Pedro Bautista, Saint. See
  Peter Baptist, Saint, 1545-1597.

Pedro Claver, Saint. See
  Peter Claver, Saint, 1580-1654.

Pedro de Alcantara, Saint. See
  Peter of Alcantara, Saint,
  1499-1562.

Pedro Nolasco, Saint. See
  Peter Nolasco, Saint,
  ca. 1189-1258.

Pelletier, Marie de Sainte Euphrasie,
  Saint. See Mary Euphrasia Pelletier, Saint, 1796-1868.

Pereira, João Heitor de Britto. See
  John de Britto, Saint, 1647-1693.

Perpetua, Saint, d. 202.

Peter, Saint, Apostle.
  x Petrus, Saint, Apostle.

Peter I, Saint, Abbot of Cava,
    c. 1122.
  x Petrus I, Saint, Abbot of Cava.
  x Pietro I, Saint, Abbot of Cava.

Peter, Saint, of Trevi, 1027(ca.)-
    1052.
  x Petrus, Saint, of Trevi.
  x Pietro, Saint, of Trevi.

Peter Baptist, Saint, 1545-1597.
  x Blasques Villacastén, Pedro.
  x Pedro Bautista, Saint.

Peter Canisius, Saint, 1521-1597.
  x Canisius, Peter, Saint.
  x Petrus Canisius, Saint.

Peter Celestine, Saint. See
  Celestine V, Saint, Pope,
  1215(ca.)-1296.

Peter Chanel, Saint, 1803-1841.
  x Chanel, Pierre Louis Marie,
    Saint.
  x Petrus Aloisius Maria Chanel,
    Saint.
  x Pierre Louis Marie Chanel,
    Saint.

Peter Chrysologus, Saint,
    ca. 400-ca. 450.
  x Chrysologus, Peter, Saint.
  x Petrus Chrysologus, Saint.

Peter Claver, Saint, 1580-1654.
  x Claver, Peter, Saint.
  x Pedro Claver, Saint.
  x Petrus Claver, Saint.

Peter Damian, Saint, 1007?-1072.
  x Damian, Peter, Saint.
  x Damiani, Pietro, Saint.
  x Petrus Damiani, Saint.
  x Pietro Damiani, Saint.

Peter Fourier, Saint, 1565-1640.
  x Fourier, Peter, Saint.
  x Petrus Forerius, Saint.
  x Pierre Fourier, Saint.

Peter Julian Eymard, Saint,
    1811-1868.
  x Eymard, Pierre Julien, Saint.
  x Petrus Julianus Eymard,
    Saint.
  x Pierre Julien Eymard, Saint.

Peter Martyr, Saint. See
  Peter of Verona, Saint,
  1206?-1252.

Peter Nolasco, Saint, ca. 1189-1258.
  x Nolasco, Peter, Saint.
  x Pedro Nolasco, Saint.
  x Petrus Nolasco, Saint.

Peter of Alcantara, Saint, 1497-1562.
  x Alcantara, Peter of, Saint.
  x Garavito, Pedro.
  x Pedro de Alcantara, Saint.
  x Petrus de Alcantara, Saint.

Peter of Verona, Saint, 1206?-1252.
  x Peter Martyr, Saint.
  x Petrus Martyr, Saint.
  x Petrus Veronensis, Saint.
  x Pietro da Verona, Saint.

Peter Parenzo, Saint, d. 1199.
  x Parenzo, Peter, Saint.
  x Petrus Parenzo, Saint.

Peter Thomas, Saint, 1305-1366.
  x Petrus Thomasius, Saint.
  x Pierre de Thomas, Saint.

Petrus, Saint, Apostle. See
  Peter, Saint, Apostle.

Petrus I, Saint, Abbot of Cava. See
  Peter I, Saint, Abbot of Cava,
  d. 1052.

Petrus, Saint, of Trevi. See
  Peter, Saint, of Trevi,
  1027(ca.)-1052.

Petrus Aloisius Maria Chanel, Saint.
  See Peter Chanel, Saint, 1803-1841.

Petrus Canisius, Saint. See
  Peter Canisius, Saint, 1521-1597.

Petrus Chrysologus, Saint. See
  Peter Chrysologus, Saint,
  ca. 400-ca. 450.

Petrus Claver, Saint. See
  Peter Claver, Saint, 1580-1654.

Petrus Coelestinus, Saint. See
  Celestine V, Saint, Pope,
  1215(ca.)-1296.

Petrus Damiani, Saint. See
  Peter Damian, Saint, 1007?-1072.

Petrus de Alcantara, Saint. See
  Peter of Alcantara, Saint,
  1499-1562.

Petrus Forerius, Saint. See
  Peter Fourier, Saint, 1565-1640.

Petrus Julianus Eymard, Saint. See
  Peter Julian Eymard, Saint,
  1811-1868.

Petrus Martyr, Saint. See
  Peter of Verona, Saint, 1206?-1252.

Petrus Nolasco, Saint. See
  Peter Nolasco, Saint, ca. 1189-1258.

Petrus Parenzo, Saint. See
  Peter Parenzo, Saint, d. 1199.

Petrus Thomasius, Saint. See
  Peter Thomas, Saint, 1305-1366.

Petrus Veronensis, Saint. See
  Peter of Verona, Saint,
  1206?-1252.

Philip, Saint, Apostle.
  x Philippus, Saint, Apostle.

Philip Benizi, Saint, 1233-1285.
  x Benizi, Philip, Saint.
  x Filippo Benizi, Saint.
  x Philippus Benitius, Saint.

Philip Neri, Saint, 1515-1595.
  x Filippo Neri, Saint.
  x Neri, Philip, Saint.
  x Philippus Nerius, Saint.

Philippus, Saint, Apostle. See
  Philip, Saint, Apostle.

Philippus Benitius, Saint. See
  Philip Benizi, Saint, 1233-1285.

Philippus Nerius, Saint. See
  Philip Neri, Saint, 1515-1595.

Pierozzi, Antonino, Saint. See
  Antoninus, Saint, Abp. of
  Florence, 1389-1459.

Pierre de Thomas, Saint. See
  Peter Thomas, Saint, 1305-1366.

Pierre Fourier, Saint. See
  Peter Fourier, Saint, 1565-1640.

Pierre Julien Eymard, Saint. See
  Peter Julian Eymard, Saint,
  1811-1868.

Pierre Louis Marie Chanel, Saint.
  See Peter Chanel, Saint,
  1803-1841.

Pietro I, Saint, Abbot of Cava.
  See Peter I, Saint, Abbot of
  Cava, d. 1122.

Pietro, Saint, of Trevi. See
  Peter, Saint, of Trevi,
  1027(ca.)-1052.

Pietro da Verona, Saint. See
  Peter of Verona, Saint,
  1206?-1252.

Pietro Damiani, Saint. See
  Peter Damian, Saint, 1007?-1072.

Pietro di Morrone. See
  Celestine V, Saint, Pope,
  1215(ca.)-1296.

Pignatelli, Giuseppe Maria, Saint.
  See Joseph Pignatelli, Saint,
  1737-1811.

Pius V, Saint, Pope, 1504-1572.
  x Ghislieri, Michele.

Pius X, Saint, Pope, 1835-1914.
  x Sarto, Giuseppe Melchiorre.

Placidus, Saint, ca. 515-ca. 550.

Placidus, Saint, d. 720.

Polycarp, Saint, Bp. of Smyrna,
  69-155.
  x Polycarpus, Saint, Bp. of Smyrna.

Polycarpus, Saint, Bp. of Smyrna.
  See Polycarp, Saint, Bp. of
  Smyrna, 69-155.

Porres, Martín de, Saint. See
  Martin de Porres, Saint, 1579-1639.

Possenti, Gabriel, Saint. See
  Gabriel Possenti, Saint, 1838-1862.

Postel, Marie Madeleine, Saint. See
  Mary Magdalene Postel, Saint,
  1756-1846.

Prosper, Tiro, Aquitanus, Saint.
  See Prosper of Aquitaine, Saint,
  5th century.

Prosper of Aquitaine, Saint,
  5th century.
  x Prosper, Tiro, Aquitanus, Saint.

Ptolomaeus, Bernardus, Saint. See
    Bernard Tolomei, Saint, 1272-1348.

Queranus, Saint. See
    Kieran, Saint, d. ca. 530.

Rabutin, Jeanne François de, baronne
    de Chantal. See Jane Frances de
    Chantal, Saint, 1572-1641.

Raimundo de Peñafort, Saint. See
    Raymund of Pennafort, Saint,
    1175(ca.)-1275.

Raphael, Saint, Archangel.

Raymund of Pennafort, Saint,
    1175(ca.)-1275.
    x Raimundo de Peñafort, Saint.
    x Raymundus de Pennaforte, Saint.

Raymundus de Pennaforte, Saint. See
    Raymund of Pennafort, Saint,
    1175(ca.)-1275.

Redi, Teresa Margaret, Saint. See
    Teresa Margaret Redi, Saint,
    1747-1770.

Regis, Jean François, Saint. See
    John Francis Regis, Saint,
    1597-1640.

Rembert, Saint, Abp. of Hamburg and
    Bremen, d. 888.
    x Rembertus, Saint.
    x Rimbert, Saint.

Rembertus, Saint. See
    Rembert, Saint, Abp. of Hamburg
    and Bremen, d. 888.

Remi, Saint, Bp. of Reims, 437?-533?
    x Remigius, Saint, Bp. of Reims.
    x Remy, Saint, Bp. of Reims.

Remigius, Saint, Bp. of Reims. See
    Remi, Saint, Bp. of Reims,
    437?-533?

Ribera, Juan de, Saint. See
    John de Ribera, Saint, 1532-1611.

Rimbert, Saint. See
    Rembert, Saint, Abp. of Hamburg
    and Bremen, d. 888.

Rita, Saint, 1386-1456.
    x Margarita de Cascia, Saint.

Robert Bellarmine, Saint, 1542-1621.
    x Bellarmine, Robert, Saint.
    x Bellarmino, Roberto Francesco
        Romolo, Saint.
    x Matthaeus Tortus, pseud.
    x Robertus Bellarminus, Saint.
    x Tortus, Matthaeus, pseud.

Robertus Bellarminus, Saint. See
    Robert Bellarmine, Saint, 1542-1621.

Roch, Saint, 14th century.
    x Rochus, Saint.

Rochus, Saint. See
    Roch, Saint, 14th century.

Rodat, Marie Emilie de, Saint. See
    Emily de Rodat, Saint, 1787-1852.

Rodriguez, Alonso, Saint. See
    Alphonsus Rodriguez, Saint,
    1532-1617.

Romola, Alessandra Lucrezia. See
    Catherine de' Ricci, Saint,
    1525-1617.

Romuald, Saint, 952(ca.)-1027.
    x Romualdo, Saint.
    x Romualdus, Saint.

Romualdo, Saint. See
    Romuald, Saint, 952(ca.)-1027.

Romualdus, Saint. See
    Romuald, Saint, 952(ca.)-1027.

Rosa de Lima, Saint. See
    Rose of Lima, Saint, 1586-1617.

Rosa de Viterbo, Saint. See
    Rose of Viterbo, Saint, d. ca. 1252.

Rose of Lima, Saint, 1586-1617.
x Rosa de Lima, Saint.

Rose of Viterbo, Saint, d. ca. 1252.
x Rosa de Viterbo, Saint.

Rossello, Maria Giuseppa, Saint. See
Maria Giuseppa Rossello, Saint,
1811-1880.

Rossi, Giovanni Battista de, Saint.
See John Baptist de Rossi, Saint,
1698-1764.

Rossi, Julius Caesar de. See
Lawrence of Brindisi, Saint,
1559-1619.

Sales, Francis de, Saint. See
Francis de Sales, Saint, 1567-1622.

Sarto, Giuseppe Melchiorre. See
Pius X, Saint, Pope, 1835-1914.

Saul of Tarsus. See
Paul, Saint, Apostle.

Savio, Domenico, Saint. See
Dominic Savio, Saint, 1842-1857.

Sebastian, Saint, 3d century.
x Sebastianus, Saint.

Sebastianus, Saint. See
Sebastian, Saint, 3d century.

Segni, Agnese de'. See
Agnes of Montepulciano, Saint,
1268(ca.)-1317.

Seton, Elizabeth see Elizabeth Ann SETON, St.

Severinus, Saint, d. 482.

Sigebert, Saint. See
Sigisbert, Saint, 8th century.

Sigisbert, Saint, 8th century.
x Sigebert, Saint.

Simeon, Stylites, Saint, 6th century.

Simon, Saint, Apostle.

Simon Stock, Saint, 1165?-1265.
x Stock, Simon, Saint.

Solano, Francis, Saint. See
Francis Solano, Saint, 1549-1610.

Soubirous, Bernadette, Saint. See
Bernadette Soubirous, Saint,
1844-1879.

Stanislaus, Saint, Bp., 1030-1079.
x Szczepanowski, Stanisław, Saint.

Stanislaus Kostka, Saint, 1550-1568.
x Kostka, Stanislaus, Saint.
x Stanisław Kostka, Saint.

Stanisław Kostka, Saint. See
Stanislaus Kostka, Saint,
1550-1568.

Stephanus I, Saint, Pope. See
Stephen, Saint, Pope, d. 257.

Stephanus I, Saint, King of Hungary.
See Stephen I, Saint, King of
Hungary, 975-1038.

Stephanus, Saint, Martyr. See
Stephen, Saint, Martyr, 1st
century.

Stephanus Harding, Saint. See
Stephen Harding, Saint, d. 1134.

Stephen I, Saint, Pope, d. 257.
x Stephanus I, Saint, Pope.

Stephen I, Saint, King of Hungary,
975-1038.
x István I, Saint, King of Hungary.
x Stephanus I, Saint, King of
Hungary. ·

Stephen, Saint, Martyr, 1st century.
x Stephanus, Saint, Martyr.

Stephen Harding, Saint, d. 1134.
    x Harding, Stephen, Saint.
    x Stephanus Harding, Saint.

Stock, Simon, Saint. See
    Simon Stock, Saint, 1165?-1265.

Strambi, Vincenzo Maria, Saint. See
    Vincent Strambi, Saint, 1745-1824.

Sturmius, Saint, Abbot of Fulda,
    d. 779.

Szczepanowski, Stanisław, Saint.
    See Stanislaus, Saint, Bp.,
    1030-1079.

Teresa, Mother (Agnes Boyaxhui)

Teresa d'Avila, Saint. See
    Teresa of Avila, Saint, 1515-1582.

Teresa de Jesús, Saint. See
    Teresa of Avila, Saint, 1515-1582.

Teresa Margaret Redi, Saint, 1747-1770.
    x Redi, Teresa Margaret, Saint.
    x Teresa Margherita del Sacro Cuore
        di Gesù, Saint.
    x Teresia Margarita Redi, Saint.

Teresa Margherita del Sacro Cuore di
    Gesù, Saint. See Teresa Margaret
    Redi, Saint, 1747-1770.

✓Teresa of Avila, Saint, 1515-1582.
    x Davila y Ahumada, Teresa Sanchez
        Cepeda.
    x Teresa d'Avila, Saint.
    x Teresa de Jesús, Saint.
    x Teresa of Jesus, Saint.
    x Teresia a Jesu, Saint.
    x Theresa of Avila, Saint.

Teresa of Jesus, Saint. See
    Teresa of Avila, Saint, 1515-1582.

✗Teresa of Lisieux, Saint, 1873-1897.
    x Martin, Marie Françoise Thérèse.
    x Teresa of the Child Jesus, Saint.
    x Teresia a Jesu Infante, Saint.
    x Theresa of Lisieux, Saint.
    ✓ x Theresa of the Child Jesus, Saint.
    x Thérèse de l'Enfant Jésus, Saint.

Teresa of the Child Jesus, Saint. See
    Teresa of Lisieux, Saint, 1873-1897.

Teresia a Jesu, Saint. See
    Teresa of Avila, Saint, 1515-1582.

Teresia a Jesu Infante, Saint. See
    Teresa of Lisieux, Saint, 1873-1897.

Teresia Margarita Redi, Saint. See
    Teresa Margaret Redi, Saint,
    1747-1770.

Thecla, Saint, 1st century.

Theodore, Saint, Abp. of Canterbury,
    602-690.
    x Theodorus, Saint, Abp. of
        Canterbury.

Theodore of Sukeon, Saint, Bp. of
    Anastacinopolis, d. 613.
    x Theodorus Siceota, Saint.

Theodore Studites, Saint, 759?-826.
    x Theodorus Studita, Saint.

Theodore the Holy, Saint, ca. 314-
    ca. 368.
    x Theodorus, Saint, Abbot of
        Tabennisi.

Theodorus, Saint, Abp. of Canterbury.
    See Theodore, Saint, Abp. of
    Canterbury, 602-690.

Theodorus, Saint, Abbot of Tabennisi.
    See Theodore the Holy, Saint,
    ca. 314-ca. 368.

Theodorus Siceota, Saint. See
    Theodore of Sukeon, Saint, Bp. of
    Anastacinopolis, d. 613.

Theodorus Studita, Saint. See
    Theodore Studites, Saint, 759?-826.

Theophilus of Corte, Saint, 1676-1740.
    x Arrighi, Biagio.

Theresa of Avila, Saint. See
    Teresa of Avila, Saint, 1515-1582.

Theresa of Lisieux, Saint. See
   Teresa of Lisieux, Saint, 1873-1897.

Theresa of the Child Jesus, Saint. See
   x Teresa of Lisieux, Saint, 1873-1897.

Thérèse de l'Enfant Jésus, Saint. See
   Teresa of Lisieux, Saint, 1873-1897.

Thomas, Saint, Apostle.

Thomas à Becket, Saint, Abp. of
   Canterbury, 1118?-1170.
   x Becket, Thomas, Saint.
   x Thomas of Canterbury, Saint.
   Thomas a Kempis
Thomas Aquinas, Saint, 1225?-1274.
   x Aquinas, Thomas, Saint.

Thomas de Villanova, Saint. See
   Thomas of Villanova, Saint,
   1488-1555.

Thomas More, Saint, 1478-1535.
   x More, Sir Thomas, Saint.
   x Morus, Thomas, Saint.

Thomas of Canterbury, Saint. See
   Thomas à Becket, Saint, Abp. of
   Canterbury, 1118?-1170.

Thomas of Villanova, Saint, 1488-1555.
   x Thomas de Villanova, Saint.
   x Tomás de Villanueva, Saint.

Thouret, Joan Antida, Saint. See
   Joan Antida Thouret, Saint,
   1765-1826.

Timotheus, Saint. See
   Timothy, Saint, Bp. of Ephesus, d. 97.

Timothy, Saint, Bp. of Ephesus, d. 97.
   x Timotheus, Saint.

Tolomei, Bernard, Saint. See
   Bernard Tolomei, Saint, 1272-1348.

Tomás, Catalina de, Saint. See
   Catherine Tomas, Saint, 1533-1574.

Tomás de Villanueva, Saint. See
   Thomas of Villanova, Saint,
   1488-1555.

Tortus, Matthaeus, pseud. See
   Robert Bellarmine, Saint,
   1542-1621.

Udalricus, Saint, Bp. of Augsburg.
   See Ulric, Saint, Bp. of Augsburg,
   890-973.

Udalricus Cellensis, Saint. See
   Ulric of Zell, Saint, 1029-1093.

Ulric, Saint, Bp. of Augsburg,
   890-973.
   x Udalricus, Saint, Bp. of Augsburg.
   x Ulrich, Saint, Bp. of Augsburg.

Ulric of Cluny, Saint. See
   Ulric of Zell, Saint, 1029-1093.

Ulric of Zell, Saint, 1029-1093.
   x Udalricus Cellensis, Saint.
   x Ulric of Cluny, Saint.
   x Ulrich von Zell, Saint.

Ulrich, Saint, Bp. of Augsburg. See
   Ulric, Saint, Bp. of Augsburg,
   890-973.

Ulrich von Zell, Saint. See
   Ulric of Zell, Saint, 1029-1093.

Ursula, Saint, 5th century.

Valentine, Saint, 3d century.
   x Valentinus, Saint.

Valentinus, Saint. See
   Valentine, Saint, 3d century.

Valerius, Saint, Abbot of San Pedro
   de Montes, fl. 655.

Vedruna de Mas, Joaquina, Saint.
   See Joaquina de Vedruna, Saint,
   1783-1854.

Veronica de Julianis, Saint. See
  Veronica Giuliani, Saint,
  1660-1727.

Veronica Giuliani, Saint, 1660-1727.
  x Giuliani, Veronica, Saint.
  x Veronica de Julianis, Saint.

Vialar, Emilie, Saint. See
  Emilie de Vialar, Saint, 1797-1856.

Vianney, Jean Baptiste Marie, Saint.
  See John Baptist Vianney, Saint,
  1786-1859.

Viator, Saint, d. 390.

Victor I, Saint, Pope, d. ca. 198.

Victor, Saint, 3d century.

Vigri-Mammolini, Caterina. See
  Catherine of Bologna, Saint,
  1413-1463.

Vincent de Paul, Saint, 1576?-1660.
  x Vincentius a Paulo, Saint.

Vincent Ferrer, Saint, 1350(ca.)-1419.
  x Ferrer, Vincent, Saint.
  x Vincentius Ferrerius, Saint.

Vincent of Lerins, Saint, 5th century.
  x Vincentius Lerinensis, 5th century.

Vincent Pallotti, Saint, 1795-1850.
  x Pallotti, Vincent, Saint.
  x Vincentius Pallotti, Saint.
  x Vincenzo Pallotti, Saint.

Vincent Strambi, Saint, 1745-1824.
  x Strambi, Vincenzo Maria, Saint.
  x Vincentius Maria Strambi, Saint.
  x Vincenzo Maria Strambi, Saint.

Vincentius a Paulo, Saint. See
  Vincent de Paul, Saint, 1576-1660.

Vincentius Ferrerius, Saint. See
  Vincent Ferrer, Saint, 1350(ca.)-
  1419.

Vincentius Lerinensis, Saint. See
  Vincent of Lerins, Saint,
  5th century.

Vincentius Maria Strambi, Saint. See
  Vincent Strambi, Saint, 1745-1824.

Vincentius Pallotti, Saint. See
  Vincent Pallotti, Saint, 1795-1850.

Vincenza Gerosa, Saint, 1784-1847.
  x Gerosa, Vincenza, Saint.

Vincenzo Maria Strambi, Saint. See
  Vincent Strambi, Saint, 1745-1824.

Vincenzo Pallotti, Saint, See
  Vincent Pallotti, Saint, 1795-1850.

Virgin Mary, Blessed. See
  Mary, Blessed Virgin.

Voitech, Saint, Abp. of Prague. See
  Adalbert, Saint, Abp. of Prague,
  956(ca.)-997.

William of Vercelli, Saint, 1085-1142.
  x Guglielmo da Vercelli, Saint.
  x Gulielmus Vercellensis, Saint.

Winifried (Saint Boniface) See
  Boniface, Saint, Abp. of Mainz,
  680-755.

Wulfstan, Saint, 1012?-1095.
  x Wulstanus, Saint.

Wulstanus, Saint. See
  Wulfstan, Saint, 1012?-1095.

Xavier, Francis, Saint. See
  Francis Xavier, Saint, 1506-1552.

Yepes, Juan. See
  John of the Cross, Saint, 1542-1591.

Zaccaria, Antonio Maria, Saint. See
  Anthony Zaccaria, Saint, 1502-1539.

Zita, Saint, d. 1271.